Houghton Mifflin Science

HOUGHTON MIFFLIN   BOSTON

Program Authors

William Badders
Elementary Science Teacher
Cleveland Public Schools
Cleveland, Ohio

Douglas Carnine, Ph.D.
Professor of Education
University of Oregon
Eugene, Oregon

James Feliciani
Supervisor of Instructional
Media and Technology
Land O' Lakes, Florida

Bobby Jeanpierre, Ph.D.
Assistant Professor, Science Education
University of Central Florida
Orlando, Florida

Carolyn Sumners, Ph.D.
Director of Astronomy and Physical Sciences
Houston Museum of Natural Science
Houston, Texas

Catherine Valentino
Author-in-Residence
Houghton Mifflin
West Kingston, Rhode Island

Content Consultants

Dr. Robert Arnold
Professor of Biology
Colgate University
Hamilton, New York

Dr. Carl D. Barrentine
Associate Professor Humanities
and Biology
University of North Dakota
Grand Forks, North Dakota

Dr. Steven L. Bernasek
Department of Chemistry
Princeton University
Princeton, New Jersey

Dennis W. Cheek
Senior Manager
Science Applications International
Corporation
Exton, Pennsylvania

Dr. Jung Choi
School of Biology
Georgia Tech
Atlanta, Georgia

Prof. John Conway
Department of Physics
University of California
Davis, California

Printed in the U.S.A.

ISBN:13: 978-0-618-49227-5
ISBN-10: 0-618-49227-5

4 5 6 7 8 9-DW-14 13 12 11 10 09 08 07

Content Consultants

Contents

UNIT A The Life Processes

UNIT B

Interactions Among Living Things

Contents

UNIT C · Earth Systems

UNIT D Atmosphere and Solar System

Contents

UNIT E
Kinds of Matter

UNIT F Forms of Energy

Features

UNIT A

UNIT B

UNIT C

Using Your Textbook

Science is an adventure. People all over the world do science. You can do science, too. You probably already do.

The Nature of Science

In this section in the front of your book, you will be introduced to scientists and to ways of investigating science.

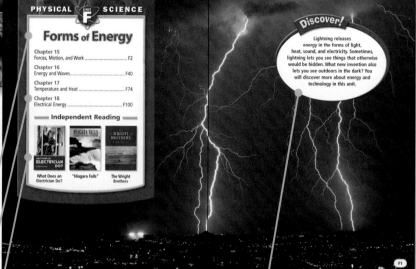

Units

The major sections of your book are units.

Unit Title is what the unit is about.

Chapters are part of a unit.

Independent Reading are books you can read on your own.

Discover! Information in this unit will help you answer this interesting question.

Chapters

Chapter Title tells what the chapter is about.

Lesson Preview gives information about each lesson.

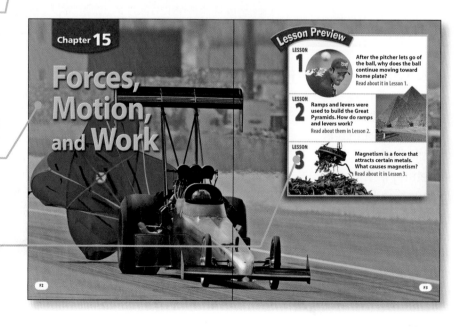

Every lesson in your book has two parts.
Lesson Part 1: Investigate Activity

Why it Matters tells why the science you will learn in each lesson is important.

Inquiry Skill tells about the main inquiry skill for the Investigate activity.

Materials lists what you will need to conduct your investigation.

Science And Math Toolbox references additional information in your book to help with your investigation.

Procedure lists the steps you will follow to conduct your Investigation.

Conclusion guides you in thinking about your investigation.

Visuals give more information about the investigation.

Investigate More! lets you take your investigation further.

Lesson Part 2: Learn by Reading

Vocabulary lists the new science words that you will learn.

Main Idea tells you what is important.

Visuals help you to understand the text.

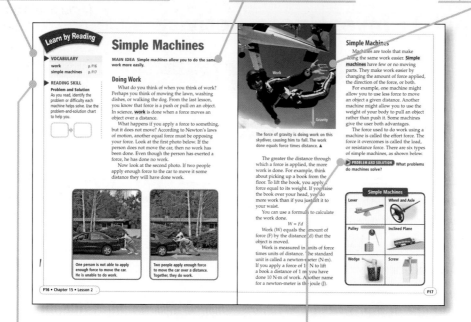

Reading Skill helps you understand and organize information as you read.

Reading Skill Check helps you check your understanding of the text.

Lesson Wrap-Up

Visual Summary shows you different ways to summarize what you've read.

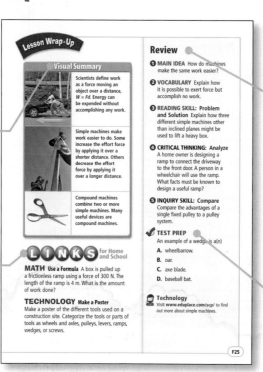

Links connects science to math and other subjects.

Review lets you check your understanding after you read.

Test Prep helps you meet standards. Standards are important goals for your learning.

Focus On

Focus On lets you learn more about a key concept in a chapter.

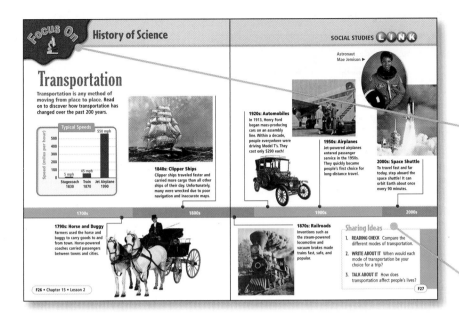

Focus On types include: Biography, History of Science, Technology, Primary Source, Literature, and Readers' Theater.

Sharing Ideas has you check your understanding and write and talk about what you have learned.

Extreme Science and Careers

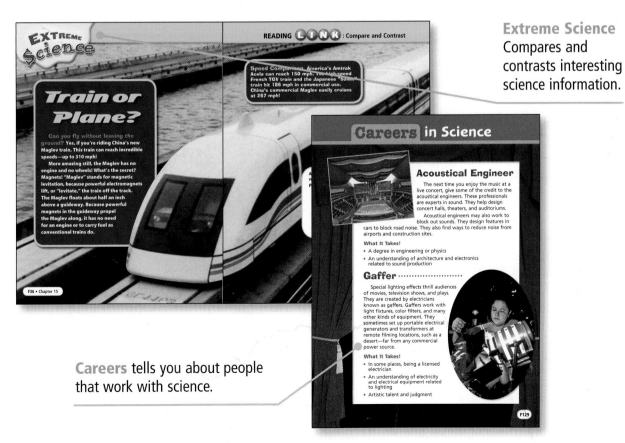

Extreme Science Compares and contrasts interesting science information.

Careers tells you about people that work with science.

Chapter and Unit Review and Test Prep

These reviews help you to know you are on track with learning science and reading standards.

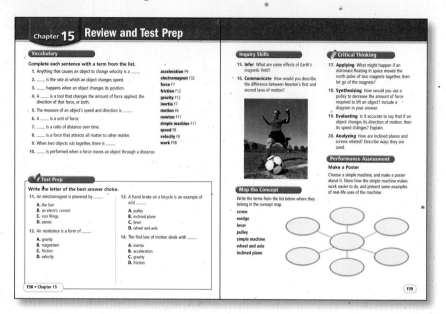

Unit Wrap-Up

Learn more about the **Discover!** question that started the unit. Also find a link to a simulation on the EduPlace web site.

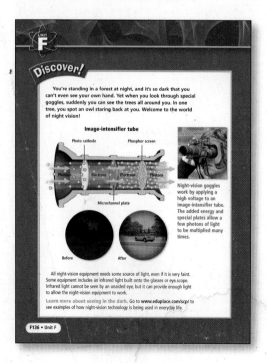

References

The back of your book includes sections you will refer to again and again.

The Nature of Science

Science is an adventure.
People all over the world do
science. You can do science, too.
You probably already do.

National Education Science Standards

Science Content Standards

Grades 5–8.A. ABILITIES NECESSARY TO DO SCIENTIFIC INQUIRY

- Identify questions that can be answered through scientific investigations.

- Design and conduct a scientific investigation.

- Use appropriate tools and techniques to gather, analyze, and interpret data.

- Develop descriptions, explanations, predictions, and models using evidence.

- Think critically and logically to make the relationships between evidence and explanations.

- Recognize and analyze alternative explanations and predictions.

- Communicate scientific procedures and explanations.

- Use mathematics in all aspects of scientific inquiry.

GRADES 5–8.A. UNDERSTANDINGS ABOUT SCIENTIFIC INQUIRY

- Different kinds of questions suggest different kinds of scientific investigations. Some investigations involve observing and describing objects, organisms, or events; some involve collecting specimens; some involve experiments; some involve seeking more information; some involve discovery of new objects and phenomena; and some involve making models.

- Current scientific knowledge and understanding guide scientific investigations. Different scientific domains employ different methods, core theories, and standards to advance scientific knowledge and understanding.

- Mathematics is important in all aspects of scientific inquiry.

- Technology used to gather data enhances accuracy and allows scientists to analyze and quantify results of investigations.

- Scientific explanations emphasize evidence, have logically consistent arguments, and use scientific principles, models, and theories. The scientific community accepts and uses such explanations until displaced by better scientific ones. When such displacement occurs, science advances.

- Science advances through legitimate skepticism. Asking questions and querying other scientists' explanations is part of scientific inquiry. Scientists evaluate the explanations proposed by other scientists by examining evidence, comparing evidence, identifying faulty reasoning, pointing out statements that go beyond the evidence, and suggesting alternative explanations for the same observations.

- Scientific investigations sometimes result in new ideas and phenomena for study, generate new methods or procedures for an investigation, or develop new technologies to improve the collection of data. All of these results can lead to new investigations.

GRADES 5–8.E. ABILITIES OF TECHNOLOGICAL DESIGN

- Identify appropriate problems for technological design.

- Design a solution or product.

- Implement a proposed design.

- Evaluate technological designs or products.

- Communicate the process of technological design.

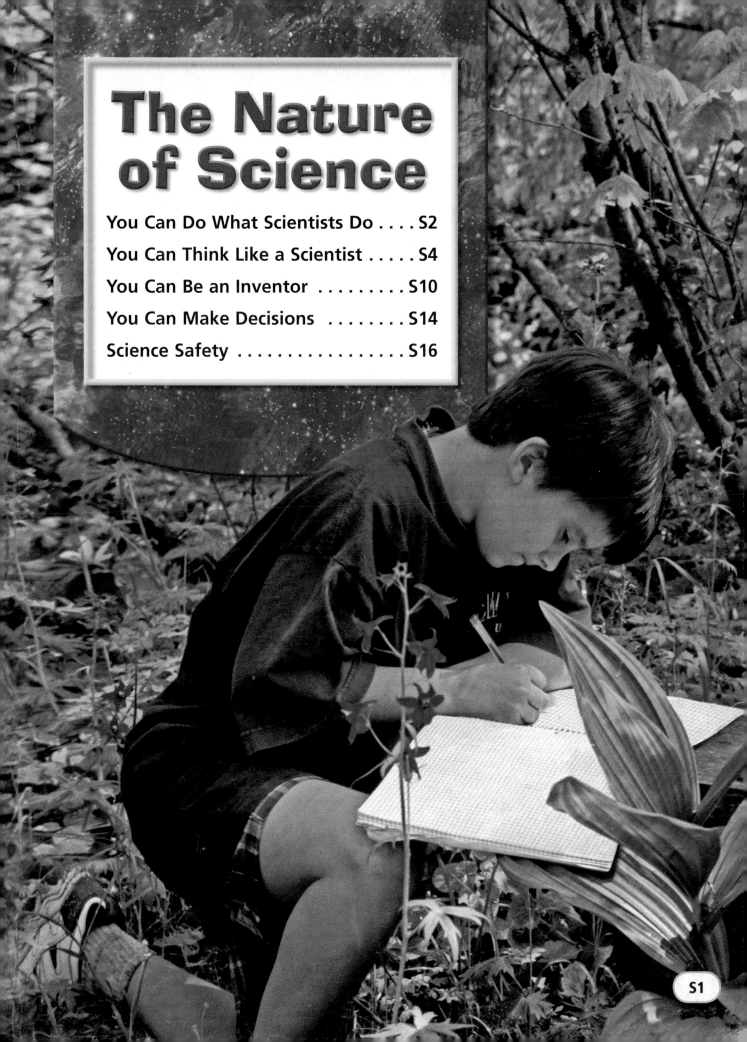

The Nature of Science

You Can...

Do What Scientists Do

Meet Dr. Dale Brown Emeagwali. She works as a teacher and researcher at Morgan State University in Baltimore, Maryland. Dr. Emeagwali is a microbiologist, which is a biologist who specializes in studying single-celled organisms, or microorganisms. The goal of her investigations is to gain a better understanding of the processes that take place inside cells. Depending on the question she is investigating, Dr. Emeagwali may observe these living things in nature or conduct an experiment in the laboratory.

Scientists ask questions. Then they answer the questions by investigating and experimenting. Dr. Emeagwali has asked many questions about how microorganisms carry out their life processes, as well as how they affect human health.

In one investigation, she demonstrated that a certain chemical exists in a type of bacteria called *Streptomyces parvulus.* Such discoveries add to the basic knowledge of microbiology. Dr. Emeagwali is pleased, though, when her work has practical applications in medicine. In another experiment, she demonstrated that certain molecules could be used to stop the formation of tumors in people with cancer.

Dr. Emeagwali understands that for each investigation she carries out she must repeat the procedure many times and get the same results before she can conclude that her results are true.

Science investigations involve communicating with other scientists.

In addition to laboratory research, Dr. Emeagwali spends time writing papers about her work in order to communicate with other scientists. She wants other scientists to be able to repeat her investigations in order to check that her results are valid. Dr. Emeagwali also spends time reading about the work of other scientists to keep informed about the progress others have made in microbiology.

Think Like a Scientist

The ways scientists ask and answer questions about the world around them is called **scientific inquiry.** Scientific inquiry requires certain attitudes, or approaches to thinking about a problem. To think like a scientist you have to be:

- curious and ask a lot of questions.

- creative and think up new ways to do things.

- able to keep an open mind. That means you consider the ideas of others.

- willing to use measurement, estimation, and other mathematics skills.

- open to changing what you think when your investigation results surprise you.

- willing to question what other people tell you.

What kind of rock is this? How did this rock form? Where did the different materials that make up the rock come from?

Use Critical Thinking

When you think critically, you make decisions about what others tell you or what you read. Is what you heard on TV or read in a magazine a fact or an opinion? A *fact* can be checked to make sure it is true. An *opinion* is what someone thinks about the facts.

Did you ever hear a scientific claim that was hard to believe? When you think, "What evidence is there to support that claim?" you are thinking critically. You'll also think critically when you evaluate investigation results. Observations can be interpreted in many ways. You'll judge whether a conclusion is supported by the data collected.

> The book states that a sedimentary rock forms when rock fragments and other sediments are pressed and cemented together.

> It looks like fragments of different kinds of rock came together to make this rock. This must be a type of sedimentary rock.

Science Inquiry

Applying scientific inquiry helps you understand the world around you. Suppose you have decided to investigate which color is easiest to see clearly in the dimmest light.

Observe In the evening, as daylight fades, you observe the different colored objects around you. As the light becomes dimmer and dimmer, you notice which color remains clear to your eyes.

Ask a Question When you think about what you saw, heard, or read, you may have questions.

Hypothesis Think about facts you already know. Do you have an idea about the answer? Write it down. That is your *hypothesis*.

Experiment Plan a test that will tell if the hypothesis is true or not. List the materials you will need. Write the steps you will follow. Make sure that you keep all conditions the same except the one you are testing. That condition is called the *variable*.

Conclusion Think about your results. What do they tell you? Did your results support your hypothesis or show it to be false?

Describe your experiment to others. Communicate your results and conclusion.

My Color Experiment

Observe As the light dims, dark colors such as dark blue seem to disappear from sight first.

Ask a question I wonder which color can be seen most clearly in the dimmest light?

Hypothesis Yellow is the color that can be seen most clearly in the dimmest light.

Experiment I'm going to observe several differently colored objects as I dim the light. Then I'm going to observe which color I can see most clearly in the dimmest light.

Conclusion The results support my hypothesis. Yellow is the color that can be seen most clearly in the dimmest light.

Inquiry Process

The methods of science may vary from one area of science to another. Here is a process that some scientists follow to answer questions and make new discoveries.

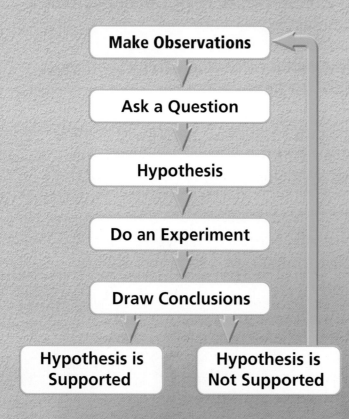

Make Observations

Ask a Question

Hypothesis

Do an Experiment

Draw Conclusions

Hypothesis is Supported

Hypothesis is Not Supported

Science Inquiry Skills

You'll use many of these skills of inquiry when you investigate and experiment.

- Ask Questions
- Observe
- Compare
- Classify
- Predict
- Measure

- Hypothesize
- Use Variables
- Experiment
- Use Models
- Communicate
- Use Numbers

- Record Data
- Analyze Data
- Infer
- Collaborate
- Research

Try It Yourself!

Experiment With Energy Beads

When you hold Energy Beads in your fist for a while and then go outdoors and open your hand, the beads change from off-white to many different colors.

1 What questions do you have about the Energy Beads?

2 How would you find out the answers?

3 How could you use Energy Beads to test a hypothesis?

4 Write your plan for an experiment with one variable using Energy Beads. Predict what will happen.

Be an Inventor

Cassandra "Cassie" Wagner became an inventor when she was 11 years old. At that time, she was in middle school. During the summer, she wanted to make a toy for her pet cat. Cats are attracted to catnip, a plant with a strong odor. Cassie considered including catnip as part of her toy.

When Cassie researched about catnip on the Internet, she discovered that some people thought an oil in the plant will repel insects. She could find no proof of that hypothesis, and so she decided to test it herself. In her first experiment, Cassie put a small amount of the oil from catnip onto a cotton ball. She then observed whether mosquitoes were repelled by the ball. They were.

With the help of a University of Florida professor, Cassie ran further experiments in a laboratory. She proved that the spray she made with the catnip oil repelled insects just as well as bug sprays sold in stores.

Cassie called her bug repellent Bugnip, and she planned to have it produced and sold to consumers. In the future, her efforts may lead to other inventions and better ways of repelling bothersome bugs.

"It was over the summer, and I didn't have much going on. I was just fooling around."

What Is Technology?

The tools people make and use, the things they build with tools, and the methods used to accomplish a practical purpose are all technology. A toy train set is an example of technology. So is a light rail system that provides transportation in a major city.

Scientists use technology, too. For example, a telescope makes it possible for scientists to see objects far into space that cannot be seen with just the eyes. Scientists also use measurement technology to make their observations more exact.

Many technologies make the world a better place to live. Sometimes, though, a technology that solves one problem can cause other problems. For example, burning coal in power plants provides power for generators that produce electricity for homes, schools, and industries. However, the burning of coal also can cause acid rain, which can be very harmful to living things.

A Better Idea

"I wish I had a better way to _____." How would you fill in the blank? Everyone wishes he or she could do a job more easily or have more fun. Inventors try to make those wishes come true. Inventing or improving an invention requires time and patience.

A company in Canada had a better idea in 1895. It invented the first power tool. Today, many other tools are powered by electricity—including this cordless power screwdriver. Today, inventors are still improving power tool technology, including using lasers and microwaves to drill into steel, stone, and glass. Maybe, someday, you will have a better idea for a new power tool.

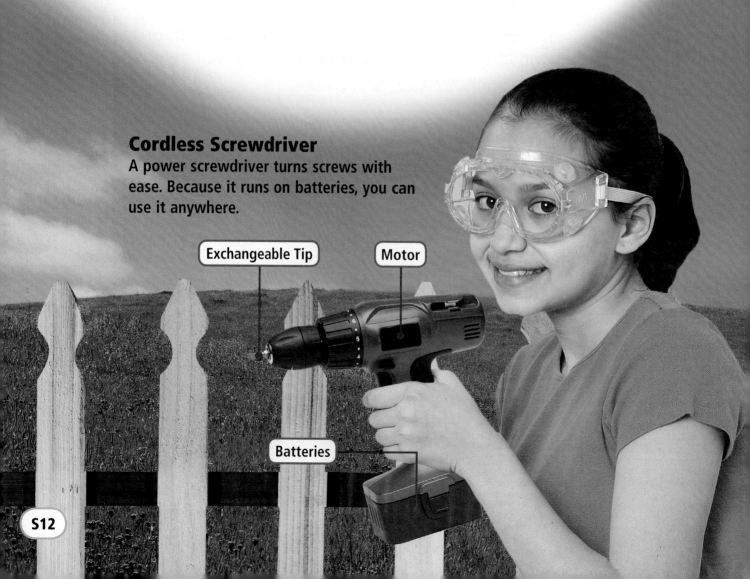

Cordless Screwdriver
A power screwdriver turns screws with ease. Because it runs on batteries, you can use it anywhere.

Exchangeable Tip

Motor

Batteries

How to Be an Inventor

1. **Identify a problem.** It may be a problem at school, at home, or in your community.

2. **List ways to solve the problem.** Sometimes the solution is a new tool. Other times it may be a new way of doing an old job or activity.

3. **Choose the best solution.** Decide which idea you predict will work best. Think about which one you can carry out.

4. **Make a sample.** A sample, called a *prototype*, is the first try. Your idea may need many materials or none at all. Choose measuring tools that will help your design work better.

5. **Try out your invention.** Use your prototype, or ask some else to try it. Keep a record of how it works and what problems you find. The more times you try it, the more information you will have.

6. **Improve your invention.** Use what you learned to make your design work better. Draw or write about the changes you made and why you made them.

7. **Share your invention.** Show your invention to others. Explain how it works. Tell how it makes an activity easier or more fun. If it did not work as well as you wanted, tell why.

You Can...

Make Decisions

Trouble for Manatees

Manatees are large, slow-moving marine mammals. An average manatee is about 3 meters long and has a mass of about 500 kilograms. Manatees are gentle plant eaters.

In summer, manatees can be seen along the ocean coasts of Alabama, Georgia, Florida, and South Carolina. In winter, they migrate to the warm waters of bays and rivers along the Gulf Coast of Florida. Living near the coast protects the manatees from diseases they might catch in colder waters. However, there are dangers in living so close to land. The great majority of manatee deaths are caused by collisions with boats. Almost all manatees have scars on their backs from being hit by fast-moving boats.

Deciding What to Do

What can be done to protect manatees from harm?

Here's how to make your decision about the manatees. You can use the same steps to help solve problems in your home, in your school, and in your community.

1 LEARN Learn about the problem. Take the time needed to get the facts. You could talk to an expert, read a science book, or explore a website.

2 LIST Make a list of actions you could take. Add actions other people could take.

3 DECIDE Think about each action on your list. Identify the risks and benefits. Decide which choice is the best one for you, your school or your community.

4 SHARE Communicate your decision to others.

Boat Slow Speed Zone!

Science Safety

☑ Know the safety rules of your school and classroom and follow them.

☑ Read and follow the safety tips in each Investigate activity.

☑ When you plan your own investigations, write down how to keep safe.

☑ Know how to clean up and put away science materials. Keep your work area clean, and tell your teacher about spills right away.

☑ Know how to safely plug in electrical devices.

☑ Wear safety goggles when your teacher tells you.

☑ Unless your teacher tells you to, never put any science materials in or near your ears, eyes, or mouth.

☑ Wear gloves when handling live animals.

☑ Wash your hands when your investigation is done.

Caring for Living Things

☑ Learn how to care for the plants and animals in your classroom so that they stay healthy and safe. Learn how to hold animals carefully.

The Life Processes

LIFE — UNIT A — SCIENCE

The Life Processes

Independent Reading

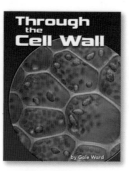

Barbara McClintock

The Amazing Amoeba

Through the Cell Wall

Discover!

Cells perform the most basic functions of life. Tiny bacteria and most protists live as single cells. Yet large plants and animals use trillions of cells to survive. Why aren't any single-celled organisms as big as you? Learning how cells function will help you answer this question.

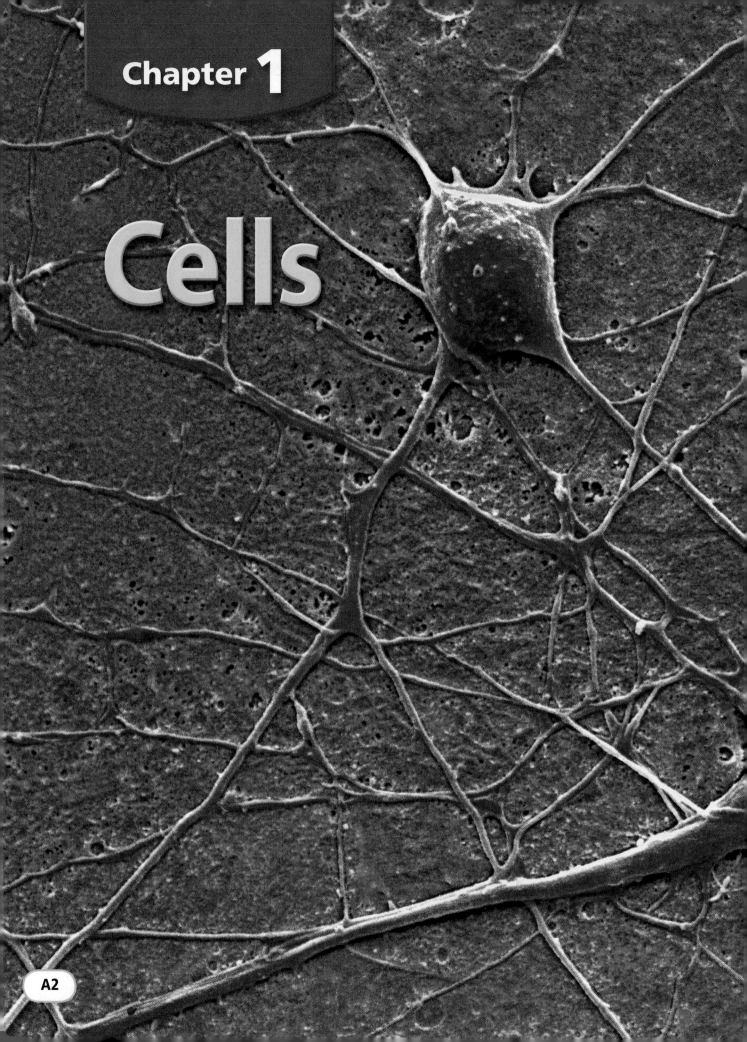

Chapter **1**

Cells

Lesson Preview

LESSON 1

Cells are tiny fluid-filled chambers with parts that never stop moving. Why are cells so important?

Read about them in Lesson 1.

LESSON 2

Some organisms exist as single cells. How do they survive?

Read about them in Lesson 2.

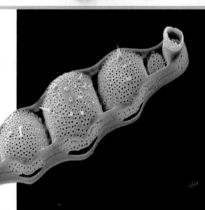

LESSON 3

All living organisms can be grouped into six kingdoms. What are the kingdoms?

Read about them in Lesson 3.

LESSON 4

Blood, muscles, bones, and nerves—are they made of different types of cells?

Read about it in Lesson 4.

What Are the Parts of a Cell?

Why It Matters...

All living things, from water plants to hippos, are made of cells. When you learn about the parts of cells and their functions, you can better understand how organisms like this hippopotamus live and interact with their environments.

PREPARE TO INVESTIGATE

Inquiry Skill

Communicate You can share science results by making sketches, charts, graphs, or models, and by speaking and writing.

Materials

- microscope
- prepared slides of various plant and animal tissues

Science and Math Toolbox
For step 2, review **Using a Microscope** on page H2.

Get Closer!

Procedure

STEP 1

1. **Observe** Work in a small group. Take turns looking through a microscope at each slide. Note the titles of the slides, which tell the sources of the samples.

2. **Communicate** Draw a picture of the cells in each sample. Next to the picture write the name of the sample, and whether it comes from a plant or an animal.

STEP 2

3. **Compare** Compare drawings with the other members of your group. Discuss how all the plant cells are similar. Discuss how all the animal cells are similar.

4. **Use Models** After you discuss the cells with your group, draw a diagram of a typical plant cell and a diagram of a typical animal cell.

Conclusion

1. **Communicate** Discuss how your diagrams of typical cells show the differences between plant and animal cells.

2. **Infer** Compare the outer boundaries of an animal cell and a plant cell. What differences between plants and animals do the cell boundaries help explain?

3. **Hypothesize** Do you think the cells of all plants and animals share the characteristics you identified? How could you test your hypothesis?

Investigate More!

Use Models Cells vary a great deal in size. Your cells are almost 100 times bigger than a bacteria cell. Build or draw a model to show the difference in size between a human and a bacteria cell.

VOCABULARY

cell	p. A6
nucleus	p. A8
organelle	p. A8

READING SKILL

Compare and Contrast
Use a Venn diagram to list similarities and differences between animal cells and plant cells.

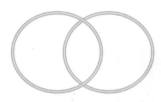

Year 1665 ▶
Hooke used a microscope to study thin slices of cork. He observed thin, boxy sections that he called cells.

Cells

MAIN IDEA Cells are the basic units of living things. Microscopes allow scientists to learn about the parts and functions of cells.

Building Blocks of Life

The basic unit that makes up living things is the **cell.** All living things, from tiny bacteria to the largest whale, are made of cells.

When you look at most living things, you cannot see individual cells. That is because most cells are much too small to be seen with the unaided eye. The invention of the microscope made it possible for scientists to discover cells and the structures within them.

In 1665, English scientist Robert Hooke studied a slice of cork under a microscope. He observed that cork was divided into many tiny, box-shaped sections. Hooke called these sections cells because they reminded him of the small rooms in which monks of the time lived.

All of Hooke's observations about cells involved the remains of dead cells. Dutch microscope maker Anton van Leeuwenhoek became the first person to observe living cells. He observed tiny living things within a drop of water.

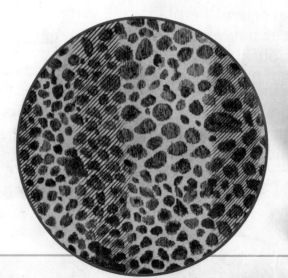

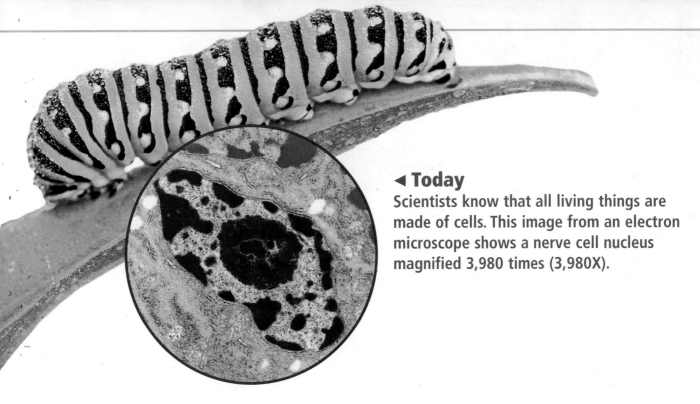

◀ Today
Scientists know that all living things are made of cells. This image from an electron microscope shows a nerve cell nucleus magnified 3,980 times (3,980X).

The Cell Theory

By using new and improved microscopes, scientists were able to observe cells in more detail. In 1838, German scientist Matthias Schleiden compared different plants and plant parts. He concluded that all plants are made of cells. Another scientist drew the same conclusion about animals. Twenty years later, German physician Rudolf Virchow reasoned that cells come only from other cells.

These conclusions were eventually organized into a single theory known as the cell theory. The theory states:

- All living things are made of one or more cells.
- The cell is the smallest unit of a living organism.
- Cells come from other cells.

Today, scientists continue to use new equipment and techniques to study cells. The additional evidence continues to support the cell theory.

Microscope Development

The earliest microscopes used a single lens to collect and focus light. In time, two lenses were combined to form a compound light microscope. Its magnifying power is the power of each lens multiplied together.

Modern light microscopes can magnify objects up to 2,000 times, or 2,000X. That's powerful enough to see not just cells, but structures within cells.

The electron microscope (EM) came into use during the 1930s. EMs use rapidly moving electrons instead of light to make images of objects. EMs may magnify objects 40,000X or more. Today, the scanning electron microscope (SEM) has taken this technology still further. SEMs allow scientists to study the three- dimensional structure of the surfaces of cells and other tiny things.

▶ **COMPARE AND CONTRAST** How does Hooke's microscope compare to microscopes today?

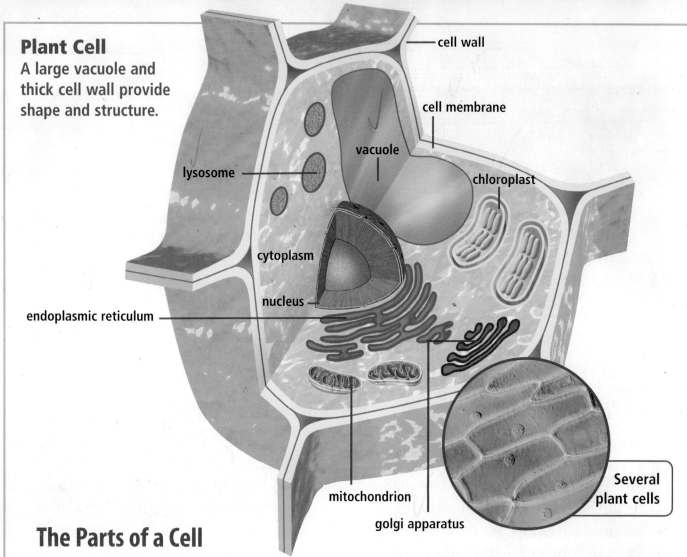

Plant Cell
A large vacuole and thick cell wall provide shape and structure.

cell wall

cell membrane

vacuole

chloroplast

lysosome

cytoplasm

nucleus

endoplasmic reticulum

mitochondrion

golgi apparatus

Several plant cells

The Parts of a Cell

Cells contain even smaller structures called **organelles.** These structures perform specific functions in the cell.

Animal cells and plant cells have many of the same organelles, but some are quite different. As you read through this section, refer to the organelle or cell part in the illustrations.

Nucleus The **nucleus** directs the activities of the cell. It stores a molecule called DNA, which determines an organism's traits. DNA stores genetic information, which is passed from parents to their offspring.

Cell Membrane The cell membrane is a thin, flexible covering that surrounds all types of cells. It allows food, water, and gases to enter the cell and wastes to leave.

Cell Wall In plant cells only, the cell wall is a rigid outer layer that surrounds the cell membrane. The cell wall protects the cell and helps the plant stand upright. Pores in the cell wall allow materials to pass in and out.

Cytoplasm Between the nucleus and the cell membrane is the cytoplasm. All of the remaining organelles are located within the cytoplasm. They are suspended there in a thick fluid.

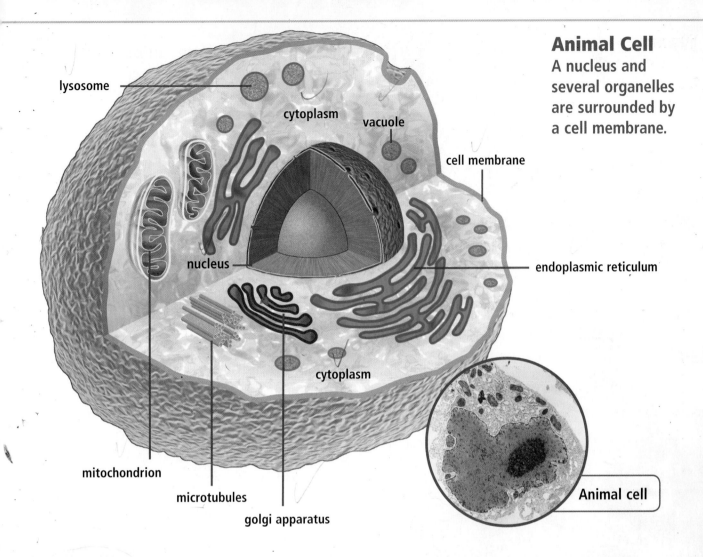

lysosome

cytoplasm

vacuole

cell membrane

nucleus

endoplasmic reticulum

cytoplasm

mitochondrion

microtubules

golgi apparatus

Animal cell

Ribosomes Tiny ribosomes are scattered throughout the cell. Unlike most other organelles, ribosomes are not surrounded by membranes. Ribosomes assemble compounds called proteins. Proteins make up the structural components of cells, and they allow the cell to perform nearly all chemical reactions.

Lysosomes Lysosomes are small, ball-shaped organelles that help the cell break down nutrients and old cell parts. Lysosomes are common in animal cells, but rare in plants.

Vacuoles Vacuoles are membrane-bound sacs that are filled with fluid. They store water, food, waste, and other substances the cell processes.

Animal cells may have small vacuoles. Plant cells, however, often have one large, central vacuole. When the vacuole in a plant cell is full, the cell is rigid. If the vacuoles in many cells lose water, the plant will wilt.

Golgi apparatus The Golgi apparatus receives proteins, then processes them for "shipment" outside the cell. This organelle is a system of membranes. It modifies and refines proteins, sometimes adding compounds that will protect them from being broken apart.

▶ **COMPARE AND CONTRAST** Describe differences between plant cells and animal cells.

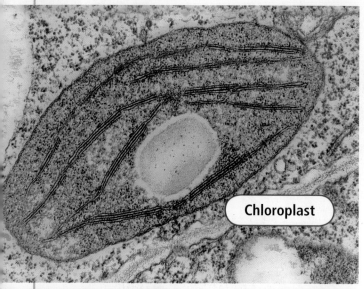

Chloroplast

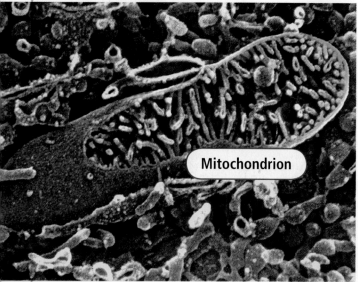

Mitochondrion

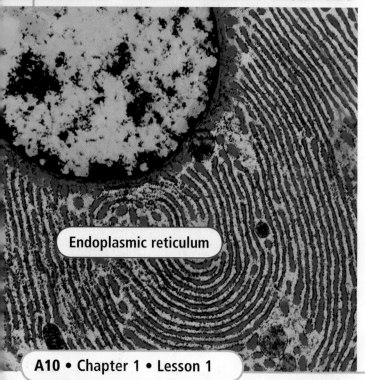

Endoplasmic reticulum

Chloroplasts Found only in plants and some protists, chloroplasts contain pigments that absorb sunlight. They use the energy to make food—a unique process among the organelles! The pigment chlorophyll gives plants their green color.

Mitochondria Large, peanut-shaped organelles, called mitochondria, are known as the "power plants" of the cell. Inside them, sugars break apart as they react with oxygen. The process releases carbon dioxide, water, and a lot of energy

In both plant and animal cells, the number of mitochondria depends on the amount of energy the cell needs. For example, a muscle cell requires a great deal of energy, and so it has a large number of mitochondria.

Endoplasmic reticulum The endoplasmic reticulum (ER) is a system of membranes and tubes. The membranes twist and turn through the cell, creating passages through which materials can pass.

A cell usually contains two kinds of ER, called rough and smooth. Rough ER is dotted with ribosomes. This type of ER is common in cells that secrete lots of proteins. Smooth ER is not covered by ribosomes. Its activities include breaking down toxic substances and controlling the levels of certain chemicals.

▶ **COMPARE AND CONTRAST** How is smooth ER different from rough ER?

Visual Summary

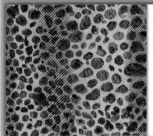

Cells were first discovered more than 300 years ago.

Microscopes allow scientists to look at and study cells.

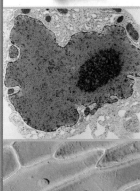

Cells contain smaller structures called organelles. Each performs a specific function.

Unlike animal cells, plant cells are surrounded by cell walls. They typically have a boxy shape.

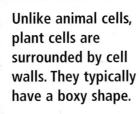

LINKS for Home and School

MATH **Make a Table** A picture from a microscope has a width of 8 cm. The power of the microscope is 100X. What is the width of the specimen that the picture shows?

TECHNOLOGY **Make a Diagram** Research the history and design of the light microscope, the electron microscope, and the scanning electron microscope. Choose one and create a diagram to show how it works.

Review

① MAIN IDEA What are the three main points of the cell theory?

② VOCABULARY Write a sentence using the terms *cell* and *nucleus.* Explain the role of the nucleus in the cell.

③ READING SKILL: Compare and Contrast How are the uses of a light microscope and a scanning electron microscope similar? How are they different?

④ CRITICAL THINKING: Evaluate How would you determine whether a cell came from an animal or a plant? Discuss cell parts in your answer.

⑤ INQUIRY SKILL: Communicate Write a paragraph explaining how a cell membrane is similar to a cell wall? How is it different?

✓ TEST PREP Which of these organelles is part of a plant cell but not an animal cell?

A. mitochondria

B. cell membrane

C. chloroplast

D. nucleus

 Technology
Visit **www.eduplace.com/scp/** to find out more about the parts of a cell.

A11

Lesson 2

How Do Single-Celled Organisms Live?

Why It Matters...

Single-celled organisms like this dinoflagellate produce much of the food and oxygen that sustain life on Earth. Other single-celled organisms are a major cause of disease.

PREPARE TO INVESTIGATE

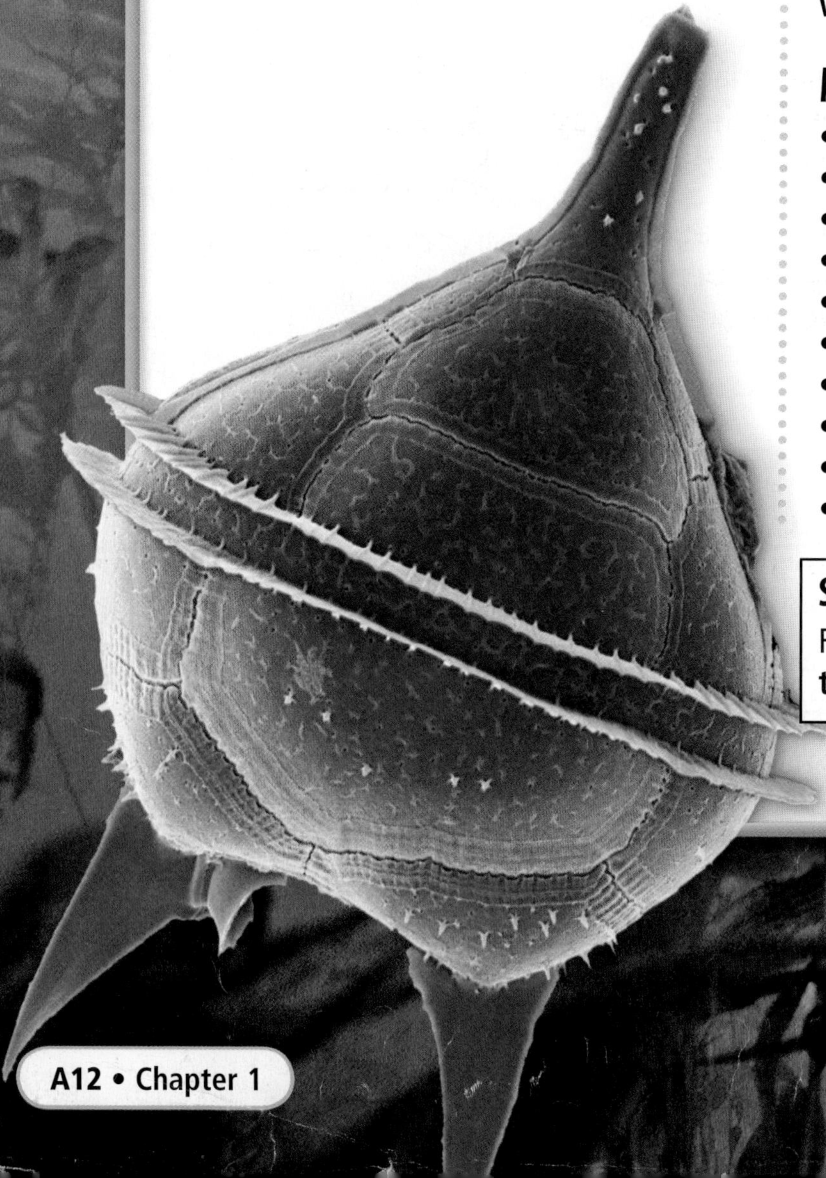

Inquiry Skill

Hypothesize When you hypothesize, you suggest a reason for what you have observed and describe how you will test your reasoning.

Materials

- measuring cup
- warm water
- cup or bowl
- teaspoon
- sugar
- packet of yeast
- 2 sealable plastic bags
- cafeteria tray
- paper towels
- lamp

Science and Math Toolbox
For step 1, review **Making a Chart to Organize Data** on page H11.

Watch Yeast Feast!

Procedure

1 **Collaborate** Work in a small group. In your *Science Notebook,* make a chart like the one shown.

2 **Experiment** Pour 3/4 cup of warm water (not hot) into a cup or bowl. Stir in 3 teaspoons (tsp.) of sugar and 1 tsp. of yeast. Pour the mixture into a sealable plastic bag. Squeeze out as much air as you can. Seal the bag completely. Rinse out the bowl.

3 **Experiment** Repeat Step 2 using a second bag, but this time do not include sugar.

4 **Experiment** Place both sealed bags on a tray lined with a paper towel. Set the tray on a shelf or tabletop under a lit lamp.

5 **Record Data** Check the bags at regular intervals over the next day. Record what you observe. Use either words or pictures to describe what you see.

Conclusion

1. **Compare** Describe how the contents of the two bags changed over time. Note important differences in the bags that you observed.

2. **Hypothesize** What do you think might have caused the effects you observed? Propose a hypothesis. Describe how you could test this hypothesis.

3. **Compare** Share your hypothesis with the class. Compare it with those of other students.

STEP 1

Time	Yeast + Water + Sugar	Yeast + Water
1 hour		
2 hours		
4 hours		
8 hours		
24 hours		

STEP 2

STEP 4

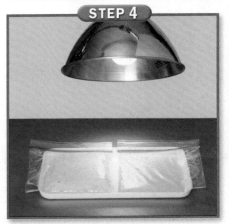

Investigate More!

Design an Experiment Do yeast grow better in warm or cold temperatures? Do they need light to grow? Design an experiment to answer a question about yeast growth.

VOCABULARY

cilia	p. A16
diffusion	p. A17
flagellum	p. A17
osmosis	p. A17

READING SKILL

Draw Conclusions Use a chart like the one shown to organize information about how single-celled organisms move. Then use the chart to draw conclusions.

Shape	Movement

Single-Celled Organisms

MAIN IDEA In single-celled organisms, all life processes are carried out in just one cell.

Life as a Single Cell

All living things have the same basic needs. They need to take in food and get rid of wastes. They need to digest nutrients so they can use and store energy. They also need to grow and reproduce. Single-celled organisms carry out all of their life processes within one cell.

Most single-celled organisms can be seen only with the aid of a microscope. For this reason, they are also known as microorganisms. Bacteria, amoebas, and paramecia are examples.

The photograph below shows a diatom, which also is made of one cell. The cell is housed inside a shell that it makes. Diatoms are classified as protists, a large and diverse group. Diatoms are an important food source for fish, whales, and other organisms that live in water.

When diatoms die, their shells do not break down. Instead, they eventually form a soft, chalky material. Deposits of this material are found all over the world. They are used as insulating products, cleaning products, and explosives. Much of Earth's petroleum came from diatoms.

◄ Diatoms
Diatoms live in fresh and salty water. Their shells are made of silica, which is like glass. Some diatoms may live together in a group called a colony.

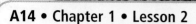

Interactions With Larger Organisms

Single-celled organisms are all around you! Sometimes their effects are helpful, while at other times they are harmful.

Bacteria, for example, do the important job of breaking down the remains of dead plants and animals. They return materials from dead organisms back to the environment, where new organisms can use them.

Bacteria also help produce and process some foods. Bacteria are used to produce yogurt, sour cream, and buttermilk, as well as cottage cheese, sauerkraut, and pickles. Did you know that helpful bacteria live inside you? In fact, your body needs certain bacteria to digest food properly and to make vitamins.

Bacteria can also be harmful. Strep throat, Lyme disease, and tuberculosis are just a few diseases that come from different bacterial infections. Other bacteria cause disease by producing poisons called toxins.

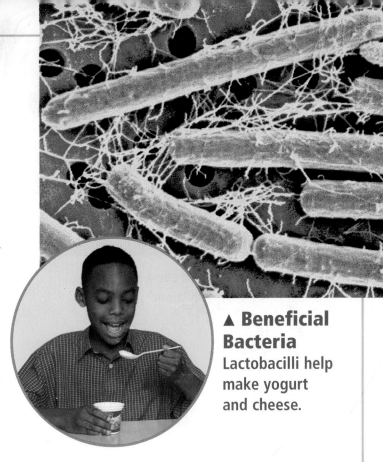

▲ **Beneficial Bacteria**
Lactobacilli help make yogurt and cheese.

Antibiotics are drugs that treat bacterial infections. They interfere with the life processes of the bacteria while not harming human cells.

Many algae are also single-celled organisms. Like plants cells, algae can make their own food using energy from the Sun. In the process, they give off oxygen. Much of the oxygen in the air comes from algae in the oceans. Algae are also a food source for many ocean animals.

Yeasts are another type of single-celled organism. Yeasts are used to make bread, vinegar, and ethanol, an important gasoline additive. Of the roughly 600 different types of yeasts, a few cause diseases in plants, animals, and humans.

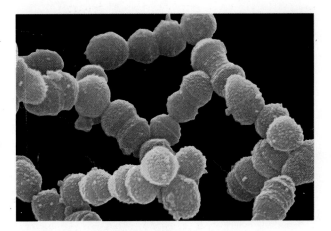

▲ **Harmful Bacteria**
These streptococci can cause illnesses such as strep throat.

▶ **DRAW CONCLUSIONS** Why are bacteria important for all living things?

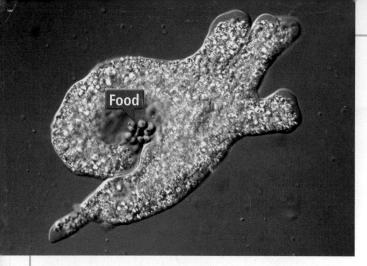

Food

▲ An amoeba takes in food by surrounding it with a membrane sac.

Getting Food

All organisms need energy. Some, like plants, make their own food. Others take in or eat food from the outside.

Single-celled organisms get food in different ways. For example, an amoeba stretches its membrane into arms that surround a food particle. As it closes in, the membrane forms a sac, or vacuole, around the food. Food is digested in the vacuole, then absorbed into the cytoplasm.

Undigested food particles are moved to the cell membrane. These wastes are washed away as the amoeba moves through the water.

A paramecium gets food very differently. Its body has a funnel called an oral groove. Small hairs called **cilia** surround the opening to the groove. The cilia move back and forth, sweeping food particles inside.

At the bottom of the oral groove, a membrane expands to form a vacuole around the food. When the vacuole breaks off, food is carried throughout the cell.

After it delivers food, the vacuole collects waste products. It then returns to the cell membrane and releases the wastes outside the cell.

The cilia of a paramecium sweep food particles toward the oral groove on the outer surface of the cell. ▼

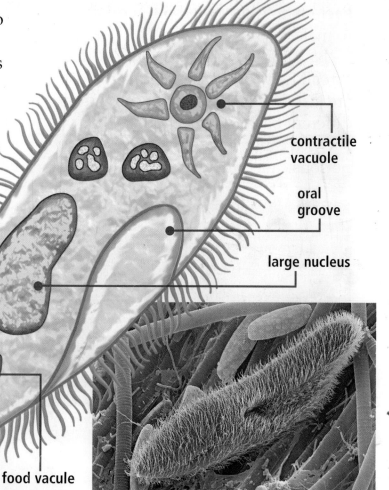

contractile vacuole

oral groove

large nucleus

cell membrane

cilia

food vacule

Diffusion

Some materials move directly through the organism's cell membrane. One way this occurs is by **diffusion.** Diffusion is the movement of particles from an area of higher concentration to an area of lower concentration. This means that particles travel from areas where they are crowded to areas where they are less crowded.

One of the most important substances that passes through the cell membrane is water. Diffusion in which water passes through the cell membrane is called **osmosis.**

Sometimes, osmosis alone is not enough to control the flow of water into or out of a cell. If too much water flows into a cell, the cell will swell. This can damage or kill the cell.

As a result, some single-celled organisms also use vacuoles to remove excess water. In an amoeba, large vacuoles release water through the cell membrane.

In a paramecium, small channels direct excess water into a contractile vacuole. When the vacuole is full, it pumps water out the cell membrane.

Diffusion and osmosis help explain why cells have such small sizes. To stay alive, cells need food, gases, and other materials that diffuse through the cell membrane. Yet beyond a certain cell size, diffusion could not take place fast enough. The area of the cell membrane would be too small to supply the cell's larger volume.

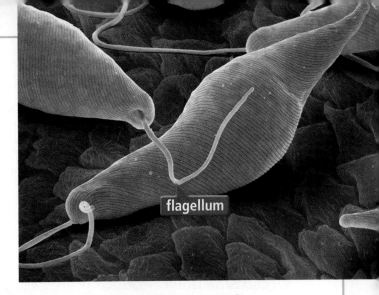
flagellum

▲ Most euglena are green, single-celled organisms that live in ponds. They swim by spinning their long whip-like structures, called flagella.

Movement

Some single-celled organisms are able to move from place to place, much like animals do. Movement enables an organism to find food and shelter, or to escape predators. The amoeba moves by pushing its membrane forward. This creates a pseudopod, or "false foot."

The paramecium moves by using cilia. The cilia beat back and forth like oars on a boat.

Another single-celled organism, the euglena, has a long structure that acts like a whip. The structure is called a **flagellum.** It spins like the propeller of a boat.

▶ **DRAW CONCLUSIONS** Why do amoebas and paramecia need moving parts?

Binary Fission

Bacteria reproduce through fission.

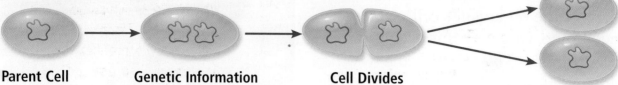

Parent Cell   Genetic Information Copied   Cell Divides   Two Identical Cells

Reproduction

Organisms must produce more of their kind if the species is to survive. The process is called reproduction. Single-celled organisms reproduce in different ways.

One very simple type of reproduction is called binary fission. A bacterial cell reproduces in this way. Recall that a cell contains genetic information that is transferred from one generation to the next. Before it divides, the parent cell makes a copy of its genetic information.

Once the cell grows longer and its genetic information is copied, the cell pinches in the middle. The two sections break apart to form two new cells. The genetic information in each cell is the same so both cells will have the same exact traits.

Budding is another form of reproduction. In budding, a small knob, or bud, forms on the parent cell. The bud contains the same genetic information as the parent cell. When the bud grows to the size of the parent cell, it breaks off. The new cell is identical to the parent. Many yeast cells reproduce through budding.

Binary fission and budding are forms of asexual reproduction. Only one parent is involved in this type of reproduction. The offspring of asexual reproduction are identical to the parent.

Some single-celled organisms can also reproduce through sexual reproduction. Two parent cells are involved in this type of reproduction. The offspring have a combination of traits from both parents. Depending on their environment, yeast and algae switch between these types of reproduction.

▶ **DRAW CONCLUSIONS** How do yeast and bacteria reproduce?

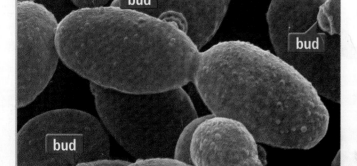

bud

bud

bud

◀ **Budding**
Yeast is just one of the single-celled organisms that reproduce by forming buds and branches.

Visual Summary

Bacteria are single-celled organisms. They can be harmful or beneficial.

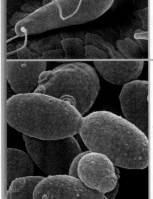

To stay alive, single-celled organisms take in food and other materials. Many move from place to place.

Some single-celled organisms reproduce through binary fission, and others reproduce through budding.

LINKS for Home and School

MATH **Make a Graph** Suppose you have one amoeba that reproduces every hour, as do all its offspring. Draw a graph to show the population growth over five hours. Assume that no amoebas die. Do you think such growth could continue without end?

WRITING **Expository** Research a harmful or beneficial bacteria species, such as one described in this lesson. Write a report about the effects of the species on people's lives. Do the bacteria affect your life? If so, how?

Review

1 MAIN IDEA Which needs do single-celled organisms have in common with organisms that have more than one cell?

2 VOCABULARY Write a sentence or short paragraph using the terms *diffusion* and *osmosis*.

3 READING SKILL: Draw Conclusions Suppose you discover a microbe that has both cilia and a flagellum. What might you conclude about the purpose of the cilia?

4 CRITICAL THINKING: Apply What might happen if you take a medicine that is strong enough to kill almost all of the bacteria in your body?

5 INQUIRY SKILL: Hypothesize Do yeast need air to grow? Propose a hypothesis to answer this question. Describe an experiment to test it.

 TEST PREP

Single-celled organisms use flagella, cilia, or pseudopods to

A. move from place to place.

B. break down food.

C. reproduce.

D. pump out water.

 Technology
Visit **www.eduplace.com/scp/** to find out more about single-celled organisms.

Louis Pasteur

What causes food to spoil? Two hundred years ago, people believed that tiny living things arose from the food. This idea was called spontaneous generation. It meant that life could assemble itself from nonliving parts.

French scientist Louis Pasteur (1822–1899) argued that microorganisms came only from their own kind, just as larger organisms do. He proved the case against spontaneous generation with the experiment shown to the right.

How can spoilage be stopped? Pasteur found that heating beverages kills or slows the tiny creatures inside them, a process now called pasteurization in his honor. Pasteur also identified bacteria and viruses that cause human diseases, and suggested ways to prevent infections. In Pasteur's time, the typical surgeon might not even wash his hands!

Pasteur's Proof Against Spontaneous Generation

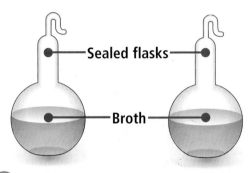

1 Pasteur prepared two sealed flasks, each holding clear broth. He boiled the broth to kill bacteria in them.

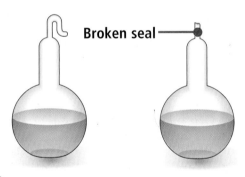

2 After a few days, the broth remains clear in both flasks. Pasteur breaks the seal of one flask.

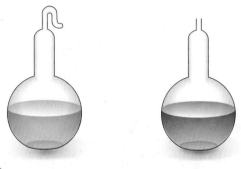

3 Days later, the broth in the sealed flask remains clear. The broth in the unsealed flask becomes brown and cloudy.

◀ Pasteur's experiment shows that the bacteria that clouded the broth must have come from the air, not the broth itself.

▲ At a pasteurization plant, milk is heated in large vats. The temperature is high enough to kill bacteria, but not too high to damage the milk.

Pasteurization helps protect milk from bacteria.

Sharing Ideas

1. **READING CHECK** According to the idea of spontaneous generation, why does food spoil? Is this explanation correct?

2. **WRITE ABOUT IT** Describe pasteurization.

3. **TALK ABOUT IT** Compare physicians' approaches to cleanliness in Pasteur's time and today.

How Do the Cells of Organisms Compare?

Why It Matters...

By comparing organisms, scientists learn more about them. Comparing and classifying organisms also helps scientists understand and make accurate predictions about newly-discovered life forms.

PREPARE TO INVESTIGATE

Inquiry Skill

Classify When you classify, you group objects by their characteristics.

Materials

- index cards
- colored pencils or markers

Science and Math Toolbox

For step 1, review **Making a Chart to Organize Data** on page H11.

Sort What You See

Procedure

STEP 1

Organism	What does it look like?	What does it do?

1 **Collaborate** Work in a small group. In your *Science Notebook*, list 15 different living organisms.

2 **Use Models** Write the name of each organism on a separate index card. Include a drawing or photo of the organism on the card.

3 **Classify** Group the index cards according to common characteristics of the organisms. Name and describe each group.

Mushroom

Flower

Frog

Conclusion

1. **Analyze Data** With your group, create a chart or diagram that shows your classification scheme.

2. **Compare** Share your classifications with another group. How is their classification scheme different from yours?

3. **Classify** Work with your group and reclassify the living organisms. Chose a different characteristic to classify them by.

Investigate More!

Research Use the Internet or books at the library to research other organisms, perhaps some you have never seen before. How do these organisms fit into your classification scheme?

VOCABULARY

fungi	p. A26
kingdom	p. A24
protist	p. A25

READING SKILL

Classify Use a chart to organize and classify information about organisms.

Classifying Living Things

MAIN IDEA Scientists classify living things by comparing and contrasting their physical characteristics.

Six Kingdoms

You probably sort your clothes into separate groups. Perhaps you put socks in one drawer and shirts in another. You might also sort books, magazines, or CDs. The process of sorting things by how they are alike and how they are different is known as classification.

Scientists use a system of classification to sort living things. Originally, people sorted living things into two groups—plants and animals. The differences between the two groups seemed clear. Animals could move around, whereas plants could not. The two groups reproduced in different ways and usually looked quite different from each other.

Once the microscope was invented, however, classification became more complicated. As scientists quickly discovered, many tiny organisms had some traits of plants and some traits of animals. Their cells did not exactly match either of the cells you explored in Lesson 1.

Today, most scientists recognize six **kingdoms** of living things. A kingdom is a large group into which organisms are organized according to their traits. Three of the six kingdoms are made up mostly of organisms that are microscopic!

◀ In this picture, you can see organisms from the animal (squirrel), plant (moss), and fungi (mushroom) kingdoms. You can't see the protists or the bacteria, but they're there!

Kingdoms of Life

Kingdom	Cell characteristics	Other characteristics
Bacteria (two kingdoms)	single-celled	• live alone or in colonies • cannot move independently • lack a nucleus
Protists	mostly single-celled	• live alone or in colonies • some can move independently, some cannot • some must find food, some make food
Fungi	mostly multi-celled	• live alone or in colonies • do not move independently • feed on decaying matter or living organisms
Plant	multi-celled	• specialized cells • do not move from place to place • produce food using sunlight
Animals	multi-celled	• specialized cells organized into complex systems • can move independently • feed on all other kingdoms

Bacteria

Earth is home to a huge number of bacteria. The cells of bacteria are described as prokaryotic. This means that they do not contain a nucleus or organelles surrounded by membranes.

There are two bacteria kingdoms: eubacteria and archaebacteria. Most of the bacteria that affect you are eubacteria. Archaebacteria are usually found in harsh environments, such as hot vents along the ocean floor, salty lakes, and hot springs.

Protists

Most **protists** are microscopic, single-celled organisms. Unlike bacteria, however, protist cells are eukaryotic. This means they have a nucleus and membrane-bound organelles. The cells of a few protists have a cell wall. Some protists can make their own food.

The protist kingdom includes protozoa (such as amoebas and paramecia), most types of algae (including diatoms and seaweed), and slime molds. Protists may be the most diverse kingdom.

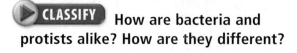 **CLASSIFY** How are bacteria and protists alike? How are they different?

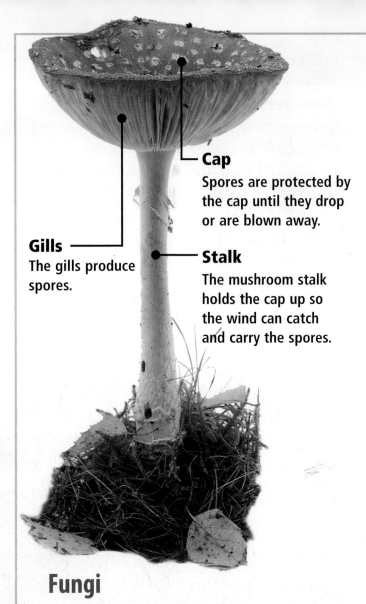

Cap
Spores are protected by the cap until they drop or are blown away.

Gills
The gills produce spores.

Stalk
The mushroom stalk holds the cap up so the wind can catch and carry the spores.

Fungi

Most organisms in the fungi kingdom are multicellular, which means they consist of more than one cell. **Fungi** absorb food, and they help break down dead plant and animal matter. Their cells have organelles and a nucleus, which makes them eukaryotic cells. Like plant cells, they also have cell walls, but they do not have chloroplasts.

Fungi range in size from microscopic yeast to larger varieties. You might see shelf fungi on tree branches. Fungi include yeasts, molds, mildews, rusts, and mushrooms.

Some fungi are harmful. They cause disease and spoil food. Other fungi are used as foods or to make foods and medicines. Fungi do an important job in nature by breaking down once-living matter. In this way, fungi recycle materials and enrich the soil.

Mushrooms develop from tiny spores that are small enough to be spread by the wind. The spores become buried under leaves or soil. There they grow into long, branching structures called filaments.

As the filaments gather nutrients from the soil, a button appears above the ground. This button grows into a full mushroom with a stalk and a cap at the top. The smooth top of the cap protects the gills underneath.

The gills release spores when the mushroom is full grown. The wind blows the spores away and the process begins all over again.

▼ Some mushrooms, like this morel, are edible. Others contain deadly toxins. Only an expert should pick wild mushrooms!

▲ Mosses are among the simplest and smallest plants. They live in moist places, usually down along the ground.

Plants

Plants are complex, multicellular organisms. They vary in size from the tiniest mosses to the tallest trees. As you learned earlier, plant cells contain a nucleus and organelles. This makes plant cells eukaryotic cells.

The characteristic that almost all plants have in common is the ability to use sunlight to make food. This process is called photosynthesis. In this process, organelles called chloroplasts absorb energy from sunlight. Plants use that energy to convert carbon dioxide and water into sugar and oxygen.

Plants, and the animals that eat them, use the energy stored in the sugar to carry out their life processes. So, when you eat plants, you are gaining energy that was stored during photosynthesis.

In addition, all animals depend on the oxygen that plants produce in order to survive. When you breathe, you take in oxygen and release carbon dioxide. Plants take in the carbon dioxide you release and produce more oxygen that you need. Plants are an essential part of this cycle.

In addition to containing chloroplasts, plant cells have other characteristics that make them different from organisms in other kingdoms. Recall that plant cells have a cell wall and a large, central vacuole. These structures provide strength and support, and they allow plants to grow much taller than protists or fungi.

▶ **CLASSIFY** What are three structures that can be found in plant cells?

▲ Baobab trees can live for several thousand years. These live on the island of Madagascar.

A27

Animals

Look in the mirror and you will see an organism from the animal kingdom. It's you! Animals range in size from almost microscopic insects to gigantic whales.

Animals are complex, multicellular organisms. Most animals can move independently, at least at some point in their lives. All respond to stimuli, such as touch or the smell of food. Unlike plants, animals cannot make their own food, because their cells lack chloroplasts. Animals get food by eating other organisms.

Scientists divide the animal kingdom into smaller groups in many different ways. One way is by separating animals that have internal skeletons from animals that do not.

Animals that do not have internal skeletons or a backbone are called invertebrates. They include insects, clams, worms, snails, and crabs. To support their bodies, invertebrates have strong muscles or thick outer coverings.

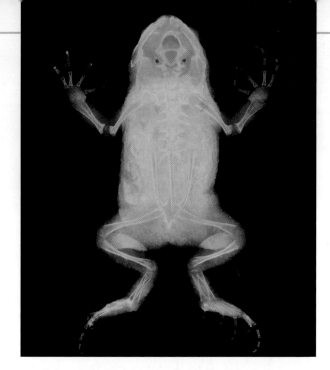

▲ Internal skeletons allow vertebrates to support larger, more complex internal organs.

Animals that have internal skeletons and backbones are called vertebrates. They include fish, frogs, snakes, birds, and horses. Humans are vertebrates as well. An internal skeleton gives support to an animal and protects its internal organs.

Vertebrates are the largest animals. They are not, however, the most numerous. Most animals are invertebrates. In fact, about 99 out of every 100 animals are invertebrates. Why do you think this is so?

▶ **CLASSIFY** In what ways are invertebrates and vertebrates alike and different?

◀ Invertebrates, such as this sea slug, do not have a backbone or an internal skeleton.

Lesson Wrap-Up

Visual Summary

```
                Kingdoms of Life

        prokaryotes          eukaryotes
         (bacteria)

    archaebacteria    eubacteria

  protists    fungi     plants     animals

                    invertebrates    vertebrates
```

 **LINKS** for Home and School

ART **Create a Poster** Research one vertebrate group such as amphibians, fish, reptiles, birds, or mammals. Make a poster that shows the unique characteristics of the group.

WRITING **Poetry** Write a poem about one of the kingdoms of living things. Include facts about the kingdom in the poem.

Review

1 **MAIN IDEA** What are the six kingdoms into which living things are classified?

2 **VOCABULARY** Define the term *kingdom.* Describe how scientists use kingdoms to classify living things.

3 **READING SKILL:** **Classify** How do fungi cells differ from plant cells? How are they alike?

4 **CRITICAL THINKING:** **Apply** List two ways in which animals and plants differ from one another. Relate these differences to the cells of plants and animals.

5 **INQUIRY SKILL:** **Classify** Explain why scientists use cell structure to classify living things.

 TEST PREP Which kingdom is made mostly of single-celled eukaryotes?

  A. eubacteria

  B. archaebacteria

  C. protists

  D. fungi

 Technology Visit **www.eduplace.com/scp/** to find out more about classifying organisms.

How Are Cells Organized?

Why It Matters...

How are you able to digest food, or move from place to place? How are you able to catch a baseball, or dance in time to music, or solve a math problem? In humans and other multicellular organisms, cell organization makes all the processes of life happen.

PREPARE TO INVESTIGATE

Inquiry Skill

Ask Questions Scientists ask questions about organisms, objects, and events. Science inquiry helps test the answers.

Materials

- microscope
- prepared slides of various animal tissues

Science and Math Toolbox

For step 2, review **Using a Microscope** on page H2.

Exploring Tissues

Procedure

1. **Collaborate** Work in a small group. In your *Science Notebook,* draw a chart like the one shown. Use the chart to record your observations of different types of tissues.

2. **Observe** Take turns looking through the microscope at each type of tissue.

3. **Record Data** Record your observations by drawing one cell in the tissue. Then draw several cells, showing how they are arranged.

4. **Communicate** With the group, discuss the function of each type of tissue you studied. What part of the body did the tissue come from? What was the shape of the cells in the tissue?

Conclusion

1. **Analyze Data** How do all the cells in a single kind of tissue compare?

2. **Infer** What can you infer about the functions of all the cells in one kind of tissue? How would you define *tissue?*

3. **Draw Conclusions** Humans and other animals have a wide variety of tissues in their bodies. What advantage does this variety provide?

STEP 1

Slide Number	Type of Tissue	Observations

STEP 2

Investigate More!

Ask Questions You have seen several examples of animal tissues. Make a list of questions you have about what you saw. Share your list with your class. Choose one question to find the answer to in this book, the library, or on the Internet.

Cell Organization

MAIN IDEA Cells join together to perform basic life functions in multicellular organisms.

VOCABULARY

organ	p. A33
organ system	p. A33
tissue	p. A33

READING SKILL

Main Idea and Details
Use a graphic organizer like the one shown to organize the main idea and details.

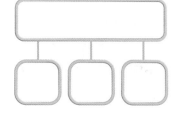

Multicellular Organisms

Unlike a single-celled organism, a multicellular organism is made up of more than one cell. In these organisms the cells work together to perform life processes. The cells are specialized, which means that they perform only certain functions. By working together, these cells meet the needs of the organism as a whole.

Cells come in many shapes and sizes. The shape of a cell often relates to its function. Nerve cells, for example, are long and have many branches. This shape allows them to deliver electrical impulses over long distances. Skin cells are generally flat and arranged close together. In this way, they form a protective layer around the body. Muscle cells are larger than other cells. Their many fibers can contract and relax to cause movement.

Cells in multicellular organisms are organized at different levels. First, they are organized into

In most multicellular organisms, cells are organized as the chart shows. ▼

Cells → Tissues → Organs → Organ Systems → Organism

Relaxed

Contracted

▲ **Cell**
Long, thin filaments allow muscle cells to contract and relax.

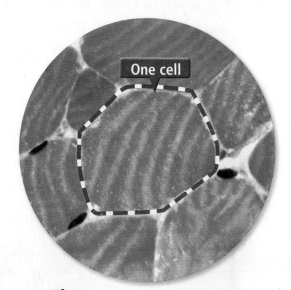

One cell

▲ **Tissue**
Muscle cells are bundled to create a strong, contracting tissue.

tissues. A **tissue** is a large group of similar specialized cells. Muscle tissue, for example, consists of long bundles of muscle cells. Each bundle of muscle tissue is held together by its own covering. Like their component cells, muscle tissues contract and relax.

Similarly, nerve cells form nerve tissue, bone cells form bone tissue, and skin cells form the tissues of the skin. A tissue gets its characteristics from the particular type of specialized cell that forms it.

Together, tissues of different types make up organs. An **organ** is a group of related tissues that perform a specific function. The heart, brain, stomach, and liver are examples of organs.

Even if two organs are made from the same kind of tissue, they can be very different in appearance and function. For example, bones in the middle ear look and function much differently from the bones in arms and legs.

Organs are organized into organ systems. An **organ system** is a group of related organs that work together to perform a specific function. Most multicellular organisms have several organ systems.

Organ systems combine to form the entire organism. On the next pages, you will read about different organ systems in humans. They work together to keep you alive and healthy.

Plants have organs and organ systems, too. Roots, stems, leaves, and fruits are organs of a plant. Specialized tubes that run through a plant form an organ system called the vascular system.

 **MAIN IDEA** What is an organ system?

Organism
The muscular system works with other systems to help the girl live and grow.

Organ System
All of the skeletal muscles make up a complex system that moves the body.

Organs
Muscle tissues make up organs called muscles, which pull bones and other parts of the body.

Circulatory System

The circulatory system is responsible for bringing oxygen and nutrients to all the cells of an animal's body. It also takes carbon dioxide and wastes away from the cells.

The heart is the central organ of the circulatory system. The heart is made of muscle tissue that pumps blood. The blood travels to the rest of the body through a network of arteries, veins, and capillaries.

Arteries carry blood away from the heart, while veins carry blood back to the heart. Capillaries are tiny tubes that connect arteries to veins. The capillaries are thin enough to let gases, nutrients, and wastes pass between the blood and body cells.

In humans, the heart is divided into four sections, or chambers. Veins from the body drain into the right atrium. The blood passes to the right ventricle, which pumps it to the lungs. There, the blood takes in oxygen and releases carbon dioxide.

The blood returns to the heart through the left atrium, then passes to the left ventricle. The left ventricle is the largest and thickest chamber. It pumps blood into the arteries that travel to all parts of the body.

Most animals have some type of heart and circulatory system, but the structure can vary. A frog's heart, for example, has three chambers instead of four. Fish hearts have only two chambers. An earthworm has five hearts, each with only one chamber.

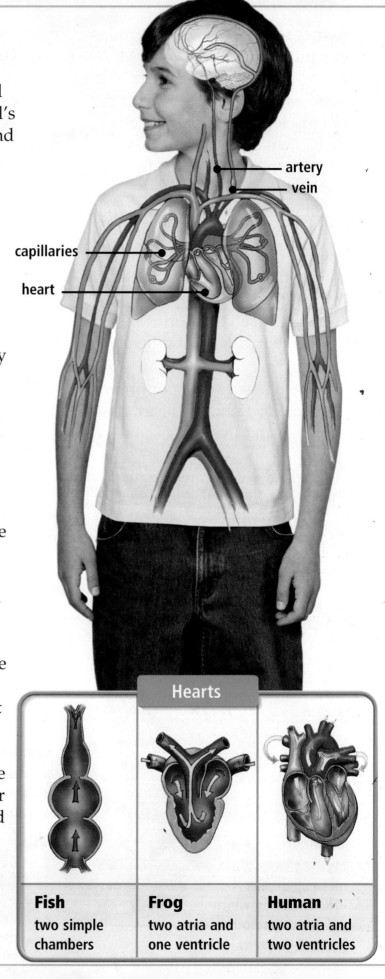

artery

vein

capillaries

heart

Hearts

Fish	**Frog**	**Human**
two simple chambers	two atria and one ventricle	two atria and two ventricles

Respiratory System

The respiratory system brings oxygen to the blood, and removes carbon dioxide from it. In humans and other land animals, the central organs are the lungs.

When you inhale, air is brought into the lungs through two tubes called bronchi (singular: bronchus). Each bronchus branches into smaller and smaller tubes. The smallest tubes lead to grapelike sacs called alveoli (singular: alveolus).

The alveoli are surrounded by capillaries. Oxygen passes from the alveoli into the blood, while carbon dioxide passes from the blood into the alveoli.

Air moves in and out of the lungs so well because of the changing size of the chest. When you inhale, muscles attached to your ribs tighten and pull upward. The diaphragm, which is located at the bottom of your chest, contracts and pulls downward. These actions expand your chest, making more space. Air flows into your body as a result.

The opposite process occurs when you exhale. When the chest muscles and diaphragm relax, the space in the chest decreases. This forces air out of your body.

All animals need oxygen, so all animals have some sort of respiratory system. Insects take in air through tiny holes in the exoskeleton called spiracles. Fish take in oxygen through organs called gills.

▶ **MAIN IDEA** How do the respiratory system and circulatory system work together?

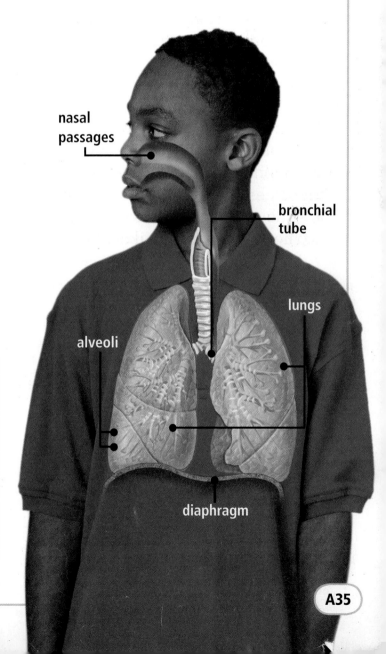

nasal passages

bronchial tube

lungs

alveoli

diaphragm

Respiratory Systems

Caterpillar
Insects let in air through holes called spiracles.

spiracles

Fish
Fish breathe through organs called gills.

gill

A35

Digestive System

Your body cannot use the foods you eat in their original forms. Instead, they must be broken down. The digestive system breaks down food into simpler substances.

Digestion begins in the mouth. There, food is chewed and mixed with a fluid called saliva. The chewed food then passes into the esophagus and on to the stomach.

When food enters the stomach, cells release gastric fluids that break down the food further. At the same time, the stomach muscles contract to mix and grind the food. Food then passes into the small intestine.

Chemicals from the liver and the pancreas enter the first part of the small intestine, where they break down food even further. Cells in the lining of the small intestine produce additional chemicals that complete the digestion process.

The small intestine is lined with millions of tiny, fingerlike projections called villi (singular: villus). Nutrients from the digested food pass from villi into the blood.

Undigested food, along with water, mucus, and other substances, pass to the large intestine. The large intestine absorbs most of the remaining water. In addition, bacteria in the large intestine make substances the body can use, such as vitamins K and B. Any remaining material leaves the body as waste.

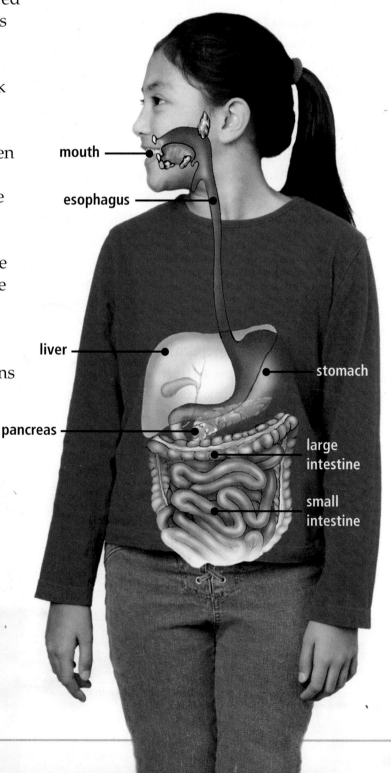

mouth

esophagus

liver

stomach

pancreas

large intestine

small intestine

Small Intestines

Mammal	Length
Horse	21 meters
Cat	1.7 meters
Human	7 meters

Nervous System

Have you ever used your big toe to test the temperature of bath water? In such a case, the toe sends a message up to the brain. The brain interprets the message, then sends a new message to muscles in the arms and hands to adjust the hot or cold water tap!

Your nervous system takes actions like this all the time. It receives and processes information, and it controls how the body reacts and moves.

The nervous system is made of specialized cells called neurons. Neurons receive and send information in the form of electrical impulses. In some ways, neurons act like electric wires, although the impulse they carry are very different from electricity.

The brain is the central organ of the nervous system. The human brain is composed of more than 100 billion neurons! Individually, those neurons do very little. Yet working together, they allow your brain to think, remember, learn, interpret information from the senses, and control movement of your body.

Extending down from the brain is a thick cord of nerve cells called the spinal cord. Nerves fan out from this cord to the rest of the body. The spinal cord is protected by a thick series of bones called vertebrae. These bones make up your backbone.

▶ **MAIN IDEA** What are the important functions of the human brain?

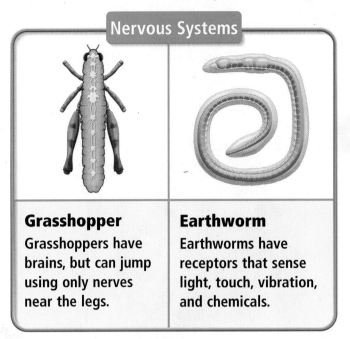

Nervous Systems

Grasshopper
Grasshoppers have brains, but can jump using only nerves near the legs.

Earthworm
Earthworms have receptors that sense light, touch, vibration, and chemicals.

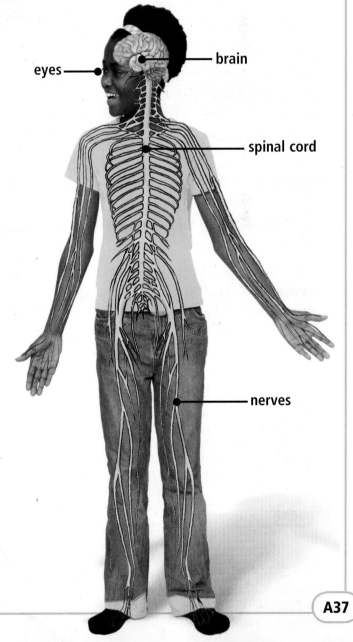

eyes

brain

spinal cord

nerves

skull

joint

bone

cartilage

spinal column

muscle

tendon

Muscular and Skeletal Systems

The muscular system of the human body has three types of muscle tissue:

Smooth Smooth muscles look smooth under a microscope. They are also called involuntary muscles because they contract without your conscious control. Smooth muscles control breathing, blood pressure, and movements in the digestive system.

Cardiac Cardiac muscle is found only in the heart, where it makes the heart beat. Like smooth muscle, cardiac muscle is involuntary.

Skeletal Skeletal muscles, also called voluntary muscles, are attached to the bones. They pull on bones and move them. Skeletal muscles also help shape the body and protect its internal organs.

Bones are held together by stringy tissues called ligaments, and they are attached to muscles by tough tissues called tendons. Bones, ligaments, and tendons make up the skeletal system.

The skeletal system provides shape and support, protects tissues and organs, and lets the body move. In addition, blood cells are made inside many bones.

Vertebrates have an internal skeleton and a backbone. Many invertebrates have hard external skeletons called exoskeletons.

◄ A hard exoskeleton covers this ghost crab.

Endocrine and Excretory Systems

The rush of energy you feel when you are frightened or excited is produced by the endocrine system. The endocrine system consists of glands. A gland is an organ that sends chemical messengers called hormones to other parts of the body.

Hormones affect the activity of cells far from where they are produced. They diffuse into the blood and are carried to where they are needed. The body produces many types of hormones. Each one acts on a specific type of cell.

Endocrine glands are located throughout the body. The thyroid gland, which is located in the neck region, controls the body's metabolism, or how cells provide energy. The adrenal glands, which are located above each kidney, are involved in the body's reaction to dangerous or frightening situations. And the pancreas, which is in the abdomen, maintains blood sugar levels.

The excretory system is responsible for removing wastes from the body and maintaining the body's water balance. Recall that undigested food is removed from the large intestine. It is the excretory system that takes over from the digestive system and flushes the waste from the digestive tract.

The kidneys are another important part of the excretory system. They are bean-shaped organs located near the middle of the back. As blood passes through the kidneys, waste and excess water are filtered out of it. They then travel from the kidneys to the bladder and then out of the body.

The excretory system plays a very important role. Without it, wastes would quickly poison the body.

▶ MAIN IDEA **What is the role of the excretory system?**

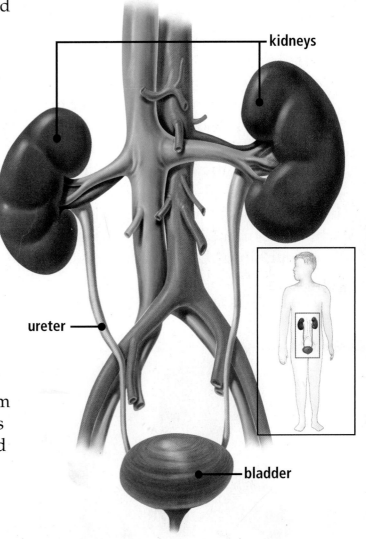

kidneys

ureter

bladder

Excretory System
The excretory system is responsible for ridding the body of waste.

Other Systems

The human body contains other organ systems as well. For example, the lymphatic system circulates a fluid called lymph. This helps keep tissues free of excess fluid.

The integumentary system includes the skin, fingernails and hair. The skin has inner and outer layers of specialized tissues.

The immune system defends the body from bacteria and other disease-causing agents. It produces antibodies and distributes them through the blood. Antibodies are proteins that help fight disease.

All body systems work together in many ways. When you exercise, for example, your nerves and muscles work together to move your skeletal system. Nerves also increase your heart rate and slow your digestion, while a hormone helps move sugar into your blood. Usually, all of this happens without you even realizing it. The body is an amazing machine!

Doctors use x-ray images to view some organs. ▶

Keeping Healthy

You can follow many simple steps to stay healthy. To kill harmful bacteria, wash your hands often. Always cover your mouth and nose when coughing and sneezing. This will help stop the spread of harmful microorganisms.

Eating fresh foods that are rich in vitamins gives cells the nutrients they need. Refusing to smoke or take drugs keeps cells strong so that they can resist infection. Exercising keeps muscles flexible. Exercise also helps you breathe more deeply and your body work efficiently.

▶ **MAIN IDEA** **What is the function of antibodies?**

Types of Doctors	
Speciality	**Responsibilities**
Pediatrician	• cares for young people • administers vaccinations • treats illnesses
Dermatologist	• cares for the skin • treats skin conditions, such as acne
Orthopedist	• cares for bones, joints, and their related muscles • treats injuries and disease
Ophthalmologist	• cares for the eyes • checks vision • treats diseases of the eye

Visual Summary

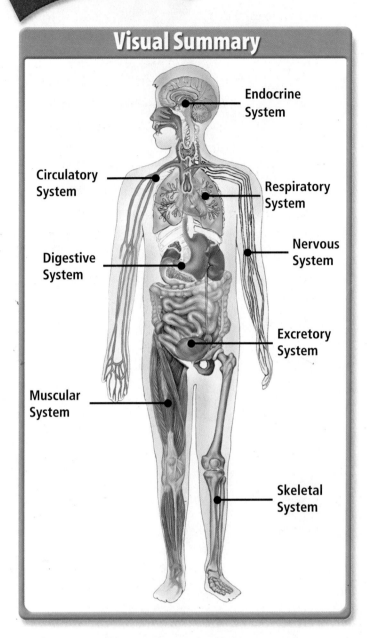

Endocrine System

Circulatory System

Respiratory System

Nervous System

Digestive System

Muscular System

Excretory System

Skeletal System

LINKS for Home and School

MATH **Make a Graph** Research the average body length of horses, cats, and humans. Make a bar graph to compare body lengths to the lengths of the small intestine, listed on p. A36.

HEALTH **Write a Report** Research one of the human organ systems covered in this lesson. Write a report on common diseases that affect the system. Share your findings with the class.

Review

❶ MAIN IDEA What processes take place in the capillaries?

❷ VOCABULARY Write a sentence or short paragraph using the terms *tissue* and *organ*.

❸ READING SKILLS: Main Idea and Details Choose two human body organ systems. Describe the main function of each.

❹ CRITICAL THINKING: Apply How are vertebrates and invertebrates different from each other?

❺ INQUIRY SKILL: Ask Questions Give examples of questions that scientists might ask about a cell, a tissue, an organ, an organ system, and an organism.

✔ TEST PREP

A major organ of the nervous system is the

A. stomach.

B. brain.

C. kidney.

D. lung.

 Technology

Visit **www.eduplace.com/scp/** to find out more about cell organization.

Cells in Glass Houses

Did you brush your teeth with fossils today? If you used toothpaste, you probably did! Fossil diatoms, ancestors of the diatoms shown here, are used in many types of toothpaste. They provide the fine grit that helps scrub and polish your teeth. But there's much more to diatoms than toothpaste!

Diatoms are an important part of Earth's ecosystem. They create much of Earth's oxygen and are the foundation of the ocean's food chain. The diatom is also one of the greatest architects in the world. These single-celled organisms build amazingly beautiful structures out of silica, which is the main ingredient of glass.

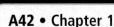

Based on their symmetry, diatoms are classified into two Orders.

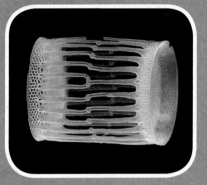

One consists of diatoms that have radial symmetry.

The other is made up of diatoms that have bilateral symmetry.

Diatoms are tiny. One hundred would fit across the head of a pin!

Vocabulary

Complete each sentence with a term from the list.

1. Examples of a(n) ____ include the skeletal system, respiratory system, and circulatory system.

2. A(n) ____ is made up of a group of related cells that work together to perform a function.

3. In many cells, genetic information is stored in the ____.

4. Water diffuses through the cell membrane by a process called ____.

5. Structures called ____ move a paramecium much as oars move a boat.

6. Animals and plants are classified in separate ____.

7. Single-celled organisms with nuclei are most likely ____.

8. Mushrooms and other ____ get their energy by decaying dead organisms.

9. Unlike other ____, ribosomes are not surrounded by membranes.

10. A group of related tissues that work together form a(n) ____.

cell A6
cilia A16
diffusion A17
flagellum A17
fungi A26
kingdoms A24
nucleus A8
organ A33
organelles A8
organ system A33
osmosis A17
protists A25
tissue A33

Test Prep

Write the letter of the best answer choice.

11. According to the cell theory, cells are the ____.

   A. same in plants and animals
   B. largest parts of the body
   C. smallest units of life
   D. smallest particles on Earth

12. The kidneys and the bladder form part of an important ____.

   A. level of organization
   B. organ system
   C. cellular structure
   D. kingdom

13. Protists are usually single-celled and are always ____.

   A. specialized
   B. like animals in structure
   C. prokaryotic
   D. eukaryotic

14. Oxygen from the air you breathe is transferred to blood in the ____.

   A. alveoli of the lungs
   B. nose and nasal passages
   C. heart
   D. bone marrow

15. Classify Photo A shows a bacterium. Photo B shows a protist. Name one similarity and one difference between the two.

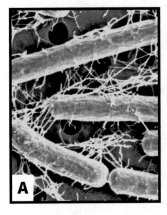

16. Infer Describe how a disease of the circulatory system could harm another system of the body. Give examples of different kinds of damage.

Map the Concept

The chart shows four categories. Place each word or term within a category.

alveoli
chromosome
digestive
endocrine
esophagus
immune
neuron
nucleus
smooth muscle
villi

cell	tissue	organ	organ system

Critical Thinking

17. Evaluate Suppose someone discovers a new form of bacteria that eats plastic. What might be the good and bad effects of this discovery?

18. Analyze What other body systems does the circulatory system affect? Describe the role of the circulatory system in the body.

19. Synthesize What are four characteristics that scientists can use to compare organisms? List specific examples of organisms that have these characteristics.

20. Apply Smoking damages the respiratory system, sometimes by thickening the walls of alveoli. What health problems would a smoker experience as a result?

Performance Assessment

Diagram Levels of Organization

Draw a diagram that shows the relationship among cells, tissues, organs, and organ systems in an organism.

Chapter 2

Plant Systems

LESSON 1

Tiny structures inside these plant cells use energy from the Sun to make food. How do they do it?

Read about it in Lesson 1.

LESSON 2

Plants defy gravity by making water go up. How do plants move water up stems?

Read about it in Lesson 2.

LESSON 3

Wild animals and even family pets can help plants to grow. How do animals help plants?

Read about it in Lesson 3.

How Do Plants Produce Food?

Why It Matters...

Almost all living things need plants to survive. Plants make food and give off oxygen. Animals, including people, eat food and breathe oxygen. The process through which plants use energy from the Sun to make food makes life as you know it possible.

PREPARE TO INVESTIGATE

Inquiry Skill

Experiment When you conduct an experiment, you plan and carry out an investigation to test a hypothesis.

Materials

- geranium plant with at least 4 leaves
- squares of cotton cloth (10 cm x 10 cm)

Science and Math Toolbox
For step 1, review **Making a Chart to Organize Data** on page H11.

Keeping Green

Procedure

1 **Collaborate** Work in a small group. In your *Science Notebook,* draw a chart like the one shown. Use the chart to help you test this hypothesis: Plant leaves need sunlight to stay green.

2 **Experiment** Place your plant in a sunny window or plant it outside in a sunny, sheltered spot. Use the cloth squares to cover at least three leaves. Leave at least one leaf uncovered to serve as a control.

3 **Predict** How do you think the different leaves will change over time? Record your prediction.

4 **Record Data** Check the plant every day and give it water if the soil is dry. Every two days, remove the cover from one or more leaves. Record your observations, then cover the leaves again.

5 **Analyze Data** Discuss the differences that you observed and recorded. Compare the effects of blocking sunlight for two days, four days, and six days.

Conclusion

1. **Use Variables** What was the variable in this investigation? How did you change it? What was the control?

2. **Analyze Data** Review the hypothesis and your prediction. Did you find evidence to support the hypothesis? Explain why or why not.

STEP 1

Time	Uncovered Leaves	Covered Leaves
2 days		
4 days		
6 days		

STEP 2

STEP 4

Investigate More!

Design an Experiment
Plan and conduct an experiment on plants that tests another variable, such as water or soil quality. Describe the control in your experiment.

Producing Food

VOCABULARY

chlorophyll	p. A51
chloroplast	p. A51
photosynthesis	p. A50
stomata	p. A52

READING SKILL

Sequence Use a chart to show the sequence of steps in photosynthesis.

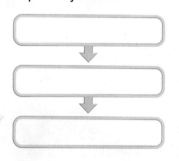

MAIN IDEA Plants use energy from the Sun to make food. They combine carbon dioxide and water to make sugar, and release oxygen in the process.

Photosynthesis

You are constantly using energy to conduct all of your life processes. You need energy to breathe, eat, move, think, and even sleep.

The energy you use ultimately comes from the Sun. Recall from Chapter 1 that plants transform the energy of sunlight into chemical energy stored in food. Plants, along with some protists and bacteria, accomplish this through a process called **photosynthesis.**

During photosynthesis, plants combine water and carbon dioxide into compounds called sugars. They release oxygen in the process.

A vine called kudzu can grow very quickly. Like almost all other plants, it uses photosynthesis to make food.

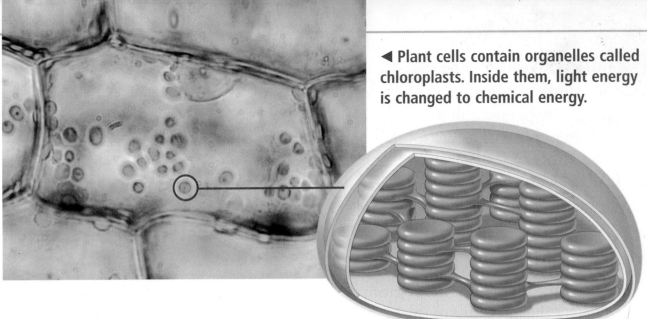

◄ Plant cells contain organelles called chloroplasts. Inside them, light energy is changed to chemical energy.

▲ Inside a chloroplast, stacks of membranes called grana contain chlorophyll, which absorbs sunlight.

Sugars are a plant's food. The plant stores sugars in its tissues and breaks them down when it needs energy. When an animal eats the plant, it can use the stored sugars. And when a larger animal eats the plant-eater, it too obtains energy originally stored in plants. In this way, all animals depend on plants for energy.

In Chapter 1 you learned that photosynthesis takes place in organelles called **chloroplasts.** The number of chloroplasts in a cell depends on the organism. Some tiny algae cells have only one chloroplast, while the cells in the leaves of a tree may each contain more than fifty.

Most chloroplasts have the same basic structure. Each is surrounded by two membranes. Another system of membranes courses through the interior of the chloroplast. These membranes look like flat sacs arranged in stacks called grana.

Inside the membranes are a variety of pigments. A pigment is a substance that absorbs light. The most important pigment in a chloroplast is **chlorophyll.**

Chlorophyll absorbs most colors of light, but not green. This means that when sunlight hits chlorophyll, green light is reflected to your eye. This is why plant parts that contain large amounts of chlorophyll look green.

How does photosynthesis work? When light strikes chlorophyll, the energy is used to split apart water molecules into hydrogen and oxygen. Later, during a series of chemical reactions, the hydrogen joins with carbon from carbon dioxide to form sugars. The oxygen gas is released.

Photosynthesis is a unique process, and it's hard to imagine life on Earth without it. The next time you look at a tall tree or other plant, remember that almost all of its matter came from only water and carbon dioxide.

▶ **SEQUENCE** What happens during the process of photosynthesis?

Plant Leaves

In almost all plants, leaves hold most of the plants' chloroplasts. You can think of leaves as the food factory for a plant.

Plant leaves come in many different shapes and sizes. They can be round or heart-shaped. They can be smooth or have jagged edges.

The broad, flat portion of a leaf is called the blade. Scientists group leaves by the structure of the blade. A simple leaf has a blade that is one piece. Oak trees and apple trees have simple leaves. A compound leaf has a blade that is divided into parts. Rose bushes and palm trees have compound leaves.

Leaves are made of different tissues. The outer layer is called the epidermis. The cells in this tissue have a waterproof coating that prevents water loss.

Remember that a plant needs to exchange gases with its environment. Small openings in the epidermis allow oxygen and carbon dioxide to enter or leave the cells. They also allow water vapor to leave. These openings are called **stomata,** and are scattered about the underside of the leaf. The word stomata comes from the Greek word *stoma*, which means mouth. You can see from the picture that stomata look like small mouths.

Specialized structures that act like gates control the opening and closing of the stomata. When they open, carbon dioxide enters the leaf while oxygen and water vapor exit.

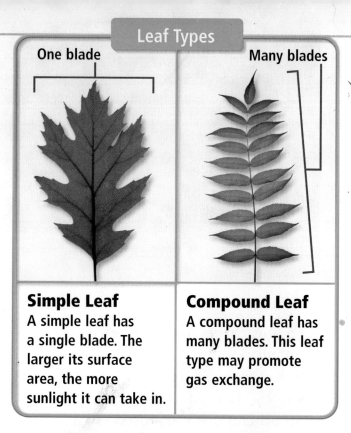

Leaf Types

One blade

Many blades

Simple Leaf
A simple leaf has a single blade. The larger its surface area, the more sunlight it can take in.

Compound Leaf
A compound leaf has many blades. This leaf type may promote gas exchange.

Stomata often open during daylight when photosynthesis occurs. At night, stomata usually close to keep water in. Stomata can also open and close in response to changes in the environment. During dry spells or on hot days, a plant's stomata might stay closed to conserve water.

Most of the cells that perform photosynthesis lie just below the epidermis. These cells are arranged with many air spaces between them so that carbon dioxide, oxygen, and water can flow freely.

Coursing through leaves are long, thin structures called veins. Veins carry materials in and out of the leaf, serving to connect the leaf's cells to the rest of the plant. You will read more about this structure later in this chapter.

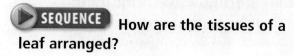 **SEQUENCE** How are the tissues of a leaf arranged?

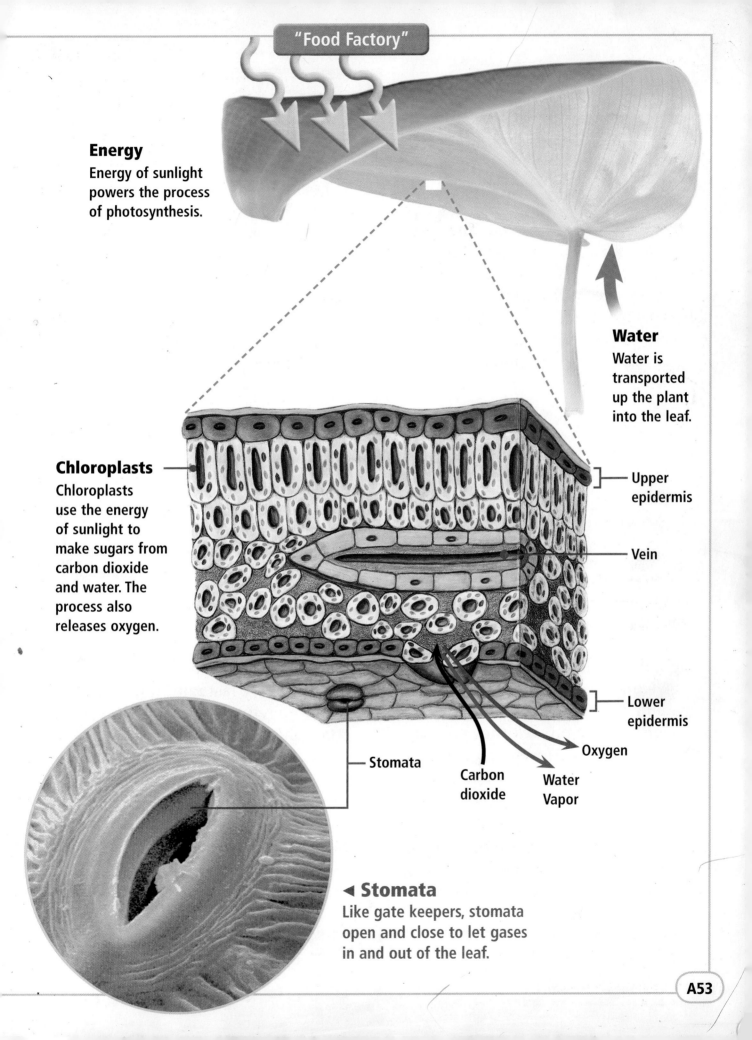

"Food Factory"

Energy
Energy of sunlight powers the process of photosynthesis.

Water
Water is transported up the plant into the leaf.

Chloroplasts
Chloroplasts use the energy of sunlight to make sugars from carbon dioxide and water. The process also releases oxygen.

Upper epidermis

Vein

Lower epidermis

Oxygen

Carbon dioxide

Water Vapor

Stomata

◄ Stomata
Like gate keepers, stomata open and close to let gases in and out of the leaf.

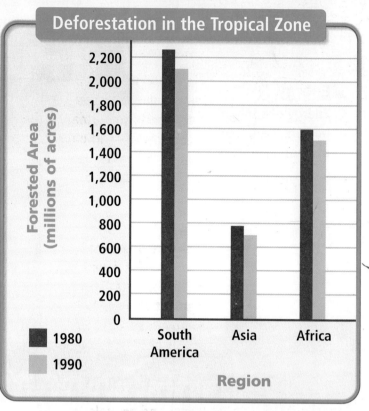

Deforestation in the Tropical Zone

Forested Area (millions of acres)

■ 1980
■ 1990

South America   Asia   Africa

Region

► Both carbon dioxide and oxygen cycle through plants, animals, and Earth's atmosphere. Cutting down forests can upset the balance that this cycle provides. Unfortunately, deforestation continues all over Earth.

Carbon and Oxygen Cycles

Why doesn't the air run out of oxygen, or fill up with carbon dioxide? The reason is that oxygen and carbon dioxide cycle through the environment. As you have read, plants take in carbon dioxide and give off oxygen. Both plants and animals use oxygen to break down sugars. In the process, they release carbon dioxide. Together, plants and animals recycle the gases they both need.

Human activities can upset the carbon and oxygen cycles. Fossil fuels, for example, contain stored carbon. When people burn these fuels, including coal, oil, and natural gas, the carbon is released as carbon dioxide.

Today, people are burning fossil fuels at a very fast rate. The result is a rapid return of carbon to the atmosphere. In addition, people are also cutting down forests, including wide tracts of rain forests in South America and other places. This means that fewer trees are available to remove carbon and release oxygen.

► **SEQUENCE** How do carbon and oxygen cycle through the atmosphere?

Visual Summary

During photosynthesis, plants and some other organisms use carbon dioxide and water to make sugars and release oxygen.

The green pigment chlorophyll is found in chloroplasts. This pigment absorbs the energy in sunlight to power photosynthesis.

Plants and animals cycle carbon and oxygen through the environment.

LINKS for Home and School

MATH Create a Formula Suppose that a forest produces *x* amount of oxygen per day. Write a formula for the amount of oxygen a forest half the size would produce in a year.

SOCIAL STUDIES Make a Map

Rain forests and other forests contain a large percentage of the green plants that live on dry land. Research more about the world's forest resources. Create a map showing where they are, how big they are, and how quickly they are disappearing.

Review

1 MAIN IDEA What are the two main products of photosynthesis?

2 VOCABULARY Write a short paragraph using the terms *chloroplast* and *stomata*. Describe the role of these structures in photosynthesis.

3 READING SKILL: Sequence Describe the purpose and steps of photosynthesis. Why is this process important to all life on Earth?

4 CRITICAL THINKING: Infer A typical cactus has a green stem and thin, spike-like needles that are not green. In which of its parts does a cactus perform photosynthesis? Explain.

5 INQUIRY SKILL: Experiment Do house plants affect the quality of air in a house? Describe an experiment to answer this question. What gases would you want to measure?

TEST PREP

In leaves, what do cells just below the epidermis do?

A. Produce hydrogen gas

B. Store nutrients

C. Perform photosynthesis

D. Create fossil fuels

Technology
Visit **www.eduplace.com/scp/** to find out more about plants and photosynthesis.

THE WORLD OF PLANTS

How do people use plants? The setting is the Chung family living room. Ben reaches for the remote control to find something worth watching. However, just as he's about to change channels . . .

Characters

TV Announcer

Ben Chung:
A fifth-grade boy

Julia Chung:
Ben's sister

Dr. Luisa Galvez:
A research chemist

Emily:
A girl at a desert farm

Dr. George Washington Carver:
Scientist

Dad:
Ben and Julia's father

Announcer: Stay tuned for our next program, "The World of Plants."

Ben: (*yawning*): Do you mind if I find something else to watch?

Julia: Go ahead. This show sounds really boring.

Announcer: You're quite wrong, Ben and Julia Chung of 333 Portland Road!

Ben: Julia! Did you hear that? He's talking to us! (*Ben and Julia lean toward the TV.*)

Announcer: That's right. Plants aren't boring at all. In fact, some are quite surprising.

Julia: Surprising? I doubt it. I already know all about plants and how important they are. Plants make the food we eat and add oxygen to the air we breathe.

Ben: And trees give us wood and paper products. So you see, we already know everything. Can we please change the channel now?

Announcer: Hold on! Do you know that rubber comes from trees, too?

Scene switches quickly to a grove of rubber trees. Birds, monkeys, and other animals chatter in the background.

Julia: Where are we?

Announcer: We're at a rubber tree plantation in Brazil. You can find farms like this in tropical regions all over the world.

Ben: (*pressing on a tree*): These trees don't seem bouncier than other trees.

Dr. Galvez: (*entering*): That's because rubber comes from the sap of a rubber tree, not from the wood.

Ben: Who are you?

Dr. Galvez: I'm a research chemist. I study ways to change raw rubber into sturdy, useful products.

Julia: Like what? Car tires?

Dr. Galvez: Yes. And many other things, too—escalators, rain gear, windshield wipers, and even pencil erasers.

Ben (*looking around*): I'm glad you're putting these rubber trees to good use.

Rubber
The rubber in most tires begins as sap in rubber trees.

Dr. Galvez: Oh, yes. Today, people use more rubber than ever before. To meet the demand, scientists are mixing natural rubber with rubber made in laboratories.

Announcer: Thanks, Dr. Galvez. Time to meet another interesting plant.

Scene switches to a desert.

Julia: Now what?

Announcer: Welcome to Arizona. Meet the jojoba plant.

Ben: It looks like an ordinary shrub to me.

Announcer: Maybe so, but take a look at these seeds. They're filled with a very unusual oil.

Julia: What's so unusual about it?

Emily *(entering):* Allow me to answer. I'm Emily, and this is my farm. Oil from jojoba seeds is used in shampoo and makeup. Researchers are studying how to use it as a fuel, too.

Ben: Like gasoline or diesel fuel?

Emily: Yes. Think how useful that might be! Instead of digging up fossil fuels, we might raise plants like the jojoba.

Julia: I bet the seeds grow year after year, too. We'd never run out of them!

Announcer: Aha! Maybe now you believe me when I say plants can be surprising! Did you know that citronella oil comes from dried grasses? People use it to repel insects, especially mosquitoes.

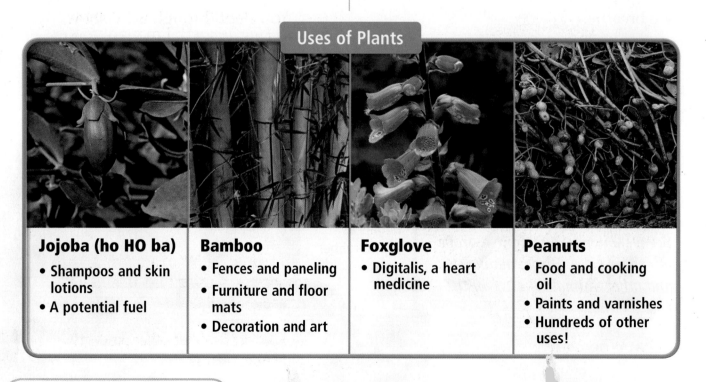

Uses of Plants

Jojoba (ho HO ba)
- Shampoos and skin lotions
- A potential fuel

Bamboo
- Fences and paneling
- Furniture and floor mats
- Decoration and art

Foxglove
- Digitalis, a heart medicine

Peanuts
- Food and cooking oil
- Paints and varnishes
- Hundreds of other uses!

Emily: Don't forget sap from the chicle tree. It's used to make chewing gum!

Dr. Galvez: How about soapwort? It's used to make soap that cleans delicate fabrics.

Soapwort plant

Dr. Carver: (*entering*): Hello, everyone. I'm Dr. George Washington Carver. I'd like to remind you about another important plant: peanuts. Why, I invented more uses for peanuts than anyone ever imagined! Today, peanuts are used to make ink, grease, shaving cream, paint, construction materials—

Ben: OK, OK! I'm convinced! Plants aren't boring!

Julia: They're downright amazing!

▲ Soap from the soapwort plant is used to clean valuable tapestries.

Dad (*shaking Ben and Julia gently*): Hey, wake up, kids!

Ben and Julia: What? What happened?

Dad: You slept through a TV show about plants. I came in part way. I thought plants were dull, but I was wrong! Why, did you know . . .

(*Ben and Julia laugh.*)

Dr. George Washington Carver
(1864–1943)

Sharing Ideas

1. **READING CHECK** What are three unusual uses for plants?

2. **WRITE ABOUT IT** What are the advantages of using fuels from plants instead of fossil fuels?

3. **TALK ABOUT IT** What other products come from plants?

How Do Plants Move Materials?

Why It Matters...

Plant leaves need water and minerals that are found in soil. Without them, photosynthesis could not occur. Almost all plants have a way to move materials upwards, against the downward pull of gravity.

These pails catch sap from maple trees.

PREPARE TO INVESTIGATE

Inquiry Skill

Predict When you predict, you tell what you think will happen, based on your knowledge of previous cause-and-effect patterns.

Materials

- a plant with at least 4 broad leaves
- petroleum jelly
- 4 plastic sandwich bags with twist ties

Science and Math Toolbox

For step 1, review **Making a Chart to Organize Data** on page H11.

Losing Water

Procedure

1. **Collaborate** Work in a small group. In your *Science Notebook,* draw a chart like the one shown.

2. **Experiment** Carefully smear petroleum jelly on the top and underside of one of the plant leaves. Coat another leaf on the top surface only. Coat a third leaf on the underside only.

3. **Experiment** Slide a bag over each of the coated leaves and close it with a twist tie. Cover a fourth, uncoated leaf with a bag, to serve as a control. Label each bag. Place the plant in a sunny window and, if needed, water it.

4. **Predict** Based on what you have learned about leaf structure, predict what will happen inside each bag.

5. **Record Data** Check the leaves every hour for three hours. Use the chart to record your observations.

Conclusion

1. **Analyze Data** With others in your group, discuss reasons for your results. Consider different explanations.

2. **Predict** Based on your results, discuss with your group what will happen if you leave the bags on the leaves for two more days. Give reasons for your prediction.

3. **Experiment** Continue the experiment for two days or longer. See if your prediction holds true.

STEP 1

Time	Uncoated	Coated on Top	Coated on Underside	Coated on Both Sides
1 hour				
2 hours				
3 hours				
1 day				
2 days				

STEP 2

Investigate More!

Design an Experiment
Plan a similar experiment with a different kind of plant. For example, you might choose a cactus or an evergreen plant.

VOCABULARY

nonvascular plant p. A62
phloem p. A63
transpiration p. A64
vascular plant p. A63
xylem p. A63

READING SKILL

Text Structure Use the headings in this lesson to identify the main ideas of the text.

Moving Materials

MAIN IDEA Plants have specialized tissues and use natural forces to transport water, minerals, and nutrients.

Nonvascular Plants

If you have ever observed moss on the side of a tree, you know that not all plants have the same structures. Mosses are examples of **nonvascular plants,** which lack true leaves, stems, and roots. They also lack structures that transport food, water, and other materials between plant parts.

In addition to mosses, nonvascular plants include liverworts and hornworts. They have few specialized cells and no complex organs.

Nonvascular plants are almost always small. Their size is limited because they lack ways to deliver water to distant parts. Instead, most of their cells must be close to the outside environment. Gases, water, and minerals move directly between the environment and the cells.

Although they are small, nonvascular plants fill important roles in their environments. Because they absorb water, they help hold soil in place and keep it from drying out.

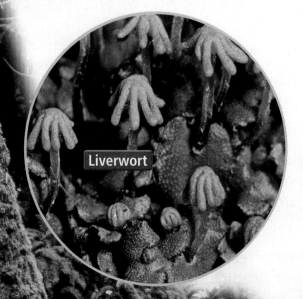

Liverwort

Moss

Mosses and Liverworts
Nonvascular plants have no complex organs. Some of their leaf-like tissues are only one cell thick.

Vascular Plants

Most plants you can name, including evergreen trees, flowering plants, and ferns, are examples of vascular plants. A **vascular plant** has specialized tissues that transport materials throughout it. Veins, which you read about in Lesson 1, carry materials in and out of leaves. Veins are examples of vascular tissues.

The organs of vascular plants include roots, stems, and leaves. Roots anchor a plant in the ground. They also absorb water and minerals from the soil. Some roots store food for the plant as well.

The stem supports the plant and holds its leaves up in the air so they can receive sunlight. The stem also provides a way for water, minerals, and food to move between the roots and the leaves.

Stems contain two important kinds of tissues: xylem and phloem. **Xylem** tissues conduct water and minerals upward from the roots. **Phloem** tissues conduct food materials downward from the leaves to the rest of the plant.

A typical plant stem has a ring of bundles containing both xylem and phloem. A strip of tissue called the vascular cambium lies between the xylem and phloem. Here, xylem and phloem cells are produced.

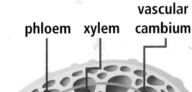
Trunks and Stems

phloem   xylem

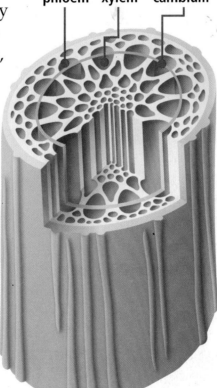

phloem   xylem   vascular cambium

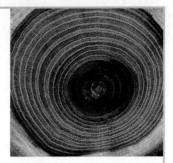

Trunks
Growth rings mark each year's new xylem, or wood tissue. The darker parts show where growth slowed at the end of each season.

Stems
Stems grow wider by adding new layers of xylem and phloem. New layers grow on either side of the vascular cambium.

 **TEXT STRUCTURE** What are two types of vascular tissue?

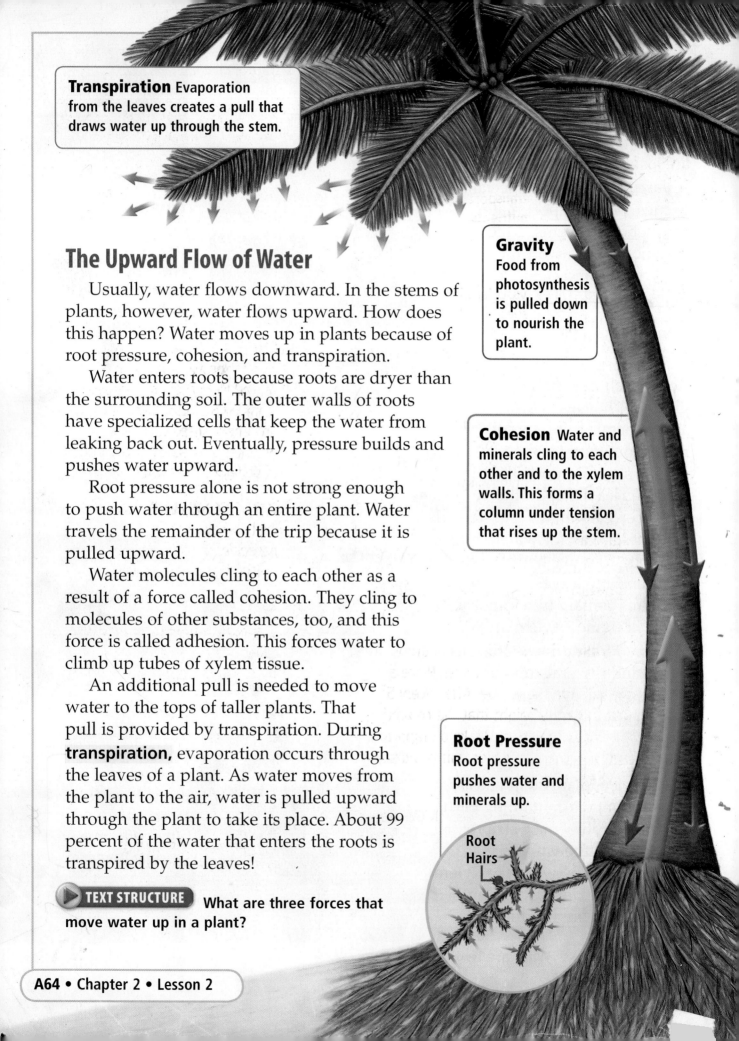

Transpiration Evaporation from the leaves creates a pull that draws water up through the stem.

The Upward Flow of Water

Usually, water flows downward. In the stems of plants, however, water flows upward. How does this happen? Water moves up in plants because of root pressure, cohesion, and transpiration.

Water enters roots because roots are dryer than the surrounding soil. The outer walls of roots have specialized cells that keep the water from leaking back out. Eventually, pressure builds and pushes water upward.

Root pressure alone is not strong enough to push water through an entire plant. Water travels the remainder of the trip because it is pulled upward.

Water molecules cling to each other as a result of a force called cohesion. They cling to molecules of other substances, too, and this force is called adhesion. This forces water to climb up tubes of xylem tissue.

An additional pull is needed to move water to the tops of taller plants. That pull is provided by transpiration. During **transpiration,** evaporation occurs through the leaves of a plant. As water moves from the plant to the air, water is pulled upward through the plant to take its place. About 99 percent of the water that enters the roots is transpired by the leaves!

Gravity Food from photosynthesis is pulled down to nourish the plant.

Cohesion Water and minerals cling to each other and to the xylem walls. This forms a column under tension that rises up the stem.

Root Pressure Root pressure pushes water and minerals up.

Root Hairs

▶ **TEXT STRUCTURE** What are three forces that move water up in a plant?

Visual Summary

Nonvascular plants do not have vessels to transport water and nutrients.

Vascular plants have specialized tissues called xylem and phloem for transporting water and nutrients.

Water is moved upward in a vascular plant by root pressure, cohesion, and transpiration.

LINKS for Home and School

MATH **Make a Graph** Mix several drops of food coloring into a beaker of water. Place a tall celery stalk into the beaker. After every 5 minutes, measure the height that the colored water traveled up the celery. Make a graph to show the data. What conclusion can you draw from your results?

WRITING **Expository** Research the story of maple syrup. Write an essay that shows how maple syrup is made, packaged, and delivered to your table.

Review

❶ **MAIN IDEA** How do forces push and pull materials through a plant?

❷ **VOCABULARY** Write a short paragraph using the terms *xylem* and *phloem.*

❸ **READING SKILL: Text Structure** List three details about either xylem or phloem.

❹ **CRITICAL THINKING: Hypothesize** Suppose you coated the leaves of a vascular plant with a substance that prevents transpiration. How would this affect the movement of water up the plant?

❺ **INQUIRY SKILL: Predict** Explain how materials in pesticides in the ground might end up in a plant's leaves.

 TEST PREP

Evaporation from plant leaves is called

A. root pressure.

B. transpiration.

C. osmosis.

D. cohesion.

 Technology

Visit **www.eduplace.com/scp/** to find out more about vascular and nonvascular plants.

How Do Plants Reproduce?

Why It Matters...

Many people enjoy flowers for their beautiful shapes and colors, and for their pleasant scents. Such qualities are no accident. Plants use their flowers to attract animals, and the animals help the plants reproduce.

PREPARE TO INVESTIGATE

Inquiry Skill

Analyze Data When you analyze data, you study the information you collect, looking for patterns that might lead to a hypothesis or to a conclusion.

Materials

- flower
- white paper or paper towels
- plastic knife
- hand lens

Inside a Flower

Procedure

1 **Collaborate** Work in small groups. In your *Science Notebook,* make a chart like the one shown here.

2 **Observe** Place the flower on the white paper and observe it carefully. Use the hand lens to see details.

3 **Record Data** Sketch the outside of the flower. Add labels to show colors, textures, and the numbers of each kind of structure.

4 **Experiment** Using the plastic knife, carefully slice the flower in half from top to bottom.

5 **Record Data** Sketch the inside of the flower. Add labels to record details.

6 **Communicate** Compare sketches with other group members. Discuss any differences you see. You may revise your sketch to make it more accurate.

Conclusion

1. **Analyze Data** Were the same structures visible on the outside and inside of the flower? Explain.

2. **Infer** Why do you think plant scientists study the insides as well as the outsides of plants?

STEP 1

Drawing of Outer Structures	Drawing of Inside Structures

STEP 2

STEP 4

Investigate More!

Design an Experiment
Plant seeds of field mustard plants or other fast-growing plants. Provide the plants light, water, and warmth. Observe and record the stages of their life cycle.

Plant Reproduction

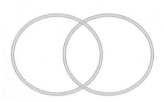
MAIN IDEA Plants reproduce using spores or seeds. They are dispersed in different ways.

Seedless Plants and Conifers

A plant's pattern of generation, growth, and reproduction is known as its life cycle. Scientists classify plants into two major groups according to their life cycles. One group is the seed plants, which reproduce with seeds. The second group is the seedless plants, which reproduce with **spores** or other structures.

Fern Life Cycle

Spores
The wind scatters mature spores from the sporangia.

Gametophytes
Some spores grow into structures that produce gametes, or male and female cells.

Sporangia
Spores are produced in sporangia on the undersides of fronds.

Fern
The zygote will grow into a mature fern.

Zygote
Male and female cells join to form the zygote, a process called fertilization. A new plant begins.

One common seedless plant is the fern. Ferns grow throughout the United States, but they grow best in warm, moist climates such as in tropical rain forests. Let's take a close look at its life cycle.

Most large plants are seed plants. Scientists further divide the seed plants into two large groups.

Plants with seeds that are not covered by a protective fruit are called gymnosperms, which means "naked seeds." Conifers, such as pine, spruce, cedar, and redwood trees, are the most common of the **gymnosperms.** The seeds of these conifers develop inside cones.

Conifers produce both male and female cones. Male cones are smaller. They are often located near the tips of the branches. Female cones are generally larger. Some types of conifers produce both male and female cones on the same plant. Other types of conifers have male and female plants that each produce only one type of cone.

Male cones produce pollen. Pollen is reproductive material that contains male gametes, or sperm cells. Female cones, called seed cones, contain ovules. Ovules contain female gametes, or eggs.

In the spring, pollen cones release millions of tiny pollen grains into the wind. Many pollen grains fall to the ground or land on water. But some are blown onto seed cones. Any process that delivers pollen to eggs is an example of **pollination.** With conifers, the wind or air is the agent of pollination.

Once the pollen grain lands on a seed cone, it releases sperm cells. These sperm cells can fertilize the ovules. This forms a new zygote, which can divide and develop into seeds. When the seeds mature, they are released from the cone. If the conditions are right, a seed will develop into a new conifer.

▶ **COMPARE AND CONTRAST** How are ferns different from conifers?

Pine cones produce pollen (in the male cones) and ovules (in the female cones). Seeds develop in the female cone.

male cone

female cone

A69

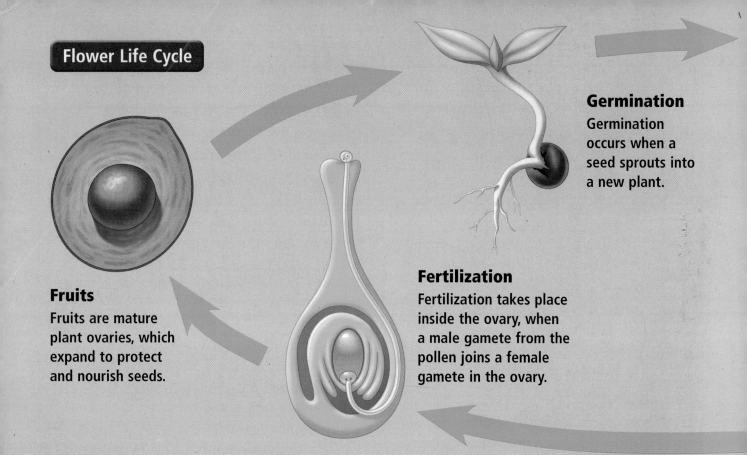

Flower Life Cycle

Germination
Germination occurs when a seed sprouts into a new plant.

Fertilization
Fertilization takes place inside the ovary, when a male gamete from the pollen joins a female gamete in the ovary.

Fruits
Fruits are mature plant ovaries, which expand to protect and nourish seeds.

Flowering Plants

The second large group of seed plants are the angiosperms. An **angiosperm** produces seeds within a protective covering. Angiosperms are also called flowering plants because they store seeds inside flowers and fruits. The flowering plants make up the largest group of plants in the world. In fact, nine out of ten plant species are flowering plants.

Flowers are the reproductive organs of angiosperms. They have many parts, and each has a purpose related to reproduction.

The male reproductive organ is called a stamen. Two parts make up the stamen: a thin filament, or stalk, and a rounded anther. The anther produces pollen, or male gametes.

The female reproductive organ of a flower is called the pistil. Pistils are found in the center of a flower. Three parts make up the pistil: the stigma, the style, and the ovary. The stigma is the sticky tip of the pistil. The style connects the stigma to the ovary. The ovary contains one or more ovules.

Keep in mind that not all flowering plants are identical. Some flowering plants make both male and female reproductive organs in the same flower. In other plants, they are made in different flowers.

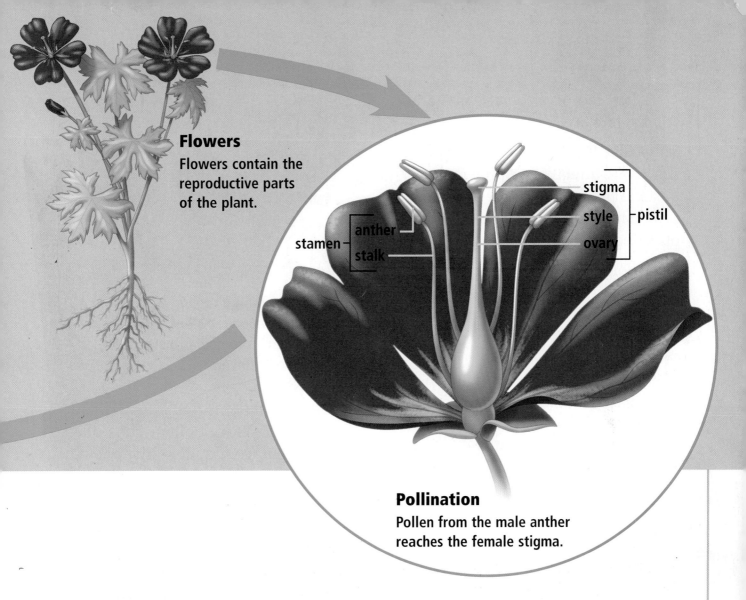

Flowers

Flowers contain the reproductive parts of the plant.

stamen — anther
stalk

stigma
style
ovary
— pistil

Pollination

Pollen from the male anther reaches the female stigma.

The colorful, leaflike structures of a flower are called petals. Flower petals surround and protect the male and female reproductive organs. They also play an important role in pollination, as you will find out soon.

In flowering plants, pollination occurs soon after a grain of pollen lands on the sticky stigma. If the pollen is from the right type of plant, the pollen produces a tube that grows through the style and into the ovule. A sperm cell is released from the tube to fertilize the egg cell in the ovule. The resulting zygote develops into a seed that may eventually become a new plant.

As the seed develops, the ovary changes to become a fruit. The fruit protects and nourishes the seeds. Fruits also attract animals that help spread the seeds.

The fruits you eat are mature ovaries that surround the seeds inside. These fruits include apples, oranges, cherries, and berries. They also include some foods you may not think of as fruits, such as tomatoes, peppers, and cucumbers.

▶ **COMPARE AND CONTRAST** How do angiosperms differ from gymnosperms?

Pollination

Pollen can be dispersed in many ways. Here are some examples.

Self-pollination In some plants pollen can move directly from the male parts to the female parts. In peas and beans, for example, a single flower contains both parts.

Wind Some plants release pollen into the wind. These plants usually produce large amounts of pollen because much of it will be wasted on the ground or in water.

Plants that depend on the wind often have structures that expose the pollen to the air. For example, some plants have very long stamens that reach into the open air. They also may have stigma with feathery arms that catch pollen from the air.

Corn is one example of a wind-pollinated plant. Male parts are located near the top of the plant, where the wind can catch the pollen. Female parts are located farther down the plant.

▲ Hummingbirds have long, thin beaks that allow them to reach the nectar inside narrow flowers.

Water Some plants live in water and use water to carry pollen. The pollen grains float from male parts to female parts. Sea grasses use this method of pollination.

Animals Flowers that have bright colors or strong fragrances are usually pollinated by animals. The colors and scents attract animals that come to feed on a sugary nectar that the flower produces.

As the animals gather nectar, pollen becomes stuck on their bodies. The pollen is deposited in different flowers as the animals move among them. Hummingbirds, bats, bees, and butterflies all pollinate flowers in this way.

Farmers who grow fruits often raise bees as well. Bees help pollinate the trees and they make honey.

◄ Honeybees have thick leg hairs that pollen clings to.

Seed Dispersal

Like pollen, plant seeds are also dispersed by different means.

Wind Have you watched the feathery seeds of a dandelion float through the wind? Dandelions, orchids, and other plants have small, light seeds that winds easily carry. The seeds of black maple trees are covered by thin, dry fruits that act as propellers.

Water Some plant seeds and fruits are spread by water. These fruits and seeds contain air chambers that help them to float. The large fruits of the coconut palm, for example, can float great distances on ocean currents. This is why coconut palms often grow on small tropical islands.

Animals If you have ever had a burr stuck on your clothing, you may have helped to disperse plant seeds. Burrs are fruits that stick to the fur of animals. As an animal moves around, it spreads the seeds to new locations.

▲ Do you see the burrs on this dog? Each burr holds seeds. The dog helps spread them away from the parent plants.

Many animals are attracted to the sweet taste of many fruits. As the animal eats the fruit, it may disturb some of the seeds. The seeds drop to the ground where they may grow into new plants.

Animals can also help spread seeds by eating fruits. Some seeds pass through an animal intact, and thus become part of its waste. Fruit-eating birds often spread plant seeds in this way.

▶ **COMPARE AND CONTRAST** What are different ways that pollen and seeds are dispersed?

◀ Seed dispersal can depend on wind, but animals are also efficient at spreading seeds.

Plant Structure

Flowers	Fruits and Seeds
Grasses • many small flowers clustered together • flowers can be arranged in many different ways	**Avocado** • fleshy fruit • one large seed • seed inside fruit
Sunflower • head is made up of many small flowers • each flower produces one seed	**Orange** • fleshy fruit • many small seeds • seeds located in center
Corn • clusters of male flowers called tassels • female flowers contained in ears • grains made by female flowers	**Strawberry** • fleshy fruit • many tiny seeds • seeds spread throughout surface

Variety in Flowering Plants

Angiosperms grow in most places on Earth. A few species even live in ocean water. Angiosperms around the world have developed an amazing variety of structures to help them reproduce in their environments.

Flowers exist in many different sizes, shapes, and colors. Water lilies have some of the largest flowers. Clover, sedges, and grasses have some of the smallest. The most common flower colors are red, yellow, white, and blue.

Fruits also exist in many sizes, from tiny berries to large coconuts. Fruits grow around different kinds and numbers of seeds. Pomegranates have many tiny seeds. A grape or apple might have two or three seeds. A cherry or avocado has only one seed.

People have learned to take advantage of this variety in flowers, fruits, and seeds. Humans eat not only seeds and plants, but also flowers. Cauliflower and broccoli are examples of flowers that people eat.

Farmers plant seeds at the start of each growing season. The ability to grow crops from seeds has helped humans thrive and flourish for thousands of years.

▶ **COMPARE AND CONTRAST** How do people take advantage of the variety in flowers, fruits, and seeds?

Lesson Wrap-Up

Visual Summary

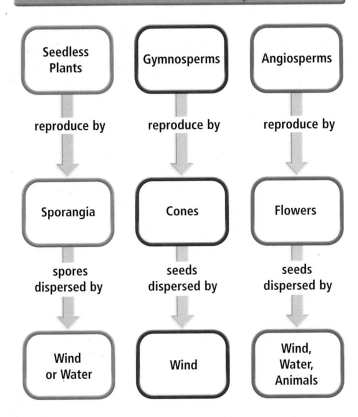

Seedless Plants	Gymnosperms	Angiosperms
reproduce by	reproduce by	reproduce by
Sporangia	Cones	Flowers
spores dispersed by	seeds dispersed by	seeds dispersed by
Wind or Water	Wind	Wind, Water, Animals

LINKS for Home and School

MATH **Make a Scale Drawing** Suppose a beekeeper has 180 acres of clover and 9 honeybee hives. How many acres must each hive pollinate in order for the clover to reproduce? Make a scale drawing of the farmer's land, showing the location of each hive and the size of the plot of land it is on.

TECHNOLOGY **Make a Poster** Research ways that farmers depend on insects to help in crop pollination and reproduction. Make a poster that features one kind of insect. Show how it helps farmers.

Review

❶ MAIN IDEA What are the most numerous types of plants?

❷ VOCABULARY Write a sentence or short paragraph using the terms *gymnosperms* and *angiosperms*.

❸ READING SKILL: Compare and Contrast What do sporangia, cones, and flowers have in common? How are they different?

❹ CRITICAL THINKING: Apply Explain why many gardeners plant flowers that attract bees and butterflies.

❺ INQUIRY SKILL: Analyze Data Give three reasons why angiosperms are the most successful plants on Earth.

 TEST PREP
All flowering plants produce seeds and

A. fruits.

B. other edible parts.

C. brightly colored petals.

D. sporangia.

 Technology
Visit **www.eduplace.com/scp/** to find out more about plant reproduction.

A75

Stuck On You

Is it a giant worm from outer space? An undersea creature? No, you're looking at a magnified burr—a tiny seed with hooks. Many plants depend on wind and water to scatter their seeds. Others rely on animals to leave them in droppings. But burrs are hitchhikers. They travel by hooking themselves onto animals' fur—and people's clothing!

Through a microscope, you can see a strong resemblance between a burr and a strip of the hooked fastener called Velcro™. This is no coincidence. Inventor George de Mestral got the idea for the tiny hooks of Velcro™ from studying the clingy burrs that he plucked from his dog's fur.

Grab a ride! Some plant species, like cockle burrs, have literally hitchhiked across North America and Europe.

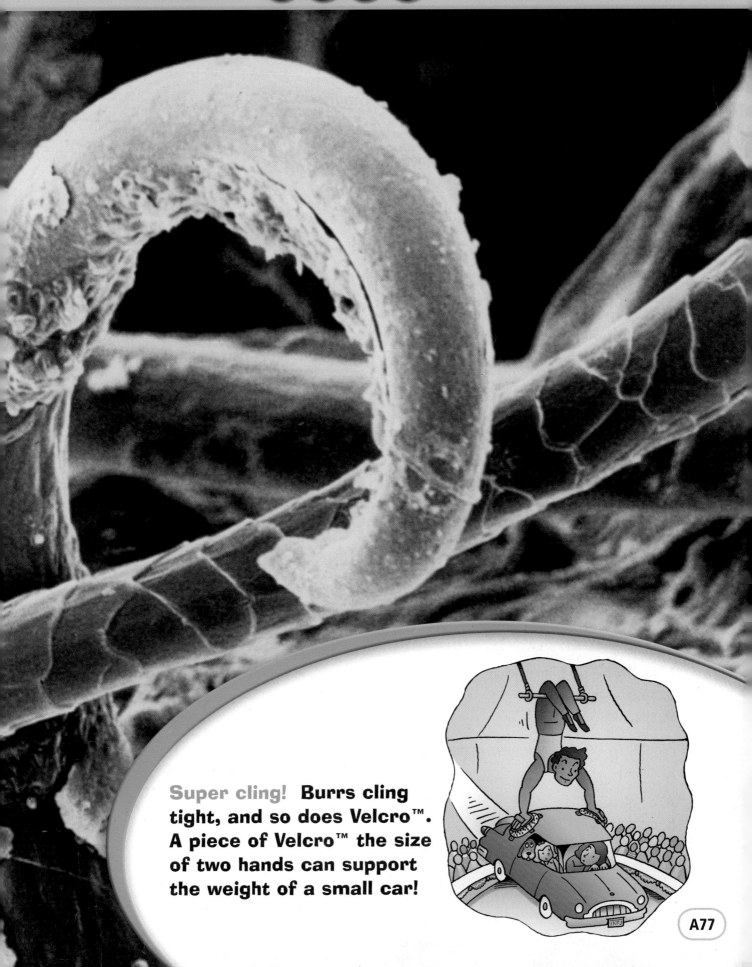

Super cling! Burrs cling tight, and so does Velcro™. A piece of Velcro™ the size of two hands can support the weight of a small car!

Vocabulary

Complete each sentence with a term from the list.

1. The green pigment in plants is called ____.

2. The process by which plants use solar energy to make food is ____.

3. Openings called ____ let air and water in and out of leaves.

4. A ____ has vessels to carry water, minerals, and nutrients.

5. Tissues known as ____ transport water from a plant's roots to its leaves.

6. The plant tissues that transport nutrients away from the leaves are ____.

7. The process of ____ takes place when evaporation occurs through the leaves of a plant.

8. Seedless plants reproduce by releasing ____.

9. The process of delivering pollen to eggs is called ____.

10. ____ are plants that produce seeds with a protective covering.

angiosperms A70
chlorophyll A51
chloroplast A51
gymnosperm A69
nonvascular plant A62
phloem A63
photosynthesis A50
pollination A69
spores A68
stomata A52
transpiration A64
vascular plant A63
xylem A63

Test Prep

Write the letter of the best answer choice.

11. Chlorophyll has the ability to ____.

    A. transport carbohydrates
    B. protect the cell from the Sun
    C. absorb light energy
    D. build cell walls

12. People rely on photosynthesis in plants for food and ____.

    A. oxygen
    B. carbon dioxide
    C. chlorophyll
    D. minerals

13. Some nonvascular plants have the ability to ____.

    A. transport water and minerals through vessels
    B. help control moisture in their environments
    C. develop strong stems and leaves
    D. produce xylem and phloem

14. Angiosperms produce their gametes inside ____.

    A. flowers
    B. sporangia
    C. cones
    D. stems

15. **Synthesize** Identify at least two functions for each of these plant parts.

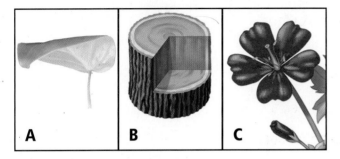

A   B   C

16. **Experiment** Describe an experiment that would help show which plants attract butterflies. Propose an hypothesis about whether butterflies are attracted to a specific color or shape of flower.

Map the Concept

The chart shows three processes. Place each word or term in the correct column. Some words go in more than one category.

chloroplasts   stomata
fruit   cohesion
gametes   evaporation
germination   water
oxygen   fertilization
solar energy   root pressure
                  transpiration

Photosynthesis	Upward Movement	Reproduction

Critical Thinking

17. **Apply** Why do moss plants grow best in damp places, such as the floor of a forest? Would mosses grow well in dry, sandy soil? Explain.

18. **Analyze** List three different ways that seeds are spread from place to place, and include one example of each. Why is seed dispersal important to plants? Why is it important to humans?

19. **Synthesize** A perfect flower has both male and female parts. An imperfect flower has either male or female parts, but not both. How would a plant that makes imperfect flowers be able to reproduce?

20. **Experiment** A student mixes a few drops of food coloring in a glass of water. She places a stalk of celery in the glass, and observes the colored water climb slowly up the stalk's tissues. What does this show about the way water travels through a plant?

Performance Assessment

Diagram a Plant

Draw and label a diagram that shows the major parts of a flowering plant. Then draw the same diagram, but write labels to show functions instead of names of parts.

Traits of Living Things

LESSON 1

This flamingo was born with some traits and it acquired others. What determines traits?

Read about it in Lesson 1.

LESSON 2

Certain traits help organisms to survive. Why are some traits more common than others?

Read about them in Lesson 2.

How Are Traits Inherited?

Why It Matters...

A trait is a physical or behavioral characteristic of an organism. Every person has a unique combination of traits. You have a set of traits that belongs to you alone. You also have traits you have acquired from interacting with your environment.

PREPARE TO INVESTIGATE

Inquiry Skill

Analyze Data When you analyze data, you look for patterns in information you have collected.

Materials
- index cards
- pencils

Science and Math Toolbox
For step 3, review **Making a Chart to Organize Data** on page H11.

Trait Tabulation

Procedure

1. **Collaborate** Work in a small group. Your team will get a letter. Assign a number to each person in your group. For example, your group letter might be C and your number might be 5, or C5.

2. **Observe** Copy the chart shown at right onto an index card. Write your number-letter code, not your name, on your card. Answer the questions in the chart.

3. **Collaborate** Collect your team's cards and exchange them with the cards from another team. Then work with your team to count the number of people with each trait. Work in the same way with each of the other teams.

4. **Record Data** Tally the results for everyone in the class. Prepare a circle graph, bar graph, or appropriate chart of your choice to show the data.

Conclusion

1. **Use Numbers** How did the data change as you counted more people in the class? Why is it important that scientists use a large number of samples when doing research, such as you did in this activity?

2. **Evaluate** Of the five traits you studied, which could change as a person grows older? Which always stay the same?

3. **Analyze Data** For each trait, which form did you find to be the most common?

STEP 2

Letter and Number: _____	
Questions:	Answers:
1. What color are your eyes?	
2. Are your earlobes attached or detached?	
3. Do you write with your left hand, right hand, or both?	
4. Do you know how to ride a skateboard?	
5. Can you recite the alphabet backwards very quickly?	

STEP 3

Detached lobe   Attached lobe

Investigate More!

Design an Experiment
With your teacher's permission, survey students in other classes about the five traits. Is the additional data consistent with the data from your class? What conclusions can you draw from your results?

READING SKILL

Sequence Use a chart like the one below to show the order of events in DNA replication.

Traits

MAIN IDEA Living things inherit many traits from their parents. They acquire others from their environment.

Traits of Organisms

Do you look like anyone in your family? People tend to look like their parents and grandparents because of heredity. **Heredity** is the process through which traits are passed from parents to offspring.

Human traits that are passed by heredity—or inherited traits—include face shape, hair color, and blood type. The color of an animal's fur, the shape of its ears, and the arrangement of its teeth are also examples of inherited traits. The colors of a flower or the shape of a fruit are examples among plants. An inherited trait can also be a behavior, such as the way a spider spins a web.

Not every trait that you can observe is passed down by heredity. Some traits are acquired. An **acquired trait** is one that an organism develops after it is born. Some acquired traits come from the environment, others are learned, and still others are brought about purposely.

Inherited traits are passed on from generation to generation through chromosomes.

Acquired Traits

Flamingos are known for their beautiful pink color, which sets them apart from other large, long-legged water birds. The color comes from pigments in shrimp and certain algae that flamingos eat.

The pink color of flamingos is an example of an acquired trait. This kind of trait comes from interactions with the environment. In a similar way, organisms can acquire traits from food, soil, water, and other elements in their environment.

Some acquired traits are learned. You were not born knowing how to ride a bicycle or a skateboard—you learned how to ride. All types of animals learn behaviors. Dogs can learn to follow commands, lions can learn to hunt, and birds can learn how to sing songs. An acquired trait of this kind is called a learned trait.

Manipulated traits are traits that people deliberately change. Plants and animals have been manipulated for thousands of years. Breeders mate animals or cross plants with the most desirable traits. Gardeners also control the shape and design of a plant to keep some plants small or to give others interesting shapes.

Some traits arise from combinations of inherited and acquired features. For example, a person may inherit the capacity to be tall. However, the trait will show itself only if combined with proper nutrition and exercise.

▶ **SEQUENCE** How might a plant develop an acquired trait?

Learned ▲
Organisms can acquire traits, like the ability to ride a skateboard, by learning and remembering skills and information.

Environmental ▲
Organisms can acquire traits from their environments. A flamingo is pink because it eats pink food.

Manipulated ▶
Manipulated traits, such as coiled bamboo, are created by human design. People can change both inherited and acquired traits.

A85

Chromosomes and Genes

What determines the inherited traits of an organism? The information is stored within the cell nucleus in a molecule called deoxyribonucleic acid, **DNA.** A DNA molecule consists of two, long parallel strands. The strands coil around each other like edges of a twisted ladder.

Molecules of DNA are passed from one generation to the next during reproduction. Recall that reproduction is the process through which organisms make offspring. For DNA to be passed to offspring, a copy of the molecules must first be made.

In cells that are not dividing, DNA and protein are found in a loose form that is spread out within the nucleus. This form of DNA, called chromatin, is difficult to see even under a light microscope.

As the cell gets ready to divide, however, the double strands of DNA coil tightly. These shorter, thicker coils of DNA form rod-shaped structures called **chromosomes.** Chromosomes are visible under a microscope.

As a cell is dividing, each chromosome consists of two identical halves called chromatids. The central region that holds the chromatids together is called the centromere.

In the bodies of most organisms, all cells have an even number of chromosomes. In fact, they form pairs. The chromosomes in each pair are similar, but not identical.

The number of chromosomes per cell is different in different species. Humans, for example, have 46 chromosomes in each cell. Dogs have 78, cats have 38, and fruit flies have 8 chromosomes.

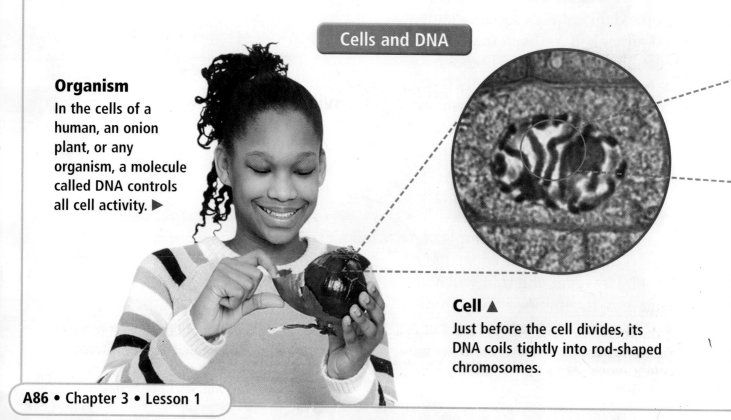

Cells and DNA

Organism

In the cells of a human, an onion plant, or any organism, a molecule called DNA controls all cell activity. ▶

Cell ▲

Just before the cell divides, its DNA coils tightly into rod-shaped chromosomes.

In every plant and animal, one type of cell is made with only half the chromosomes of other cells. These are the cells used for reproduction. They are called gametes, or egg and sperm cells. Human gametes, for example, contain only 23 chromosomes.

When two gametes combine, their chromosomes become part of the nucleus of a cell of a new individual. The cell has a complete set of chromosomes.

There are many more traits than there are chromosomes. The reason is that the information in one chromosome can determine many traits. Each trait of an organism is determined by a short segment of DNA known as a **gene.** One chromosome can have hundreds of genes on it.

The Structure of DNA

The basic units of DNA are called **nucleotides.** Each nucleotide is made up of a phosphate, a sugar, and a nitrogen base. There are four possible nitrogen bases.

Recall that a molecule of DNA resembles a ladder. The phosphate groups and sugar molecules make up the sides of the ladder. Pairs of nitrogen bases make up the steps. Pairs form only between specific bases.

The order of the nitrogen bases determines the genes of the organism. Because the bases can be arranged in a great number of ways, a great number of genes are possible.

▶ **SEQUENCE** Why do body cells have twice as many chromosomes as gametes?

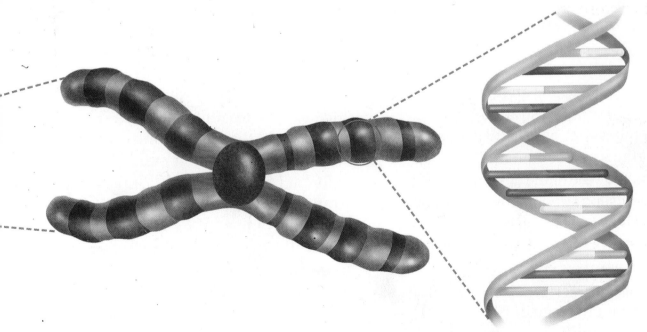

Chromosome ▲
A chromosome is made of two identical strands, called chromatids, joined at the centromere. The DNA is organized into units called genes.

DNA ▲
The information in DNA is coded by its arrangement of nitrogen bases. A single DNA molecule may have billions of base pairs!

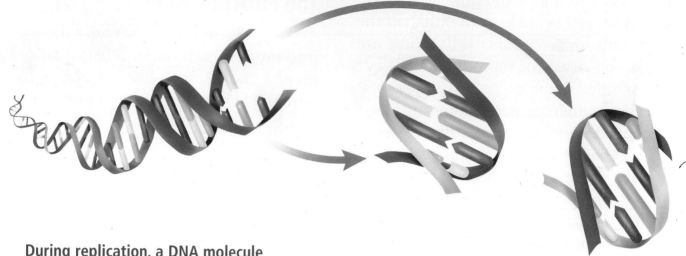

During replication, a DNA molecule separates. Each strand is used to form a new DNA molecule. ▲

The two new molecules are identical to the original. ▲

DNA Replication

Before a cell divides, an exact copy of its DNA is made. This process is called DNA replication. To begin the process, the strands of the DNA molecule separate along their nitrogen bases. This part of the process resembles unzipping a zipper.

Quickly after, bases floating around the nucleus attach to the bases of unzipped strands of DNA. Remember that bases always pair up in the same combinations. That means that the same type of base that just separated from one strand attaches to take its place.

This process happens to both of the unzipped strands. When all the bases are in place, a new strand has formed on each of the original strands. In this way, two new DNA molecules are formed, each identical to the original.

Protein Synthesis

What is so important about the order of bases in the DNA molecule? DNA directs the production of substances called proteins. Proteins control most of the life processes in cells. They are also necessary for building and maintaining cells. It is the proteins that cause certain traits to be expressed in an organism.

Proteins are made up of smaller units known as amino acids. There are 20 different amino acids that can be arranged in many different combinations. The specific arrangement of amino acids determines the nature of the protein.

Recall from Chapter 1 that proteins are formed on cell organelles called ribosomes. By means of intermediate molecules, DNA directs the order in which amino acids are arranged to form these proteins. Through this action, DNA controls all cell activities!

Can you find the mutation?

Mutations

Occasionally, an error occurs during the process of DNA replication. This kind of change is called a **mutation.**

A mutation may cause a change in the proteins formed in a cell. Many mutations are harmful because they decrease an organism's chances for survival. In rare cases, mutations are helpful because they result in desirable traits.

Some mutations are neither harmful nor helpful. Even if they result in changes to the organism's proteins, the changes are less obvious and do not directly affect the survival of the organism.

Many mutations occur by chance. Other mutations are caused by environmental factors called mutagens. Ultraviolet radiation from the Sun and certain chemicals, such as some pesticides, can act as mutagens.

Can a mutation be passed to an organism's offspring? This depends on the cell in which the mutation occurs. If the mutation affects a gamete—a sperm cell or an egg cell—the mutation may be passed on to the next generation. Mutations that affect body cells only are not passed along.

▶ **SEQUENCE** How does a mutation affect the traits of an organism?

Do you see the different streaks and colors on the corn kernels? They came from mutations—changes to the normal replication of genes. ▲

A89

Genes and Health

Some human diseases are inherited because they result from mutations in one or more genes. Sickle cell anemia is a disorder that results when a person inherits a mutated gene for the production of hemoglobin. In blood, hemoglobin is the protein that carries oxygen.

In this disorder, one of the nitrogen bases in the gene for hemoglobin is changed. This error results in the production of protein that causes red blood cells to be shaped like sickles instead of the normal donut shape. The sickle shape prevents the cells from working properly.

Cystic fibrosis is another inherited disorder. This is a disease that results from genes that produce a defect in proteins that control the flow of certain materials into and out of cells.

Some other inherited diseases include hemophilia and muscular dystrophy. Hemophilia is a disease in which the blood does not clot properly. Muscular dystrophy causes the muscles to break down over time.

Another type of genetic disorder occurs when chromosomes do not separate properly during reproduction. Recall that chromosomes are copied before a cell divides. The copies split apart, and one copy goes to each new cell. Down syndrome occurs when a specific pair of chromosomes does not separate properly. The extra chromosome results in physical problems and some mental retardation.

▶ **SEQUENCE** How does sickle cell anemia affect human health?

Inherited Diseases

Disorder	Description
Cystic fibrosis	Makes mucus extra thick and sticky, clogging lungs and digestive track.
Hemophilia	Prevents body from producing clotting factors, resulting in uncontrolled bleeding.
Muscular dystrophy	Prevents body from making protein for muscle cells, resulting in muscle weakness.
Sickle cell anemia	Creates red blood cells shaped like sickles. Sickle cells block other cells in the bloodstream and do not carry as much oxygen.

Sickle cell anemia produces blood cells in an abnormal sickle shape. Sickle cells block other blood cells. ▼

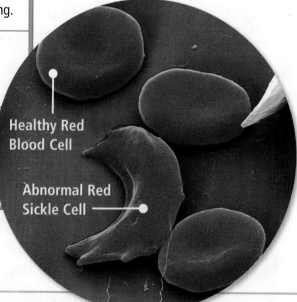

Healthy Red Blood Cell

Abnormal Red Sickle Cell

Lesson Wrap-Up

Visual Summary

Traits can be inherited from parents or acquired from the environment.

DNA in chromosomes contains genes that determine the traits of an organism.

Mutations occur when the bases in a genetic sequence change.

LINKS for Home and School

MATH **Make a Bar Graph** Research the number of chromosome pairs in five different species. Create a bar graph that compares them. Does the number of chromosomes per cell relate to the complexity of the organism? Draw a conclusion from your data.

TECHNOLOGY **Write a Documentary** Scientists continue to develop new technology to study and manipulate DNA. Research the Human Genome Project, genetic engineering, or other scientific advances. Present your findings in the style of a television documentary.

Review

1. **MAIN IDEA** What material carries the information that determines genetic traits?

2. **VOCABULARY** Write a sentence or short paragraph using the terms *genes* and *DNA*.

3. **READING SKILL: Sequence** What steps take place during DNA replication?

4. **CRITICAL THINKING: Apply** How do mutations affect an organism? Why can some mutations have no effect?

5. **INQUIRY SKILL: Analyze Data** What information would a scientist need to discover whether a disorder had a genetic cause, an environmental cause, or a combination of the two?

 TEST PREP

Human traits are most accurately described as

A. almost entirely genetic in origin.

B. both inherited and acquired.

C. almost entirely learned from other humans.

D. like those of plants.

 Technology
Visit **www.eduplace.com/scp/** to find out more about heredity.

Rosalind Franklin

(1920–1958)

In 1962, James Watson, Francis Crick, and Maurice Wilkins were awarded the Nobel Prize for discovering the structure of DNA. Yet their achievement relied greatly on a woman who was not so honored. Alas, Rosalind Franklin had died four years earlier.

As a young girl, Franklin was energetic and talkative, often arguing politics with her father. She excelled in school, especially at science. She became the first woman in her family to graduate from college with a science degree.

Her most famous works are her x-ray pictures of DNA, such as the one shown here. Other scientists had tried to take pictures like this. However, Franklin recognized that DNA changed its shape in water. She carefully and precisely added just the right amount of water to her specimens. From her pictures and other data, she determined much about the shape and composition of the DNA molecule.

One of Franklin's colleagues described her with these words: "…Miss Franklin was distinguished by extreme clarity and perfection in everything she undertook. Her photographs are among the most beautiful of any substances ever taken."

X-ray Picture of DNA

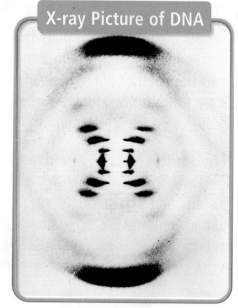

Compare Franklin's X-ray picture to the illustration of DNA on page A87. ▶

Lynn Margulis

(1938–)

In the 1980s, scientists studying cells discovered something they did not expect. Mitochondria, the cell parts that produce energy, have their own DNA! This DNA controls only the mitochondria. It works apart from the DNA in the nucleus.

Yet, the discovery did not surprise everyone. Years earlier, biologist Lynn Margulis predicted just such a finding. The prediction was part of a larger idea she proposed about cell history. It is called the endosymbiont hypothesis.

According to this hypothesis, mitochondria and chloroplasts were once small, free-living cells, much like bacteria. At some point, a larger, amoeba-like cell engulfed some of them. Yet, instead of breaking apart, the small cells stayed alive inside the larger cell. After many cycles of reproduction, they became cell parts.

The endosymbiont hypothesis explains much about mitochondria. As for Margulis, she now is recognized as an insightful and dedicated scientist.

Animal Cell

Mitochondrion

Nucleus

Unique features of mitochondria

- Able to use oxygen
- Surrounded by a double membrane
- Divides separately from the rest of the cell
- Has its own DNA that resembles bacterial DNA

Sharing Ideas

1. **READING CHECK** What did Franklin and Margulis show about DNA?

2. **WRITE ABOUT IT** What does Margulis' hypothesis explain about cells?

3. **TALK ABOUT IT** Which science skills did Franklin and Margulis practice?

A93

Why Are Some Traits Very Common?

Why It Matters...

For a species to continue, its members must reproduce. Sometimes, new individuals are exact copies of one parent. Other times, they are similar to two parents, but not exactly like them. When the two young giraffes become adults, they may pass traits to young of their own.

PREPARE TO INVESTIGATE

Inquiry Skill

Use Models When you use models, you make an object that helps you understand a concept or process.

Materials

- 4 each of 3 shapes of beads or buttons, with each shape in 2 colors (12 beads total)
- chenille stems

Science and Math Toolbox

For step 2, review **Making a Chart to Organize Data** on page H11.

Chromosome Combinations

Procedure

1 **Use Models** Model genes on chromosomes by stringing three beads on each chenille stem. Refer to the chart to find the meaning of each type of bead. Thread the ear shape gene first, then the eye color gene, and then the gene for hair color. Separate the chromosomes into two pairs to represent two parents.

2 **Record Data** In your *Science Notebook*, draw the bead shapes and colors on the chromosomes for each parent. Create a chart to organize your data.

3 **Experiment** Take one chromosome from the first parent to form a gamete chromosome. Repeat for the second parent. Draw the gamete chromosomes in the chart. Then combine them to form the chromosomes for a new cell called a zygote. Draw the chromosomes of the zygote in the chart.

Conclusion

1. **Analyze Data** Is it possible to predict the offspring's chances of having a certain hair color, eye color, and ear shape? Why or why not?

2. **Use Models** Make a model of two parents whose traits are exactly alike and model the offspring's chromosomes. Are the traits of this offspring more predictable than those of the first offspring you modeled?

STEP 1

Trait	A	B
ear shape	Attached	Not Attached
eye color	Blue	Brown
hair color	Brown	Black

STEP 1

STEP 3

Investigate More!

Design an Experiment
Find out what happens when you add more choices of traits. Make models with several choices for eye color, hair color, and one other trait.

READING SKILL

Cause and Effect Use a chart like the one below to show the effects of selective breeding.

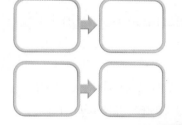

How Traits Are Passed

MAIN IDEA Over many generations, species develop traits that help them to survive.

Asexual Reproduction

You learned in Chapter 1 that some organisms need only one parent to reproduce. In **asexual reproduction,** offspring are produced from one parent. Bacteria and many protists typically reproduce asexually.

Recall that fission and budding are the simplest types of asexual reproduction. Spore formation, which you read about in Chapter 2, is another kind of asexual reproduction. Yeast, for example, may produce spores that are spread by water and wind. Each spore can grow into a new yeast organism.

When an organism reproduces asexually, an exact copy of DNA is passed from parent to offspring. Generation after generation, the offspring have the same genetic material, or DNA. Mutations are the only sources of new traits in this type of reproduction.

Plantlets are offspring that break off or are cut away from the parent plant. Each plantlet can become a separate plant without fertilization. ▼

Plantlet

New Roots

Original Arm

Four New Arms

Regeneration

Starfish, or sea stars, can grow new arms to replace those that have been cut off. This regeneration is a form of asexual reproduction.

In the simplest organisms, such as bacteria, most or all reproduction is asexual. Other organisms use asexual reproduction part of the time. Many fungi and plants, for example, alternate between asexual reproduction and sexual reproduction.

Yeast also alternate. A yeast produces buds asexually. The bud breaks off from the yeast cell and begins to grow. At other times, the yeast produces male and female gametes. These cells can combine to make a new yeast cell.

Plants have several different asexual structures. Some plants produce long stems or roots that then grow plantlets, or baby plants, that break off from the parent. Other kinds of plants can grow from root cuttings or from stem fragments.

Budding

Hydra are animals that reproduce asexually by budding. They can also reproduce using female and male gametes. ▶

Another asexual process in some animals is regeneration. For example, flatworms called *planaria* can regenerate. If a planaria is cut in half, each half will grow to produce two whole worms.

Cells divide during both asexual reproduction and regeneration. In both processes, the new cells have exactly the same DNA as the original cells. Replicating and passing on the same DNA helps ensure that traits will stay the same.

▶ **CAUSE AND EFFECT** How many parent cells are needed for asexual reproduction?

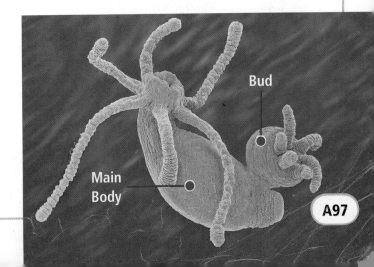

Bud

Main Body

A97

Sexual Reproduction

Sexual reproduction occurs when a female gamete joins with a male gamete to form a new organism. In addition to yeast and algae, animals and plants also practice sexual reproduction.

A flowering plant has male and female reproductive structures in its flowers. Pollination occurs when pollen is transferred from the male part, a stamen, to the female part, a pistil. A sperm cell released by the pollen then fertilizes an egg cell.

In Lesson 1, you learned that gametes contain half the number of chromosomes as in the organism's other cells. When a sperm cell combines with an egg cell, the chromosomes become part of the same cell. The result is a cell with a complete set of chromosomes.

In this way, the offspring receives one chromosome in each pair from each parent. Each chromosome contains genes that determine the traits of the offspring. The offspring receives two genes for each trait.

Different genes may code for different forms of the same trait. For example, suppose a bee carries pollen from a red flower to a yellow flower. The offspring may receive a gene for red flower color and a gene for yellow flower color. Red and yellow are two forms of the same trait—flower color.

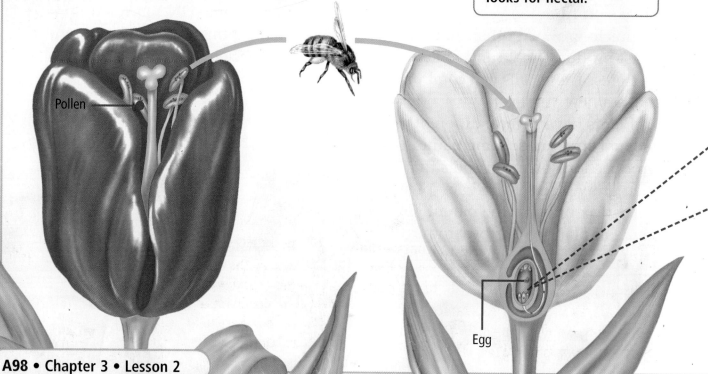

1 **Pollen**
Pollen contains male sex cells that have the male genes.

2 **Pollination**
A bee or other pollinator transports male genetic material from flower to flower.

3 **Egg**
The egg is located deep in the flower. The bee brushes the pollen onto the female parts as it looks for nectar.

Pollen

Egg

The form of a trait that is expressed depends on the characteristics of the genes. Some forms of a trait are dominant and others are recessive. If an offspring receives genes for two different forms of a trait, the trait of the **dominant** gene is expressed. The **recessive** gene is not expressed.

Suppose red flowers are dominant for a particular plant. An offspring plant that receives a gene for red flowers from each parent will have red flowers. So will an offspring plant that receives a gene for red flowers from one parent and a gene for yellow flowers from the other parent. The dominant trait is expressed instead of the recessive trait. Only offspring that receive a gene for yellow flowers from each parent will have yellow flowers.

An organism that has two identical genes for a trait is said to be purebred. A purebred organism can have two dominant genes or two recessive genes. An organism that has two different genes for the same trait is called a **hybrid.**

The offspring of hybrids may express traits that are different from either parent. Think again about the red and yellow flowers. Suppose a bee carries pollen from a red flower to a red flower. Because red flowers are dominant, you might think that all of the offspring will have red flowers. If the parents are hybrids, however, they each carry a gene for yellow flowers—even though you don't see it. If an offspring happens to receive a gene for yellow flowers from each parent, it will express the recessive trait of yellow flowers.

▶ **CAUSE AND EFFECT** In sexual reproduction, how many cells create a new organism?

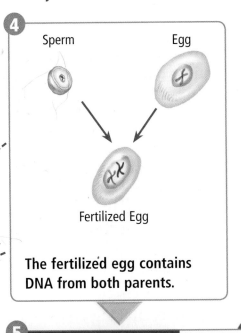

4

Sperm   Egg

Fertilized Egg

The fertilized egg contains DNA from both parents.

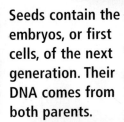

5

Seeds contain the embryos, or first cells, of the next generation. Their DNA comes from both parents.

6

These flowers display the traits of their species and the dominant traits of their particular variants.

Broccoli

Cauliflower

Brussels sprouts

Ancestral Plant?

Broccoli, cauliflower, and Brussels sprouts are just a few of the variants derived by **selective breeding** from an ancient cabbage plant.

Selective Breeding

For thousands of years, humans have identified and worked to increase desirable traits in plants and animals. Long before scientists knew about chromosomes and genes, farmers and shepherds were breeding plants and animals to obtain offspring with useful traits.

The practice of breeding plants and animals for desirable traits is known as **selective breeding.** Through selective breeding, humans try to plan the arrangement of genes in offspring without actually changing the genetic material in any way.

One method of selective breeding involves combining parents with two or more different traits. This method is known as hybridization. The goal of hybridization is to produce a hybrid organism with the best traits from both parents.

For example, a plant breeder might cross a rose plant that produces large, fragrant flowers with a rose bush that does not have thorns. The desired result would be a plant that produces large, fragrant flowers and does not have thorns.

Selective breeding may produce plants and animals that survive specific environments. For example, red winter wheat is a hybrid that grows in cold weather. It allows farmers to harvest two wheat crops a year, even in cold climates.

Another method of selective breeding involves combining plants and animals with the same or similar traits. In this way, a breeder can predict that the traits of the offspring will be very similar to the traits of the parents.

This method, known as inbreeding, is in some ways opposite to hybridization. Breeders sometimes practice inbreeding to keep a breed pure. Horses and dogs, for example, are often bred pure so that offspring maintain the same traits as their parents.

One drawback of inbreeding is that it reduces the chances that an offspring will inherit new combinations of genes. This means that the genetic information among a generation is very similar.

If similar organisms are exposed to changes in their environment, such as harsh weather or disease, all may suffer. In a population where some of the organisms have a different genetic makeup, at least some may survive such conditions.

Why do you think people breed thornless roses? ▶

Today, farmers and ranchers use technology to improve crops and animals. For example, food additives can stimulate hens to lay more eggs or cows to make more milk. Some crop plants release compounds that kill insect pests. Also, computers make it easier to document selective breeding procedures and to identify patterns in the results.

▶ **CAUSE AND EFFECT** **What is the intended result of selective breeding?**

Beef Cow

Dairy Cow

Some cows are bred to produce beef. Others are bred to produce milk.

Adaptations

In nature, favorable traits are not necessarily those traits that are preferred by humans. They are traits that help an organism to survive. Any trait that helps an individual to survive in its environment is called an **adaptation.**

For example, flowers of pond plants will be exposed to many water insects. Those plants that can be pollinated by water insects have an advantage over other plants. This trait makes these plants more likely to survive and reproduce in their environment.

A favorable trait in one environment may not be favorable elsewhere. The same plant that is pollinated by water insects would suffer in a dry, desert environment.

Some adaptations help organisms to find food. The shape of a pelican's beak is an adaptation that allows the bird to scoop up fish. A hummingbird's long, thin beak is adapted to feed on nectar inside flowers. A parrot's beak is short and thick, which lets it crack open seeds.

Other adaptations help organisms defend themselves. Spines or stinging rays keep predators away or wound those that get too close. Thorns, spines, or tough leaves protect plants from being eaten.

▲ Air bladders keep this seaweed floating, letting its leaves bask in the Sun.

▲ A long, deep beak helps a pelican scoop up fish.

▲ Porcupine quills are adaptations that defend against predators.

Camouflage
The walking stick is an insect that looks like a twig. It is well hidden.

Warning coloration
The red and yellow pattern of the poison arrow frog signal predators that it is toxic.

Mimicry
The king snake gets extra protection from looking like a coral snake.

Camouflage Many adaptations protect organisms from predators. The ability to blend into the surroundings is known as camouflage. Organisms with camouflage can hide from predators.

For example, some insects look very much like the flowers of their favorite plants. Bees typically gather honey at the times of day when shadows are deepest. Their black stripes blend into the shadows.

Warning Coloration Bright colors often indicate that an organism is poisonous. The colors warn predators to stay away. The bright colors of many frogs warn other organisms that the frogs are poisonous. A predator that eats one poisonous frog is not likely to eat any others!

Did you know that many birds avoid eating red insects? Red insects often are poisonous.

Mimicry The ability to look like another species is known as mimicry. An organism might mimic another species that is more threatening to a predator. The king snake, for example, is not a poisonous snake. However, it mimics the poisonous coral snake, which most predators will avoid.

Sometimes two species have adaptations that work together. Butterflies, for example, are attracted to plants that have many flowers in large clusters. The butterflies can eat nectar without using too much energy flying from flower to flower. In return, the butterflies help the plants by transferring pollen from one flower to another.

▶ **CAUSE AND EFFECT** What is an adaptation?

Lesson Wrap-Up

Visual Summary

Organisms reproduce in one of two main ways: asexually with only one parent or sexually with two parents.

Through selective breeding, people create offspring that have desirable traits.

Adaptations help individuals to survive in their environments.

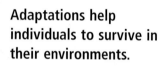 **for Home and School**

MATH Make a Chart Research an endangered species, such as the bald eagle or Florida panther. Make a chart that shows the known population of the species at different times over the last 50 years.

WRITING Explanatory Research the history of horses in the United States. Find out when horses arrived, how they were used, and how people have changed horses. Write a report to show what you learned.

Review

① MAIN IDEA What process do humans use to influence the traits of a species?

② VOCABULARY Write a sentence or short paragraph using the terms *asexual* and *adaptation*.

③ READING SKILL: Cause and Effect What are two possible effects that changes in environment can have on a species?

④ CRITICAL THINKING: Synthesize Compare the benefits and drawbacks of asexual reproduction and sexual reproduction.

⑤ INQUIRY SKILL: Use a Model How could you create a model to show the passing down of a recessive trait through three generations?

 TEST PREP

An adaptation is best described as

A. a series of learned or acquired traits.

B. the result of experimentation by humans.

C. a trait that is favorable to survival.

D. an attempt to grow stronger than other organisms.

 Technology

Visit **www.eduplace.com/scp/** to find out more about adaptations.

Chef

Chefs prepare all kinds of creative and tasty dishes for restaurants. They also work at schools, office buildings, and other places that serve food. Chefs must have excellent cooking skills. Because foods come from living things, chefs need to know the nutritional value of different plants, animals, and fungi. They also need to know how to make different foods look appealing and taste delicious.

What It Takes!

- A certificate from a cooking school or training on the job
- Keen senses of taste and smell
- An artistic flair, to prepare attractive dishes

Botanist

Botany is the scientific study of plants. Botanists may work to develop heartier crops or cures for plant diseases. Or they may research new drugs from plants of the rain forest.

Some botanists travel the world to study unusual plants. Others work in laboratories, conducting experiments on plant parts and plant cells. Still others work with farmers, dieticians, landscape designers, or other people who work with plants.

What It Takes!

- A degree in botany, biology, or ecology
- An interest in plants
- An appreciation for nature

EXTREME Science

Check Out These Chickens

Take a look at these birds. Believe it or not, they really are chickens! They've been bred to bring out certain traits, such as curly feathers or special colors.

How is this done? Selective breeding. Breeders understand that certain traits of the parent are passed through DNA to the offspring. To produce a bird with long, curly feathers, they look for chickens that already have these traits. By selecting only those birds that have long, curly feathers, they gradually develop a new breed of chicken. This same method has created many types of dogs, cats, and other domesticated animals.

This breed of Polish chicken has been raised for at least 500 years. Today people raise fancy chickens like these for fun, profit, and competition.

This hen is the offspring of a Polish rooster and an Araucana frizzle hen. She got her tufted head from Dad and her fluffed-up body feathers from Mom.

The Polish crested ▶ rooster is famous for the umbrella-like crest of feathers on its head.

Review and Test Prep

Vocabulary

Complete each sentence with a term from the list.

1. A trait developed through learning is a(n) _____.

2. A chemical sequence of DNA, or _____, determines a trait of an organism.

3. A(n) _____ is made of a phosphate, a sugar, and a base.

4. The reproductive material known as _____ appears in two strands coiled around each other.

5. A(n) _____ is a change in the arrangement of bases in a gene.

6. Bacteria multiply by _____.

7. A _____ trait is expressed even if only one gene for that form of the trait is inherited.

8. A(n) _____ trait is only expressed if an organism has two genes for that form of the trait.

9. Farmers practice _____ when they mate organisms with desirable traits.

10. Any trait that helps an individual to survive in its environment is a(n) _____.

acquired trait A84
adaptation A102
asexual reproduction A96
chromosome A86
DNA A86
dominant A99
gene A87
heredity A84
hybrid A99
mutation A89
nucleotide A87
recessive A99
selective breeding A100
sexual reproduction A98

Test Prep

Write the letter of the best answer choice.

11. Both traits from the environment and learned traits are _____.

    A. passed down through the chromosomes
    B. taught by parents to offspring
    C. always the result of human intervention
    D. acquired by individuals in each generation

12. In organisms that reproduce sexually, the number of chromosomes in body cells is _____ the number in gametes.

    A. one-half   C. twice
    B. one-third   D. four times

13. In asexual reproduction, _____.

    A. nucleotides join to form genes
    B. the offspring has exactly the same DNA as the parent
    C. male and female gametes join
    D. the offspring inherit traits from two parents

14. Humans can change the traits of other organisms through _____.

    A. selective breeding
    B. introducing new predators or prey
    C. changing the environment
    D. all of the above

Inquiry Skills

15. Analyze Data Copy or trace the diagram below. Choose labels from the list below to label the parts of the diagram.

chromosome   DNA
nitrogenous bases   gene
centromere

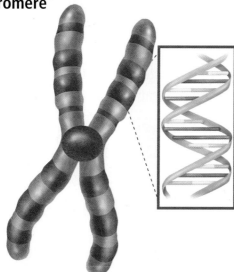

16. Use a Model Draw a diagram that traces one person's chromosomes back through at least three generations (parents, grandparents, and great-grandparents).

Map the Concept

Draw a Venn diagram like the one shown here. Write each term listed below in the space for asexual reproduction, sexual reproduction, or both.

budding   one parent
DNA   pollination
fertilization   regeneration
mutations   two parents

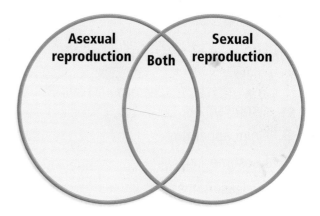

Critical Thinking

17. Synthesize Explain why it is necessary in sexual reproduction for the gametes to have half the number of chromosomes found in body cells.

18. Apply Botanists and farmers save seeds in a seed bank. Explain the purpose of a seed bank. How can two seeds from the same plant species be different?

19. Synthesize Explain why asexual processes are important to organisms that reproduce from two parents.

20. Apply List three inherited or acquired traits that help you survive, and explain why each trait is an advantage.

Performance Assessment

Describe Selective Breeding

Use beads and chenille stems to model the process of selective breeding. Describe how gene numbers change from generation to generation.

Write the letter of the best answer choice.

1. Which shows the mature ovary of an angiosperm?

   A.

   B.

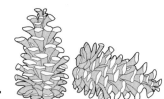

   C.

   D.

2. Which organelle directs the activities of a cell?

   A. cytoplasm

   B. Golgi apparatus

   C. lysosome

   D. nucleus

3. Water and nutrients from soil flow to the leaves of a vascular plant through _____ .

   A. phloem.

   B. spores.

   C. stomata.

   D. xylem.

4. The "master molecules" that determine an organism's traits are called _____ .

   A. amino acids.

   B. chromatids.

   C. DNA.

   D. genes.

5. Which is NOT a trait that this girl probably inherited from her parents?

   A. hairstyle

   B. eye color

   C. nose size

   D. mouth shape

6. Which organ system includes the thyroid gland, adrenal glands, and pancreas?

   A. nervous system

   B. excretory system

   C. endocrine system

   D. circulatory system

7. Which is NOT used during photosynthesis to make food?

   A. carbon dioxide

   B. sugar

   C. sunlight

   D. water

8. Which organism belongs to the fungi kingdom?

A.

B.

C.

D.

Answer the following in complete sentences.

9. Name two diseases caused by single-celled organisms. Explain how each disease makes people sick.

10. Some traits help animals to survive. Name a trait you have that helps you survive. Explain how this trait benefits you.

Discover!

Everything the cell takes in and lets out must pass through the cell membrane. Cells may grow larger as they receive food and oxygen. The larger the cell grows, however, the more nutrients it needs to stay healthy. Beyond a certain cell size, the cell membrane cannot take in nutrients quickly enough.

You can compare a cell to a sugar cube. In this cube, the ratio of surface area to volume is 6 to 1.

If the sugar cube doubles in width, the ratio of surface area to volume decreases to 3 to 1. If a cell grew like this, food and oxygen could not diffuse quickly enough for the cell to survive.

Instead of growing larger and larger, cells divide into new cells. To survive, however, each new cell must continue to border a supply of food and oxygen.

1 cm

Volume: 1 cm³
Surface Area: 6 cm²

2 cm

Volume: 8 cm³
Surface Area: 24 cm²

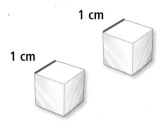

1 cm

1 cm

Volume: 2 cm³
Surface Area: 12 cm²

In all living things, cell size is limited by the ratio of surface area to volume. Should cell volume increase too much, the demand for food and oxygen would be greater than the amount that diffusion can supply. This explains why each of your cells is about the size of an amoeba. You just have many more of them!

Learn more about cell sizes and the ratio of surface area to volume.
Go to **www.eduplace.com/scp/** to run a simulation.

LIFE UNIT B SCIENCE

Interactions Among Living Things

LIFE · UNIT B · SCIENCE

Interactions Among Living Things

Independent Reading

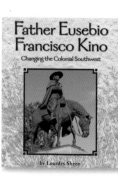

Life on the Serengeti

Biomes

Father Eusebio Francisco Kino

The ears of a jackrabbit measure one-third the length of its body! How do long ears help a jackrabbit survive in hot places? In this unit, you'll learn how certain characteristics help animals survive in their native habitats.

Chapter 4

Ecosystems, Communities, and Biomes

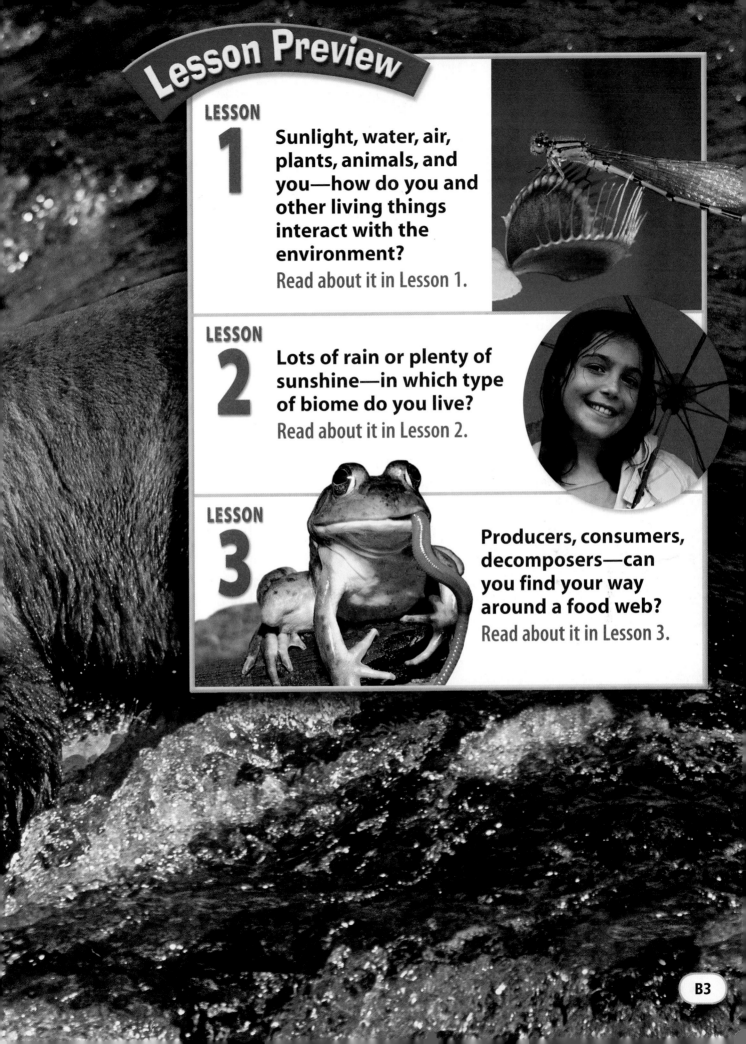

Lesson Preview

LESSON 1

Sunlight, water, air, plants, animals, and you—how do you and other living things interact with the environment?

Read about it in Lesson 1.

LESSON 2

Lots of rain or plenty of sunshine—in which type of biome do you live?

Read about it in Lesson 2.

LESSON 3

Producers, consumers, decomposers—can you find your way around a food web?

Read about it in Lesson 3.

How Do Living Things Form Communities?

Why It Matters...

You live in a community made up of trees and grasses, pets and people, and all the other living things in your area. Living things interact with one another and with nonliving things. In nature, everything an animal needs to survive—including food, air, and shelter—comes from the living and nonliving things in its environment.

PREPARE TO INVESTIGATE

Inquiry Skill

Observe When you observe, you use your senses to determine and describe the properties of objects and events.

Materials

- soil
- 500 ml beaker
- terrarium
- organic matter, such as peat moss or decayed leaves
- food scraps
- water
- earthworms

Look at Life

Procedure

Safety: Wash your hands after setting up the terrarium.

STEP 1

1. **Collaborate** Work in a small group. Measure 500 ml of soil in the beaker. Pour the soil into the terrarium. Spread a thin layer of organic matter over the soil. Add earthworms and a handful of food scraps, such as apple peels, to the terrarium.

2. **Predict** Add water to one side of the terrarium until the soil is slightly wet. In your *Science Notebook,* predict how the earthworms will react to the water. Loosely place the lid on the terrarium. Place it out of the sunlight.

STEP 3

Terrarium Ecosystem	
Living Things	Nonliving Things

3. **Classify** Make a chart in your *Science Notebook* like the one shown. Classify the things in the terrarium as living or nonliving.

4. **Observe** Each day for one week, carefully observe the earthworms and their environment.

STEP 4

5. **Record Data** Write down your observations in your *Science Notebook.* Include the time and day of each observation.

Conclusion

1. **Observe** What interactions did you observe between the earthworms and their environment?

2. **Infer** Based on your observations, what do earthworms need to survive?

Investigate More!

Design an Experiment
Predict whether earthworms grow largest in fine, coarse, or rocky soil. How could you test your prediction? Run an experiment with your teacher's approval.

Ecosystems

VOCABULARY

community   p. B7
ecosystem   p. B6
population   p. B8

READING SKILL

Main Idea and Details
As you read, write down details that describe ecosystems.

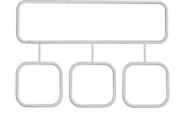

MAIN IDEA An ecosystem is a community of different plants and animals, as well as the water, soil, and other nonliving things in the area.

What Is an Ecosystem?

If you put your head on the ground of a forest, what would you see? You might notice ants marching in line, or worms burrowing through the soil. Fuzzy mosses might tickle your nose, and twigs and bits of leaves might stick in your hair.

A section of forest floor is one example of an ecosystem. An **ecosystem** is made up of all the living and nonliving things that interact in one place. In a forest, the living things range from tiny bacteria and earthworms to trees towering above. Nonliving things include sunlight, soil, water, and air.

Scientists define and study small ecosystems, such as a rotting log or a patch of soil under a tree. They also study large ecosystems, such as a large forest or prairie. Regardless of size, everything in an ecosystem interacts.

Small Ecosystems
Soil, a rotting log, fungus, moss, and a lizard are all part of this small ecosystem.

The Florida Everglades is a large ecosystem in southern Florida. The land is swampy, covered by a thin layer of muddy water. Grasses grow tall because only a few cypress trees block the sunlight.

Closer to the ocean, salt water mixes with fresh water in shallow lands called estuaries. Mangrove trees thrive in estuaries, as do newly hatched fish and shrimp. Many birds nest in the mangroves and fish the waters for food.

The plants, birds, fish, and other organisms of the Everglades make up a community. A **community** is the group of living things found in an ecosystem. These living things depend upon one another for food, shelter, and other needs. They also depend upon the nonliving things in the ecosystem.

Organisms that live well in one ecosystem might not survive in another. Alligators, for example, find food and shelter only in warm, wet places. They also must drink lots of water to flush wastes from their blood.

Like the alligator, the roseate spoonbill is well suited for life in the Everglades. Its tall legs and strong feet are ideal for wading. It shakes its open bill through the water to capture small fish and other animals.

▶ **MAIN IDEA** Describe some interactions among living things in the Everglades.

Roseate spoonbill

Florida panther

Alligator

Large Ecosystem
The Florida Everglades includes a community of many living things, including cypress, birds, panthers, and alligators.

Populations

You can learn a great deal by studying an individual plant, animal, or other organism. But to understand how an ecosystem functions, you need to study populations. A **population** consists of all the members of the same type of organism that live in an ecosystem.

The Everglades ecosystem includes populations of mangrove and cypress trees, alligators and spoonbills, and a wide variety of other species. The birth or death of one plant or animal is not likely to change the Everglades very much. But what if a disease killed all the mangrove trees? Or a new animal species began nesting where the spoonbills nest? Events like these can affect the entire community.

To evaluate ecosystems, scientists consider factors that affect the whole community. One major concern for the Everglades is the water supply. The Everglades depends on fresh water flowing from the north. Yet human needs are draining that supply, and those needs are growing every year.

In an ocean ecosystem, which fish would you suspect are most important in the community? Arguably, the answer is the smallest fishes, including herring and mackerel. These fish are food for bigger fish, which in turn are food for sharks, killer whales, and other big animals. Without large numbers of small fish, many other animals would starve.

▶ **MAIN IDEA** Why are small fish important in ocean ecosystems?

Populations in the Ocean

Feeding Relationships
Small fish eat algae and other plant life, and they are food for larger fish. Feeding relationships like these are a part of all ecosystems.

Visual Summary

Ecosystems are made up of all the living and nonliving things that interact in a given place.

A community is made up of different populations of living things in an ecosystem.

A population consists of all the members of the same type of organism that live in a community.

LINKS for Home and School

MATH Make an Estimate A stable population of small beach crabs is the primary food source for a certain type of sea bird. The crabs support a population of about 500 birds. Changes in the environment result in a 30 percent increase in the crab population. About how many individuals might one expect to find in the sea bird population in later years?

TECHNOLOGY Make a Poster Use the Internet or library to explore which types of technology scientists use to study ecosystems. Share your results with the class by making a poster. Use words and images to explain how the technology works and how it is used.

Review

1 MAIN IDEA How do scientists classify the parts of an ecosystem?

2 VOCABULARY Use the terms *ecosystem, community,* and *population* to describe the area where you live.

3 READING SKILL: Main Idea and Details What nonliving things are found in ecosystems? Why are they important?

4 CRITICAL THINKING: Apply What might happen if one population in an ecosystem disappeared? Give an example.

5 INQUIRY SKILL: Observe Go outside with a partner and carefully observe a small patch of grass. Classify the things you observe as living or nonliving.

 TEST PREP

What makes up an ecosystem?

A. plant and animals only

B. water, air, and other nonliving things

C. all the living and nonliving things and their interactions

D. one population only

 Technology
Visit **www.eduplace.com/scp/** to find out more about ecosystems.

What Are Biomes?

Why It Matters...

Is your area usually hot and wet, or cold and dry? Are there thick forests or tall grasses? These types of factors affect many parts of your life, including the kind of home you live in and the clothes that you wear.

All plants and animals are affected by their environments. The prairie dogs shown below live very well on the grasslands, but would not survive on the tundra or in a rainforest. Earth's different regions support different kinds of living things.

PREPARE TO INVESTIGATE

Inquiry Skill

Analyze Data When you analyze data, you look for patterns in the information to make inferences, predictions, and other generalizations.

Materials

• different-colored pencils
• calculator

Science and Math Toolbox
For step 1, review **Making a Line Graph** on page H13.

Compare Climates

Procedure

Des Moines, Iowa

Equator

Iquitos, Peru

1 **Use Numbers** In your *Science Notebook* make a line graph using data in the temperature chart for Des Moines, Iowa and Iquitos, Peru. Plot the months on the *x*-axis and temperature on the *y*-axis.

2 **Use Numbers** Use the data in the precipitation chart to make a bar graph in your *Science Notebook.* Plot the months on the *x*-axis and precipitation on the *y*-axis.

3 **Use Numbers** Calculate average annual rates of precipitation and temperature for both places.

Average Temperature												
	Jan.	Feb.	Mar.	Apr.	May	Jun.	Jul.	Aug.	Sep.	Oct.	Nov.	Dec.
Des Moines	−7°C	−5°C	−3°C	3°C	7°C	21°C	23°C	22°C	18°C	11°C	2°C	−4°C
Iquitos	27°C	26°C	25°C	25°C	25°C	24°C	24°C	25°C	25°C	25°C	26°C	26°C

Average Precipitation												
	Jan.	Feb.	Mar.	Apr.	May	Jun.	Jul.	Aug.	Sep.	Oct.	Nov.	Dec.
Des Moines	4 cm	3 cm	5 cm	6 cm	11 cm	13 cm	8 cm	9 cm	7 cm	6 cm	4 cm	2 cm
Iquitos	24 cm	26 cm	25 cm	35 cm	26 cm	13 cm	16 cm	12 cm	27 cm	19 cm	24 cm	26 cm

Conclusion

1. **Analyze Data** Describe temperature and precipitation patterns in both places. Which place receives more precipitation? Is precipitation constant throughout the year?

2. **Compare** Use the data to compare Des Moines and Iquitos to your community.

— Investigate More! —

Design an Experiment
Study a globe to find a city of the same latitude as Des Moines. Research climate data for that city. How do their climates compare? Make a chart or graph to show data.

Biomes

VOCABULARY

biome	p. B12
climate	p. B12
desert	p. B14
grasslands	p. B14
taiga	p. B15
temperate forests	p. B13
tropical rain forests	p. B13
tundra	p. B15

READING SKILL

Text Structure As you read, use the heads and subheads to outline the lesson.

MAIN IDEA Biomes are large regions of Earth. Each biome has a characteristic climate that determines its communities of living things.

Earth's Major Biomes

A **biome** is a large group of ecosystems that have similar characteristics. Study the map below to find the six major land biomes.

What makes biomes different from one another? The most important factor is climate. **Climate** refers to the type of weather that occurs in an area over a long period of time. Some climates are rainy, while others are quite dry. Some have a variety of temperatures, while others are almost always hot or cold. Different climates support different populations of living things.

Earth is home to six major land biomes. In each biome, climate affects the kinds of plants and animals that live there. ▼

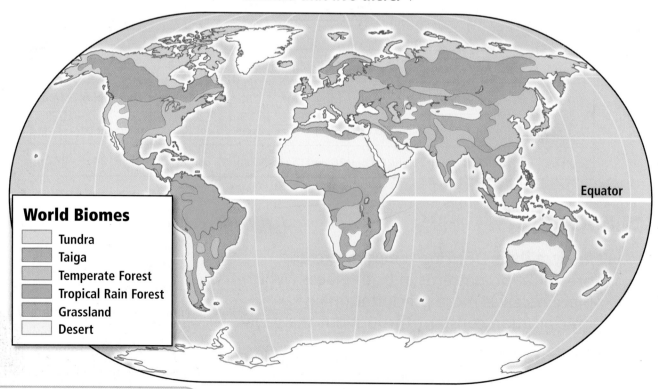

Equator

World Biomes
- Tundra
- Taiga
- Temperate Forest
- Tropical Rain Forest
- Grassland
- Desert

Forest Biomes

Forests are home to tall trees and the animals that live in them. Forests are part of two biomes. **Tropical rain forests** are very rainy and hot. Some rain forests get more than 600 cm (240 in.) of rain each year! Temperatures range from about 18°C to 35°C (64°F to 95°F), which is like a hot summer that lasts all year.

Because of the moisture and warmth, tropical rain forests are teeming with life. In fact, more kinds of plants and animals live in this biome than in any other. Its huge mass of plants produces much of Earth's oxygen. Some of these plants might supply new medicines and other useful products.

The other type of forest biome, **temperate forests,** experiences four distinct seasons: summer, fall, winter, and spring. Temperatures range from a chilly –30°C (–22°F) to a warm 30°C (86°F). A temperate forest receives perhaps one-fifth the rainfall of a tropical forest.

These forests are home to animals such as white-tailed deer, rabbits, skunks, squirrels, and black bears. The trees include maple, oak, hickory, and beech. These trees lose their leaves in the fall and are dormant through winter. The fallen leaves decay on the ground and add nutrients to the soil.

▶ **TEXT STRUCTURE** Compare the climates of both forests.

Tropical Rain Forest

Location: near the equator
Climate: warm and wet

Temperate Forest

Location: eastern North America and other places
Climate: four distinct seasons

B13

Grasslands

Location: central Africa, central U.S., and other regions

Climate: distinct dry season

Desert

Location: varies

Climate: extremely dry

Grasslands and Deserts

Grasses cover the land in the **grasslands** biome. Trees are few and far between.

There are two main types of grasslands: prairies and savannas. Prairies are found in temperate regions, such as the central United States. Temperatures may dip as low as −40°C (−40°F) in winter and soar to 38°C (100°F) in summer. Prairie animals include prairie dogs, coyotes, hawks, and grouse.

Most savannas are found in warmer regions, such as central Africa. Yearly temperatures typically remain above 18°C (64°F). Elephants, giraffes, lions, and zebras call the savanna home.

A savanna receives as much as 100 cm (40 in.) of rain each year. But the savanna has a dry season, as do other grasslands. That's partly why trees are scarce in this biome—they do not thrive for long periods without water.

The **desert** is the driest biome. Most deserts receive less than 25 cm (10 in.) of rain each year. In fact, some deserts may not see a drop of rain all year long.

Cacti, sagebrush, and other plants are found in many deserts. Desert plants and animals are adapted to live with little water. Cacti, for example, have a waxy coating and spiny leaves to help reduce water loss. Earth's driest deserts contain little life. These deserts are filled with sandy dunes that stretch seemingly without end.

Taiga and Tundra

The **taiga** biome has long, severe winters and short, cool summers. Temperatures may reach 10°C (50°F) during only one to three months each year. The taiga is fairly dry, each year receiving only about 50 cm (20 in.) of precipitation, mostly snow.

The most common trees in the taiga are conifers, such as pines, firs, and spruces. The leaves of these trees are thin, waxy needles that help keep in water. Their leaves do not fall all at once when the weather turns cold. Animals of the taiga include moose, deer, and wolves.

As harsh as the taiga can be, it is mild compared to the tundra. The **tundra** is Earth's coldest biome, having an average winter temperature of –34°C (–29°F). The ground is frozen for hundreds of meters down, and lower layers stay frozen all year long. This frozen ground is called permafrost.

In summer, temperatures hover just under 10°C (50°F). As the ground thaws, the tundra becomes swampy and covered with mosses, lichens, and dwarf-like trees. Mosquitoes thrive in the short summer.

Other tundra animals include polar bears, caribou, and reindeer. These animals have adaptations that help them survive in this cold biome. Polar bears, for example, have a thick layer of fat to keep them warm.

▶ **TEXT STRUCTURE** How do temperatures compare in the taiga and tundra?

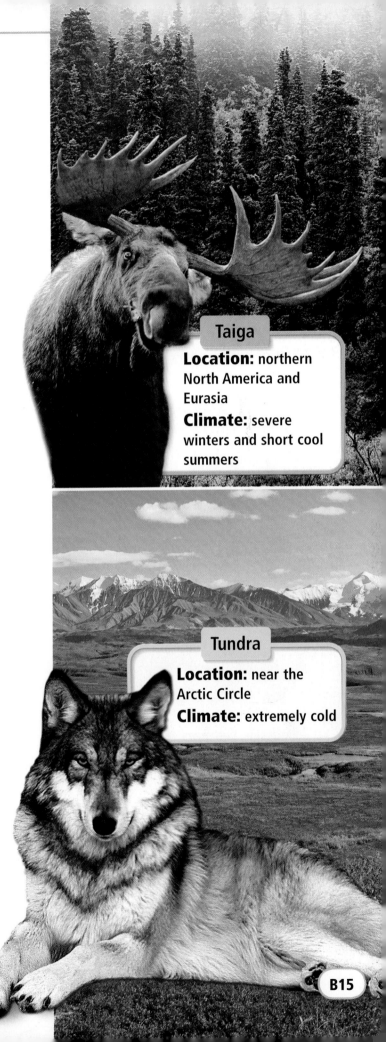

Taiga
Location: northern North America and Eurasia
Climate: severe winters and short cool summers

Tundra
Location: near the Arctic Circle
Climate: extremely cold

Marine Biomes

Look back at the map on page B12. Oceans cover about 70 percent of Earth's surface! They are home to the marine biomes.

Living things need special adaptations to live on or near the ocean shore. This is because the water level keeps changing with the tides. The intertidal zone is the area that ocean tides cover and uncover in a regular cycle. Sometimes this zone is under water, and other times it is exposed to the Sun and air.

In this zone, animals such as clams and mussels attach sticky threads to rocks so the waves won't wash them away. Other animals, including many kinds of crabs and some snails, can move about over land and underwater.

Just beyond the shore is the near-shore zone. In some places, this zone is home to an underground forest of tall, brown seaweed called kelp. Otters and other animals live among the swaying stalks.

The presence of water and sunlight defines the zones of marine biomes. Different plants and animals live in each. ▼

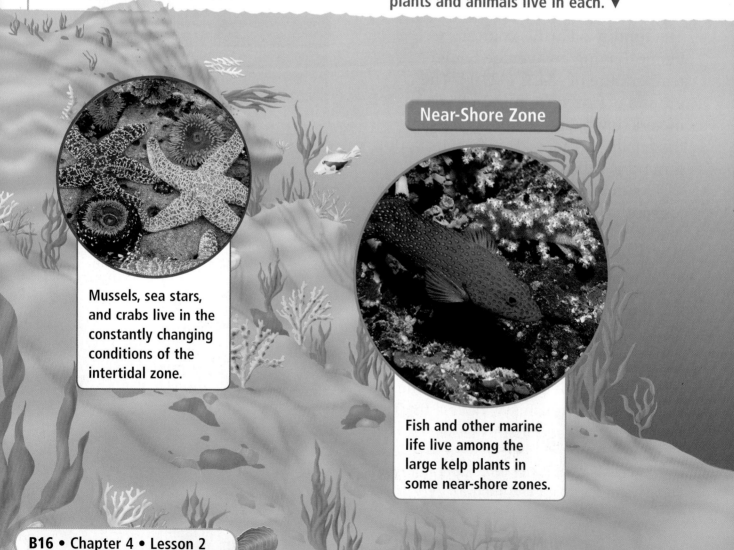

Intertidal Zone

Mussels, sea stars, and crabs live in the constantly changing conditions of the intertidal zone.

Near-Shore Zone

Fish and other marine life live among the large kelp plants in some near-shore zones.

Still farther out to sea is the open ocean zone. Here, the water is deep and cold. Tiny algae float near the surface. Algae are plant-like organisms, and most are single-celled. Because algae are so numerous, they produce most of Earth's oxygen! They also provide food for ocean animals.

Even when the water is clear, sunlight mostly reaches a depth of only about 200 meters (660 ft). So, the floor of the open ocean is very cold and dark. Organisms here use special adaptations to survive such a harsh environment. Some fish produce their own light, just as lightning bugs do on land. The light helps them to hunt for food.

Other unusual organisms include the giant tubeworms that live by vents on the ocean floor. These vents release heat and gases from Earth's interior. The tubeworms are unusual because the vents—not the Sun—are the source of their energy. Bacteria near the vents make food using heated chemicals, a process unlike any other on Earth.

▶ **TEXT STRUCTURE** **Compare the conditions in the three zones of the ocean.**

Dolphins, whales, and jellyfish spend much of their time near the surface in open ocean zones.

Open Ocean Zone

Huge schools of herring, tuna, and other fish live in the middle depths of the open ocean.

Fangtooth fish and other creatures have adapted to the cold and darkness of the deepest parts of the ocean.

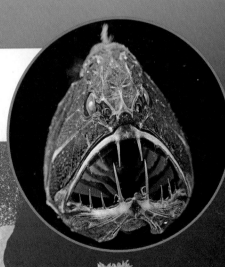

Freshwater Ecosystems

Other bodies of water are made up of fresh water. These ecosystems include streams, rivers, ponds, lakes, and wetlands.

Streams and rivers contain flowing water. Near the beginning of a river, the current is usually fast and the water is clear. Trout and other fast-swimming fish live in this zone. Farther downstream, the current slows and the river widens. Plants are able to take root in the muddy bottom. Fish, beavers, and waterfowl may find homes here.

Kingfishers hunt for fish in fresh water. ▼

As the river flows, it picks up sediments. Near the end of the river, called the mouth, the water drops its sediments and becomes murky. Catfish and carp may live in these dark waters.

Ponds and lakes are made of still water. Some are small and may disappear during dry spells. Others, such as the Great Lakes, are huge.

Deep ponds and lakes have three different zones. Algae, plants, insects, and fish live near the sun-warmed surface. Farther down, the water is cooler, but some sunlight shines through. Here live plankton, which is a general term for many kinds of tiny organisms that live in water. Fish and other larger animals feed on the plankton.

Still farther down is a zone that is deep and cold. Bacteria and other decomposers break down dead plants and animals.

▶ **TEXT STRUCTURE** What are three types of freshwater ecosystems?

Visual Summary

Different biomes have different climates and types of plants. Climate is influenced by temperature and precipitation.

Land biomes include tropical rain forests, temperate forests, grasslands, deserts, taiga, and tundra.

Water covers much of Earth's surface. Many organisms live in marine biomes and freshwater ecosystems.

LINKS for Home and School

MATH Find an Average Annual rainfall in a particular rain forest is shown in the table below. What was the average rainfall over the five-year period?

Year 1	Year 2	Year 3	Year 4	Year 5
250 cm	240 cm	230 cm	260 cm	250 cm

TECHNOLOGY Gather Data Set up a rain gauge and record precipitation levels for one week. During the same period, use a thermometer to record temperatures. Explain how your data relate to the type of climate found in your biome.

Review

1 MAIN IDEA What factors distinguish one biome from another?

2 VOCABULARY What is a biome? List six examples of biomes.

3 READING SKILL: Text Structure Use your outline of this lesson to summarize the biome of your choice.

4 CRITICAL THINKING: Analyze Why aren't marine algae found at depths below 200 meters? How does this influence life at these depths?

5 INQUIRY SKILL: Analyze Data Which land biomes have a greater temperature range during the year, those near the equator or those in temperate regions?

 TEST PREP

Unlike freshwater ecosystems, marine biomes are

A. salty.

B. dry.

C. sunny.

D. full of life.

 Technology

Visit **www.eduplace.com/scp/** to find out more about biomes.

Earth's ecosystems inspire writers of both fiction and science. Compare these two selections about the Everglades of Florida.

Some Rivers
by Frank Asch

Some rivers rush to the sea.
They push and tumble and fall.
But the Everglades is a river
with no hurry in her at all.
Soaking the cypress
that grows so tall;
nursing a frog,
so quiet and small;
she flows but a mile
in the course of a day,
with plenty of time
to think on the way.

But how can she cope
with the acres of corn
and sorrowful cities that drain her?
With hunters and tourists and levees
that chain and stain and pain her?
Does the half of her that's left
think only of the past?
Or does she think of her future
and how long it will last?
Some rivers rush to the sea.
They push and tumble and fall.
But the Everglades is a river
with no hurry in her at all.

The River of Grass

Prologue to Everglades: Buffalo Tiger and the River of Grass, **by Peter Lourie**

In the early sixteenth century the Spanish explorer Ponce de León searched the coast of Florida for the Fountain of Youth. He never discovered the mythical fountain, but if he had penetrated deeper into the peninsula that the Spaniards called "the land of flowers," he might have found something else: the Everglades, a slow-moving swamp that is in fact a huge, silent river.

The Everglades, called Pa-hay-okee, or "Grassy Water," by the Miccosukee Indians, is often only inches deep, yet it runs a hundred miles from Florida's Lake Okeechobee to the Gulf of Mexico and Florida Bay. In places it is seventy miles wide. It has been called a river of grass because of the dense waves of tawny sawgrass arcing gently to the south, pointing in the direction of the sluggish flow of the water.

The Miccosukee Indians have lived in the Everglades for more than a hundred years. When they first arrived they found the river of grass to be a kind of paradise. Even today, the Grassy Water dazzles the eye with its abundance of birds and other wildlife. Yet, unlike a hundred years ago, there is sadness in this bright spot on the planet. Great pressures from pollution and overdevelopment threaten to destroy the river of grass.

Sharing Ideas

1. **READING CHECK** According to both passages, what major problems threaten the Everglades?

2. **WRITE ABOUT IT** Why is the Everglades a special, unique place? Express your ideas.

3. **TALK ABOUT IT** What do you think should be done to protect the Everglades?

What Is a Food Web?

Why It Matters...

What did you have for breakfast? Like this owl, you get the energy you need from food. Food energy comes ultimately from the Sun. It is then passed through an ecosystem by living things.

Inquiry Skill

Use Models When you use models, you make and analyze a structure or picture representing a real-world process to better understand how the process works.

Materials

- different-colored pencils
- Investigate photo card

Science and Math Toolbox
For step 2, review **Making a Chart to Organize Data** on page H11.

Model Energy Flow

Procedure

STEP 1

1. **Hypothesize** Look at the photo card of living things. It includes grass, zebras, and a lion. Form a hypothesis about how each organism obtains its energy.

2. **Use Models** In an ecosystem, energy from food passes from one organism to another. Producers get their energy from the Sun. In your *Science Notebook,* make a chart like the one shown. Which organisms in the photo are producers? Draw the producers in the bottom level of the chart.

3. **Use Numbers** Producers get 100 units of energy from the Sun. Write this number of units on the chart. Note that producers use 90 percent of these units for their own life processes.

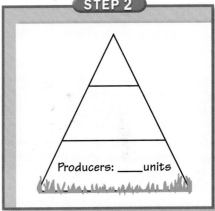

STEP 2

Producers: _____ units

4. **Use Models** Which consumers eat the producers? Draw the consumers in the next level of the chart. Record the amount of energy available to them. They will use 90 percent of this energy.

5. **Use Models** Which consumer eats other consumers? Draw this consumer in the top level of the chart. Record its available energy.

Conclusion

1. **Use Numbers** How much energy is left for the living things that eat the producers? How much is left for the last consumer?

2. **Infer** Why aren't there more levels in the chart? Explain.

Investigate More!

Research The model you used is called an energy pyramid. Use the Internet or library to research energy pyramids. What happens to energy as it is passed from one living thing to another?

Energy Flow

VOCABULARY

food chain   p. B25
food web   p. B26

READING SKILL

Classify As you read, sort groups of living things according to their role in a food web.

MAIN IDEA In an ecosystem, energy flows from producers to consumers to decomposers.

Energy from Food

Would you like to make food from a gas in the air and water from the ground? You could do that—if you were a plant. Plants are Earth's producers, as are algae and certain bacteria. A producer makes its own food from raw materials and energy.

Plants and other producers use the energy of sunlight, changing it into chemical energy. Water and carbon dioxide combine into sugars and oxygen. Sugars are the food for the plant. Plants use some of these sugars to grow, and store the rest in their tissues.

When you eat a plant, you take in energy the plant stored. You and all other animals are consumers. A consumer gets energy by eating food, not producing it.

First-Level Consumer

The caterpillar is a first-level consumer that eats leaves.

Producer

Grass and other plants are producers. They make up the first link in most food chains.

Food Chains

To better understand feeding relationships, scientists organize the living things of a community into food chains. A **food chain** describes how energy in an ecosystem flows from one organism to another.

Almost all food chains begin with the Sun. Producers, such as green grass, capture the Sun's energy to make food. Animals that eat plants, such as a caterpillar, are called first-level consumers or primary consumers. These animals eat plants or other producers.

The birds are second-level consumers. They eat other consumers. The cat is a third-level consumer. Notice that all the consumers rely on plants. Without plants, there would not be a food chain.

Which other organisms play a role in a food chain? If plants and animals die without being eaten, organisms called decomposers will break down the remains. Decomposers include bacteria, some protists, and fungi, as well as earthworms and other small animals. They serve to return an organism's tissues back to the soil for new organisms to use again.

In every ecosystem, different producers, consumers, and decomposers are constantly filling their roles in food chains. You, too, are part of food chains. When are you a primary consumer? Are you also a second-level consumer?

▶ **CLASSIFY** Compare a producer and a consumer.

Second-Level Consumer

The bird is a second-level consumer that eats the caterpillar.

Third-Level Consumer

The cat is a third-level consumer that eats the bird.

Decomposers

Decomposers break down the decaying remains of dead producers and consumers.

Food Webs

Like you, most animals take part in more than one food chain. For example, do cats eat only birds? No, cats also eat mice and fish.

A **food web** shows how food chains combine in an ecosystem. Look at the food web on the opposite page. The algae, trees, and smaller plants are producers. The mouse eats plant seeds, and it also eats insects. The snake eats insects, too, but it also eats mice. The hawk hunts both mice and snakes, and so does the fox.

By studying food webs, scientists can explain how ecosystems function. They also can predict the effects of changes to an ecosystem. If the hawks all left the ecosystem shown here, how do you think the other animals would be affected?

Classifying Consumers Most consumers play a similar role in every food chain they are a part of. A rabbit, for example, is always a primary consumer. It is an herbivore, meaning "plant eater."

Other consumers are second- or third-level consumers. Examples include hawks and snakes. These animals are called carnivores. The word *carnivore* means "meat eater." Many carnivores are predators, animals that hunt and kill prey.

A few animals, such as bears, eat both plants and animals. They are omnivores—the prefix *omni-* meaning "all." If you eat both plant and animal products, you are an omnivore, too.

Cycles in Nature

Food chains and food webs show how energy flows through an ecosystem. Ecosystems have many other interactions, too.

For example, as you learned in Chapter 2, plants take up carbon dioxide from the air and release oxygen. Animals do just the opposite—they release carbon dioxide and take in oxygen. In this way, plants and animals provide one another with the gases each needs.

Another important cycle is the water cycle. All living things need water. Water leaves Earth's surface through evaporation. It returns through rain, sleet, and snow.

Nitrogen also cycles through ecosystems. Nitrogen is a gas that makes up almost four-fifths of Earth's atmosphere. All living things need nitrogen, but in a form different than nitrogen gas from the air. Fortunately, certain bacteria are able to "fix" nitrogen gas into a form that plants can use. Animals obtain nitrogen by eating plants.

Bug-eating Plants Marshy soils typically have little fixed nitrogen. To get the nitrogen they need, some plants take an interesting approach— they "eat" animals!

When an insect touches the tooth-like fringes on a Venus flytrap, for example, the plant closes its leaves over it. These plants trap insects not for their energy, but for the fixed nitrogen in their bodies.

▶ **CLASSIFY** How do consumers and producers interact in an ecosystem?

Food Web
Energy is transferred from one organism to another in a food web. The arrows show the direction of energy flow.

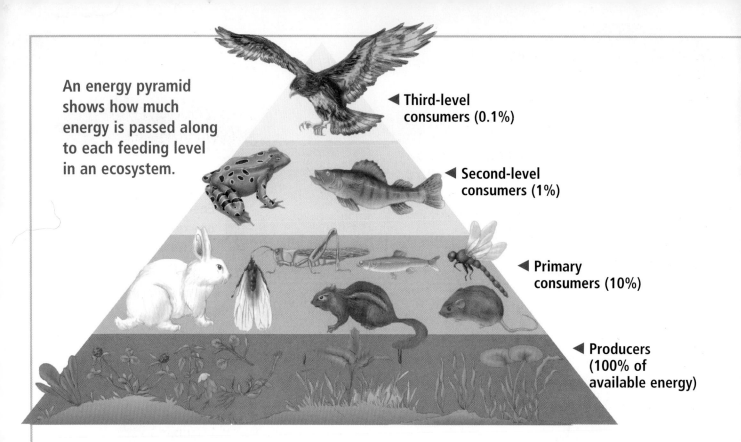

An energy pyramid shows how much energy is passed along to each feeding level in an ecosystem.

◄ Third-level consumers (0.1%)

◄ Second-level consumers (1%)

◄ Primary consumers (10%)

◄ Producers (100% of available energy)

Energy Pyramid

What happens to the food you eat? You use the energy stored in food to walk, run, and engage in many other activities. A lot of this energy leaves your body in the form of heat. Any leftover energy is stored in your body tissues. You, like all living things, use some energy, lose some as heat, and store some energy in tissues.

An energy pyramid shows how energy flows through an ecosystem. Notice that each level is larger than the level above it. In general, only about 10 percent of the energy in one level is passed on to the next.

Producers, such as plants, make up the base of the energy pyramid. Primary consumers make up the next level. Second- and third-level consumers make up the next levels.

An energy pyramid explains a great deal about the populations of ecosystems. As a general rule, producers have the largest populations because they have the most energy available to them. Next in numbers are the primary and second-level consumers. An ecosystem can support only a few third-level consumers.

The higher an animal's level on the energy pyramid, the wider the range of land it must cover for food. This explains the large hunting ranges of animals such as eagles, lions, and snakes. These animals all have adaptations to move quickly and to catch smaller animals.

The energy pyramid also explains why food chains last only for three or four links. Beyond that, little energy remains for an animal to use.

 **CLASSIFY** **What is an energy pyramid?**

Lesson Wrap-Up

Visual Summary

Producers get their energy from the Sun. All other living things get their energy from producers.

A food chain shows the flow of energy from one organism to another. A food web shows overlapping food chains in an ecosystem.

Energy is lost as heat at each step of a food chain. An energy pyramid shows how much energy is available for producers and consumers.

LINKS for Home and School

MATH Make a Graph Only 10 percent of the energy in one level of a food chain is passed on to the next. Make a graph showing energy movement in a four-level food chain. Assume 100 units of energy at the lowest level.

HEALTH Make a Food Pyramid Humans need to eat different types of foods to stay healthy. Research the basic food groups and serving suggestions. Make a food pyramid that shows what you should eat each day.

Review

1 MAIN IDEA Describe how energy flows through an ecosystem.

2 VOCABULARY Compare a food chain with a food web. Use both terms to explain how animals interact and depend on one another.

3 READING SKILL: Classify Give one example each of a producer, herbivore, carnivore, omnivore, and decomposer.

4 CRITICAL THINKING: Apply What would happen to an ecosystem if a drought killed half of the plants that lived there?

5 INQUIRY SKILL: Use Models List the things you ate for breakfast today. Use the list to construct one or more food chains for each food.

 TEST PREP

Unlike a carnivore, an herbivore

A. makes its own food.

B. eats only producers.

C. eats other animals.

D. eats both plants and animals.

 Technology
Visit **www.eduplace.com/scp/** to find out more about food webs.

Blushing Giants

Walruses blush a lot, but not because they're embarrassed! It's just their way of staying comfortable in their cold Arctic biome. Walruses have a thick layer of blubber that keeps them warm in the ocean. Out in the Sun, all that padding makes them hot. So when they sunbathe, their hot blood rushes to the surface to let off some heat. The walruses turn bright pink.

Hippopotamuses turn pink too, but in a very different way. Hippo skin oozes reddish slime. This slime is an adaptation to the hot climate of their African biome. The slime keeps the hippos' skin from drying out under the powerful tropical sun. It works as a sunscreen too. The best part is that the hippo never has to remember to put it on!

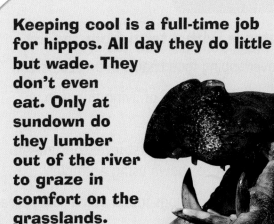

Keeping cool is a full-time job for hippos. All day they do little but wade. They don't even eat. Only at sundown do they lumber out of the river to graze in comfort on the grasslands.

These overgrown teeth are no use at all for chewing, but they make handy tools in a frozen world. After a huge meal of clams on the ocean floor, walruses use their sharp tusks to haul themselves onto the slippery ice.

Vocabulary

Complete each sentence with a term from the list.

1. A(n) _____ shows overlapping food chains in an ecosystem.

2. Zebras are an example of a(n) _____ of living things in an ecosystem.

3. The flow of energy from producer to first-level consumer to second-level consumer can be shown using a simple _____.

4. Different populations of living things found in the same area at the same time form a(n) _____.

5. A(n) _____ includes living and nonliving things interacting together.

6. Ecosystems with similar climate and vegetation make up a(n) _____.

7. Temperature and precipitation determine the _____ of an area.

8. The _____ biome has long, severe winters and short, cool summers.

9. Prairies and savannas are the two main types of _____.

10. _____ has a layer of frozen ground called permafrost.

biome B12
community B7
climate B12
desert B14
ecosystem B6
food chain B25
food web B26
grasslands B14
population B8
taiga B15
temperate forests B13
tropical rain forests B13
tundra B15

Test Prep

Write the letter of the best answer choice.

11. About _____ percent of the energy available at one level of an energy pyramid passes to the next level.

   A. 10
   B. 30
   C. 60
   D. 90

12. Tropical rain forests are _____ year round.

   A. cold and dry
   B. cold and wet
   C. warm and dry
   D. warm and wet

13. Very limited populations survive in Earth's driest _____.

   A. tropical rain forests
   B. grasslands
   C. taigas
   D. deserts

14. Trees that lose their leaves in cool fall weather are common in _____.

   A. tropical rain forests
   B. temperate rain forests
   C. taigas
   D. deserts

15. Classify How do scientists classify a marine biome into three zones? In which zone must populations survive both above and below the water? What happens in this zone?

16. Analyze Data The table below shows climate data for two cities in the United States. What biome do you suspect each city is a part of? Explain. You may choose to graph the data to organize it.

Temp: Average monthly temperature (°F)
Precip: Total precipitation (inches)

Month	City A Temp/Precip.	City B Temp/Precip.
Jan.	54/0.7	24/2.7
March	62/0.9	34/2.7
May	79/0.1	57/3.1
July	94/0.8	71/3.1
Sept.	86/0.9	62/3.5
Nov.	62/0.7	41/3.8

17. Apply Describe four ways that you interacted with living and nonliving things in ecosystems today.

18. Analyze If you wanted to show energy flow in an ecosystem, would it be best to use a food chain or a food web? Explain your answer.

19. Evaluate Your friend comments that bacteria are all unhealthy. What could you say to improve his understanding of bacteria?

20. Analyze Which animal receives more energy from a producer: a first-level consumer or a second-level consumer? Explain.

Performance Assessment

Display a Biome

Make a display that shows a typical scene from a biome. Include at least four different types of living things. The display may be a detailed drawing, poster, or diorama. Write a paragraph or short essay to accompany the display.

Map the Concept

Fill the terms below into the concept map. Each oval represents a larger group than the oval inside it.

Biome
Community
Ecosystem
Organism
Population

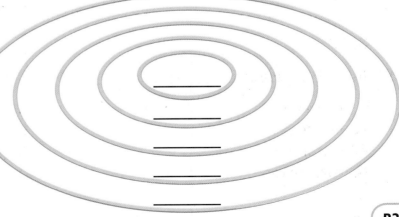

Chapter 5

Life in Ecosystems

LESSON 1

Living things live on the highest mountains and in the deepest oceans. How do they survive in such different places?

Read about it in Lesson 1.

LESSON 2

Decreases in food supply, changes in climate, relocated species—how do these factors upset the balance of an ecosystem?

Read about it in Lesson 2.

LESSON 3

Swamps turn into meadows, meadows turn into forests—how do living things respond to changes in ecosystems?

Read about it in Lesson 3.

What Are Habitats and Niches?

Why It Matters...

How can a clownfish live so close to the stinging tentacles of a sea anemone? The fish rubs against the anemone, coating its scales with a kind of slime. The anemone doesn't recognize the coated fish as food.

Living things interact with one another in all sorts of ways. These interactions are key to understanding how they survive.

PREPARE TO INVESTIGATE

Inquiry Skill

Observe When you observe, you use your senses to describe the properties of objects and events.

Materials

- safety goggles
- earthworms
- goldfish
- 2 aquariums
- soil
- organic matter
- apple peels
- fish food

Worm and Fish Habitats

Procedure

Safety: Wear goggles when handling soil.

STEP 1

1. **Collaborate** Work in a small group. Half fill one aquarium with soil. Spread a thin layer of decayed leaves or other organic matter over the soil. Add some earthworms and a handful of apple peels. Moisten the soil. Wash your hands afterwards.

2. **Measure** Fill the second aquarium with water at room temperature, almost to the top. Add the goldfish and fish food. You may also add small rocks and plastic plants. Wash your hands afterwards.

STEP 2

3. **Observe** Each day for a week, observe the earthworms and fish. How do they move? What do they eat? How do they affect their environment?

4. **Record Data** In your *Science Notebook,* write your observations in a chart like the one shown.

STEP 4

Observations		
	Worms	Fish
Physical Properties		
Type of Food		
Interactions		

Conclusion

1. **Infer** What body parts make the fish well suited to their environment? How are the earthworms suited to their environment?

2. **Predict** Could the fish live in the earthworms' environment? Could the earthworms live in the fish's environment? Why or why not?

Investigate More!

Research Learn about an interesting plant or animal that lives in the wild in your state. Where does it live? What role does it fill in its ecosystem?

VOCABULARY

adaptation	p. B40
habitat	p. B38
niche	p. B39
symbiosis	p. B42

READING SKILL

Compare and Contrast
As you read, compare and contrast relationships among different organisms and their environments.

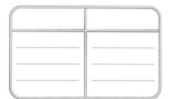

Habitats and Niches

MAIN IDEA Each kind of organism occupies a particular niche in its habitat.

Habitats

To tell people where you live, you probably use a street address. An address is a simple way to describe the location of your home.

All living things have an "address," a place they live in. This place is called a habitat. A **habitat** is the area where an organism lives, grows, and develops. Everything that an organism needs to survive can be found in its habitat.

Many different living things may live in the same habitat. The African savanna, for example, is home to zebras, lions, and many other animals.

Savanna Habitat

Lion
The niche of a lion in a savanna includes hunting zebras.

Niches

Have you seen pictures or movies of workers at an automobile factory? Every worker has a place to be and a job to do. If one of them fails to do his or her job, everyone else's job is affected.

Organisms in a habitat have specific functions, too. A **niche** describes what an organism does in its habitat. You can think of a niche as a job at a factory or a role in a play. Each organism plays a certain role in its habitat.

Look at the savanna habitat shown below. The zebras are consumers. They eat producers, such as grass. They drink water from the watering hole. These are parts of their niche.

Zebras are also food for lions. That is another part of their niche. Zebras and lions share the same habitat, but have different niches.

Niches describe more than just feeding relationships. A niche includes exactly where in the habitat an organism lives, how it reproduces, how it protects itself, and how it behaves. For example, birds in the savanna may live in nests. They may use sticks, mud, and other materials. Part of their niche includes recycling such materials from their habitat.

Each group of organisms in a habitat uses resources in different ways. Zebras, for example, eat the grass. Lions do not eat grass, but they lie in the grass. Birds use the grass to build nests. Because each group uses the same resources in different ways, there are enough resources for everyone. However, changes in ecosystems can upset this balance, as you'll learn in the next lesson.

▶ **COMPARE AND CONTRAST** How do habitats and niches compare?

Zebra
The niche of a zebra in a savanna includes eating grass.

Adaptations

What if you see a drawing of a large, white polar bear crossing a hot, sandy desert? Something's wrong with this picture! Can you explain what it is?

The thick fur and heavy padding of a polar bear help it stay warm in its cold, arctic habitat. Desert animals, on the other hand, have body parts that help them stay cool. These characteristics are called adaptations. An **adaptation** is any characteristic that helps an organism survive.

Sometimes adaptations are physical. The turtles in the pictures on this page are good examples of similar animals with different adaptations. The desert tortoise has legs that help it move easily across the sand. The sea turtle has flippers that help it move through water. Each animal's body is physically adapted to its habitat.

Plants have adaptations, too. For example, a cactus's leaves are thin, pointed spines. Its body, or stem, has a very thick outer layer. These adaptations help the cactus conserve water in its dry habitat.

Other adaptations are behavioral. This means that the organism has certain behaviors that help it survive in its habitat. A bat, for example, might sleep through the winter. This adaptation, called hibernation, allows the bat to live in cold climates.

Sea Turtle ▲
The flippers of a sea turtle are adapted for swimming.

Desert Tortoise ▲
The feet of a desert tortoise are adapted for walking in sand.

Cacti
Most plants would wilt and die in a hot desert. Cacti survive because of their waxy stems, long roots, and other adaptations. ▶

Natural Selection

How do organisms develop adaptations? In the mid-1800s, British naturalist Charles Darwin proposed a theory to help explain the process. According to Darwin, some members of a species have characteristics better suited to the environment than other members. These individuals are more likely to survive and pass on their characteristics to their offspring.

This process is known as natural selection. Let's examine how it works.

Picture a rocky beach. A population of birds searches among the rocks for food. Some of the birds have long, pointed beaks and can easily pick up pieces of food from cracks between the rocks. Other birds have shorter, more rounded beaks and cannot reach food.

Which birds are more likely to survive on the rocky beach? Which birds are more likely to reproduce? The birds with the pointed beaks are more likely to do both. Thus, their characteristics are passed on to their offspring. After several generations, many more of the birds on the beach will have pointed beaks.

Most scientists believe that natural selection accounts for the amazing variety of living things and their adaptations. Scientists also use the theory to predict how species might change in the future.

▲ Why does a sandpiper have such a long, thin beak? According to the theory of natural selection, traits that help an animal survive become more common in the population.

The dense, shaggy hair of these yaks helps them survive the bitterly cold weather of the Himalaya Mountains. ▼

> **COMPARE AND CONTRAST** What is an adaptation? Compare adaptations among different organisms.

Types of Symbiosis

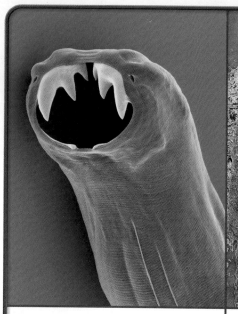

Parasitism
A hookworm takes blood and nutrients from its host. It benefits, and the host is harmed.

Commensalism
An elf owl makes its nest in a hole in a cactus. The owl benefits, and the cactus is not affected.

Mutualism
Cleaner shrimp eat parasites attached to fish. Both the shrimp and the fish benefit from this relationship.

Symbiosis

All living things depend on and affect one another. Sometimes the relationship is very close. **Symbiosis** describes a close, long-lasting relationship between two different kinds of organisms. This word means "living together."

Parasitism is one type of symbiosis. One organism, called the parasite, benefits from living off the body of another organism, the host. For example, a hookworm benefits from living inside the digestive tract of a larger host, such as a dog. The dog may become ill, but it usually doesn't die. If it did, the hookworm would die, too.

In commensalism, one organism benefits and the other organism is not affected. Birds called cattle egrets, for example, follow cattle as they move through a field. The birds eat the insects that jump from the grass as the cattle graze. The birds benefit, while the cattle are neither harmed nor helped.

In mutualism, both organisms benefit. Cleaner shrimp, for example, eat parasites off fish. The shrimp get food and the fish stay healthy. This relationship helps both the shrimp and the fish.

▶ **COMPARE AND CONTRAST** How do the three types of symbiosis compare?

Visual Summary

A natural habitat is the area where an organism lives. It provides everything the organism needs to survive. A niche describes the role of an organism in its habitat.

Adaptations are traits that help organisms survive in their habitats. Adaptations can be physical or behavioral.

Symbiosis is a close, long-lasting relationship between organisms. The three main types of symbiosis are parasitism, commensalism, and mutualism.

LINKS for Home and School

MATH Make a Line Graph The table lists the bird population on an island for 4 years. Plot the data on a line graph. Describe the changes you observe.

Year	'00	'01	'02	'03	'04
Pop.	40	92	160	152	148

TECHNOLOGY Use a Map Find a topographic map of your state or community. Use the map key to describe the physical features of habitats near you.

Review

1 MAIN IDEA Describe two different niches in a savanna habitat.

2 VOCABULARY Give an example of an adaptation. Describe how the adaptation helps the organism.

3 READING SKILL: Compare and Contrast According to natural selection, how do differences among organisms help develop adaptations?

4 CRITICAL THINKING: Apply How would you describe your niche in your family? How does it compare to an animal's niche in nature?

5 INQUIRY SKILL: Observe Describe a type of symbiotic relationship that you have observed. Identify which organisms benefit and which are harmed, if any.

 TEST PREP

An organism's niche includes

A. where it lives.

B. how it protects itself.

C. how it reproduces.

D. all of the above.

 Technology

Visit **www.eduplace.com/scp/** to find out more about habitats and niches.

What Factors Affect Ecosystems?

Why It Matters...

How many wolves can live in a forest? The answer depends on the size of the forest and the amount of food it provides for the wolves. Temperature can affect the population, and so can pollution. In any population—of wolves, trees, birds, or people—the size is limited by the available resources.

PREPARE TO INVESTIGATE

Inquiry Skill

Hypothesize When you hypothesize, you use prior knowledge or observations to suggest a cause-and-effect relationship that can be tested.

Materials

- measuring cup
- 3 plastic cups
- 32 lima bean seeds
- soil
- water
- marker
- safety goggles

Science and Math Toolbox
For step 4, review **Making a Chart to Organize Data** on page H11.

Limits to Growth

Procedure

Safety: Wear goggles while handling soil.

STEP 1

1. **Collaborate** Work with a partner. Label the three cups A, B, and C. Place soil into the cups until they are nearly full. Each cup should contain roughly the same amount of soil.

2. **Use Variables** Place 2 seeds in cup A. Place 10 seeds in cup B. Place 20 seeds in cup C.

STEP 2

3. **Measure** Measure and pour 25 mL of water into each cup.

4. **Record Data** Place all three cups in a sunny spot. In your *Science Notebook,* make a chart like the one shown for each cup.

5. **Observe** Over the course of the next three weeks, water the cups when the soil is dry and measure growth. Be certain that all the cups receive the same amount of water and sunlight. Record the date, height, and your observations at least twice a week.

STEP 4

Cup ___		
Date	Height	Observations

Conclusion

1. **Observe** What differences did you observe in the growing seeds?

2. **Hypothesize** What factor might have caused these differences?

3. **Use Variables** Why was it important to give each cup the same amount of sunlight and water?

Investigate More!

Design an Experiment Design an experiment to determine how sunlight affects plant growth. Remember to keep other variables constant, and to include a control.

▶ VOCABULARY

extinction	p. B51
population	p B46
predator	p. B47
prey	p. B47

▶ READING SKILL

Cause and Effect As you read, look for cause-and-effect relationships in populations and ecosystems.

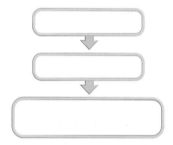

Changes in Population

Main Idea The size of any population can vary over time. It responds to changes in climate and resources.

A Balanced Ecosystem

Different living things use the resources of an ecosystem in different ways. They take some resources from ecosystems and add others to it. A balanced ecosystem has enough resources for all of its living things.

Every ecosystem supports many populations. A **population** is all the organisms of a given species that live together in the same area. Any change in one part of an ecosystem can upset the balance. For example, suppose a fungus kills many of the plants that rabbits eat. Such an event could lower the rabbit population. This would affect the hawks, owls, and other animals that eat the rabbits.

On the other hand, if a population of rabbits becomes too large, they might crowd out other species that live in the area. Because ecosystems have limited resources, they can support only a limited number of living things.

Predators that consume frog eggs help keep the frog population from growing too large.

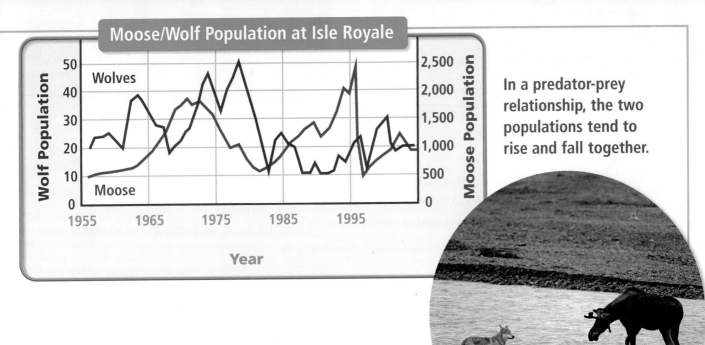

Moose/Wolf Population at Isle Royale

Wolf Population — Wolves — Moose — Moose Population

1955   1965   1975   1985   1995

Year

In a predator-prey relationship, the two populations tend to rise and fall together.

Limits on Populations

In any ecosystem, populations are always changing. Old animals die, and new ones take their place. When a tree falls, plants that thrive in sunlight can begin to grow. Other changes, however, can upset the balance of the ecosystem.

Consider the relationship between predators and their prey. **Predators** are animals that hunt and eat other animals. **Prey** are animals hunted and eaten by predators.

In a healthy ecosystem, the population densities of predators and prey are balanced. But certain factors can upset this balance. One example comes from an actual ecosystem—Isle Royale, an island in Lake Superior.

Moose first appeared on the island around 1900. They may have crossed on ice that formed a temporary bridge from the mainland. The island had plenty of plants for the moose to eat, and no predators.

The population of the moose had skyrocketed by 1930. Then it fell sharply. Why? The moose did not have enough food. Food is a limited resource in an ecosystem. So, the limited food supply on the island helped slow population growth.

In 1950, wolves appeared on the island. Wolves are predators of moose, so the moose population dropped while the wolves increased. Yet after a while, the wolf population dropped because not enough moose remained to support them. With fewer wolves, the moose population rose again. As the graph shows, the populations of these two species continued to rise and fall.

Lack of predators can make an ecosystem unbalanced as prey populations grow unchecked. Adding predators is one way to restore the balance.

▶ **CAUSE AND EFFECT** How might a decrease in predators affect prey?

Changing the Balance

Once changed, an ecosystem may take hundreds of years to recover. In some cases, it is changed forever.

Some factors that cause big changes in ecosystems are living. Alien species are good examples. Alien species are plants, animals, or other organisms that are not native to a given ecosystem.

In some cases, an alien species has no natural predators in its new home. It may thrive and "steal" resources from native plants and animals, or feed directly off them.

How do alien species enter new ecosystems? Often, they are brought in by accident. Zebra mussels, for example, traveled from western Russia to North America during the 1980s in water stored on a boat. The

▲ Zebra mussels anchor themselves to solid surfaces, including other organisms such as freshwater clams.

zebra mussels were dumped into the Great Lakes with the water. By the 1990s, the mussels had spread throughout many lakes and rivers.

The tiny zebra mussels can clog water pipes used by power plants and water treatment facilities. Zebra mussels also harm native organisms. They grow in large groups on clams, mussels, and crayfish. This growth can smother the native species.

Another problem is that zebra mussels filter the water, clearing it of plankton. Plankton are tiny producers. With fewer plankton to eat and to provide oxygen, many native species die.

It can be very difficult to get rid of an alien species. However, many states are working together to control the spread of these troublesome organisms.

◄ The Asian long-horned beetle entered the United States in wooden shipping crates in the 1990s. It burrows under the bark of trees, slowly killing them.

Nonliving things can also change the balance of an ecosystem. These include natural events, such as volcanic eruptions.

For example, Mount St. Helens is a volcano in the state of Washington. For many years, it was like a sleeping giant—it caused no trouble. Hemlock and fir thrived on the mountainside, as did many animals.

Everything changed in May 1980, when the volcano violently erupted. In a matter of minutes, hot lava burned and destroyed trees over an area of 500 square kilometers. Thick deposits of ash covered ground hundreds of kilometers away. The area surrounding the volcano became almost barren.

Within a few years of the Mount St. Helens eruption, flowers bloomed again on nearby slopes.

Yet life slowly returned to the mountain and neighboring areas. Some plants survived the eruption. Wind blew in seeds for grasses and shrubs, which sprouted a year or so after the eruption. Then larger plants moved in, followed by animals that ate those plants.

In 2004, the volcano turned active once again, although the damage was not nearly as severe as before. If the volcano stays quiet for many more years, the forest will return as before.

Other natural events include forest fires, floods, and droughts. Each can cause long-lasting changes in ecosystems. What do you think animals do when ecosystems change?

▶ **CAUSE AND EFFECT** **Describe one way that a nonliving factor may change an ecosystem.**

1983

1980

When a new lizard moved into part of its habitat, the green anole of Florida moved to the treetops. ▲

Adapting to Change

What if your home suddenly lost heat during a cold winter? What would you and your family do? You might move to a new home. Or you might adapt to the cold house, meaning you would find a way to still live there. Maybe you would build a fire or wear warm clothes.

In nature, living things also respond to dramatic changes in their environment. Sometimes they relocate, meaning they move to a new home.

The move need not be far. For example, in recent years a lizard from Cuba invaded part of the Florida habitat of another lizard, the green anole. The green anole used to live close to the ground. When it lost resources to the Cuban lizard, the green anole moved to the treetops.

A living thing can also adapt to changes in its environment. For example, many animals grow thicker coats when the weather turns cold.

If the change is too dramatic, however, the animal might perish, meaning it would die. Perishing is the consequence when living things can neither adapt nor relocate to survive a change.

Living things have relocated, adapted, and perished for as long as they have been on Earth. Fossils give clues to how this happened. Fossils are the remains or traces of once-living things.

Fossils may not show how individual organisms changed, but they do show that different species have lived at different times. Look at the fossil dinosaur shown below. No animal alive today has a skeleton just like this. Because dinosaurs could not survive changes in their environment, they perished.

Fossils help scientists determine how species have changed. ▶

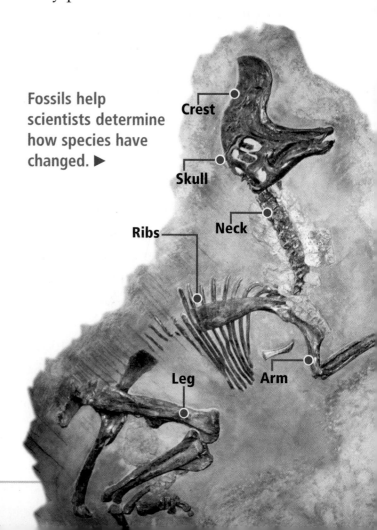

Crest

Skull

Neck

Ribs

Leg

Arm

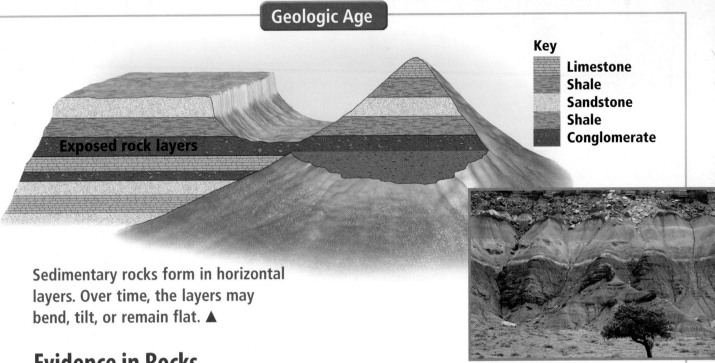

Key
Limestone
Shale
Sandstone
Shale
Conglomerate

Sedimentary rocks form in horizontal layers. Over time, the layers may bend, tilt, or remain flat. ▲

Evidence in Rocks

Change in ecosystems can occur very rapidly and can affect vast areas. For many animals, perishing is often the result. Throughout Earth's history, not only have countless individual organisms perished, but so have entire species.

When this happens, the species becomes extinct. **Extinction** occurs when all members of a species die out. Many different events can cause extinction, even among very successful species.

How do scientists draw conclusions about species that went extinct long ago? They do so by studying both fossils and the rocks in which the fossils were found.

The illustration above, for example, shows layers of rocks from a hillside. These layers formed on top of one another over time. The oldest rocks are on the bottom, the youngest on top. Any fossils in the rocks must have formed at the same time as the rocks around them.

Taken together, fossils and rocks show that species and ecosystems have changed a great deal throughout Earth's history. For example, fossil shells or fish show the land once was underwater. Fossil ferns show a wet, warm climate. Both kinds of fossils have been found in mountains!

Scientists are also able to estimate the age of a fossil, typically through a process called radioactive dating. The oldest fossils are billions of years old.

Sometimes the absence of fossils is key information. For example, Earth's rocks hold a wide variety of dinosaur fossils, yet none in layers younger than 65 million years old. Scientists conclude that all the dinosaurs died at once at this time.

Such an event is called a mass extinction. Earth has experienced several mass extinctions throughout its history.

▶ **CAUSE AND EFFECT** What can scientists learn by studying fossils and rocks?

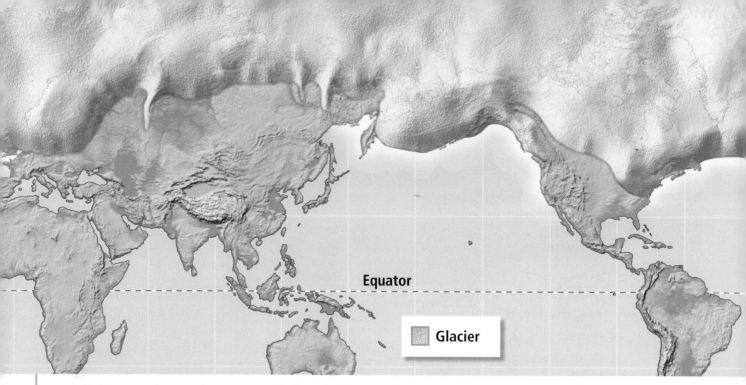

Equator

Glacier

▲ This map shows the extent of the glaciers in the Northern Hemisphere during the most recent ice age, from about 20,000 years ago.

Climate Change

Do you live in New York? Or Minnesota or Michigan? If you could travel back in time—say, 20,000 years—you would not recognize these states. They would be covered under a thick sheet of ice.

Over the last two million years, large parts of North America and Europe have been covered several times by huge ice sheets, or glaciers. These periods are called ice ages. The last ice age ended about 11,000 years ago.

During an ice age, much of Earth's water is locked up in glaciers, causing sea levels to fall. During the last ice age, the drop in sea level exposed a land bridge between Asia and North America. Many living things, humans included, may have crossed this bridge to settle in North America.

Many animals were already in North America at this time. Some were very large, like the woolly mammoth and the saber-toothed cat. With their thick, furry coats, they were well adapted to the cold conditions. When the ice age ended, however, they became extinct.

Some scientists believe that these animals could not adapt to the warmer climate. Other scientists think that both climate and humans caused the extinctions. Humans may have overhunted the great animals.

The exact reasons why some animals became extinct may never be known. But Earth's climate does change periodically. These changes greatly affect the living things upon it.

▶ CAUSE AND EFFECT How might climate change affect living things in the future?

Lesson Wrap-Up

Visual Summary

Ecosystems have limited resources. A balanced ecosystem has enough resources to support all living things.

Both living things, such as alien species, and nonliving things, such as volcanic eruptions, can upset the balance of an ecosystem.

Living things can respond to changes in ecosystems by relocating, adapting, or perishing.

LINKS for Home and School

MATH Calculate Population Density
Measure the area of your classroom. Determine the number of students in the class. Then calculate the population density of students in the classroom per square meter.

HISTORY Create a Time Line Research major mass extinctions that have occurred throughout Earth's history. Make a time line showing when each extinction occurred and what types of organisms were affected.

Review

❶ MAIN IDEA What factors can cause the size of a population of living things to change?

❷ VOCABULARY Use the terms *predator* and *prey* in a sentence.

❸ READING SKILL: Cause and Effect Why do alien species often thrive in their new ecosystems?

❹ CRITICAL THINKING: Apply Does your classroom have unlimited resources? Explain.

❺ INQUIRY SKILL: Hypothesize What changes in living and nonliving things might be brought about by the onset of another ice age?

 TEST PREP
A mass extinction occurs when

A. one animal species dies out.

B. one plant species dies out.

C. many species die out at roughly the same time.

D. many species die out at different times.

 Technology
Visit **www.eduplace.com/scp/** to find out more about populations.

DINOSAUR EXTINCTION

Scientists have dug up dinosaur fossils all over the world. Yet the fossils always are in rock layers older than 65 million years. Younger layers lack them.

What killed the dinosaurs so quickly? Scientists continue to debate this question! Two theories are outlined on the next page.

Whatever killed the dinosaurs also seems to have killed more than half the species of the time—a mass extinction. Earth's climate changed, too. It changed from warm and mild to cool and more varied.

Fortunately, mammals survived the mass extinction. The success of today's mammals—including humans— might stem from this long-ago event.

The asteroid theory of dinosaur extinction was put forth by father- and-son scientists: Luis Alvarez (left) and Walter Alvarez (right). ▼

What killed the dinosaurs?

Asteroid Theory

An unusual amount of iridium is found in rock layers from the time of the mass extinction. Iridium metal is rare on Earth's surface, but more common in asteroids. An asteroid strike might have filled the air with dust and debris. If sunlight was blocked, plants would have died, and dinosaurs would have followed.

Volcano Theory

Volcanic eruptions may have filled the air with soot and ash, blocking the Sun. The volcano theory argues that extinction took place more gradually, perhaps over several million years. The theory also explains the iridium deposits, because Earth's interior is high in iridium.

Sharing Ideas

1. **READING CHECK** How do scientists infer that dinosaurs went extinct quickly?

2. **WRITE ABOUT IT** Compare the two theories about the extinction of the dinosaurs.

3. **TALK ABOUT IT** Do you think Earth is in danger of another mass extinction?

B55

How Can Humans Change Ecosytems?

Why It Matters...

Huge numbers of bison once roamed the Great Plains of North America. Yet in the 1800s, humans hunted them almost to extinction. Hunting and other human activities changed not only the bison, but the ecosystems of which they were part.

Changes like this continue today. By understanding how and why ecosystems change, people can manage those changes wisely.

PREPARE TO INVESTIGATE

Inquiry Skill

Predict When you predict, you use observations, facts, or patterns to anticipate results.

Materials

- plastic container with lid
- ice cubes
- modeling clay
- water
- metric ruler

Science and Math Toolbox

For step 2, review **Measurements** on page H16.

Rising Sea Level

Procedure

1. **Use Models** Work with a partner. Use clay to make a model slope inside a shallow plastic container. The slope represents a coastal area. It should be placed at one end of the container.

STEP 1

2. **Measure** Add water to a depth of 2 cm inside the container. The water represents the ocean. It should cover only the edge of the slope.

STEP 2

3. **Predict** Add four ice cubes to the container. The ice cubes represent glaciers. Cover the container. In your *Science Notebook,* predict what will happen to the level of the water when the ice cubes melt.

STEP 3

4. **Record Data** The next day, measure the depth of the water in the container. Record your measurements in a chart.

Conclusion

1. **Observe** What happened to the depth of the water in the container?

2. **Observe** How was the model land affected by the change in the depth of the water?

3. **Predict** How might a rise in sea level affect coastal areas?

Investigate More!

Research Is Earth's average temperature increasing? Research this question. Prepare a report that includes a graph or map to display data.

VOCABULARY

endangered   p. B59
  species
pollution   p. B60
threatened species p. B59

READING SKILL

Draw Conclusions As you read, draw conclusions about the impact of humans on ecosystems.

Tropical rain forests are being cleared for farming and logging. Many species are lost along with the forests. ▼

Human Impact on Ecosystems

Main Idea Human activities impact ecosystems in both positive and negative ways.

Human Activities

Rain forests are among the most valuable resources on Earth. They are home to a vast variety of plants and animals. Yet rain forests are destroyed every day. By one account, almost 200,000 square kilometers (77,000 square miles) are lost each year. That's about 37 city blocks per minute!

People clear rain forests for land to grow crops, raise livestock, and build homes and businesses. Lumber that comes from the trees is valuable, too.

Why should you be concerned about the loss of rain forests? One reason is that plants and animals may become extinct when their habitats are destroyed. Scientists believe that some rain forest plants may contain substances that could be used as medicines. In addition, rain forest plants release oxygen and take in carbon dioxide from the atmosphere.

▲ Developers cut the top off a hillside to build these houses in California.

▲ In the United States alone, more than 4 billion kg (9 billion lbs) of fish are caught each year. Many popular fish are now threatened.

Humans have a huge effect on ecosystems by destroying habitats. In fact, habitat loss is the main reason why rates of extinction are rising. Not only rain forests are affected. Other ecosystems are impacted, too.

Wetlands, for example, are sometimes drained and filled in to provide land for farms, businesses, and housing developments. Until recently, people did not understand the importance of wetlands. These ecosystems help filter harmful chemicals from groundwater.

The spongy grasses in wetland areas also absorb excess water during heavy rains. This action helps reduce flooding. Many animal species hatch in wetlands. Later, as adults, they live in the sea. Wetlands are important nurseries for these animals.

Excessive hunting and fishing practices pose another threat to many ecosystems. In the early 1800s, for example, more than 60 million bison roamed the Great Plains. Yet by 1890, fewer than a thousand were left. Overhunting was the biggest reason. People killed the bison for their hides or tongues.

When a species is close to becoming extinct, it is called an **endangered species.** When a species is close to becoming endangered, it is called a **threatened species.** These categories are important. They let everyone know which species need the most protection.

▶ **DRAW CONCLUSIONS** Is habitat destruction a serious problem? Explain.

Types of Pollution

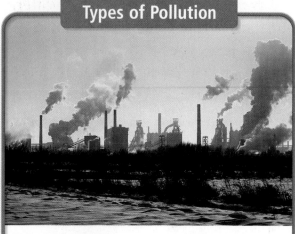

Air Pollution
Factories that burn fossil fuels can release harmful substances into the air.

Water Pollution
Oil spills can harm plants and animals that live in or near the water.

Land Pollution
Trash and garbage are often carelessly discarded, polluting the land.

Pollution

What other human activities can impact ecosystems? Burning fossil fuels is one example. Fossil fuels include oil, gas, and coal. These fuels contain a lot of energy and are easy to use. However, burning them can cause pollution. **Pollution** is the addition of harmful substances to the environment.

When fossil fuels are burned, certain gases and solid particles are released into the air. These pollutants can make the air unhealthy to breathe. Some combine with water droplets to form acids. They fall to the ground as acid rain.

Fossil fuels don't have to be burned to pose a threat to the environment. Oil, for example, is often transported on big ships called tankers. Accidental spills can damage the environment and be expensive to clean. About 300,000 birds died following a major oil spill in Alaska in 1989.

Human activities can also pollute the land. Each year, people in the United States produce hundreds of millions of tons of solid waste, including paper, plastics, and metals. Most solid waste is buried in sanitary landfills, and some is burned. However, people sometimes carelessly dump solid waste along roadsides or in bodies of water.

Some farming and lawn-care practices can also cause pollution. Rain can wash fertilizers into rivers and streams, where they may damage the ecosystem.

Growth of Human Population

Hundreds of years ago, the effects of human activities were relatively small. There were no power plants or motor vehicles. And the human population was much smaller than it is today. As the graph shows, today's human population is very large, and growing larger all the time.

In 1800, only about 1 billion people lived on Earth. By 1930, that number had doubled. A mere 30 years later, the population had increased to 3 billion. Today, more than 6 billion people live on the planet.

Modern humans have been around for thousands of years. Yet our population growth remained fairly steady until the last 200 years. Why has the human population grown so fast in such a short time? Advances in medicine and technology have made it possible for more people to survive diseases and accidents. These same factors help people live longer lives.

Everyone needs food, clean water, clean air, shelter, and other resources. As you've learned, however, ecosystems have limited resources. If the human population continues to grow, not enough resources will be available. In fact, in many parts of the world, food and water are already scarce or poorly managed.

Remember that human activities can harm ecosystems. A growing human population will take up more space. More natural habitats will be lost. More species will be threatened with extinction. Can anything be done to help this situation? Read on to find out how people are protecting the environment.

▶ **DRAW CONCLUSIONS** **How has the growth in human population affected ecosystems around the world?**

A growing human population must compete for a limited amount of resources, such as food, land, and water.

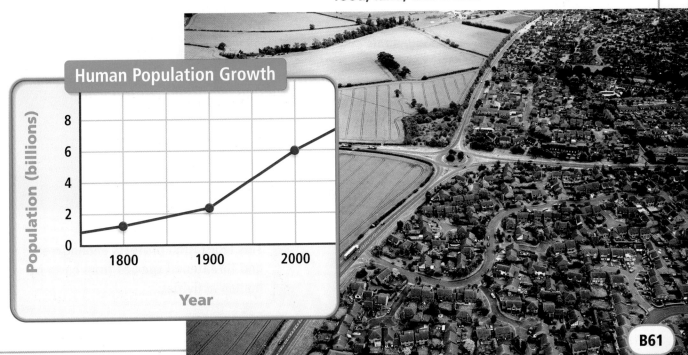

Human Population Growth

Graph: Population (billions) vs. Year, showing population rising from about 1 billion in 1800 to over 6 billion in 2000.

Good News

All around the world, people are working to reduce pollution and restore damaged ecosystems. Governments are passing laws. Industries are taking action. And people like you are making a difference everywhere!

▶ **DRAW CONCLUSIONS** How can individual actions help protect the environment?

Wildlife Refuges

In the United States, wildlife refuges cover nearly 40 million hectares (15 million acres). Development and hunting are limited in these refuges.

Cleaner Cars

The Clean Air Act, revised in 1990, limits the pollutants from new cars. Some manufacturers have designed cars that use alternative fuels.

Endangered Species Act

This legislation protects endangered and threatened species from harm by human activities.

Community Actions

Many people work to clean up trash, plant trees, or carpool to school and work. Individuals can make a big difference!

Clean Technology

New technology reduces pollutants at coal-burning power plants.

Protecting Wetlands

The Environmental Protection Agency (EPA) works with state and local governments to protect bogs, swamps, and other wet places.

Environmental Legislation

Many states have passed laws to protect or support local species. In Florida, funds from license plates help protect manatees.

Visual Summary

Many habitats are destroyed by logging, development, and other human actions. Overharvesting can reduce the populations of certain species.

Pollution affects air, water, and land. A growing human population means that more people are competing for limited resources.

Governments have passed laws to protect the environment. Many industries use new technology to reduce pollution. Individuals can help clean up ecosystems.

LINKS for Home and School

MATH **Make a Table** Read the information about human population on B61 and make a table to show this data. About when was the world population at 4 billion?

WRITE **Explanatory** Use the library or Internet to research how individuals can help the environment. Make a "Help the Environment" booklet. Share the booklet with classmates.

Review

1 MAIN IDEA What are some ways that people affect ecosystems?

2 VOCABULARY What can happen to a threatened species if its population continues to decrease?

3 READING SKILL: Draw Conclusions Can the actions of one person help the environment? Explain your answer.

4 CRITICAL THINKING: Synthesis A plant in a tropical rain forest becomes extinct. Why should this concern you?

5 INQUIRY SKILL: Predict How will Earth's resources be affected if the human population continues to grow?

 TEST PREP

During the past 200 years, the human population has

A. decreased.

B. stayed the same.

C. increased slightly.

D. increased greatly.

Technology
Visit **www.eduplace.com/scp/** to find out more about pollution.

Entomologist

Between 7,000 and 10,000 new species of insects are discovered every year! Entomologists study insects to learn how they behave, function, and relate to other organisms in different ecosystems.

Entomology is important for many reasons. Insects recycle nutrients, pollinate crops, and provide food for larger animals. Other insects threaten food supplies or spread diseases.

What It Takes!

- A degree in entomology or biology
- An interest in insects and their environments

Ship's Captain

Boats and ships are visitors to water ecosystems. Sometimes their visits can cause great changes. Fishing boats, oil tankers, and even passenger liners can damage ecosystems if they are not run properly.

A ship's captain needs to understand the ship and its cargo, as well as the environment through which they travel. The job comes with great responsibility.

What It Takes!

- An understanding of sea-going vessels and ocean navigation
- Leadership and management skills

Fastest Claw in the West

Wham! What a punch! Call it a shrimp, but for its size, it's the hardest hitter on Earth. The mantis shrimp socks a punch that approaches the force of a bullet! It can smash through the armor of the toughest prey in the blink of an eye.

In an aquarium, a mantis shrimp can spell trouble for the ecosystem. Why? It rapidly shatters and eats all the snails and other shelled creatures in the tank. And good luck getting rid of this powerful puncher! The mantis shrimp is smart. It knows how to hide and strike out from behind cover. It can easily break a person's finger—or even the tough safety glass of a public aquarium.

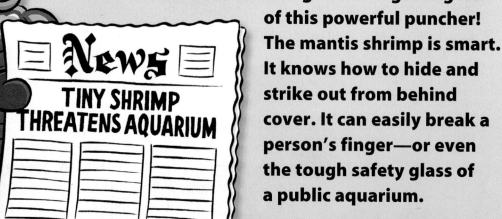

News

TINY SHRIMP THREATENS AQUARIUM

Sock it to 'em!
A human boxer is no match for the mantis shrimp. In the blink of an eye, the shrimp's club-shaped front leg can reach 50 mph. That's two or three times faster than the fastest human puncher!

Vocabulary

Complete each sentence with a term from the list.

1. A(n) ____ is the area where an organism lives.

2. When a species is very close to becoming extinct, it is called a(n) ____.

3. Predators hunt and eat ____.

4. ____ is the number of living things of a certain species in a given area.

5. A(n) ____ is an organism's role in its habitat.

6. Burning fossil fuels and dumping trash can cause ____.

7. A lion is an example of a(n) ____ that hunts zebras.

8. The flippers on a sea turtle are an example of a physical ____.

9. ____ occurs when all the members of a certain species die off.

10. Parasitism, commensalism, and mutualism are types of ____.

adaptation B40
endangered species B59
extinction B51
habitat B38
niche B39
pollution B60
population B46
predator B47
prey B47
symbiosis B42
threatened species B59

Test Prep

Write the letter of the best answer choice.

11. What best describes a species that would be classified as endangered if it lost more members?

   A. extinct
   B. thriving
   C. alien
   D. threatened

12. Potentially harmful organisms that are not native to a given ecosystem are called ____.

   A. predators   **C.** parasites
   B. alien species   **D.** threatened species

13. In the process of ____, organisms that are best suited to their environments survive and pass on their traits to their offspring.

   A. natural selection
   B. mass extinction
   C. niches and habitats
   D. behavioral adaptation

14. Which of the following is NOT a way that humans affect ecosystems?

   A. pollution   **C.** earthquakes
   B. development   **D.** overharvesting

15. Observe Look around the area in which you live for examples of how humans have changed local ecosystems. Write a short paragraph describing these changes.

16. Predict A fire destroyed a forest. After a year, grasses began to grow back in the area. Soon after that, rabbits moved in to eat the grass. The rabbits had no major predators, so their population grew. Recently, foxes and hawks returned to the area. Predict how the population of the rabbits will change.

Fill in the concept map by writing definitions for each term.

17. Synthesizing What might be done to stop the spread of harmful alien species? List three ideas and discuss why they could work.

18. Applying What are some things you can do to help the environment? How could you encourage people to join you?

19. Evaluating Is it helpful to classify organisms as endangered or threatened? Why or why not?

20. Analyzing Humans, other mammals, and birds can maintain a constant body temperature. Why is this a useful adaptation? How does this explain the spread of these animals around Earth?

Make a Fossil

Use clay to make a model fossil. Select an object such as a leaf and press it into the clay. Or, trace the outline of an animal's footprint in the clay. Exchange your model with another student. What can you infer about the plant or animal from studying the fossil?

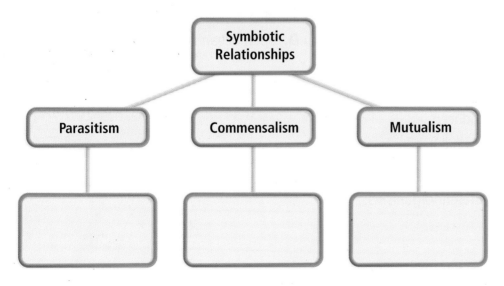

Write the letter of the best answer choice.

1. A hookworm lives by using the nutrients in a dog's digestive system. Which type of symbiosis is this?

hookworm

   A. commensalism
   B. mutualism
   C. organism
   D. parasitism

2. Which is the second-level consumer in this food chain?

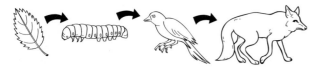

   A. bird
   B. caterpillar
   C. fox
   D. leaf

3. Which is NOT a reason that rain forests should be preserved?

   A. They contain many producers.
   B. They are home to many habitats.
   C. They are good for growing crops.
   D. They contain many different organisms.

4. Which factor is MOST important in creating the difference in biomes?

   A. physical features
   B. temperature
   C. plant life
   D. climate

5. Which is Earth's largest land biome?

   A. desert
   B. grasslands
   C. tundra
   D. taiga

6. The marine organism shown lives in the _____ .

   A. shore zone.
   B. intertidal zone.
   C. near-shore zone.
   D. open ocean zone.

7. The illustration below shows part of a forest ecosystem. Which is part of the ecosystem but not part of the forest community?

    A. rock

    B. grass

    C. mouse

    D. bird

8. The illustration below is MOST likely a _____ .

    A. taiga biome.

    B. tundra biome.

    C. desert biome.

    D. grassland biome.

Answer the following in complete sentences.

9. What is a mass extinction? Give two examples of what might cause a mass extinction.

10. Explain what an alien species is and how the introduction of an alien species can affect ecosystems.

Discover!

Grasslands can be hot and dry in the summer, with temperatures sometimes climbing over 38°C (100°F). Animals that live in hot places must find a way to keep cool. The jackrabbit's long ears are adapted not only for hearing, but to help cool its body.

A jackrabbit's ears are about 20 cm long. The wind cools the ear's thin skin, which cools blood vessels lying closely beneath.

Other kinds of rabbits cannot survive high temperatures. They would suffer fatal heat strokes at temperatures of around 25°C (77°F) or higher.

Snowshoe hares live in cold, Arctic climates. Small ears help trap body heat inside.

All organisms have adaptations to help them survive in their natural habitats. Adaptations include physical features, such as ear shape and length, as well as behaviors, such as feeding at night instead of the day. Many organisms are adapted to very specific habitats. If their habitat is destroyed, they may not survive elsewhere.

Learn more about adaptations. Go to **www.eduplace.com/scp/** for examples of other adaptations that help animals and plants survive.

Earth Systems

Earth Systems

Independent Reading

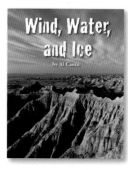

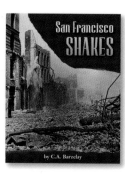

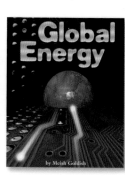

Wind, Water, and Ice

San Francisco Shakes

Global Energy

Discover!

Earth's surface is constantly changing. When a strong earthquake strikes, the surface shakes and rolls. Other earthquakes are hardly felt at all. How do scientists measure the strength of earthquakes? You will have the answer to this question by the end of the unit.

Chapter 6

Earth's Changing Surface

Lesson Preview

LESSON 1

Features of Earth's surface range from deep ocean trenches to tall mountains. What are these features like?

Read about them in Lesson 1.

LESSON 2

Wind, water, ice, and gravity—how do these agents wear down Earth's surface?

Read about it in Lesson 2.

LESSON 3

Shifting sand, bubbling lava, moving crust, and flowing ice— how do they build up Earth's surface?

Read about it in Lesson 3.

What Makes Up Earth's Surface?

Why It Matters...

The next time you're at the shore, take a close look at the sand along the water's edge. At one time, those tiny grains may have been part of the rocks that made up a hilltop or mountainside. Understanding Earth's different features can help you identify, enjoy, and protect them.

PREPARE TO INVESTIGATE

Inquiry Skill

Compare When you compare, you describe how two or more things are similar and how they are different.

Materials

- modeling clay
- 1 shallow square pan
- paper
- dental floss
- plastic knife

Model a Map

Procedure

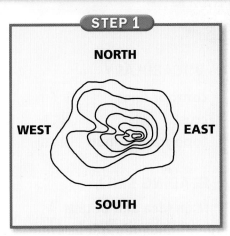

STEP 1

NORTH

WEST   EAST

SOUTH

1. **Compare** A topographic map has contour lines. These lines connect points that have the same elevation, which is distance above sea level. Study the topographic map of a hill shown here.

2. **Use Models** Add clay to the pan and make a model of the hill. Refer to the picture and the map.

STEP 2

3. **Measure** With a pencil, mark contour lines on the model hill. Use the topographic map as a guide. Then use a plastic knife or dental floss to slice the hill in layers along the lines. Set each layer aside.

4. **Communicate** Place the largest layer on a sheet of paper and trace around the edges. Then trace the other layers to create a topographic map.

STEP 4

Conclusion

1. **Compare** How are the sliced layers of your model like the contour lines in the map?

2. **Use Models** Look at the topographic map. Where is the steepest slope? Where is the flattest plain?

3. **Infer** How are topographic maps useful? When might you use such a map?

Investigate More!

Design an Experiment
Use clay to model another landform. Cut and trace its layers to make a topographic map.

Earth's Features

VOCABULARY

contour lines   p. C10
crust   p. C7
topographic map p. C10

READING SKILL

Main Idea and Details As you read, write details about Earth's surface features.

MAIN IDEA Earth's surface includes water and solid landforms. You can identify surface features by their location, shape, and elevation.

A Watery Planet

Earth is the only planet in our solar system with a large amount of water on its surface. Most of that water is found in the oceans, which are vast bodies of salt water. All of Earth's oceans are connected, forming one great world ocean. Most of the world ocean is in the southern part of the planet.

The world ocean surrounds the continents, which are huge landmasses that rise above the ocean surface. Most of the water on the continents, called inland water, is not salty. Water with little salt is called fresh water. Lakes and rivers are the major surface features that hold or carry fresh water. Rivers, streams, ponds, and other smaller features also hold fresh water.

Plants, humans, and other animals all need fresh water. Yet only about three percent of Earth's water is fresh water. And most of this is found underground or locked in glaciers or ice sheets near Earth's poles. For these reasons, fresh water is a very important resource.

Mountains stand above all other solid surface features.

Earth's Solid Surface

Earth's rocky outer layer is called the **crust.** Different features make up the surface of the crust. These features are found on the continents and on the ocean floor. Continental features are often called landforms.

Mountains are the tallest of Earth's landforms. Their steep slopes rise to tall peaks. Mountains can be found as single peaks or in chains, ranges, and mountain systems. Six major mountain ranges form the Rocky Mountain system.

Hills are smaller than mountains. Although hills do not rise as high as mountains, their rounded crests still stand above the land around them.

Mountain valleys are long, narrow regions of low land between ranges of mountains or hills. Canyons are deep valleys with steep sides. Often a river or stream runs along the bottom of a valley or canyon.

Plateaus are high landforms with fairly flat surfaces. Plateaus are often found along the tops of canyons and can extend for many miles on either side of a canyon. Mesas are similar to plateaus, but are much smaller. The word mesa means "table" in Spanish.

Like plateaus, plains are broad and flat. Unlike plateaus, plains are lower than their surroundings. The Midwest region of the United States contains wide-ranging plains.

As the name suggests, a river valley has a river flowing through it, usually in the center of the valley. The river moves along a channel in the valley floor.

A flood plain is the floor of a river valley on either side of the river. Water covers a flood plain when a river overflows its banks. The flood plains of some river valleys are hundreds of kilometers wide.

▶ **MAIN IDEA** **Name six of Earth's landforms.**

Plateaus How do plateaus compare to mountains and hills?

River valleys occur in mountains, hills, and plains.

Coastal Features

As you travel from the middle of a continent toward the coast, different landforms appear. In North America, the Atlantic Coastal Plain extends from Canada all the way to Florida. This coastal plain slopes gently from the Appalachian Mountains to the shores of the Atlantic Ocean.

Beaches and marshlands are found at shorelines, where dry land meets the ocean. Beaches are flat landforms along an ocean or large lake. Beach material varies in texture and shape. Some beaches are rocky or pebbly, while others are sandy.

The west coast is very different. There is no coastal plain along the shores of the Pacific Ocean. In many places, the coastline is rocky. Steep cliffs and mountains extend to the water's edge.

Along both coasts, ocean waves pound against the rocky coastline to make many interesting features. These features include beaches, sea caves, sea cliffs, and sea arches.

Pocket beaches form along a rocky coastline. These beaches are small and curve landward, with sand filling spaces, or "pockets," between rocky cliffs. They are common in New England and the Pacific Northwest.

Mainland beaches are quite different from pocket beaches. They are found along straight shorelines that are free of large rocks. Some mainland beaches stretch for miles.

Long, sandy beaches are also found along barrier islands. These islands are separated from the mainland by a narrow, shallow body of water. Barrier beaches may be quite large. Florida's Miami Beach is a large barrier beach. So is the beach at Atlantic City, New Jersey.

Sand dunes are mounds or ridges of sand that the wind often forms along coastlines. They often form in long, irregular rows set back from the water.

Beaches may be rocky, pebbly, or sandy—or a combination of all three.

Coastal plains are low-lying areas that slope gently from the mainland toward the shore.

Ocean Floor Features

Starting at the water's edge, the continental margin extends to the deep ocean floor. This feature consists of three parts: the continental shelf, the continental slope, and the continental rise.

The continental shelf forms the edges of a continent. A shelf normally slopes gradually down from sea level to a depth of less than 200 m (660 ft). The width can range from less than 80 km (48 mi) to more than 1,000 km.

Beyond the shelf is the steeper continental slope. It can fall to depths of 3 km (1.8 mi) and range from 20 km to 100 km wide. The slope forms the sides of the continents. At the bottom of the slope is the continental rise. This region stretches out about 1,000 km across the ocean floor.

The ocean floor has a variety of features, some similar to those found on dry land. For example, Hudson Canyon slices southeast through the continental shelf starting from a point near New York City. Such canyons are known as submarine canyons.

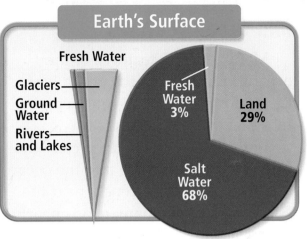

Earth's Surface

Fresh Water

Glaciers
Ground Water
Rivers and Lakes

Fresh Water 3%

Land 29%

Salt Water 68%

As the graph shows, oceans cover most of Earth's surface.

Mountains and plains are present underwater, too. Seamounts are huge, steep-sided mountains rising from the ocean floor.

Some seamounts have flat tops. They are known as guyots (GEE ohs). They once may have risen above the water's surface. Over time, they were worn down and covered by rising water.

Seamounts occur mainly on the deep ocean floor. This vast area is known as the abyssal plain.

▶ **MAIN IDEA** From the shore to the ocean floor, what are the three parts of the continental margin?

Seamounts may rise thousands of meters above the ocean floor.

Mid-Ocean Features

Many striking features of the ocean floor occur in the ocean basin, the region beyond the continental margin.

In the ocean basin, deep canyons called trenches plunge into the ocean floor. The Mariana Trench, near the Pacific island of Guam, drops nearly 11 km (6.6 mi) below the ocean floor.

Mid-ocean ridges form a mountain chain that runs more than 56,000 km (33,600 mi) through the world ocean. Parts of the chain have different names. These names include the Mid-Atlantic Ridge, the East Pacific Rise, and the Mid-Indian Ridge.

Most mountains in the mid-ocean ridges reach more than 1,500 m (4,950 ft) high. Some peaks stick out of the water as islands.

A number of the ridges have deep, steep-sided valleys down their centers. These valleys create a ragged, rough surface on the ridges. The sides of the ridges slope down to the abyssal plain.

Mapping Surface Features

A **topographic map** is a map that shows the shape of surface features and their elevations, or heights above sea level. **Contour lines** connect points on the map that have the same elevation. By studying contour lines, you can learn the shape and steepness of the land.

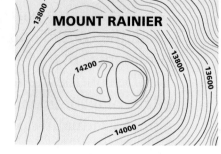

This topographic map shows Mount Rainier in Washington State. The numbers on the contour lines show elevation in feet. The spacing of the lines shows how steeply the land slopes.

▶ **MAIN IDEA** What do contour lines show about landforms?

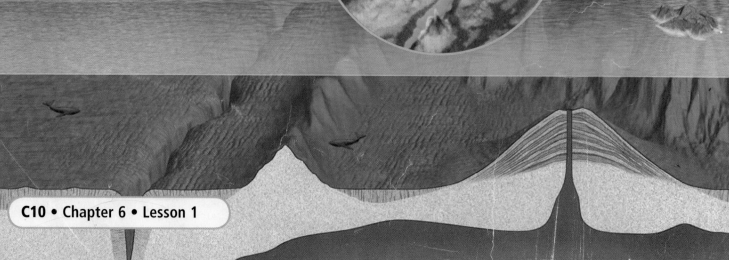

Mid-Ocean Ridge The slopes of mid-ocean ridges extend to the abyssal plain.

mid-ocean ridge

Visual Summary

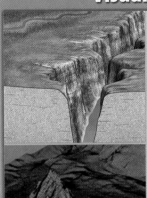

Earth has many types of surface features both on dry land and under water.

Oceans cover most of Earth's surface.

MOUNT RAINIER

13800

14200

14000

Topographic maps help picture Earth's features. Contour lines show elevation.

LINKS for Home and School

MATH **Calculate and Compare** The mountain chain formed by mid-ocean ridges stretches for more than 56,000 km. How many miles is that? (1 km = 0.6 miles)

TECHNOLOGY **Mapping the Ocean** Scientists map the ocean floor by using sonar, a technology that uses sounds to measure distances. Research sonar and its many uses.

Review

1 MAIN IDEA What three properties are used to identify surface features?

2 VOCABULARY How do contour lines help you visualize a feature of Earth's solid surface?

3 READING SKILL: Main Idea and Details Name and describe the three parts of the continental margin.

4 CRITICAL THINKING: Analyze Earth has lots of water. Water covers more than 70 percent of Earth's surface. Even so, water is a critical resource for all living things. Explain why.

5 INQUIRY SKILL: Compare Describe how plateaus and plains are similar and how they are different.

 TEST PREP
The Mariana Trench is a feature of the floor of the Pacific Ocean. What land feature does its shape most resemble?

A. river valley

B. canyon

C. mountain range

D. beach

 Technology
Visit **www.eduplace.com/scp/** to find out more about Earth's features.

Lesson 2

How Is Earth's Surface Worn Down?

Why It Matters...

Weathering and erosion change Earth's surface every day. Sometimes these changes take place very quickly, but often they are very slow. The rock formation shown here took thousands of years to form. Understanding how and why Earth changes is the key to preventing or influencing the changes.

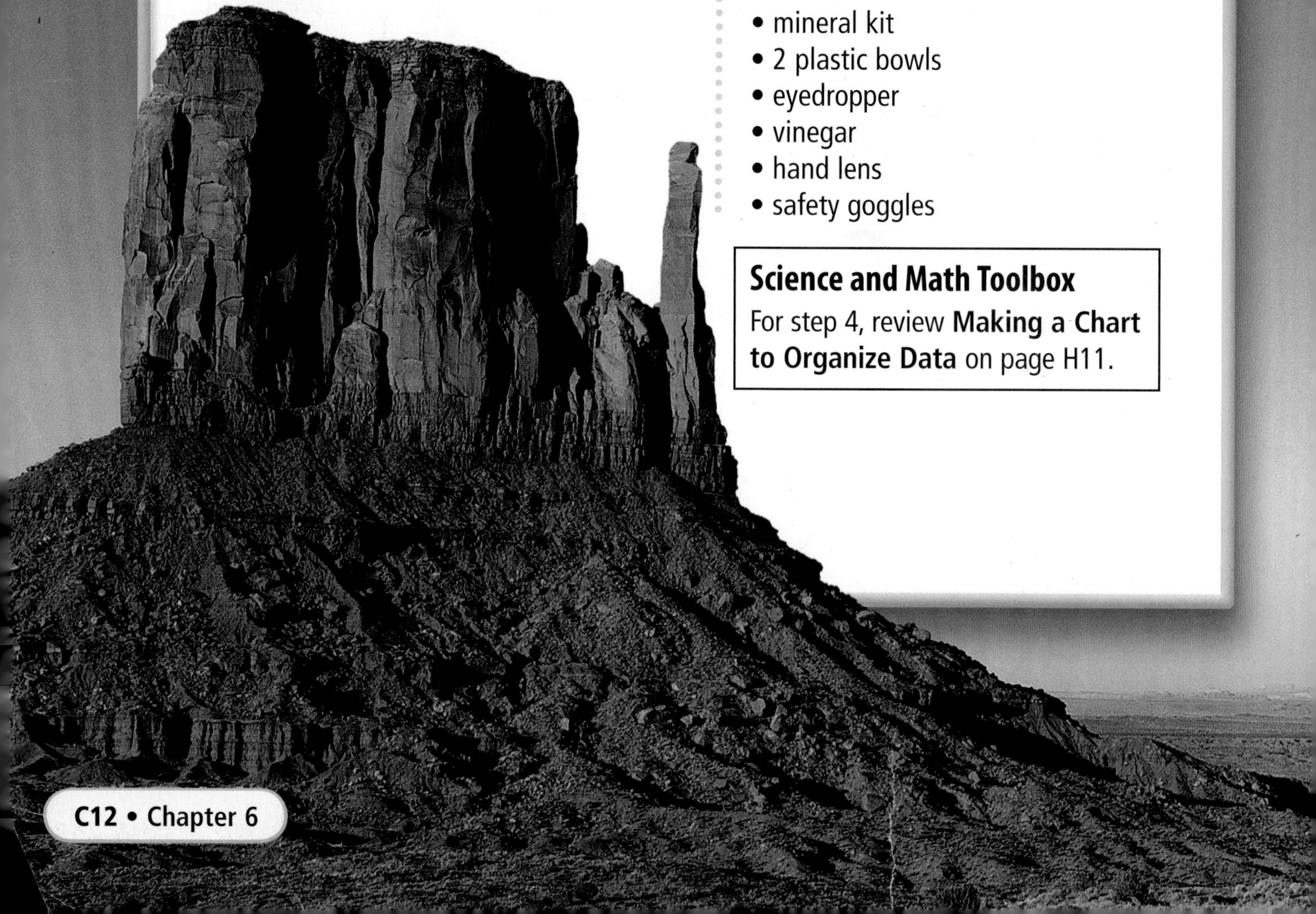

PREPARE TO INVESTIGATE

Inquiry Skill

Predict When you predict, you apply facts you know, observations you have made, and cause-and-effect relationships you understand.

Materials

- nail
- mineral kit
- 2 plastic bowls
- eyedropper
- vinegar
- hand lens
- safety goggles

Science and Math Toolbox

For step 4, review **Making a Chart to Organize Data** on page H11.

Rock Erosion

Procedure

Safety: Wear goggles during this activity.

1. **Experiment** Using a nail, scratch the calcite over a plastic bowl. In a separate bowl repeat the procedure with halite. There should be a small pile of dust in each bowl.

2. **Predict** What do you think will happen to the minerals when they come in contact with vinegar? Write your predictions in your *Science Notebook.*

3. **Observe** Using an eyedropper, add 3–6 drops of vinegar to the calcite. Using the hand lens, observe the reaction. Do the same in the bowl containing halite. Then wash your hands.

4. **Record Data** Draw a picture of the calcite and halite reactions in your *Science Notebook.*

Conclusion

1. **Compare** How do the reactions of the calcite and the halite differ?

2. **Predict** Based on your data, predict how acid rain can break down or weather rocks. How do your results support this prediction?

3. **Infer** Why are most caves and caverns formed in limestone, a kind of rock made from calcite?

Investigate More!

Design an Experiment
Can water break apart rocks when it freezes into ice? Find out in an experiment with chalk, water, a plastic bag, and a freezer.

VOCABULARY

erosion   p. C16
sediment   p. C14
weathering   p. C14

READING SKILL

Sequence Use a diagram to record the sequence of steps in weathering and erosion.

Wearing Down Earth's Surface

MAIN IDEA Destructive forces, such as weathering and erosion, wear down Earth's surface features.

Weathering

Earth's crust is mostly solid rock. The rocks are broken into pieces by processes of **weathering.** Weathering is a destructive force, or a force that breaks down something. There are two types of weathering: mechanical and chemical.

Mechanical weathering is the breaking of larger rocks into smaller pieces of rock, called **sediment.** In cold climates, ice plays a major role in this process. As water freezes, it expands. When water trickles into the cracks of rocks, it can break the rocks apart when it freezes.

Moving air and water also cause mechanical weathering. As blown sand or rushing water hits rocks, the rocks weaken. Over time, they crack or crumble. Even living things can cause mechanical weathering. Plant roots can grow through cracks and break apart rocks. Burrowing animals push against rocks and allow water to move deeper into rocks and soil, where freezing and thawing can weather rocks.

Sometimes rocks will peel into sheets. As soil and rocks are removed from a buried rock, pressure on the rock is reduced. This may allow minerals in the rock to expand. An outer layer of the rock will peel away. Eventually, other layers may also crack and flake.

Trees have the power to move or split rocks as they grow.

Cave Formation

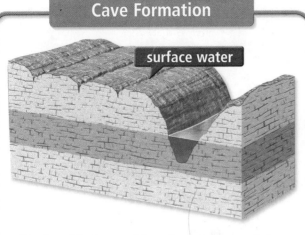

surface water

Weak acids formed in rainwater seep into the ground, where they weather rock.

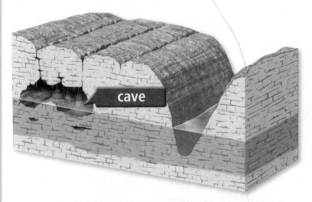

cave

Over time, holes are produced. Eventually, the holes grow into caves.

Caves are a result of weathering. ▲

Although mechanical weathering breaks rocks, it does not change the type of rock. In chemical weathering, rocks change into other materials.

Water is the main factor that causes chemical weathering. Water can dissolve some minerals that make up rocks. Water also dissolves certain chemicals from the air and soil to form a weak acid. This acidic water can easily dissolve certain minerals.

The type of minerals in rock also affects weathering. For example, weak acids dissolve limestone and marble more easily than some other minerals.

Generally, a combination of different types of weathering is at work in a region. Most weathering takes place at or near Earth's surface. However, water trickling through the ground can affect rocks far beneath the surface. Caves are underground hollow areas created by weathering. Large caves are often called caverns.

Most caverns are made from limestone. Weak acids seep into the ground until they reach a zone soaked with water. As the ground water becomes more acidic, it dissolves minerals in the rock.

Over time, holes are produced in the rock. The holes grow, creating passages, chambers, and pits, and eventually become caves. At first, the caves are full of water. Over time, the water drains away.

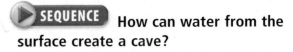 **SEQUENCE** How can water from the surface create a cave?

River Valley Formation

1 A shallow stream gradually erodes its channel.

2 The stream grows into a river, which carries sediment away from its banks.

3 In time, the river cuts a V-shaped valley.

Erosion

Weathering is the process that breaks down rock into smaller pieces called sediments. The carrying away of sediments by moving water, wind, or moving ice is called **erosion.**

A common agent of erosion is water moving down a river. The river begins as a shallow stream, often at a high elevation. Gravity moves the water downhill. As it flows, the rushing water erodes the ground, dissolving minerals and picking up sediments from the streambed. Over time, the river channel becomes wider and deeper.

Usually a stream joins other streams to become a river. The increasing flow of water and tumbling rocks further erode the river channel. This process may carve out a steeper or wider valley. In some cases, rapid cutting of the valley floor in the upper part of a river can create a canyon.

Further along its course, the river gains more water. The water broadens and deepens the river channel.

A mountain stream in California weathers rocks as it rushes over them. It carries sediment downstream. ▲

Over time, rivers create the deep V-shaped valleys known as canyons. ▲

Frozen water also wears down and shapes Earth's surface features. Thousands of years ago, glaciers helped to shape the rolling plains in the northern United States. They also carved out the Great Lakes.

In arctic regions and in high mountains, glaciers continue to shape Earth today. Gravity moves rivers of ice downhill toward the sea. Although glaciers move very slowly, their weight and size give them great power. Mountain glaciers can transform V-shaped river valleys into U-shaped valleys.

Glaciers can also move enormous amounts of soil and rock. These sediments are carried along the bottoms and sides of the ice. As the ice inches forward, sediments in the ice grind against the surface below.

Glaciers often carve out hollows in the land they erode. When the glaciers melt, these hollows fill with water to form lakes. Glaciers created more than 10,000 such lakes in Minnesota.

Ocean waves and currents also erode Earth's surface. Crashing waves break down rock along coastlines. The sediments are dragged back and forth, slowly turning to sand.

Wind and waves from the open ocean also batter headlands. Headlands are narrow sections of land that jut out into the ocean. Usually they are cliffs of hard rock.

Waves curve around the headland, throwing up salty water and pebbles. Gradually this movement erodes cracks in the headlands, forming sea caves. Sea caves on both sides of a headland may join to form a sea arch.

As erosion continues, the top of the arch may collapse. The ocean side of the arch is left standing alone. This single column is called a sea stack.

▶ **SEQUENCE** **Describe one way that erosion wears down Earth's surface.**

A sea arch forms when sea caves on both sides of a headland join. ▼

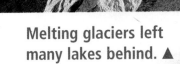

Melting glaciers left many lakes behind. ▲

C17

Slow and Fast Changes

The ongoing process of erosion keeps the landscape changing. In general, such destructive forces act very slowly. However, sometimes such changes happen much faster.

You read that chemical weathering creates caves in certain types of rock beneath Earth's surface. This process can take thousands of years. However, after a cave has formed, the rock above the cave often has little support. At some point, this rock may collapse, forming a sinkhole.

Sinkholes can form very suddenly. One large sinkhole formed in a single day in Winter Park, Florida. The city sealed it and made an urban lake.

Sinkhole is a very descriptive term: Land above weathered rock sinks into a hole. This sinkhole affected central Florida. ▲

When sediments slide down a steep slope, buildings on them slide, too. This landslide took place in southern California. ▼

Landslides also occur suddenly as the result of erosion. In fact, they can happen in minutes. Landslides are large movements of land that tumble down a steep slope. Mudslides, rock falls, and avalanches are examples of landslides.

Although gravity is the main cause of a landslide, other destructive forces are involved. Erosion from rivers, rain, glaciers, or ocean water may steepen a slope and loosen sediments. If the sediments become soaked with water, they may slide more easily. Any disturbance, such as a minor earthquake, can create cracks or shake rocks loose. This action can start landslides.

Volcanoes can also cause landslides. Volcanic eruptions can deposit ash and other materials on steep slopes. Heavy rains added to this material can cause a landslide.

▶ **SEQUENCE** How does a landslide occur?

Lesson Wrap-Up

Visual Summary

Earth's surface features are worn down by destructive forces, such as weathering and erosion.

Water, wind, and the actions of plants and animals all can cause weathering.

In erosion, weathered rock is moved by wind, water, ice, or gravity.

Destructive forces usually act to change Earth's surface slowly but can also cause rapid changes to Earth's surface.

LINKS for Home and School

MATH **Solve a Problem** You observe a giant wave crash on the rocks. After 1.5 seconds, you hear the sound of the crashing wave. How far are you from the rocks? (Speed of sound in air is 340 m/sec.)

WRITING **Narrative** Plan a trip to the Grand Canyon, Glacier National Park, or Carlsbad Caverns. Research your chosen park. What activities will you participate in? What sights will you see?

Review

❶ **MAIN IDEA** Why are weathering and erosion considered destructive forces?

❷ **VOCABULARY** What are sediments? Give an example of sediments and how they form.

❸ **READING SKILL: Sequence** Describe the sequence of events in the formation of a cave.

❹ **CRITICAL THINKING: Infer** How could you tell if a glacier had once moved across a region?

❺ **INQUIRY SKILL: Predict** Would the features of a marble statue last longer in a dry desert region or in a warm, moist region that has heavy industry? Explain your reasoning.

✓ **TEST PREP** Which of these is the strongest agent of chemical weathering?

A. plant roots

B. acidic water

C. burrowing animals

D. freezing water

 Technology Visit **www.eduplace.com/scp/** to find out more about erosion and weathering.

Cleopatra's Needle

How can weathering and erosion change rock? One ancient stone obelisk—a kind of tall statue—provides a very interesting example.

In appreciation for help in building the Suez Canal, the ruler of Egypt presented the United States an obelisk that was more than 3,000 years old. This obelisk is now called Cleopatra's Needle. It was installed in Central Park in New York City in 1881.

The obelisk remains in the same spot today, but it has changed drastically. Much of the outer surface of the stone has worn away, blurring inscriptions that were clear when the statue arrived.

Look at the photos of Cleopatra's Needle and a similar obelisk that remained in Egypt. In 1881, the two looked much alike. How are they different now? How do you explain these differences? For a hint, compare the graphs of temperature and precipitation in the two locations.

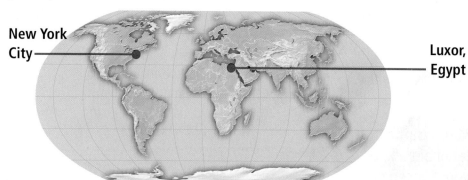

New York City

Luxor, Egypt

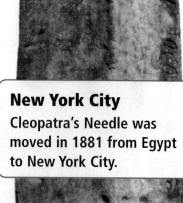

New York City
Cleopatra's Needle was moved in 1881 from Egypt to New York City.

Egypt
The Obelisk of Ramesses II has remained in Egypt since ancient times.

The graphs show average temperature and precipitation for New York City and Luxor, Egypt. How do the climates of the two places compare? ▶

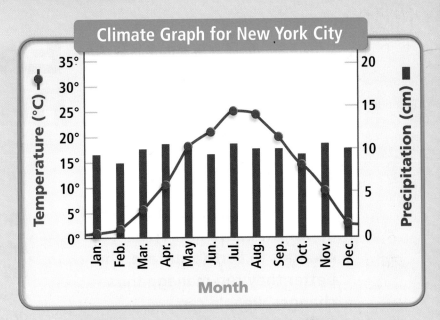

Climate Graph for New York City

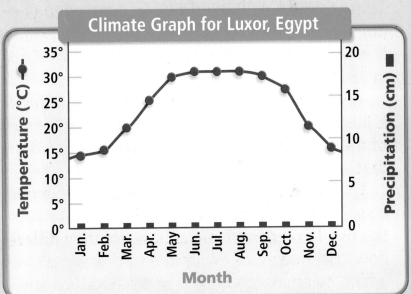

Climate Graph for Luxor, Egypt

Sharing Ideas

1. **READING CHECK** How has Cleopatra's Needle changed since it came to New York City? Compare it to the obelisk that stayed in Egypt.

2. **WRITE ABOUT IT** Study the climate graphs. Compare the climates of the two places.

3. **TALK ABOUT IT** How do you explain the differences between the two statues?

How Is Earth's Surface Built Up?

Why It Matters...

The more people understand about the cause and effect of changes to Earth's surface, the better they can manage those changes. People can work with nature to take care of Earth's surface and enjoy its features.

PREPARE TO INVESTIGATE

Inquiry Skill

Infer When you infer, you use facts you know and observations you have made to draw a conclusion.

Materials

- soil
- aluminum pan
- pencil
- paper cup
- bottle of water

Set Up a Streaming Slope

Procedure

STEP 1

1. **Use Models** With a partner, build a soil slope on one end of an aluminum pan. The slope can be steep or gentle.

2. **Record Data** Draw a picture of the soil slope in your *Science Notebook.*

3. **Predict** You will drip water from a paper cup onto the soil at the top of the slope. Predict what you think will happen. Record your prediction.

STEP 4

4. **Experiment** With a pencil, poke a small hole in the bottom of a paper cup. Cover the hole in the cup with your finger. Have your partner fill the cup with water from a water bottle. Hold the cup 3 to 4 cm above the soil at the top of the slope. Remove your finger and let the water flow over the soil slope.

5. **Observe** What happened to the soil? Draw a picture and describe the changes in your *Science Notebook.*

Conclusion

1. **Compare** Look at the two pictures you drew of the soil slope. How are they alike and different? Do the pictures support your prediction about what would happen when you poured water onto the slope?

2. **Infer** What can you infer about the way water and gravity wear down and build up Earth's surface?

Investigate More!

Design an Experiment
Make another soil slope. This time, pour water from the bottle down the slope. How do the speed and amount of water affect a soil slope?

▶ **VOCABULARY**

deposition   p. C24

▶ **READING SKILL**

Cause and Effect Use a chart to show the effects of constructive forces on Earth's surface.

Building Up Earth's Surface

MAIN IDEA Forces such as deposition and volcanic activity build up Earth's surface features.

Deposition

Have you seen waves gently lapping at a sandy beach? Waves are part of the reason that beaches have sand. Ocean waves and currents drop sand on a beach in a process called deposition.

Deposition is the dropping, or releasing, of sediments that have been moved from one place to another. Sand is sediment made from rocks or shells that have been ground into fine grains.

Both erosion and deposition are gradual processes. However, erosion is a destructive force, meaning that it wears down the land. Deposition is a constructive force, meaning that it builds up the land.

Wind sweeps sand into sand dunes. Sand dunes are sediment deposits that form on the inland part of beaches.

Deposition helps create a variety of surface features. Several of these features occur as part of river systems.

Recall that the source of a river is usually inland at some high elevation. The water flows downhill, swiftly at first, picking up sediment. At the mouth of the river, the water usually empties into a large body of water, such as a lake or ocean.

As it nears the mouth, the land gradually levels out. The leveling causes the water to lose energy and slow down. Sediment drops out of the water.

When a river moves across wide, flat regions, the river begins to wind in smooth curves called meanders. Meanders increase in size as water erodes the outside of each curve and deposits sediment on the inside.

Flooding of rivers on lowlands also deposits sediment. This sediment builds up on the flood plains.

When the flow of river water decreases quickly, special kinds of deposits are formed. An alluvial fan is a fan-shaped land mass that forms after a river rushes down a steep slope, then slows over a flat plain.

A delta is a low plain that forms where a river enters an ocean. If the river is large, the delta will be large, too. The mighty Mississippi River has a vast delta that extends well out into the Gulf of Mexico.

CAUSE AND EFFECT Why is sediment deposited as the slope of a river bed levels out?

Alluvial fans and deltas are formed when rivers slow suddenly and their sediments are deposited. ▲

As a river flows across a flat plain, its course begins to wind in curves called meanders. ▲

Pushing Up Earth's Surface

Surface features can be pushed up from below as well as built up from above. Not far below Earth's surface, temperatures are quite high. In some places, the conditions are hot enough to melt rock!

Melted rock below Earth's surface is called magma. Magma originates in a layer of Earth just below the crust. Pressure below the surface can cause magma to push up on Earth's crust, creating round, dome-shaped mountains.

In some places, magma can work its way up through the crust and flow out onto Earth's surface as lava. As lava flows, it cools and hardens into rock.

In some places, enough lava will build up to form a huge deposit with gently sloping sides. Such deposits are called shield cones. Shield cones often form on the ocean floor. For example, the Hawaiian Islands are actually the tops of several giant shield cones. The base of Mauna Loa, the largest of these cones, is about 4,500 m (15,000 ft) below the surface of the Pacific Ocean. Its peak rises over 4,100 m (14,000 ft) above the ocean's surface.

Compare this view of Hawaii from the International Space Station to the illustration below. ▶

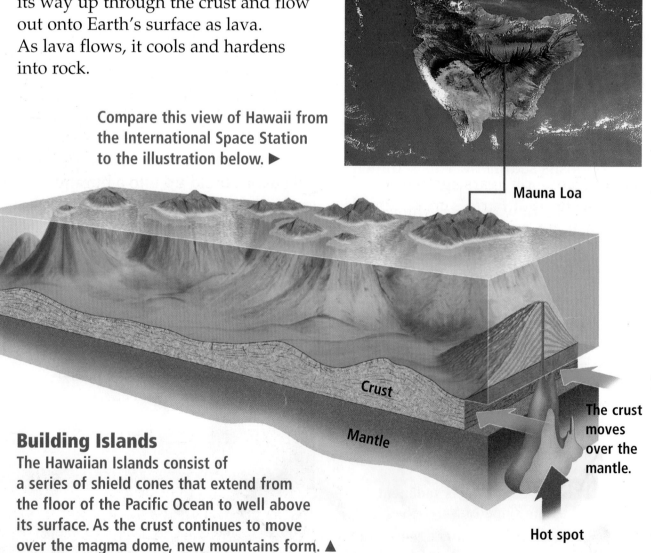

Mauna Loa

Crust

Mantle

The crust moves over the mantle.

Hot spot

Building Islands

The Hawaiian Islands consist of a series of shield cones that extend from the floor of the Pacific Ocean to well above its surface. As the crust continues to move over the magma dome, new mountains form. ▲

1 The Himalayas began forming when one plate of Earth's crust crashed into another plate.

2 For millions of years, the plates have continued to push together, folding and uplifting to form mountains.

Crust

Mantle

Crust

Mantle

A different constructive force created the Himalaya Mountains. These mountains in Central Asia are among the highest on Earth.

The Himalayas began forming about 65 million years ago when huge sections of Earth's crust moved into each other. The pressure caused the crust to fold.

Other features of Earth are made from the remains of living things. For example, the chalk cliffs of Dover, England, are made up of shells of tiny sea animals. These shells were deposited on the sea floor millions of years ago. When forces below the crust raised the sea floor, the chalk deposits became chalk cliffs.

Coral reefs are another type of formation produced from the remains of living things. In shallow tropical waters, tiny animals called corals gather in colonies. As corals die, their skeletons build up into a bumpy ridge called a reef.

In some Pacific Ocean waters, reefs are built around volcanic islands. Sometimes an island will sink, but the coral continues to grow. This creates a barrier reef separate from the island.

▶ **CAUSE AND EFFECT** How were the Himalaya Mountains formed?

Atolls are ring-shaped islands formed from deposits of coral skeletons called coral reefs. ▶

Glacial Deposits

Thousands of years ago, snow fell year-round over large areas of Asia, Europe, and North America. Over time, the weight of snow from the top added pressure below. Slowly, the snow turned to ice. Glaciers were formed.

The ice in some of these glaciers was almost a thousand meters thick. The ice's weight became so great that it pushed and dented the land.

These moving masses of ice were tremendous forces of erosion. Huge amounts of soil and rock were pushed ahead of the ice and carried along in the glacier's bottom layers.

After thousands of years, the ice began to melt. The glaciers reached their present positions about 11,000 years ago. As the ice melted, it left behind a changed landscape.

The rock material deposited by a glacier is known as till. Till may be silt, sand, gravel, boulders, or sharp rocks. Some till is picked up as a glacier scrapes Earth's surface. The glacier drags till along its icy base.

Eskers form from streams that flow along the bottoms of melting glaciers. ▲

A glacier also deposits till at its front, or snout. Such deposits are called moraines. Long Island, New York, is the terminal moraine left when the last ice sheet melted. The melting water carried sand and clay away from the snout. Today, the southern portion of Long Island is sandy, while the northern portion is rocky.

Streams flowing through tunnels in melting glaciers deposit sand and gravel in ridges, too. These winding ridges are called eskers.

CAUSE AND EFFECT How do glaciers deposit sediment?

Cirque

In high mountains, glaciers can carve out bowl-shaped hollows called cirques. ◄

Visual Summary

Deposition builds up surface features such as sand dunes, alluvial fans, and river deltas.

Magma pushing up from Earth's mantle can create islands and mountains.

Mountains can also form when tectonic plates collide, folding and lifting upward.

Cirques, moraines, and eskers are formed by glacial deposits.

LINKS for Home and School

MATH Solve a Problem A particular glacier moves about eight centimeters a year. At this rate, how long will it take the glacier to move one kilometer?

SOCIAL STUDIES Make a Map

The state of Hawaii is made up of a chain of islands. Research Hawaii. What unusual plants and animals live there? What are some benefits and challenges of living on an island? Create a poster to present your findings.

Review

1 MAIN IDEA Compare Earth's constructive forces and destructive forces.

2 VOCABULARY Why is deposition described as the opposite of erosion? Give examples of these processes.

3 READING SKILL: Cause and Effect What causes the creation of dome mountains?

4 CRITICAL THINKING: Synthesizing In Hawaii, some beaches are covered in black sand. What can you conclude from this fact?

5 INQUIRY SKILL: Infer What can the size and shape of a sand dune tell you about how it was formed?

 TEST PREP

When a river meets an ocean, sediments drop out of the river because the river

A. speeds up.

B. slows down.

C. becomes saltier.

D. flows uphill.

 Technology
Visit **www.eduplace.com/scp/** to find out more about building up Earth's surface.

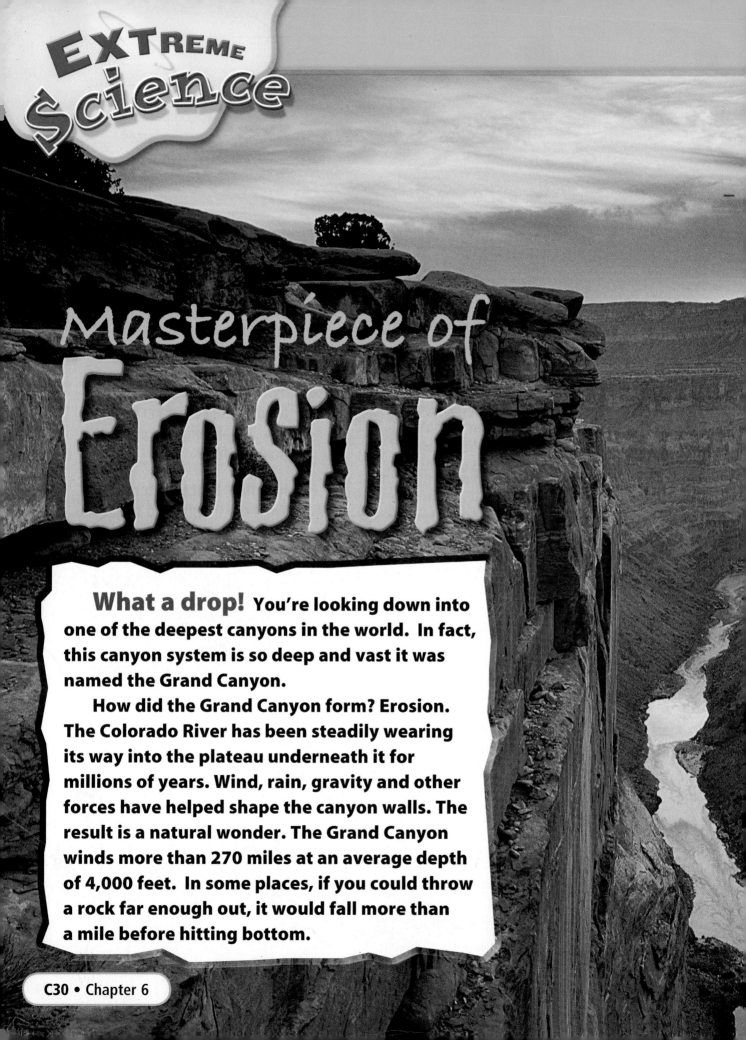

EXTREME Science

Masterpiece of Erosion

What a drop! You're looking down into one of the deepest canyons in the world. In fact, this canyon system is so deep and vast it was named the Grand Canyon.

How did the Grand Canyon form? Erosion. The Colorado River has been steadily wearing its way into the plateau underneath it for millions of years. Wind, rain, gravity and other forces have helped shape the canyon walls. The result is a natural wonder. The Grand Canyon winds more than 270 miles at an average depth of 4,000 feet. In some places, if you could throw a rock far enough out, it would fall more than a mile before hitting bottom.

Vocabulary

Complete each sentence with a term from the list. You may use each term more than once.

1. _____ is a constructive force.

2. A map that shows the shapes of Earth's landforms is a _____.

3. The rocky outer layer of Earth is called the _____.

4. A topographic map has _____ that connect places that have the same elevation.

5. Weathering and _____ are destructive forces.

6. Moving water, wind, and ice carry weathered rocks away in a process called _____.

7. Sand and other tiny pieces of rock are moved by erosion and settled by _____.

8. Tiny pieces that form from the weathering of rocks are _____.

9. Water is a common agent of both weathering and _____.

10. The process known as _____ can be mechanical or chemical.

contour lines C10
crust C7
deposition C24
erosion C16
sediment C14
topographic map C10
weathering C14

Test Prep

Write the letter of the best answer choice.

11. Location, shape, and elevation help define Earth's _____.

   A. constructive forces
   B. destructive forces
   C. surface features
   D. sediments

12. Erosion and weathering are examples of _____.

   A. constructive forces
   B. destructive forces
   C. surface features
   D. land buildup

13. Volcanic activity is an example of _____.

   A. erosion
   B. constructive force
   C. weathering
   D. alluvial plain formation

14. Thanks to wind and water, the products of one place's weathering become materials for another place's _____.

   A. volcanoes
   B. glacial till
   C. coral reefs
   D. deposition

15. Make a Model Suppose you have a lump of sugar, water, a spray bottle, and a cake pan. Describe how you could use those items to construct a working model of erosion and deposition.

16. Infer The icy sidewalk in front of your school was treated with salt to help the ice melt. In the spring, you noticed the cement was crumbly and falling apart. What type of weathering did you observe? Explain.

Map the Concept

Complete the concept map using words from the list below. Some words belong in more than one category.

glaciers   deposition   plateau
acids   volcanoes   lava
weathering   sediments   beaches
erosion   continental shelf
waves   mountains

Destructive Forces	Surface Features	Constructive Forces

Critical Thinking

17. Apply What features on the ocean floor are similar to features on Earth's surface?

18. Synthesize Formations called stalactites and stalagmites grow in caves where the water evaporates. A mineral deposit, calcium carbonate, is left behind. Describe another location in nature where a similar process takes place.

19. Apply Look at the photograph of the meandering river on page C25. Water flows at different speeds through a meander. Where do you think the water flows the fastest? Explain your reasoning.

20. Evaluate Two statues were put up in the center of a busy industrial city. One is made from marble and the other is made from granite. Predict what the statues may look like 50 years from now. Explain your reasoning.

Performance Assessment

Draw a Map

Illustrate four of the following terms with a drawing. Your drawing should accurately represent the main characteristics of these features.

continental slope	continental shelf	continental rise
barrier island	seamount	ocean
shoreline	marsh/swamp	sand dune
beach	sand	mid-ocean ridge

Earth's Structure

Lesson Preview

LESSON 1

Cool and crusty on the outside, hot on the inside—what is Earth's structure like?

Read about it in Lesson 1.

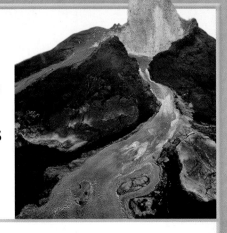

LESSON 2

Shaking earthquakes and erupting volcanoes—what forces of nature cause these dramatic events to occur?

Read about them in Lesson 2.

LESSON 3

Some mountains are tall and jagged. Others are rounded and covered in trees. How do mountains form?

Read about it in Lesson 3.

What Is Earth's Structure?

Why It Matters...

Earth has a layered structure, with solid rock at the surface and partly liquid rock material below. Understanding Earth's structure can help scientists predict when a geyser or volcano will erupt, or how a river will change course over time.

PREPARE TO INVESTIGATE

Inquiry Skill

Use Models When you use models, you study, make, or operate something that stands for a real-world process or action. Models can help you to understand better or show how a process or action works.

Materials

- modeling clay, 2 colors
- a small marble
- metric measuring tape
- aluminum foil
- plastic knife

Science and Math Toolbox

For step 4, review **Using a Tape Measure** on page H6.

A Model World

Procedure

1. **Collaborate** Working with a partner, roll modeling clay into two balls of different colors. Make one the size of a golf ball and the other the size of a baseball.

2. **Use models** The smaller clay ball represents Earth's outer core. The marble represents its inner core. Push the marble into the center of the smaller clay ball and reshape the clay around it. You now have a model of Earth's two-part core.

3. **Observe** The larger clay ball represents Earth's mantle. Using the plastic knife, cut this clay ball in half. Reshape the clay so that this ball can be wrapped around the two-part core. You now have a model of Earth's core and mantle.

4. **Measure** Use a measuring tape to find the distance around your model at its "equator." Cut a rectangle of foil equal to that distance in length and one-third of that distance in width. Wrap the foil around the mantle and smooth it out. This thin layer of foil represents Earth's crust.

STEP 1

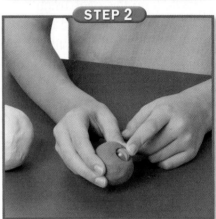
STEP 2

STEP 4

Conclusion

1. **Use Models** In your *Science Notebook*, draw what your model of Earth would look like if you could slice it in half. Label the layers.

2. **Infer** How would you describe the layers that make up Earth's structure? Write about them in your *Science Notebook*.

Investigate More!

Design an Experiment
List some materials you could use to model Earth's layered structure. Describe how you would arrange them.

Earth's Structure

MAIN IDEA Earth has a layered structure. Its outer layer is made up of moving plates.

VOCABULARY

core	p. C41
crust	p. C40
lithosphere	p. C41
mantle	p. C41
plate tectonics	p. C42

READING SKILL

Text Structure Outline the text on this page using an outline form. Select key words and phrases as topic headings.

Hot Inside

In many parts of the world, columns of steaming hot water can be found shooting up from Earth's surface. These boiling fountains are known as geysers. Geysers form in places where water drains down a deep channel in Earth's surface. At the bottom of the channel, hot rocks heat the water until steam forms, pushing boiling water up onto the surface. Finally, the built-up pressure forces the remaining water to erupt in a sudden explosion. The existence of geysers suggests that Earth is extremely hot inside.

Yellowstone National Park in Wyoming is well known for its numerous geysers and hot springs. Long before this region became a tourist attraction, Jim Bridger explored its wonders. Bridger was a fur trader, scout, and mountain man. He told everyone he met about the many geysers and amazing sights of the region.

Visit Yellowstone today, and you too can see evidence of Earth's hot interior. But just how hot is it inside Earth?

66 Geysers spout up 70 feet, with a terrible hissing noise, at regular intervals. In this section are the great springs, so hot that meat is readily cooked in them.... **99**

Jim Bridger (1804–1881)
Geyser Gazer

Yellowstone National Park's hot springs, geysers, and mudpots are evidence of Earth's hot interior. ▲

Temperature of Earth's Interior

Earth's Center

Earth's temperature increases about 25°C per km in the crust, then more gradually from the upper mantle to its center. ▶

Scientists cannot travel very far below Earth's surface to measure temperatures directly. By studying mines and holes drilled in the crust, scientists know that the temperature increases about 2 to 3°C for every 0.1 km (300 ft) below the surface. However, the deepest drill holes reach less than 15 km (9 mi) below the surface. So scientists depend on other, less direct evidence.

Scientists study geysers and volcanic activity to learn what Earth is like inside. They also conduct experiments on surface rocks and minerals under conditions of high pressure and temperature.

More information about Earth's interior can be gained by observing seismic waves. These waves are vibrations that travel through the solid Earth during earthquakes. Seismic waves change as they travel deeper and as they move through different kinds of materials at different temperatures.

▶ **TEXT STRUCTURE** What information does the graph on this page present?

Layers of the Earth

Crust
Earth's thin outermost layer is solid rock. It is about five times thicker under the continents than it is under the oceans.

Mantle
This thick layer is between the crust and the outer core. The solid upper mantle combines with the crust to form the lithosphere.

Outer Core
Formed mostly of molten metal, this is Earth's only liquid layer.

Inner Core
Pressure keeps this super-hot metallic region in a solid state.

Earth's Layers

Earth has a layered structure. Most of these layers are made up of solid or partly melted rock. The innermost layers are mostly a mixture of metals.

Earth's layers vary in thickness. The **crust,** the uppermost layer, is much thinner than the other layers. The crust is nearly all solid rock. Under the continents, the crust is mostly granite and other light rocks.

Below the oceans, the crust is mostly made of basalt—a dark, dense rock.

The crust is by far the thinnest of Earth's layers. Under the continents, the average thickness of the crust is about 40 km (24 mi), but it may be as much as 70 km (42 mi) in mountainous regions. The crust is even thinner under the oceans. The ocean-floor crust has a thickness of about 7 km (4 mi).

As discussed earlier, temperature increases as you go deeper into the Earth. So, the deeper that rocks are located, the hotter they are.

The layer just below Earth's crust is the **mantle.** The mantle is about 2,900 km (1,800 mi) thick and makes up more than two-thirds of Earth's mass. At the boundary where the upper mantle meets the crust, the mantle rock is solid. This solid upper mantle and crust combine to form a rigid shell called the **lithosphere.**

Below the lithosphere, much of the rock material in the mantle is partially melted. This material can flow very slowly, like plastic that has been heated almost to its melting point. The solid lithosphere can be thought of as "floating" on this thick lower mantle.

The innermost of Earth's layers is the **core,** which extends to the center of the Earth. The core is divided into two regions, or layers—the outer core and the inner core. The outer core is about 2,200 km (1,400 mi) thick, and is the only layer that is in a liquid state. It is made up mostly of molten iron and nickel, with some sulfur and oxygen also present.

The inner core, about 1,200 km (720 mi) thick, is even hotter than the outer core. It is probably made up of iron and nickel as well. However, the extremely high pressure so deep inside Earth keeps this metal from melting.

Many scientists believe that the presence of molten iron and nickel in Earth's core explains why Earth is surrounded by a magnetic field. According to one theory, convection currents move slowly throughout the liquid outer core. Electric currents are produced as Earth rotates, setting up Earth's magnetic field.

A hard-boiled egg is often used to model Earth's structure. The hard, thin shell of the egg is the crust. The egg white is the mantle, and the yolk is the core. Others compare Earth to a peach or similar fruit with a thin skin and a pit in the center.

▶ **TEXT STRUCTURE** Use an outline form to organize the information about Earth's layered structure.

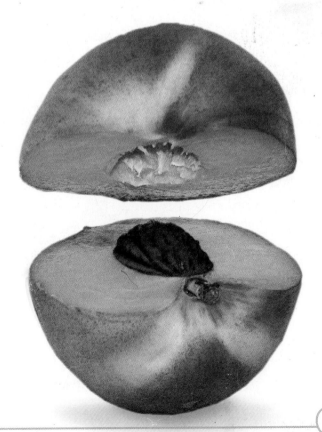

When a peach is used as a model of Earth, what does the peach pit represent? ▶

Moving Plates

Have you ever wondered if Earth's surface always looked as it does today? Alfred Wegener wondered. Wegener was a German meteorologist and geologist. In 1915, he suggested that the continents were moving very slowly across Earth's surface.

Known as the theory of continental drift, Wegener's ideas were based on evidence that included fossils and rock formations. However, he could not explain how the continents could move through the solid crust of the sea floor or what force could move them. So, his theory was rejected by most scientists.

In the 1950s, scientists discovered that molten rock from the mantle was rising to Earth's surface in the ocean basins. As this rock cooled and hardened, it was being added to Earth's crust.

This discovery led scientists to suggest that the lithosphere is not one solid shell of rock. In fact, they now believe that the lithosphere is broken up into giant slabs of rock called plates. These plates seem to "float" on top of the mantle, much like giant ships floating on a sea of thick molten rock.

The idea of giant plates of rock moving slowly across Earth's surface is called **plate tectonics.** As you might expect, the plates move very slowly. Their average speed is about 10 cm (4 in.) a year. However, over millions of years, plates can move thousands of kilometers.

There are two kinds of plates. Oceanic plates consist almost entirely of dense ocean-floor material. Continental plates are made up of lighter continental rock "riding" on top of denser rock.

This map shows Earth's major plates. Plates interact along their boundaries. ▼

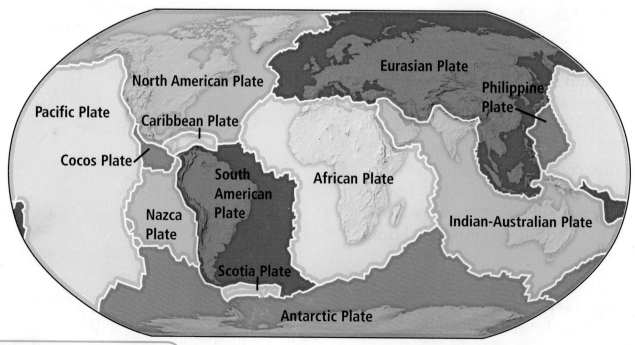

Plates interact at their edges, or plate boundaries. The pictures show the interaction that takes place at each type of boundary.

At converging boundaries, two plates converge, or move toward each other. Eventually they collide. When plates collide, one may ride up over the other. The upper plate forces the edge of the lower plate under the surface. This is called subduction.

Subduction usually occurs when a continental plate and an oceanic plate converge. The dense rock of the oceanic plate slides under the lighter rock of the continental plate.

At diverging boundaries, two plates move away, or diverge, from each other. Molten rock rises up in the gap between the plates, forming new crust. This usually happens in the middle of the ocean floor, so it is called sea-floor spreading.

In some places, plates simply slide past each other in opposite directions. These are known as sliding boundaries. Whether converging, diverging, or sliding, Earth's plates never stop moving and changing. New rock is added to Earth's crust in some places, while old rock is "lost" to the mantle in other places.

The moving, separating, and merging of the continents has been happening for billions of years. You can learn more about plate tectonics in the Readers' Theater feature on pages C46–C49.

▶ TEXT STRUCTURE Describe three ways in which Earth's plates interact at their boundaries.

Types of Plate Boundaries

Converging Boundaries
Two plates move toward each other. One plate may move under the other in a process called subduction.

Diverging Boundaries
Two plates move away from each other. Molten rock rises to fill the gap, creating new crust.

Sliding Boundaries
Two plates slide past each other, moving in opposite directions.

◄ A fossil of a tropical fern like the one shown below was found here. Since the fossil formed, the region is believed to have moved 3,200 km (2,000 mi) on a section of a continental plate.

Evidence for Moving Plates

Scientists conclude that Earth's plates have been moving for at least two billion years. They base this conclusion on evidence found in rocks at Earth's surface. These rocks have been eroded and deposited since the planet first took shape.

As you learned in Chapter 6, all rock at Earth's surface is subject to weathering and erosion. Weathered rock, or sediment, is deposited in layers. In turn, the layers eventually change into sedimentary rocks.

Layers of sedimentary rocks provide clues to changes that were taking place at the time the layers were forming. For example, the layers can show the mineral content of the rocks and how the sediment was deposited. The layers may also contain fossils.

A **fossil** is the physical remains or traces of a plant or animal that lived long ago. Fossils are usually found in layers of sedimentary rock.

By studying fossils in rock layers, scientists can get an idea of how plates moved in Earth's past. For example, fossils of similar species have been discovered on opposite sides of an ocean along the edges of different continents. Scientists believe that the fossils come from a period when those continents were joined. Over time, the continents separated, taking the fossils to new locations.

Some fossils seem to be very far from where they were deposited. Fossils of tropical plants and animals have been found in polar regions. Fossils of fish have been found near the tops of mountains. Scientists believe that the fossils were carried to their present locations by the movement of tectonic plates.

▶ **TEXT STRUCTURE** Use an outline form to organize information about the evidence supporting the idea of moving plates.

Visual Summary

Earth has a layered structure consisting of the crust, mantle, outer core, and inner core.

The crust and upper mantle make up the rigid lithosphere, which is broken into large sections called plates.

Plates interact in three ways at their boundaries: they may converge, diverge, or slide past one another.

Fossils and other material in layers of rock provide evidence of Earth's moving plates.

LINKS for Home and School

MATH **Calculate Diameter** Earth's inner and outer core combined are about the size of Mars. Using the measurements on page C41, calculate the diameter of Mars in kilometers.

ART **Build a Sculpture** Build a movable sculpture that models one or more plate boundaries. Use modeling clay, fabric, or other available materials. Write a paragraph that explains what the model shows.

Review

1 **MAIN IDEA** What parts of a hard-boiled egg are used to model Earth's structure?

2 **VOCABULARY** What parts of Earth's structure combine to form the lithosphere?

3 **READING SKILL: Text Structure** Outline the text under the head "Moving Plates" on page C42.

4 **CRITICAL THINKING: Applying** At a converging boundary, why do ocean plates usually subduct beneath continental plates?

5 **INQUIRY SKILL: Use Models** Describe how you would use small rocks, pieces of board, and a tub of water to model Earth's lithosphere.

 TEST PREP

The thinnest layer of Earth's structure is the

A. crust.

B. lithosphere.

C. inner core.

D. mantle.

 Technology
Visit **www.eduplace.com/scp/** to find out more about Earth's structure.

Alfred Wegener and Pangaea

What is Pangaea? Scientist Alfred Wegener (1880–1930) believed that long ago the seven continents were joined together, forming a supercontinent he called Pangaea.

Characters

Alfred Wegener

The Seven Continents:
Africa, Antarctica, Asia, Australia, Europe, North America, South America

The setting is planet Earth, and Wegener is taking the stage.

Wegener (*to audience*): Good afternoon. I am German scientist Alfred Wegener.

Europe (*aside*): His name is pronounced "VAY-guh-ner."

Wegener: My friends and I are here to present my theory of continental drift, which I published in the year 1915.

North America (*shocked*): Did you say "continental drift?" Are you suggesting that continents move?

Wegener: Don't act so surprised! Surely you know that continents move during earthquakes and volcanic eruptions.

North America: Yes, but—

Wegener (*holding up one hand at North America*): Let me tell you my story. Then you will understand. It all started when I was a young man fascinated by maps. One day I noticed that the coasts of two continents appear to fit together, like pieces of a jigsaw puzzle. Africa and South America, will you demonstrate?

Africa (*moving toward South America*): If I turn a little this way, and South America rotates that way . . .

South America: Yes, we *could* fit together, couldn't we?

Wegener: Yes! That got me thinking. I found out that nearly identical fossils have been discovered on both sides of the Atlantic Ocean, as well as identical rock layers. There are similar pairs of mountain ranges, too, such as the Scottish Highlands in Europe and the Appalachians in North America.

Asia: What are you driving at? Are you saying that some of the continents were once joined together?

Wegener: Not *some* of the continents— *all* of the continents! That's my theory.

Antarctica: Incredible!

Wegener: Isn't it? I call this joined continent *Pangaea.* That's Greek for "all the Earth." Might the seven of you demonstrate what Pangaea looked like?

Wegener waves directions. The continents move together to form Pangaea.

Australia (*stumbling*): This is terribly disorienting. Am I still Down Under?

South America: Hey, someone's stepping on my Galápagos Islands!

Antarctica: It's getting a bit too warm around here.

Wegener: Stop right there! Perfect! As you can see, the continents fit together into one supercontinent. According to my theory, this is how Earth looked about 200 million years ago.

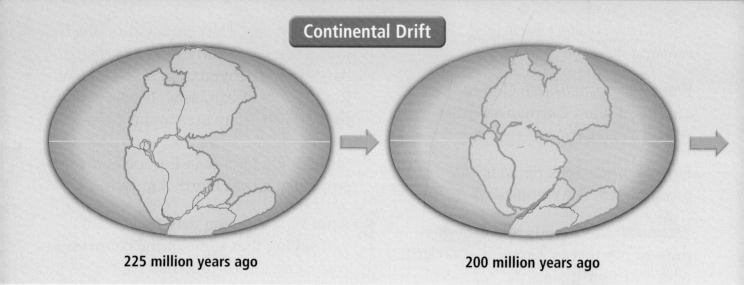

Continental Drift

225 million years ago   200 million years ago

Africa: So animals could wander from me to South America, is that right?

South America: Plant seeds could travel easily, too.

Wegener: Right and right. But over the years, slowly but surely, the continents drifted apart.

Wegner gestures at the continents. They drift apart, back to their modern-day positions.

Australia: Well, it was fun while it lasted!

Europe *(to the others)*: Maybe I'll see you again in another 200 million years or so.

Wegener: Perhaps, perhaps. My theory about Pangaea explains a great deal about Earth's geography. For example, have you noticed that mountain ranges are found mostly near the edges of continents?

South America: Now that you mention it, I have a rugged mountain range running along my west coast.

North America: That's funny, so do I!

Asia: And I have the Himalayas, that tall mountain range just north of India.

Wegener: According to my theory, mountains arise when continents move into each other. For example, the Himalayas rose when India slammed into the rest of Asia.

Asia: Ouch!

North America: Well, Mr. Wegener, you seem to have solved all the mysteries of our planet. So tell us: Just how *did* continents move around the planet?

Wegener *(shaking his head)*: Well, you've hit upon the weakness of my theory. I could only guess at how the continents moved. Many of my critics enjoyed pointing this out.

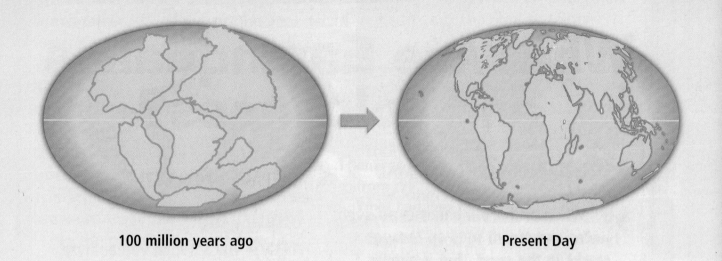

100 million years ago → **Present Day**

Continents gather around Wegener and pat him on the back in consolation.

Wegener: It's okay. After my time, people decided that I was correct. You see, scientists began studying the ocean floor.

Asia: What do oceans have to do with anything?

Wegener: A great deal! Scientists have discovered giant mountain chains, called mid-ocean ridges, in the ocean's depths. In these ridges, molten rocks rise from below Earth's surface and become part of the ocean floor.

Europe: So what does that mean?

Wegener: It means that the ocean floors are moving, too! Oceans and continents move in giant slabs that scientists call tectonic plates. If I'd lived long enough, I would have studied tectonic plates myself.

Australia: I'd like to thank Mr. Wegener for proposing new ideas that challenged old ones. That's very important in science!

Africa: Plus, he used evidence from many different branches of science.

North America: A keen observer and a logical thinker—that's our Mr. Wegener!

Wegener: Why thank you, my friends. I am truly—moved!

All laugh.

Sharing Ideas

1. **READING CHECK** What is Wegener's theory of continental drift?

2. **WRITE ABOUT IT** Describe facts about Earth's geography that Wegener's theory explains.

3. **TALK ABOUT IT** What lessons about science does Wegener's story illustrate?

C49

What Are Earthquakes and Volcanoes?

Why It Matters...

When a fruit pie bakes in an oven, juices and steam seep up through cracks in the crust. That is similar to how a volcano forms. Volcanic eruptions and earthquakes can be violent events. By learning more about them, people may be able to avoid some of the dangers they represent.

PREPARE TO INVESTIGATE

Inquiry Skill

Analyze Data When you analyze data, you look for patterns in information you collect. Those patterns can lead you to draw conclusions, make predictions, and state generalizations.

Materials

- world atlas
- blank world map
- red pencil
- green pencil

◀ A volcanologist is a scientist who studies volcanoes.

Picking a Pattern

Procedure

1 **Compare** Read and compare the lists of earthquake and volcano locations below. What similarities do you find?

STEP 2

Earthquakes	Year		Volcanoes	Year
Banda Sea, East Indonesia	1938		Mt. Pinatubo, Phillippines	1991
Concepción, Chile	1751		Mt. St. Helens, Washington	1980
Esmeraldas (offshore), Ecuador	1906		Krakatau, Indonesia	1883
Kamchatka Peninsula, Russia	1952		Mt. Fuji, Japan	1707
Kobe, Japan	1995		Arenal, Costa Rica	1968
Prince William Sound, Alaska	1964		Momotombo, Nicaragua	1609
San Francisco, California	1906		Mt. Hood, Oregon	1865
Tangshan, China	1976		Tiatia (Kurile Islands), Russia	1973

STEP 3

2 **Use Models** Use an atlas to find the locations of the earthquakes and volcanoes.

3 **Record Data** Mark each location on the blank world map. Draw a red triangle for a volcano. Draw a green circle for an earthquake. Check your work.

Conclusion

1. **Analyze Data** In your *Science Notebook,* draw conclusions about the pattern you see.

2. **Predict** Using what you know about Earth's structure, predict the relationship between the planet's plates and the places where most volcanoes and earthquakes occur.

Investigate More!

Research Use the Internet or other reference sources to research a recent major earthquake or volcanic eruption. Where did it take place? What damage did it cause? Report your findings.

READING SKILL

Cause and Effect Track the general causes and effects of faulting.

Earthquakes and Volcanoes

MAIN IDEA Earthquakes and volcanoes change Earth's surface, usually at plate boundaries.

At the Faults

As you have learned, Earth's crust moves very slowly. Typically, this motion can hardly be felt. But at times, it can cause sudden and unexpected changes to Earth's surface.

Most major surface changes occur at or near plate boundaries. Recall from the last lesson that plates may push together (converge), move apart (diverge), or slide past each other at plate boundaries.

Faults are cracks in Earth's crust along which movement takes place. At a fault, rocks often bend and fold. Sometimes, they lock together and jam along the fault. Over many years, stress builds up on the rocks as the plates strain against each other. Finally, the rocks break. The plates shudder and jolt into a new position. This sudden movement causes Earth's crust to shake.

The wavy lines from a seismograph indicate the strength of seismic waves moving through Earth's crust. ▼

▼ The San Andreas fault extends almost the full length of California.

As the crust shakes, it sends out shock waves of energy known as **seismic waves.** A seismograph has sensors that detect and measure vibrations of Earth's crust. The seismograph produces a record of seismic waves called a seismogram.

The movement of rocks along a fault is called faulting. During faulting, the rocks crack or split into blocks. The blocks then continue to move in relation to each other, sometimes leading to further faulting.

The drawings show the three main types of faults. Each is caused by a different type of force applied in the region where movement takes place.

At diverging boundaries, the force stretches rock. Eventually the rock breaks and one block moves down along a sloping crack. Mid-ocean ridges are typical locations for these types of faults.

Other faults occur at converging boundaries. Here, the force squeezes rock. When the rock breaks, one block moves up along a sloping crack while the other moves down. Often this occurs in regions of subduction, where one plate plunges below the other.

The third type of fault occurs in regions where blocks move horizontally past each other. These faults are common at sliding boundaries, such as the San Andreas Fault in California.

▶ **CAUSE AND EFFECT** What happens when stress builds up along a fault?

Fault at Diverging Boundary
As sections of the crust move apart, rocks are stretched until they snap, causing one block to move down along a sloping crack.

Fault at Converging Boundary
Rocks are compressed as they come together, causing one block to move up along a sloping crack as the other moves down.

Fault at Sliding Boundary
Rocks grind against each other as they move horizontally past each other in opposite directions. Pressure builds up along the fault until the rocks break.

C53

▲ The city of Taipei in Taiwan suffered a devastating earthquake on September 21, 1999.

Earthquakes

An **earthquake** is a violent shaking of Earth's crust. The release of built-up energy along a fault is what makes Earth shake, or quake. The energy released depends on how much rock breaks and how far the blocks of rock shift.

With the records produced by seismographs, scientists can measure an earthquake's energy. This measurement expresses its size, or magnitude, using a scale called the Richter scale. For example, an earthquake with a magnitude of less than 3.5 may not even be felt, although it is recorded by the seismograph. An earthquake measuring 7.5 is a major earthquake.

The surface effects, or intensity, of an earthquake vary from place to place. Intensity is measured by what can be seen and felt on the surface.

What people see and feel often depends on how far they are from the earthquake's focus. The **focus** of an earthquake is the point underground where the faulting occurs. Most focus points are less than 72 km (45 mi) below Earth's surface.

The point on the surface directly above the focus is an earthquake's **epicenter.** That is where the intensity is strongest. Why? The epicenter is the closest point to the focus, where seismic waves are strongest.

The shaking is caused by the energy of the seismic waves. Long after the initial earthquake occurs, continued seismic wave activity can cause miniquakes, or aftershocks.

Seismic Waves

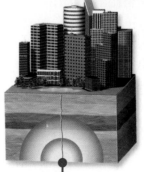

focus

epicenter   wave

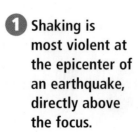

1 Shaking is most violent at the epicenter of an earthquake, directly above the focus.

2 Seismic waves spread out from the focus, decreasing in energy as they travel.

There are two general types of seismic waves—body waves and surface waves. Waves that travel through Earth's interior are called body waves. The deeper they extend, the faster they travel.

Body waves called P waves can travel through Earth's interior in less than an hour. They can pass through solid and liquids. As P waves pass into and out of the liquid outer core, they change direction. They return to Earth's surface, where they cause back-and-forth motions of rock.

Body waves called S waves travel slightly slower than P waves. When S waves reach the surface, they cause it to move up and down. However, S waves can travel only through solids. So, S waves that pass from the mantle into the liquid outer core lose their energy and do not return to the surface.

Surface waves, or L waves, travel along Earth's surface. These waves travel more slowly than body waves. Surface waves do not travel too far from the epicenter of an earthquake. However, surface waves cause the most damage, because they make the ground swell and roll like ocean waves.

The damage caused by surface waves can be extensive. Buildings fall down and roads heave up. Bridges collapse. Glass breaks. Rivers change course or flood their banks. Trees topple and cliffs crumble. Out at sea, massive waves are set in motion. These waves, often 30 m high (90 ft), can reach speeds of 500 km/h (300 mi/h). Such waves can cause great amounts of damage when they crash onshore.

▶ **CAUSE AND EFFECT** Why do surface waves cause great damage?

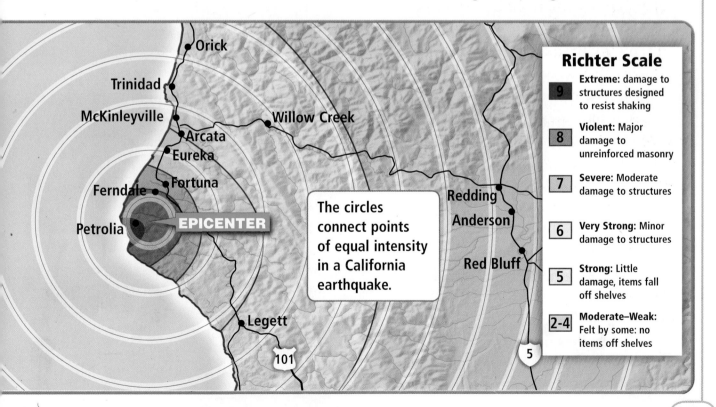

The circles connect points of equal intensity in a California earthquake.

Richter Scale

9	**Extreme:** damage to structures designed to resist shaking
8	**Violent:** Major damage to unreinforced masonry
7	**Severe:** Moderate damage to structures
6	**Very Strong:** Minor damage to structures
5	**Strong:** Little damage, items fall off shelves
2-4	**Moderate–Weak:** Felt by some: no items off shelves

Volcanoes

A volcano is an opening in Earth's surface through which melted rock, hot gases, rock fragments, and ash burst forth, or erupt. A violent eruption can release rivers of red-hot molten rock, hissing jets of poisonous gas, curling clouds of thick gray ash, and explosions of scorched rock.

You can see why volcanoes are sometimes referred to as mountains of fire. In fact, the word *volcano* comes from the ancient Roman god of fire, Vulcan.

How do such mountains of fire form? Volcanoes come from Earth's hot interior. Most volcanoes start 37 to 100 miles below the surface. At these depths, rock can become so hot it melts. Melted rock below Earth's surface is called **magma.**

When rock melts, it releases gases. These gases mix with the magma, making it lighter than the solid rock around it. Slowly, the gas-filled magma rises toward the surface. As it rises, it melts rock around it, gradually forming a large chamber. This chamber may be only a few kilometers below the surface.

Under pressure from the weight of surrounding rock, the magma is forced to find an escape. It melts or forces a channel into weak or cracked rock. Within this channel, it pushes upward. Once near the surface, gas and magma burst through a central opening, or vent. The erupting material builds up, forming a volcanic mountain, or volcano.

After an eruption, a volcano usually collapses into a bowl-shaped mouth called a crater. At the bottom of the crater lies the central vent. Many volcanoes have repeated eruptions. In these later eruptions, some of the volcanic material in the channel may remain below the surface. It may also push out through side vents.

Lava Flows

Volcanoes have been called mountains of fire.

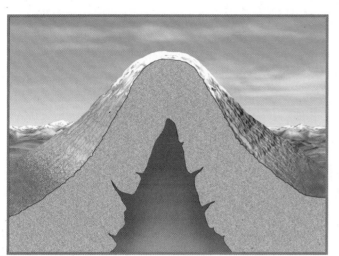

1 Hot, gas-filled magma rises, melting rock along the way, until it forms a chamber near the surface.

2 Pressure builds until the gas and magma force open a channel leading to the surface. Volcanic material moves through this channel and erupts through the vent.

Three main types of volcanic material are ejected during an eruption. The main one, magma, is called lava once it reaches the surface. It may be fast-flowing and liquid-like or thick and slow-flowing.

As it comes from a volcano, flowing lava may be hotter than 1,100°C (2,000°F). As it cools, lava hardens into formations such as boulders, domes, cones, tubes, and smooth or jagged sheets.

Rock fragments may form when gas in sticky magma cannot escape. Pressure builds up until the gas blasts the magma apart.

The fragments erupt into dust, ash, and large chunks called bombs. Small bombs, called cinders, may be no larger than a baseball. The largest bombs can be more than 1 m (3 ft) wide and weigh 100 tons!

Gases are also released during a volcanic eruption. Mostly steam, volcanic gases often contain poisonous chemicals. These gases mix with ash to form a deadly black smoke.

There are different classes of volcanoes and volcanic cones. Shield volcanoes form when a lot of lava flows smoothly from a vent and spreads out to cover a wide area. This action creates a broad, low, dome-shaped volcano.

Cinder cones form when mostly rock fragments erupt and are deposited around the vent. This creates a cone-shaped volcano with steep sides.

Composite volcanoes are also cone shaped. The sides of these volcanoes are steeper than those of a shield cone, but not as steep as a cinder cone.

▶ **CAUSE AND EFFECT** What causes magma to rise to the surface?

C57

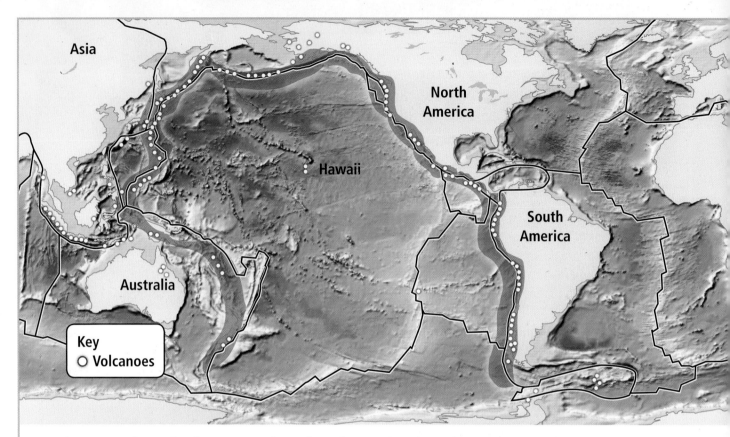

A large number of volcanoes and earthquakes strike along the edge of the Pacific Ocean. This explains why this zone is called the Ring of Fire. ▲

Ring of Fire

Many earthquakes and volcanoes occur in a zone that borders the Pacific Ocean. For that reason, this zone has been named the Ring of Fire.

The Ring of Fire outlines Earth's subduction zones, places where one of Earth's plates is forced under another. The Pacific Plate converges with several continental plates to form the Ring of Fire.

Faulting during subduction causes earthquakes and can also lead to volcanic activity. As the subducting plate sinks into the mantle, it melts to form magma. The magma may later rise to the surface as a line of volcanoes.

On the ocean floor, a deep narrow valley called an ocean trench may form along a subduction zone. Resulting volcanoes often parallel the trench, usually in an arc.

Faulting at diverging boundaries also causes earthquakes and creates volcanoes. Diverging boundaries are usually located near the middle of ocean basins. At these boundaries, magma rises to the surface between separating plates, creating volcanic mountain ranges known as ocean ridges. Faulting at the ridges leads to earthquakes.

▶ **CAUSE AND EFFECT** Why is the Pacific rim a region of earthquakes and active volcanoes?

Lesson Wrap-Up

Visual Summary

An earthquake is a violent shaking of Earth's crust caused by faulting, which shifts rock and sends out seismic waves.

Volcanoes form when gas-filled magma rises through Earth's interior. This forces volcanic materials to burst through a vent.

Many volcanoes and earthquakes occur in a subduction zone around the Pacific Ocean called the Ring of Fire.

LINKS for Home and School

MATH Make a Graph Research three recent earthquakes. Make a bar graph that shows the Richter scale readings for each earthquake. Share your graph with the class.

TECHNOLOGY Prepare a Report How can old buildings be reinforced to withstand earthquakes? Research this question on the Internet or at the library. Write a report to present your findings.

Review

❶ **MAIN IDEA** Why do earthquakes and volcanoes usually occur at plate boundaries?

❷ **VOCABULARY** Define *epicenter* and *focus* and describe their relationship.

❸ **READING SKILL: Cause and Effect** Describe the cause-and-effect relationship that creates volcanoes in the Ring of Fire.

❹ **CRITICAL THINKING: Analyze** How would Earth be different if its crust did not move and it lacked tectonic plates?

❺ **INQUIRY SKILL: Analyze Data** Research at least five recent earthquakes or volcanic eruptions. Add them to the list on Page C51. Do the additional data support the conclusions that this lesson presents about earthquakes and volcanoes?

 TEST PREP

Seismic waves that cause the most damage are

A. P waves.

B. surface waves.

C. ocean waves.

D. body waves.

 Technology

Visit **www.eduplace.com/scp/** to find out more about the most famous volcanic eruptions in recorded history.

How Do Mountains Form?

Why It Matters...

Have you ever wondered why mountains often form along a coastline? Or why those mountains look like wrinkled land? Understanding how mountains form allows people to understand what Earth's surface was like in the past. It also helps them predict future changes in Earth's surface.

Inquiry Skill

Observe When you observe, you use your senses to accurately describe things, making sure to distinguish between facts and opinions or guesses.

Materials

- shoebox lid
- moist sand
- scissors
- measuring cup
- wax paper
- goggles

Science and Math Toolbox

For step 2, review **Measurement** on page H16.

Make a Mountain!

Procedure

Safety: Be careful when using scissors. Wear goggles for this investigation.

STEP 1

1. **Collaborate** Work with a partner. Place a shoebox lid upside down on a flat surface. Then carefully cut a narrow slit along one end of the lid where it bends up.

2. **Measure** Line the top of the lid with wax paper. It should be the width of the slit and about 2.5 cm (1 in) longer than the lid.

3. **Use Models** Place the wax paper in the lid. Pull one end of the paper about 2.5 cm (1 in) through the slit. Spread half of the sand at the end of the lid near the slit.

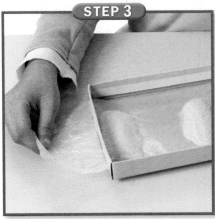
STEP 3

4. **Use Models** Spread the other half near the center of the lid. Each pile of sand represents the crust on one of Earth's plates. Draw the model setup in your *Science Notebook*.

5. **Use Models** Slowly pull the wax paper through the slit to model the movement of one of Earth's plates.

Conclusion

1. **Observe** In your *Science Notebook*, draw what happened to the sand as accurately as you can.

2. **Compare** How does what happened to the sand compare to what happens to rocks in the crust when two plates collide?

Investigate More!

Design an Experiment
Select materials to model what happens along a diverging boundary.

Mountain Formation

VOCABULARY

dome mountains   p. C64

fault-block   p. C63
   mountains

fold mountains   p. C62

READING SKILL

Categorize/Classify Use a chart to list the types of mountains and the forces that build them.

MAIN IDEA Mountains are formed by various processes, usually at plate boundaries. They can be classified by how they form and by their height.

Folding and Faulting Forces

Awesome! That is what you might think as you look down from a high mountain peak or gaze at mountains along a horizon. Indeed, mountains are awe-inspiring. Not only are they Earth's highest surface features, but they are some of its most beautiful. From the Alps in Central Europe to the Rockies in North America, mountains make up the backdrop to many of the world's scenic spots.

Grand in scale and great in mass, mountains may seem permanent. However, like Earth's other surface features, they are continually being created and destroyed.

Most mountains form at or near plate boundaries. In fact, most of the largest mountain ranges form where two plates collide and force layers of rock into folds. These are known as **fold mountains.** The Andes shown below are examples.

Folding
Folding often occurs at the edge of a continent and results in long, narrow mountain ranges, such as the Andes along South America's west coast.

Faulting

Faulting can produce dramatic cliffs when a large section of rock is forced upward or downward, as in this formation in the Rocky Mountains.

Fold mountains often form where an oceanic plate collides with a continental plate. Sediment from the ocean floor becomes attached to the edge of the continent. The sediment and continental rock crumple together, creating rolling folds. As the layers of rock wrinkle, they may also crack. This creates faults, or fractures, in the crust.

Erosion softens the folds over time. For that reason, some of the oldest fold mountains, like Arkansas's Ouachita Mountains, have rounded peaks. These mountains formed before dinosaurs lived!

Fault-block mountains may form wherever faulting occurs. They may even occur at faults within fold mountains. You know that during faulting, rocks break into blocks at a fault. The blocks may move in several ways along one or more faults to create mountains.

Most fault-block mountains appear to form at converging or diverging boundaries. However, mountain-building activity also occurs at sliding faults. The mountains may split and slip sideways like a stack of magazines falling to one side. The new range may then shift along the sliding fault. This is what has happened to some mountain ranges bordering Death Valley in California.

As with fold mountains, erosion helps shape fault-block mountains. Many of the large isolated mountains in the Southwest are fault-block mountains. They are separated by wide plains filled with eroded material from those mountains.

▶ **CLASSIFY** Which type of mountain is usually formed at converging boundaries?

Volcanic Forces

Sometimes volcanic activity forms mountains. This type of mountain usually forms at plate boundaries.

Volcanic activity may happen at converging boundaries when the edge of one plate sinks beneath another and melts into magma. If the magma rises and bursts through the crust, it generally forms a volcanic mountain. This process may even happen within mountains formed by other processes. For example, many of the mountains in the Andes chain in South America are volcanoes.

At diverging boundaries, magma rises up in the gap between the two plates. It then cools on the surface into ridges of new plate material. Recall that mid-ocean ridges form on the ocean floor at diverging boundaries. These underwater mountains make up the world's longest mountain chain.

Volcanic mountains can form away from plate boundaries as well. Magma plumes rising in the mantle create hot spots in the crust. As a plate moves over a hot spot, volcanic material erupts through the plate, creating a chain of volcanic mountains. Sometimes magma rises toward the surface but doesn't break through the crust. It may push up under Earth's crust, creating a dome-shaped mound. The molten rock then cools and hardens. This is how **dome mountains** are formed.

Erosion often continues to shape dome mountains. Irregular peaks and valleys may result. The Black Hills in South Dakota and the Adirondack Mountains in New York are examples of dome mountains.

Some mountains are formed entirely by erosion. The Catskills in New York are an example. These mountains formed when erosion carved out peaks and valleys from a plateau.

▶ **CLASSIFY** How are dome mountains different from other mountains?

hardened magma

Dome
Dome mountains form when volcanic material bulges upward under the crust, hardening as it cools. A number of dome mountains lie to the east of the Rocky Mountain range.

Visual Summary

Mountain Formation

- Fold Mountains

- Fault-block Mountains

- Volcanic Mountains

- Dome Mountains

 **LINKS** for Home and School

MATH **Convert Units** One of the highest mountains in the Alps is Mont Blanc, which is 4,810 m high. How many kilometers is that?

WRITING **Write a Story** The Navajo in the southwestern United States honor the mountains that surround them. Tibetans honor the Himalayan peak Kang Rimpoche. Choose a culture that lives near mountains and research their beliefs about mountains. Write a story about the people and their mountains.

Review

❶ MAIN IDEA Name and describe the four types, or classes, of mountains.

❷ VOCABULARY How does a dome mountain form?

❸ READING SKILL: Categorize/ Classify Which two types of mountains are formed by volcanic activity?

❹ CRITICAL THINKING: Synthesizing What might you conclude if you notice sections of warped and wrinkled rock layers on the side of a mountain?

❺ INQUIRY SKILL: Observe If someone described a dome mountain as "beautiful," would that be an accurate scientific observation? Why or why not?

✓ **TEST PREP**
Which of these is not a type of mountain?

A. fault-block

B. fold

C. dome

D. diverging

 Technology
Visit **www.eduplace.com/scp/** to find out more about mountain formations.

SLEEPING GIANT ERUPTS!

Talk about waking up on the wrong side of the bed! Snow-capped Mount St. Helens slept for a hundred years. Then on May 18, 1980, the volcano blew its top in one of the greatest explosions in recorded history. The sideways blast blew down enough trees to build 300,000 homes. Debris from the volcano was 600 feet deep and even blocked nearby rivers!

Before the eruption, the mountain was 9,677 feet tall. Afterward it was 1,314 feet shorter! Recently, the volcano has shown new signs of activity. Scientists are monitoring it closely to determine if another major eruption will occur.

In 1980, plumes of ash reached a height of 80,000 feet, ▶ blocking air traffic. In three days, the ash traveled all the way across the United States.

The View From Inside
This picture is taken from inside the blown-out top of Mount St. Helens. Here you can see the inner walls of the volcano's cone. ▼

steam plume

Danger Mounting This rising, steaming lump is called a lava dome. As magma pushes up from underneath it rises higher and higher—until the next big eruption. When will it be?

Review and Test Prep

Vocabulary

Complete each sentence with a term from the list.

1. The outermost layer of Earth is called the ____.

2. The ____ is composed of the solid upper mantle and the crust.

3. The ____ of an earthquake is the point underground where faulting occurs.

4. The layer of Earth between the crust and the outer core is called the ____.

5. Shock waves of energy released in an earthquake are called ____.

6. The release of energy along a fault causes an ____.

7. Earth's innermost layer is the ____.

8. Molten rock, or ____, that flows on the surface is called lava.

9. A crack in the crust along which rocks move is called a ____.

10. ____ form when magma pushes up from beneath Earth's crust.

core C41
crust C40
dome mountains C64
earthquake C54
epicenter C54
fault C52
fault-block mountains C63
focus C54
fold mountains C62
lithosphere C41
magma C56
mantle C41
seismic waves C53

Test Prep

Write the letter of the best answer choice.

11. Earth's rigid outer layers are broken up into ____.

    A. diverging boundaries
    B. tectonic plates
    C. the crust and the lithosphere
    D. the inner and outer core

12. What instrument measures the strength of an Earthquake?

    A. Thermometer
    B. Anemometer
    C. Spring Scale
    D. Seismograph

13. The temperature of Earth's interior ____.

    A. increases with depth
    B. decreases with depth
    C. is the same throughout
    D. is highest near the equator

14. Where does most mountain formation take place?

    A. at diverging boundaries
    B. at mid-ocean ridges
    C. along ocean trenches
    D. at plate boundaries

15. Use Models What kind of fault is shown here? Describe what is happening.

16. Analyze Data Describe the information that the Richter scale indicates about an earthquake.

Map the Concept

Complete the concept map using the words listed below.

converging	Earth
core	mantle
diverging	sliding

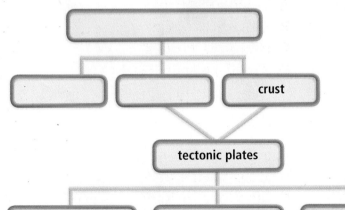

17. Apply The Himalaya Mountains lie on the northern border of India, which is also a plate boundary. Use plate tectonic theory to explain why Mt. Everest is increasing in height. What types of mountains are the Himalayas?

18. Synthesize As Alfred Wegener hypothesized, Pangaea was a supercontinent that ran north to south across the equator. North America was positioned over the equator. How might the climate of the United States have been different from today? What was the climate like in Antarctica?

19. Apply Why do tall mountains form at converging and diverging boundaries, but not typically at sliding boundaries?

20. Synthesizing During a strong earthquake, is the most damage done at the epicenter? Explain.

Performance Assessment

Make Mountains

Create a poster diagramming the three different types of mountains. Indicate the type of plate boundary, the type of mountain, and an example of where they occur.

Chapter 8

Using Resources Wisely

Lesson Preview

LESSON 1

Cars, planes, and trucks—where do people get the energy to power vehicles?

Read about it in Lesson 1.

LESSON 2

Every day, wind and rain carry away soil. What problems can soil loss cause?

Read about it in Lesson 2.

LESSON 3

Reduce, reuse, recycle—how can you conserve Earth's valuable resources?

Read about it in Lesson 3.

How Do People Use Resources?

Why It Matters...

You depend on natural resources for almost every activity of your life. Some resources, like the petroleum used to make gasoline, exist in limited supplies. When they are used up, they are gone forever. If people use resources wisely, everyone will have them for years to come.

PREPARE TO INVESTIGATE

Inquiry Skill

Use Models When you use models, you can see what happens in a real-world process.

Materials

- 3 plastic cups
- sand
- measuring cup
- teaspoon
- tablespoon
- goggles
- marking pen

Science and Math Toolbox

For step 3, review **Measuring Volume** on page H7.

Just a Spoonful

Procedure

Safety: Wear goggles for this activity.

1. **Collaborate** Work with a partner. Label one cup "Natural Resource." Fill this cup with 100 ml of sand. Label a second cup "Resource Supply." Fill it with 100 ml of sand. In your *Science Notebook*, make a chart like the one shown.

2. **Use Models** One partner will be the "resource user" and will use a tablespoon to remove sand from the Natural Resource cup. The other will be the "resource supplier" and use a teaspoon to add sand to the cup. Spoon sand in and out of the cup at the same rate for 30 seconds.

3. **Measure** Measure and record the amount of sand remaining in the cup.

4. **Use Models** Refill the cup with 100 ml of sand. Repeat steps 2 and 3, but this time, only the resource user should spoon sand out of the cup. Do not add sand to the cup.

Conclusion

1. **Compare** What is the difference in the amount of sand in the Resource cup for the two trials? Explain the difference.

2. **Hypothesize** Based on the data, what do you think would happen in step 2 if both students were using the same size spoons?

3. **Use Models** What do the results show about natural resources?

STEP 1

Use of Resources	Result
One student removing natural resource and one student supplying natural resource	
One student removing natural resource	

STEP 2

STEP 3

Investigate More!

Design an Experiment
Repeat the activity, this time varying the speeds that you add or remove the sand. How does changing the rate affect the final amount of sand in the cup? Report your results in a chart, graph, or diagram.

Earth's Resources

VOCABULARY

conservation   p. C78

fossil fuel   p. C75

natural resource   p. C74

nonrenewable resource   p. C75

renewable resource   p. C76

READING SKILL

Problem and Solution
Use a diagram like the one below to compare possible solutions to the problem of limited natural resources.

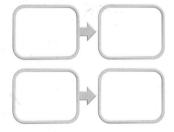

MAIN IDEA The Earth provides many resources that people need and use. Some resources are found only in limited quantities. Other resources are almost unlimited.

Natural Resources

The natural world provides everything that people need to stay alive, and many things that people find useful or helpful. These resources include air, water, minerals, and soil. They are called **natural resources.**

Humans have found many ways to take advantage of natural resources. We use them to build houses, grow crops, and raise livestock. We also use natural resources as a source of fuel and electrical energy. Natural resources that are used to produce energy are called energy resources.

Nuggets
Copper sometimes is found in pure nuggets like these. ▶

Mining
Copper comes from mines like the one here. Copper usually is found in combination with other elements. ▶

Nonrenewable Resources

Some natural resources are not easily replaced. These resources are called **nonrenewable resources.** Once a nonrenewable resource is used up, natural processes take millions of years to replace it.

Nonrenewable resources include oil, natural gas, and coal, which are examples of **fossil fuels.** They are called fossil fuels because they come from the remains of ancient plants and animals. Oil, which is also called petroleum, formed from the remains of plants and animals that once lived in the oceans.

How did plants and animals change into oil? After they died, their remains settled on the ocean floor. Over time, sediments built up on top of the remains, which were pressed under the building weight of the sediments. This pressure, along with heat from Earth's interior, changed the appearance and chemical makeup of the remains. Further pressure squeezed the remains into liquid. That liquid is oil.

Other nonrenewable resources include minerals and some rocks, such as ores of aluminum, iron, and copper. These materials are used for building materials and for making a wide range of products, from automobiles to jewelry.

Because nonrenewable resources cannot be replaced, it is important to use them wisely. If people are not careful, these resources will not be available for future generations.

▶ **PROBLEM AND SOLUTION** Why are fossil fuels examples of nonrenewable resources?

Petroleum Formation

As marine plants and animals died, their remains were sometimes buried before they completely decomposed.

Over millions of years, heat and pressure turned this organic matter into oil.

The oil collected in fractured rocks or in spaces between sediment particles. Today, oil pumps remove the oil from these spaces.

Renewable Resources

Not all natural resources are nonrenewable. Resources that are easily replaced or that can be used over and over again are called **renewable resources.** Farm crops and animals are examples. So are oxygen and fresh water.

Trees are renewable resources because new ones can always be grown. People use trees to make paper products and for lumber. Wood from trees can also be burned as fuel. Many companies operate tree farms. For each tree that is cut down, a young tree is planted. Thus, the supply of trees is constantly renewed.

Trees are a valuable natural resource. By replacing cut-down trees, a tree farm can provide wood over and over again. ▼

Renewable resources that are used to produce energy are called alternative energy sources. They provide options to using fossil fuels.

Wind Windmills have been used for hundreds of years to move water and to grind grain. Today, wind farms use rows of wind turbines to power electric generators.

Like old-fashioned windmills, the turbines have blades that turn as the wind blows. The energy from the moving blades is converted into electricity.

Solar Energy from the Sun is called solar energy. Solar panels can collect sunlight and convert it to thermal energy. This energy can be used to heat homes. Other devices, called solar cells, convert the Sun's energy into electricity. Today, solar cells power calculators and electronic road signs. In the future, people may be driving solar-powered cars!

Water Power plants that use moving water to generate electricity are called hydroelectric plants. At these plants, water is held behind a dam and slowly released. The falling water turns turbines, similar to the way wind turns turbines. The energy is converted into electricity.

Today, people still use fossil fuels for much of their energy needs. Yet these fuels are becoming scarcer and more expensive. Developing alternative energy resources makes sense for the future!

▶ **PROBLEM AND SOLUTION** How can people reduce their use of fossil fuels?

Wind

In windy places, wind turbines can generate electricity very efficiently.

Solar

Cars powered by solar energy must have a large surface area for solar cells. The solar cells collect the Sun's energy and convert it to electricity to power the car.

Water

Hydroelectric plants use the force of moving water to turn turbines. The energy from the spinning turbines is converted into electricity.

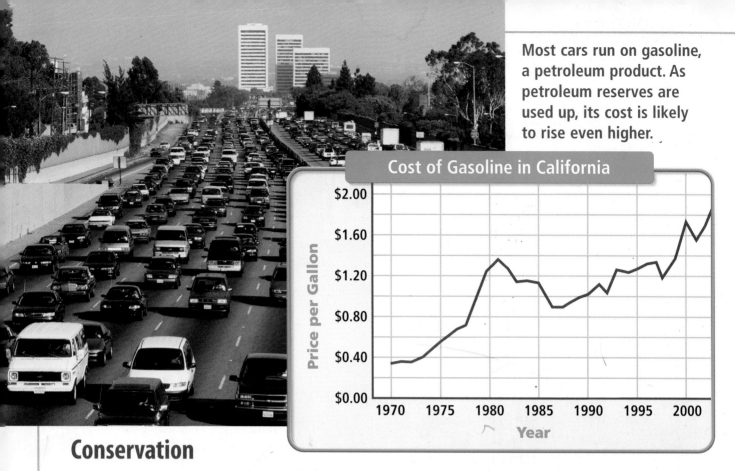

Most cars run on gasoline, a petroleum product. As petroleum reserves are used up, its cost is likely to rise even higher.

Cost of Gasoline in California

Price per Gallon

$2.00
$1.60
$1.20
$0.80
$0.40
$0.00

1970 1975 1980 1985 1990 1995 2000

Year

Conservation

The efficient use of resources is called **conservation.** Conserving nonrenewable resources is very important, because they cannot be replaced. By not wasting fossil fuels, you can save them for the future.

Another reason to conserve fossil fuels is to reduce pollution. Smoke from burning these fuels can mix with water in the air to form smog, which is not healthy to breathe.

Burning fuels adds a gas called carbon dioxide to the atmosphere. This action may be slowly warming Earth's temperature, an event called global warming. Scientists are studying this potential problem.

Other waste gases from fossil fuels mix with water in the air to form acid rain, another environmental problem. Acid rain can kill trees and fish, and damage buildings and statues.

What might be the most important natural resource to conserve? In many places, the answer is water. People need clean, fresh water for drinking, bathing, and growing crops. Although nature renews fresh water, the world's demand for water increases every year as the population grows.

You and your family can help to conserve Earth's important resources by following some simple, common-sense practices. Use public transportation, or form carpools. Turn off electric lights and appliances when not in use. Fix leaky faucets. What other ideas can you think of to practice conservation?

▶ **PROBLEM AND SOLUTION** **What problem can conservation help to solve?**

Lesson Wrap-Up

Visual Summary

Natural resources are nonrenewable if they cannot be replaced in a person's lifetime.

Natural resources are renewable if they can be quickly and naturally replaced.

Alternative energy sources help people to conserve fossil fuels, a nonrenewable resource.

LINKS for Home and School

MATH Create a Graph Suppose a gasoline-powered car can travel 40 km (25 mi) on a gallon of gasoline. A car that uses a combination of gasoline and electricity can travel 96 km (60 mi) on a gallon of gasoline. Make a bar graph to show how far each car can travel on 25 gallons of gas.

TECHNOLOGY Draw a Diagram
Research new technology that uses an alternative energy resource. Draw a diagram or illustration of the technology and present your display to the class.

Review

❶ **MAIN IDEA** Why is solar energy called a renewable resource?

❷ **VOCABULARY** Write a short paragraph using the terms *natural resource* and *energy resource.*

❸ **READING SKILL: Problem and Solution** Which alternative energy resource do you think is most likely to replace fossil fuels in the future?

❹ **CRITICAL THINKING: Evaluate** Where are the best places to build wind farms? Explain your reasoning.

❺ **INQUIRY SKILL: Use Models** A student constructs a model of a natural resource using a can with a small hole in the bottom. With the hole plugged, the can is filled with sand. When the plug is removed, the sand drains out. What kind of resource does this model illustrate?

 TEST PREP
Which of the following is a renewable resource?

A. oil

B. natural gas

C. lumber

D. aluminum

 Technology
Visit **www.eduplace.com/scp/** to find out more about natural resources.

Hybrid Cars

In many ways, hybrid cars look and operate much like other modern cars. The difference is inside. Hybrids are powered by a combination of gasoline and electricity!

As you read about hybrid cars, compare them to conventional cars that run on gasoline only. What advantages do you think hybrid cars provide?

Instruments
This gauge shows the volume of gas in the tank and the charge of the battery. ▼

Gasoline Engine
The engine is smaller and more fuel-efficient than the engines of most cars. It pollutes less, too.

Electric Motor
The motor draws energy from the batteries to accelerate the car. Yet it also can act as a generator, using the energy of the moving car to recharge the batteries.

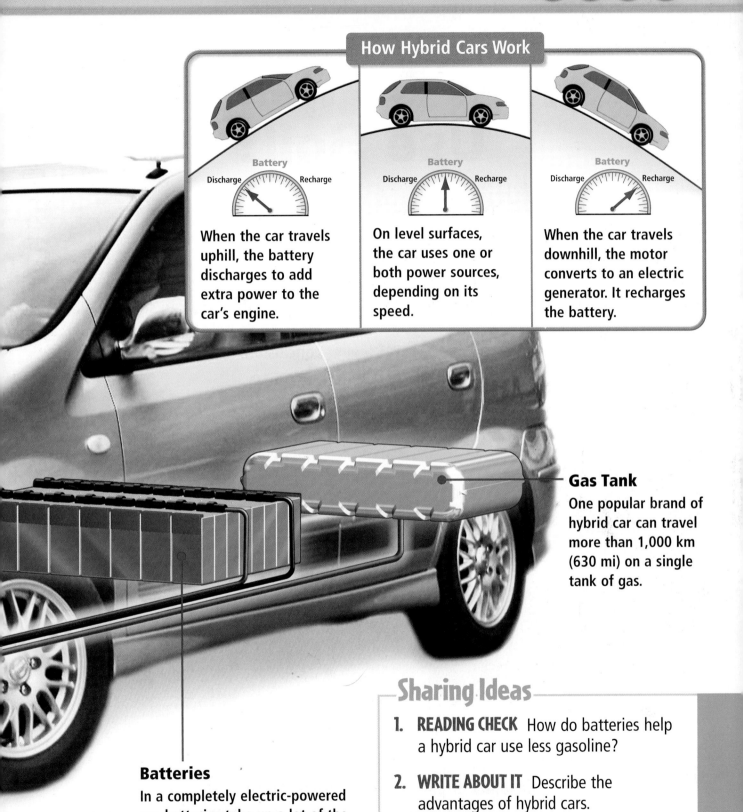

How Hybrid Cars Work

Battery
Discharge · Recharge

When the car travels uphill, the battery discharges to add extra power to the car's engine.

Battery
Discharge · Recharge

On level surfaces, the car uses one or both power sources, depending on its speed.

Battery
Discharge · Recharge

When the car travels downhill, the motor converts to an electric generator. It recharges the battery.

Gas Tank
One popular brand of hybrid car can travel more than 1,000 km (630 mi) on a single tank of gas.

Batteries
In a completely electric-powered car, batteries take up a lot of the car's volume. Because a hybrid car needs less battery power, its batteries take up less space.

Sharing Ideas

1. **READING CHECK** How do batteries help a hybrid car use less gasoline?

2. **WRITE ABOUT IT** Describe the advantages of hybrid cars.

3. **TALK ABOUT IT** How do hybrid cars compare to cars that run on gasoline only?

How Do People Use Soil?

Why It Matters...

Plants need mature, nutrient-rich soil in order to grow. Plants in turn protect and enrich soil. By studying how plants and soil interact, you can help protect both.

PREPARE TO INVESTIGATE

Inquiry Skill

Observe When you observe, you use what you can see or measure to help you draw a conclusion.

Materials

- 2 plastic bowls
- measuring cup
- moist soil
- plastic wrap
- goggles

Science and Math Toolbox

For steps 2 to 4, review **Making a Chart to Organize Data** on page H11.

A Mighty Wind!

Procedure

Safety: Wear goggles for this activity.

STEP 1

Soil Quality	Sample A	Sample B
Day 1		
Day 2		

1. **Collaborate** Work with a partner. Place 250 mL (1 cup) of moist soil in each of the two plastic bowls. Label the soil samples A and B. In your *Science Notebook*, create a chart like the one shown.

2. **Observe** Test the soil samples to determine their characteristics. For example, feel the consistency, dampness, and texture of the soil. Blow on it to see what effect wind might have on it. Record your observations.

STEP 2

3. **Experiment** Securely cover soil sample A with plastic wrap. Make sure there are no holes or gaps in the wrap. Leave soil sample B open. Place the two bins in a warm, sunny window and leave them overnight.

STEP 3

4. **Observe** Remove the plastic wrap from sample A. Repeat step 2 with both samples and record your observations.

Conclusion

1. **Compare** Compare your data about the two soil samples. What similarities and differences do you notice? How do you explain them?

2. **Infer** How do you think your observations might explain soil conditions in nature?

3. **Hypothesize** Do you think that growing plants affect the way that soil holds water? How could you test your hypothesis?

Investigate More!

Design an Experiment
Will soil, sand, and gravel dry out at different rates? Design an experiment to find out. Conduct the experiment with your teacher's approval.

Uses of Soil

MAIN IDEA Soil supports the growth of crops and other plants. Soil must be protected because mature, nutrient-rich soil takes a long time to form.

What is Soil?

Soil is a natural resource that is made up of minerals and small rocks, water, gases, and organic matter. The minerals and small rocks are weathered bedrock. The organic matter, called humus, is decayed plant and animal material.

Not all soils are alike. Different geographic areas have different types of soil. For example, the soil in a desert will be very different from soil in a forest. The type of soil that forms depends on several factors. These factors include climate and the types of rocks and organic matter present in the area. The size of the particles in soil may describe the soil's texture. Study the types of soil shown below. How do you think the quality of soil affects the plants that grow in it?

Sandy Soil
In sandy soil, particles are medium-sized and very hard. ▲

Clay soil
Clay soil is made up of very small, tightly-packed mineral particles. ▲

Rocky soil
Rocky soil, or gravel, includes relatively large fragments of rock. ▲

How Soil Is Formed

Soil forms in a process that takes thousands of years. This process begins with weathering. As you learned in Chapter 6, weathering is the breaking down of rock into smaller pieces of rocks and minerals.

If you were to dig a hole deep enough, you would hit bedrock. Bedrock is unweathered rock beneath the soil and other loose material on Earth's surface.

As the upper part of the bedrock weathers, it breaks into smaller pieces. These pieces eventually become part of the mixture called soil. Soil that forms from the bedrock beneath is called **residual soil.**

Sometimes, the soil in an area has minerals that are different from those in the bedrock below. This soil, called **transported soil,** has been carried from some other location by wind and water.

As soil forms, plants begin to grow. After plants and animals die, their remains decay. Rain carries the decayed organic material, or humus, from the surface into the developing soil. Humus adds nutrients to soil.

Plant roots, insects, worms, and other organisms also help in the development of nutrient-rich soil. Roots grow into the soil, and insects and worms burrow in it. They create spaces between the soil particles. These spaces allow air to circulate and more humus to collect.

▶ **DRAW CONCLUSIONS** How does the bedrock affect the type of soil in an area?

Earthworms, bacteria, and fungi break down dead plant and animal material. The remains add nutrients to the soil.

Profile of Mature Soil

Over time, as soil develops, definite layers can be observed. These layers are called soil horizons. A mature soil has four horizons. Young or immature soil has fewer horizons.

All of the soil horizons together are called a **soil profile.** In a mature soil profile, from the top down, the horizons are called topsoil, subsoil, parent material, and bedrock. The layers are also given letter names, as shown in the diagram.

Horizon A is the **topsoil.** Topsoil contains humus, minerals and rock fragments, as well as insects and earthworms. This part of the soil has the most nutrients and is important for growing plants. Most plant seeds germinate, or sprout, in topsoil.

Horizon B is the **subsoil.** Subsoil usually contains very little humus. However, water washes down some nutrients and organic matter from the topsoil. Some plant roots may reach down into the subsoil, and some earthworms and other organisms may be found here.

The next layer, horizon C, is made up of chunks of partly weathered bedrock. This rock is sometimes called the parent material, because the soil comes from it.

Below the parent material is the bedrock, or horizon D. This thick layer of rock is the foundation for the soil.

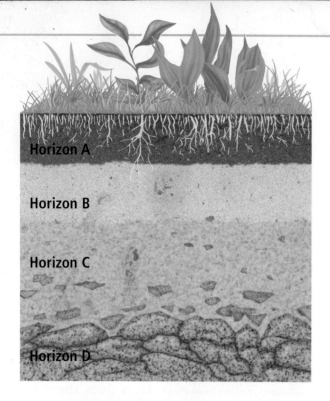

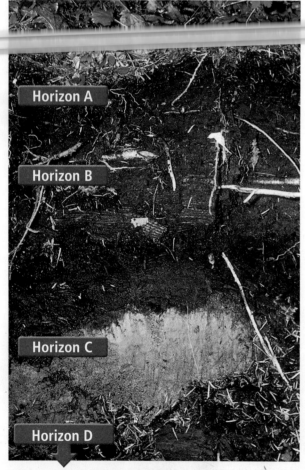

The action of water, plants, and animals created the mature soil profile shown here. ▲

▶ **DRAW CONCLUSIONS** What can you learn from studying a soil profile?

Crop Rotation Schedule

	Field 1	Field 3	Field 5
Year 1	Wheat	Wheat	Wheat
Year 2	Canola	Canola	Corn
Year 3	Barley	Corn	Canola
Year 4	Flax	Sunflower	Flax
Year 5	Soybean	Barley	Alfalfa

▲ These crops are different from those that were grown in the same fields a season ago.

◀ This table shows several recommended crop rotation schedules for northeast North Dakota.

Protecting Topsoil

As you have learned, topsoil is the layer of soil that has the most nutrients. Plants use these nutrients in a way that is comparable to how your body uses vitamins. While the nutrients are not food for plants, they are necessary for healthy growth.

The nutrients are passed on to animals that eat the plants, and to animals that eat the plant-eaters. Organic material from these plants and animals then returns the nutrients to the soil. This cycle is important to all living things.

Farmers must meet the challenge of maintaining nutrients in the soil. Growing crops take nutrients out of the soil. When the crops are harvested, the nutrients are removed with them.

How do farmers solve this problem? One solution is to add fertilizer to the soil to replace the nutrients. This solution is not perfect, however, because some of the fertilizer washes away when it rains.

Another way of returning nutrients to the soil is through crop rotation. Crop rotation is the planting of different crops during different growing seasons. Each type of plant uses different sets of nutrients.

If the same crop is grown in the same field for many years, the same nutrients are removed from the soil. With crop rotation, the soil is naturally replenished.

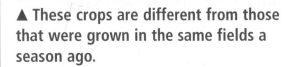 **DRAW CONCLUSIONS** According to the chart, if corn is grown in a field in Year 3, what crop should be planted in Year 4?

Conserving Topsoil

Farmers have found ways to prevent soil from losing nutrients. However, topsoil also needs to be protected from wind, water, and other agents of erosion.

What can be the result of excessive soil erosion? People learned the hard answer in the 1930s. Up until then, many farmers in the Great Plains practiced poor soil management. As a result, crops sometimes were poor and the topsoil was left bare. Conditions worsened during a long drought, which dried the topsoil. Winds simply picked up the topsoil and carried it away.

The region where this happened became known as the Dust Bowl. Huge dust storms swept across the area, and winds carried soil far from the farmlands. Without topsoil,

Experts estimate that about 850 million tons of topsoil were lost in the dust storms of 1935. Today, in part because of better soil conservation, that land is fertile again. ▼

farmers were unable to grow crops for many years. Without crops, a food shortage set in.

Today, farmers follow much smarter soil conservation plans. One way farmers prevent wind erosion of the topsoil is by creating windbreaks, or shelterbelts. A windbreak is a line of trees planted along the edge of a field. The trees help block the wind and prevent or reduce soil erosion.

Water is another factor in soil erosion. When water moves down the slopes of a plowed field, it picks up soil and carries it away. To reduce this type of erosion, farmers practice contour plowing. They follow the contours of their fields as they plow. These winding furrows slow water down as gravity moves it down the slope.

Another approach to preventing soil erosion is to plant cover crops, such as clover or alfalfa. The roots of these plants hold soil in place and prevent it from being carried away.

▶ **DRAW CONCLUSIONS** How do plants help protect soil?

Visual Summary

Soil is made up of weathered rock material, gases, water, and humus. Decaying plants and animals add nutrients to the soil.

Topsoil is important because it provides most of the nutrients for growing plants.

Conservation practices help farmers prevent the loss of topsoil through erosion. "Dust Bowls" can be prevented.

L I N K S for Home and School

MATH Estimate Using Fractions A farmer practices crop rotation to conserve soil nutrients. She grows wheat one year in every five. About what fraction of her total crop output is wheat?

WRITING Narrative Find out more about the Dust Bowl of the 1930s. Write a short story describing what it must have been like to be a farmer in the Great Plains during the 1930s.

Review

❶ MAIN IDEA What layers make up a mature soil profile?

❷ VOCABULARY In your own words, define the term *soil profile.*

❸ READING SKILL: Draw Conclusions You notice that the steep sides of a highway road cut are covered in tightly woven netting. What might be the reason for this practice?

❹ CRITICAL THINKING: Analyze Why do farmers need to understand the nutrients required by the crops that they plant?

❺ INQUIRY SKILL: Observe You dig up part of your yard in hopes of planting a garden. You see that the uppermost layer of soil is thin, and you find a lot of rocks near the surface. What does this tell you about how your garden will grow?

 TEST PREP

The layer of mature soil that contains only a few nutrients is the

A. bedrock.

B. parent material.

C. subsoil.

D. topsoil.

 Technology
Visit **www.eduplace.com/scp/** to find out more about soil.

Lesson 3

How Can People Use Resources Wisely?

Why It Matters...

Why should you recycle old bottles and cans? One reason is to conserve Earth's resources. Recycling plastics, metals, and other materials means they can be used to make new products.

Inquiry Skill

Collaborate When you collaborate, you work with other people to find solutions by considering the suggestions, findings, and ideas of others.

Science and Math Toolbox
For steps 2 to 4, review **Making a Chart to Organize Data** on page H11.

Recycling!

Procedure

1. **Collaborate** As a class, identify all the materials that your family, your school, and your community recycle.

2. **Record Data** In your *Science Notebook*, list the materials that the class identified. Create a chart like the one shown.

3. **Predict** Review your list and choose two types of recyclable materials that your household uses. Predict how many of these recyclable items your household uses in a week. Then predict how many of the goods will be recycled. Record your predictions.

4. **Observe** For one week, monitor your household's use of the selected recyclable goods. Record how many items are recycled and how many are thrown in the trash.

STEP 2

	Predicted data		Observed data	
	Used	Recycled	Used	Recycled
Glass bottles				
Newspaper				
Plastic				
Aluminum cans				

STEP 4

Conclusion

1. **Analyze Data** Use your data to calculate the total amount of your chosen recyclable goods used in your household that week. Then, calculate the percentage of those materials that were set aside to be recycled. Did your household recycle more or less than it threw in the trash?

2. **Collaborate** Work in a small group to develop a plan that would encourage people in your community to recycle more.

Investigate More!

Solve a Problem
From your data or other observations, choose a resource that you think is wasted in your community. How could this resource be used wisely? Present your ideas in a letter, poster, or skit.

Learn by Reading

VOCABULARY

recycling   p. C92

READING SKILL

Problem and Solution
Use a chart to compare the pros and cons of one of the conservation solutions discussed in this lesson.

Conservation

MAIN IDEA By reducing, reusing, and recycling, people can help ensure that important resources used to make everyday items will be available in the future.

Using Resources Wisely

Think about some of the things you used today—a plastic water bottle, an aluminum can, a paper towel. These are very useful items, and all come from natural resources. Plastic is a petroleum-based product. Aluminum comes from a mineral ore that is mined. Paper is made from trees.

When you finished using these items, what did you do with them? Did you throw them away in the trash? If so, the resources used to make those items are lost. But it doesn't have to be that way.

Recycling means recovering a resource from one item and using that resource to make another item. Recycling saves energy and conserves resources.

Recycling Rates in the United States (2002-2003)

Recyclable Item	Percent
Beverage Cans	54%
Plastic Bottles	21%
Newspapers	73%
Glass Containers	33%

▲ How do you think the trash that you throw out compares to the data shown here?

◄ **Recycle**
The triple-arrow symbol means that this can should be recycled.

The Three Rs of Conservation

There are three main ways to conserve resources: reduce, reuse, and recycle. People refer to these as the three Rs of conservation. You have already learned how recycling helps conserve resources.

Reducing simply means using less material. For example, when you use one paper towel to wipe up a spill instead of using two, you reduce your use of paper. If you choose not to use a straw in your drink, you reduce the amount of plastic you use. Every time you walk or ride a bike instead of riding in a car, you reduce the amount of fossil fuels that you use.

Reusing is another way to conserve resources. Reusing can be as simple as using a glass cup again and again instead of throwing away a plastic cup after a single use.

Reusing also means putting things to new uses. For example, you could wash an empty plastic pickle jar and keep it on your desk as a pencil holder. This keeps the jar from ending up in the garbage. It also saves the material that would have been used to make a pencil holder that you otherwise might have bought at a store.

In general, reducing and reusing are more effective than recycling. Both save more resources and energy than recycling does. But recycling resources is still much better than wasting them.

▶ **PROBLEM AND SOLUTION** How does recycling help to conserve natural resources?

▲ **Reduce**
Insulation helps reduce the amount of energy used in buildings. This fiberglass insulation helps keep a house cool in the summer and warm in the winter.

Reuse
These containers and cloth diapers can be used over and over again. What other reusable items can you name? ▶

Landfills

Have you ever wondered what happens to the trash that you throw away? You may know that a truck picks it up, but where does the truck take it?

Most trash ends up in a landfill. A landfill is a place where trash is deposited and then covered with plastic or clay. The plastic or clay seals the trash in the landfill and keeps the wastes contained.

Landfills are carefully designed to keep waste in and water and air out. This design has both benefits and drawbacks. The sealing of landfills keeps materials in the waste from polluting the environment. Harmful chemicals are stopped from seeping into the groundwater. Yet the lack of air and water slows the rate that the wastes decompose, or break down.

Most organic matter, such as paper or leather, will decompose fairly quickly when exposed to air and water. However, when sealed in a landfill, they might take several years to break down. Other wastes can take hundreds of years to decompose. Trash you throw out today may remain in landfills for a very long time.

Each landfill is designed to take up a certain amount of space. Once it is filled, it must be closed. Some communities have no more space to create new landfills. They must ship their trash to other areas for disposal.

When we reduce, reuse, and recycle items that would otherwise be thrown out as trash, we decrease the amount of material that is sent to landfills. Not only are resources conserved, but space in landfills is also conserved.

▶ **PROBLEM AND SOLUTION** **Why must landfills be carefully designed?**

Landfills take up valuable land resources. Practicing the three Rs reduces the trash that goes to the landfill.

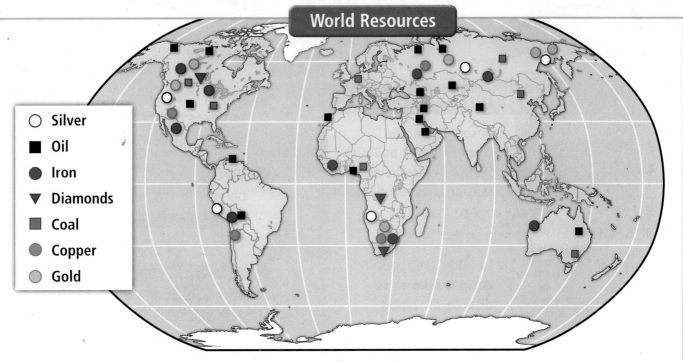

○	Silver
■	Oil
●	Iron
▼	Diamonds
■	Coal
●	Copper
●	Gold

This map shows where natural resources are found. When resources are not located near where they are used, other resources must be used to transport them. ▲

Where the Resources Are

The map on this page shows places around the world that have large deposits of different natural resources. You can see that many resources are found only in certain parts of the world.

In the past, people often settled in areas where important resources were found. The natural resources available in an area shaped the lives and businesses of communities in the region. While this is still true to some extent, modern transportation and technology make it much easier for people to use and rely on resources from all over the world.

Today, people commonly transport resources. A resource such as silver may be taken from the place it is mined and shipped to another place to be processed. Pure silver is then shipped all over the world to jewelers and other manufacturers.

Oil is one resource that is used everywhere, but found in large supplies in only a few places. Every day, ships carry millions of gallons of oil across the oceans.

These ships sometimes have accidents, and their cargoes spill into the water. Oil spills can be deadly to fish, whales, seals, and other marine life. Eventually, the oil can wash up on land and damage ecosystems along the shore.

Transporting resources around the world brings many benefits. However, it can also be costly and harm the environment. When people conserve natural resources through the three Rs of conservation, fewer resources need to be shipped around the world.

▶ **PROBLEM AND SOLUTION** What is one solution to the problems caused by transporting oil?

Visual Summary

Resources can be conserved and pollution reduced by reducing, reusing, and recycling.

Landfills are specially designed places to dispose of wastes.

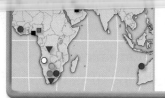

Natural resources are transported regularly from regions where they are found to other regions where they are used.

LINKS for Home and School

MATH **Make a Graph** Use newspapers, almanacs, and the Internet to find out the average amount of trash produced by a nearby city each year for the last five years. Make a line graph showing the data. Analyze the trends you find.

TECHNOLOGY **Write a Report**
Research developments in the design and location of landfills. Write a report explaining what you learned.

Review

1 MAIN IDEA What are three practices that help conserve natural resources?

2 VOCABULARY Write a short paragraph that explains how recycling conserves natural resources.

3 READING SKILL: Problem and Solution Landfills are lined with plastic or clay. What problem does this help to solve?

4 CRITICAL THINKING: Apply Cobalt is a metal used in making powerful magnets. The United States imports all its cobalt from other countries. If large cobalt deposits were found in the Rocky Mountains, how might that affect the United States and other countries?

5 INQUIRY SKILL: Collaborate Work with a partner to list three ways of reducing the use of natural resources at your school.

TEST PREP
Which of the following is NOT a method of conserving resources?

A. replace

B. recycle

C. reuse

D. reduce

Technology
Visit **www.eduplace.com/scp/** to find out more about how resources can be used wisely.

Cartographer

Cartographers are map makers. They map many types of surface features, from the highest mountain to the ocean floor. Maps may present natural features, such as elevation and climate, or human-made ones, such as cities, roads, and crops.

Cartographers rely on physical surveys, as well as images from airplanes and satellites. They often use computers, too.

What It Takes!

- A degree in geography, geology, or art
- Drawing and computer skills

Farmer

Is farming the most important job in the world? Nearly all of the world's food comes from crops and livestock raised by farmers and ranchers. So do many other products, such as cotton, leather, and wool.

Farmers must do many tasks: operate and care for farm machinery, monitor weather conditions, prevent crop and animal diseases, care for the soil, and manage a business.

What It Takes!

- Courses in agriculture and business
- Energy for strenuous work outdoors

EXTREME Science

TIRED!

What a waste! It took millions of gallons of fossil fuel and many other nonrenewable resources to make the tires in this picture. Every year hundreds of millions of tires are thrown away. Experts estimate there are at least 1 *billion* scrap tires in the United States!

Because tires take up to 80 years to decompose, they aren't going away soon. Fortunately, recycling tires has become big business. Each year, more and more old tires are processed to produce fuel. Tires are also ground up and used to create safe, sturdy surfaces for roads, sidewalks, and playgrounds.

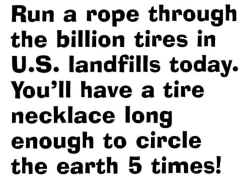

Run a rope through the billion tires in U.S. landfills today. You'll have a tire necklace long enough to circle the earth 5 times!

Tire Doctor

Dr. Jagdish Dhawan, shown here, worked with fellow chemistry professor Richard Legendre to develop a new process that recycles scrap tires into high-grade oil without any waste.

Vocabulary

Complete each sentence with a term from the list.

1. Sending aluminum cans to a plant to be made into other aluminum products is an example of _____.

2. A(n) _____ is anything found in nature that is necessary or useful to humans.

3. Coal is called a(n) _____ because it formed from the remains of ancient living things.

4. The layers that make up a mature soil represent the _____.

5. Humus is most commonly found in _____.

6. The layer of soil with little or no organic matter is called _____.

7. _____ is soil that is located where it formed.

8. A(n) _____ may only be used once because it cannot be replaced.

9. Soil that has been carried by wind or water from where it formed is called _____.

10. A(n) _____ may be used repeatedly, because it can be replaced.

conservation C80
fossil fuel C77
natural resource C76
nonrenewable resource C77
recycling C94
renewable resource C78
residual soil C87
soil C86
soil profile C88
subsoil C88
topsoil C88
transported soil C87

Test Prep

Write the letter of the best answer choice.

11. The practice of using all resources wisely is called _____.

    A. conservation
    B. using renewable resources
    C. using nonrenewable resources
    D. composting

12. Which is NOT a common part of soil?

    A. humus   C. minerals
    B. water   D. fossil fuels

13. What is one example of capturing a renewable energy source?

    A. mining for coal
    B. mining for oil
    C. installing wind turbines
    D. drinking a glass of water

14. Using china dishes instead of paper plates is an example of _____ paper use.

    A. reducing   C. recycling
    B. reusing   D. unwise

Inquiry Skills

15. **Observe** How could you use the appearance of a creek after a rainstorm to determine if soil erosion is taking place?

16. **Collaborate** How might people work together to reduce the amount of trash that is sent to a landfill? Discuss positive steps that families, businesses, and communities can take.

Map the Concept

This chart shows two categories. Classify each of these natural resources.

coal
oil
trees
solar energy
natural gas
wind energy
moving water

Renewable Resource	Nonrenewable Resource

Critical Thinking

17. **Evaluate** How would you respond to people who say it is not necessary to conserve fossil fuels, because the supply of fossil fuels will not run out during their lifetime?

18. **Apply** Name three different types of resources that people mine from Earth. Describe uses for these resources.

19. **Apply** If you were interviewing a company to pick up your materials for recycling, what are three questions you would ask?

20. **Analyze** What natural resources are especially common in your state? How do people collect or use them? Research your state's resources at the library or on the Internet.

Performance Assessment

Plowing a Field

Suppose a farmer wanted to check on the quality of his soil from one year to the next. Make a list of steps he could take to gather this information. Explain how each action would help him detect any changes in soil quality.

Write the letter of the best answer choice.

1. Rosa keeps her pens and pencils in an old tennis ball can. Which conservation strategy is this?

   A. recycle

   B. reduce

   C. resource

   D. reuse

2. Which surface feature do living organisms build up?

   A. coral reef

   B. river delta

   C. shield cone

   D. terminal moraine

3. The diagram shows which type of plate boundary?

   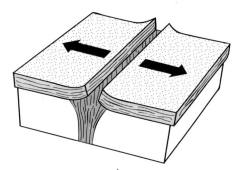

   A. converging

   B. diverging

   C. sliding

   D. subducting

4. Soil that forms from the bedrock below it is called _____ .

   A. humus.

   B. rocky soil.

   C. residual soil.

   D. transported soil.

5. Which is a nonrenewable energy source?

   A.

   B.

   C.

   D.

6. Which of the following provide evidence to support the theory of continental drift?

   A. atolls

   B. caves

   C. deltas

   D. fossils

7. Which of the following is NOT a feature of the deep ocean floor?

    A. guyot

    B. seamount

    C. abyssal plain

    D. continental margin

8. Which represents a destructive force on Earth's surface?

A.

B.

C.

D.

Answer the following in complete sentences.

9. Hybrid cars run on gasoline some of the time and on electric power the rest of the time. What conservation strategy applies to hybrid cars? Explain your answer.

10. Earthquakes generate three kinds of waves: S waves, P waves, and L waves. Which wave type causes the MOST damage? Explain your answer.

Discover!

On January 17, 1994, a strong earthquake struck southern California. The epicenter was near the community of Northridge, and the magnitude was 6.7 on the Richter scale. The map shows how strongly the shaking was felt in different communities.

Richter Scale

1	2	3	4	5	6	7	8	9
	Typically not felt	**MINOR** felt but no damage	**LIGHT** shaking and rattling	**MODERATE** damage to some buildings	**STRONG** serious damage < 100 km away	**MAJOR** serious damage > 100 km away	**GREAT** serious damage over large region	

Earthquakes strike when rocks suddenly break deep below Earth's surface. In a severe earthquake, the shock waves can topple buildings and collapse bridges. Earthquakes are common along the edge of the Pacific Ocean, where tectonic plates are slowly sliding against one another.

See an earthquake in action. Go to **www.eduplace.com/scp/** to view a Flash™ movie and to learn more about earthquakes.

Atmosphere and Solar System

EARTH SCIENCE

UNIT D

Atmosphere and Solar System

Independent Reading

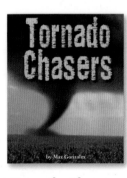

Tornado Chasers   **Space Wardrobe**   **15 Facts About Stars**

You look up at the night sky and see countless numbers of twinkling stars. Some stars appear larger and brighter than others. And some seem more twinkly than their neighbors. What makes stars appear to twinkle? You'll have the answer to this question by the end of the unit.

Chapter 9

Weather and Climate

Lesson Preview

LESSON 1

Winter—or summer—wonderland? Why is the Arctic always cold?

Read about it in Lesson 1.

LESSON 2

How does hi-tech equipment in space help you decide what clothes you should wear?

Read about it in Lesson 2.

What Factors Affect Climate?

Why It Matters...

All organisms, including humans, are affected by the climate of the part of the world they live in. Understanding the factors that affect climate helps people predict and prepare for changes in weather.

PREPARE TO INVESTIGATE

Inquiry Skill

Compare When you compare, you describe how two or more objects or events are the same and how they are different.

Materials

- graph paper, 2 sheets
- meter stick
- protractor
- large flashlight

Science and Math Toolbox

For step 5, review **Measurements** on page H16.

Lighten Up!

Procedure

Safety: Do not shine the light into anyone's eyes, including your own.

1. **Collaborate** Work with a partner. Place a sheet of graph paper on the floor in your work area.

2. **Measure** Hold the flashlight 1/2 meter above the graph paper and pointed directly at it. When the room has been darkened, shine the flashlight directly onto the center of the graph paper at an angle of 90 degrees.

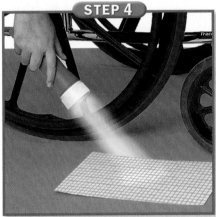

3. **Record Data** While you hold the light steady, have your partner carefully trace the lighted area of the graph paper. Label the drawing. Pick up the graph paper and replace it with a clean piece.

4. Now tilt the flashlight at an angle of 45 degrees to the graph paper. Use a protractor to help you determine the angle. Repeat steps 2 and 3.

5. **Use Numbers** Count the squares inside each shape traced in the sheets of graph paper to find the areas of the two shapes. Record the areas in your *Science Notebook.*

Conclusion

1. **Compare** What differences did you notice between the two lighted areas? How do the two areas compare?

2. How might the difference in the lighted areas explain why Earth's surface is not evenly heated by the Sun?

Investigate More!

Design an Experiment
Design an experiment to show how striking a curved surface, such as a large ball, affects the angle of the Sun's rays. Predict what will happen, then test your prediction.

Climate

Uneven heating of Earth's surface affects the climate of an area.

MAIN IDEA Climate is the normal pattern of weather in an area over many years. Earth's shape, the tilt of its axis, and its geographic features affect the climate of an area.

Uneven Heating

In summer, would you wear a bathing suit at the North Pole? Would you wear a down jacket in Egypt? No, you would not. The North Pole would be too cold and Egypt too hot. Why? Earth's shape and the tilt of its axis cause the Sun's rays to strike different parts of Earth's surface at different angles. So, energy from the Sun heats the surface unevenly.

Egypt is located near the equator, where the Sun's rays strike the surface at an angle near 90 degrees. This causes these areas to be warm year round. Near the poles, the rays strike the surface at angles much less than 90 degrees, resulting in much cooler temperatures. What kinds of temperatures might you expect to find in areas between these two regions?

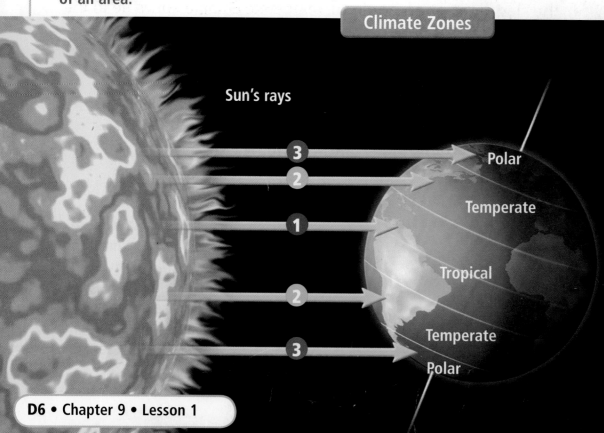

Climate Zones

Sun's rays

3 Polar
2
Temperate
1
Tropical
2
Temperate
3
Polar

1 **Tropical climates** are very warm and often very rainy.

2 **Temperate climates** have warm summers and cool to very cold winters.

3 **Polar climates** have cold temperatures year round, even during summer months.

Major Climate Zones

Climate is the normal pattern of weather in an area over many years. Uneven heating of Earth's surface by the Sun creates three major climate zones: tropical, temperate, and polar.

The major difference among the climate zones is their yearly average temperature and amount of precipitation. Precipitation, as you might already know, is any type of water—rain, snow, sleet, or hail—that falls from clouds.

Tropical climates occur at the equator and in areas just north and south of it. The temperatures in these climates are very warm year round. The coldest month in this type of climate is often no cooler than 15°C (59°F). Tropical climates can receive up to 250 cm (100 in.) of rain per year. However, some tropical areas receive very little rain.

Temperate climate zones lie to the north and south of the tropics. Some temperate climates have mild winters and mild summers. Others have very warm summers and very cold winters. In temperate climates, much of the precipitation in summer is rain. In winter, it is snow.

Places close to Earth's North Pole and South Pole have polar climates. Temperatures in these areas are very cold year round. Most of the precipitation falls as snow.

Study the figure on page D6. In which climate zone do you live?

▶ **CAUSE AND EFFECT** How does uneven heating by the Sun affect climate on Earth?

D7

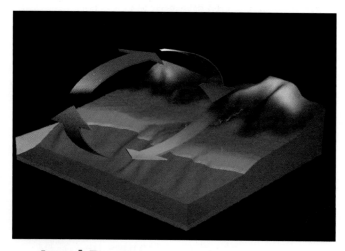

Sea Breeze
A sea breeze flows from the water toward the land. ▲

Land Breeze
A land breeze flows from the land toward the water. ▲

Land and Sea Breezes

If you've ever been to the shore, you may have noticed that land and water heat up and cool down at different rates. The unequal heating of the two different surface types causes local winds known as land breezes and sea breezes.

During the day, land heats faster than water. As warm air rises over the land, cool air moves in from the water to take its place. This creates a sea breeze.

At night, air moves in the opposite way. Land cools faster than water, so the air over the water is warmer. Warm air rises over the water, and cool air moves from land to water. This creates a land breeze.

② **Condensation** The mountains force the warm, moist air to rise into cooler parts of the atmosphere, causing the water vapor to condense.

① **Evaporation** The Sun provides the energy for liquid water to become water vapor, an invisible gas.

Mountain Effect

Why are some places rainier than others? Mountains near oceans hold part of the answer. These mountains affect the water cycle—the movement of water between Earth's atmosphere and land.

Recall that most of Earth's water is in oceans. When water evaporates from oceans, it becomes water vapor in the air. The warm, moist air rises and moves over land.

Air that meets mountains is forced higher, where temperatures are colder. Cold air can hold less water vapor than warm air. So, the water condenses into tiny water droplets.

The droplets form clouds that can drop rain or snow along one side of the mountain. This side, which faces the wind, is called the windward side of a mountain. Some of the wettest places on Earth are on the windward sides of mountains.

When the air finally crosses to the other side of the mountain, it usually has very little moisture left. Dry winds sweep down this side of the mountain, which is called the leeward side. These dry areas on the leeward slopes are called rain shadows. Desert climates are common in rain shadows.

▶ **CAUSE AND EFFECT** Describe the difference in precipitation on the leeward side and windward side of a mountain.

Mountain Effect Precipitation

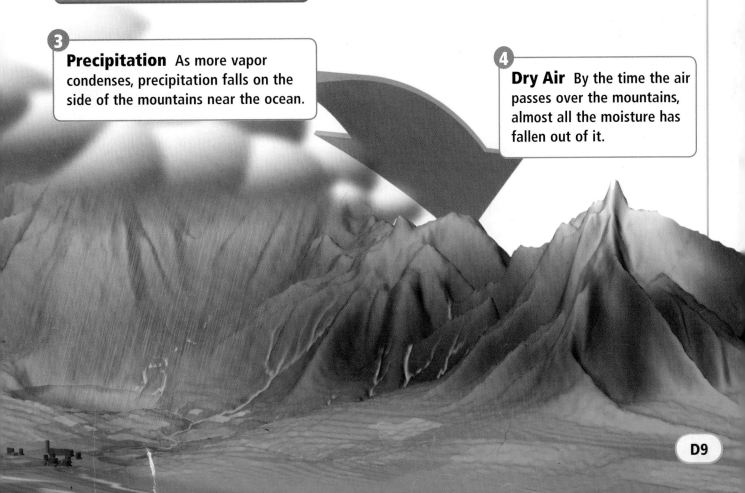

3
Precipitation As more vapor condenses, precipitation falls on the side of the mountains near the ocean.

4
Dry Air By the time the air passes over the mountains, almost all the moisture has fallen out of it.

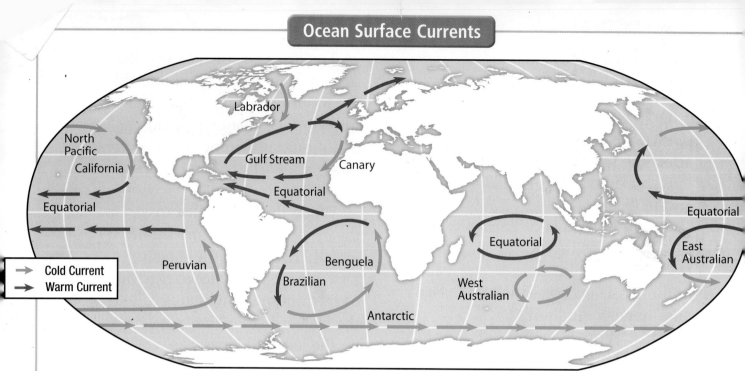

Ocean currents move water and energy from place to place.

Oceans and Climate

As the map above shows, about 70 percent of Earth's surface is covered by water. Most of this is ocean water. Ocean waters absorb huge amounts of energy from the Sun.

Recall that regions near the equator absorb more energy than those near the poles. So, ocean waters are warmest near the equator and coldest near the poles.

Air just above warm ocean water is warmed by the water below. The warm air rises and cooler air moves in to take its place. This exchange of air near Earth's surface creates winds. Winds blowing across the ocean create moving streams of water called **ocean currents.**

The currents shown on the map above are surface currents. As you can see, some currents are warm and others are cold. Warm currents move warm ocean water toward polar regions. Cold currents move cold ocean water toward the equator. These currents have a moderating effect on world climates.

Like many patterns in nature, the pattern of ocean currents can change from time to time. **El Niño** is a name given to a periodic change in direction of warm ocean currents across the Pacific Ocean. El Niño events occur every five to seven years, and can cause temporary changes in climate around the globe.

▶ **CAUSE AND EFFECT** How do ocean currents affect climate?

Lesson Wrap-Up

Visual Summary

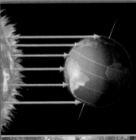
Uneven heating by the Sun causes some parts of Earth to be warmer than others.

Climate is the normal pattern of weather in an area over many years.

Bodies of water, mountains, and ocean currents can affect climate.

LINKS for Home and School

MATH **Find an Average** This table shows the amount of precipitation in Portland, Oregon, during a five-year period. Find the average yearly rainfall during this period.

Precipitation (cm)

Year 1	Year 2	Year 3	Year 4	Year 5
83.3	85.1	74.9	77.0	88.7

WRITING **Expository** Research El Niño. What do scientists think is its cause? How does it affect fishing, ocean transportation, or other human activities? Write a short essay to present your findings.

Review

❶ MAIN IDEA What are some factors that affect climate?

❷ VOCABULARY What are ocean currents? What sets them in motion?

❸ READING SKILL: Cause and Effect Describe two ways in which bodies of water can affect climate. Use these words in your answer: *land breeze, sea breeze,* and *ocean currents.*

❹ CRITICAL THINKING: Synthesize Study the illustrations on pages D6 and D10. What kind of climate do you think Miami, Florida, has? Explain.

❺ INQUIRY SKILL: Cause and Effect What factors help to account for the differences among tropical, temperate, and polar climates?

✔ TEST PREP
Ocean currents affect climate because they

A. are always cold.

B. are always warm.

C. move water and energy from one place to another.

D. cause winds to move air from one place to another.

Technology
Visit **www.eduplace.com/scp/** to find out more about climate.

Luke Howard (1772-1864)

Luke Howard earned his living as a businessman. He ran a company in England that made and sold medicines. Yet today he is remembered for his favorite hobby, which was studying clouds.

Among Howard's influences was Carolus Linnaeus, the scientist who developed the classification scheme for living things. Howard decided that clouds could be classified as well. In a speech he delivered in 1802, Howard described four classes of clouds. The classes are listed in the table. Howard chose Latin names because Latin was known to all scientists of the time.

Howard presented his essay not at a university or other formal institution, but to a discussion group that met at a private home. Nevertheless, his essay was published, and his names for clouds became very popular.

Cumulus (Heap)
Heaps that pile over a flat base

Stratus (Layer)
Widely extended horizontal sheet

Nimbus (Rain)
Cloud system that produces rain

Cirrus (Curl)
Fibers that spread in any and all directions

June Bacon-Bercey (1934-)

As a young woman, June Bacon-Bercey was not sure if she would live out her dream of becoming a meteorologist. "I was discouraged, and other women were, too," she said. One of the problems was paying for the education she needed.

Yet Bacon-Bercey persevered, raising funds however she could. And over time, she was rewarded for her efforts. For many years, she worked as a professional meteorologist and reporter for a television station in Buffalo, New York. In 1979, she was hired as Chief Administrator of television activities for the National Oceanic and Atmospheric Agency (NOAA). As her career progressed, she became recognized as an international expert on the weather.

Yet success for herself was not enough. In 1977, Bacon-Bercey won thousands of dollars on a television quiz show. She used the money to establish a scholarship for women who want to become meteorologists.

"If [women] feel they've got some money behind them, it might be better," she said.

Bacon-Bercey and other scientists at NOAA work to forecast the weather, study oceans and coastlines, and protect the environment.

Sharing Ideas

1. **READING CHECK** How did Luke Howard classify clouds?

2. **WRITE ABOUT IT** Compare the stories of Luke Howard and June Bacon-Bercey.

3. **TALK ABOUT IT** In what ways are Howard and Bacon-Bercey good role models to follow?

Lesson 2

How Are Weather Forecasts Made?

Why It Matters...

Who depends on the weather forecast? Farmers need to know the weather before plowing fields or harvesting crops. Airplane pilots need to plan the best routes. And many businesses, from outdoor restaurants to baseball teams, make plans based on the weather.

Sometimes everyone depends on the forecast. When a severe storm approaches, the correct forecast can save people's lives.

Inquiry Skill

Collaborate When you collaborate, you work with others to conduct experiments, exchange information, and draw conclusions.

Materials

- 2 round uninflated balloons
- scissors
- small baby food jar
- 2 thick rubber bands
- toothpick
- transparent tape
- large wide-mouth jar

The Pressure's On!

Procedure

Safety: Be careful when using scissors.

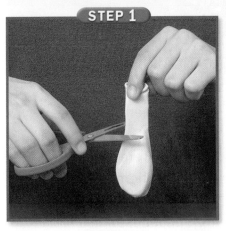

STEP 1

1. **Collaborate** Work with a partner. Cut the top off of two balloons. Then, cut one of the balloons 1/3 of the way down.

2. Stretch the smaller balloon over the mouth of the smaller jar until it is tight. Secure it with a rubber band. Tape a toothpick on the balloon over the center of the mouth of the jar. Leaving the toothpick hanging over the lip of the jar.

STEP 2

3. Carefully place the small jar inside the larger jar. Stretch the larger balloon tightly over the mouth of the large jar. Secure it with a rubber band.

4. **Experiment** While one partner holds the large jar, the other partner should push down on the balloon to increase the air pressure inside the large jar.

STEP 3

5. **Observe** In your *Science Notebook,* record what happens to the toothpick when the balloon is stretched downward.

6. **Experiment** Repeat step 4, this time pulling up on the balloon. Record what happens to the toothpick.

Conclusion

1. **Infer** How does pulling up on the balloon affect the air pressure inside the jar?

2. **Hypothesize** What does your model show about how changes in air pressure can be observed?

Investigate More!

Design an Experiment
How could you modify this experiment to detect actual changes in atmospheric air pressure? Compare your observations with air pressures listed in the newspaper.

Earth's Atmosphere

VOCABULARY

air mass	p. D18
atmosphere	p. D16
front	p. D19
mesosphere	p. D17
stratosphere	p. D17
thermosphere	p. D17
troposphere	p. D17

READING SKILL

Draw Conclusions Select one of the air masses described in the lesson. Draw a conclusion about the kind of weather it might produce.

Main Idea Earth's atmosphere is a mixture of gases that surrounds the planet. Changes in this blanket of air cause changes in weather. Weather can be forecast using different tools.

Composition of Earth's Atmosphere

Earth's **atmosphere** is a mixture of gases that surrounds the planet. This ocean of air is made mostly of nitrogen and oxygen. Other gases are present in very small amounts. As you can see from the graph below, argon makes up about 0.93 percent of dry air. Carbon dioxide makes up about 0.03 percent of dry air. Neon and helium each make up a tiny percentage of our atmosphere.

The amount of any one gas in the atmosphere can vary. In dry air, for example, there is little or no water vapor. In the moist air over an ocean, water vapor can make up four percent of the air.

Carbon dioxide is another gas that is present in the atmosphere in varying amounts. You might already know that the amount of this gas in the atmosphere increases when fossil fuels are burned.

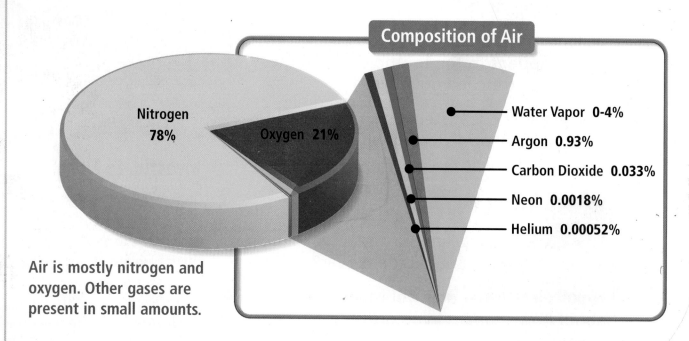

Composition of Air

Nitrogen 78%
Oxygen 21%
Water Vapor 0-4%
Argon 0.93%
Carbon Dioxide 0.033%
Neon 0.0018%
Helium 0.00052%

Air is mostly nitrogen and oxygen. Other gases are present in small amounts.

Structure of the Atmosphere

Earth's atmosphere can be divided into four main layers. The layer closest to Earth, where almost all weather occurs, is the **troposphere.** Although it is the thinnest layer, the troposphere contains about 75 percent of the gases that make up the atmosphere.

Temperature and air pressure decrease with distance from Earth's surface. Air pressure, which is an important element of weather, is caused by the weight of the gases in the atmosphere. Air pressure affects the water cycle which, in turn, affects the weather.

The **stratosphere** lies above the troposphere. Air in this layer is much colder and drier than air in the troposphere. The stratosphere contains most of our planet's ozone, a form of oxygen. Ozone absorbs certain types of radiation from the Sun that can harm living things.

The **mesosphere** lies above the stratosphere. The top of the mesosphere is the coldest part of Earth's atmosphere.

The very thin air of the **thermosphere** is the first part of the atmosphere struck by sunlight. Temperatures in the thermosphere can reach 1,700°C.

▶ **DRAW CONCLUSIONS** Why does most weather occur in the troposphere?

Earth's atmosphere is a mixture of gases that form four main layers.

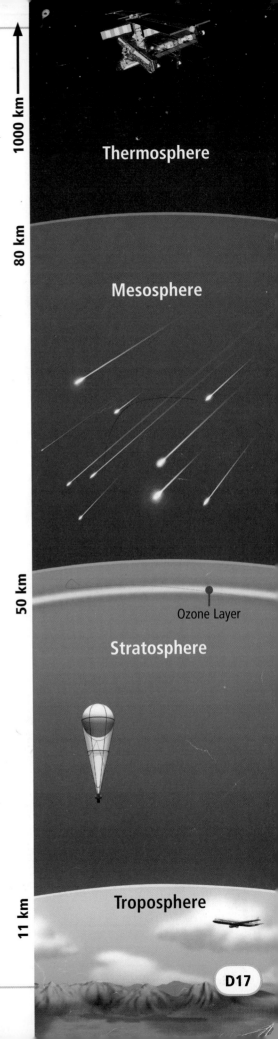

1000 km

80 km

50 km

11 km

Thermosphere

Mesosphere

Ozone Layer

Stratosphere

Troposphere

D17

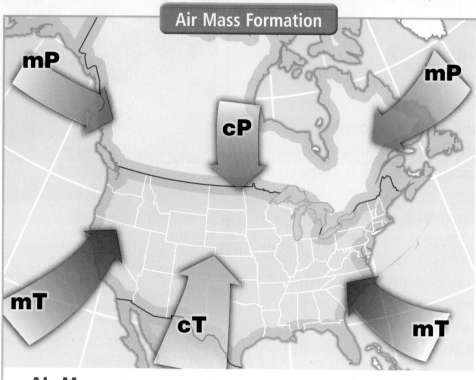

◄ Different air masses bring air of different temperatures and water content to North America.

Key

mP	maritime polar
cP	continental polar
mT	maritime tropical
cT	continental tropical

Air Masses

In the troposphere, where almost all weather occurs, large volumes of air called air masses are always moving. An **air mass** is a body of air that has about the same temperature and moisture throughout.

The temperature and moisture properties of an air mass depend on where it develops. Polar air masses form at middle to high latitudes and are generally cold. Tropical air masses form at low latitudes and tend to be warm. Continental air masses form over land and are generally dry. Maritime air masses form over water and are moist.

The map above shows the types of air masses that affect most of North America. Notice that pairs of letters are used to identify the different air masses. Taken together, each pair identifies the moisture and temperature properties of the air mass.

Lower-case letters m and c are used to represent *maritime* (moist) and *continental* (dry). Upper-case, or capital, letters P and T are used for *polar* (cold) and *tropical* (warm).

Find the mP and mT air masses on the map. These moist air masses are responsible for fog and drizzle in coastal regions. They also bring moisture to the center of the country.

Now locate and cP and cT air masses. These air masses, which form over land, contain little moisture. When such air masses move into an area, they generally bring fair weather.

Now look at the map to find the type of air mass responsible for much of the weather in your area. What are its properties? Is it humid or dry? Warm or cold? Does this agree with the type of weather your area experiences?

Fronts

When two air masses meet, a front forms. A weather **front** is the boundary between two air masses with different properties. The approach of a front is usually marked by a change in the weather. Such changes occur because cold air is denser than warm air.

A warm front forms when a warm air mass moves into an area of colder air. The warm air slides up and over the colder air, forming a gently sloping front. A warm front generally brings a large area of clouds and precipitation. On a weather map, a warm front is shown by a red line with red half circles along one side.

A cold front forms when cold air pushes its way into a warmer air mass. The dense cold air forces warmer air to rapidly rise high into the atmosphere. Clouds, heavy rain, and thunderstorms are produced along cold fronts. On a weather map, a cold front is shown by a blue line with blue triangles.

Sometimes when two air masses meet, neither mass moves forward. This type of front is called a stationary front. On a weather map, a stationary front is shown by a line with both red half circles and blue triangles.

▶ **DRAW CONCLUSIONS** How do air masses affect weather?

Warm Front

A warm front forms when warm air moves into an area. Light rains are associated with warm fronts.

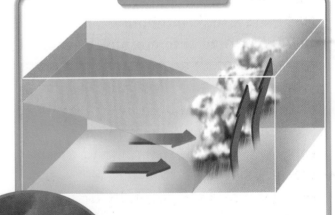

Cold Front

A cold front forms when cold air moves into an area. Heavy rains often form along a cold front.

Observing Weather

Weather is the overall condition of the atmosphere at a given time and place. Meteorologists are scientists who study weather. They make observations and collect data. Every few hours they record their findings on a weather map like the one below. By studying a series of maps, meteorologists are able to forecast future weather conditions.

Like all maps, weather maps use symbols. A key is provided to help understand the map. Study the map and look for the symbols for fronts as described on page D19. Identify and locate the warm fronts and cold fronts. Symbols are also used to indicate certain conditions, such as cloud cover, type of precipitation, and the occurrence of thunderstorms.

Notice that colors are used to represent air temperatures. In the United States, temperature is usually reported in degrees Fahrenheit.

Weather maps also identify areas of high and low air pressure. In a high-pressure system, indicated by an H, air sinks to the surface and moves away from the center. High-pressure systems usually have clear weather.

In a low-pressure system, shown by an L, air at the center of the system rises. Air around the system moves in towards the center to take the place of the rising air. Cloudy and rainy weather is usually present in a low-pressure system.

Most weather systems move from west to east across the United States. Look at the map below. What kind of weather might you expect in Texas in a few days?

Data from many sources are combined on maps that can be used to forecast the weather. ▼

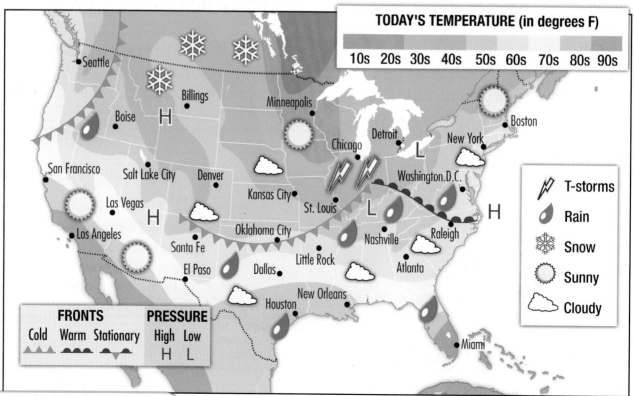

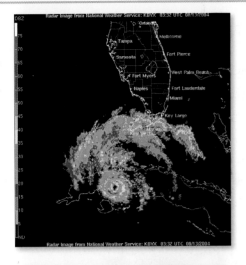

1 **3:32 A.M.**
Hurricane Charley first struck Florida in the early morning.

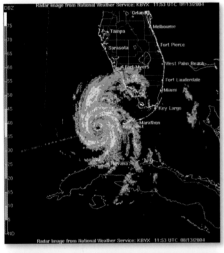

2 **11:53 A.M.**
Hurricane Charley continued to move up the western coast.

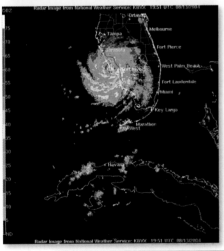

3 **7:51 P.M.**
Heavy rains fell over much of Florida as the storm moved across the state.

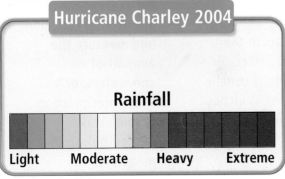

Hurricane Charley 2004

Rainfall

Light   Moderate   Heavy   Extreme

Radar

A useful tool for observing and forecasting weather is radar. A weather radar transmitter sends out radio signals. When these signals hit rain, snow, or other forms of precipitation, the signals bounce back to the transmitter and are recorded.

These radar signals can be used to create an image of a storm. You may have seen radar images, which look like fuzzy patches, used in weather reports on television.

Study the three images to the left. They are some of the early radar images of Hurricane Charley, which struck Florida in 2004. Note the different colors in the images. The colors indicate the strength of the rain brought by the hurricane. Where is the rainfall light? Where in the storm system is the rainfall the heaviest?

Radar can also be used to determine how large a storm is, how fast it is moving, and where it is headed. With this information, forecasters can warn people when severe storms are approaching. In the case of large, destructive storms, such as hurricanes, early warnings can save lives and property.

Look again at the radar images on this page. In what direction did Charley move as it passed over Florida?

▶ **DRAW CONCLUSIONS** What are two types of weather data that can be observed with radar?

Other Weather Instruments

Weather satellites are another important tool used in observing and forecasting weather. Satellites orbit high above Earth and use instruments to gather data from the upper atmosphere.

Information from these instruments can be used to determine temperatures and wind speeds on Earth. Using satellites, weather forecasters can monitor the motion of clouds and track hurricanes and other large storms.

In addition to maps, radar, and satellites, other tools are used to measure weather conditions. As you probably already know, thermometers measure temperature. Look at the other instruments described below. Which one seems the most interesting to you?

DRAW CONCLUSIONS Why are weather satellites an important tool for weather forecasters?

Weather vanes are used to indicate the direction from which wind is blowing. ▲

Thermometers are used to measure temperature. They may report degrees Fahrenheit (°F), degrees Celsius (°C), or both. ▲

Anemometers measure wind speed. Some also indicate the direction of the wind. ▲

Barometers measure air pressure. In the United States, air pressure is usually reported in inches of mercury. ▲

Rain gauges are used to collect and measure the amount of rain, snow, sleet, or hail. If the precipitation is solid, it is melted before it is measured. ▲

Lesson Wrap-Up

Visual Summary

The atmosphere is a blanket of air that surrounds Earth.

cP

cT

Large bodies of air, called air masses, form in the layer of the atmosphere closest to Earth. These air masses meet to form fronts, along which weather changes occur.

Different kinds of instruments can be used to make observations about the weather.

LINKS for Home and School

MATH Make a Table Research an extreme weather event that has occurred in your area. Make a table to compare temperatures, wind speeds, and precipitation during the storm with the normal values for that time of year.

TECHNOLOGY Be a Forecaster Use the Internet to prepare today's weather forecast. Include satellite images that show the weather in your area, and relate them to the forecast. Present your forecast to the class.

Review

1 MAIN IDEA What are the four main layers of Earth's atmosphere?

2 VOCABULARY What is an air mass and what determines its properties?

3 READING SKILL: Draw Conclusions Suppose your area is experiencing thunderstorms. What kinds of changes in the atmosphere led to the formation of the storms?

4 CRITICAL THINKING: Apply How might radar images help to reduce damage from an approaching storm?

5 INQUIRY SKILL: Collaborate How might sharing data gathered in different regions allow scientists to better predict the weather?

TEST PREP

Weather fronts form when

A. air masses meet.

B. air masses form.

C. cold air rises.

D. warm air sinks.

 Technology
Visit **www.eduplace.com/scp/** to find out more about weather.

Twister!

It can rumble like an avalanche. It can roar like a freight train. It can scream like a jet engine. Few things can withstand its fury. It's the mightiest wind on earth— the tornado!

Tornadoes are concentrated, twisting columns of air. They hang from the bottom of special, rotating thunderstorms called supercells. Tornadoes contain the fastest winds on earth. The most powerful reach over 300 miles per hour!

In April of 1974, the United States had the biggest tornado outbreak in its history. A total of 148 tornadoes hit 13 states. Called the Super Outbreak, this storm system produced 30 devastating F4 and six incredible F5 tornadoes.

Wedge The most powerful tornadoes often have a wedge shape. The largest wedges can span a mile or two across.

Rope Many tornadoes end their lives in what is called the rope stage. Although thin and strung out, the winds of a roped-out tornado can still do great damage.

Fujita Scale

F0	40-72 mph	light
F1	73-112 mph	moderate
F2	113-157 mph	considerable
F3	158-206 mph	severe
F4	207-260 mph	devastating
F5	261-318 mph	incredible

The Fujita scale gives scientists a way to classify tornadoes based on wind damage.

Vocabulary

Complete each sentence with a term from the list. Some terms may be used more than once.

air mass D18
atmosphere D16
climate D6
El Niño D10
front D19
mesosphere D17
ocean currents D10
stratosphere D17
thermosphere D17
troposphere D17

1. _____ is the range of normal weather conditions in an area over a long period of time.

2. A large body of air that has similar properties of temperature and moisture is a(n) _____.

3. A(n) _____ forms when two air masses with different properties meet.

4. Movements of large volumes of ocean water are called _____.

5. Earth's _____ is a mixture of gases that surrounds the planet.

6. The layer of Earth's atmosphere where most weather takes place is the _____.

7. The coldest layer of the atmosphere is the _____.

8. The hottest layer of the atmosphere is the _____.

9. A layer of ozone in the _____ protects Earth's surface from dangerous radiation.

10. During an event called _____, warm ocean currents change direction in the Pacific Ocean.

Test Prep

Write the letter of the best answer choice.

11. Near the poles, energy from the Sun _____.

    A. doesn't strike Earth
    B. strikes Earth at a sharp angle
    C. strikes Earth directly
    D. is very concentrated

12. A land breeze is a local wind that blows _____.

    A. only over land
    B. only over water
    C. from land toward water
    D. from water toward land

13. _____ are the two most abundant gases in Earth's atmosphere.

    A. Oxygen and helium
    B. Oxygen and hydrogen
    C. Nitrogen and oxygen
    D. Nitrogen and carbon dioxide

14. A(n) _____ forms when warm air moves into an area of cooler air.

    A. warm front
    B. cold front
    C. polar air mass
    D. maritime air mass

Inquiry Skills

15. **Compare** Use maps and information from this chapter to compare the climate of Florida with the climate of Ohio. What effect do bodies of water have on the climates of these two states?

16. **Predict** Suppose you lived in Tampa, Florida, and were planning a picnic. The morning weather report includes the radar image below. Decide whether or not the weather will affect your plans.

Critical Thinking

17. **Inferring** Look at the photo on page D4. What kind of climate does this area have? Describe the average temperature and amount of precipitation.

18. **Applying** Where would you expect to find hot, dry climates in the United States? Explain your answer.

19. **Drawing Conclusions** The amounts of a specific gas in the atmosphere can change from time to time. Why do you think this is so?

20. **Evaluating** Would you expect weather forecasts made weeks in advance to be more or less accurate than short-term forecasts? Explain.

Performance Assessment

Study today's weather map from the newspaper or the Internet. Predict tomorrow's weather for a specific area on the map. Compare your prediction to the actual weather that place experiences.

Map the Concept

The chart shows three pairs of terms. Complete the chart to compare and contrast the terms.

Tropical climate	Polar climate	Land breeze	Sea breeze	Warm front	Cold front

Chapter 10

Earth and Its Moon

LESSON 1

Day or night? This picture was taken near midnight. Why is the Sun shining?

Read about it in Lesson 1.

LESSON 2

The Moon is Earth's only natural satellite. Why does it appear to change shape?

Read about it in Lesson 2.

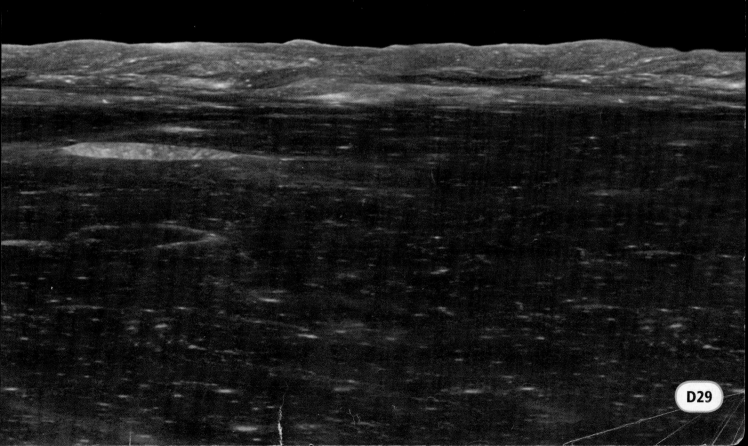

What Causes Earth's Seasons?

Why It Matters...

Winter, spring, summer, fall—the seasons repeat year after year. Yet seasons are very different in different places. In October, when it is fall in the United States, it is springtime in Australia. Understanding how Earth moves through space is the key to understanding seasons.

PREPARE TO INVESTIGATE

Inquiry Skill

Use Models You can change a model, observe the results, and then suggest how the real thing would work if the change was made.

Materials

- fine-tipped black marker
- small plastic foam ball
- pencil
- large yellow ball or inflated round balloon

Science and Math Toolbox
For step 3, review **Measurements** on page H16.

Reasons for Seasons

Procedure

STEP 1

1. **Use Models** Draw a line around the middle of the foam ball, as shown in the diagram. The foam ball represents Earth, and the line represents the equator.

2. **Use Models** Carefully push a pencil completely through the foam ball at a right angle to the equator. The pencil represents Earth's imaginary axis.

STEP 2

3. **Collaborate** The yellow ball or balloon represents the Sun. Working with a partner, hold the Sun and Earth about 1 meter (3 feet) apart. Hold Earth so the North Pole tilts slightly toward the Sun.

4. **Use Variables** Move Earth in a circle around the Sun, making sure that the North Pole always points in the same direction.

STEP 3

5. **Communicate** Repeat step 4, this time stopping at each quarter trip around the Sun. At each position, discuss how the Sun's rays hit Earth. Have your partner record the positions and observations.

Conclusion

1. **Compare** When did Earth's northern half receive the most sunlight? When did the southern half receive the most sunlight?

2. **Analyze Data** How does Earth's tilt affect the seasons where you live?

Investigate More!

Design an Experiment What if Earth's axis were not tilted? Or what if its tilt increased? Use models to predict how Earth would be affected.

Earth's Seasons

MAIN IDEA Earth's rotation and its revolution cause day and night as well as seasons.

Earth's Tilted Axis

Although you can't feel it, Earth is moving at close to 1,600 km (1,000 mi) per hour. That is because Earth is spinning, or rotating, around an imaginary line called an **axis.** Picture Earth's axis as a line that goes from the North Pole through the center of Earth to the South Pole. In relation to Earth's orbit around the Sun, the axis is not vertical, or straight up and down. It is titled at an angle of $23\frac{1}{2}°$.

It takes 23 hours and 56 minutes—one day—for Earth to make one full rotation on its axis. As Earth rotates, different parts face the Sun. It is daytime on the side of Earth facing the Sun. It is nighttime on the side facing away from the Sun.

Earth's tilted axis is why Earth has seasons. ▼

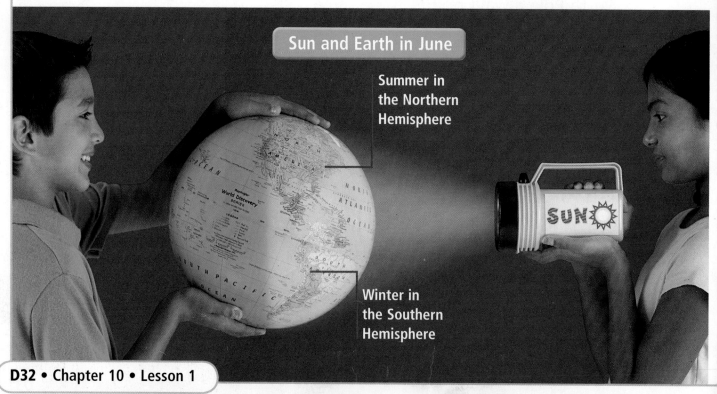

Sun and Earth in June

Summer in the Northern Hemisphere

Winter in the Southern Hemisphere

As Earth spins on its axis, it also moves around the Sun. One full trip around the Sun is called a **revolution.** Earth takes 365 $\frac{1}{4}$ days, or one year, to complete one revolution. The path of Earth's revolution is called its orbit. The orbit is a kind of oval shape called an ellipse.

Because of Earth's tilted axis, different parts of Earth tilt toward or away from the Sun during its trip around the sun. This tilt causes seasons.

In the photograph on page D32, Earth's northern half is tilted toward the Sun. In this position, it is summer in the Northern Hemisphere and winter in the Southern Hemisphere.

In the photo below, six months have passed. Earth is at the opposite end of its orbit. Now Earth's southern half tilts toward the Sun, so the seasons are reversed.

Why does a tilt toward the Sun bring warmer weather? There are two reasons. First, when a hemisphere tilts toward the Sun, the Sun appears to rise higher in the sky. The higher the Sun's position, the more concentrated its rays are as they strike Earth. Second, daylight lasts longer. More hours of daylight means more heating time.

Together, concentrated sunlight and longer days bring warm weather in summer. Likewise, the combination of less concentrated sunlight and shorter days bring cold weather in winter.

Regions near the equator do not have noticeable seasons. They receive about the same amounts of sunlight all year long.

▶ **CAUSE AND EFFECT** Why do the Northern and Southern hemispheres have opposite seasons?

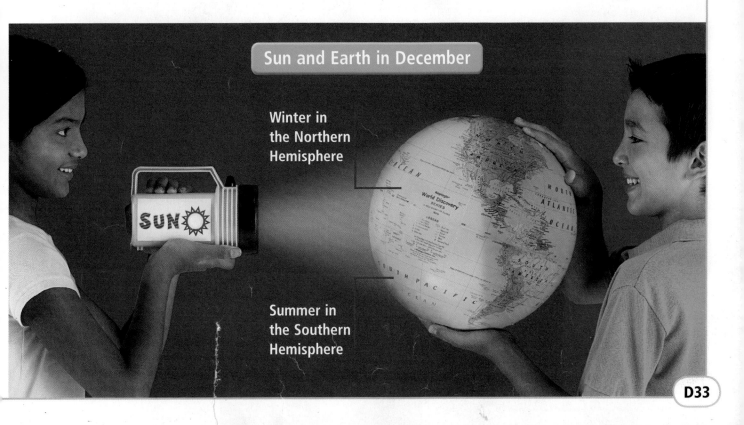

Sun and Earth in December

Winter in the Northern Hemisphere

SUN

Summer in the Southern Hemisphere

Solstices and Equinoxes

On June 21 or 22, the North Pole of Earth's axis tilts toward the Sun. This event marks the **summer solstice** and the beginning of summer in the Northern Hemisphere. On this longest day of the year, the hemisphere receives more sunlight than on any other day of the year.

Six months later, on December 21, or 22, the North Pole points directly away from the Sun. This event marks the **winter solstice** and the beginning of winter in the Northern Hemisphere. On this shortest day, the hemisphere receives less sunlight than on any other day of the year.

Twice a year, neither hemisphere is tilted toward the Sun. Such events are called equinoxes. Periods of daylight and darkness are each 12 hours long every place on Earth.

One of those events occurs on March 20 or 21. This marks the **vernal equinox,** which is the first day of spring in the Northern Hemisphere. The second of these events occurs six months later, on September 22 or 23. This event marks the **autumnal equinox,** which is the first day of fall in the Northern Hemisphere.

▶ **CAUSE AND EFFECT** How do the lengths of day and night compare during a solstice? During an equinox?

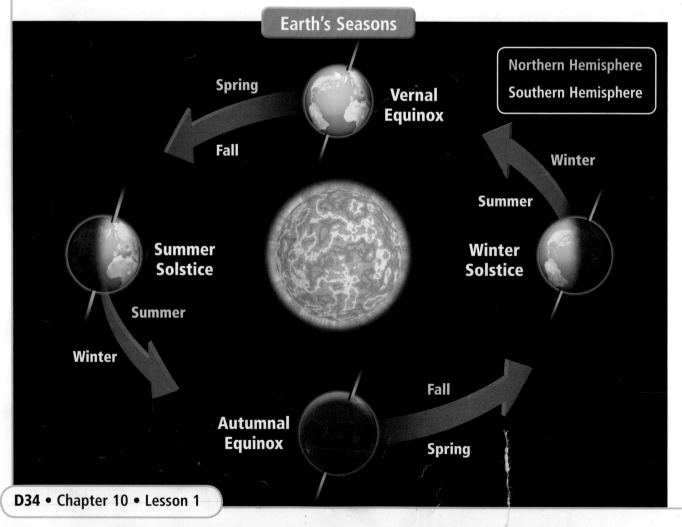

Earth's Seasons

Northern Hemisphere
Southern Hemisphere

Spring

Fall

Vernal Equinox

Winter

Summer

Summer Solstice

Winter Solstice

Summer

Winter

Autumnal Equinox

Fall

Spring

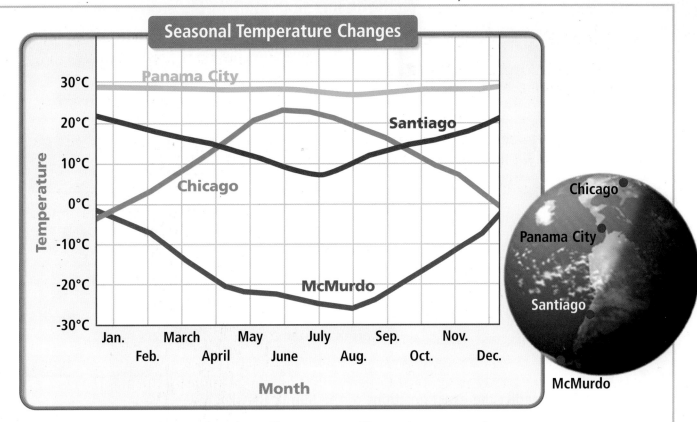

Seasonal Temperature Changes

The angle at which the Sun's rays strike an area affects the seasonal temperatures.

Seasons

In everyday life, seasons are periods of a particular kind of weather. Earth scientists, however, define seasons by the position of Earth in its orbit. By this definition, all places on Earth have four seasons: spring, summer, fall, and winter. Yet the effects of these seasons are extreme in some places, while they hardly exist in others.

Near the equator, the Sun's rays arrive at almost right angles. This causes the Sun's energy to be more concentrated. Near the poles, the rays arrive at much sharper angles. This causes the same amount of sunlight to be spread out. This difference affects average temperatures. Look at the graph above.

Places close to the poles, such as McMurdo in Antarctica, have cold weather all year long. Compare its temperatures to those of Panama City, which is near the equator.

Other places have wide variations in temperature throughout the year. Compare the temperatures of Chicago, Illinois, and Santiago, Chile. These cities are both about halfway between the equator and a pole, but are on opposite hemispheres. How do their yearly temperatures compare?

A place's position on Earth is the most important factor affecting its temperature and seasonal changes. As you have read in other chapters, other factors affect climate as well.

▶ **CAUSE AND EFFECT** Why do places near the equator have higher year-round temperatures than places near the poles?

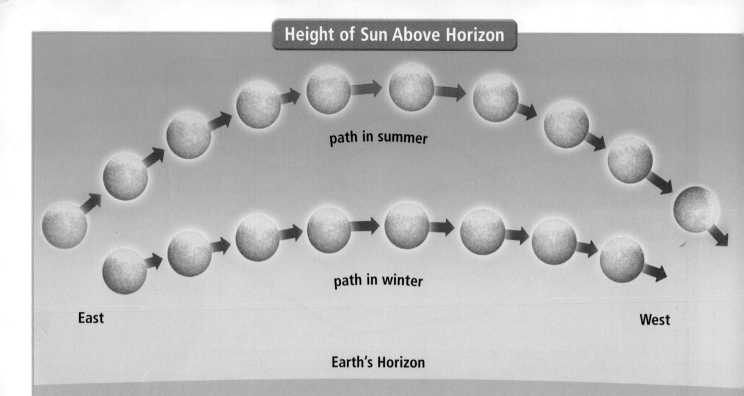

Height of Sun Above Horizon

path in summer

path in winter

East

West

Earth's Horizon

Scientists can predict the exact positions of the Sun in the sky. Why does the Sun rise higher in summer than in winter?

Ideas About the Sun

Hundreds of years ago, people believed many false ideas about Earth and Sun. As they looked up at the sky, they thought that Earth was the center of the universe. The Sun and other objects appeared to revolve around it.

In the 1600s, Italian astronomer Galileo published a book about the universe called *Dialogue*. The book presented evidence that the Sun lay in the center, while Earth and other planets revolved around it.

Galileo was arrested for promoting this idea! Today, he is recognized for his courage and for being correct. Having built on the work of Galileo and others, scientists now can predict the positions of Earth, the Sun, and other objects in space.

Another false idea is that seasons come from Earth's changing distance from the Sun. In fact, Earth's elliptical orbit brings it slightly closer to the Sun in December than in June. However, the effects of the changing distance are very minor.

As you have read, seasons result from Earth's tilted axis and revolution around the Sun. The tilt causes the Sun to rise higher in the sky and makes the days last longer during the summer.

The illustration shows how the Sun appears to travel across the sky in the Northern Hemisphere. Its higher path in the summer provides more daylight and warmer temperatures.

▶ **CAUSE AND EFFECT** Describe some false ideas people held about Earth.

Visual Summary

Earth rotates on its axis as it revolves around the Sun. It takes one day to rotate and one year to revolve. Earth revolves in an elliptical path called an orbit.

Earth's axis is slightly tilted. This causes parts of Earth to point toward or away from the Sun during its orbit. The result is four seasons: spring, summer, fall, and winter.

The concentration and amount of sunlight a region receives determines the characteristics of its seasons.

LINKS for Home and School

MATH Make a Line Graph Research local temperatures over the last four weeks. Calculate the average high temperature and the average low temperature for each week. Then create a line graph similar to the one on page D35.

TECHNOLOGY Write a Report
Hundreds of years ago, astronomers studied the skies with astrolabes, sextants, and other tools. Research tools such as these and how they were used. Write a report to show your findings.

Review

❶ MAIN IDEA What causes day and night? What causes seasons?

❷ VOCABULARY Compare a solstice with an equinox. What seasons do these events mark?

❸ READING SKILL: Cause and Effect Chicago, Illinois, lies midway between the North Pole and the equator. Why does Chicago have a wide range of yearly temperatures?

❹ CRITICAL THINKING: Apply Explain why summer in the Northern Hemisphere occurs when winter occurs in the Southern Hemisphere.

❺ INQUIRY SKILL: Use Models How would you create a three-dimensional model to explain Earth's cycle of seasons?

✔ TEST PREP
During an equinox, the number of hours of daylight is

A. greater than the number of hours of darkness.

B. less than the number of hours of darkness.

C. the same as the number of hours of darkness.

D. sometimes less than and sometimes greater than the number of hours of darkness.

Technology
Visit **www.eduplace.com/scp/** to find out more about Earth's motion.

Midnight SUN

If you like sunshine, maybe you should visit Fairbanks, Alaska, in June. That's because the Sun stays in the sky almost all day long! Of course, you may want to leave before winter. During the middle of December, the Sun appears for only a few hours around noon.

Why is Fairbanks' cycle of day and night so extreme? The reason is because of its high latitude, meaning its northern position on Earth. The higher the latitude, the more severe the effects of Earth's tilted axis.

Several kilometers north of Fairbanks is the Arctic Circle. This is an imaginary circular line around Earth that is $23\frac{1}{2}$ degrees away from the North Pole, the same degree that Earth tilts. At the Arctic Circle, the Sun never sets for a single day—the day of the summer solstice. Darkness prevails six months later during the winter solstice.

Blame the Tilt!
During summer, Earth's tilt points Alaska toward the Sun. For at least one day, the Sun does not set north of the Arctic Circle.

As the summer solstice approaches, the Sun sets later and later at night. When could this photograph have been taken?

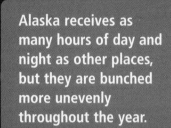

Alaska receives as many hours of day and night as other places, but they are bunched more unevenly throughout the year.

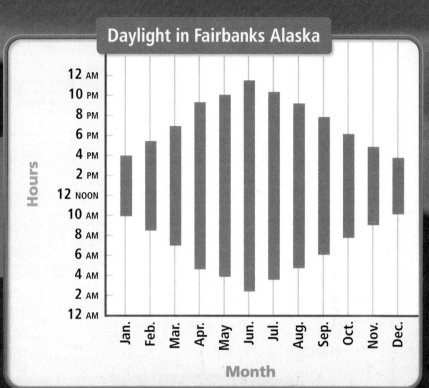

Daylight in Fairbanks Alaska

Hours

12 AM
10 PM
8 PM
6 PM
4 PM
2 PM
12 NOON
10 AM
8 AM
6 AM
4 AM
2 AM
12 AM

Jan. Feb. Mar. Apr. May Jun. Jul. Aug. Sep. Oct. Nov. Dec.

Month

Sharing Ideas

1. **READING CHECK** What is the Arctic Circle?

2. **WRITE ABOUT IT** Why does Alaska have such extreme lengths of day and night?

3. **TALK ABOUT IT** How do you think Alaskans cope with long summer days and long winter nights?

Why Does the Moon Have Phases?

Why It Matters...

Do you look at the Moon? Would you like to visit it, as some astronauts have done? The Moon has fascinated observers for thousands of years. Many civilizations built calendars around the Moon's phases. How do you think today's calendar reflects the Moon?

PREPARE TO INVESTIGATE

Inquiry Skill

Compare When you compare objects or events, note both similarities and differences.

Materials

- small foam ball
- flashlight

Science and Math Toolbox

For step 1, review **Using a Tape Measure or Ruler** on page H6.

It's Just a Phase!

Procedure

Safety: Do not shine the flashlight directly at someone's eyes.

1. **Collaborate** Dim the lights in the room. Hold the small ball slightly above your head, as shown in the photo. Have your partner hold a flashlight about a meter (3 feet) away. Shine the flashlight on the ball.

2. **Use Models** Your head represents Earth, the ball is the Moon, and the flashlight is the Sun. Observe how the Moon appears to you in this position.

3. **Observe** As you hold the Moon steady, slowly rotate in a circle. Your partner should not move the flashlight. Observe how the Moon appears to change.

4. **Communicate** In your *Science Notebook,* draw how the Moon appeared in at least four different positions. Organize your drawings to best show the process they model.

5. **Experiment** Switch roles with your partner and repeat the procedure.

Conclusion

1. **Compare** Describe what the Moon looked like at each of the four positions.

2. **Analyze Data** Using your data, explain why you think the Moon appears to change shape from night to night.

Investigate More!

Design an Experiment
How does Earth appear when viewed from the Moon? Does Earth appear to change shape, or does it always look the same? Design an experiment to find out.

Earth's Moon

VOCABULARY

lunar eclipse   p. D46
Moon phases   p. D44
solar eclipse   p. D46

READING SKILL

Sequence Use a graphic organizer such as the one shown to track the sequence of the phases of the moon.

MAIN IDEA The Moon revolves around Earth, and together they revolve around the Sun. The same side of the Moon always faces Earth, but the Sun lights different parts of it at different times.

The Moon

Earth has one natural satellite, an object that revolves around it through space. This satellite is the Moon. The Moon is a sphere that is about one-fourth the size of Earth. The Moon's surface is rocky and includes large and small craters, or holes. From Earth, large craters appear as dark areas on the Moon.

The Moon's mass is about 80 times lighter than the mass of Earth. Because of its smaller mass, the Moon's surface gravity is about one-sixth of Earth's gravitational pull. Its weak gravity prevents the Moon from having much of an atmosphere. However, its pull of gravity is strong enough to affect tides on Earth.

◄ Earth has one natural satellite—the Moon.

Viewing the Moon

If you've ever gazed at the Moon, you know that it appears to be the biggest and brightest object in the night sky. The Moon appears so large because it is very close to Earth. However, the Moon is actually smaller than other objects in the sky. For instance, the planet Venus appears as a dot in the sky, only a little larger than a star. Yet it is about the same size as Earth! Because the Moon is closer, it appears bigger.

Although the Moon can look very bright, it does not produce any light. Instead, sunlight reflects off the Moon's surface. This is why you can see the Moon from Earth. Like Earth, the Moon rotates on an imaginary axis. Also like Earth, the Moon revolves. While Earth revolves around the Sun, the Moon revolves around Earth.

The Moon takes $27\frac{1}{3}$ days to complete one revolution around Earth. Some time in the distant past, the gravitational pull of Earth affected the Moon's period of rotation. Now the Moon's rotation takes the same amount of time as its revolution around Earth. So, the same side of the Moon always faces Earth.

▶ **SEQUENCE** Why can you see the Moon from Earth?

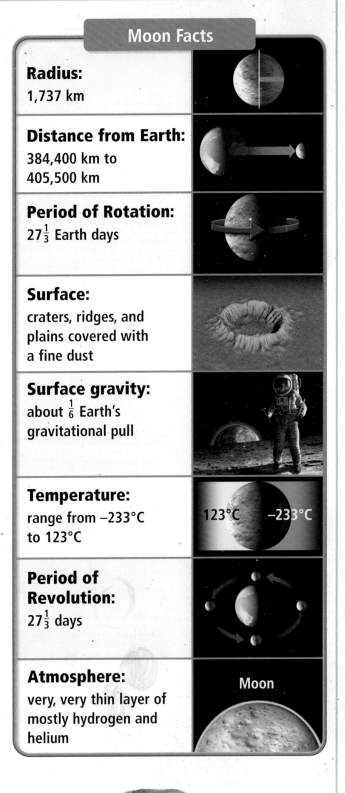

Moon Facts

Radius: 1,737 km	
Distance from Earth: 384,400 km to 405,500 km	
Period of Rotation: $27\frac{1}{3}$ Earth days	
Surface: craters, ridges, and plains covered with a fine dust	
Surface gravity: about $\frac{1}{6}$ Earth's gravitational pull	
Temperature: range from −233°C to 123°C	123°C −233°C
Period of Revolution: $27\frac{1}{3}$ days	
Atmosphere: very, very thin layer of mostly hydrogen and helium	Moon

Most of the rocks on the surface of the Moon formed about 4.6 billion years ago when lava cooled and hardened. ▶

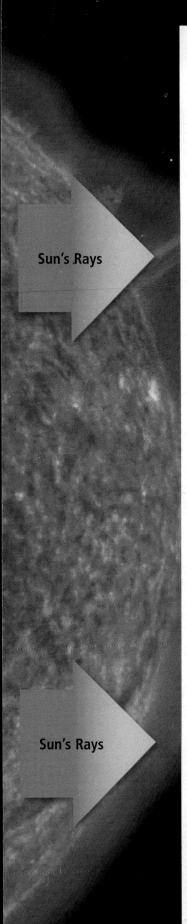

Sun's Rays

Sun's Rays

Phases of the Moon

The Sun always lights one half of the Moon. As the Moon orbits Earth, different amounts of the lighted half are visible from Earth. The shapes created by the changing amounts of the visible lighted areas are called **Moon phases.** A complete cycle of Moon phases takes about one month.

The first phase in the cycle is the new Moon. Find the new Moon in the photos to the right. During this phase, the Moon is between Earth and the Sun. Because its lighted side is facing away from Earth, the Moon appears dark when viewed from Earth.

As the Moon continues in its orbit, more of the lighted area becomes visible. During this time, the Moon is described as waxing, or growing. The waxing crescent phase appears after the new Moon phase. Later, when half of the Moon's lighted area is visible, the Moon is in its first quarter phase.

The portion of the lighted area continues to grow until the full Moon phase is reached. During this phase, the entire lighted side of the Moon is visible from Earth. At this point, the Earth is between the Moon and the Sun.

After the full Moon phase, the area of the lighted side that is visible from Earth begins to get smaller. The Moon is said to be waning. Phases during this half of the Moon's revolution include waning gibbous, last quarter, and waning crescent.

The visible lighted area continues to decrease in size as the Moon finishes its revolution around Earth. It takes about 29 days for a complete cycle of the phases of the Moon—from one new Moon to the next.

Look again at the circle of photographs. Remember that these apparent changes in shape depend on the Moon's position in space relative to Earth and the Sun.

Now look at the drawings in the inner circle. They show what the Moon looks like to an observer above the system in space. All of the drawings are alike because the side of the Moon facing the sun is always lighted. It is only the area visible from Earth that seems to change shape.

 **SEQUENCE** **Why does the Moon go through phases?**

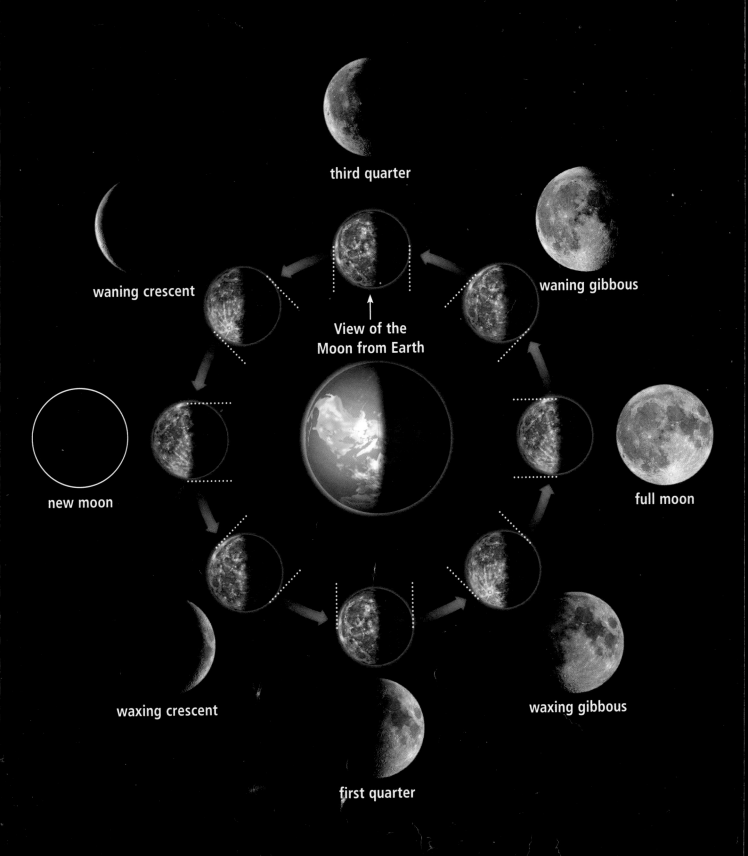

third quarter

waning crescent

waning gibbous

View of the
Moon from Earth

new moon

full moon

waxing crescent

waxing gibbous

first quarter

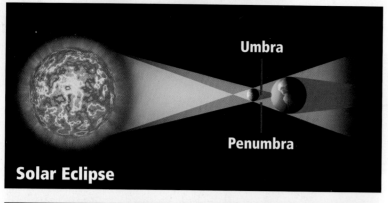

Umbra

Penumbra

Solar Eclipse

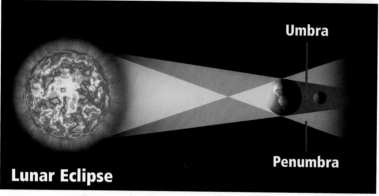

Umbra

Penumbra

Lunar Eclipse

Eclipses occur when Earth, the Sun, and the Moon form a straight line in space. ▲

Eclipses

An eclipse occurs when one object passes into the shadow of another object. When Earth, the Sun, and the Moon form a straight line, two kinds of eclipses can occur.

A **solar eclipse** occurs when the Moon passes between the Sun and Earth. The Moon casts a shadow on Earth's surface. The darker area of the shadow is called the umbra. The lighter area is the penumbra. The part of Earth's surface within the umbra experiences a total solar eclipse, as shown in the photograph at the top right. The part of Earth's surface in the penumbra experiences a partial solar eclipse.

A **lunar eclipse** takes place when Earth passes directly between the Sun and the Moon, as shown in the bottom illustration. When this happens, the Moon moves into Earth's shadow.

During a total lunar eclipse, the entire Moon passes into the umbra of Earth's shadow. The Moon is still visible, but has a reddish appearance, as shown in the photograph at the bottom right above. During a partial lunar eclipse, only part of the Moon passes into the umbra. The rest is in the penumbra.

▶ **SEQUENCE** Compare the positions of Earth, the Sun, and the Moon during a solar eclipse and during a lunar eclipse.

Visual Summary

The Moon is Earth's only natural satellite.

The same side of the Moon is always seen from Earth. The Moon appears to change shape as it revolves around Earth.

During a solar eclipse, the Moon passes directly between Earth and the Sun. During a lunar eclipse, Earth passes directly between the Moon and the Sun.

LINKS for Home and School

MATH **Apply a Formula** The radius (r) of Earth's Moon is 1,737 km and the diameter (d) is two times the radius ($d = 2r$). Use the equation $C = \pi d$ to determine the Moon's circumference (C).

WRITING **Narrative** How has the Moon influenced you? Do you notice its phases? Would you like to visit the Moon? Discuss the Moon in a story or poem.

Review

1 MAIN IDEA Why is the same side of the Moon always visible from Earth?

2 VOCABULARY Explain what is meant by *Moon phases*.

3 READING SKILL: Sequence List the sequence of the phases of the Moon starting with waxing gibbous and ending with the first quarter.

4 CRITICAL THINKING: Apply How would you determine what the phase of the Moon will be 10 days from today?

5 INQUIRY SKILL: Compare Compare a solar eclipse with a lunar eclipse.

✓ TEST PREP What happens during a total solar eclipse?

A. The Moon blocks out all of the Sun.

B. The Sun blocks out all of the Moon.

C. The Moon blocks out part of the Sun.

D. The Sun blocks out part of the Moon.

Technology
Visit **www.eduplace.com/scp/** to find out more about Earth's Moon.

Lunar Extremes

Everything about the Moon is extreme. Because the Moon has no atmosphere to even out the Sun's radiant energy, temperatures vary from blistering hot to frigid cold. The surface is pockmarked by micrometeorites, which bombard like tiny bullets from space. Dangerous radiation fries everything. It's about as unfriendly a place for life as you could imagine.

Nevertheless, over the course of three years in the 20th century, life was there—human life. The Apollo missions to the Moon were among the greatest scientific achievements in history. Six separate times astronauts landed on the Moon, where they walked, hopped, and even drove around, gathering samples and doing experiments. Talk about extreme science!

The only thing standing between the astronauts and death was their remarkable space suits. The suits supplied air, kept them cool, and protected them from radiation and micrometeorites.

Hot and Cold

On the sunny side of the Moon, temperatures reach 260° F. On the dark side, they can drop to - 280° F!

High Jump

Because there is less gravity on the Moon, you can jump six times higher than you can on Earth.

Super Throw

You can throw an object six times farther too!

D49

Vocabulary

Complete each sentence with a term from the list. You may use each term more than once.

1. A(n) _____ is an imaginary line about which a body rotates.

2. During the _____, the North Pole is at its greatest tilt away from the Sun.

3. During a(n) _____, Earth passes directly between the Moon and the Sun.

4. Apparent changes in the shapes of the Moon throughout the month are called _____.

5. When _____ occurs, spring begins in the Northern Hemisphere.

6. The North Pole is tilted directly toward the Sun during the _____.

7. When the Moon passes directly between the Sun and Earth, a(n) _____ occurs.

8. The first day of fall in the Northern Hemisphere marks the _____.

9. During a total _____, the Sun is in the umbra of the Moon's shadow.

10. The path of Earth's _____ is elliptical.

autumnal equinox D34
axis D32
lunar eclipse D46
Moon phases D44
revolution D33
solar eclipse D46
summer solstice D34
vernal equinox D34
winter solstice D34

Test Prep

Write the letter of the best answer choice.

11. During a solstice, _____.

   A. one of Earth's poles is tilted toward the Sun
   B. neither pole is tilted toward the Sun
   C. spring begins in the Northern Hemisphere
   D. fall begins in the Northern Hemisphere

12. Places near the equator tend to be warm year-round because _____.

   A. of solar eclipses
   B. of lunar eclipses
   C. the Sun's rays strike this part of Earth directly
   D. the Sun's rays are slanted over this part of Earth

13. Day and night are the same length during _____.

   A. winter solstice
   B. a total solar eclipse
   C. vernal equinox
   D. a total lunar eclipse

14. The same side of the Moon is always visible from Earth because _____.

   A. the Moon is smaller than the Sun
   B. the Moon is Earth's only satellite
   C. the Moon's rotation takes a shorter amount of time than its revolution
   D. the Moon's rotation takes the same amount of time as its revolution

15. **Cause and Effect** How does Earth's tilt on its axis cause seasons to change in different parts of the world?

16. **Sequence** Identify the Moon phase shown below and explain how it will change over the next two weeks. Include drawings in your answer.

The chart shows three pairs of science terms. Complete the chart to explain how they differ.

17. **Analyze** Explain why the Northern and Southern Hemispheres have opposite seasons at the same time.

18. **Synthesize** Explain why the shortest day of the year in the Northern Hemisphere is on December 21 or 22. Where is this the longest day?

19. **Evaluate** Look again at the illustration and photos on pages D45 and D46. What type of eclipse occurs when the Moon is in its full Moon phase? In its new Moon phase? Explain.

20. **Hypothesize** Why do you think few people have witnessed a total solar eclipse while many people have observed lunar eclipses?

Observe the Moon

Observe and draw the Moon on five or six consecutive nights. Identify the phases you observe and predict what the Moon will look like over the next two weeks.

Solstice	Equinox	New Moon	Full Moon	Solar eclipse	Lunar eclipse

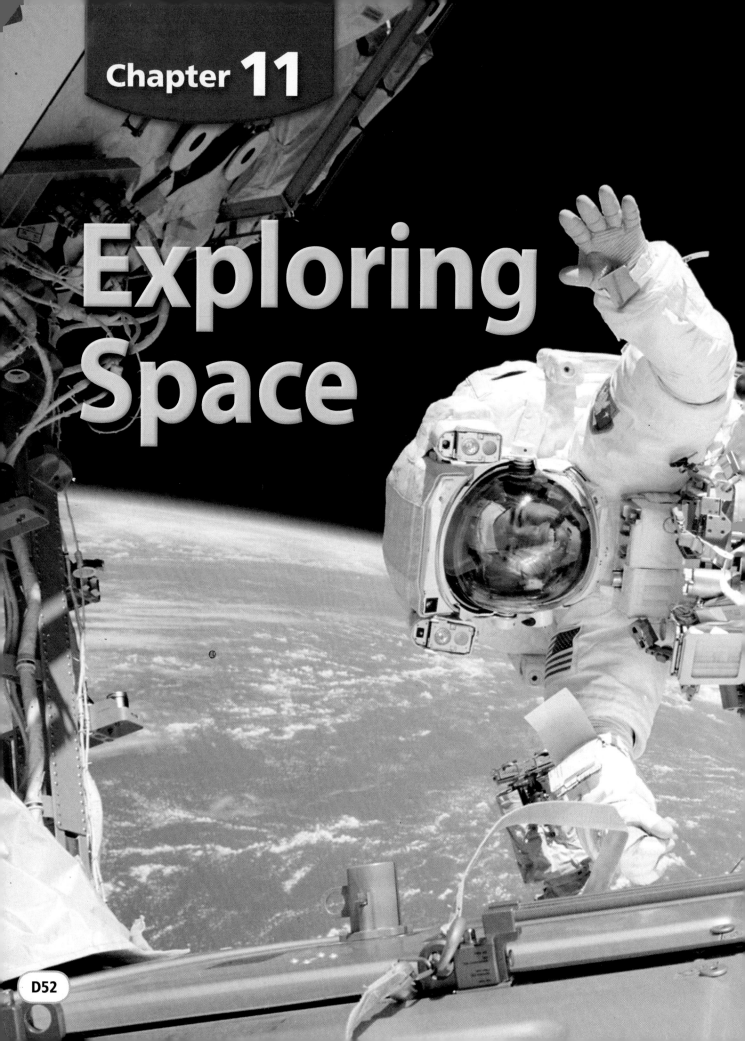

Chapter 11

Exploring Space

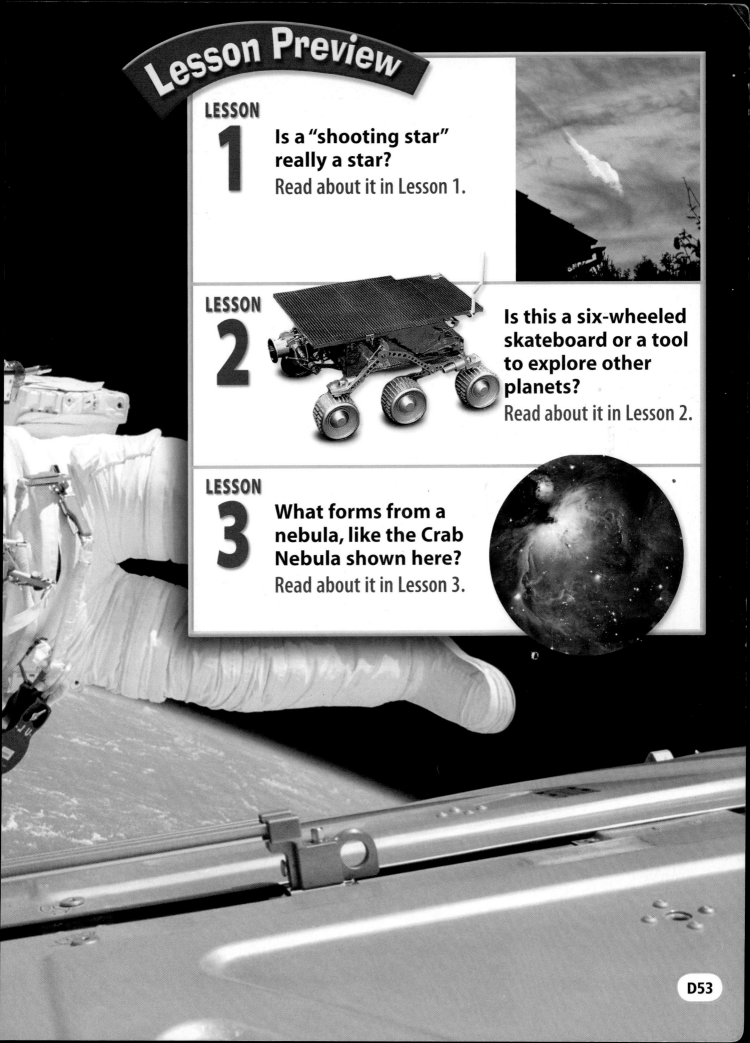

Lesson Preview

LESSON 1

Is a "shooting star" really a star?
Read about it in Lesson 1.

LESSON 2

Is this a six-wheeled skateboard or a tool to explore other planets?
Read about it in Lesson 2.

LESSON 3

What forms from a nebula, like the Crab Nebula shown here?
Read about it in Lesson 3.

What Orbits the Sun?

Why It Matters...

Earth is only one small part of the solar system. The Sun, eight other planets, and thousands of smaller bodies belong to this system, too. Yet only Earth is able to support life, at least as far as scientists can tell. Understanding Earth's position in the solar system is one key to understanding why it supports life.

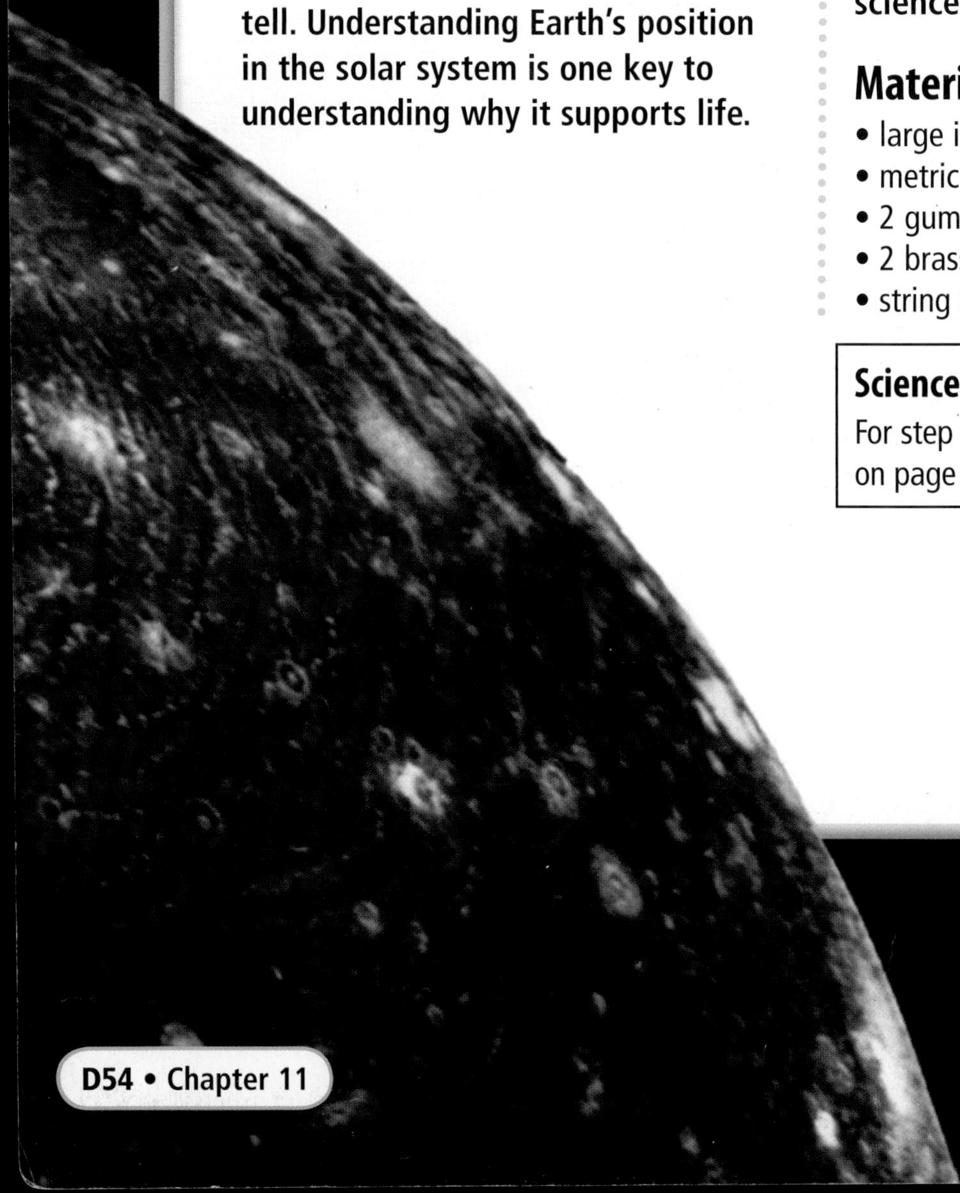

PREPARE TO INVESTIGATE

Inquiry Skill

Research When you research, you use library reference materials, search the Internet, and talk to experts to learn science information.

Materials

- large index card
- metric ruler
- 2 gummed reinforced rings
- 2 brass fasteners
- string (30 cm long)

Science and Math Toolbox
For step 1, review **Measurements** on page H16.

A Very Long Trip!

Procedure

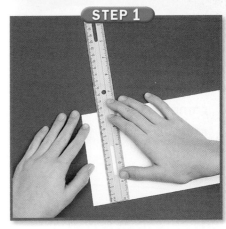
STEP 1

1. **Measure** Use a ruler to find the midpoint of the short side of a large index card. Draw a straight line across the center of the card.

2. **Measure** Mark two points, each 2 cm in from the edge of the card. Then measure 2 cm in from one of the points and draw a small circle. Label the circle "Sun."

3. **Use Models** Attach reinforced rings over the two marked points on the card. Carefully push the brass fasteners through the rings and the card. Spread the prongs of each fastener.

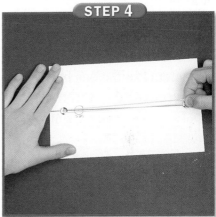
STEP 4

4. Tie the ends of the string to form a circle with a circumference of about 25 cm. Loop the string around the brass fasteners.

5. **Collaborate** Have a partner hold the edges of the card while you insert the tip of a pencil inside the string loop. Keeping the string tight, draw an ellipse by moving the pencil around the inside of the string. The ellipse models the orbit of a comet.

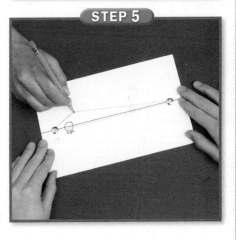
STEP 5

Conclusion

1. **Observe** How does the orbit of a comet compare with the orbits of the planets?

2. **Predict** What do you think happens to a comet when it reaches the point in its orbit closest to the Sun?

Investigate More!

Research Find out more about comets by researching at the library or on the Internet. Use your findings to make a poster.

The Solar System

MAIN IDEA The Sun and the bodies that revolve around it make up the solar system. The solar system is a small part of a much larger system called the Milky Way galaxy.

▶ **VOCABULARY**

asteroid	p. D58
comet	p. D59
meteor	p. D60
meteorite	p. D60
meteoroid	p. D60
planet	p. D56
solar system	p. D56

▶ **READING SKILL**

Text Structure Use a diagram like the one below to record details about the parts of the solar system.

The Sun and Its Neighbors

In your neighborhood, your neighbors are the people who live near you. Earth's neighborhood is the solar system. The **solar system** is the Sun and all bodies that travel, or revolve, around it. Earth is one of nine **planets,** large bodies that revolve around the Sun. The planets do not make their own light, but shine by reflecting the Sun's light.

The Sun is by far the largest and most massive part of the solar system. Its gravity holds the other parts in their positions. Many planets, including Earth, have one or more moons. Smaller members of the solar system include asteroids, comets, and meteoroids.

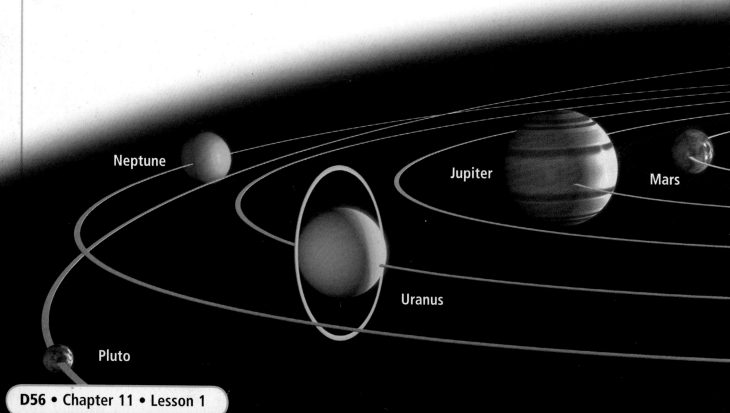

Neptune

Jupiter

Mars

Uranus

Pluto

Even with its thousands of parts, the solar system is a very small part of a much larger system called the Milky Way galaxy. You'll learn more about galaxies in Lesson 3.

Scientists believe that the solar system is about 4.6 billion years old. It formed from a hot, spinning cloud of gases and dust. Over time, gravity pulled the gas and dust toward the center of the cloud, causing the cloud to collapse. As it continued to spin, the cloud flattened and its temperature rose. Eventually, great heat and pressure built up near the center of the cloud. Nuclear reactions produced a star now called the Sun.

Away from the center of the spinning cloud, temperatures were cooler. Matter in this cooler part of the cloud began to come together to form the planets and their moons.

Planets closest to the Sun formed from heavy, rocky material. Farther from the Sun, planets were able to hold onto lighter gases and form much larger planets. Moons eventually formed around all but two of the planets.

Along with the planets and their moons, other small bodies formed in the solar system. These include asteroids, comets, and meteoroids.

The paths, or orbits, of all of the bodies that travel around the Sun are shaped like slightly flattened circles called ellipses. The strong gravitational force of the Sun holds all the objects in the solar system in their orbits.

▶ **TEXT STRUCTURE** **What does the illustration show about the planets in the solar system?**

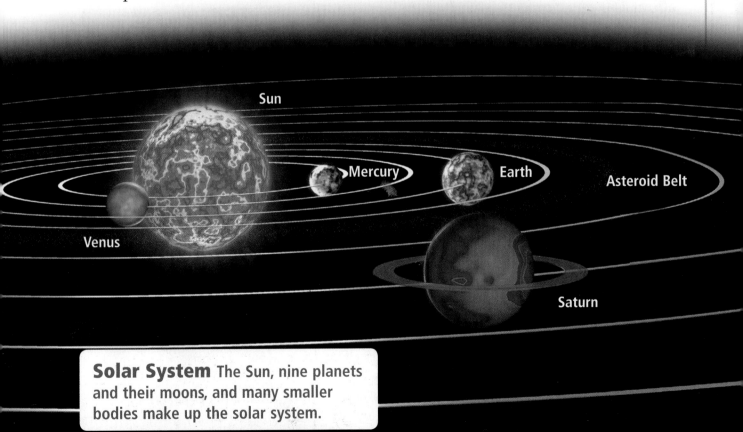

Sun

Mercury

Earth

Asteroid Belt

Venus

Saturn

Solar System The Sun, nine planets and their moons, and many smaller bodies make up the solar system.

Earth's Moon

Io

Io is one of the moons of Jupiter. Many volcanoes dot its surface.

Enceladus

Saturn's moon Enceladus has an icy surface of smooth plains, craters, and long cracks and ridges.

Ariel

The valleys of Ariel, a moon of Uranus, may have formed during violent moonquakes.

Moons are natural satellites that orbit a planet.

Moons

In Chapter 10, you learned about Earth's moon—the satellite that is often called the Moon. Did you know that astronomers have discovered about 140 other moons in the solar system? All these moons are held in their orbits by the gravitational attraction of their planets.

Unlike Earth's Moon, some moons have atmospheres surrounding them. Others show evidence that water or ice may lie deep beneath their surfaces. One moon has active volcanoes, and another has geysers!

Asteroids

An **asteroid** is a relatively small, rocky object that orbits the Sun. Scientists estimate that millions of these chunks of rock and metal exist in the solar system. Most of them orbit in a band called the asteroid belt, located between the orbits of Mars and Jupiter.

Asteroids range in size from hundreds of kilometers in diameter to only a few meters across. Many asteroids have very peculiar shapes. Some even look like baked potatoes!

One theory about the origin of the asteroids is that Jupiter's strong pull of gravity prevented them from coming together to form a planet. Another, less likely idea is that the asteroids are remnants of several planets that collided and broke apart.

◀ Asteroids are small, rocky bodies that orbit the Sun, many in a belt between Mars and Jupiter.

Comets

A **comet** is a small, orbiting body made of dust, ice, and frozen gases. The solid center of a comet is its nucleus. Like all objects in the solar system, comets orbit the Sun. However, most comets travel in very long, elliptical paths similar to the one shown on this page.

When a comet approaches the Sun, frozen solids in its nucleus vaporize. Gases and dust are released, producing a glowing region called a coma. Energy from the Sun causes the coma to grow. Charged particles streaming from the Sun push particles out of the coma, producing a glowing tail that can reach millions of kilometers into space.

The orbits of some comets extend to just beyond the planet Neptune. These comets make one complete trip around the Sun in fewer than 200 years. They are called short-period comets. The best known comet, Halley's comet, is a short-period comet that orbits the sun about once every 76 years. It will next be visible from Earth in the year 2061.

The orbits of other comets extend much farther from the Sun. Some scientists believe that most of these comets are found beyond Pluto. As many as a trillion comets may exist in this region. These comets can take up to 30 million years to orbit the Sun! They are called long-period comets. Hale-Bopp, a long-period comet identified in 1995, takes nearly 2,500 years to orbit the Sun.

▶ **TEXT STRUCTURE** What causes the "tail" of a comet to form?

Named for its discoverer, Yuji Hyakutake, this comet was one of the brightest to approach the Sun in the 20th century. ▼

Comet Orbit

A comet's tail always points away from the Sun, regardless of the direction the comet is moving.

Meteors

Have you ever seen a "shooting star" sweep across the night sky? It produces bright, short-lived streak of light. But such streaks are not moving stars at all. They are meteors.

A **meteor** is a streak of light caused by a chunk of matter that enters Earth's atmosphere and is heated by friction with the air. These chunks of matter are called **meteoroids.** For a few moments, the meteoroids burn as they fall, appearing as streaks of light against the night sky. A few meteoroids are the size of asteroids. But most are much smaller. Many are smaller than a grain of sand.

Sometimes more meteors are visible in the sky than usual. These

Meteor showers occur when Earth passes through particles that were shed from the tails of comets. ▼

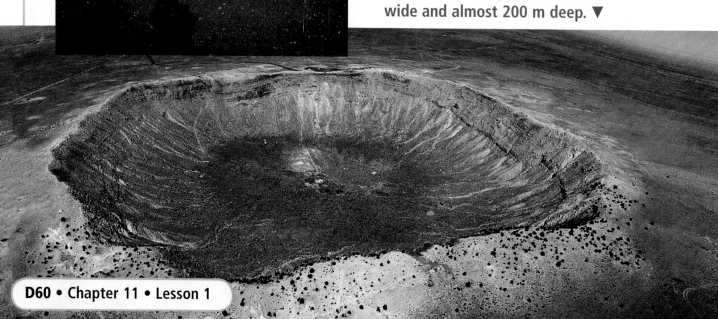

Meteor

events are called meteor showers. During the meteor shower shown in the photo below, an average of 50 meteors per hour could be seen.

Meteor showers can last from a few hours to a few days. Most showers occur when Earth passes through clouds of dust left orbiting the Sun by a passing comet.

Sometimes, the falling rocks stay intact during their trip through Earth's atmosphere. When these objects strike the ground, they are called **meteorites.** Most meteorites are believed to come from the asteroid belt.

When large meteorites strike Earth's surface, they form bowl-shaped depressions called impact craters. The impact crater shown below is the Barringer Crater in Arizona. It formed sometime between 20,000 and 50,000 years ago.

▶ **TEXT STRUCTURE** How is a meteorite different from a meteor?

The Barringer impact crater is over 1 km wide and almost 200 m deep. ▼

Visual Summary

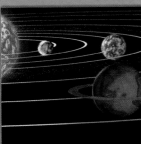

The solar system consists of the Sun, nine planets, their moons, and many other smaller bodies that revolve around the Sun.

All but two planets in the solar system have at least one moon. Moons, comets, and asteroids are among the smaller bodies in the solar system.

Meteoroids are bits of matter that burn up when they enter Earth's atmosphere.

LINKS for Home and School

MATH Calculate Circumference The average radius of Earth's orbit around the Sun is approximately 150 million km (93 million mi). Using the formula $C = 2\pi r$, calculate the circumference (C) of Earth's orbit. Suppose Earth's orbit to be circular for this calculation.

ART Make a Poster Learn more about one of the moons of Jupiter, Saturn, Neptune, or Uranus. Make a color drawing of the moon, labeling its interesting features. Include a paragraph describing the moon and what makes it unique.

Review

1 MAIN IDEA What different types of bodies make up the solar system?

2 VOCABULARY Write a sentence using the words *asteroid* and *comet*.

3 READING SKILL: Text Structure Make a brief outline that shows how these terms are related: *planets, moons, asteroids, the Sun.*

4 CRITICAL THINKING: Apply Earth and its Moon formed at about the same time and from the same processes. Why do you think Earth's surface has fewer craters than the surface of the Moon?

5 INQUIRY SKILLS: Research How could you find out more about collecting meteorites?

 TEST PREP
Small rocky objects that orbit the Sun between Mars and Jupiter are called

A. meteors.

B. meteorites.

C. comets.

D. asteroids.

 Technology
Visit **www.eduplace.com/scp/** to find out more about the solar system.

What Are the Planets Like?

Why It Matters...

By studying other planets and their moons, scientists have learned a lot about Earth and its Moon. Studying the solar system also provides clues about the stars and galaxies that lie beyond it.

PREPARE TO INVESTIGATE

Inquiry Skill

Use Models Some models are scale models. All parts of a scale model are larger or smaller than the size of the actual object being modeled, but are in exact proportions.

Materials

- marker
- metric tape measure
- piece of string (40 m)
- 10 wooden stakes (30 cm long)
- masking tape
- 10 cardboard rectangles
- modeling clay

Science and Math Toolbox
For step 1, review **Using a Tape Measure or Ruler** on page H6.

Scaling the Solar System

Procedure

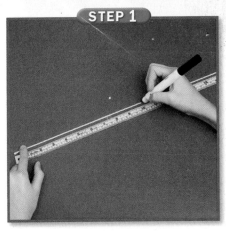
STEP 1

1 **Measure** Work with three other students. Obtain the scale distance values from your teacher and write them in your *Science Notebook*. Using the marker and the measuring tape, mark off along the string the positions of the Sun and planets.

2 **Use Models** Label one of the rectangles as the Sun. Tape the sign to a stake. Gently push the stake into the ground, if outdoors. If you are indoors, make a small clay ball and push the stake into the clay.

STEP 2

3 **Collaborate** Work with the members in your team to label the rest of the rectangles with the planet names and tape each to a stake.

STEP 4

4 **Use Numbers** Have one team member hold the end of the string that represents the Sun while another student stretches the string so that it is taut. The other students in your team should place the planet stakes in their correct positions along the stretched string.

Conclusion

1. **Analyze Data** Which group of planets—the inner planets or the outer planets—is closer together?

2. **Use Numbers** Study the distances between the first four planets from the Sun. Is there a pattern? If so, what is the pattern? Then describe distances among the outer planets.

Investigate More!

Design an Experiment
Find the diameters of the planets on pages D65–D66. Use these diameters to make a scale-size model of the Sun and each of the nine planets. Use a scale of 1 cm to 1,000 km.

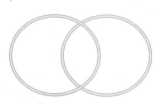

The Planets

READING SKILL

Compare and Contrast
Use a diagram like the one below to compare and contrast the inner and outer planets.

MAIN IDEA There are nine planets in our solar system. The four planets closest to the Sun are called the inner planets. The remaining five are called the outer planets.

The Inner Planets

The first four planets from the Sun are Mercury, Venus, Earth, and Mars. These planets are called the **inner planets** because they are closer to the Sun than the other planets in the solar system. The inner planets have certain characteristics in common. They are rocky and much smaller than most of the other planets. Yet, if you could travel to the inner planets, you would find them very different from Earth and from each other.

Mercury is the smallest of the inner planets and the one closest to the Sun. Mercury's surface temperature varies widely between its day and its night. During the planet's slow rotation, the side facing the Sun becomes extremely hot, while the side facing away becomes extremely cold.

Mercury
Mercury's surface has many craters. Some of these may contain frozen water. ▼

Sun

Venus ▶
Venus has a few craters on its surface. A thick, poisonous atmosphere surrounds this planet.

The surface of Venus, the second planet from the Sun, is hidden below a thick layer of clouds made up mostly of sulfuric acid! The atmosphere itself is 96 percent carbon dioxide, creating tremendous pressure and a strong greenhouse effect.

Temperatures at the surface are hot enough to melt lead. The pressure exerted by the atmosphere is bone-crushing—about the same as that found one km beneath the ocean's surface on Earth.

You are familiar with conditions on Earth, the third planet from the Sun. It is the only planet known to have liquid water. Earth's atmosphere and oceans help keep its surface temperature within a range that supports life.

Mars, the red planet, is smaller than Earth, but has about the same amount of land area. Compared to other planets, Mars has been extensively observed and explored. The Mars Expedition rovers, named Spirit and Opportunity, have recently visited the surface and sent information back to Earth.

Mars ▲
Mars is home to the largest volcano in the solar system.

The surface of Mars shows sign of water erosion, indicating that it may once have been more like Earth. While much of its surface is flat and rocky, Mars has deep canyons and the highest volcanic mountain known in our solar system. Olympus Mons stands 24 km, or almost 80,000 ft, above the Martian surface.

COMPARE AND CONTRAST What are some similarities among the inner planets?

Earth ▲
Earth's temperature and its atmosphere make it the only planet in the solar system known to support life.

Inner Planets		
Planet	**Diameter (km)**	**Distance from Sun (million km)**
Mercury	4,880	57.9
Venus	12,100	108.2
Earth	12,756	149.6
Mars	6,800	227.9

The Outer Planets

The **outer planets** are Jupiter, Saturn, Uranus, Neptune, and Pluto. Except for Pluto, these planets are larger than the inner planets and their volume consists mostly of gases.

Jupiter, the fifth planet from the Sun, is one of the brightest objects in the night sky. Jupiter takes only about 10 hours to rotate once on its axis. Winds reaching speeds of 670 km/hr (400 mph) form clearly visible bands.

Jupiter is famous for its Great Red Spot. This gigantic storm system has been visible from Earth for more than 300 years.

In addition to its many moons, Jupiter also has rings. The rings are made up of small particles that may have been produced by meteor collisions with Jupiter's moons.

The planet best known for its rings is Saturn, the sixth planet from the Sun. Saturn's band of rings is 250,000 km wide, but only 1 km thick. The rings consist mostly of ice particles.

Saturn is the least dense of any planet. If you could put Saturn in water, it would float! Yet it is as massive as 95 Earths.

Jupiter ▼
Jupiter is a giant—it is the biggest, most massive planet in the solar system. It has more than 60 moons!

Outer Planets		
Planet	**Diameter (km)**	**Distance from Sun (million km)**
Jupiter	142,800	778
Saturn	120,000	1,427
Uranus	50,800	2,870
Neptune	48,600	4,500
Pluto	2,300	5,900

Saturn ▲
Thousands of particles make up the rings that surround Saturn.

Uranus, the seventh planet from the Sun, was once called "Herschel" after the astronomer who discovered it. Like other planets, the axis of Uranus is tilted. Yet its axis is tilted so much it is nearly parallel to the plane of its orbit. Compared to other planets, Uranus is "lying" on its side.

Like Jupiter and Saturn, Uranus consists mostly of gases with a core of rock and ice. Uranus has at least 27 moons and a system of 11 rings.

Neptune, the eighth planet in the solar system, is similar in color and composition to Uranus. Scientists predicted its existence based on observations of the motion of Uranus, but it was not discovered until 1846.

Like all gas giants, Neptune is a windy planet, but its winds are the fastest yet observed in the solar system. They reach velocities of 2,700 km/hr (1,500 mph)!

Pluto ▶
Pluto has ice caps at its poles and large dark spots near its equator.

Neptune has at least 11 moons and a system of rings. One of Neptune's rings appears braided, and scientists are trying to understand this unusual observation. Neptune's largest moon is Triton.

Pluto is usually the farthest planet from the Sun. However, its orbit sometimes brings it closer to the Sun than Neptune. Unlike the other outer planets, Pluto is small, icy, and rocky. Not surprisingly, it is very cold. Pluto has one moon, called Charon.

▶ **COMPARE AND CONTRAST** What do most of the outer planets have in common?

Neptune ▼
Neptune and its largest moon, Triton, are getting closer to each other. The two probably will collide within the next 100 million years.

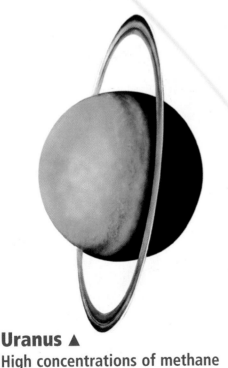

Uranus ▲
High concentrations of methane give Uranus a greenish color.

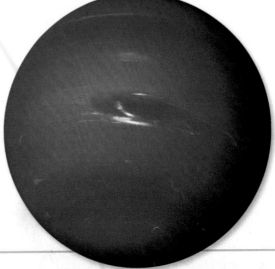

◄ The European Space Agency launched the Mars Express space probe in June of 2003.

Exploring Space

Many early observations of the solar system were made with simple optical telescopes. With these tools, an observer looked through lenses that made objects appear larger and brighter. Such telescopes could be used only to observe nearby objects in space.

Optical telescopes are still used to explore the solar system and beyond. Today, though, many are equipped with cameras and computers that produce images and collect and process data. Other types of telescopes gather invisible radiation, such as radio or x-ray waves, to form images.

Telescopes are affected by Earth's atmosphere. Clouds and gases in the air may prevent users from seeing objects clearly in space. Thus, many telescopes are set up on mountain peaks. Others are launched into space and orbit Earth!

The space shuttle is a vehicle that takes equipment and people into space. While the shuttle orbits Earth, experiments can be carried out. After a certain time, a shuttle returns to Earth. A space station stays in space for long periods of time. It has areas in which astronauts and scientists live, sleep and conduct experiments.

A space probe is a spacecraft that carries special instruments into space. Some probes are launched into Earth's upper atmosphere. Other probes go much farther. The Mars rovers Spirit and Opportunity have explored Mars, moving across its surface and analyzing samples of rocks and dirt.

▶ **COMPARE AND CONTRAST** How does the space shuttle differ from a space probe?

◄ The Mars rovers have taken many photographs and analyzed Martian rocks.

Visual Summary

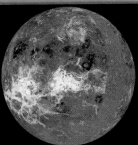

Mercury, Venus, Earth, and Mars, make up the inner planets. The inner planets are small and rocky and have few or no moons.

Jupiter, Saturn, Uranus, Neptune, and Pluto, are the outer planets. With the exception of Pluto, the outer planets are large and gaseous, and have many moons.

Space probes can be used to explore regions of space that are too dangerous or difficult for humans to explore directly.

LINKS for Home and School

MATH **Estimate Circumference** Earth's circumference is about 41,660 km. The circumference of Uranus is about 188,400 km. About what fraction of Uranus's circumference is Earth's?

TECHNOLOGY **Create a Photo Essay** Find out about a spacecraft that is currently being used to explore space. Write several paragraphs on the craft and its mission. Illustrate your essay with images from magazines or the Internet.

Review

1 **MAIN IDEA** How are the planets of the solar system grouped?

2 **VOCABULARY** Contrast space stations and space probes.

3 **READING SKILL: Compare and Contrast** Compare and contrast the characteristics of Earth with those of its two nearest neighbors.

4 **CRITICAL THINKING: Hypothesize** Why do you think the outer planets have so many moons?

5 **INQUIRY SKILLS: Use Models** Why are models useful to study the solar system?

 TEST PREP

The inner and outer planets are separated by

A. the asteroid belt.

B. Jupiter's great storm.

C. Earth and its Moon.

D. Saturn and its rings.

 Technology
Visit **www.eduplace.com/scp/** to find out more about planets.

Lisa Westberg Peters studied science carefully for her book of poems about Earth. Compare her poem about meteors to the work of a non-fiction writer.

Earth Charged in Meteor's Fiery Death

by Lisa Westberg Peters

The earth was charged Wednesday
in connection with the fiery death
of a large meteor.

"It was a combination of gravity
and thick air," police said.
"That meteor didn't have a chance."

The meteor fell out of orbit
early Tuesday and was vaporized
as it plunged toward the earth.

"It was a fireball!"
said Jose Martinez of Sacramento.
"It lit up my whole backyard."

A hearing will be held next week.

EARTHSHAKE
Poems from the Ground Up

BY Lisa Westberg Peters ★ PICTURES BY Cathie Felstead

Meteors

**Excerpt from *Comets, Meteors, and Asteroids,*
by Seymour Simon**

Meteors flash in the sky every night. They happen every
day, too, but we usually can't see them in the Sun's glare.

Meteor flashes are also called falling or shooting stars.
But meteors are not stars. Stars are suns far beyond our Solar
System. Meteors begin as meteoroids, bits of rock or metal that
orbit around the Sun. We can't see them in space because they
are too small and too dark.

But sometimes meteoroids plunge into Earth's atmosphere
at speeds faster than a bullet. The friction produced by
rubbing against air particles makes them glow red-hot, and
they are then called meteors. We see the bright flash for only a
few seconds.

Meteors come much closer to the Earth than comets. Some
are brighter than the brightest star and are called fireballs.

Several times each year you can see more than a dozen
meteors in an hour in the same part of the night sky. This is
called a meteor shower. It occurs when Earth passes through
an old comet orbit and collides with some of the particles
remaining from the comet's nucleus. Each year, Earth passes
through the old comet path
at about the same date. The
Leonids, for example, are
meteors from rocks left behind
in the orbit of Comet Temple-
Tuttle. When the Leonids appear
in mid-November, they seem to
come from the direction of the
constellation (a group of stars)
named Leo.

Sharing Ideas

1. **READING CHECK** Why do meteors burn as
   they enter Earth's atmosphere?

2. **WRITE ABOUT IT** Why do meteor
   showers appear at certain times every
   year?

3. **TALK ABOUT IT** Is it reasonable to
   suggest that Earth causes the death of
   meteors, as the poem suggests?

What Are Stars Like?

Why It Matters...

Earth revolves around a star called the Sun. Without this star, Earth would be a cold, lifeless body. Reactions in the Sun's core give off energy needed by almost all the living things on Earth.

Inquiry Skill

Use Numbers You can use numbers and your math skills to understand objects, events, and ideas in science.

Materials

- 7 long, black chenille stems
- 7 round beads that fit snugly onto the chenille stems
- piece of black poster board (about 8.5 in. x 11 in.)
- gel pen (silver, gold, or white)
- scissors
- metric ruler

Science and Math Toolbox

For step 1, review **Using an Equation or Formula** on page H10.

Star Search!

Procedure

STEP 1

Star	Actual Distance (Ly) from Earth	Scale Distance (cm)
Alkaid		
Mizar		
Aloith		
Megrez		

1. **Use Numbers** Refer to the table on page D75. Using a scale of 1 cm equals 10 light-years, compute the scale distances in cm to each of the stars in the Big Dipper, a star group that is part of a constellation. In your *Science Notebook,* record your values in a table like the one shown.

2. **Analyze Data** Look at the photo on page D75. Use it to mark positions for the stars of the Big Dipper on the black poster board. Connect the dots with the gel pen. Carefully use scissors to poke holes into the poster board at each star location.

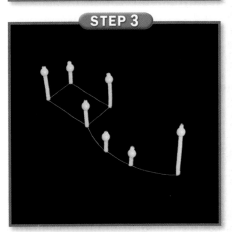

STEP 3

3. **Use Numbers** Cut each of the chenille stems to the correct scale length from your table. Insert each chenille stem into its correct place in the model constellation. Place a bead at the end of each chenille stem.

STEP 4

4. **Observe** Observe your model from different positions.

Conclusion

1. **Use Models** How did this scale model aid in your understanding of distances to stars in a constellation? What questions about stars does it help answer?

2. **Hypothesize** How might the star group you modeled look from a different part of the galaxy? Use your model to make a sketch that answers this question.

Investigate More!

Design an Experiment On a clear night, sit facing north and observe the sky. Sketch the brightest stars and organize them into groups. The next day, exchange sketches with a classmate. That night, try to identify your classmate's star groups.

Stars

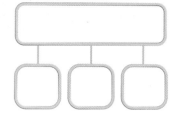

MAIN IDEA A star is a large sphere of glowing gases. Stars change as they go through their life cycles. The Sun is a medium-sized star that is about halfway through its life cycle.

Earth's Star: the Sun

Have you ever wondered what a star is? Why do stars twinkle, and how far are they from Earth?

A **star** is a large sphere of glowing gases. Nuclear reactions in the star's core produce energy that eventually reaches the star's atmosphere and radiates into space. The twinkle of starlight is caused by movement of particles in Earth's atmosphere.

Recall from Lesson 2 that everything in the solar system orbits a star called the Sun. The Sun is a yellow star made mostly of hydrogen and helium. Its volume is more than one million times the volume of Earth! The surface temperature of the Sun is about 5,500°C (9,932°F).

In many ways, the Sun is a typical star. Yet many stars are hotter and larger than the Sun, while others are smaller and cooler. Some are even larger and *cooler*!

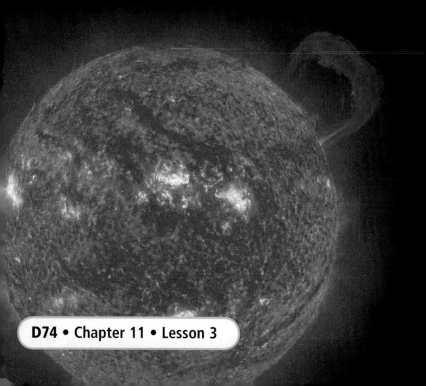

The diameter of the Sun is about 1.4 million km. The Sun appears small from Earth because it is so far away. Other stars appear even smaller because they are much, much farther away.

Stars in the Big Dipper

Star Name	Distance from Earth
1 Alkaid	108 Ly
2 Mizar	59 Ly
3 Alioth	62 Ly
4 Megrez	65 Ly
5 Phecda	75 Ly
6 Merak	62 Ly
7 Dubhe	75 Ly

▲ The stars that form the Big Dipper are many light-years from Earth. The Big Dipper is a star group that is part of a constellation called Ursa Major.

The Sun is about 150 million km (93 million mi) from Earth. While this distance may seem very large, it is actually small compared to distances between other objects in space.

Because distances beyond the solar system are so large, astronomers often use a special unit to measure them. A **light-year,** which is abbreviated Ly, is the distance that light travels in one year—about 9.5 trillion km! For reference, the Sun is about 0.00001 Ly from Earth. The next closest star is Proxima Centauri. It is about 4.3 Ly from Earth.

For centuries, people have arranged stars into patterns called constellations. Look at the table on this page. How far from Earth are the stars that form the Big Dipper?

Most of the billions of stars in the universe are very, very far from Earth. You are able to see some of these stars because they are so bright. The brightness of a star is called its **magnitude.** In general, bigger stars have greater magnitudes than smaller stars. Also, stars that are closer to Earth appear brighter than those farther away. Very hot stars appear brighter than cooler stars unless the cooler star is very large.

▶ **MAIN IDEA** What is a light-year?

A Star is Born

Although stars are not alive, scientists think of them as having a life cycle. A star's path through its life cycle depends on its mass. Every star begins its life as a rotating cloud of dust and gases called a nebula. Over time, gravity causes the matter in a nebula to collapse in toward the center.

As the cloud rotates faster and faster, it forms a protostar. A **protostar** is the first stage in the formation of a star. Temperatures in the protostar increase until they are high enough for nuclear reactions to take place. When these reactions occur, the protostar begins to glow. It is now a star.

After nuclear reactions have stabilized the newly formed star, it becomes a main sequence star. This kind of star will continue to release energy for millions or even billions of years. The time a star remains on the main sequence depends on its original mass.

The hottest, brightest main sequence stars are blue or white in color. The surface temperatures of these stars are between about 10,000 and 40,000°C! Medium-size main sequence stars, like the Sun, are generally yellow or orange. Their surface temperatures range from about 5,000°C to about 8,500°C. The coolest, dimmest main sequence stars are red. Their surface temperatures are only 3,000°C to 4,000°C.

The Sun is a medium-sized star that is about midway through its life cycle. Scientists estimate that it will continue burning for another 4 to 5 billion years.

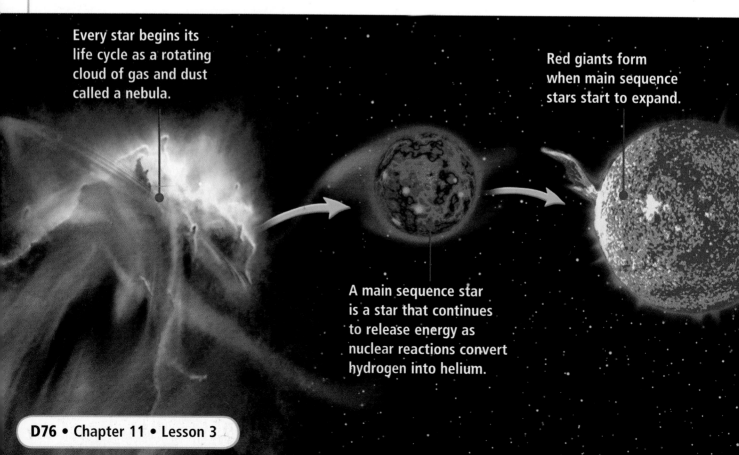

Every star begins its life cycle as a rotating cloud of gas and dust called a nebula.

A main sequence star is a star that continues to release energy as nuclear reactions convert hydrogen into helium.

Red giants form when main sequence stars start to expand.

When a star has reached the end of the main sequence stage, its core is no longer stable and begins to shrink. At the same time, the outer part of the star expands. This phase in a star's life cycle is called the red giant phase. As you can see from the diagram, a red giant can follow one of two paths, depending on its mass.

For a medium-size star in the red giant phase, the outer part of the star continues to release energy. The core continues to heat up until the hydrogen supply in the core is used up. Once the star runs out of "fuel" it collapses and becomes a white dwarf. Gradually, a white dwarf cools and becomes a black dwarf.

For a very massive star in its red giant phase, the temperature in the core rapidly increases as gravity pulls matter in toward the center.

These changes cause the star to explode. This explosion is called a supernova. Some supernovas leave behind colorful remnants called nebulae.

Sometimes after a supernova, a red giant becomes a rapidly spinning star that is very dense. Such a star is called a neutron star. If the remnant of the red giant is very large, it collapses in on itself to form a black hole. A black hole has such a powerful gravitational pull that it is able to pull in any energy or matter that comes too near it. Not even light can escape.

▷ **MAIN IDEA** What characteristic determines which path a star will follow along the main sequence?

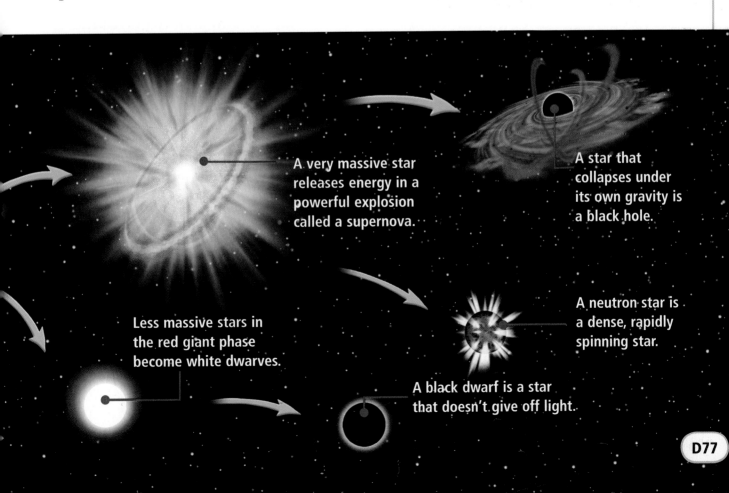

A very massive star releases energy in a powerful explosion called a supernova.

A star that collapses under its own gravity is a black hole.

Less massive stars in the red giant phase become white dwarves.

A neutron star is a dense, rapidly spinning star.

A black dwarf is a star that doesn't give off light.

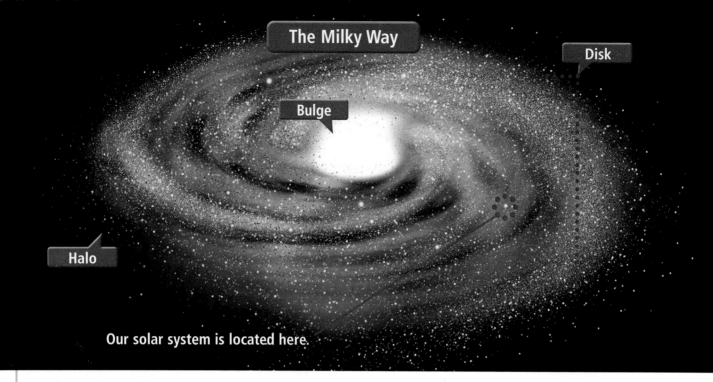

The Milky Way

Disk

Bulge

Halo

Our solar system is located here.

The spiral swirls that stretch out from the Milky Way's central bulge are called the disk.

Galaxies

A **galaxy** is an enormous system of gases, dust, and stars, all held together by gravity. Small galaxies consist of hundreds of thousands of stars. Large galaxies contain billions of stars. Scientists keep revising the estimated number of galaxies as they gather more data. Recently, scientists who work with the Hubble Space Telescope estimated that the universe is home to about 125 billion galaxies.

Most galaxies have two main parts: a bulge and a halo. The bulge is a region of old stars, gases, and dust. The outer part of a bulge often fades into a galaxy's halo. The halo, like the bulge, contains old stars, but also has a lot of dark matter. Dark matter is matter that can't be observed directly, but it makes up much of the mass of the universe.

The Milky Way

You probably already know that the solar system is part of to the Milky Way galaxy. However, did you know that the Sun is only one of the more than 200 billion stars in this galaxy? If you could view the Milky Way galaxy from above, it would look like the drawing on this page.

Most of the stars, gas, and dust in the Milky Way are found in a region called the disk. This flattened region of young stars and dust is about 100,000 Ly across and lies just beyond the bulge. The solar system is located in the disk about 28,000 Ly from the center of the galaxy.

Outside the central bulge is the galaxy's halo. The Milky Way's halo may be more than 130,000 Ly across.

Types of Galaxies

Look again at the drawing of the Milky Way on the facing page. Now look at the photos on this page that show the three major types of galaxies. You will note that the Milky Way is a spiral galaxy. All spiral galaxies have three main parts—a bulge, a disk, and a halo.

In some spiral galaxies, like the Milky Way, arms extend directly from the bulge. Another example of this type of spiral galaxy is shown at the top of this page. In other spirals, the arms extend from a bar-shaped mass of matter that runs through the bulge.

Elliptical galaxies are the second major type of galaxy. They are shaped like a flattened ball, and they have no arms. Elliptical galaxies are brighter toward the central bulge.

Irregular galaxies are collections of stars, gases, and dust that have no real shape or structure. Irregular galaxies have large regions of hydrogen gas and young hot stars. An irregular galaxy is shown in the bottom photograph on this page.

To learn about distant galaxies, scientists are observing and studying them with the Hubble Telescope and other telescopes in space. The galaxies are too far away to explore with spacecraft.

▶ **MAIN IDEA** Describe the three major types of galaxies.

Spiral Galaxy
A spiral galaxy has arms that extend outward from its central bulge.

Elliptical Galaxy
An elliptical galaxy is shaped like a flattened ball or sphere.

Irregular Galaxy
An irregular galaxy has no real shape or structure.

Visual Summary

Stars are enormous spheres of glowing gases. The apparent brightness of a star depends on its size, its temperature, its real brightness, and its distance from Earth.

A star goes through a life cycle that includes several stages. The initial mass of the star determines which of two different paths it follows.

A galaxy is an enormous collection of stars, gases, and dust. Most galaxies can be classified according to shape.

LINKS for Home and School

MATH Make a Model Use the measurements given in this lesson to make a scale model of the Milky Way galaxy. Indicate the position of the solar system in your model.

WRITING Creative With a few classmates, write a script and perform a three-minute skit on the life cycle of a star. Be creative, but scientifically accurate, in your production.

Review

1 MAIN IDEA What is a star?

2 VOCABULARY What three factors determine the magnitude of a star?

3 READING SKILL: Main Ideas/ Details Provide details from this lesson that support the following main idea: Stars change as they go through their life cycles.

4 CRITICAL THINKING: Apply Which path will Earth's Sun probably follow after it reaches the red giant phase? Explain.

5 INQUIRY SKILL Use Numbers Suppose the surface temperature of a main sequence star is about 20,000°C. What color is this star and how does it compare with Earth's Sun?

 TEST PREP

Possible stages in the life cycle of a very massive star, in order, are

A. red giant, blue hole, white dwarf.

B. neutron star, black hole, black dwarf.

C. red giant, supernova, black hole.

D. supernova, white dwarf, neutron star.

 Technology
Visit **www.eduplace.com/scp/** to find out more about stars.

Astronaut

Astronauts work for NASA, the government agency that explores space. They pilot spacecraft, conduct scientific experiments, conduct needed repairs, and perform other tasks in space. Much of their work is done under conditions of very small gravity, which NASA calls microgravity.

What It Takes!

- A degree in engineering or other scientific field
- Rigorous training in simulated spaceflight
- The ability to work in enclosed spaces
- Excellent physical condition

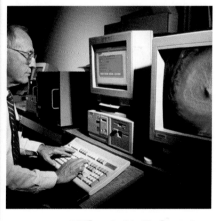

Computer Systems Technician

A computer systems technician takes care of computer hardware and software. This work includes installing and maintaining networks of computers, trouble-shooting problems, and updating equipment.

What It Takes!

- Training at a technical institute or on the job
- The ability to think logically and to solve problems
- Learning new developments and products

Out With a Bang!

What can suddenly outshine an entire galaxy of *billions* of stars? A supernova! Towards the end of their lives, enormous stars called super-giants die in colossal explosions that rip them apart. The dying stars blast out hot, glowing gases that expand and become huge nebulas.

Shown here is the Crab Nebula. It is the remnant of a supernova that Chinese astronomers observed in 1054. They called it a "guest star." It was so bright that for three weeks it could be seen in broad daylight. Then it faded away. Over 650 years later, the supernova's nebula was discovered by telescope. Only much later did astronomers realize that the "guest star" of 1054 was the supernova that created the Crab Nebula we see today.

Planetary Nebulas

The Ring Nebula was one of the first planetary nebulas to be discovered.

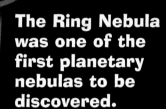

Can you see why this nebula is known as the Cat's Eye Nebula?

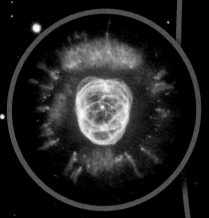

This is the Eskimo Nebula. Can you see the head surrounded by a furry hood?

Vocabulary

Complete each sentence with a term from the list.

1. A star's brightness is called its ____.

2. A(n) ____ is a huge system of stars, dust, and gases in space.

3. The first stage in the formation of a star is a(n) ____.

4. Saturn is one of the five ____.

5. Pluto is usually the outermost ____ of the solar system.

6. A(n) ____ has a frozen nucleus and can develop a glowing tail.

7. The Sun, nine planets, and thousands of other bodies make up the ____.

8. ____ are often called "shooting stars."

9. The Sun is a giant sphere of glowing gases called a(n) ____.

10. ____ are small rocky bodies found in a belt between Mars and Jupiter.

asteroids D58
comet D59
galaxy D78
inner planets D64
light-year D75
magnitude D75
meteors D60
meteorites D60
meteoroids D60
outer planets D66
planet D56
protostar D76
solar system D56
star D74

 Test Prep

Write the letter of the best answer choice.

11. The gravitational pull of ____ holds objects in the solar system in their orbits.

    A. the Sun
    B. the outer planets
    C. Jupiter
    D. the Milky Way

12. All objects in the solar system travel around the Sun in ____.

    A. about 24 hours
    B. about 1 year
    C. elliptical orbits
    D. circular orbits

13. Which of these is NOT a small, rocky planet?

    A. Earth
    B. Mercury
    C. Uranus
    D. Pluto

14. Mercury and Venus ____.

    A. are inner planets
    B. are outer planets
    C. give off their own light
    D. are gaseous giants

Inquiry Skills

15. Use Models Would a physical model be a good choice to model the life cycle of a star? Explain your answer.

16. Use Numbers What units would you use to express distances within the solar system? Explain your choice.

Map the Concept

Complete the chart to compare and contrast meteors, meteoroids, meteorites, comets, and asteroids.

Similarities	Differences

Critical Thinking

17. Analyze What is another way you might divide the planets into two groups other than inner planets and outer planets?

18. Sequence Describe the life cycle of a very massive star from the red giant phase onward.

19. Apply Use what you have learned in this chapter to write a paragraph about Earth's location in the universe.

20. Synthesize What are some advantages of conducting experiments from a space station rather than a space shuttle?

Performance Assessment

Make a Scale Model

Choose one planet in the solar system. Use references and information given in this chapter to make a scale drawing of the planet in relation to Earth. Include a key to the scale.

Write the letter of the best answer.

1. Which is NOT found within the solar system?

   A. asteroid

   B. comet

   C. nebula

   D. satellite

2. Almost all weather occurs in the _____ .

   A. mesosphere.

   B. stratosphere.

   C. thermosphere.

   D. troposphere.

3. During which phase of the Moon shown below is Earth located between the Sun and the Moon?

   A.

   B.

   C.

   D.

4. In the diagram of Earth shown below, what season is it at point A?

   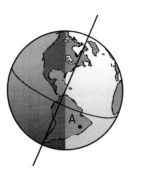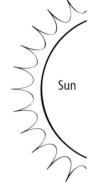

   Sun

   A. summer

   B. spring

   C. winter

   D. fall

5. Which BEST describes the inner planets?

   A. They are very cold.

   B. They are gas giants.

   C. They have dozens of moons.

   D. They are small and rocky.

6. A continental polar air mass is _____ .

   A. dry and cold.

   B. dry and warm.

   C. wet and cold.

   D. wet and warm.

7. According to the diagram, which stage in the life cycle of a star likely has the highest density?

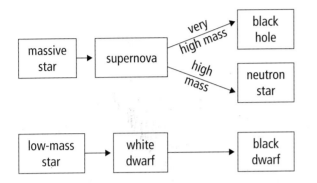

A. black hole

B. black dwarf

C. neutron star

D. white dwarf

8. Which BEST describes Earth's motions?

A. Earth revolves on its axis and rotates around the Sun.

B. Earth rotates on its axis and revolves around the Sun.

C. Earth rotates around the Sun and revolves around the Moon.

D. Earth revolves around the Moon and rotates around the Sun.

Answer the following in complete sentences.

9. Explain why Earth is cold near the poles and warm near the equator.

10. Which of the outer planets is most like the four inner planets? Explain your answer.

Discover!

Because stars are many light-years away from Earth, it takes a long time for their light to reach Earth. What happens to that light when it finally passes through Earth's atmosphere? The answer explains why stars appear to twinkle, or scintillate.

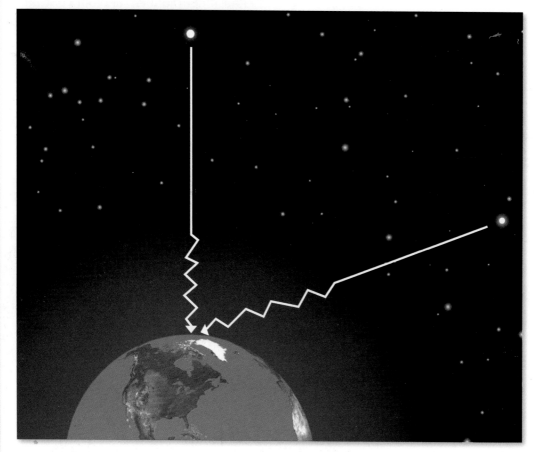

Starlight bends as it passes through Earth's atmosphere. Since the atmosphere is constantly moving and changing, starlight can bend many times! Stars closer to the horizon twinkle more because the starlight passing through the horizon to reach your line of sight travels through more of the atmosphere than starlight passing from directly above. The more atmosphere the starlight passes through, the more it is bent and the more the star appears to twinkle.

See a star twinkling. Go to **www.eduplace.com/scp/** to view a Flash ™ movie and to learn more about stars.

Kinds of Matter

Kinds of Matter

Independent Reading

Marie Curie

Marvelous Metals

It's in the Air

Discover!

The stars in the night sky, the sand that you dig your toes into, even the air that you breathe—all come from only about 100 elements. What is the most common element in the universe? In this unit, you'll learn the answer to this question and many others about matter and the elements.

Chapter 12

The Structure of Matter

LESSON 1

Every thing you've ever touched—a pencil, a rock, a button, even the air you breathe—is made of atoms. What are these basic building blocks of matter?

Find out in Lesson 1.

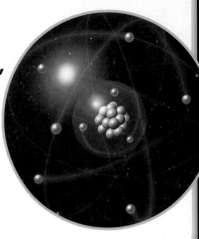

LESSON 2

Some art made of metals has lasted thousands of years. What are metals, and why are they different from other substances?

Find out in Lesson 2.

LESSON 3

The exhaust produced by the space shuttle is almost entirely water vapor. How can burning fuel produce water?

Find out in Lesson 3.

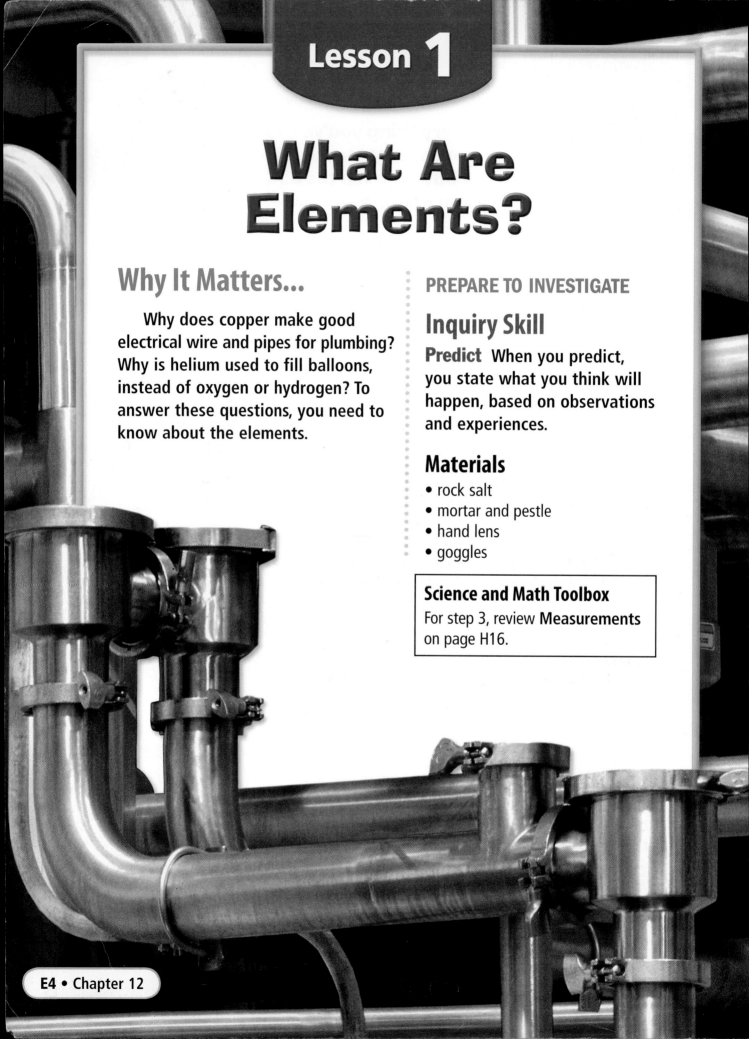

What Are Elements?

Why It Matters...

Why does copper make good electrical wire and pipes for plumbing? Why is helium used to fill balloons, instead of oxygen or hydrogen? To answer these questions, you need to know about the elements.

PREPARE TO INVESTIGATE

Inquiry Skill

Predict When you predict, you state what you think will happen, based on observations and experiences.

Materials

- rock salt
- mortar and pestle
- hand lens
- goggles

Science and Math Toolbox
For step 3, review **Measurements** on page H16.

Smash It!

Procedure

Safety: Wear goggles as you perform the procedure.

STEP 1

1. **Observe** Use the hand lens to look at a chunk of rock salt. Record your observation.

2. **Collaborate** Place a chunk of rock salt into the mortar. With a partner, use the pestle to crush the rock salt into smaller pieces. Make the pieces about the size shown in the photograph at right.

STEP 2

3. **Observe** Use the hand lens to look at the crushed rock salt. Record what the salt looks like.

4. **Record Data** Now grind the rock salt into even smaller pieces. Look at the pieces with the hand lens. Record what they look like.

STEP 4

5. **Ask Questions** Grind the salt into fine powder. Look at the powder with your hand lens and record what you see. Do you think the powder is as small as a pestle could grind the rock salt?

STEP 5

Conclusion

1. **Analyze Data** Compare your observations of the different-size pieces of rock salt. Compare and contrast how it looked at each size.

2. **Predict** What do you think the salt would look like under a microscope if you could grind it into even finer pieces?

Investigate More!

Design an Experiment Try this experiment with other substances, such as sugar cubes, cereal, or table salt. Compare the different particles that result.

READING SKILL

Compare and Contrast
Use a chart to help you compare and contrast the properties of different forms of carbon.

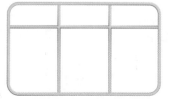

Elements

MAIN IDEA All matter is made up of elements. The smallest piece of an element is called an atom.

Elements and Atoms

All matter is made up of elements. An **element** is a substance that cannot be broken apart into other substances. You can think of elements as the building blocks of matter.

Some substances are made from a single element. Diamond, for example, is made from only the element carbon. Most substances are made from two or more elements. Table salt is made of two elements—sodium and chlorine.

What would you get if you could grind a diamond into the smallest carbon pieces possible? You would get carbon atoms. An **atom** is the smallest particle of an element that still has the properties of that element.

Atoms are so tiny that they can be seen only with special microscopes. If you lined up 100 million atoms end-to-end, they might measure as long as 1 centimeter!

Ancient Greek philosophers were the first to suggest that all matter is made up of very tiny particles. In about 430 B.C., the Greek philosopher Democritus named these particles *atomos,* which means "indivisible." He believed that atoms were solid and could not be changed or destroyed.

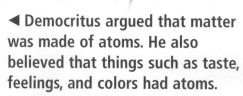

◀ Democritus argued that matter was made of atoms. He also believed that things such as taste, feelings, and colors had atoms.

Models of the Atom

Not all of Democritus' ideas about atoms were correct. Over time, scientists have questioned and revised the model of the atom they use. Look at the diagrams at right.

In 1803, English chemist John Dalton suggested the first atomic theory of matter based on scientific observations. Dalton's model showed atoms as solid spheres of different sizes and masses.

In 1897, another English scientist, J.J. Thomson, discovered that atoms contain negatively charged particles called **electrons.** Thomson proposed that the electrons were distributed evenly through the atom. His model is sometimes called the plum-pudding model, after a dessert it resembles.

In 1911, New Zealand physicist Ernest Rutherford showed that atoms have a small central core, called the **nucleus.** Surrounding the nucleus is mostly empty space. He argued that electrons moved somewhere in that space. In 1913, Danish scientist Niels Bohr suggested that electrons travel in specific orbits around the nucleus.

In 1926, Austrian scientist Erwin Schrödinger developed the electron cloud model. In this model, the "clouds," or orbitals, represent the probability of finding an electron in a certain location. It is the most widely accepted model of the atom today.

▶ **COMPARE AND CONTRAST** How are atoms and elements related?

Atom Models

Dalton (1803)
Atoms are solid spheres of different sizes and masses.

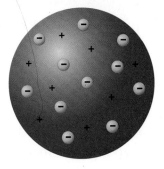

Thomson (1897)
A ball of positive charge has negatively charged electrons located throughout it.

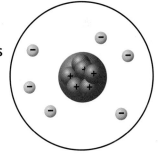

Rutherford (1911)
The small, dense nucleus is surrounded by mostly empty space. Electrons move through that space.

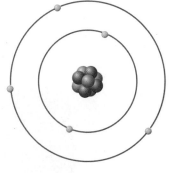

Bohr (1913)
Electrons travel in specific orbits around the nucleus.

Schrödinger (1926)
Electron clouds or orbitals show the probability of finding an electron in a particular location.

Organization of Atoms

Electrons move rapidly around the nucleus. They have a negative charge and extremely small mass. Most of an atom's mass is in the nucleus, which is made of protons and neutrons. A **proton** is a particle with a positive electrical charge. A **neutron** is a particle with no charge.

Any atom of a given element has the same number of protons in its nucleus. However, the number of neutrons may vary. For example, a carbon atom always has 6 protons in its nucleus. And while most have 6 neutrons, some have 7 or 8 neutrons.

A carbon atom also has 6 electrons. Atoms have an equal number of protons and electrons. The positive and negative charges balance each other so the atom is neutral.

Carbon atoms can group together in different ways, as shown below. Coal is a hard, black substance that is mostly carbon. Coal is a very important fossil fuel that forms underground from dead plants.

Graphite is another form of carbon. The "lead" in most pencils is actually graphite mixed with clay. Graphite is gray or black and has a slippery feel. It leaves a black mark when it is rubbed.

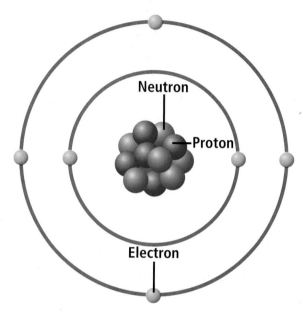

Carbon Atom All carbon atoms have 6 protons and 6 electrons. Groups of carbon atoms can be arranged in several different ways. Each form has different properties.

Forms of Carbon

Coal
Anthracite coal contains 90 to 98 percent pure carbon. ▲

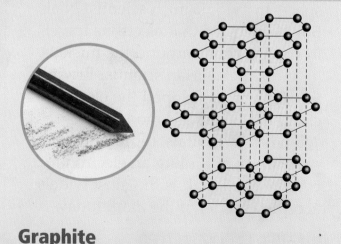

Graphite
The atoms in graphite are arranged in sheets that separate easily. ▲

Diamond is another form of pure carbon. Diamonds are formed at high temperature and pressure deep in Earth's crust. They are beautiful, valuable, and made of the hardest natural substance found on Earth. Diamonds that are not "perfect" enough for jewelry are put in tools used for cutting and grinding.

As you can see, carbon is found in nature in a variety of forms with different properties. How can one element have so many different properties? The answer lies in the different ways in which carbon atoms can be arranged.

In the diagrams below, notice that the arrangements of the atoms are all different. In graphite, the atoms are arranged in rings of six atoms each. These rings form sheets that can slide past each other. That's why graphite feels slippery.

The carbon atoms in diamond are packed very tightly together, with each atom bonded to four other atoms. The arrangement gives diamond its hardness.

Another form of carbon has a very unusual shape and an even more unusual name. Buckminsterfullerene is made up of 60 carbon atoms. They form a sphere in which carbon atoms are joined in hexagons and pentagons.

This form of carbon was discovered in 1985. It was named after architect Buckminster Fuller, who built domes that used hexagons and pentagons to give them great strength.

▶ **COMPARE AND CONTRAST** Why do the different forms of carbon have different properties?

Diamond
Diamond is the hardest natural substance found on Earth. ▲

Buckyball
A buckyball or buckminsterfullerene is made up of 60 carbon atoms, arranged in a pattern that looks like a soccer ball. ▲

Helium
The helium in these balloons is less dense than air, so they float.

Aluminum
Aluminum is a metallic element that is strong but lightweight.

Copper
Copper can be stretched into wires. It also conducts electricity well.

Silver
Silver is a shiny metal that is soft enough to be formed into jewelry.

Elements Alone and Joined

As you have seen, carbon atoms can join together in several different ways. In fact, most atoms join with other atoms to form molecules. A **molecule** is two or more atoms joined together by certain forces of attraction called chemical bonds. In a molecule, the atoms in some ways act as a single unit.

Some molecules consist of atoms of a single element. For example, the oxygen you breathe is made of molecules of two oxygen atoms.

Other molecules are made up of atoms of a combination of elements. A molecule of water, for example, contains two hydrogen atoms and one oxygen atom. Other molecules are larger. Some molecules in your body are made of thousands, millions, or even billions of atoms!

Scientists have identified more than 100 different elements. Yet only about half of them are common on Earth, and only about 90 are found in nature. The others have been produced by scientists in laboratories.

An element's properties stem from the atoms that make it up. Examples of properties are color, hardness, and density. Look at the photos on this page. What are some of the properties of the elements shown?

▶ **COMPARE AND CONTRAST** How do atoms, molecules, and elements differ?

Lesson Wrap-Up

Visual Summary

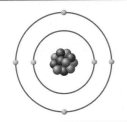	Atoms are the building blocks of matter. They are made up of smaller particles—electrons, protons, and neutrons.
	An element is a form of matter made up of only one kind of atom. Different elements have different properties that can be measured.
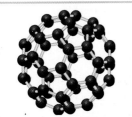	Most atoms can combine with other atoms to form molecules.

LINKS for Home and School

MATH Make a Model The atoms in diamond are arranged so that each atom bonds to four other atoms. Together, these four atoms form a tetrahedron. Research this shape. What unique qualities does this structure have? Build a model tetrahedron to share with the class.

WRITING Expository Research Buckminster Fuller's geodesic dome. Write a report that compares Fuller's design with the molecular shape of Buckminsterfullerene. Include diagrams in your report.

Review

1 MAIN IDEA What are the tiny particles that make up an atom?

2 VOCABULARY Write a sentence using the terms *atom* and *element*.

3 READING SKILL: Compare and Contrast Explain how diamond and graphite are similar and how they are different.

4 CRITICAL THINKING: Apply Suppose you want to build a kite for a kite-flying contest. You need to find building materials. Explain what properties you would want the materials to have.

5 INQUIRY SKILL: Predict A uranium atom has 92 protons in its nucleus. Use what you know about atoms to predict how many electrons a neutral uranium atom has.

 TEST PREP

The atoms in a diamond

A. have no electrons.

B. are all carbon atoms.

C. are carbon and oxygen atoms.

D. are like tiny, solid balls.

 Technology
Visit **www.eduplace.com/scp/** to find out more about atoms.

What Is the Periodic Table?

Why It Matters...

Neon signs contain helium, neon, argon, and other elemental gases that are made to glow. These gases are among the more than 100 known elements. Scientist have grouped all the elements into a table based on their properties.

PREPARE TO INVESTIGATE

Inquiry Skill

Classify When you classify, you sort things into groups according to their properties.

Materials

- goggles
- hand lens
- copper wire
- samples of aluminum, carbon, and sulfur

Science and Math Toolbox

For step 1, review **Making a Chart to Organize Data** on page H11.

Compare Elements

Procedure

Safety: Wear goggles for this investigation.

1 **Collaborate** Work with a partner. Gather the materials listed. In your *Science Notebook,* make a chart like the one shown.

2 **Observe** Look at the samples of copper, aluminum, carbon, and sulfur. Test each sample to find some of its properties. You may observe it closely, feel it, and rub it lightly on a piece of paper. Try to find properties that two or more of the samples have in common.

3 **Record Data** As you examine each element, record the properties you observe in your chart. For example, is the element hard or soft? Stiff or bendable? Dull or shiny?

4 **Classify** How would you classify the elements into two groups? Below your chart, list and describe the two groups.

Conclusion

1. **Analyze Data** Compare your observations of the elements. How are copper and aluminum similar? How are carbon and sulfur similar?

2. **Infer** Based on your observations, what do you think might be some properties of metals and some properties of nonmetals?

STEP 1

Element	Properties
Copper	
Aluminum	
Carbon	
Sulfur	

STEP 2

STEP 2

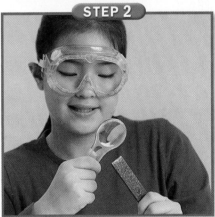

Investigate More!

Design an Experiment
How would you compare the ability of each element to conduct electricity? Make a plan. Choose a graph, diagram, or chart to display your results.

The Periodic Table

VOCABULARY

chemical symbol	p. E16
metal	p. E17
noble gas	p. E20
nonmetal	p. E17
periodic table	p. E15
semimetal	p. E17

READING SKILL

Categorize Use a chart to categorize elements into metals and nonmetals.

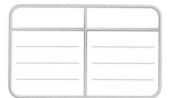

MAIN IDEA Scientists have identified more than 100 elements. The elements are organized in the periodic table.

Organizing the Elements

The idea that all matter is made up of elements goes back at least as far as ancient Greece. Around 450 B.C., the Greek philosopher Empedocles (ehm PEHD uh kleez) suggested that all matter is made up of four elements: earth, air, fire, and water.

By the Middle Ages, people began to realize that there must be more than just those four elements. In the 1600s, English chemist Robert Boyle argued that earth, air, fire, and water could not be real elements. Later, in the late 1700s, French chemist Antoine-Laurent Lavoisier made one of the first modern lists of chemical elements.

By the 1800s, scientists had begun to identify many new elements. Scientists were also learning that some elements had similar properties. They began to organize elements into families, or groups, with similar properties. However, there was no standardized way of classifying elements.

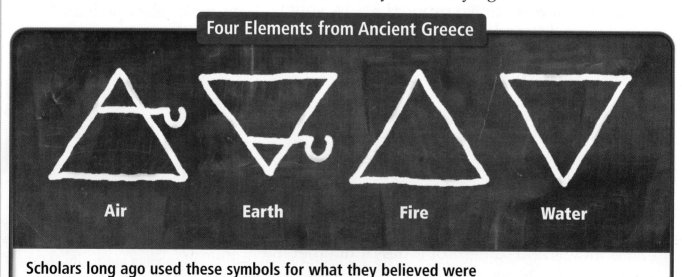

Four Elements from Ancient Greece

Air   Earth   Fire   Water

Scholars long ago used these symbols for what they believed were the four elements—air, earth, fire, and water.

ПЕРИОДИЧЕСКАЯ СИСТЕМА ЭЛЕМЕНТОВ

ПЕРИО	РЯДЫ	I	II	III	IV	V	VI	VII	VIII	0
1	I	H 1 1,008								He 2 4,003
2	II	Li 3 8,940	Be 4 9,02	B 5 10,82	C 6 12,010	N 7 14,008	O 8 16,000	F 9 19,00		Ne 10 20,183
3	III	Na 11 22,997	Mg 12 24,32	Al 13 26,97	Si 14 28,06	P 15 30,98	S 16 32,06	Cl 17 35,457		Ar 18 39,944
4	IV	K 19 39,096	Ca 20 40,08	Sc 21 45,10	Ti 22 47,90	V 23 50,95	Cr 24 52,01	Mn 25 54,93	Fe 26 55,85 Co 27 58,94 Ni 28 58,69	
	V	Cu 29 63,57	Zn 30 65,38	Ga 31 69,72	Ge 32 72,60	As 33 74,91	Se 34 78,96	Br 35 79,916		Kr 36 83,7
5	VI	Rb 37 85,48	Sr 38 87,63	Y 39 88,92	Zr 40 91,22	Nb 41 92,91	Mo 42 95,95	Ma 43	Ru 44 101,7 Rh 45 102,91 Pd 46 106,7	
	VII	Ag 47 107,88	Cd 48 112,41	In 49 114,76	Sn 50 118,70	Sb 51 121,76	Te 52 127,61	J 53 126,92		Xe 54 131,3
6	VIII	Cs 55 132,91	Ba 56 137,36	La 57 138,92	Hf 72 178,6	Ta 73 180,88	W 74 183,92	Re 75 186,31	Os 76 190,2 Ir 77 193,1 Pt 78 195,23	
	IX	Au 79 197,2	Hg 80 200,61	Tl 81 204,39	Pb 82 207,21	Bi 83 209,00	Po 84 210	85		Rn 86 222
7	X	87 —	Ra 88 226,05	Ac 89 227	Th 90 232,12	Pa 91 231	U 92 238,07			

* ЛАНТАНИДЫ 58–71

| Ce 58 140,13 | Pr 59 140,92 | Nd 60 144,27 | 61 — | Sm 62 150,43 | Eu 63 152,0 | Gd 64 156,9 |
| Tb 65 1?3,2 | Dy 66 162,46 | Ho 67 164,94 | Er 68 167,2 | Tu 69 169,4 | Yb 70 173,04 | Cp 71 174,99 |

▲ Dmitri Mendeleyev left blank spaces in his table for elements that he predicted were yet to be discovered. The photo shows one of his revised tables.

Mendeleyev's Table

In 1869, Russian chemist Dmitri Mendeleyev developed a way to arrange and classify the elements. First he listed the elements in order of increasing mass. By studying the list, he noticed that the properties of the elements in his list showed a repeating pattern.

Next he rearranged the list so that elements with similar properties would appear in the same columns of his table. When arranging the elements this way, he had to leave some blank spaces in his table.

Mendeleyev predicted that, sometime in the future, scientists would discover the elements that fit in the blank spaces. He thought these elements would have properties similar to those elements above and below them in the table. These predictions were correct, and scientists saw the value of the table.

Today, scientists use a table of the elements very similar to Mendeleyev's table. Like his table, the modern **periodic table** is a table in which the elements are arranged by their properties. The periodic table is standardized. This means that scientists all over the world use the same one.

Why is the table called periodic? Recall that Mendeleyev discovered that the properties of elements have a repeating pattern. The word *periodic* means "repeating."

Although Mendeleyev recognized the pattern among the elements, he could not explain why the pattern should exist. Scientists now can explain how elements in the same column of the table form chemical bonds in similar ways.

▶ CLASSIFY **How is the periodic table different from an alphabetical list of elements?**

The Periodic Table

In the modern periodic table, elements are arranged in order of increasing atomic number, which is the number of protons in their nuclei.

One example of the periodic table is shown below. The box for each element lists the atomic number, chemical symbol, and name. The **chemical symbol** is an abbreviation of the element's name, sometimes from Latin or Greek.

Each column in the periodic table is called a group. Elements within a group have similar properties. For example, look at the group that contains copper (Cu), silver (Ag), and gold (Au). These three elements are all soft, shiny metals.

The horizontal rows in the table are called periods. Notice that the periods have an increasing number of elements. Do you see the two rows that seem to have been pulled out of the table? This is done to keep the table from being too wide.

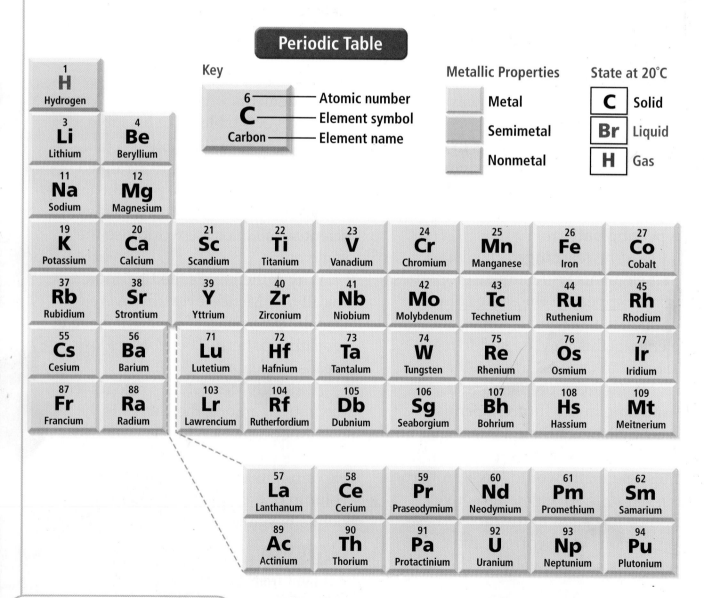

Periodic Table

Key
6 — Atomic number
C — Element symbol
Carbon — Element name

Metallic Properties
Metal
Semimetal
Nonmetal

State at 20°C
C Solid
Br Liquid
H Gas

Classification of Elements

Elements can be classified in different ways. Below the colors of the boxes show whether elements are metals, nonmetals, or semimetals.

Metals are usually shiny, can be bent or stretched, and conduct electricity. Most elements are metals.

Many **nonmetals** are gases. Solid nonmetals are usually dull in color, do not conduct electricity, do not bend or stretch very much, and break easily. **Semimetals** are like metals in some ways and like nonmetals in other ways.

Can you find the pattern of metals, nonmetals, and semimetals in the table?

Also note that the chemical symbols are different colors. The color tells you whether the element is a solid, liquid, or gas at room temperature. Most elements are solids.

In the periodic table below, elements with black symbols are solids. Only two elements, mercury (Hg) and bromine (Br), are liquids at room temperature. Their symbols are blue. Elements with red symbols are gases.

▶ **CLASSIFY** What is the difference between groups and periods in the periodic table?

								2 He Helium
			5 B Boron	6 C Carbon	7 N Nitrogen	8 O Oxygen	9 F Fluorine	10 Ne Neon
			13 Al Aluminum	14 Si Silicon	15 P Phosphorus	16 S Sulfur	17 Cl Chlorine	18 Ar Argon
28 Ni Nickel	29 Cu Copper	30 Zn Zinc	31 Ga Gallium	32 Ge Germanium	33 As Arsenic	34 Se Selenium	35 Br Bromine	36 Kr Krypton
46 Pd Palladium	47 Ag Silver	48 Cd Cadmium	49 In Indium	50 Sn Tin	51 Sb Antimony	52 Te Tellurium	53 I Iodine	54 Xe Xenon
78 Pt Platinum	79 Au Gold	80 Hg Mercury	81 Tl Thallium	82 Pb Lead	83 Bi Bismuth	84 Po Polonium	85 At Astatine	86 Rn Radon
110 Ds Darmstadtium	111 Uuu Unununium*							

63 Eu Europium	64 Gd Gadolinium	65 Tb Terbium	66 Dy Dysprosium	67 Ho Holmium	68 Er Erbium	69 Tm Thulium	70 Yb Ytterbium
95 Am Americium	96 Cm Curium	97 Bk Berkelium	98 Cf Californium	99 Es Einsteinium	100 Fm Fermium	101 Md Mendelevium	102 No Nobelium

*Temporary name

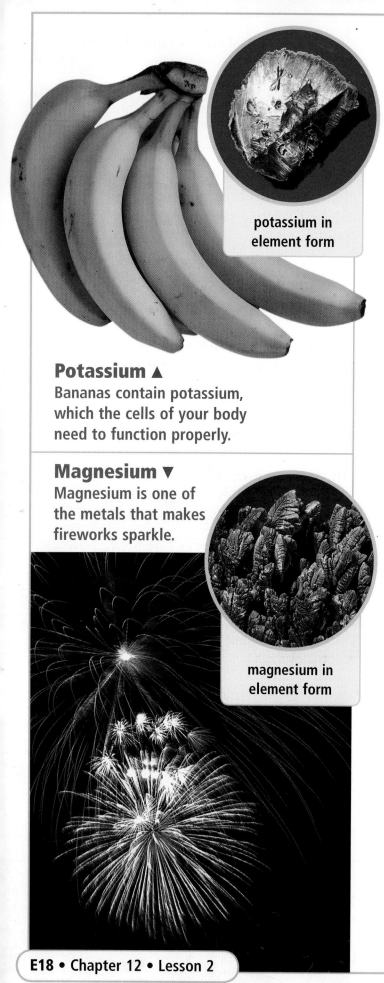

Potassium ▲
Bananas contain potassium, which the cells of your body need to function properly.

potassium in element form

Magnesium ▼
Magnesium is one of the metals that makes fireworks sparkle.

magnesium in element form

Metals

In the periodic table on pages E17 and E18, find the red line that runs through the semimetals. All the metals fall to the left of this line. Metals include familiar elements, such as iron, gold, and aluminum. Rarer metals include technetium and francium.

When you think about something made of metal, you probably think of a shiny, silver- or gold-colored object. One of the properties that most metals have is luster, the ability to reflect light.

Can you think of some other properties of metals? For example, how are metals shaped? Metal workers can hammer metals into thin sheets and bend a metal by using force or by heating it. The ability to bend is a property of most metals.

Think of how electricity comes into your home. Most likely it travels through copper electrical wires. Electrical wires make use of two properties of metals. These properties are the ability to be stretched or pulled into thin wires and the ability to conduct electricity.

Look around you and you'll see many things made of metals. Your drink can is probably made out of the metals aluminum and manganese. Your desk might contain steel, which is made from iron. The coins in your pocket are made from copper and nickel. You may be wearing a silver necklace.

Calcium ▲
The calcium in milk helps keep your bones strong and healthy.

calcium in element form

Metals are also found in foods and in your body. For example, your bones and teeth contain calcium. Your blood contains iron. In fact, a healthy body depends on small amounts of many different metals.

Metals found in living things are usually combined with other elements in chemical compounds. The calcium in your body, for example, does not look like the chips of pure calcium shown in the photograph above. Instead, it forms compounds with carbon, oxygen, hydrogen, and other elements.

Silicon ▶
Computer chips are made from silicon.

Semimetals

In the periodic table, semimetals are located between the metals and the nonmetals. These elements have properties of both metals and nonmetals.

One semimetal is silicon. About 28 percent of Earth's crust is silicon, making it Earth's second most common element. Sand is a compound of silicon and oxygen. Silicon is found in most rocks, in water, and even in your body.

Like all semimetals, silicon is a semiconductor. That means that under some circumstances silicon conducts electricity and at other times it does not.

Adding other elements to silicon can change its conductivity. Because of these properties, silicon is used to make electric circuits found in computer chips.

▶ **CLASSIFY** Which two properties of metals are useful in making wires for electric circuits?

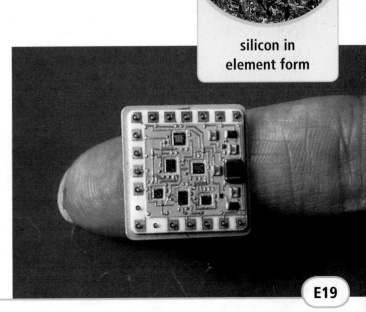

silicon in element form

Nonmetals and Noble Gases

Recall that solid nonmetals are dull in color and do not conduct electricity. They are usually brittle, which means they break easily. One example of a nonmetal is sulfur.

Sulfur is a very important element in the chemical industry. It is used as an ingredient in chemicals such as sulfuric acid, a very strong acid that is found in car batteries. Another nonmetal is phosphorus, which is used to make the striking surfaces of safety matches.

Many nonmetals are gases. Nitrogen makes up about 78 percent of the air you breathe. It is also important in making fertilizers. Oxygen is the most abundant element on Earth. About 21 percent of the air you breathe and 47 percent of the Earth's crust is oxygen. Oxygen reacts with many metals. Have you ever seen an old, rusty car? Rust is iron oxide—a combination of iron and oxygen.

Compounds of fluorine are added to drinking water to help prevent tooth decay. Chlorine is also often added to drinking water in small amounts to kill bacteria or any other organisms that may be in the water. Chlorinating water can help prevent certain diseases that have troubled people for centuries.

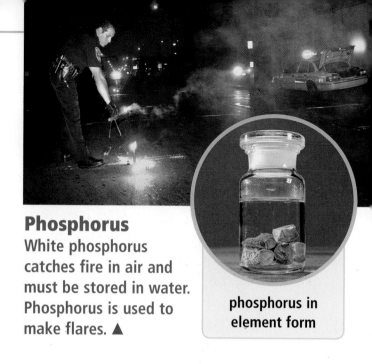

Phosphorus
White phosphorus catches fire in air and must be stored in water. Phosphorus is used to make flares. ▲

phosphorus in element form

The last column, or group, of the periodic table is made of nonmetals only. These are the **noble gases,** the elements that hardly ever combine with other elements to form molecules.

The noble gas helium is used to fill balloons and airships because it is lighter than air. Helium and other noble gases are also used in welding.

Noble gases will glow if an electric current is passed through them. For this reason, they are used to make what are called neon lights, even though neon is not the only gas that is used. Different mixtures of the gases glow in different colors.

Neon
Neon and other noble gases are used to make colorful signs. ▶

Visual Summary

Dmitri Mendeleyev created the first periodic table. He left blank spaces for elements that he believed would later be discovered.

6
C
Carbon

The periodic table contains basic information for each element: its name, chemical symbol, and atomic number.

5 B Boron	6 C Carbon	7 N Nitrogen
13 Al Aluminum	14 Si Silicon	15 P Phosphorus

29 Cu Copper	30 Zn Zinc	31 Ga Gallium	32 Ge Germanium	33 As Arsenic
47 Ag Silver	48 Cd Cadmium	49 In Indium	50 Sn Tin	51 Sb Antimony
79 Au Gold	80 Hg Mercury	81 Tl Thallium	82 Pb Lead	83 Bi Bismuth

The elements in the periodic table can be classified as metals, semimetals, and nonmetals.

LINKS for Home and School

MATH Prepare a Kit You have been hired to build a modeling kit. The kit should contain enough model protons, electrons, and neutrons to model one atom each from the first 10 elements. How many of each particle must you provide?

HEALTH Write a Report Research the element fluorine to find out why it is often added to drinking water and toothpaste. Write a report about what you learn. Do you think adding fluoride to water is a wise practice?

Review

1 MAIN IDEA What are elements?

2 VOCABULARY What information about each element is contained in its box in the periodic table?

3 READING SKILL: Compare and Constrast How are metals and semimetals alike? How are they different?

4 CRITICAL THINKING: Analyze Suppose you are given a sample of an element. You are asked to identify the element as a metal or a nonmetal. What are some properties you would look for? Explain.

5 INQUIRY SKILL: Infer A scientist has an unknown gas in a container. By experimenting, she has found that the gas will not combine with any other element. This gas is most likely which type of element? Explain.

✓ TEST PREP

The properties of semimetals are

A. more like metals.

B. more like nonmetals.

C. somewhat like metals and somewhat like nonmetals.

D. somewhat like noble gases.

 Technology

Visit **www.eduplace.com/scp/** to find out more about the elements.

People and the Periodic Table

What kinds of scientists work with elements of the periodic table? Read these stories to find out!

1 **H** Hydrogen	
3 **Li** Lithium	4 **Be** Beryllium
11 **Na** Sodium	12 **Mg** Magnesium
19 **K** Potassium	20 **Ca** Calcium
37 **Rb** Rubidium	38 **Sr** Strontium
55 **Cs** Cesium	56 **Ba**
87 **Fr** Francium	

Lu **Hf** **Ta** **W** **Re** **Os** **Ir** Iridium

109 **Mt** Meitnerium

62 **Sm** Samarium

94 **Pu** Plutonium

Hazel Juanita Harper, D.D.S

Is calcium important for strong teeth? Dr. Hazel Harper would tell you that it is. She treats patients in Washington, D.C., and she advocates for oral health. In 1997, she became the first woman president of the National Dental Association.

"What excites me about dentistry is being able to change a smile and shape a personality," said Dr. Harper about her work.

Otto Hahn and Lise Meitner

In the 1930s, chemists Hahn and Meitner showed how an atom's nucleus could split apart. Meitner named this process nuclear fission. Years after her death, a new element was named in her honor.

Mario Molina

Chlorine and fluorine are parts of chemicals called chlorofluorocarbons (CFCs). CFCs were once used in refrigerators, spray cans, and other devices.

Yet CFCs are no longer used, thanks in part to Dr. Mario Molina. He showed how CFCs can damage the ozone layer in the upper atmosphere. This layer protects Earth's surface from harmful radiation. Dr. Molina's work led to an international ban on CFCs.

"I am heartened and humbled that I was able to do something that . . . had a profound impact on the global environment," said Dr. Molina.

2 **He** Helium					
5 **B** Boron	6 **C** Carbon	7 **N** Nitrogen	8 **O** Oxygen	9 **F** Fluorine	10 **Ne** Neon
13	14 **Si** Silicon	15 **P** Phosphorus	16 **S** Sulfur	17 **Cl** Chlorine	18 **Ar** Argon
	32 **Ge** Germanium	33 **As** Arsenic	34 **Se** Selenium	35 **Br** Bromine	36 **Kr** Krypton
	50 **Sn** Tin	51 **Sb** Antimony	52 **Te** Tellurium	53 **I** Iodine	54 **Xe** Xenon
	82 **Pb** Lead	83 **Bi** Bismuth	84 **Po** Polonium	85 **At** Astatine	86 **Rn** Radon

Katharina Lodders

Dr. Katharina Lodders has arranged the elements in a new way. Her periodic table is organized to show how abundant, or common, an element is in the universe. She expects the table will help scientists study how planets form.

67 **Ho** Holmium

99 **Es** Einsteinium

Sharing Ideas

1. **READING CHECK** What contribution did Dr. Molina make to the global environment?

2. **WRITE ABOUT IT** Choose an element from the table. How does it affect you?

3. **TALK ABOUT IT** What kinds of scientists work with the elements?

Lesson 3

What Are Compounds?

Why It Matters...

Elements combine into countless numbers of different chemical substances. Most of these substances, like the water in this snow sculpture, are compounds. Your body is made of chemical compounds, and you depend on compounds for goods of all kinds.

PREPARE TO INVESTIGATE

Inquiry Skill

Infer When you infer, you use logical reasoning to draw conclusions from observations and data.

Materials

- goggles
- water
- plastic cup
- plastic spoon
- baking soda
- 2 pieces of insulated wire with the ends stripped
- tape
- 9-volt battery

Science and Math Toolbox
For step 4, review **Making a Chart to Organize Data** on page H11.

Splitting Water

Procedure

Safety: Wear goggles. Use a low-voltage battery only. Never place wires from an electrical outlet into water.

1. **Collaborate** Work with a partner. Fill the cup at least halfway with water. Stir in a spoonful of baking soda.

2. **Experiment** Tape one end of each piece of wire to the battery terminals. Make sure the bare metal ends touch the terminals.

3. **Experiment** Place the other ends of the two wires in the water. Tape the wires to the sides of the cup, so that they do not touch each other.

4. **Observe** Observe the ends of the two wires in the water. Record your observations in your *Science Notebook*. Note any differences you see at the end of each wire.

5. **Predict** Predict what would happen if you removed one of the wires from the water. Record your prediction, then test it.

Conclusion

1. **Hypothesize** Water is made up of the elements hydrogen and oxygen, which are gases at room temperature. What do you think the electric current does to the water? How do you know?

2. **Infer** Each molecule of water has two hydrogen atoms and one oxygen atom. How does this explain any differences that you observed?

STEP 1

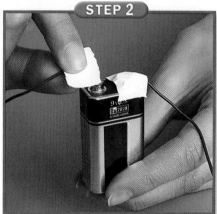

STEP 2

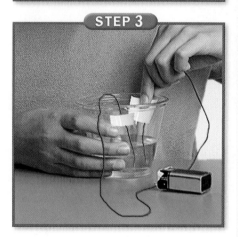

STEP 3

Investigate More!

Design an Experiment
Run the investigation without baking soda. Then try dissolving salt or sugar in place of the baking soda. Compare your results. Hypothesize what the role of the baking soda was.

VOCABULARY

chemical formula   p. E29
chemical reaction   p. E28
compound   p. E26

READING SKILL

Compare and Contrast
Use a Venn diagram to compare and contrast the properties of two compounds in this lesson.

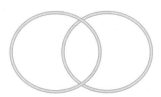

Compounds

MAIN IDEA Two or more elements can combine to form a compound. Compounds have different properties from the elements that make them up.

Combining Elements

At one time, water was thought to be an element. Recall that an element cannot be broken down into other substances. How did scientists discover that water is not an element? They broke it down into other substances by passing an electric current through it.

Water is a compound. A **compound** is a pure substance made up of two or more elements that are chemically combined. Water is made up of the elements hydrogen and oxygen.

A compound has its own chemical properties. In many compounds, atoms combine to form molecules. Each molecule of a compound acts identically to every other molecule of that compound. They all have the same chemical properties.

All water molecules are made up of two hydrogen atoms and one oxygen atom. Every molecule of water has the properties of water. When a molecule of water is broken apart, the resulting particles no longer have those properties. They have the properties of hydrogen and oxygen.

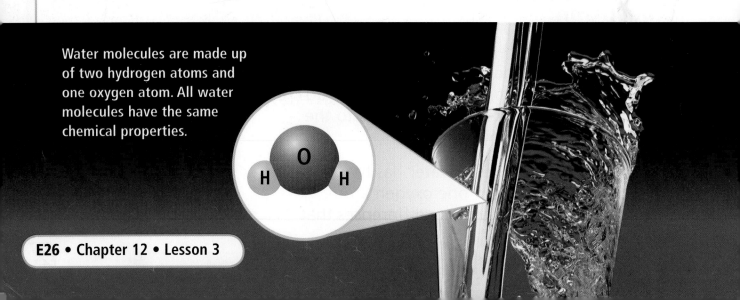

Water molecules are made up of two hydrogen atoms and one oxygen atom. All water molecules have the same chemical properties.

Many Compounds

Countless compounds are found in nature. Many more have been created in the laboratory.

There are many two-element compounds other than water. Each time you exhale, your breath contains the compound carbon dioxide. Molecules of carbon dioxide are made up of one carbon atom and two oxygen atoms.

Other compounds are made of more than two elements. Look at the unusual limestone formations in the photo of the cave. Limestone rock is mostly a compound called calcium carbonate. This compound is not made of molecules. Instead, the atoms are arranged in a rigid pattern called a crystal.

Another familiar compound is rust. Many items, like the old truck in the photo above, are made of steel. Steel contains the element iron. When iron is left outdoors, it will rust.

Rust is a compound of iron and oxygen called iron oxide. Iron oxide forms when iron reacts with oxygen in the air. Water speeds up the reaction. That's why iron rusts more quickly when it is wet. Salt also makes iron rust more quickly.

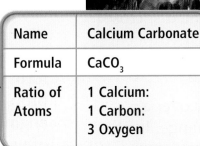

Name	Calcium Carbonate
Formula	$CaCO_3$
Ratio of Atoms	1 Calcium: 1 Carbon: 3 Oxygen

▲ Water evaporates, leaving calcium carbonate behind. This produces stalagmite and stalactite formations.

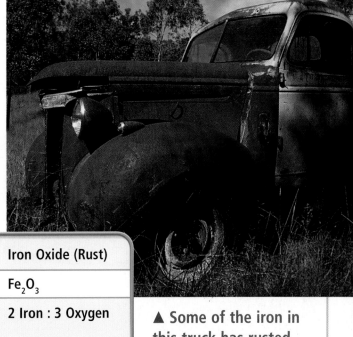

Name	Iron Oxide (Rust)
Formula	Fe_2O_3
Ratio of Atoms	2 Iron : 3 Oxygen

▲ Some of the iron in this truck has rusted. Rust is a compound called iron oxide. Rust forms when iron combines with oxygen gas.

▶ **COMPARE AND CONTRAST**

What happens when atoms of two or more elements combine chemically?

Making and Breaking Compounds

To form a compound, the atoms of the elements involved must take part in a chemical reaction. A **chemical reaction** is a process in which one or more substances are changed into one or more different substances.

Look at the photos below. The left one shows a spoonful of sugar. Table sugar is a compound called sucrose. It is made up of carbon, hydrogen, and oxygen. One molecule of sucrose contains 45 atoms!

If you heat the sugar over a flame, the sugar will change. First, it will melt—a physical change. Even though it looks different, it is still sugar. The molecules have not changed.

If you continue heating, a chemical reaction will take place. Water vapor will be released into the air, leaving a black substance behind. This substance is carbon.

In this chemical reaction, one substance—a compound—is broken down into simpler substances. Many reactions are of this type.

In another type of chemical reaction, simple substances can combine to form a more complex substance. One example of this type of reaction takes place in the main engines of the space shuttle.

Liquid hydrogen and liquid oxygen are stored in the shuttle's external tank. In the engines, hydrogen and oxygen combine to form water. Energy is released in the process. The exhaust from the main engines is steam—tiny droplets of water.

In each of these chemical reactions, energy is an important factor. Energy is required to break apart water or sugar. Energy is released when elements combine to form these compounds.

Chemical Reaction

Sugar

H_2O H_2O H_2O

Carbon

1 Sucrose ($C_{12}H_{22}O_{11}$) is a sugar, a compound of carbon, hydrogen, and oxygen.

2 When heated, the sucrose molecules break down, leaving the element carbon and releasing water molecules.

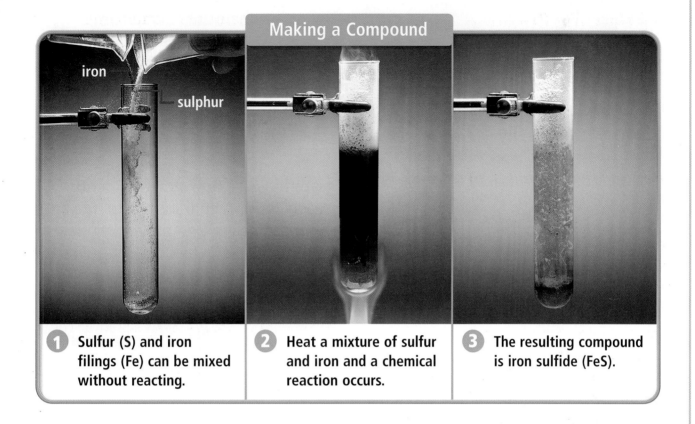

Making a Compound

1. Sulfur (S) and iron filings (Fe) can be mixed without reacting.

2. Heat a mixture of sulfur and iron and a chemical reaction occurs.

3. The resulting compound is iron sulfide (FeS).

Compounds and Formulas

Look at the photos above. When you mix black iron filings and yellow sulfur, they don't react. They are still iron and sulfur. You can use a magnet to separate the iron from the sulfur.

However, if you heat the iron-and-sulfur mixture, a chemical reaction takes place. In this reaction, the iron and sulfur atoms combine to form the compound iron sulfide.

Iron sulfide looks different from the iron and the sulfur from which it is made. It also has different properties. For example, no part of the compound is attracted to a magnet. The iron in iron sulfide has lost its magnetic property.

Scientists use chemical formulas to identify chemical compounds. A **chemical formula** is a shorthand way to describe a compound. Chemical formulas use chemical symbols and numbers to show the makeup of a compound.

For example, the chemical symbol for iron is Fe. The chemical symbol for sulfur is S. The chemical formula for iron sulfide, FeS, tells you that iron sulfide has one iron atom for every sulfur atom.

Often the elements in a compound do not form a one-to-one ratio. In such cases, the ratio is indicated by small numbers to the lower right of the symbols. Such a number is called a subscript. For example, the chemical formula for water is H_2O. In any sample of water, there are two hydrogen atoms for every one oxygen atom.

 **COMPARE AND CONTRAST** What does a subscript in a chemical formula represent?

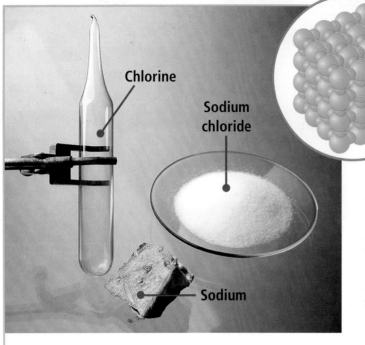

Chlorine

Sodium chloride

Sodium

Sodium Chloride

Sodium (Na) and chlorine (Cl) are the elements that make up the compound sodium chloride (NaCl), or table salt.

Everyday Compounds

Compounds, like elements, are pure substances. Only a chemical reaction will break down a compound into its component elements.

The pictures on these pages show several compounds you probably encounter every day. These compounds, like all compounds, have their own distinctive chemical properties.

For example, common table salt is used in cooking and baking to add flavor to food. Salt is a compound called sodium chloride, or NaCl. As you know, sodium chloride forms hard, whitish crystals. The properties of sodium chloride are very different from those of sodium and chlorine.

In its element form, sodium is a very soft, shiny metal. It is so soft it can be cut with a butter knife. Sodium easily reacts with many substances and must be stored in oil. When exposed to air, it reacts quickly

with oxygen. In water, it violently reacts to form sodium hydroxide and hydrogen gas.

The element chlorine is a greenish, poisonous gas. It is used to kill bacteria and other harmful organisms in drinking water and swimming pools. Chlorine has a strong smell. If you've been swimming in a pool or used bleach, you know what chlorine smells like.

When sodium and chlorine meet, a chemical reaction between them produces salt, or sodium chloride. Salt is a very stable compound, meaning it does not chemically change very quickly or easily.

On the next page, you will read about three other common compounds. All are very different from the individual elements that make them up.

Chemical Formulas	
Compound	**Chemical Formula**
sucrose	$C_{12}H_{22}O_{11}$
calcium carbonate	$CaCO_3$
iron oxide (rust)	Fe_2O_3

These are the chemical formulas for some of the compounds you've already read about in this lesson.

Carbon Dioxide Carbon dioxide (CO_2), is a gas made up of carbon and oxygen. Every time you exhale, your lungs release carbon dioxide. It is also produced when almost anything containing carbon is burned.

Carbonated drinks get their fizz from CO_2. When placed under pressure, small amounts of carbon dioxide will dissolve in water. Release the pressure, and the CO_2 will bubble out. This is why soda slowly goes "flat" if you leave its container open.

Carbon dioxide gas gives soda its fizz and tart taste.

Glass Sand and glass are made mostly of silicon dioxide (SiO_2), a very common compound. SiO_2 is only one of the compounds in glass. It is mixed with others and heated. Then the glass is shaped as it cools.

Glass is an example of an amorphous solid, meaning a solid without form. Unlike the particles of other solids, the particles of silicon dioxide are arranged in a loose, random pattern.

Glass is made of silicon dioxide (SiO_2) and other compounds.

Polymers Some compounds are made up of large molecules, called polymers. A polymer is a chain-like molecule made up of repeated units. Many polymers are important to life. For example, many fats, proteins, carbohydrates, and even DNA are polymers. Plastics are polymers that are made from fossil fuels.

▶ **COMPARE AND CONTRAST** Identify three common compounds and their uses.

The nonstick coating of this frying pan is made of a polymer.

Water: Earth's Most Abundant Compound

Water is everywhere on Earth. About three-fourths of Earth's surface is covered with water, and all organisms depend on water to live. Many organisms, such as fish and most single-celled organisms, can live only in water or in moist environments. You need water, too. Your body is about 65 percent water, and staying healthy requires water.

Not only is water abundant, it is also a unique compound. For example, water is one of the few compounds that is a liquid at room temperature.

Another interesting characteristic of water is its ability to dissolve substances. In fact, water dissolves more substances than any other liquid.

One reason for the unique properties of water is its shape. Water molecules have a bent shape, as shown in the diagram. Because of this shape, the oxygen end of the molecule has a slight negative charge and the hydrogen end has a slight positive charge. This uneven distribution of charge gives water its ability to dissolve many compounds.

The charges also cause water molecules to attract one another. The slight positive charge of the hydrogen end of a molecule attracts the slight negative charge of the oxygen end of a second molecule. This is why water is a liquid over a wide range of temperatures.

▶ **COMPARE AND CONTRAST** Name two unique properties of water.

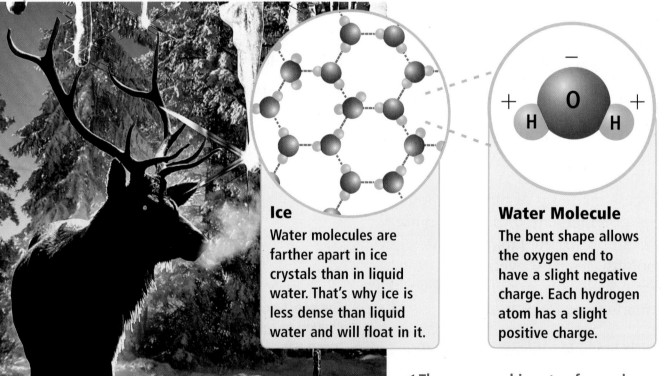

Ice
Water molecules are farther apart in ice crystals than in liquid water. That's why ice is less dense than liquid water and will float in it.

Water Molecule
The bent shape allows the oxygen end to have a slight negative charge. Each hydrogen atom has a slight positive charge.

◀ The snow and ice stay frozen because the temperature is below 0°C (32°F), the freezing point of water.

Lesson Wrap-Up

Visual Summary

Atoms of different elements combine in a chemical reaction to create a compound.

Water (H₂O)

A chemical formula tells which elements and how many atoms of each make up a molecule.

The properties of a compound are usually different from the properties of the elements that make it up.

LINKS for Home and School

MATH Calculate Total Atoms The chemical formula for baking soda, or sodium bicarbonate, is $NaHCO_3$. Calculate the total number of each type of atom in 4 molecules of this compound.

TECHNOLOGY Write a Report
Scanning tunneling microscopes (STMs) allow scientists to see three-dimensional images of molecules. Research the development and uses of STMs. Write a report that includes a diagram showing how an STM works.

Review

❶ MAIN IDEA Why are elements known as the building blocks of matter?

❷ VOCABULARY In your own words, define *chemical formula*.

❸ READING SKILL: Compare and Contrast How are elements and compounds alike? How are they different?

❹ CRITICAL THINKING: Apply Research some compounds other than the ones mentioned in this lesson. Pick one example and explain how you know it is a compound.

❺ INQUIRY SKILL: Infer Ty added water to a mixture of two other substances. A short time later, he observed that one substance had turned green and another had turned orange. What might Ty infer?

 TEST PREP
Elements and compounds

A. are pure substances.

B. are made up of atoms.

C. have specific properties.

D. are all of the above.

 Technology
Visit **www.eduplace.com/scp/** to find out more about compounds.

Space Armor

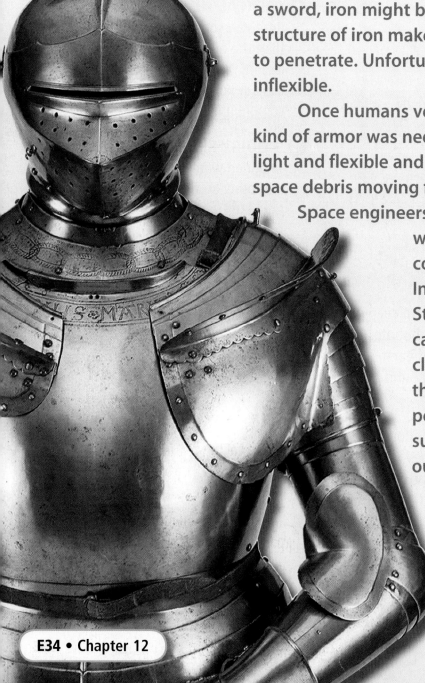

What makes better armor, cloth or metal? It depends! If you are trying to protect yourself from a sword, iron might be a better choice. The molecular structure of iron makes iron armor strong and difficult to penetrate. Unfortunately, iron is also heavy and inflexible.

Once humans ventured into space, a different kind of armor was needed. It had to be extremely light and flexible and yet protect astronauts from space debris moving faster than a bullet.

Space engineers found the material they were looking for in an amazing compound called Kevlar™. Invented by the chemist Stephanie Kwolek, Kevlar™ can be woven into a flexible cloth that is five times stronger than steel! Kevlar™ fiber is the perfect material for a modern suit of armor—one you wear in outer space!

◄ • • • • • • • • • •

Heavy and Stiff
Medieval suits of armor could weigh as much as 100 pounds and were very awkward to wear.

Flexible and Strong

Because Kevlar™ is incredibly strong for its weight, it is often used in space suits. It protects astronauts from speeding micrometeoroids and punctures that would cause the suit to lose pressure and oxygen.

Vocabulary

Complete each sentence with a term from the list.

1. The smallest particle of an element that still has the properties of that element is a(n) ____.

2. The atomic particle that has an extremely small mass compared to the others is the ____.

3. The ____ is the central part of an atom.

4. A particle with a positive charge is called a(n) ____.

5. When two or more atoms are joined together, a(n) ____ is formed.

6. An abbreviation of an element's name is its ____.

7. One of a group of elements that seldom combine with other elements is a(n) ____.

8. When two or more elements are chemically combined to form a new substance, a(n) ____ is formed.

9. When substances are changed into different substances, a(n) ____ has taken place.

10. An atomic particle with no charge is called a(n) ____.

atom E6 ✗
chemical formula E29
chemical reaction E28
chemical symbol E16
compound E26
electron E7
element E6
metal E17
molecule E10
noble gas E20
nonmetal E17
neutron E8
nucleus E7 ✗
periodic table E15
proton E8
semimetal E17

Test Prep

Write the letter of the best answer choice.

11. The Periodic Table ____.

    A. lists all known compounds.
    B. illustrates how molecules are formed.
    C. lists all known elements.
    D. organizes chemical formulas.

12. Atoms of two different elements have different numbers of ____.

    A. atoms   **C.** molecules
    B. compounds   **D.** protons

13. The properties of a compound are ____ those of the substances that make them up.

    A. exactly the same as
    B. the reverse of
    C. different from
    D. more intense than

14. In the Periodic Table, C, H, and O are examples of ____.

    A. atomic numbers   **C.** chemical symbols
    B. atomic particles   **D.** chemical reactions

15. Predict If an element were discovered that would fit at the bottom of the first column of the Periodic Table, what would its atomic number be? How many protons would be in its nucleus? Would it be a metal or a non-metal? Refer to the periodic table on E16–E17.

1	**H** Hydrogen
3	**Li** Lithium
11	**Na** Sodium
19	**K** Potassium
37	**Rb** Rubidium
55	**Cs** Cesium
87	**Fr** Francium
	?

16. Classify Examine the list below. Classify each item as representing either an element or a compound.

NaCl   Au   CaCO₃   C   Ni

Co   Ca(Mg)CO₃   SiO₂   HCO₃

Map the Concept

Fill in the flow chart with the following words. Begin with the smaller structures and work toward the larger. One word is used twice.

atom   electron   molecule
neutron   proton

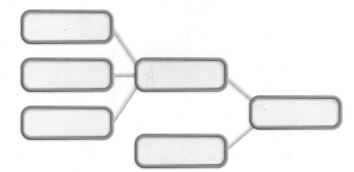

17. Apply Silicates are minerals that are composed mostly of the elements silicon and oxygen. Some silicates occur in sheet-like form and can be scratched with a fingernail. Others are blocky and so hard that they can scratch glass. How could you explain the differences in these minerals?

18. Analyze Two elements in the periodic table exist as liquids at room temperature. What are these elements? If they did occur as solids, would their placement in the Periodic Table be different?

19. Analyze Groundwater can become polluted with heavy metals, such as lead and mercury, and with many toxic compounds. Do you think the water molecules are polluted permanently? If not, how might the water become cleaner? Explain.

20. Evaluate Read the following statement: Water that is pumped from the ground is pure H_2O. Given what you've learned about water and its properties, why is this statement probably inaccurate?

Performance Assessment

Draw an Atom

Oxygen has atomic number 8. A typical oxygen atom has 8 neutrons. Draw a model of this atom. Show where the protons, electrons, and neutrons are found. Refer to the atomic model on page E8.

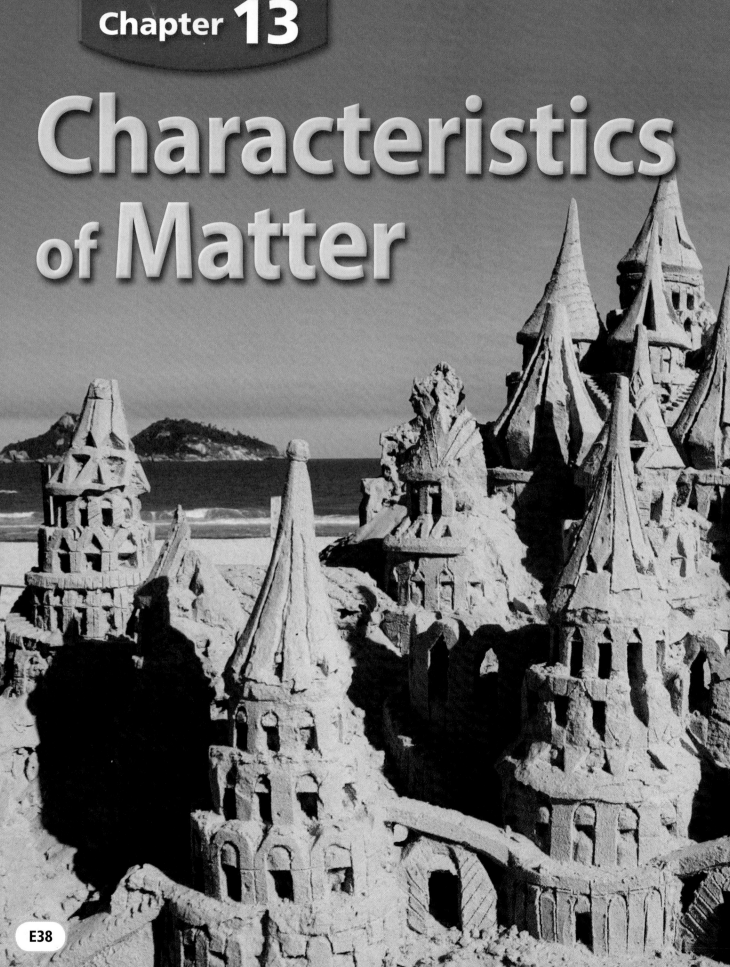

Chapter 13

Characteristics of Matter

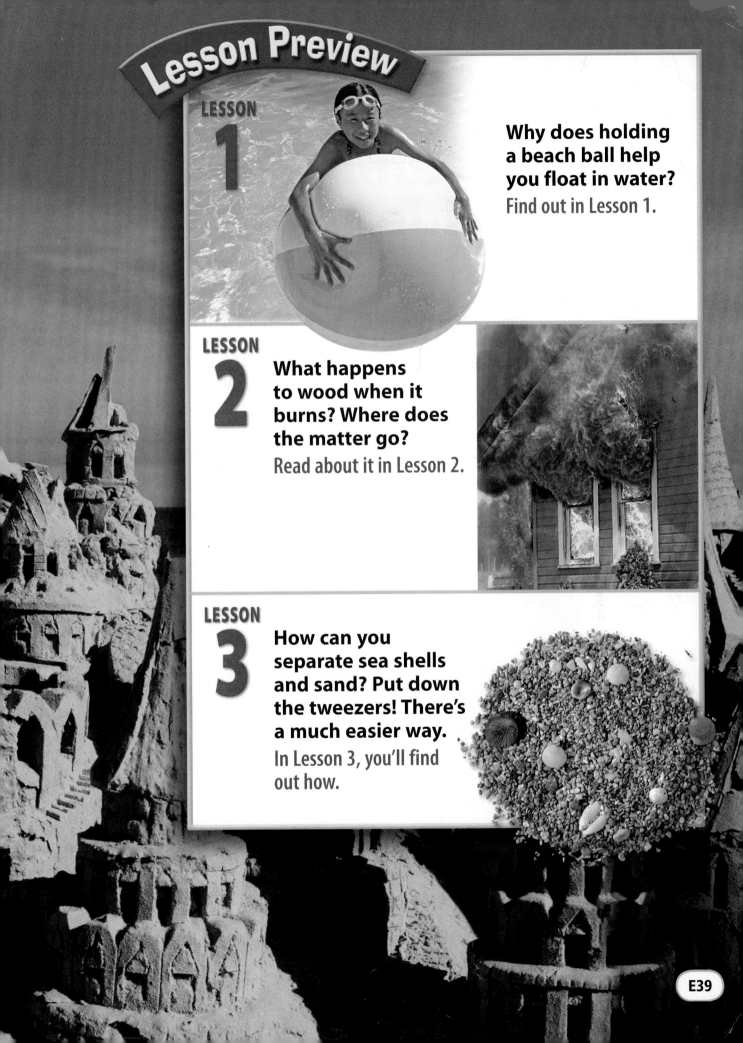

Lesson Preview

LESSON 1

Why does holding a beach ball help you float in water?

Find out in Lesson 1.

LESSON 2

What happens to wood when it burns? Where does the matter go?

Read about it in Lesson 2.

LESSON 3

How can you separate sea shells and sand? Put down the tweezers! There's a much easier way.

In Lesson 3, you'll find out how.

How Can Materials Be Identified?

Why It Matters...

Different materials each have their own unique physical and chemical properties. Different paints, for example, have different colors. The properties of a material determine ways it can be used. Discovering new properties of a material can lead to new uses and advances in technology.

PREPARE TO INVESTIGATE

Inquiry Skill

Use Numbers When you use numbers, you use numerical data, mathematical skills, and language to describe and compare objects and events.

Materials

- two 250-mL beakers
- vegetable oil
- water
- balance
- cardboard
- 2 books
- masking tape
- plastic wrap
- 2 droppers
- timer, or stopwatch

Science and Math Toolbox

For step 4, review **Measuring Elapsed Time** on page H14.

Oil and Water

Procedure

STEP 1

1 **Collaborate** Work with a partner. Using the balance, find the mass of an empty 250-mL beaker. Then add 100 mL of vegetable oil to the beaker. Find the mass of the beaker and oil. Subtract to find the mass of the oil. Record the results in your *Science Notebook*.

STEP 2

2 **Use Numbers** Repeat step 1 with the other beaker and 100 mL of water. Compare the masses of the two liquids. Then subtract to find the difference.

3 **Collaborate** Cover the cardboard with plastic wrap. Lean the piece of cardboard against a stack of books to make a ramp. Tape the ramp to the books. Place strips of tape near the top and bottom of the ramp. They are "start" and "finish" lines.

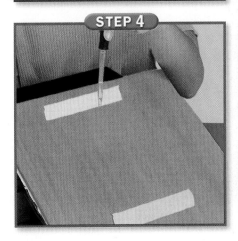
STEP 4

4 **Observe** One partner will start the timer while the other adds five drops of oil to the starting line. Time how long it takes for the oil to travel down the ramp. Record your observations. Repeat with water on the right side of the ramp.

5 **Observe** Pour the water into the oil and stir the mixture. Observe the mixture for about a minute. Record your observations.

Conclusion

1. **Use Numbers** Calculate the density (*D*) of oil by dividing its mass by its volume (*D = M/V*). Then calculate the density of water.

2. **Apply** What happens when two liquids of different densities are mixed together?

Investigate More!

Design an Experiment
Viscosity is a measure of how much a fluid resists flowing. Does a liquid's density affect its viscosity? Design an experiment to test your answer.

Properties

VOCABULARY

boiling point	p. E45
chemical property	p. E43
conductivity	p. E46
density	p. E44
melting point	p. E45
physical property	p. E43
solubility	p. E46

READING SKILL

Main Idea and Details
As you read, write down details that describe different physical properties of matter.

MAIN IDEA Physical and chemical properties are characteristics used to describe, identify, and classify matter.

Using Your Senses

Every object or material you can think of is some form of matter. And every sample of matter has properties that can be used to describe it. You can use your senses to observe certain properties. For example, you might describe an ice cube as cold, colorless, odorless, and cube-shaped. A puff of smoke from a wood fire might be gray and shapeless, with a distinct odor.

Properties can also be used to help identify pure substances—elements and compounds—and to tell one kind of matter from another. The chart on the next page compares some properties of water and glass.

You study, compare, and apply the properties of matter all the time! When you want to write a letter, you choose a piece of paper. Paper's properties are ideal for writing. When you want to play baseball, you choose a bat made of wood or metal, not paper. What other choices of matter do you make?

Water Bottle
The plastic is dark, lightweight, and flexible. Unlike glass, it won't break when you drop it. ▶

Shoes
Tough, sturdy, spikes dig into the ground. The shoe is softer inside, where the foot fits. ▼

Some Properties of Materials		
Property	**Water**	**Glass**
Color	colorless and clear	colorless and clear
State	liquid at room temperature	solid at room temperature
Melting point	0°C	greater than 1,000°C
Conductivity	conducts electricity	does not conduct electricity
Reactivity with sodium hydroxide	dissolves in sodium hydroxide to form ions	reacts with sodium hydroxide, which etches the glass

Two kinds of properties can be used to describe and classify matter—physical properties and chemical properties. Think about a sheet of paper and a sheet of aluminum foil. Both are thin, flat, and flexible, which are physical properties. Also note that paper will burn and aluminum will not. These are chemical properties.

A **physical property** can be measured or detected by the senses. Some physical properties include state, size, color, and odor. Many physical properties, such as length, volume, and mass, can be measured. In fact, matter is often defined as anything that has mass and volume.

A **chemical property** is the ability or tendency of a material to change its chemical makeup. Materials are made of smaller particles—atoms and molecules. When the arrangement of atoms or molecules changes, a new material is formed. The new material has a different identity and different properties from the original material.

You can discover a material's chemical properties by observing how it changes under different conditions. For example, when a piece of paper is held in a flame, the paper will burn. Burning is a chemical change in which matter combines with oxygen. Burning paper produces new matter that is very different from the paper and the oxygen.

▶ **MAIN IDEA** Compare the properties of two examples of matter.

Basketball
Air inside the basketball keeps it round and bouncy. Compare its size and shape to the baseball. ▶

Glove and Baseball
A glove is shaped like the hand that fits inside it. It is ideal for catching the hard, tough baseball. ▼

Mass, Volume, and Density

Mass is a measure of the amount of matter in an object or a material. It can be measured in grams (g) or kilograms (kg). A large object contains more matter than a smaller object made of the same material. So, the larger sample has a greater mass.

Volume is the amount of space a sample of matter takes up. The volume of a solid can be measured in cubic centimeters (cm^3). Liquid volumes are measured in liters (L) or milliliters (mL). One cubic centimeter is equal to one milliliter.

You can find the volume of a rectangular solid by multiplying its length, width, and height. To find the volume of an odd-shaped solid, sink it in water in a graduated cylinder. The object's volume equals the increase in the water level.

The **density** of a material is its mass per unit volume. To find the density of a sample, measure its mass and its volume, then divide. For example, a 10-mL sample with a mass of 13 g has a density of 1.3 grams per milliliter (g/mL).

All samples of a pure substance kept under the same conditions have the same density. A drop of pure water and a tub-load of pure water both have density of 1 g/mL. This is the density of pure water in the liquid state. Liquids with other densities are not pure water.

Remember that density is not the same as mass. For example, lead is much denser than aluminum. If a block of lead and a block of aluminum each have a mass of 10 g, what can you conclude about them?

Some Physical Properties

Volume
To find the volume of a solid that does not float in water, measure the volume of water that it displaces.

Mass
The mass of an object can be measured with a balance or with a scale.

Density
A bottle filled with plastic foam will float, because foam is less dense than water. A bottle filled with sand will sink, because sand is denser than water.

Boiling Point
The boiling point of water is 100°C.

Melting Point
The melting point of water is 0°C.

Melting and Boiling Points

Another physical property is state of matter. The three familiar states are solid, liquid, and gas.

Solids are rigid. They have a definite shape and volume. Liquids can flow. They take on the shape of their container, but keep the same volume. Gases have no definite shape or volume. They can expand or contract to fill any container. They typically are much less dense than solids and liquids.

When enough energy is added to a solid, it melts to form a liquid. The temperature at which a solid substance changes to a liquid is called its **melting point.** When enough energy is removed from a liquid, it freezes to form a solid. The freezing point and the melting point for a given substance are the same.

Like density, the melting point is the same for all samples of any given substance. So, this property can be used to identify different substances. For example, the melting point of water is 0°C (32°F). The melting point of gold is about 1,060°C (1,940°F).

When enough energy is added to a liquid, it changes into a gas. The temperature at which this happens is called the **boiling point.**

Boiling point can also be used to identify a substance. For example, both water and rubbing alcohol are colorless liquids. The boiling point of water is 100°C (212°F), while the boiling point of rubbing alcohol is 108°C (226°F).

 **When will a substance change state?**

E45

Solubility and Conductivity

Stir sugar in water, and you can observe the sugar dissolve in the water, that is, mix evenly with it. The mixture that results is called a solution. You will learn more about solutions later in this chapter.

The measure of how much of one substance can dissolve in another is called **solubility.** Solubility is another physical property of matter. Some substances, like salt and sugar, are very soluble in water. Other substances, like oil and sand, are not. And while salt is soluble in water, it is not soluble in alcohol. You could use this property to tell the difference between samples of salt and sugar.

Another physical property of matter is conductivity. The **conductivity** of a material is its ability to carry energy. Electrical conductivity refers to carrying electricity. Thermal conductivity refers to carrying heat.

Most metals are good conductors of both electricity and heat. For example, copper is used both in cookware and in electrical wires.

Materials that have a low conductivity, such as rubber and plastic, are used to insulate conductors. In an electric cord, insulation around a metal wire prevents both electricity and heat from escaping.

You should never use a current-carrying electrical cord that has frayed insulation. You might get an electrical shock, or heat from the cord could start a fire!

▶ **MAIN IDEA** Describe the solubility of sugar in water.

Solubility

▲ Oil and sand will not dissolve in water, so they form separate layers when mixed with water.

▲ Powdered drink mix will dissolve in water, so the two form a colored solution when mixed.

wire

insulation

◀ Metal wires have a higher electrical conductivity than plastic insulation.

Visual Summary

A physical property is a characteristic that can be measured or detected by the senses.

To find the volume of an object with an irregular shape, sink it in water.

Melting point is the temperature at which a solid changes to a liquid. Boiling point is the temperature at which a liquid changes to a gas.

LINKS for Home and School

MATH Calculate Volume A gold nugget has a mass of 380 g. The density of gold is 19 g/cm³. Calculate the volume of the nugget by using the formula: Density = Mass/Volume

ART Make a Color Wheel Many paints get their color from simple materials. For example, zinc and titanium are used as pigments in white paints. Research the pigments used in acrylic or oil paints. Make a color wheel. Indicate which material is traditionally used to produce each of the colors on the wheel.

Review

1 MAIN IDEA How are physical and chemical properties of matter useful?

2 VOCABULARY How is the density of a substance related to its mass and its volume?

3 READING SKILL: Main Idea and Details What can you conclude about two liquid samples that have different boiling points?

4 CRITICAL THINKING: Apply Don't swim outdoors during a thunderstorm! A lightning strike could send an electric charge through the water to your body. Which physical property of water explains this safety tip?

5 INQUIRY SKILL: Use Numbers What is the volume, in milliliters, of a rectangular solid that has a length of 3 cm, a width of 2 cm, and a height of 2 cm?

 TEST PREP

Which of the following is not a physical property of matter?

A. conductivity

B. density

C. reactivity

D. solubility

 Technology

Visit **www.eduplace.com/scp/** to find out more about using properties to identify substances.

Submarines

Today's submarines range from tiny, one-man crafts to huge ships powered by nuclear reactors. Yet all use the same basic principles to control their depth in water. An object sinks or floats because of its density, which is the ratio of mass to volume. Most submarines change their mass by pumping water out or letting water inside. Adding or subtracting mass changes the density, causing the ship to dive or rise.

waterline

Will it float?
Both pieces of aluminum foil have the same mass. But the piece shaped into a boat is filled with air, which is much less dense than water. So, the boat floats!

Cabin Like a space capsule, the sub's cabin is sealed from the outside. Oxygen can be supplied by pressurized tanks or by certain chemical reactions. Carbon dioxide is removed by devices called scrubbers.

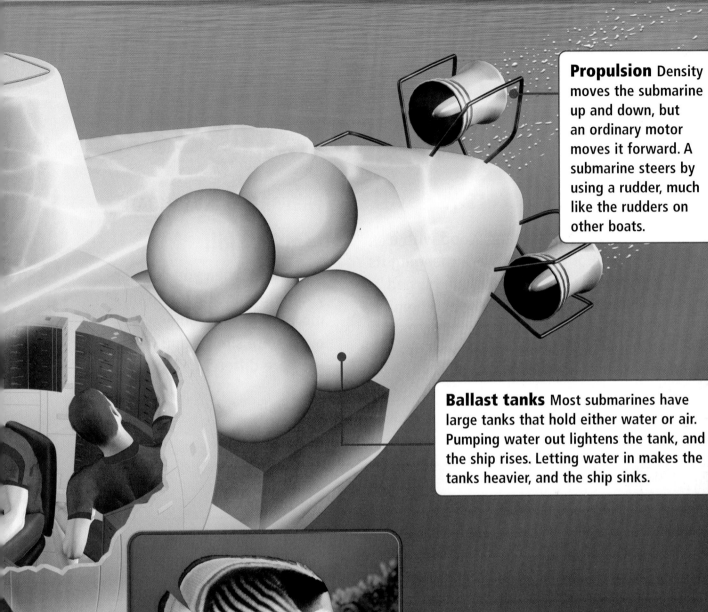

Propulsion Density moves the submarine up and down, but an ordinary motor moves it forward. A submarine steers by using a rudder, much like the rudders on other boats.

Ballast tanks Most submarines have large tanks that hold either water or air. Pumping water out lightens the tank, and the ship rises. Letting water in makes the tanks heavier, and the ship sinks.

How do fish rise and sink?

Most fish change their density by using an organ called a swim bladder. When the fish wants to move up or down, its swim bladder either fills with gas or releases it.

Sharing Ideas

1. **READING CHECK** How does a submarine rise and sink in the water?

2. **WRITE ABOUT IT** How does a swim bladder compare to ballast tanks?

3. **TALK ABOUT IT** What challenges face the crew of a submarine during a long journey?

How Does Matter Change?

Why It Matters...

When you shape wood with a plane or a saw, you are changing its physical properties. If you burned the wood, that would be a chemical change. You use physical and chemical changes every day to make matter more useful.

Inquiry Skill

Compare When you compare, you determine how two or more organisms, objects, or events are similar and how they are different.

Materials
- goggles
- two jars
- skim milk
- vinegar

Science and Math Toolbox

For step 2, review **Measuring Volume** on page H7.

Milk and Vinegar

Procedure

Safety: Wear goggles during this investigation.

1. **Collaborate** Work with a partner. In your *Science Notebook*, create a chart like the one shown. Make the chart large enough for you to include written observations.

2. **Observe** Pour 100 mL of milk into one jar and 100 mL of vinegar into the other jar. Study the properties of each liquid. Record your observations.

3. **Observe** Tightly cover the jar of milk, shake it vigorously, and set it on your work surface. Observe how the milk returns along the sides to the bottom of the jar. Record your observations.

4. **Record Data** Repeat step 3 with the jar of vinegar.

5. **Experiment** Uncover the jars and carefully pour a small amount of vinegar into the milk. Observe the interaction of the two liquids. Record your observations.

6. **Experiment** Pour the rest of the vinegar into the milk. Stir the mixture and allow it to settle. Record your observations.

Conclusion

1. **Compare** Compare and contrast the properties of milk and vinegar.

2. **Hypothesize** What happened when the milk and vinegar were mixed? Form a hypothesis that answers this question.

STEP 1

	Milk	Vinegar
Properties		
Behavior after shaking		

STEP 2

STEP 3

Investigate More!

Design an Experiment Try the experiment with different substances, such as lemon juice, baking soda, water, and salt. Compare the result with those obtained when vinegar is mixed with milk.

► **VOCABULARY**

chemical change   p. E53
chemical reaction   p. E53
physical change   p. E52

► **READING SKILL**

Classify Use a chart to show characteristics of physical and chemical changes.

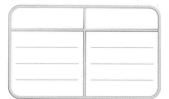

Physical and Chemical Changes

MAIN IDEA A chemical change involves a change in the identity of the matter, whereas a physical change does not.

Physical Changes

If you have ever sawed a board or sharpened a pencil, you have observed a physical change in matter. The sawdust on the floor and the shavings in the sharpener look different from the board and the pencil. But the chemical makeup of these materials hasn't changed at all.

A **physical change** is a change in the size, shape, or state of matter with no new matter being formed. In the case of the board and the pencil, only the size of the samples has been changed. The chemical properties of the sawdust and the shavings are the same as the chemical properties of the objects from which they came.

cutting

sanding

drilling

The students are changing the shape of wood in different ways. Each change is a physical change.

Chemical Changes

A **chemical change** is a change in matter that results in new substances being formed. What causes a chemical change? In any sample of matter, forces called chemical bonds hold the atoms or molecules together. Chemical changes involve breaking these bonds and forming new bonds. This creates new substances with new chemical properties.

A **chemical reaction** is a specific example of one or more chemical changes. All chemical changes occur as a result of chemical reactions. Burning wood is one example of a chemical change. Wood contains cellulose, which is made up of carbon, hydrogen, and oxygen. When wood burns, the atoms of carbon and hydrogen in the wood combine with molecules of oxygen in the air. A chemical change forms carbon dioxide gas, water, and ashes.

Chemical changes take place all around you every day. How can you recognize them? A change in color sometimes indicates a chemical change. For example, the outer shell of the Statue of Liberty is made of copper, which is a bright, shiny metal. As it was exposed to the weather, chemical changes caused

▲ Burning wood is an example of a chemical change.

the copper to change color, first to brown, then to black, and later to the greenish color it is today.

Other chemical changes give off energy in the form of heat or light. Whenever you ignite wood in a campfire, natural gas on the stove, or the wick of a candle, you are setting in motion a chemical change that gives off energy.

▶ **CLASSIFY** Crumpling a sheet of paper involves what kind of change?

When you twist a glow stick, you start a chemical change that produces a glowing light. ▶

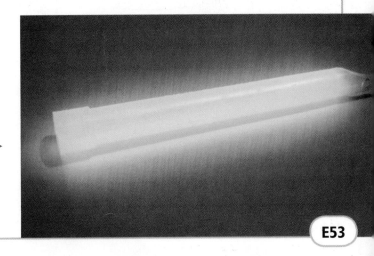

Classifying Changes

When matter changes its appearance, does that mean it has undergone a chemical change? Not necessarily. For example, a block of ice looks very different from a puddle of liquid water. But a change of state is a physical change.

Each molecule that makes up ice is made up of two hydrogen atoms and one oxygen atom. When ice melts to form water, the atoms in the molecules do not change. Instead, they break apart from one another and begin to move more freely.

When liquid water evaporates the water molecules speed up and move farther apart. Their motion has changed, but the particles are still the same as before.

Dissolving is another example of a physical change. When sugar dissolves in water, sugar molecules move apart and spread to all parts of the solution. The molecules that make up sugar and water are the same before and after the sugar dissolves. Only their motion and arrangement change, not their identity.

Natural salt is harvested from seawater through evaporation, which separates the parts of the solution. ▼

Solutions

Salt dissolves in water.

The salt seems to disappear. What kind of change has occurred?

When the water evaporates, the salt remains. Evaporation and dissolving are physical changes.

batter

muffin

Chemical Change
When you bake muffin batter, you are causing a chemical change in the ingredients.

Other examples of physical changes include cutting, tearing, and changes of position. Think of a raindrop forming in a cloud, falling to Earth, mixing in a river or lake, then evaporating into the air. All of these changes are physical changes. The substance is always water.

Recall that a chemical change creates new substances with new chemical properties. Such changes can take place slowly or quickly, loudly or quietly, or at very hot or cold temperatures.

An example of a slow chemical change is the rusting of iron. This happens when iron is exposed to moist air. The iron combines with oxygen from the air to form iron oxide, or rust. Rust is quite different from either iron or oxygen.

Other chemical reactions take place more quickly. For example, when you heat muffin batter, it undergoes chemical reactions that change it into muffins. The identities and properties of the substances are different before and after the baking.

Do you think you can change the speed that chemical changes take place? The answer is yes! For example, adding salt to iron will speed up rusting. This is why iron objects near the ocean often rust more quickly than those on land.

Raising the temperature is another way to speed up many chemical reactions, or even to change their products. Other reactions speed up in the presence of a catalyst. A catalyst is not changed during a reaction. It only increases the rate of the reaction.

Did you know that living things use chemical changes? Plants grow by using the energy of sunlight to produce food from carbon dioxide and water. By repeating this reaction over and over again, a small acorn can grow into a tall oak tree!

You use chemical reactions to digest food. The reaction between broken-down food and oxygen releases the energy your body uses.

▶ **CLASSIFY** How is a chemical change different from a physical change?

oxygen

cellulose

water vapor   carbon dioxide

Original Materials

Wood is mostly cellulose. When heated, it will react with oxygen in the air.

Chemical Change

Cellulose and oxygen combine to form two gases: carbon dioxide and water vapor. The flames are hot glowing gases.

New Materials

Most of the wood has been changed into gases. Some carbon remains in ashes.

Conservation of Matter

Regardless of the kind of change taking place in a sample of matter, the amount of matter stays the same. When matter changes, mass is always conserved, meaning that it is neither created nor destroyed.

In a chemical change, this means that the mass of the materials before a chemical change is equal to the mass afterwards. This is true even if you cannot see the materials that form, such as when a gas is produced.

Matter is also conserved in all physical changes. When you place water in the freezer, it undergoes a physical change. The water freezes and becomes ice.

As you may know, the volume of water increases when it freezes. But that does not mean that matter was created. Instead, the arrangement of the water molecules takes up more space in ice than in water.

You can use a scale to prove that mass is conserved when matter changes. For example, fruit changes chemically when it either ripens or decays. Tissues change, new materials form, and gases are released. By covering the fruit and placing it on a scale, you can observe that the mass stays the same even as the fruit changes. Try it!

Sometimes the conservation of mass is hard to see. For example, when a log burns in the fireplace, only a few ashes remain. The pictures and captions at the top of the page describe what happens when wood burns.

What if you could measure the mass of the logs and the oxygen? You would discover that their combined masses equal the total mass of the ashes and gases produced.

▶ **CLASSIFY**   **What kind of change does not involve the production of new substances?**

Lesson Wrap-Up

Visual Summary

A physical change does not involve a change in the identity of the matter undergoing change.

A chemical change involves a change in the identity and properties of the matter undergoing change.

Matter is neither created nor destroyed during chemical and physical changes.

LINKS for Home and School

MATH **Make a Line Graph** When yeast is added to a solution of sugar and water, some of the sugar is changed to ethanol. This process is called fermentation. Create a line graph that shows the following production rate of ethanol.

Time (hr)	1	2	3	4	5	6
Ethanol produced	1 unit	2 units	3 units	3 units	2 units	1 unit

TECHNOLOGY **Make a Display**
Research the process used to desalinate, or remove salt from, water. Find or draw pictures for each step in the process. Make a visual display or illustrated flow chart that explains the process.

Review

1 MAIN IDEA What happens to substances during a chemical change?

2 VOCABULARY What is a physical change? Give an example of a physical change.

3 READING SKILL: Compare and Contrast How do the particles that make up matter compare during physical and chemical changes?

4 CRITICAL THINKING: Infer When an electric current is passed through a sample of water, bubbles of gas form. Some of this gas will burn when lit. What can you infer about the type of change taking place?

5 INQUIRY SKILL: Compare Ice and liquid water are very different, yet they are made of the same molecules. Compare their physical and chemical properties.

TEST PREP
When vinegar is added to baking soda, bubbles of carbon dioxide gas form. This is a _____

A. change of state.

B. change of mass.

C. chemical change.

D. physical change.

Technology
Visit **www.eduplace.com/scp/** to find out more about changes in matter.

E57

What Are Solutions and Mixtures?

Why It Matters...

Mixtures are *everywhere*! Most rocks and the waters of Earth's oceans are mixtures. So are many foods. Knowing what ingredients to use in a mixture, from paint to trail mix, can make the difference between success and failure.

Inquiry Skill

Predict When you predict, you use observations, patterns, data, or cause-and-effect relationships to anticipate results.

Materials

- goggles
- two 250-mL beakers
- water
- teaspoon
- sand
- salt

Science and Math Toolbox

For step 1, review **Measuring Volume** on page H7.

Sand, Salt, Solutions

Procedure

Safety: Wear goggles as you perform this procedure.

STEP 1

1. **Collaborate** Work with a partner. Pour 250 mL of water into each beaker.

2. **Observe** Add two teaspoons of sand to one beaker and two teaspoons of salt to the other beaker. Observe what happens to the sand and to the salt. Record your observations in your *Science Notebook*.

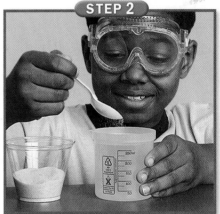
STEP 2

3. **Experiment** Use the spoon to stir the mixture of sand and water for about 15 seconds. Stop stirring and observe the mixture. Record your observations. Allow the mixture to sit quietly for several minutes. Again, observe the mixture and record your observations.

4. **Predict** Predict what will happen to the mixture of salt and water if it is stirred. Record your prediction. Then repeat step 3 with the mixture of salt and water.

STEP 3

5. **Compare** Record any similarities and differences in the two mixtures after stirring and after sitting still.

Conclusion

1. **Infer** Which material formed a solution when mixed with water? How did you reach this conclusion?

2. **Predict** What would happen if you used sugar instead of sand?

Investigate More!

Design an Experiment
Select a number of different materials to mix with water. Compare your results with those you obtained with sand and salt.

VOCABULARY

mixture	p. E60
solute	p. E62
solution	p. E62
solvent	p. E62

READING SKILL

Compare and Contrast
Use the information in this lesson to compare and contrast mixtures and solutions.

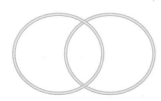

A salad is a mixture. You can see that the different parts that make up the mixture have different properties. ▼

Mixtures and Solutions

MAIN IDEA Some mixtures are uniform, meaning they are evenly mixed. Other mixtures have different amounts of materials in different places. Mixtures that are evenly mixed at the molecular level are called solutions.

Types of Mixtures

A fresh vegetable salad can be a perfect part of a healthy and tasty meal. Each type of vegetable adds to the flavor of the salad. Yet by eating different parts of the salad, you could taste each vegetable individually. That's because a salad is a mixture. A **mixture** is a physical combination of two or more substances. The substances in a mixture are not chemically combined as they are in a compound. So, a mixture is not a pure substance.

Mixtures may be classified as heterogeneous or homogeneous. In a heterogeneous mixture, like a salad, the materials that make up the mixture are distributed unevenly. Individual pieces are present in some parts and not others. A homogeneous mixture is uniform throughout. A sample taken from one part of this kind of mixture will be identical to a sample taken from any other part.

Lettuce
+ Cucumber
+ Tomato
+ Pepper
+ Other ingredients

= MIXTURE

To separate a mixture, take advantage of the physical properties of the different parts. What properties of matter are being used to separate mixtures in these two examples?

sand and pebbles

corks and marbles

Separating a Mixture

In a mixture, each substance keeps its original properties. If you separated all of the parts of a salad, the tomatoes would still be tomatoes and the lettuce would still be lettuce.

Mixtures can be separated according to different properties. Think about a mixture of corks and marbles. You could spend hours picking out the cork pieces. However, because cork floats in water, you can separate the mixture by putting it in water and skimming off the floating corks.

Now think about a mixture of sand and seashells. It would take a long time to pick out the shells. Both parts of the mixture sink in water, so adding water does not separate them. But note the different sizes of the pieces. You could use a sieve or a strainer to separate them.

Mixture or Compound?

Mixtures can have variable composition. This means that two similar mixtures may be made up of the same materials, but in different amounts. Two salads might both be made of lettuce, carrots, olives, and tomatoes. Although they have the same ingredients, one may have more carrots and less tomato than the other.

Compounds, however, always have the same composition. Every molecule of water has one oxygen atom and two hydrogen atoms that are chemically combined. The compound's chemical formula describes its composition. Because a mixture does not have a definite composition, it cannot be represented by a chemical formula.

▶ **COMPARE AND CONTRAST** Compare mixtures and compounds.

Solutions

A **solution** is a homogeneous mixture, meaning two or more substances that are evenly distributed. The materials that make up a solution mix together at the atomic or molecular level.

You make a solution when you make pink lemonade from a powdered mix. The particles that mix in the water are molecules of sugar, dye, and flavoring.

In any solution, the substance being dissolved is called the **solute.** The substance that dissolves the solute is called the **solvent.** In a solution of water and sugar, water is the solvent and sugar is the solute.

Even though you can't see the different parts of a sugar-water solution, it is still a mixture. The properties of the substances that make up the mixture are the same as they were before they were mixed together. The sugar still tastes sweet. The water is still a liquid and still allows light to pass through.

Many solutions, such as lemonade and saltwater, have a liquid solvent and a solid solute. However, solutions can have other combinations. Soda water is a solution made of carbon dioxide gas dissolved in water. Air is a solution of several different gases. Brass is a solution of two solids—zinc and copper.

Particles in a solution spread evenly throughout the solution because they mix at the atomic or

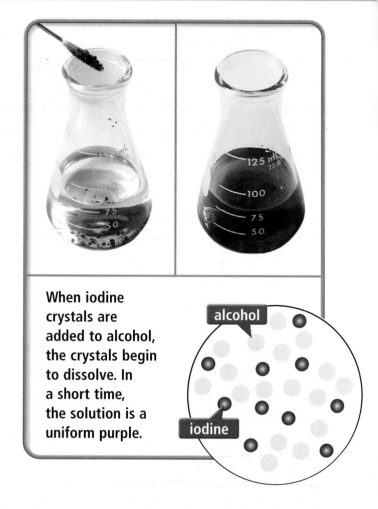

When iodine crystals are added to alcohol, the crystals begin to dissolve. In a short time, the solution is a uniform purple.

molecular level. Think about the solution of iodine and alcohol shown above. Each molecule of iodine has two atoms of the element iodine and is represented by the chemical formula I_2. Each molecule of alcohol has atoms of carbon, hydrogen, and oxygen and is represented by the chemical formula C_3H_8O.

When the two substances are mixed, the iodine dissolves in the alcohol. The particles of iodine spread throughout the mixture. If you could highly magnify a section of the solution, you would see that molecules of the two substances have become evenly mixed.

Separating a Solution

To separate a solution, you must make use of the different properties of the mixed materials. You usually cannot use the size of the particles to separate them, because only very special filters are fine enough to trap a molecule.

There are other properties you can use, however. For example, some liquids evaporate at fairly low temperatures. You often can allow a liquid solvent to evaporate, leaving the solute behind.

This happens when a sample of saltwater is left in the air over a couple of days. The water slowly evaporates, leaving behind crystals of salt.

A simple way to separate most solutions is to use the different boiling points or melting points of the substances. Sugar is collected in this way. Growers cut down the sugar cane stems and crush them. Then the sugar cane juice is collected and heated. The water boils off at 100°C (212°F), while solid sugar remains behind.

▶ **COMPARE AND CONTRAST** Describe how you could separate a mixture of sugar and water.

Sugar comes from the juice of sugar cane like that being harvested in the photo below. ▼

First, the cane is prepared for juicing.

Sugar cane juice contains a solution of sugar and water.

Water is removed from the juice and solid sugar is recovered.

E63

Alloys

Mixtures of two or more metals are called alloys. Alloys may also be mixtures of a metal and another solid. Alloys often have combinations of the properties of the materials that form them.

Bronze, for example, is an alloy of copper and tin, and combines the best properties of both. Bronze is a durable alloy and it is malleable, meaning it is easy to hammer into thin sheets. The sheets can then be formed into different shapes. Because of its useful properties, bronze has been used for centuries in tools, weapons, and sculptures.

The amounts of each material in an alloy can affect its properties. Steel is an alloy of iron, carbon, and sometimes other solids. Softer steels, made with less carbon, are used to make nails and chains. Harder steels, made with more carbon, are used to make tools and support beams.

There are many kinds of alloys with different uses. Brass is an alloy of copper and zinc, and is used to make many musical instruments. Sterling silver, an alloy of silver and copper, is used to make jewelry.

▶ **COMPARE AND CONTRAST** How do the properties of alloys compare to the properties of the materials used to form them?

The "skin" of a typical airplane is an alloy of aluminum, titanium, and other metals. ▶

Copper
+ Zinc
─────
= Brass

◀ **Brass**
Many musical instruments are made of alloys.

Visual Summary

In many mixtures, the different materials are not uniformly mixed.

Mixtures in which the particles are evenly mixed at the atomic or molecular level are called solutions.

You can use the physical properties of different parts of a mixture to separate them.

Alloys are solutions of two or more metals or of a metal and another solid.

LINKS for Home and School

MATH Make a Pie Chart Suppose a solution is made up of 10 parts water, 3 parts salt, and 2 parts sugar. Create a pie chart that shows the percentages of each material in the solution.

WRITING Expository Research the Bronze Age. Find out how the development of this important alloy changed the people who first created it. Write a report describing what you learned.

Review

❶ **MAIN IDEA** How are solutions different from other mixtures?

❷ **VOCABULARY** How do solutes differ from solvents? Include a specific solution in your answer.

❸ **READING SKILL: Draw Conclusions** A mixture is made up of evenly spaced atoms of copper and silver. Is the mixture a solution? Explain your answer.

❹ **CRITICAL THINKING: Apply** Mia makes a delicious soup broth. She wants to separate the solid ingredients from the broth. What method could she use?

❺ **INQUIRY SKILL: Predict** A student has jars containing different amounts of water. She adds salt to each jar until no more salt will dissolve. She makes the chart below. Predict how much salt will dissolve in 100 mL of water.

Water	25 mL	50 mL	75 mL	100 mL
Salt	9 g	18 g	27 g	?

 TEST PREP Which of the following is a type of alloy?

A. salt water

B. gold

C. iodine

D. bronze

 Technology Visit **www.eduplace.com/scp/** to find out more about solutions.

Colossal Crystals

Crystals the size of trees? Most mineral crystals are small enough to hold in your hand. These mammoth gypsum crystals found in caves in the Naica Mountains of Mexico can reach 50 feet! They are the largest known crystals on Earth.

How did these giant crystals form? Geologists think molten rock below the Naica Mountains pushed super-hot, mineral-filled water into the mountains' limestone. This hot water acted as a powerful solvent that dissolved the limestone and created a huge cavern. The cavern later filled with a hot, mineral-rich solution containing a kind of salt called gypsum, or calcium sulfate.

The heat, pressure, and very high concentration of minerals in the solution were ideal for enormous gypsum crystals to form. Eventually, the mineral solution drained away, leaving behind the giant crystals we see today.

Miniature Crystal Cave
The small crystals in this hand-sized geode were formed in much the same way as the colossal Naica cave crystals. A small rock cavity filled with mineral-rich water and crystals formed inside.

Vocabulary

Complete each sentence with a term from the list.

1. The _____ of a material is its ability to carry an electric charge.

2. The ability or tendency of a material to change its chemical make up is a _____.

3. The material that is being dissolved in a solution is the _____.

4. A _____ does not change the identity of the material undergoing the change.

5. A _____ is a homogenous mixture.

6. The _____ of a substance is the temperature at which the liquid form of the substance changes to a gas.

7. The _____ of a substance is the mass per unit volume.

8. A change that results in one or more new substances being formed is a _____.

9. A solute dissolves in a _____.

10. _____ is the ability of a material to go into solution.

boiling point E45
chemical change E53
chemical property E43
conductivity E46
density E44
melting point E45
physical change E52
physical property E43
solubility E46
solute E62
solution E62
solvent E62

✓ Test Prep

Write the letter of the best answer choice.

11. A characteristic of a material that can be observed with the senses is _____ .

   A. its composition
   B. a reaction time
   C. a physical property
   D. its density

12. The _____ of a material is the temperature at which it changes from a solid to a liquid.

   A. solubility
   B. melting point
   C. boiling point
   D. critical temperature

13. Which of the following involves a change in the identity of the matter undergoing change?

   A. melting   **C.** freezing
   B. boiling   **D.** burning

14. Which of the following is a mixture in which the particles are evenly mixed at the molecular level?

   A. ice cream
   B. sand and iron filings
   C. brass
   D. carbon

15. **Classify** A mixture of iodine and alcohol sits in an open beaker. Over time, purple iodine crystals form on the beaker's sides. Did they form from physical or chemical changes? Explain.

16. **Infer** Your teacher placed two different materials in each of three beakers. The materials are baking soda, vinegar, and water. Use the observations to complete the chart.

Beaker	Materials	Observations	Physical or Chemical Change?
A		evaporation leaves white powder	
B		bubbles of gas form in liquid	
C		evaporation leaves empty beaker	

The concept map below shows how changes and properties of matter can be classified. Use the terms below to complete the concept map.

boiling point   melting point
chemical change   physical change
chemical property   physical property
conductivity   solubility
density

17. **Analyze** Lava lamps contain two different liquids. As one of the liquids is heated at the base of the lamp, its density changes and it rises to the top. At the top, the liquid cools, its density changes again, and it starts to sink. Describe the density changes.

18. **Synthesis** How could you learn whether or not a material conducted electricity? Describe a procedure you could follow.

19. **Apply** Saturated fats are generally solid at room temperature. Unsaturated fats are generally liquid (oil) at room temperature. In general, which kind of fat has a higher melting point? Explain your answer.

20. **Synthesis** Milk is a mixture made up of tiny droplets of fat suspended in a liquid. The different parts of the mixture can be viewed under a microscope. Your friend states that milk is a solution. Do you agree? Explain.

Separating a Mixture

You are given a mixture of sugar, sand, and sawdust. Design a method for separating out each part of the mixture.

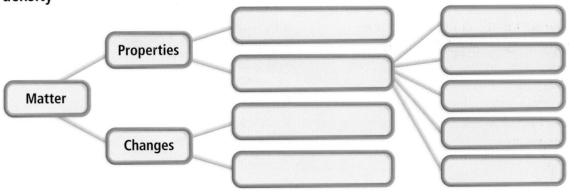

Chapter 14

Changes of State

Lesson Preview

LESSON 1

In even the largest icebergs, about 10 percent of the mass is above water. Why are ice and liquid water so different?

Read about it in Lesson 1.

LESSON 2

Why do ice pops melt when you take them out of the freezer?

Read about it in Lesson 2.

What Are Three States of Matter?

Why It Matters...

Steel is a uniform mixture of solids, mostly iron and carbon. These solids have been heated until they melt. Under the right conditions, most matter can be made to change from one state, or form, to another.

PREPARE TO INVESTIGATE

Inquiry Skill

Experiment Scientists may perform experiments to test the properties of different states of matter.

Materials

- plastic bottle
- water
- graduated cylinder
- marbles
- balance
- plastic cups

Science and Math Toolbox

For steps 3 and 4, review **Measuring Volume** on page H7.

Vanishing Volume

Procedure

STEP 1

1. **Measure** To find the volume of a bottle, fill it with water. Then pour the water into a graduated cylinder. Record the volume in your *Science Notebook*.

2. **Compare** Fill the same bottle with marbles. Compare the way marbles fill the bottle to the way the water filled it.

STEP 2

3. **Infer** What other material is in the jar besides the marbles? (Hint: The same material is all around you.)

4. **Experiment** Design a procedure to find the total volume of the open space surrounding the marbles in the bottle. Choose from the following materials: graduated cylinder, balance, water, and plastic cups. With your teacher's approval, carry out your experiment.

STEP 4

Conclusion

1. **Use Numbers** What was the total volume of the marbles in the bottle? Use the results of your experiment to calculate the answer.

2. **Hypothesize** What property allows gases and liquids to fill the spaces between solid objects?

3. **Predict** How would this investigation be different if cubes were used to fill the bottle instead of marbles?

Investigate More!

Design an Experiment
How much open space is in a plastic bottle filled with beads? Or with coarse gravel, or sand? Adapt your procedure to find and compare the answers.

States of Matter

VOCABULARY

gas	p. E78
liquid	p. E77
solid	p. E76
state of matter	p. E74

READING SKILL

Text Structure As you read, use the text headings to make an outline of the lesson.

MAIN IDEA Matter can exist in three familiar states: solids, liquids, and gases. These states are determined by the motion and arrangement of particles.

Solids, Liquids, and Gases

Picture yourself as the captain of a large fishing boat. Your crew has just finished a fishing voyage along the coast of Alaska. As you look at the icy coastline, you realize you are ready to head home to warmer temperatures. Suddenly, you hear a loud cracking and then a huge splash. You watch as a large section of ice from a giant glacier breaks off and falls into the sea.

This scene describes two states of matter interacting on a very large scale! A **state of matter** is the physical form that matter takes. Three familiar states of matter are solids, liquids, and gases.

Ice is an example of matter in the solid state. Ice is the solid form of water. The ocean water is in the liquid state. The air above the water is a mixture of invisible gases. One of these gases is water vapor. Water vapor is water in the gas state.

States of Matter
Water can exist as a solid, liquid, or gas. In each state, the particles of matter are arranged in predictable ways. ▶

Solids
In solids, particles are held together very closely. They vibrate in place.

Particles and States of Matter

You have learned that all matter is made up of atoms and molecules. These particles are always in motion.

The state of any sample of matter depends on the movement and spacing of its particles. In solids, particles vibrate back and forth, but do not move about.

For most substances, particles are most closely packed in the solid state. Water is an exception to this rule. Water molecules are slightly farther apart in solid ice than they are in liquid water. However, the molecules in ice still do not move about freely.

In liquids, the particles are also quite close together, but they have a little space in which to move around. Unlike particles in solids, particles in liquids can slip past one another.

Because of this, the arrangement of particles in liquids is disorderly and always changing.

In gases, the particles are spread very far apart compared to liquids and solids. Their arrangement is completely random, and they fill the space of their containers. They are constantly bouncing off one another and the sides of their containers.

Some substances, like water, can commonly be found in any of the three states. Others, like iron and helium, are found in only one state in nature. The properties of a substance's particles determines its state.

▶ **TEXT STRUCTURE** Compare the arrangement of particles in a solid, a liquid, and a gas.

Liquids
In the liquid state, water particles can slip past each other and move about.

Gases
The particles in gases are spread very far apart. They are constantly moving and bouncing off one another. Water forms an invisible gas called water vapor.

Solids

A **solid** is a form of matter that has a definite shape and volume. The way that particles in solids are arranged and the way that they vibrate in place give solids certain properties. One property is that solids keep their shapes. If you move a solid, or place it into a container, its shape will stay the same.

Wood is a solid. A block of wood will keep its shape wherever you put it—on a countertop, in a rectangular cardboard box, or in a circular cake tin. This property is usually described as having definite shape, meaning the shape of a solid doesn't change.

The closeness of the particles in a solid and small forces of attraction between them keep the particles from moving from place to place. Since the particles stay in position, the shape of a solid doesn't change.

Another property of solids is that they have definite volume. That is, they take up the same amount of space wherever they are. The volume of a solid object stays the same unless you remove a part of the object.

For example, consider a wood block that has a volume of 30 cm³. Wherever you move it, the volume will still be 30 cm³. You can even compress the block, which means to squeeze it. The volume will not change much, if at all.

Many solids might appear to change shape and volume. For example, you can squeeze a foam ball into a smaller volume, and a pillow dents easily when you rest your head on it. In both cases, however, solid matter is surrounded by "pockets" of air. The air changes its shape and volume, not the solid parts.

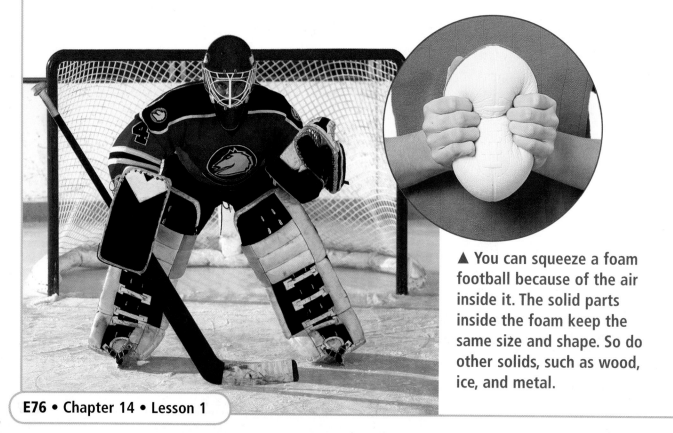

▲ You can squeeze a foam football because of the air inside it. The solid parts inside the foam keep the same size and shape. So do other solids, such as wood, ice, and metal.

Volume

A liquid poured into different containers will keep its volume, but will take the shape of each container.

Liquids

What shape is orange juice? You can't answer that question because orange juice is a liquid. A liquid is a form of matter that has a definite volume, but no definite shape. A **liquid** will change shape to match the shape of its container.

Think about what happens when you use a straw to drink apple juice from a rectangular container. The juice has one shape in the container and has a different shape when it's in the straw.

Contrast liquid water with ice, which is a solid. When you place an ice cube in a glass, it keeps its cube shape—that is, until it melts into a liquid. Then it takes on the shape of its container.

Liquids have no definite shape because their particles are not rigidly held in place. The particles of a liquid are able to flow past one another to take on the shape of its container. Any substance whose particles can flow freely is called a fluid.

Like solids, liquids have a definite volume. To prove this, pour a liquid sample into different containers. Each time, the liquid will take the shape of the container, but its volume will never change.

Also, like solids, liquids are not very compressible. Because the particles are close together, liquids do not easily compress into smaller volumes.

This property makes liquids very useful. For example, a hydraulic device uses an enclosed liquid to transmit a force. If you push on one end of the liquid in a sealed tube, the push will be transmitted by the liquid to the other end of the tube. The brake system of a car uses this property to transmit the force from the driver's foot on the pedal to the brake pad on the wheel of the car.

▶ **TEXT STRUCTURE** What will change the shape of a liquid?

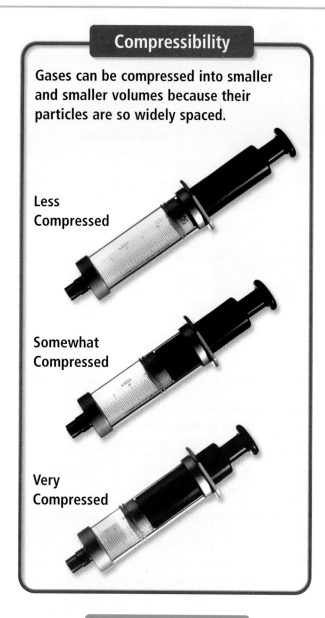

Compressibility

Gases can be compressed into smaller and smaller volumes because their particles are so widely spaced.

Less Compressed

Somewhat Compressed

Very Compressed

States of Matter

Property	Solid	Liquid	Gas
Definite Shape	yes	no	no
Definite Volume	yes	yes	no
Compressible	no	no	yes
Fluid	no	yes	yes
Particle Spacing	close	close	varies

The spacing and speed of particles determines state of matter.

Gases

A **gas** is a form of matter that has no definite shape or volume. The particles that make up gases can move about freely. Particles of a gas are constantly moving about and bouncing off one another.

When a sample of gas is placed in a closed container, the particles spread out to fill the container and take its shape. Because the particles are free to move about and flow, all gases are fluids.

Unlike solids and liquids, gases are very compressible. Their particles are so far apart that they can easily be pressed closer together into a smaller volume. For example, helium gas is often compressed and kept in metal tanks. The helium inside the tank has the shape and volume of the tank.

If you were to use the helium in a small tank to fill a large number of balloons for a party, that small volume of helium would take on the different shapes and total volume of all the balloons.

Gases have much lower densities than liquids and solids. A balloon filled with helium will float in air. This is because the helium-filled balloon is less dense than the air.

Objects with lower densities float in fluids that have higher densities. For example, ice is less dense than liquid water. So, an ice cube will float in a glass of water.

▶ **TEXT STRUCTURE** How do a solid, a liquid, and a gas fill a container?

Lesson Wrap-Up

Visual Summary

The motion and arrangement of particles in each state of matter give the states their unique properties.

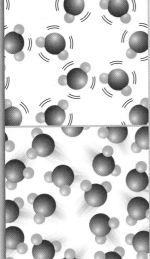

The particles in solids are arranged very close together. They vibrate in place but do not move around.

The particles in liquids are close together. They slip past one another and move about.

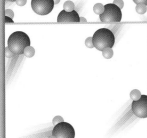

The particles in gases are spread very far apart. They are constantly moving freely.

LINKS for Home and School

MATH **Work With Decimals** The density of water is 1.000 g/cm³ at 4°C and 0.998 g/cm³ at 20°C. As water warms from 4°C to 20°C, how much does its density decrease?

TECHNOLOGY **Write a Report**
Research different ways that hydraulic devices are used in everyday life. What machines rely on hydraulics?

Review

1 MAIN IDEA What two factors determine the state of matter of an object or sample?

2 VOCABULARY What are three familiar states of matter? Describe them in terms of their shapes and volumes.

3 READING SKILL: Text Structure Look back at the structure of the lesson. The states of matter are discussed in the order of particular properties that change as you move through the lesson. Why do you think that solids are discussed first?

4 CRITICAL THINKING: Evaluate Why must a gas be kept in a closed container?

5 INQUIRY SKILL: Experiment For most substances, particles are spaced farther apart in the liquid state than in the solid state. Design a demonstration to show that this is not true for water.

✔ **TEST PREP**
Solids and liquids are similar because both

A. are fluids.

B. are compressible.

C. have no definite shape.

D. have definite volume.

 Technology
Visit **www.eduplace.com/scp/** to find out more about states of matter.

Technology

Glass

What is glass? In the past, scientists had trouble classifying glass. Glass acts like a solid. Yet its atoms are arranged quite randomly, like the particles of a liquid.

Scientists once argued that glass was a slow-moving liquid. Their evidence was 200-year-old window panes that were thicker on the bottom than on top. The scientists thought that the glass had slowly flowed downward. As they researched the windows, however, they discovered the true explanation. The windows had been built with thick bottoms to hold them in their frames.

Today, scientists classify glass as an amorphous solid, meaning a solid without form. Read on to learn how glass is made from sand. Do you agree that "without form" describes glass best?

From Sand to Glass

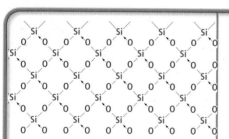

Sand

A sand grain is a crystal of silicon dioxide (SiO_2). Atoms of silicon (Si) and oxygen (O) are arranged tightly in a matrix.

Glass

When sand is heated, some of its bonds break apart. They reform when the sand cools. However, if the cooling is fast enough, the bonds reform in a random arrangement. This makes glass!

Tougher Glass

By mixing sodium carbonate with the sand, sodium ions (Na^+) become part of the glass that results. Sodium makes glass tougher and last longer. You use glass like this in windows, bottles, and other products.

Glass Blowing

In the traditional method, the glass artist blows through a long pipe, called a vessel, to shape the glass as it cools. Chemicals mixed with the melted glass tint it red, blue, purple, or other colors.

Safety Glass ▷
Automobile windshields are stronger and safer than most glass. When they do break, they typically form hundreds of tiny pieces instead of larger, more dangerous shards.

Sharing Ideas

1. **READING CHECK**
   Describe how sand turns into glass.

2. **WRITE ABOUT IT**
   What properties of matter describe glass?

3. **TALK ABOUT IT**
   Compare glass to other materials.

How Does Matter Change State?

Why It Matters...

The teakettle is on the stove. As liquid water in the kettle heats up, changes of state begin to take place. Soon steam comes out of the spout.

Water in the gas state is invisible. But when it hits the cool air, it changes to a "cloud" of tiny droplets of water you can see. The water has changed from a liquid to a gas and back to a liquid—just like that! Changes of state are part of everyday life.

PREPARE TO INVESTIGATE

Inquiry Skill

Observe You can find out more about a substance by using your senses to make careful observations of its properties.

Materials

- clear plastic cup
- warm water
- paper towel
- food coloring
- ice cube
- plastic wrap

Making Rain

Procedure

STEP 1

1. **Observe** Fill a clear plastic cup one-half full of warm water from the tap. Place the cup on a paper towel. Add 2 drops of food coloring. Observe the properties of the water. Record your observations in your *Science Notebook*.

2. **Observe** Get an ice cube from the freezer. Record your observations of the ice cube's properties.

STEP 2

3. **Predict** Cover the plastic cup tightly with plastic wrap. Place the ice cube on top of the plastic wrap. Predict what will happen. Then watch what happens and record your observations.

Conclusion

STEP 3

1. **Hypothesize** What substance collected underneath the plastic wrap? Where do you think the substance came from? Draw a diagram to explain your idea.

2. **Infer** What kind of change took place on top of the plastic wrap? What kind of change took place beneath the plastic wrap?

3. **Experiment** Design an experiment to test your hypothesis. How could you prove where the substance came from?

Investigate More!

Design an Experiment
Use what you know about ice and liquid water to design an experiment to show that mass is conserved when ice melts.

Changes of State

VOCABULARY

condensation	p. E85
deposition	p. E86
evaporation	p. E85
melting	p. E84
sublimation	p. E86
thermal expansion	p. E87
vaporization	p. E85

READING SKILL

Cause and Effect Use a chart to show how adding or removing energy affects state.

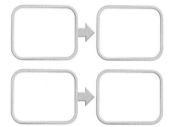

MAIN IDEA Matter can change from one state to another when energy is added or removed. Changes of state are always physical changes.

Melting and Freezing

In many places, spring brings warmer temperatures. Snow and ice begin changing state from solids to liquids. A change of state is a physical change. The substance involved keeps its identity, and matter is always conserved.

When energy is added to a solid, its temperature will rise to a certain point. The solid starts **melting,** or changing from a solid to a liquid, at its melting point.

The process is reversed when energy is removed from a liquid. The temperature drops to the freezing point. The temperature stays the same while the liquid freezes.

For any substance, the melting point and the freezing point are the same. Both the melting point and the freezing point of water are 0°C (32°F).

A change of state takes place when snow and ice begin melting in the spring.

Vaporizing and Condensing

Watch a drop of water on a hot frying pan. It sizzles, pops, and disappears. The change of state is caused by a rapid increase in temperature.

Adding energy to a substance makes its particles speed up, raising the temperature. At some point, the particles have so much energy that they break the forces that keep them in the liquid state. The water vaporizes. **Vaporization** is the change of state from a liquid to a gas.

Rapid vaporization is called boiling. The boiling point of a substance is the temperature at which rapid vaporization occurs. Boiling points can be slightly different from place to place because of air pressure. The boiling point for water at sea level is 100°C (212°F).

Slow or gradual vaporization is called **evaporation.** Evaporation takes place at the surface of a liquid. The higher the temperature of the surroundings, the faster evaporation takes place.

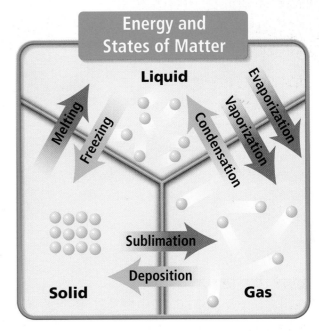

Energy and States of Matter

Liquid

Melting

Freezing

Evaporation

Vaporization

Condensation

Sublimation

Deposition

Solid

Gas

Changes in energy can cause changes in state.

When energy is removed from a gas, it will undergo **condensation,** a change of state from a gas to a liquid. You can observe condensation on a hot day when you make a pitcher of ice-cold lemonade. The pitcher will begin to "sweat," as water droplets form on the outside of the glass. The droplets come from water vapor in the air condensing on the cold glass.

You can also observe condensation on a freezing cold day. The air you breathe out contains water vapor, which condenses when it loses energy to the cold air.

▶ **CAUSE AND EFFECT** How does temperature affect the motion of particles that make up a substance?

The cold bottle removes energy from water vapor in the air that touches it. The water vapor condenses into liquid droplets on the outside of the bottle.

Instead, it sublimates into carbon dioxide gas. People use dry ice instead of ordinary ice when they want to keep something cold, but not wet.

The opposite of sublimation is deposition. **Deposition** is the change of state from gas to solid. When energy is removed from a gas, its particles slow down. Under certain conditions, the gas can change directly into a solid.

Frost is a common example of deposition. Frost forms on grass, cars, and window panes when the temperature of these surfaces is below 0°C, the freezing point of water. When water vapor in the air touches these surfaces, it changes directly from a gas to tiny crystals of ice.

Skipping a Step

Different kinds of matter will change states at different temperatures and at different rates. Each change depends on the particles that make up matter and the forces among the particles.

Sometimes, matter can skip the liquid state! When conditions are right, adding energy to a solid will change it directly to a gas. The process of changing from a solid to a gas is called **sublimation.**

Sublimation explains why dry ice is "dry." Dry ice is solid carbon dioxide. It doesn't melt into a liquid.

Sublimation ►
In sublimation, a solid changes directly to a gas without passing through the liquid state.

Expansion and Contraction

For most substances, a sample of solid matter will expand, or increase in size, when it is heated. The increase in size of a substance due to a change in temperature is called **thermal expansion.**

Remember that the particles of solids are constantly vibrating in place. When the temperature of a solid rises, its particles vibrate more rapidly and move farther apart. As a result, the entire sample expands. It's like the difference between small and large jumps: when you jump higher, you take up more space.

When a solid sample is cooled, the opposite happens. The particles vibrate more slowly. The sample contracts, or decreases in size. When a solid undergoes thermal contraction due to cooling, it takes up less space.

The molecules of water in ice take up more space than in a liquid. So, water expands when it freezes.

Thermal expansion and contraction can strain bridges. Engineers make bridges safer by adding expansion joints. These are spaces between metal parts that allow the bridge to change length without weakening or breaking.

Not all substances get smaller when they get colder. Water expands when it freezes because the molecules in ice crystals are spread farther apart than the molecules in liquid water.

Expansion of water explains why ice floats. Because a given mass of ice has a greater volume than an equal mass of liquid water, the solid ice is less dense than the liquid water.

Although heating or cooling may change the volume of matter, the mass will stay the same. One gram of any substance—solid, liquid, or gas—remains one gram at any temperature.

▶ **CAUSE AND EFFECT** Why does water expand when it freezes?

◀ Engineers add expansion joints to bridges to ease the strain of expansion and contraction.

Visual Summary

Adding energy to a liquid results in evaporation. Removing energy from a liquid results in freezing.

Removing energy from a gas can result in condensation.

Adding energy to a solid results in melting or, in some cases, sublimation.

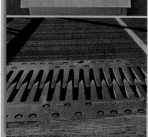

Solids expand when they are heated and contract when they are cooled.

LINKS for Home and School

MATH **Use an Equation** The boiling point of water is 100°C. Use the following equation to convert this temperature to degrees Fahrenheit: $°F = (\frac{9}{5} \times °C) + 32$.

WRITING **Write a Poem** Take the perspective of a solid, liquid, or gas substance that is undergoing a state change. Write a poem describing that change.

Review

1. **MAIN IDEA** Name three changes of state that can take place when energy is removed from a substance.

2. **VOCABULARY** Describe the processes of vaporization and condensation. How are the processes related?

3. **READING SKILL: Cause and Effect** When will a liquid evaporate, and when will it boil? Compare the two changes.

4. **CRITICAL THINKING: Apply** A scientist removes energy from a sample of gas. The matter that results has definite shape and definite volume. What change of state took place?

5. **INQUIRY SKILL: Observe** A solid has undergone a physical change. What observations can you make to determine which change of state took place?

 TEST PREP

What change of state produces fog?

A. freezing

B. condensation

C. sublimation

D. deposition

 Technology

Visit **www.eduplace.com/scp/** to find out more about changes of state.

Forensic Chemist

Hundreds of crimes every year are solved with the help of forensic chemists. These scientists carefully examine crime scenes and conduct laboratory tests on evidence.

Forensic chemists might analyze DNA, identify chemicals, or examine such evidence as broken glass, carpet fibers, and strands of hair. They often have to report their findings to lawyers and judges.

What It Takes!

- A degree in chemistry, biology, or genetics
- Good analytical and laboratory skills

Pyrotechnician

Did you ever wonder who makes the fireworks you see on the Fourth of July? That person is called a pyrotechnician. Pyrotechnicians, literally "crafters of fire," work with flammable and explosive materials. These artists create spectacular and safe visual displays and sound effects.

What It Takes!

- An understanding of basic chemistry
- Artistic creativity
- Following safety rules

Extreme Science

How Cool Is That?

You've heard of "boiling hot." Well, what about "boiling cold?" This rose was "boiled" in one of the coldest liquids known—liquid nitrogen. Liquid nitrogen boils at a temperature so cold it can instantly freeze anything that contains water, such as this rose, or even your skin.

Nitrogen (N_2) is more familiar to us as a gas. It's very familiar, in fact. About 78% of the air we breathe is nitrogen. But when nitrogen is compressed and made cold enough, it turns to liquid.

How cold is cold enough? Think about what an ice cube feels like in your hand. It aches, right? That's 32° F. Now imagine something more than 350 degrees colder! Nitrogen liquefies at -320° F. At room temperature, it boils away like water on a hot stove!

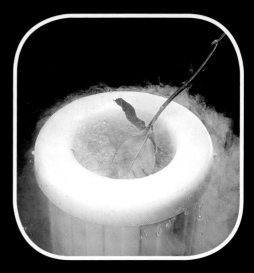

A rose, like most living tissue, is largely made of water. That's why it's soft and flexible at room temperature.

The liquid nitrogen absorbs heat from the rose and boils furiously as it returns to a gas.

After one swift dip in the liquid nitrogen, the rose is frozen solid. It's so brittle, it shatters like glass!

Vocabulary

Complete each sentence with a term from the list.

1. A baseball will remain a sphere no matter where you move it because a _____ has a definite shape.

2. When energy is added to a solid, the solid may change directly to a gas in a process called _____.

3. The same sample of oxygen will fill a small container or a large container because a _____ has no definite volume.

4. A _____ has a definite volume but no definite shape.

5. A liquid changing to a gas is an example of _____.

6. Frost forms on a window pane by the process of _____.

7. The change of a solid to a liquid is called _____.

8. A solid increases in size during _____.

9. A(n) _____ is the physical form that matter takes.

10. When enough energy is removed from a gas it can undergo _____ and change to a liquid.

condensation E85
deposition E86
evaporation E85
gas E78
liquid E77
melting E84
solid E76
state of matter E74
sublimation E86
thermal expansion E87
vaporization E85

Test Prep

Write the letter of the best answer choice.

11. The state of a sample of matter depends on the movement and _____ of particles.

    A. temperature
    B. shape
    C. size
    D. spacing

12. Solid, liquid, and gas are three _____.

    A. properties of matter.
    B. states of matter.
    C. particles of matter.
    D. laws of matter.

13. Which of the following does not involve a change in state?

    A. sublimation
    B. condensation
    C. thermal expansion
    D. freezing

14. The adding or removing of _____ can cause matter to change from one state to another.

    A. particles
    B. phases
    C. energy
    D. movement

Inquiry Skills

15. Experiment Karl's factory produces metal rods. He wants to determine how much thermal contraction occurs in the rods. Describe an experiment he could conduct to find this out.

16. Observe Annabel placed a container of ice on a hot plate for 30 minutes. She made a chart of her observations, but some of the data was erased. Fill in the chart.

Time (minutes)	States of Matter	Types of Change
0 to 1		Change in temperature
2 to 17		Melting
18 to 24	Liquid only	
25 to 35	Liquid and gas	

Map the Concept

Copy the concept map shown here. Label the arrows with the correct terms from the list.

condensation   melting
deposition   sublimation
freezing   vaporization

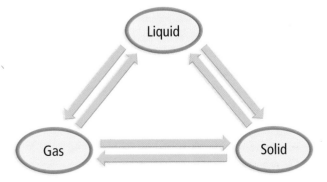

Critical Thinking

17. Analyze Powders, such as powdered sugar, consist of many tiny solid particles. You can pour powdered sugar into a container, and it will take the shape of the container, just like a liquid would. Why isn't powdered sugar classified as a liquid?

18. Evaluate Jari says that the melting point and freezing point of a substance can be different temperatures. Is this statement accurate? Why or why not?

19. Apply Describe three different kinds of matter—one of each state—that could be used to fill a mattress. Which would you prefer for your mattress? Explain.

20. Synthesis Mothballs contain a solid substance called naphthalene. When energy is added to naphthalene, it becomes a vapor without changing to the liquid state. What would likely happen to several mothballs that were left outside on a hot summer day? Explain your answer.

Performance Assessment

Melting Time

How long do ice cubes take to melt? How does their temperature change while they melt? Design and run an experiment to find out. Use ice cubes, a thermometer, and a stopwatch. Plot time and temperature in a line graph.

Write the letter of the best answer.

1. Which is NOT an element?

   A. aluminum

   B. carbon

   C. oxygen

   D. water

2. Look at this section of the Periodic Table.

28	29	30
Ni	**Cu**	**Zn**
58.71	63.55	65.8
46	47	48
Pd	**Ag**	**Cd**
106.4	107.8	112.4
78	79	80
Pt	**Au**	**Hg**
195.9	196.9	200.5

   Which element is copper (Cu) MOST likely to resemble?

   A. mercury (Hg)

   B. nickel (Ni)

   C. silver (Ag)

   D. zinc (Zn)

3. Two elements combine chemically to form a new material. This material is called a(n)
   .

   A. atom

   B. compound

   C. conductor

   D. mixture

4. Which pair of properties BEST describes a solid?

   A. compressible, fluid

   B. definite shape, fluid

   C. definite volume, compressible

   D. definite shape, definite volume

5. A solid can change directly to a gas through the process of   .

   A. condensation

   B. deposition

   C. sublimation

   D. evaporation

6. Which property of sand makes it settle to the bottom of the liquid in the jar?

   A. density

   B. mass

   C. solubility

   D. volume

7. Which shows a physical change taking place?

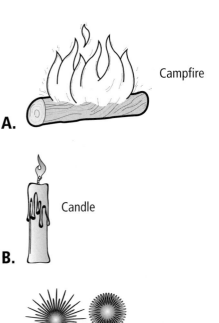

A. Campfire

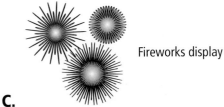

B. Candle

C. Fireworks display

D. Ice cream cone

8. Which property determines how much of a substance can dissolve in another substance?

A. conductivity

B. density

C. mass

D. solubility

Answer the following in complete sentences.

9. Sodium is a soft, silvery metal that burns vigorously when exposed to air. Chlorine is a pale green, poisonous gas. Do these properties tell you anything about the properties of the compound sodium chloride, which is made up of sodium and chlorine? Explain your answer.

10. A bucket of sand also contains a few shells, some strands of seaweed, and a small crab. Is this mixture heterogeneous or homogeneous? Explain your answer.

Discover!

What do your body, a rocket, and a star have in common? All contain hydrogen: the simplest and most common element in the Universe. Although simple in structure, hydrogen is an important building block for all sorts of matter. Read about the different examples below.

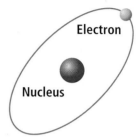

Hydrogen Atom

Fuels The space shuttle uses liquid hydrogen as a fuel. In the future, hydrogen fuel cells may be used as fuel for cars.

Stars Inside a star, hydrogen nuclei fuse to form the next simplest element, helium. The process releases huge amounts of energy.

Water Every molecule of water is made of two hydrogen atoms joined to an oxygen atom. Life could not exist without water!

Acids Fruit juice tastes tangy because of acids. Most acids release hydrogen ions when they dissolve in water.

In its element form, hydrogen exists as a molecule of two atoms. However most of Earth's hydrogen is bound into compounds with other elements, especially carbon, oxygen, and nitrogen. A countless number of hydrogen compounds form and break apart every time you cook a meal, ride in a car, or move a muscle.

Learn about hydrogen fuel cells. Go to **www.eduplace.com/scp/** to see examples of hydrogen as a fuel.

PHYSICAL  SCIENCE

UNIT
F

Forms of Energy

PHYSICAL SCIENCE
UNIT F

Forms of Energy

Independent Reading

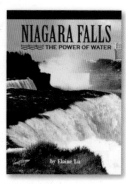

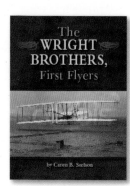

What Does an Electrician Do?

Niagara Falls

The Wright Brothers

Discover!

Lightning releases energy in the forms of light, heat, sound, and electricity. Sometimes, lightning lets you see things that otherwise would be hidden. What new invention also lets you see outdoors in the dark? You will discover more about energy and technology in this unit.

Chapter 15

Forces, Motion, and Work

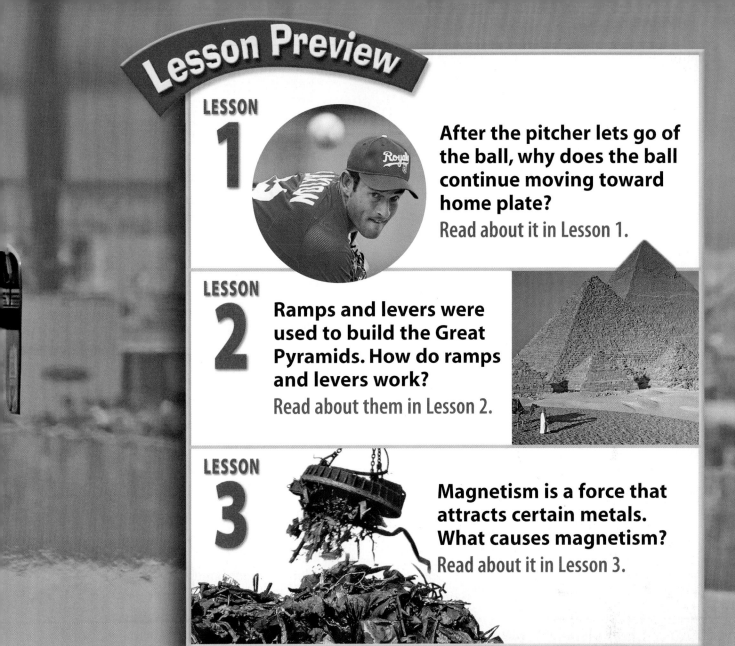

LESSON 1

After the pitcher lets go of the ball, why does the ball continue moving toward home plate?

Read about it in Lesson 1.

LESSON 2

Ramps and levers were used to build the Great Pyramids. How do ramps and levers work?

Read about them in Lesson 2.

LESSON 3

Magnetism is a force that attracts certain metals. What causes magnetism?

Read about it in Lesson 3.

What Can Change an Object's Motion?

Why It Matters...

Almost everything is moving in the world around you. If you understand the physical laws of motion, then you can understand many processes in nature and technology.

PREPARE TO INVESTIGATE

Inquiry Skill

Measure When you measure something, you compare physical characteristics, such as length, volume, and mass, to a standard unit.

Materials

- toy truck or car
- shoebox without top
- scissors
- large rubber band
- 2 rulers
- packing tape
- stopwatch
- meterstick or metric measuring tape
- small masses

Science and Math Toolbox

For step 3, review **Using a Tape Measure or Ruler** on page H6.

Monster Trucks

Procedure

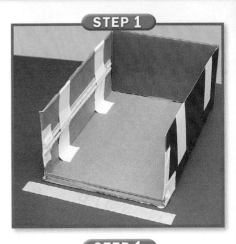

STEP 1

1. **Collaborate** Work with a partner. Cut away one short end of the shoebox. Use packing tape to tape the rulers to the long sides of the box and to attach the rubber band across the open end. In your *Science Notebook*, make a chart like the one shown.

2. **Experiment** Make a starting line on the floor. Place and hold the box so that the open end is at the line. Pull the truck against the rubber band, all the way to the back of the box. As your partner starts the stopwatch, let go of the truck. Record in your chart the time that the truck is in motion.

STEP 1

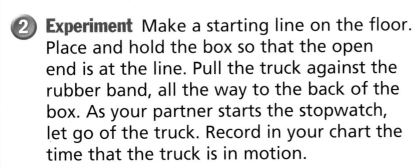

		Distance	Time	Speed
Truck alone	1			
	2			
	3			
Truck with mass	1			
	2			
	3			

3. **Measure** Use the meterstick or measuring tape to measure the distance that the truck traveled. Record the distance.

4. **Experiment** Repeat steps 2 and 3 two more times. Record the results of each trial.

STEP 2

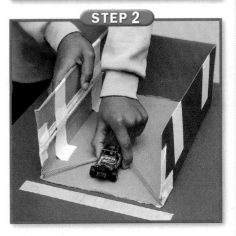

5. **Use Numbers** For each trial, find the truck's average speed by dividing the distance traveled by the time elapsed.

6. **Use Variables** Tape a block of wood or other mass to the top of the truck. Do three more trials. Repeat again, using a greater mass.

Conclusion

1. **Analyze Data** How far did the truck go in the first three trials? How did changing the mass affect the distance traveled or the truck's speed?

2. **Hypothesize** What do you think would happen if you added a second rubber band?

Investigate More!

Design an Experiment
How could you use the same equipment to make the truck travel farther? Write your ideas, then test them. What factors affect the truck's motion?

Change in Motion

MAIN IDEA A force applied to an object can change the object's motion.

VOCABULARY

acceleration	p. F9
force	p. F7
friction	p. F12
gravity	p. F12
inertia	p. F7
motion	p. F6
newton	p. F11
speed	p. F8
velocity	p. F8

READING SKILL

Main Idea and Details
Choose one paragraph of the lesson. Write the main idea and details in a chart.

Motion

When something moves, it is in motion. **Motion** is a change in an object's position. A motionless object is at rest, or stationary.

Motion is described relative to a frame of reference. In other words, to describe an object as moving or stationary, you have to compare it to another object.

Consider people standing on the street watching a bus drive past. Their frame of reference includes other objects, such as trees and houses. Relative to these objects, the people on the street are stationary and the people on the bus are moving.

To the bus passengers, their frame of reference is the bus and everything inside it. Relative to the bus, the people on the bus are not moving, unless they get up and walk around.

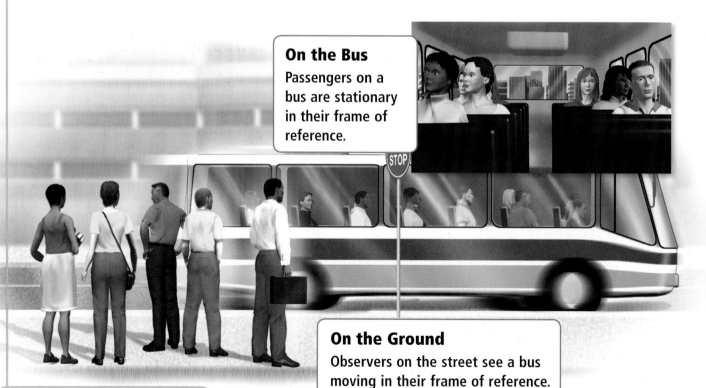

On the Bus
Passengers on a bus are stationary in their frame of reference.

On the Ground
Observers on the street see a bus moving in their frame of reference.

Newton's First Law

In any discussion of motion, the name of English scientist Sir Isaac Newton usually comes up. He was one of history's greatest scientists and mathematicians. In 1687, he presented his laws of motion. Newton's laws show the relationship between forces and motion. A **force** is a push or a pull that acts on an object.

Newton's first law of motion explains what happens to objects that are at rest or are moving. The law states that an object at rest will remain at rest unless a force acts on it. For example, this page is at rest. It will remain at rest until it is acted upon by an external force, such as your hand.

Newton's first law also states that an object in motion will continue to move at a constant speed in the same direction if no forces act on it.

This tendency of an object at rest to remain at rest or an object in motion to remain in motion is called **inertia.** So, Newton's first law is also called the principle of inertia.

You can see examples of Newton's first law in a game of soccer. A soccer ball lying on the field will remain at rest until a player kicks it. The force of the kick overcomes the inertia of the ball, setting the ball in motion.

The ball will continue to move at a constant speed until another force acts on it. A ball rolling across the grass will slow down because of friction. A ball kicked into the air will fall back to the ground because of the force of gravity.

The soccer ball will remain at rest until the force of the kicker's foot overcomes the soccer ball's inertia and sets it in motion.

Newton's first law also applies to a game of baseball. A baseball begins at rest in the pitcher's hand. The pitcher then applies a force to the ball, hurling it toward home plate. The ball's inertia keeps it moving forward, although the ball changes direction slightly because of friction against air and the force of gravity.

At home plate, two things may happen. The ball may land in the mitt of the catcher, who applies a force to stop it. Or the batter may strike the ball with a bat. If the batter's force is strong enough, the ball could travel long enough for a home run.

 **MAIN IDEA** What is inertia?

Speed, Velocity, and Acceleration

Newton's first law means that, without the action of a force, an object will move at a constant speed—the same speed all the time—in a constant direction. The **speed** of an object is a measure of the distance it moves in a given amount of time.

To calculate average speed, divide the distance traveled by the time it took the object to travel that distance. You can use a formula to relate speed (*s*), distance (*d*), and time (*t*):

$$s = \frac{d}{t}$$

For example, if a car travels 160 km (100 mi) in 2 hours, its average speed is

$$s = \frac{160 \text{ km}}{2 \text{ h}}$$

$$s = 80 \text{ km/h}$$

There are many other units of speed, but they all have the same form: units of distance per units of time. Scientists often use meters per second (m/s). Note that speed is a rate. It is the rate of change in distance over time.

Velocity is a measure of both an object's speed *and* its direction.

A jumping ice skater changes both his acceleration and velocity, as this stop-action photograph shows. If a skater moves a distance of 4 meters during 2 seconds, what is his average speed? ▼

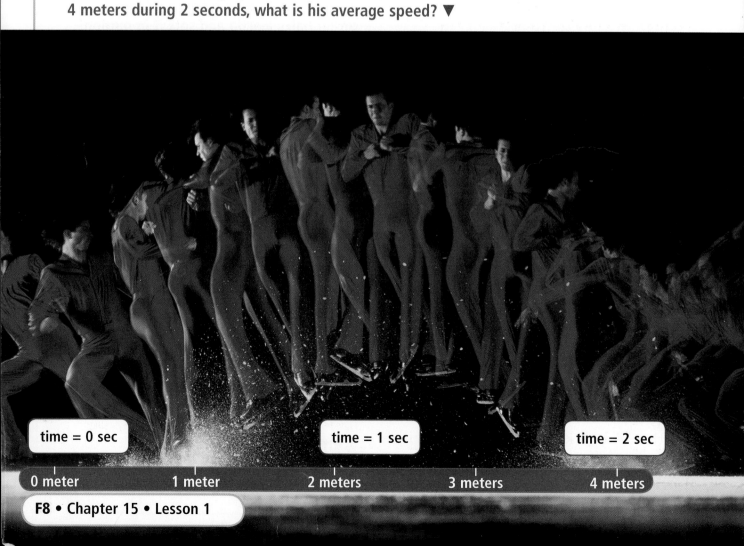

time = 0 sec   time = 1 sec   time = 2 sec

0 meter   1 meter   2 meters   3 meters   4 meters

To understand the difference between speed and velocity, think of the following example. Suppose you are jogging north at a speed of 8 km/h (5 mph) while your friend is jogging east at a speed of 8 km/h. You and your friend have the same speed but your velocities are different. This is because your directions of travel are different.

A force can change the speed of an object, its direction, or both. In each case, a force causes the object's velocity to change. Change in an object's velocity is known as **acceleration.** Since velocity describes both speed and direction, acceleration can be a change in speed, a change in direction, or both.

Acceleration is expressed as a change in velocity over a certain period of time. For example, suppose the velocity of a car changes from 13 m/s to 23 m/s in 5 seconds. The change in the car's velocity is 23 m/s – 13 m/s = 10 m/s. It takes 5 s to make this change, so the acceleration is 10 m/s ÷ 5 s = 2 m/s per second.

People usually think of acceleration as speeding up. That is why a car's gas pedal is also called an accelerator. When an object slows down, it is commonly called deceleration. In science, however, accelerating can mean speeding up, slowing down, or changing direction. In fact, any change in motion is acceleration.

Top Animal Speeds

Cheetah	100 km/h (60 mph)
Blue Whale	50 km/h (30 mph)
Peregrine Falcon	320 km/h (200 mph)
Dragonfly	60 km/h (35 mph)

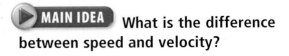 **MAIN IDEA** **What is the difference between speed and velocity?**

Balanced and Unbalanced Forces

Newton's first law applies to situations in which no forces are acting upon an object. What happens when forces do act upon an object?

Suppose you are having a tug-of-war with your dog. You are pulling on one end of the rope and your dog is pulling on the other end in the opposite direction. If each of you pulls with equal force, the rope will not move. The two forces are equal in strength, but opposite in direction. The forces are balanced.

Now suppose a friend helps you pull your end of the rope. Together, you pull with a greater force than the dog does. The forces are unbalanced. When forces are balanced, they cancel each other out, and there is no movement. In this case, the dog's force is not great enough to balance the force of two people. The difference between the two forces, called the *net* force, is acting on the rope. The rope will accelerate in the direction of the net force, toward you and your friend.

An object will accelerate, or change its motion, only when an unbalanced force acts on it. This is Newton's second law of motion.

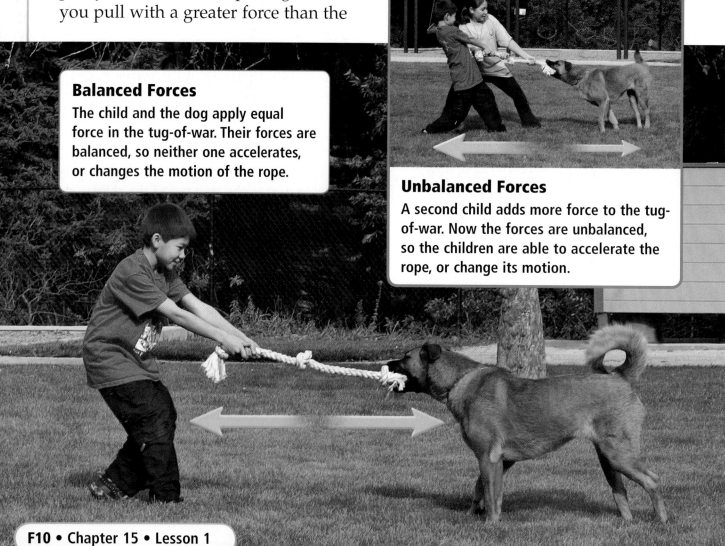

Balanced Forces
The child and the dog apply equal force in the tug-of-war. Their forces are balanced, so neither one accelerates, or changes the motion of the rope.

Unbalanced Forces
A second child adds more force to the tug-of-war. Now the forces are unbalanced, so the children are able to accelerate the rope, or change its motion.

Newton's Second Law

Newton's second law of motion describes the relationship between force, mass, and acceleration. The law can be stated as a formula,

$$F = ma,$$

where F is the applied net force, m is the mass of the object, and a is the amount of acceleration.

Look at the photos at right. In the top photo, a fifth-grader pushes the wagon, causing it to accelerate. In the second photo, an adult pushes on the same wagon. Because the adult pushes the same mass with a greater force, the acceleration is greater. The greater the net force applied to an object, the greater the acceleration of the object.

Now compare the top and bottom pictures. The fifth-grader pushes the wagon with the same force in both cases. But because the adult's mass is much greater than the mass of the child, the acceleration of the wagon is smaller. For the same applied force, an object with a greater mass will have a smaller acceleration than an object with a smaller mass.

Force is measured in a unit called the newton, in honor of Sir Isaac Newton. One **newton (N)** is the force required to accelerate a mass of 1 kg at 1 m/s per second. If you measure any two of the quantities force, mass, and acceleration, you can use the formula $F = ma$ to calculate the third.

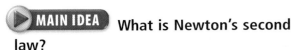 **MAIN IDEA** What is Newton's second law?

Newton's Second Law

A fifth-grader pushing the wagon causes the wagon with the child to accelerate.

An adult pushes the wagon and the child with a greater force, causing a greater acceleration.

Because of the adult's greater mass, the acceleration is small.

Gravity and Friction

Gravity is a force that causes objects with mass to be attracted, or pulled, toward one another. Gravity is a noncontact force, meaning it acts on an object without touching it.

Newton's Law of Universal Gravitation describes the attractive force between two masses. The force increases with the masses of the two objects. However, the farther apart the two objects are, the weaker the force. Earth's mass is much greater than the mass of any object on its surface. That's why you experience gravity as a downward force.

The force of gravity accelerates the skater as she moves down the hill.▼

Friction is a force that resists motion of one surface across another surface. Friction is a contact force, which means that two objects or surfaces have to touch one another. Friction is usually greater between rough surfaces than smooth ones.

In the photo, the skater slows down by using friction between the brake and the concrete. Even without the brake, she still will slow down eventually. Friction between her skate wheels and the ground will slow her movement until she stops.

Air resistance will also help slow down the skater. Air resistance, or drag, is a type of friction that opposes motion through air. Skydivers use a parachute to increase air resistance and slow down their rate of falling.

As you have seen, gravity and friction affect motion on Earth. In outer space, however, no air slows down a moving object. And far away from stars and planets there is little gravity. Objects moving through space continue in a straight line at constant velocity.

▶ **MAIN IDEA** Describe some forces that affect motion on Earth.

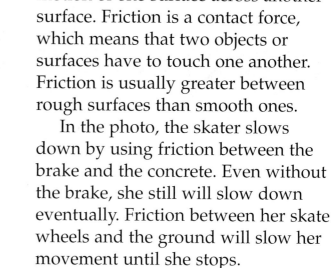

◀ To slow down, the skater uses the friction between the sidewalk and the brake on her skate.

Visual Summary

Newton's first law states that an object at rest or in motion will remain at rest or in motion unless a force acts on it.

Newton's second law states that an object will accelerate if the forces acting on it are unbalanced.

The forces of gravity and friction also affect the motion of objects.

LINKS for Home and School

MATH **Calculate Speed** If a greyhound runs 11 km in 10 minutes, what is its average speed in kilometers per hour? Do you think a greyhound could maintain this speed for an hour? Explain.

WRITING **Expository** Research major events in the life of Sir Isaac Newton. Write a report about some of his famous discoveries. Include photos or drawings of his experiments or inventions. Where would you rank him among the greatest scientists?

Review

1 **MAIN IDEA** How can an object's speed or direction be changed?

2 **VOCABULARY** What is the difference between velocity and acceleration? Give an example of each. Be sure to use the correct units.

3 **READING SKILL: Main Idea and Details** What are three ways an object may accelerate?

4 **CRITICAL THINKING: Analyze** Explain why the shoulder strap of a car seat belt is important.

5 **INQUIRY SKILL: Measure** In the United States, speed is typically measured in miles per hour (mph). To convert mph to km/h, multiply by 1.6. Calculate in km/h the speed of a train traveling 75 mph.

✔ TEST PREP

The brakes on a bicycle slow it down due to the force of

A. acceleration.

B. air resistance.

C. gravity.

D. friction.

 Technology
Visit **www.eduplace.com/scp/** to find out more about force and motion.

Lesson 2

Are Simple Machines Used?

Why It Matters...

You perform hundreds of tasks every day, and simple machines make them easier. Imagine how hard it would be to steer a bicycle without handlebars, or to cut meat without a knife. Even your arms and legs are examples of simple machines.

PREPARE TO INVESTIGATE

Inquiry Skill

Compare When you compare, you describe how two or more things or events are similar and how they are different.

Materials

- 50-g mass with hook
- spring scale
- stack of books
- tape measure
- 2 large pieces of cardboard
- scissors

Science and Math Toolbox
For step 2, review **Measurements** on page H16.

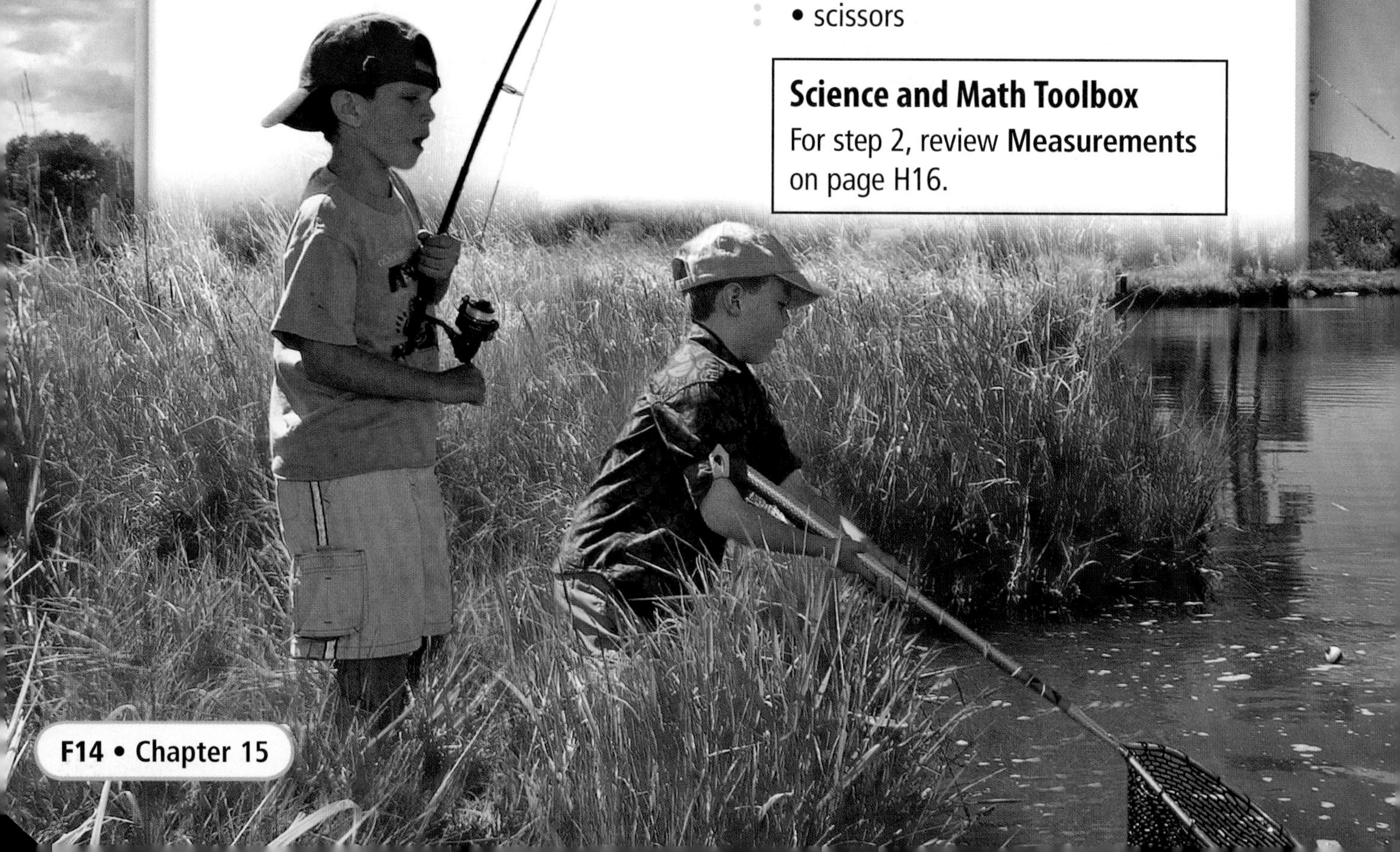

Ramping It Up

Procedure

STEP 1

Distance (cm)	Force (N)

1. **Collaborate** Work with a partner. Make a stack of books. In your *Science Notebook,* make a chart like the one shown.

2. **Experiment** Hook the mass to the spring scale. Lift the mass straight up to the height of the stack of books. Read the spring scale and record the force needed to lift the mass.

STEP 2

3. **Record Data** Use a tape measure to carefully measure the distance the mass was lifted. Record the distance.

4. **Experiment** Lean the cardboard against the stack of books to create a ramp. Align the top edge of the cardboard with the top of the books. While holding the ramp in place, use the spring scale to drag the mass to the top of the ramp. Move the mass smoothly and at a constant speed. Record the force and the length of the ramp.

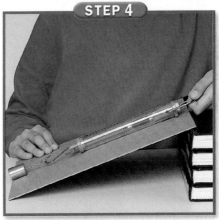

STEP 4

Safety: Be careful using scissors.

5. **Use Variables** Cut the cardboard in half to shorten it. Repeat step 4 using the shorter ramp.

Conclusion

1. **Compare** How did using the ramp affect the amount of force needed to lift the mass?

2. **Infer** How did changing the length of the ramp affect the force needed to raise the mass to the top of the stack of books?

Investigate More!

Design an Experiment
Try the experiment using the same length of cardboard but a different-sized stack of books. How does the height of the stack affect the force needed to move the mass the same distance?

Simple Machines

MAIN IDEA Simple machines allow you to do the same work more easily.

Doing Work

What do you think of when you think of work? Perhaps you think of mowing the lawn, washing dishes, or walking the dog. From the last lesson, you know that force is a push or pull on an object. In science, **work** is done when a force moves an object over a distance.

What happens if you apply a force to something, but it does not move? According to Newton's laws of motion, another equal force must be opposing your force. Look at the first photo below. If the person does not move the car, then no work has been done. Even though the person has exerted a force, he has done no work.

Now look at the second photo. If two people apply enough force to the car to move it some distance they will have done work.

One person is not able to apply enough force to move the car. He is unable to do work.

Two people apply enough force to move the car over a distance. Together, they do work.

Work

Gravity

The force of gravity is doing work on this skydiver, causing him to fall. The work done equals force times distance. ▲

The greater the distance through which a force is applied, the more work is done. For example, think about picking up a book from the floor. To lift the book, you apply a force equal to its weight. If you raise the book over your head, you do more work than if you just lift it to your waist.

You can use a formula to calculate the work done.

$$W = Fd$$

Work (W) equals the amount of force (F) times the distance (d) that the object is moved.

Work is measured in units of force times units of distance. The standard unit is called a newton-meter (N·m). If you apply a force of 10 N to lift a book a distance of 1 m, you have done 10 N·m of work. Another name for a newton-meter is the joule (J).

Simple Machines

Machines are tools that make doing the same work easier. **Simple machines** have few or no moving parts. They make work easier by changing the amount of force applied, the direction of the force, or both.

For example, one machine might allow you to use less force to move an object a given distance. Another machine might allow you to use the weight of your body to pull an object rather than push it. Some machines give the user both advantages.

The force used to do work using a machine is called the effort force. The force it overcomes is called the load, or resistance force. There are six types of simple machines, as shown below.

▶ **PROBLEM AND SOLUTION** What problems do machines solve?

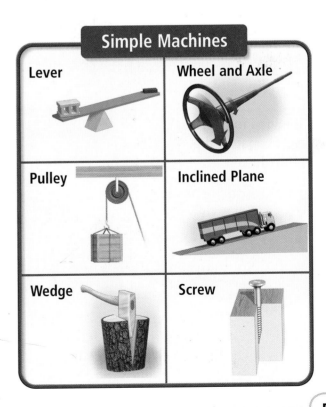

Simple Machines

Lever	Wheel and Axle
Pulley	Inclined Plane
Wedge	Screw

Levers

Levers are rigid bars that pivot around a point. Levers can change the direction of a force, change the ratio between the force and the distance an object moves, or both.

To understand a lever, consider two different forces: the effort and the load. The effort force is the force that is applied to the lever. The load is the force that works against the effort. Also look at the lever's pivot point, called the fulcrum. Different kinds of levers place the fulcrum in different positions. There are three classes of levers.

First-Class Levers Take a look at the diagram below. This lever shows the fulcrum between the effort and the load. This type of lever is called a first-class lever. A small downward force exerted by the brick on the far end of the lever can overcome the weight of the concrete block, which is the load. The block will be balanced, or will rise.

Note that the fulcrum is placed closer to the load than to the effort. With this placement, the effort end of the lever is pushed a long distance to raise the load just a short distance. The advantage is that much less force is used to push the lever down. A first-class lever always changes the direction of the force. Pushing down on the effort end raises the load.

Look at the photo of the pliers on the next page. A pliers is made of two first-class levers joined together at the fulcrum. Squeeze the handles of the pliers, and the pliers squeezes the walnut at the other end. Because of the placement of the fulcrum, the force on the walnut is much greater than the force you exert on the handles.

Other examples of first-class levers include seesaws, crowbars, and fingernail clippers. In all cases, the fulcrum is between the effort and load.

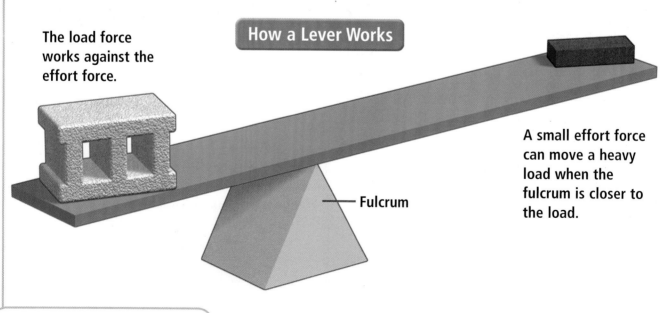

The load force works against the effort force.

How a Lever Works

Fulcrum

A small effort force can move a heavy load when the fulcrum is closer to the load.

Second-Class Levers In a second-class lever, the load is placed between the fulcrum and the effort force. A second-class lever increases the force but doesn't change its direction.

The nutcracker shown here is made of two second-class levers. Squeeze its handles, and the nut will be squeezed even harder. But unlike the forces on a pliers, the direction of the effort force on a nutcracker is the same as the direction of the resistance force.

Other examples of second-class levers are wheelbarrows and bottle openers. As with the nutcracker, these tools allow a small effort force to overcome a large load.

Third-Class Levers In a third-class lever, the effort is applied between the fulcrum and the load. This is the only type of lever that always reduces the effort force instead of increasing it.

In the photograph, each chopstick acts as a third-class lever. Notice that a force applied over a tiny distance at the fulcrum—where you hold the chopsticks—moves the food at the other end over a longer distance.

A fishing rod is another example of a third-class lever. The fulcrum is at the end of the rod that you hold steady. The resistance force is the weight of the fish at the other end. By pulling up on the middle of the fishing rod, you can lift the fish out of the water.

A shovel and a stapler are other familiar examples of third-class levers. A pair of tweezers consists of two third-class levers, joined at the fulcrum.

▶ **PROBLEM AND SOLUTION** List examples of problems a lever could solve.

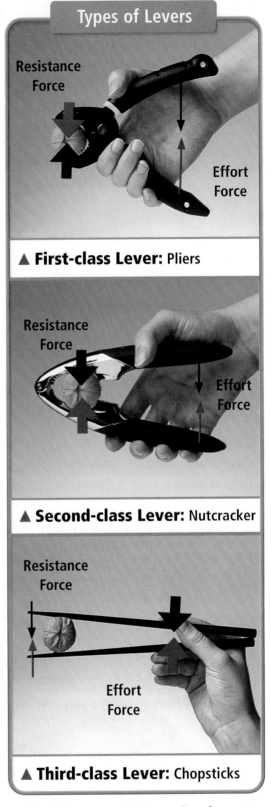

Types of Levers

Resistance Force

Effort Force

▲ **First-class Lever:** Pliers

Resistance Force

Effort Force

▲ **Second-class Lever:** Nutcracker

Resistance Force

Effort Force

▲ **Third-class Lever:** Chopsticks

Each of these tools is made of two levers joined together at their fulcrums.

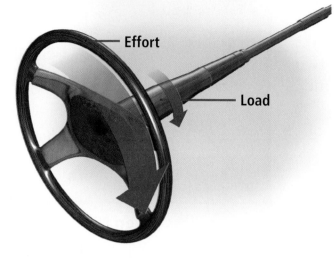

Effort

Load

▲ A car's steering wheel is an example of a wheel and axle. The axle is a cylinder attached to the center of the wheel.

Wheel and Axles and Pulleys

No one knows exactly who invented the first wheel and axle, but humans started using this machine sometime around 3300 B.C. The wheel and axle is a simple machine that changes the amount of force applied to an object. Wheel and axles are used for many things, including to steer a truck, to open a valve on a water pipe, and to seal a submarine hatch.

Examine the diagram above. The axle is attached to the wheel at the center. When the wheel is turned, the axle also turns. Likewise, if the axle is turned, the wheel turns as well.

A wheel and axle can be used two ways. When the effort force is applied to the wheel, the force is increased. When the effort force is applied to the axle, the distance over which the force acts is increased.

Look at the diagram of the car steering wheel. When a driver turns the wheel, the rim of the steering wheel travels a greater distance than the rim of the steering column. Because the steering column—the axle—travels a shorter distance, the force applied to the axle is increased.

Many other familiar items, such as doorknobs and faucets, work the same way. The wider the wheel, the less effort force required to turn it. However, you need to turn the wider wheel a greater distance to do the same amount of work.

Have you ever watched gears in action? A gear is a wheel with teeth around its rim. The teeth interlock with teeth of other gears, allowing a system of gears to transmit motion. Machines that use gears include cars, bicycles, and window cranks.

A pulley is a wheel with a groove along its edge. A single fixed pulley consists of a pulley attached to a high point, such as a tree branch or a ceiling, with a rope fed through the wheel's groove. You attach one end of the rope to an object and then pull down the other end to lift the object. This is called a fixed pulley because the pulley remains in place.

The fixed pulley changes the direction but not the size of the force needed to move an object. Pulling the rope a distance of 1 m lifts the object 1 m, so the same force must be exerted. The advantage is that you can pull down instead of lifting up. Pulling down is often much easier!

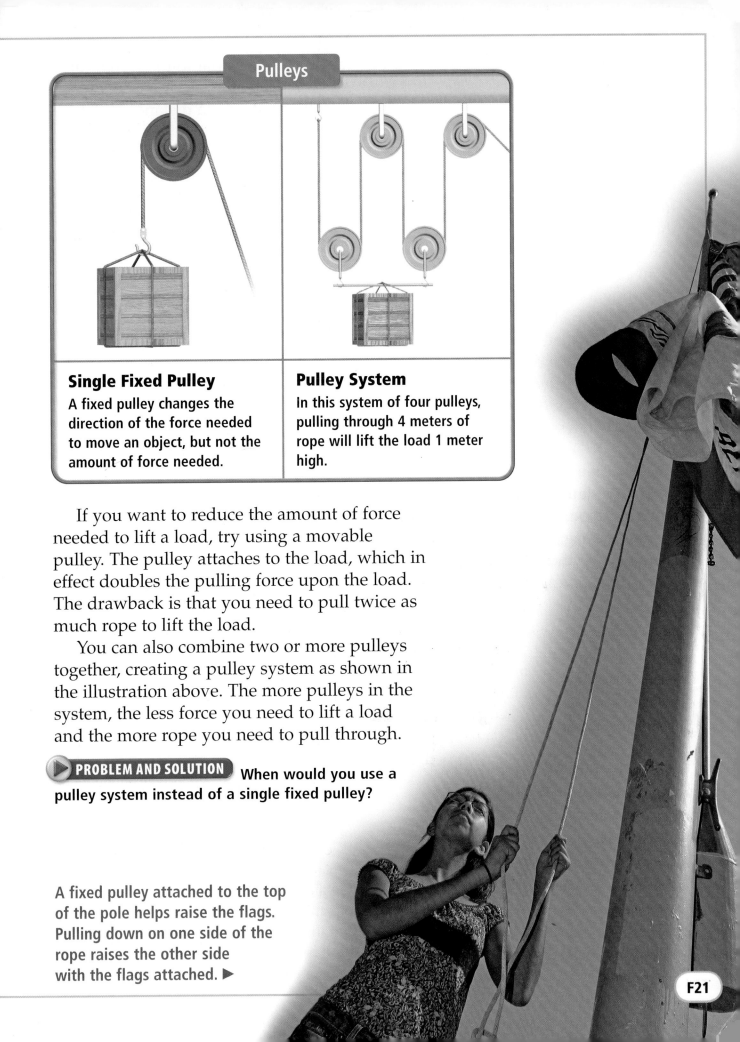

Pulleys

Single Fixed Pulley
A fixed pulley changes the direction of the force needed to move an object, but not the amount of force needed.

Pulley System
In this system of four pulleys, pulling through 4 meters of rope will lift the load 1 meter high.

If you want to reduce the amount of force needed to lift a load, try using a movable pulley. The pulley attaches to the load, which in effect doubles the pulling force upon the load. The drawback is that you need to pull twice as much rope to lift the load.

You can also combine two or more pulleys together, creating a pulley system as shown in the illustration above. The more pulleys in the system, the less force you need to lift a load and the more rope you need to pull through.

▶ **PROBLEM AND SOLUTION** When would you use a pulley system instead of a single fixed pulley?

A fixed pulley attached to the top of the pole helps raise the flags. Pulling down on one side of the rope raises the other side with the flags attached. ▶

Inclined Planes

Another simple machine that changes the ratio of force to distance is an inclined plane, or ramp. An inclined plane decreases the amount of force required to raise an object. In exchange, it increases the distance that the object must be moved to reach a given height.

In one picture below, two people are lifting a heavy box into a truck. In the other picture, one person uses an inclined plane to do a similar task. The box must be moved twice the distance, but only half the effort force is needed. If the inclined plane were longer, even less effort force would be needed.

The amount of work done on the box is the same whether it is lifted straight up or slid along the inclined plane. Look again at the example below. To lift the box straight up from the ground, the two people must apply a force equal to the weight of the box. The amount of work done to lift the 500-N box a distance of 2.0 m is $W = 500$ N $\times$ 2.0 m = 1,000 N·m.

Pushing the 500-N box up the inclined plane requires only half the force, or 250 N. The inclined plane is 4.0 m long. The work done is $W = 250$ N $\times$ 4.0 m = 1,000 N·m.

The example assumes that the inclined plane is frictionless. In the real world, the friction force between the box and the inclined plane would need to be overcome. Using a wheeled cart helps to reduce friction.

▶ **PROBLEM AND SOLUTION** What is the advantage of using an inclined plane to move a heavy object?

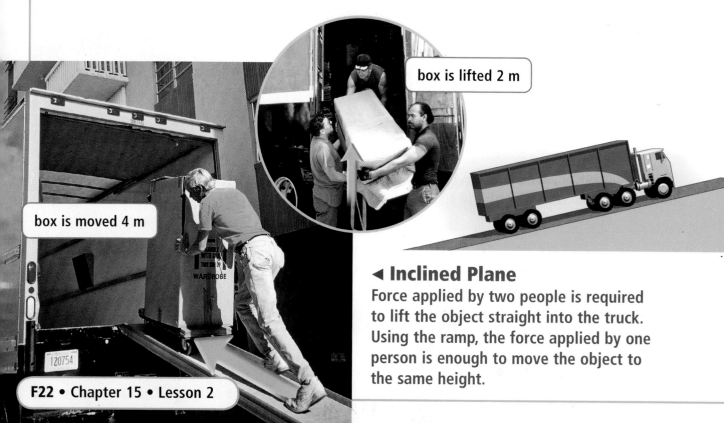

box is lifted 2 m

box is moved 4 m

◀ **Inclined Plane**
Force applied by two people is required to lift the object straight into the truck. Using the ramp, the force applied by one person is enough to move the object to the same height.

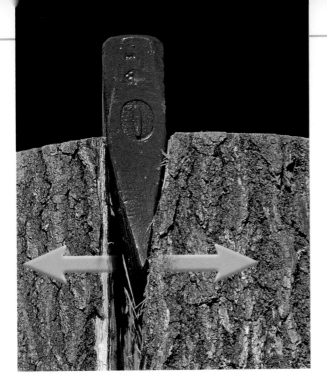

Wedge

The blade of a log-splitting maul is a wedge. When it is swung, the weight of the head drives the wedge into the wood, splitting the wood into two pieces. ▲

Wedges and Screws

A wedge is a simple machine that consists of two inclined planes back to back. Like an inclined plane, a wedge changes the direction of the force. An effort force is applied to the thick end of the wedge. As the wedge moves under or through an object, the sides of the wedge exert forces on the object that are at right angles to the direction of the applied force.

Because of its shape, a wedge must move a greater distance through an object to push it apart a much smaller distance. The sideways force exerted by the wedge is greater than the applied force. Many tools, such as chisels, knives, and even doorstops, are wedges.

A screw is an inclined plane wrapped around a cylinder or cone. The plane makes up the threads of a screw. A screw changes both the direction of force and the ratio of force to distance. When force is applied to turn the screw, the threads cause the screw to move.

Look at the car jack shown below. It takes many turns of the screw to move the car up or down only a little. A small effort force is greatly multiplied, allowing a person to slowly lift a car.

▶ **READING CHECK** List three ways you might use a wedge.

Screw

Turning the screw pulls the diagonal pieces closer together, which raises the jack and lifts the car. ▼

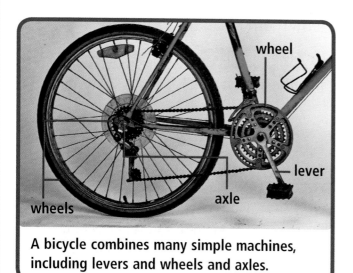

lever

fulcrum

effort

resistance

lever wedges

A pair of scissors combines two simple machines: wedges and levers.

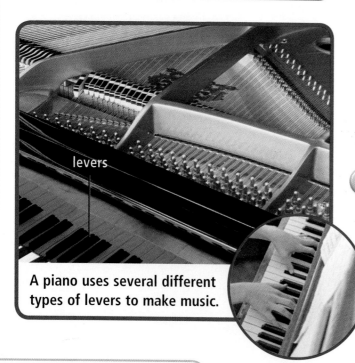

wheel

lever

axle

wheels

A bicycle combines many simple machines, including levers and wheels and axles.

A piano uses several different types of levers to make music.

levers

Compound Machines

Many of the devices that you use every day are made of two or more simple machines. Tools that are made of a combination of simple machines are called compound machines. A pair of scissors is one example. The scissors consists of a pair of levers with the fulcrum in the middle. The cutting blades of the scissors are wedges.

Another example of a compound machine is a bicycle. It uses pedals, which are levers, to apply force to the sprocket. The sprocket is a wheel and axle that uses gears to move the chain.

As the chain moves, it transfers force to a smaller sprocket attached to the axle of the rear wheel. So, the force applied to the pedal is converted through a combination of simple machines to make the back wheel turn.

A piano uses a variety of different types of levers to make the hammers strike the strings. The keys are first-class levers. Pushing down on a key causes the other end of the key to lift, pushing on a wooden post. The post pushes up into the end of the hammer, which is another first-class lever. The hammer strikes the string.

▶ **PROBLEM AND SOLUTION** What are compound machines?

Lesson Wrap-Up

Visual Summary

Scientists define work as a force moving an object over a distance, *W = Fd*. Energy can be expended without accomplishing any work.

Simple machines make work easier to do. Some increase the effort force by applying it over a shorter distance. Others decrease the effort force by applying it over a longer distance.

Compound machines combine two or more simple machines. Many useful devices are compound machines.

LINKS for Home and School

MATH **Use a Formula** A box is pulled up a frictionless ramp using a force of 300 N. The length of the ramp is 4 m. What is the amount of work done?

TECHNOLOGY **Make a Poster**
Make a poster of the different tools used on a construction site. Categorize the tools or parts of tools as wheels and axles, pulleys, levers, ramps, wedges, or screws.

Review

1 MAIN IDEA How do machines make the same work easier?

2 VOCABULARY Explain how it is possible to exert force but accomplish no work.

3 READING SKILL: Problem and Solution Explain how three different simple machines other than inclined planes might be used to lift a heavy box.

4 CRITICAL THINKING: Analyze A home owner is designing a ramp to connect the driveway to the front door. A person in a wheelchair will use the ramp. What facts must be known to design a useful ramp?

5 INQUIRY SKILL: Compare Compare the advantages of a single fixed pulley to a pulley system.

 TEST PREP
An example of a wedge is a(n)

A. wheelbarrow.

B. oar.

C. axe blade.

D. baseball bat.

 Technology
Visit **www.eduplace.com/scp/** to find out more about simple machines.

Transportation

Transportation is any method of moving from place to place. Read on to discover how transportation has changed over the past 200 years.

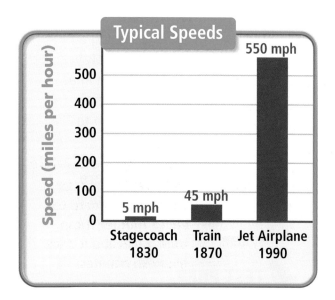

Typical Speeds

1840s: Clipper Ships

Clipper ships traveled faster and carried more cargo than all other ships of their day. Unfortunately, many were wrecked due to poor navigation and inaccurate maps.

1700s   **1800s**

1790s: Horse and Buggy

Farmers used the horse and buggy to carry goods to and from town. Horse-powered coaches carried passengers between towns and cities.

Astronaut
Mae Jemison ▶

1920s: Automobiles

In 1913, Henry Ford began mass-producing cars on an assembly line. Within a decade, people everywhere were driving Model T's. They cost only $290 each!

1950s: Airplanes

Jet-powered airplanes entered passenger service in the 1950s. They quickly became people's first choice for long-distance travel.

2000s: Space Shuttle

To travel fast and far today, step aboard the space shuttle! It can orbit Earth about once every 90 minutes.

1900s   **2000s**

1870s: Railroads

Inventions such as the steam-powered locomotive and vacuum brakes made trains fast, safe, and popular.

Sharing Ideas

1. **READING CHECK** Compare the different modes of transportation.

2. **WRITE ABOUT IT** When would each mode of transportation be your choice for a trip?

3. **TALK ABOUT IT** How does transportation affect people's lives?

What Forces Come from Magnets?

Why It Matters...

Did you know that you use a magnet every time you ring a doorbell? From refrigerator magnets to doorbells to bullet trains, magnets are an important part of today's fast-paced, technology-filled world.

PREPARE TO INVESTIGATE

Inquiry Skill

Infer When you infer, you use data and observations to draw conclusions.

Materials

- bar magnet
- iron filings
- plastic tray
- horseshoe magnet
- wax paper
- disc magnet
- goggles

Exploring Magnets

Procedure

Safety: Wear goggles for this activity.

STEP 1

1. **Experiment** Place the bar magnet in the tray. Cover the magnet with a sheet of wax paper. Sprinkle iron filings onto the paper and observe what happens.

2. **Record Data** In your *Science Notebook,* sketch the pattern of the filings around the magnet. Include a written description of how the filings are arranged.

3. **Use Variables** Pick up the wax paper with the filings. Be careful not to spill any. Replace the bar magnet with the horseshoe magnet. Put the wax paper, with the filings, on top of the horseshoe magnet.

STEP 3

4. **Compare** Sketch the pattern of the filings and include a written description. Note any differences between the two patterns.

5. **Use Variables** Repeat steps 3 and 4, replacing the horseshoe magnet with the disc magnet. Draw and record your observations.

Conclusion

1. **Compare** How were the iron filing patterns different for each magnet? How were they similar?

2. **Infer** What can you infer from the patterns about how each type of magnet attracts filings?

Investigate More!

Research Research how a battery, an iron nail, and a wire can be used to make a simple electromagnet. With your teacher's approval, build the electromagnet. Use iron filings to investigate the magnetic field it creates.

Magnets

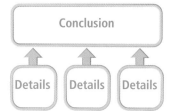
MAIN IDEA Magnetism comes from a special alignment of an atom's electrons as found in iron and many other metals. Electric currents also create magnetic fields.

Magnets and Magnetic Fields

Prehistoric people discovered magnetism when they found magnetic rocks, called lodestones. Lodestones, which are mostly iron, are able to attract or repel certain metals. They must have seemed very unusual to ancient peoples.

Today, scientists know that magnetism is a force created by the motion of electrons in atoms. Moving electrons produce magnetic fields, or areas in which a magnetic force can be observed. When electrons are aligned in the same direction, the fields around them combine to create a strong magnet. Metals such as iron, nickel, and cobalt are some materials that can act as magnets.

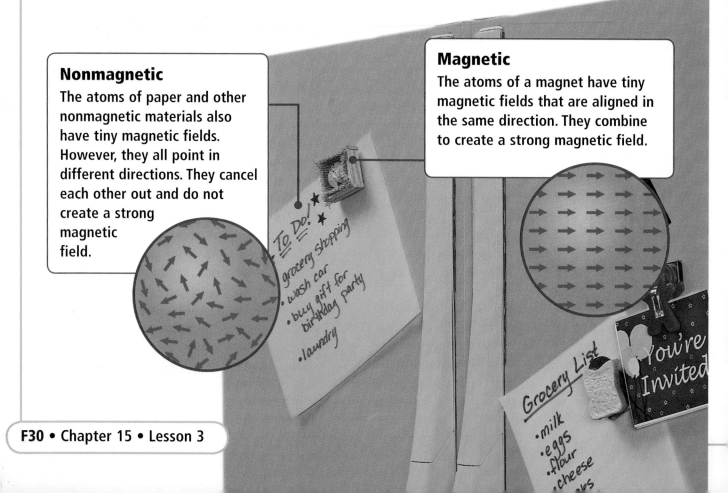

Nonmagnetic
The atoms of paper and other nonmagnetic materials also have tiny magnetic fields. However, they all point in different directions. They cancel each other out and do not create a strong magnetic field.

Magnetic
The atoms of a magnet have tiny magnetic fields that are aligned in the same direction. They combine to create a strong magnetic field.

Because the atoms in a magnet are aligned in the same direction, they form two regions called poles. The poles are named north and south.

All magnets have a north pole and a south pole. Even if you break a magnet in half, each half would still have a north pole and a south pole.

What happens if you bring the north pole of one magnet near the north pole of another magnet? Without touching, the two magnets will strongly repel, or push away from, each other. This repulsion occurs because the atoms of the first magnet are aligned in the opposite direction from the atoms in the second magnet. The same is true if you put two south poles together.

However, if you bring the north pole of one magnet near the south pole of another magnet, the magnets will strongly attract each other. In this case, the atoms of both magnets will be aligned in the same direction. They create one big magnetic field.

Each pole of a magnet is attracted to a magnetic pole of Earth. If you hang a magnet on a string, the north pole of the magnet will point to Earth's North Pole and the south pole will point to Earth's South Pole. To make a compass needle easy to understand, the north pole of the needle is labeled "N." This is a way of saying "North is this way."

When you put a magnet close to an iron object without the magnet touching it, you will see or feel a magnetic attraction. The magnet temporarily aligns the atoms in the

Like Poles Repel
The iron filings show the attraction and repulsion of the magnets' magnetic fields. With the two north poles face to face, the magnets repel each other.

Opposite Poles Attract
With opposite poles facing one another, the magnets attract each other.

iron in the same direction as the atoms in the magnet.

On the other hand, if you bring a magnet near an object that contains no magnetic material, nothing will happen. The atoms in the nonmagnetic material will not be affected.

 **DRAW CONCLUSIONS** What are some magnetic materials?

Making Magnets

There are several ways to change the alignment of atoms in magnetic materials. As you have seen, bringing a permanent magnet close to a magnetic material will temporarily change the alignment of its atoms. When you take the magnet away, however, the atoms of the magnetic material lose their alignment.

For example, if you rub a magnet along an iron nail, the nail's atoms will begin to align. Continue rubbing for a few minutes, and the nail's atoms will stay aligned for a short time after you take the magnet away. The nail itself will become a magnet for a little while. A magnet that is created this way is called a temporary magnet.

The alignment of atoms in magnets can also be changed. If you strike or heat a magnet, some of the magnet's atoms will move out of alignment. For example, if you drop a magnet on the floor, it will become weaker.

Another way to change the alignment of atoms in a magnetic material is by using an electric current. Electrons moving through a wire create a magnetic field around the wire. When magnetic materials are placed within these fields, some of their atoms will align. The greater the electric current that runs through the wire, the stronger the magnetic field will be.

A magnet created by using an electric current is called an **electromagnet.** You can construct a simple electromagnet by using a flashlight battery, a coil of insulated wire, and an iron core, such as a nail. First, coil the wire around the nail, as shown in the picture below. Make sure that the coils are all wrapped in the same direction.

Next, carefully tape one bare end of the wire to the positive terminal on the battery and the other bare end to the negative terminal. The nail will act as a magnet as long as an electric current passes through the coil.

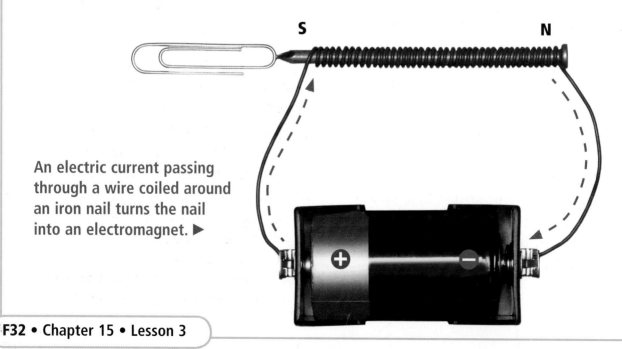

An electric current passing through a wire coiled around an iron nail turns the nail into an electromagnet. ▶

When a doorbell button is pressed, a coil of wire is magnetized, attracting the rod and causing it to hit the bell.

You can increase the strength of an electromagnet by wrapping more coils around the core, and by using a stronger battery. Be careful, however! In addition to creating magnetic fields, an electric current running through a wire can generate heat. Too much electric current could make the wire or the nail too hot to touch. Only use flashlight batteries that provide 1.5 volts.

You can conduct different experiments to create electromagnets. For example, you can try magnetic materials other than a nail, such as a paper clip, a pair of scissors, or a piece of silverware. Check the item with a magnet first to see if would make a good electromagnet. If the item is strongly attracted to the magnet, then it will probably make a good electromagnet.

Another experiment you can try is to change the number of turns on the wire coil. Test three different numbers of turns and record how many paper clips you can pick up in each case.

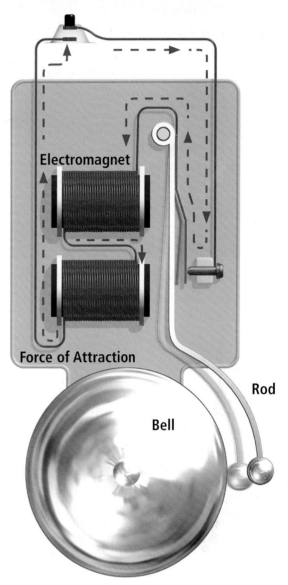

How a Doorbell Works

Switch (doorbell button)

Electromagnet

Force of Attraction

Bell

Rod

Electromagnets can create very powerful magnetic fields. These devices have many different uses, from picking up and moving cars at a junkyard to sending bullet trains speeding across the countryside. Electromagnets are also used in electric motors found in many household appliances.

▶ **DRAW CONCLUSIONS** What causes the atoms in an electromagnet to align?

▲ Aurora Borealis is Latin and means "dawn of the north."

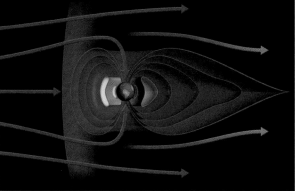

The arrows represent solar wind. These fast-moving electrons distort Earth's magnetic field and can cause auroras in the skies above both magnetic poles. ▼

Auroras

If you are far enough north and go outside on a dark night, you might see ribbons and curtains of green or red light chase across the sky. This is the aurora borealis (aw RAWR uh bawr ee AL ihs) or northern lights.

What causes the aurora? Recall that Earth is like a giant magnet. Like a bar magnet, Earth has a north magnetic pole and a south magnetic pole. The magnetic lines of force are closest together at the magnetic poles and Earth's magnetic field surrounds the planet.

Fast electrons from space are guided by Earth's magnetic field into Earth's upper atmosphere. There, at altitudes of 100 km (60 mi) or higher, the fast electrons collide with atoms and molecules of oxygen and nitrogen that make up Earth's atmosphere. In the collisions, the electrons give up their energy to the atoms and molecules, which emit light you see as an aurora.

The color of the aurora depends on the type of gas molecules that are hit by the electrons. This is just like in a neon sign, where the color of the light depends on the type of gas the sign is filled with.

Where do the fast electrons come from? They come from the Sun! The Sun continuously sends out a stream of charged particles in all directions, called the solar wind.

Auroras are also produced near Earth's South Pole. As you might have guessed, these auroras are called southern lights.

▶ DRAW CONCLUSIONS Why do auroras occur in Earth's polar regions?

Lesson Wrap-Up

Visual Summary

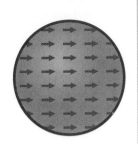 Atoms have small magnetic fields. In magnets, these fields all point in the same direction, one larger, stronger magnetic field.

 Electrons moving through a wire create a magnetic field around the wire. When a magnetic material is placed within this field, its atoms are temporarily aligned, creating a strong magnetic field.

 Technologies that use magnets and electromagnets include doorbells, bullet trains, and electric motors.

LINKS for Home and School

MATH **Angle Measures** The face of a compass represents 360°. What is the angle measure between N and S? Between N and E? Do these angles depend on the diameter of the compass?

TECHNOLOGY **Create a Poster**
Research a device that uses magnets, such as a television, computer storage disk, or mag-lev train. Prepare a poster to show how the device is used and how it works.

Review

❶ MAIN IDEA What gives magnets their magnetic properties?

❷ VOCABULARY What is an electromagnet? Describe its properties and how it works.

❸ READING SKILL: Draw Conclusions
Suppose that two electromagnets attract each other, then suddenly repel each other. What conclusion could explain this observation?

❹ CRITICAL THINKING: Apply
While on a hike, you notice that the needle of your compass suddenly points to a new direction. Aside from moving the compass, what might cause such a change?

❺ INQUIRY SKILL: Infer
Suppose you have a magnet that is losing some of its strength. What might have happened to it?

✔ TEST PREP
Magnetism is a force created by

A. gravity.

B. the motion of electrons in atoms.

C. the size of nuclei in atoms.

D. very large molecules.

 Technology
Visit **www.eduplace.com/scp/** to find out more about magnetism.

Train or Plane?

Can you fly without leaving the ground? Yes, if you're riding China's new Maglev train. This train can reach incredible speeds—up to 310 mph!

More amazing still, the Maglev has no engine and no wheels! What's the secret? Magnets! "Maglev" stands for magnetic levitation, because powerful electromagnets lift, or "levitate," the train off the track. The Maglev floats about half an inch above a guideway. Because powerful magnets in the guideway propel the Maglev along, it has no need for an engine or to carry fuel as conventional trains do.

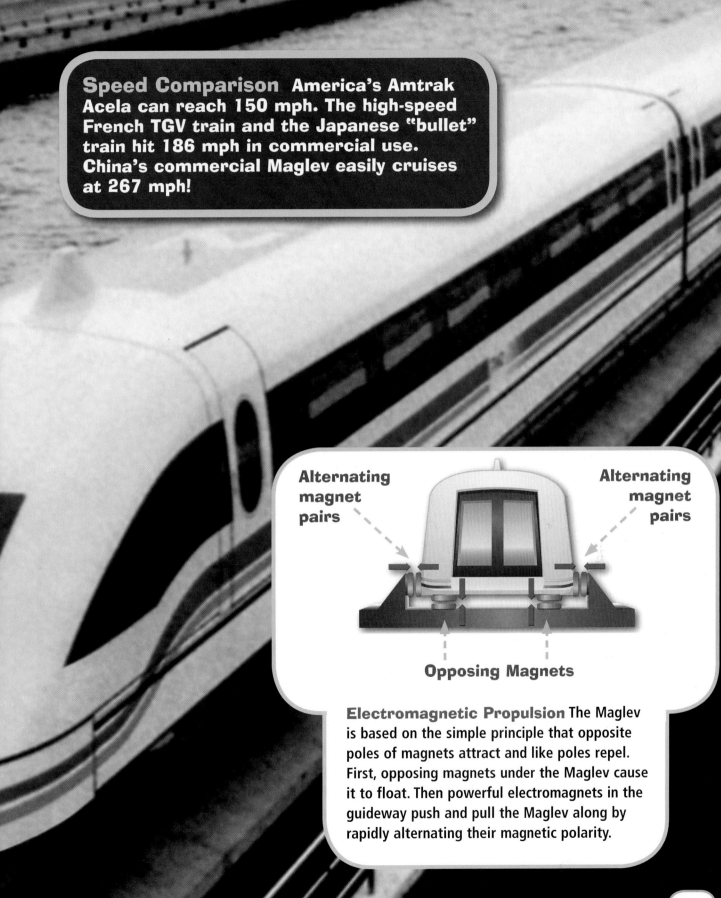

Speed Comparison America's Amtrak Acela can reach 150 mph. The high-speed French TGV train and the Japanese "bullet" train hit 186 mph in commercial use. China's commercial Maglev easily cruises at 267 mph!

Alternating magnet pairs

Alternating magnet pairs

Opposing Magnets

Electromagnetic Propulsion The Maglev is based on the simple principle that opposite poles of magnets attract and like poles repel. First, opposing magnets under the Maglev cause it to float. Then powerful electromagnets in the guideway push and pull the Maglev along by rapidly alternating their magnetic polarity.

Vocabulary

Complete each sentence with a term from the list.

1. Anything that causes an object to change velocity is a _____.

2. _____ is the rate at which an object changes speed.

3. _____ happens when an object changes its position.

4. A _____ is a tool that changes the amount of force applied, the direction of that force, or both.

5. The measure of an object's speed and direction is _____.

6. A _____ is a unit of force.

7. _____ is a ratio of distance over time.

8. _____ is a force that attracts all matter to other matter.

9. When two objects rub together, there is _____.

10. _____ is performed when a force moves an object through a distance.

acceleration F9
electromagnet F32
force F7
friction F12
gravity F12
inertia F7
motion F6
newton F11
simple machine F17
speed F8
velocity F8
work F16

✓ Test Prep

Write the letter of the best answer choice.

11. An electromagnet is powered by _____.

    A. the Sun
    B. an electric current
    C. iron filings
    D. atoms

12. Air resistance is a form of _____.

    A. gravity
    B. magnetism
    C. friction
    D. velocity

13. A hand brake on a bicycle is an example of a(n) _____.

    A. pulley
    B. inclined plane
    C. lever
    D. wheel and axle

14. The first law of motion deals with _____.

    A. inertia
    B. acceleration
    C. gravity
    D. friction

15. **Infer** What are some effects of Earth's magnetic field?

16. **Communicate** How would you describe the difference between Newton's first and second laws of motion?

Map the Concept

Write the terms from the list below where they belong in the concept map.

screw

wedge

lever

pulley

simple machine

wheel and axle

inclined plane

17. **Applying** What might happen if an astronaut floating in space moved the north poles of two magnets together, then let go of the magnets?

18. **Synthesizing** How would you use a pulley to decrease the amount of force required to lift an object? Include a diagram in your answer.

19. **Evaluating** Is it accurate to say that if an object changes its direction of motion, then its speed changes? Explain.

20. **Analyzing** How are inclined planes and screws related? Describe ways they are used.

Performance Assessment

Make a Poster

Choose a simple machine, and make a poster about it. Show how the simple machine makes work easier to do, and present some examples of real-life uses of the machine.

Chapter 16

Energy and Waves

Lesson Preview

LESSON 1

What kind of energy comes from a swinging wrecking ball?

Read about it in Lesson 1.

LESSON 2

How does striking cymbals together create energy that travels to your ear?

Read about it in Lesson 2.

LESSON 3

How does light striking glass produce such colorful light?

Read about it in Lesson 3.

What Are Kinetic and Potential Energy?

Why It Matters...

Drop a ball in water. Waves will ripple away from the place where it strikes, forming wider and wider circles. Why does this happen? Some of the energy of the falling ball is transferred to the water making waves. The waves lose energy as they spread apart.

Changes in energy take place all the time. If you understand them, you can put them to good use.

PREPARE TO INVESTIGATE

Inquiry Skill

Predict When you predict, you use observations, patterns, data, or cause-and-effect relationships to anticipate results.

Materials

- tape
- 1.5 m of clear plastic tubing
- marble

Science and Math Toolbox

For step 1, review **Making a Chart to Organize Data** on page H11.

Rollerball

Procedure

1. **Collaborate** Work with a partner to create a roller coaster for the marble. Tape one end of the tubing to the edge of your desk. This will be the start of the track. In your *Science Notebook,* create a chart like the one shown.

2. **Experiment** Tape the other end of the tubing to the seat of a chair that is lower than the desk. Let the tubing drape between the desk and the chair so that it just touches the floor.

3. **Observe** Drop the marble into the top of the tubing. Observe how the marble travels. Use a chart to record your observations of the marble's changes in speed.

4. **Use Variables** Tape the tubing that was on the chair to another desk of the same height as the first desk. Drop the marble through the tube. Record your observations of the marble's movement.

5. **Predict** Hold the end of the tube higher than the desk. Predict how far the marble will run through the tubing. Test your prediction.

Conclusion

1. **Infer** How did the height at the end of the track affect the speed of the marble through the tubing?

2. **Hypothesize** Was your prediction in step 5 correct? Propose an explanation of the results.

STEP 1

Height at Start		
Height at End		
Observations		

STEP 2

STEP 3

Investigate More!

Design an Experiment
Will twists and turns in the tubing change the height a marble can travel? Experiment with different arrangements. Choose a graph or chart to report data from the experiment.

Energy

VOCABULARY

energy	p. F44
kinetic energy	p. F46
potential energy	p. F46

READING SKILL

Classify What are some examples of potential energy and what are some types of kinetic energy?

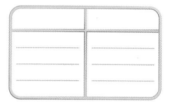

MAIN IDEA Kinetic energy and potential energy can each be transformed into the other. In all cases, energy is neither created nor destroyed.

Forms of Energy

Energy is a familiar part of your everyday life. A burning lump of coal, a falling rock, and a spinning fan all have energy. What do these examples have in common? Each describes an object that is changing. Each is an example of energy's effect on matter.

Just what is energy? **Energy** is the ability to do work. Energy and work are measured by the same unit, the joule.

Energy comes in many different forms. When coal is burned, for example, chemical energy stored in the coal is converted to light that you can see and heat that you can feel. The motor of a fan changes electrical energy into energy of the spinning blades. A falling rock has energy because it is moving.

Even objects at rest have energy. Remember that matter is made up of particles that are constantly in motion. Thermal energy is the motion of these particles, which you can feel as heat. When energy is changed from one form to another, some of it is almost always changed into thermal energy.

Energy at Mission Control

◀ Electrical energy powers the computers. Radio waves, a form of electromagnetic energy, allow controllers to talk to the astronauts.

Visible light is one type of electromagnetic energy. So are microwaves, radio waves, and x-rays.

When the electromagnetic energy in sunlight reaches Earth, some of it is absorbed and changed into thermal energy. Plants also use the energy in sunlight to produce food, which they store as chemical energy.

Matter contains chemical energy, which can be released during a chemical reaction. Chemical energy in coal is released when the coal burns. Chemical energy in a battery is used to power devices such as flashlights.

Electricity is the movement of charged particles. People use electricity to power toasters, streetlights, televisions, computers, and many other things. In each, electrical energy is changed into thermal energy, electromagnetic energy, or mechanical energy.

The energy that an object has because of its motion or its position is called mechanical energy. For example, an acorn hanging from a tree has mechanical energy because of its position above the ground. When it falls, it has mechanical energy because it is in motion.

A vibrating object has mechanical energy that may be changed to sound energy. Wind is the mechanical energy of moving air. The moving parts of a machine have mechanical energy, too.

▶ **CLASSIFY** A large rock on the edge of a cliff has what form of energy?

Chemical energy in the rocket fuel is changed to the mechanical energy of the moving rocket, as well as thermal energy and electromagnetic energy. ▶

Potential Energy and Kinetic Energy

Recall that energy is the ability to do work. Energy can be transferred from one object to another, and it can change form. How do these ideas relate to one another?

Work involves applying a force to matter over a distance. Any time that work is done, energy is either transferred from one object to another or changed from one form to another.

Think of a bowling ball rolling down a lane. Work was done to set the ball in motion. Work is done on the pin when mechanical energy from the ball is transferred to the pin.

When chemicals react in a battery, electrons move through a wire or other conductor. Chemical energy is transformed to electrical energy when work is done on the electrons.

From these examples, you can see that motion and matter are an important part of understanding energy. In fact, energy can be described by the way it relates to the motion of matter.

Any object that is in motion has **kinetic energy.** Kinetic energy is the energy of a moving object. A moving bowling ball has kinetic energy. So do the moving electrons in an electric current.

Potential energy is energy that is stored in an object. Chemical bonds in a bowler's muscles store potential energy that the bowler uses to swing the ball. The chemicals in a battery store potential energy that is used to create an electric current.

The archer in the picture used energy to pull the bowstring and bend the bow. While she holds the bowstring and takes aim, that energy is stored in the bent bow. Because of its position, the arrow has potential mechanical energy.

◄ A pulled bow has potential energy. When the bow is released, the energy is changed to the kinetic energy of a moving bow and arrow.

As soon as she releases the bowstring, the bow will return to its original shape. The potential energy stored in the bow will be transformed into kinetic energy of the moving bowstring. Some of that kinetic energy will be transferred to the arrow and send it flying forward.

The archer was able to store energy in the bow by changing the bow's shape. Potential energy can also be stored in an object by changing the object's height.

If you lift a box from the floor and set it on a table, you are applying a force to raise the box against the force of gravity. So, you do work on the box. As it rests on the table, the box has potential energy due to its height. Push the box off the table, and that potential energy would be converted to kinetic energy as the box falls.

Energy is either potential or kinetic. The charts provide examples.

▶ **CLASSIFY** Give two examples of energy changing from potential energy to kinetic energy.

Potential Energy	
Potential Energy	**Example**
Chemical	battery
Elastic	compressed spring
Mechanical	rock on a ledge

Kinetic Energy	
Kinetic Energy	**Example**
Sound	vibrating object
Thermal	hot cocoa
Mechanical	falling rock
Electrical	electrons in an electrical current

Some of the kinetic energy of the moving boat is transferred to the water, making waves. ▼

All PE

Half PE   Half KE

All KE

Calculating Mechanical Energy

When an object that has potential mechanical energy starts moving, some of its potential energy is transformed into kinetic mechanical energy. As the object's kinetic energy increases, its potential energy decreases. Another way of saying this is that the mechanical energy (ME) of an object equals the sum of its potential energy (PE) and its kinetic energy (KE).

$$ME = PE + KE$$

Look at the falling apple. As the apple is held by its stem, all of its mechanical energy is stored as potential energy, due to its height above the ground. The apple is not in motion, so it has no kinetic energy.

As the apple is released and starts to fall, it loses potential energy and gains kinetic energy. The farther the apple falls, the greater its kinetic energy and the less its potential energy. The total mechanical energy remains the same.

The instant before the apple hits the floor, all of its mechanical energy will have been converted to kinetic energy. It will have no more potential energy relative to the ground.

▶ **CLASSIFY** **How does the mechanical energy of an object change as it falls?**

◀ **In this time-lapse photograph, the energy of the falling apple is changed from potential to kinetic.**

Lesson Wrap-Up

Visual Summary

Energy has many different forms. It can be changed from one form to another, but not created or destroyed.

Potential energy is energy stored in an object. Kinetic energy is the energy of motion.

Mechanical energy of a falling object is the sum of its potential energy and kinetic energy.

LINKS for Home and School

MATH Make a Graph Calculate the potential energy, in joules, of a 5-kg ball at different heights above the ground. Use the formula $PE = mgh$, where m is the mass in kilograms, g is 9.8 m/s², and h is the height in meters. Make a line graph to show the results.

WRITING Expository Research new technologies for converting solar energy directly into electrical energy. Write a report about the new technologies.

Review

1 MAIN IDEA What is the difference between potential energy and kinetic energy?

2 VOCABULARY Explain how potential energy and kinetic energy relate to mechanical energy.

3 READING SKILL: Classify Describe the changes in energy when an apple falls.

4 CRITICAL THINKING: Evaluate When are an object's potential energy and kinetic energy equal? Give an example.

5 INQUIRY SKILL: Predict How do you think an object's speed affects its kinetic energy? Do you think mass affects kinetic energy? How might you test your answers?

✓ TEST PREP

When does a falling object have the greatest mechanical energy?

A. Just before it starts to fall.

B. Just before it hits the ground.

C. Half way through the fall.

D. The mechanical energy is the same throughout the fall.

Technology

Visit **www.eduplace.com/scp/** to learn more about kinetic and potential energy.

How Are Sounds Made?

Why It Matters...

Lions roar, winds whistle, and peals of thunder roll and bellow. You use sounds to communicate, to entertain, and to know when your classes begin or end.

If you play a musical instrument, then you know at least one way to make sounds and change them. Just how do sounds change?

PREPARE TO INVESTIGATE

Inquiry Skill

Hypothesize When you hypothesize, you use observations or prior knowledge to suggest a possible answer to a question.

Materials

- tuning forks with three different pitches
- bowl
- water
- block of wood
- sheet of metal
- rubber eraser

Science and Math Toolbox
For step 5, review **Making a Chart to Organize Data** on page H11.

Getting in Tune

Procedure

1 **Classify** Strike each tuning fork against the palm of your hand, then place it close to your ear to listen. Classify the sounds from each tuning fork as low, middle, and high. Record your observations in your *Science Notebook.*

2 **Compare** Fill the bowl with water. Again, strike each tuning fork. Each time, dip the forked end slowly in the water after striking it. Observe and compare the sizes of the ripples produced.

3 **Hypothesize** Form a hypothesis about whether sounds change when they travel through different materials, such as wood, metal, and rubber.

4 **Experiment** Strike a tuning fork and hold the end of its handle against the block of wood. Listen, then record what you hear. Repeat with the metal sheet and the rubber eraser.

5 **Communicate** Make a chart to organize the information that you recorded. Use the chart to compare your observations with those of another student.

Conclusion

1. **Analyze Data** What do the ripples in the water show about the tuning forks?

2. **Compare** Did evidence support your hypothesis from step 3? Compare your hypothesis to the results of the experiment.

STEP 1

STEP 2

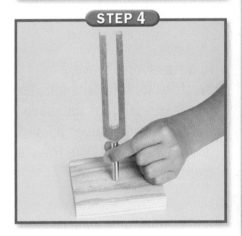

STEP 4

Investigate More!

Design an Experiment
Investigate the effect of changing tension or thickness of a vibrating object, such as a string or a rubber band. Plan an experiment. With your teacher's permission, carry it out. Record your results.

Sound Production

VOCABULARY

mechanical wave   p. F52
pitch   p. F56
vibration   p. F54
volume   p. F57

READING SKILL

Draw Conclusions Can sound be created in a vacuum?

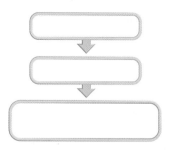

In a transverse wave, particles move perpendicular to the direction of the wave. Here, the rope moves up and down while the wave travels from left to right. ▼

MAIN IDEA Sound is produced by vibrations that transfer energy through air or another medium.

Mechanical Waves

A **mechanical wave** forms when a disturbance causes energy to be transferred through matter, such as air or water. Mechanical waves always need matter to move through. Mechanical waves cannot travel through empty space. That's why you cannot hear sounds on the Moon.

Mechanical waves can move in different ways. The rope pictured below is moving in a transverse wave. This means that the medium moves perpendicular to the direction of the wave. The rope, which is the medium, moves up and down. The wave moves from left to right.

Part of the rope moves up as the energy moves through it. As that part of the rope drops back down, it transfers the energy to the next part of the rope, which in turn moves up. In this way, the energy is transferred through the rope from left to right as the rope moves up and down.

Transverse Wave

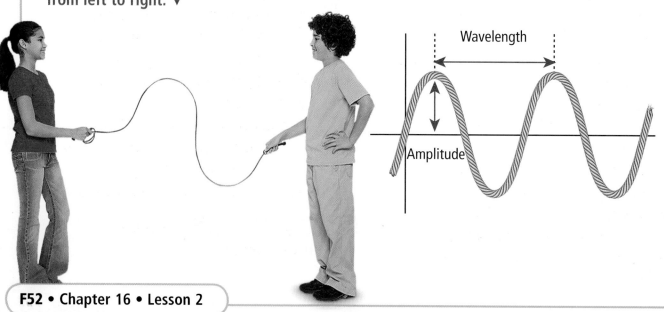

Wavelength

Amplitude

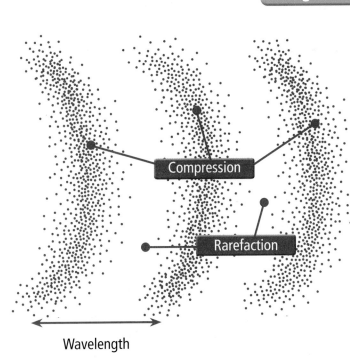

Compression

Rarefaction

Wavelength

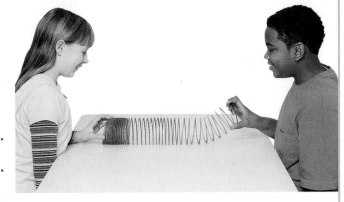

◀ In a longitudinal wave, particles move parallel to the direction in which the wave travels. They form compressions and rarefactions, transferring energy away from the source.

Water waves are transverse mechanical waves. If you drop a rock into water, ripples will spread out through the water in all directions. These ripples are created by energy passing through the water. Particles of water move up and down, forming the ripples. The energy is transferred outward from the rock, creating new ripples as it moves.

Scientists describe waves by their amplitude and wavelength. Amplitude is the height of the crests or troughs from the rest position of a transverse wave. Wavelength is the distance between two neighboring crests or troughs.

Scientists also describe a wave's frequency, which is the number of waves that pass a point per second. Frequency and wavelength are related. Waves with shorter wavelengths have higher frequencies. Waves with longer wavelengths have lower frequencies.

Longitudinal waves are also mechanical waves. In a longitudinal wave, particles in the medium move back and forth parallel to the direction the wave travels.

In the picture above, one of the students quickly pushed the spring forward and then snapped it back. Coils along the spring come together and spread apart as energy is transferred through them. The coils move back and forth only.

The part of a longitudinal wave where the particles come together is called a compression. The part where they spread out is called a rarefaction.

 **DRAW CONCLUSIONS** **What is a mechanical wave?**

Sound Waves

Sound waves are longitudinal mechanical waves that move through air or another medium. These waves are produced by vibrations. A **vibration** is a rapid back-and-forth movement of an object.

When an object vibrates, it transfers energy to its surroundings. The energy of those vibrations travels through the surrounding medium as longitudinal waves.

Most of the sounds that you hear are transferred through air. If a pencil is tapped against a desk, both the pencil and the desk vibrate. The vibrations are too tiny to see, but they are there.

The vibrations compress and spread apart the air molecules around them. As the first molecules are pushed away, they bump into molecules next to them. These molecules then bump into other nearby molecules, while the first molecules return to where they were.

This pattern continues, spreading out from the desk and the pencil like ripples in a pond. However, the desk and pencil do not vibrate for very long. That's why the sound that they create doesn't last very long.

Other types of materials, such as metals, vibrate more easily. Consider a metal tuning fork. When struck, its vibrations are easy to see. It makes a sound that lasts much longer than the sound made by the pencil hitting the desk.

Look at the sousaphone. It produces sound when air travels through it. When the player's lips vibrate, the air inside the sousaphone vibrates, too. As the vibrating air moves through the instrument, the metal itself vibrates and magnifies the sound.

Sousaphone
A sousaphone is much like a tuba. Its coiled shape makes it easier to carry. ▶

Waves travel at different speeds through different materials. This is true of all types of mechanical waves, including sound waves.

For example, sound waves generally move faster through solids and liquids than through gases. The temperature of the medium, especially gases, also affects the speed. The chart shows the speeds of sound through some different materials.

How can the different speeds of sound be put to use? Railroad workers have been known to put their ears to the track to listen for oncoming trains. Woodpeckers listen to trees to hear the bugs inside them. Long ago, Native Americans on the plains put their ears to the ground to listen for buffalo hoofbeats.

▶ **DRAW CONCLUSIONS** Through which state of matter—solids, liquids, or gases—do sounds travel the fastest?

Speed of Sound in Different Materials

Material	Speed (m/s)
Dry air (25°C)	346
Fresh water	1,500
Wood (oak)	1,850
Gold	3,240
Steel	5,200

Sound waves
Sound waves cause compressions and rarefactions of the air. Your eardrums vibrate in response. Your brain interprets those vibrations as sound. ▲

Oscilloscope
An oscilloscope can picture a sound wave. Although sound waves are longitudinal, the oscilloscope produces a picture of a transverse wave. ▲

Pitch

Sound waves have different properties depending on the vibrations of the object that produced them. **Pitch** is how high or low you perceive the sound to be.

The pitch of a sound depends on the sound wave's frequency. The higher the frequency of a wave, the higher the pitch of the sound. You can change the pitch of a sound by changing the frequency at which the object making the sound vibrates.

Whistles make high-pitched sounds because they vibrate at a high frequency. Tubas and sousaphones make low-pitched sounds because they vibrate at a low frequency.

A piano has many strings that vary in thickness and length. When you strike a piano key, the pitch of the sound produced depends on the properties of the string that vibrates. Long, thick strings produce low-pitched sounds. Short, thin strings produce high-pitched sounds.

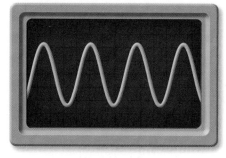

Low-frequency, loud sound

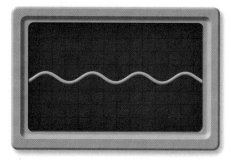

Low-frequency, soft sound

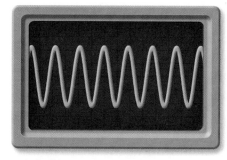

High-frequency, loud sound

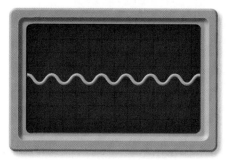

High-frequency, soft sound

Sound Waves ▲

Digital recording software produces graphs like these. They represent sound waves as transverse waves. The amplitude shows volume. The frequency or wavelength shows pitch.

Volume

Another property of sound is volume. **Volume** is how loud or soft a sound is. It is a measure of the intensity, or strength, of the vibrations that produce a sound. Intensity is determined by the amplitude of the sound waves.

Like the strings of a piano, the strings on a guitar produce sounds of different pitch. The fifth string on a guitar is tuned to a pitch called low A. When you pluck this string, it will always vibrate at a frequency of 440 times per second. So, it will always produce a sound with the same pitch.

The volume, or loudness, of the sound produced by this string depends on how much force you use to pluck it. Pluck it lightly and it will vibrate back and forth across a short distance. Air particles will be displaced a smaller distance from their rest positions, producing a soft sound with low-A pitch.

What happens if you use a stronger force to pluck the string? The string will vibrate back and forth across a greater distance. Air particles will be displaced a greater distance from their rest positions, producing a louder sound. The sound will, however, have the same pitch.

▶ **DRAW CONCLUSIONS** What is the difference between pitch and volume?

Decibel Levels of Common Sounds	
Sound	**Decibels**
Softest sound you can hear	1
Whisper	20
Normal speaking	60
Music through headphones	100
Thunder	120
Jet plane (from 30m)	140

▲ Scientists measure the loudness of sound in units called decibels. Continuous sound above 85 decibels can damage hearing.

Without protective ear mufflers, a jet engine, at 140 decibels, can cause permanent hearing damage within a few minutes of exposure. ▼

This is one of the world's quietest rooms! The pyramid shapes help to prevent echoes and keep outside sounds from entering the room. ▼

This concert hall is designed to allow both the audience and the musicians on stage to hear the music clearly. ▲

Acoustics

Like other types of waves, sound waves behave in different ways when traveling from one material into another. When a sound wave strikes a surface, it may reflect off it, travel through it, or be absorbed by it. Acoustics is the study of how materials affect sound waves.

When a sound wave in air hits a concrete wall, most of the sound wave will be reflected, or bounced off the surface. Sound waves behave this way when they strike most hard, smooth surfaces. This is why you hear an echo when you yell into a canyon.

When a sound wave hits something soft or porous, most of it will be absorbed. Cotton and other fabrics are examples of materials that absorb sounds well.

Some materials reflect or absorb sound differently, depending on the frequency of the sound. Architects take this into account when they design concert halls and auditoriums. The goal is to project a balance of sound frequencies to the audience.

For example, if the wall behind an orchestra reflected mostly high-pitched frequencies, the music would sound thin and squeaky. If it reflected mostly low-pitched frequencies, the music would sound muffled. As for the back and side walls, they usually are designed to absorb sound. If they were reflective, the music would not sound very clear.

▶ **DRAW CONCLUSIONS** Why does your voice sound different in the living room than in the shower?

Visual Summary

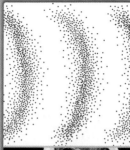

Mechanical waves require a medium to move through. They may travel as transverse waves or longitudinal waves.

Pitch is a measure of the frequency of sound waves. Amplitude is a measure of their volume.

Sound waves behave differently when they encounter different materials. Some materials reflect sound, while others absorb sound.

LINKS for Home and School

MATH **Make a Graph** Choose three different musical instruments. Find the frequencies of the lowest and highest pitches that the instruments can play. Create a graph to show the range of pitch for the instruments.

TECHNOLOGY **Make a Poster**
Research how a stereo speaker detects electrical currents and turns them into sound waves. Make a poster to show the different parts of the speaker and how they produce sound waves.

Review

1 MAIN IDEA What are sound waves and how do they travel?

2 VOCABULARY What are vibrations? Give an example of an object that vibrates and the effect of the vibrations.

3 READING SKILL: Draw Conclusions Why is it important to wear ear protection if you are working with a loud device such as a jackhammer?

4 CRITICAL THINKING: Synthesize How could you change the area around your home stereo so that you could hear the music more clearly?

5 INQUIRY SKILL: Hypothesize How might sound reflect off a hard, curved surface? Propose a hypothesis.

 TEST PREP
Waves observed in a moving rope are examples of

A. longitudinal waves.

B. transverse waves.

C. compression waves.

D. electromagnetic waves.

 Technology
Visit **www.eduplace.com/scp/** to find out more about sound.

The Sound Barrier?

In 1947 Chuck Yeager and the X-1 showed that the sound barrier was not a real barrier at all.

Sound travels through air at about 340 meters per second, which is about 760 miles per hour. Could an airplane fly this fast? In the years shortly after World War II, pilots and engineers tried to find out.

Several experimental planes shook violently as they approached the speed of sound. Some crashed. Pilots began to speak of a sound barrier, a natural speed limit that might not be breakable.

One pilot did not believe in this barrier. In 1947, U.S. Air Force pilot Chuck Yeager was setting speed records in a rocket-powered airplane called the X-1. During one October morning that year, Yeager accelerated the X-1 to greater speeds than ever before. Suddenly a loud boom and the airplane's dials indicated the same event: Yeager had "broken" the sound barrier. He was flying faster than the speed of sound! And he experienced hardly any bumps or jolts at all.

How a Sonic Boom Forms

Below the Speed of Sound

As an airplane moves faster, sound waves bunch closer together in front of it.

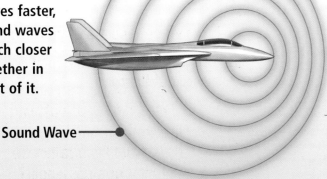

Sound Wave

At the Speed of Sound

The sound waves travel as fast as the airplane itself and run into each other in front of the airplane.

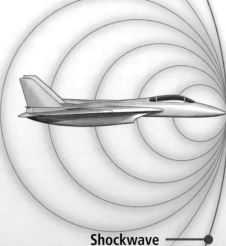

Shockwave

A fast-moving airplane creates a wave of air pressure around it. When it passes the speed of sound, the pressure is so great that water vapor condenses into a temporary cloud.

Today The F/A-18 Hornet is one of the fastest airplanes in the sky. It can fly as fast as Mach 1.8, meaning 1.8 times the speed of sound. Today, it is common for military jets to fly faster than the speed of sound.

Beyond the Speed of Sound

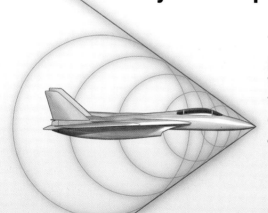

The sound waves produce a shock wave that reaches the ground and can be heard as a sonic boom.

Sonic Boom heard here

Sharing Ideas

1. **READING CHECK** Why did some pilots think that airplanes could not fly faster than the speed of sound?

2. **WRITE ABOUT IT** Describe what happens when a plane accelerates past the speed of sound.

3. **TALK ABOUT IT** Would you like to fly faster than sound? If so, would you rather be the pilot or a passenger?

Lesson 3

What Are Some Properties of Light?

Why It Matters...

Light waves make it possible to see. By understanding the way light waves behave, scientists have been able to develop such important technologies as eyeglasses, cameras, microscopes, telescopes, lasers, and fiber optics.

PREPARE TO INVESTIGATE

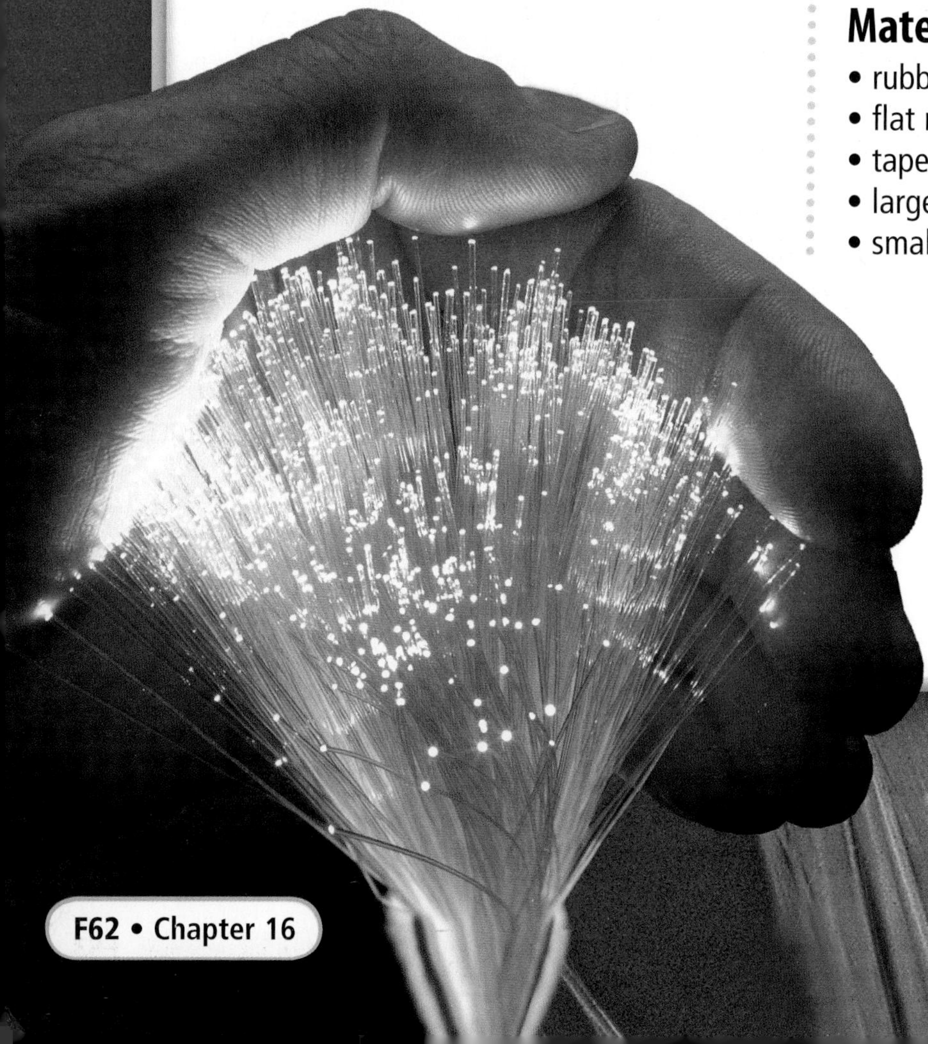

Inquiry Skill

Analyze Data When you analyze data, you look for patterns in observations and other information. These patterns can help you to make inferences, predict, and hypothesize.

Materials

- rubber ball
- flat mirror
- tape
- large cardboard box
- small penlight

Bouncing Beam

Procedure

1. **Collaborate** Stand a few feet from a partner and bounce a ball back and forth. Observe the angle at which the ball strikes the floor and the angle at which it bounces up. Record your observations in your *Science Notebook.*

2. **Experiment** Change the distance between partners several times. Repeat step 1 at each new distance.

3. **Experiment** Inside the box, center the mirror on one end and tape it in place. Position the penlight as shown so that it faces the center of the mirror.

4. **Observe** In a darkened classroom, turn on the penlight and observe the angle at which the light strikes the mirror and the angle at which it bounces off. Record your observations.

5. **Experiment** Tilt the penlight slightly to change the angle at which the light strikes the mirror. Observe the path of the beam as it bounces off the mirror. Change the tilt of the penlight several times and record your observations.

STEP 1

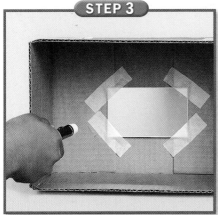
STEP 3

Conclusion

1. **Analyze Data** Compare the way that the ball bounced and the way that the beam behaved.

2. **Infer** Based on your data, make an inference about the angle at which light bounces, or reflects, off a flat mirror.

Investigate More!

Design an Experiment
How might a curved mirror affect the path of a light beam striking its surface? Experiment with a curved mirror to find out. You may design a curved mirror from aluminum foil.

Properties of Light

MAIN IDEA Light waves are electromagnetic waves. Light can travel through a vacuum or through a medium. White light can be separated into colors.

READING SKILL

Cause and Effect As you read, look for what causes light to be refracted.

Electromagnetic Waves

Mechanical waves, such as sound waves, always need a medium like air or water to travel through. Electromagnetic waves are waves that can travel through a medium or through a vacuum. Visible light, radio waves, gamma rays, microwaves, infrared rays, ultraviolet rays, and x-rays are all examples of electromagnetic waves. Together, these waves make up the electromagnetic spectrum, as shown in the chart on the facing page.

Different kinds of electromagnetic waves have different frequencies and wavelengths. Remember that wavelength is the distance between the wave's crests. Frequency is the number of wavelengths that pass a given point per second.

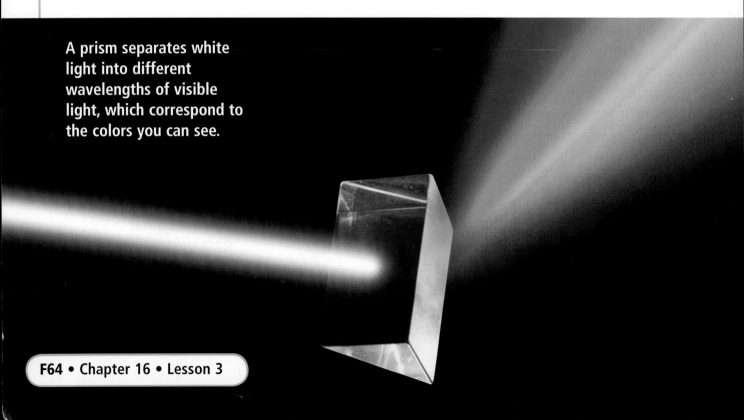

A prism separates white light into different wavelengths of visible light, which correspond to the colors you can see.

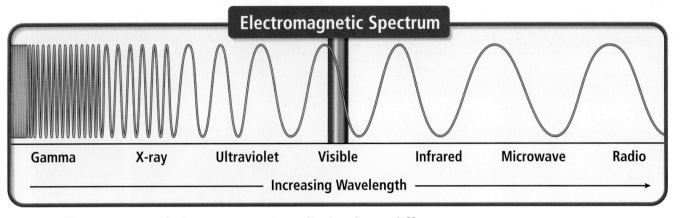

Electromagnetic Spectrum

Gamma   X-ray   Ultraviolet   Visible   Infrared   Microwave   Radio

— Increasing Wavelength →

▲ Different types of electromagnetic radiation have different properties, depending on their wavelengths and frequencies.

Visible light is radiation that humans can see. It is in the middle of the spectrum. Visible light consists of seven different colors of light, each with its own range of wavelengths.

The Sun and other stars constantly emit visible light, which is why we can see them. However, they also emit all of the other wavelengths of electromagnetic waves.

Some of these waves can be harmful to living things. Fortunately, Earth's atmosphere blocks many of the harmful x-rays from the Sun.

Sunlight reaching Earth's surface still contains ultraviolet (UV) radiation. Long exposure to UV radiation has been proven to cause skin cancer. That is why you should wear sunscreen to block UV radiation and protect your skin.

Like sound waves, electromagnetic waves interact differently with different materials. Radio waves can travel short distances through most materials. Visible light passes through transparent materials, such as glass, but can be blocked by most

other materials. Ozone in Earth's atmosphere absorbs UV rays. X-rays and gamma rays can penetrate most materials, but are stopped or slowed down by thick concrete, lead, or steel.

▶ **CAUSE AND EFFECT** How do electromagnetic waves differ?

▲ Different materials will reflect certain wavelengths of light and absorb others. The apple reflects red wavelengths and absorbs other wavelengths.

F65

Reflection and Refraction

Electromagnetic waves behave in different ways when they strike different materials. Sometimes the waves are absorbed. Absorbed light is converted into thermal energy. Other wavelengths may be reflected. **Reflection** occurs when a wave bounces off of a material. Light reflecting from objects is what makes them visible.

The metal used to coat the back of a mirror is an example of a material that reflects almost all light that strikes it. When you look at a mirror, you see all the different wavelengths of light reflected. The image you see is almost like looking at the object itself!

Like sound waves, light waves travel at different speeds through different materials. When light waves pass from one material into another, they usually change speed. This change causes the light to refract, or bend. **Refraction** occurs when the path of a light wave changes as it moves from one material to another.

Refraction ▲
Refraction causes the pencil to appear broken, even though it is not.

For an example, look at the picture of the pencil in the glass. The pencil appears to be broken, although it is not. It appears broken because light travels through water and glass at different speeds than through air. The light waves refract, or bend, as they pass from water to glass to air on their way to the lens of the camera that took the picture.

How can refraction be put to good use? Devices that refract light include eyeglasses, contact lenses, cameras, microscopes, and telescopes.

◄ Reflection
A mirror reflects most of the light coming from an object. The image you see in the mirror closely resembles the object itself.

All of these devices use lenses. A **lens** is a curved piece of clear material, typically glass or plastic, that refracts light in a predictable way. Lenses can refract light to create useful images of an object.

There are many kinds of lenses. A convex lens is thicker at the center than at its edges. This type of lens bends light rays toward one another.

A concave lens is thinner at its center. It bends light rays away from one another.

By combining convex and concave lenses in different ways, people can make all sorts of different devices. For example, many telescopes use two convex lenses to make faraway objects look larger. Microscopes use lenses to make small objects appear larger.

Your eyes also have lenses. In an eye with perfect vision, the lens focuses images onto a structure called the retina. Sometimes, images form slightly in front of or behind the retina, and vision is blurry. The remedy is corrective lenses, which bend light rays just enough to focus the image correctly.

▶ **CAUSE AND EFFECT** How can eyeglasses correct vision?

Normal Eyesight

Light that passes through the the lens of an eye is refracted so that it focuses an image at the back of the eye, or retina.

Corrected Eyesight

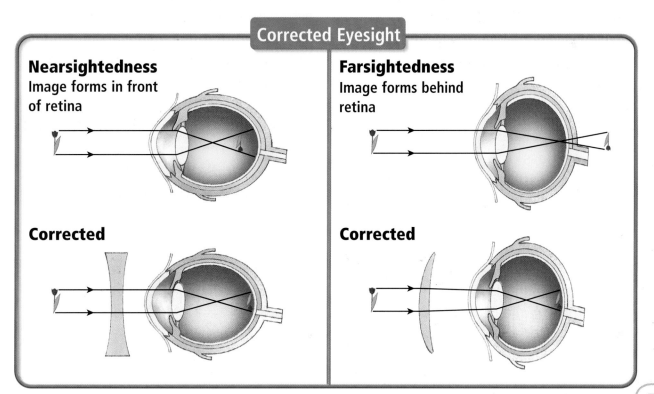

Nearsightedness
Image forms in front of retina

Corrected

Farsightedness
Image forms behind retina

Corrected

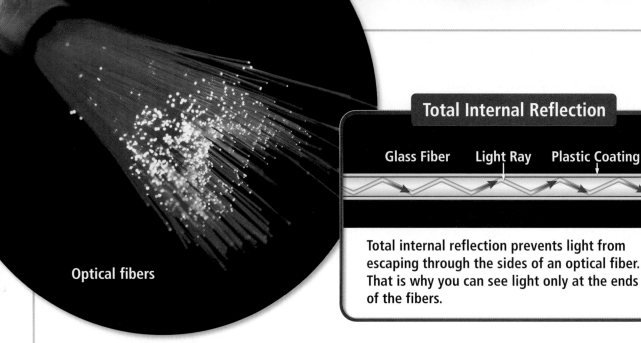

Optical fibers

Total Internal Reflection

Glass Fiber   Light Ray   Plastic Coating

Total internal reflection prevents light from escaping through the sides of an optical fiber. That is why you can see light only at the ends of the fibers.

Fiber Optics

Reflection of light lies at the heart of an important technology called fiber optics. In fiber optics, special fibers carry light waves along a flexible cable. The technology has improved communications over telephones and the Internet. Doctors use fiber optics to look down a patient's throat and into the stomach.

Remember that light typically travels in a straight line. How can it follow the looping path of an optical fiber? The answer depends on a property called total internal reflection.

When light strikes the inner surface of glass or plastic, it usually passes right through. However, when light strikes a surface at a wide enough angle, it will reflect, as if it hits a mirror.

If you look straight down into a lake, you will see through the water. But look at the surface at a wide enough angle, and the light will be reflected. ▶

Optical fibers use a special coating that reflects light. Light waves continuously reflect off the interior of the fiber as they travel along it. In this way, the fibers can transmit light over long distances.

▶ **CAUSE AND EFFECT** What property of light is used in optical fibers?

Lesson Wrap-Up

Visual Summary

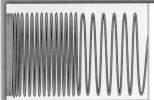

X-rays are examples of electromagnetic waves, forms of energy that can travel through a vacuum.

Gamma   X-ray

The colors that you see are different wavelengths of visible light. White light contains all of the different wavelengths of visible light.

Light can be transmitted, absorbed, reflected, or refracted.

LINKS for Home and School

MATH **Use a Protractor** With a partner, use a mirror to view an object around a corner. Note the positions of the viewer, the mirror, and the object. Use a protractor to measure the angle formed by the viewer, mirror, and object.

TECHNOLOGY **Make a Poster** Find out how certain types of microscopes or telescopes use mirrors and lenses to reflect and refract light. Make a poster that labels the parts of the device and shows the path of the light.

Review

❶ MAIN IDEA How are electromagnetic waves different from mechanical waves?

❷ VOCABULARY Write a paragraph about light using the terms *reflection* and *refraction*.

❸ READING SKILL: Cause and Effect What causes light to refract? Give an example from everyday life.

❹ CRITICAL THINKING: Apply What might cause an overhead projector image to be out of focus? How might you correct the problem?

❺ INQUIRY SKILL: Analyze Data A material's index of refraction indicates how greatly light is refracted by that material. Based on the data below, which material refracts light the most?

Material	Index of Refraction
Air	1.0
Glass	1.5
Water	1.3

 TEST PREP

Electromagnetic waves differ from mechanical waves in that they

A. can be reflected.

B. contain less energy.

C. can travel through a vacuum.

D. can travel through matter.

 Technology

Visit **www.eduplace.com/scp/** to find out more about light.

Extreme Beam

Imagine an operation where the doctor doesn't have to touch the patient. Impossible? Not with lasers!

Every year, thousands of people have surgery using laser light. Lasers cut with such amazing exactness that doctors can use them to perform the most delicate of operations, such as the eye surgery shown here.

What's so special about a laser beam? Unlike regular light, laser light is extremely concentrated and tightly organized. In a laser beam, the light is one wavelength, and the waves move in time with each other, like people marching in rows. These properties make laser light an extremely useful tool for making precision measurements and such products as computer chips.

Lasers are both precise and powerful. Here one is used to cut a length of pipe.

Laser Surgery

Doctors use laser beams to make a microscopic cut through the eye's transparent lens cover, or cornea. The laser will then shave off parts of the lens to reshape it. When the cornea heals, the patient will enjoy better vision.

Vocabulary

Complete each sentence with a term from the list.

1. The ____ of a sound is how high or low it is.

2. ____ includes all of the wavelengths of each color.

3. A rapid back-and-forth movement is a ____.

4. A ____ requires a medium to travel through.

5. ____ is the ability to do work.

6. Stored energy is called ____.

7. A ____ occurs when a wave bounces off a material.

8. ____ is a measure of a sound wave's intensity.

9. Energy an object has due to its motion is called ____.

10. ____ occurs when the path of light is changed by passing from one material into another.

energy F44
kinetic energy F46
lens F67
mechanical wave F52
pitch F56
potential energy F46
reflection F66
refraction F66
vibration F54
visible light F65
volume F57

Test Prep

Write the letter of the best answer choice.

11. An example of kinetic energy is ____.

    A. a rock held above the ground
    B. a bowstring pulled back
    C. a barrel of oil
    D. a moving roller coaster

12. Thermal energy can be described as ____.

    A. potential energy
    B. the movement of electrons
    C. the refraction of light
    D. the motion of particles in matter

13. A device that refracts light in a predictable way is ____.

    A. a mirror
    B. a lens
    C. an optical fiber
    D. a tuning fork

14. Which of the following is part of the electromagnetic spectrum?

    A. mechanical energy
    B. potential energy
    C. sound waves
    D. radio waves

15. **Analyze** What if light of only one frequency was passed through a prism? Would it separate into different colors? Explain your answer.

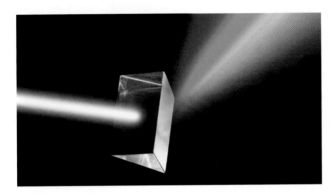

16. **Hypothesize** Can a dog see different colors? Form a hypothesis. How could you test it?

Map the Concept

Copy the concept map shown here. Then enter words into the map from the list below.

electromagnetic waves
light
mechanical waves
radio waves
sound waves
water waves
x-rays
ultraviolet waves

17. **Apply** How might you improve the sound quality in a concert hall where the music sounds high-pitched and squeaky?

18. **Synthesize** Explain why matter is necessary for sound to travel through. Where could no sounds be heard?

19. **Sequence** A golf ball is dropped in water. In what way does energy change?

20. **Analyze** Explain how wavelength relates to the energy of electromagnetic waves. Give examples of high- and low-energy waves.

Performance Assessment

Make a Diagram

Draw a diagram of how transverse and longitudinal waves travel. Show how differences in wavelength affect pitch in sound waves and color in light waves.

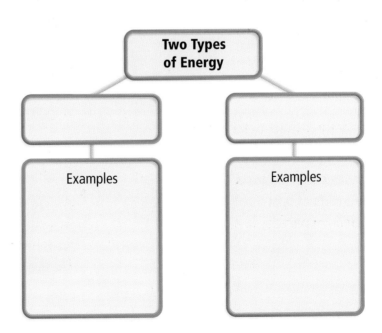

Two Types of Energy

Examples

Examples

Chapter 17

Temperature and Heat

LESSON 1

When cold water splashes over a hot fire, what happens to the temperatures of both?

Read about it in Lesson 1.

LESSON 2

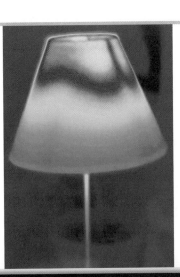

From red to yellow to blue, this lamp shade changes color with temperature. Different parts of the shade receive more thermal energy from the light bulb.

Read about it in Lesson 2.

What Is Thermal Energy?

Why It Matters...

To shape a piece of metal, a blacksmith heats it in a fire to soften it. The metal becomes hot enough to glow!

All matter has thermal energy, which it gains or loses through heat. As a blacksmith knows, heat can affect the properties of matter.

PREPARE TO INVESTIGATE

Inquiry Skill

Measure When you measure, you select and use appropriate tools and units to accurately describe and compare organisms, objects, or events.

Materials

- large plastic container
- small plastic container
- hot water
- 2 thermometers
- ice cubes
- stopwatch

Science and Math Toolbox

For step 3, review **Using a Thermometer** on page H8.

Melting the Ice

Procedure

1 **Experiment** Fill the large and small containers with hot tap water. Leave a little room in each container. Use the thermometers to measure the temperature in each container. Record your measurements in your *Science Notebook.*

STEP 1

2 **Observe** Choose two ice cubes that are about the same size. Carefully place one ice cube into each container at the same time and start the stopwatch. Record how long each cube takes to melt in its container.

STEP 2

3 **Measure** Measure the temperature of the water in each container immediately after its cube has completely melted. Record the time and temperature.

4 **Use Numbers** Calculate the change in temperature for each container. Subtract the temperature of the water after the cube melted from the original temperature of the water.

Conclusion

1. **Analyze Data** Explain the difference in the temperature changes in the two containers.

2. **Infer** What can you infer about the amount of thermal energy in each container before the cubes were added?

3. **Predict** How would the temperature change if you used a much larger container of water?

--- **Investigate More!** ---

Design an Experiment
Investigate what happens if you use two ice cubes or half as much water in each container. Compare your results with the results of this investigation.

Thermal Energy

VOCABULARY

heat	p. F80
temperature	p. F78
thermal energy	p. F78

▶ **READING SKILL**

Compare and Contrast
How are thermal energy and temperature related? How are they different?

MAIN IDEA Thermal energy is the total kinetic energy of the particles that make up a substance.

Temperature and Thermal Energy

All matter is made up of tiny particles, such as atoms and molecules. These particles are constantly moving, which means they have kinetic energy. **Thermal energy** is the total kinetic energy of the particles that make up a material.

Each cup below contains the same amount of soup, but the cup of hot soup contains much more thermal energy. This is because the particles of the hot soup are moving faster than those of the cold soup. The faster particles have more kinetic energy.

Words such as hot and cold describe temperature. **Temperature** describes the average kinetic energy of the particles that make up a material. The temperature of the hot soup is higher because its particles have a greater kinetic energy.

Comparing Thermal Energy

Cold Soup ▲
Slow-moving particles have little kinetic energy.

Hot Soup ▲
Fast-moving particles have lots of kinetic energy.

Thermometers are marked with temperature scales that are divided into units called degrees. The symbol for a degree is a small raised circle. The two most widely used temperature scales are the Fahrenheit scale and the Celsius scale. Both are shown on the thermometer at right.

The Fahrenheit scale is commonly used in the United States. This scale, indicated by the letter *F*, is shown on the right side of the thermometer. Notice that water freezes at 32°F and boils at 212°F.

Scientists use the Celsius scale for measuring temperature. People also use this scale in daily life in most countries around the world. The Celsius scale, indicated by a *C*, is shown on the left side of the thermometer. Water freezes at 0°C and boils at 100°C.

Many thermometers consist of a thin glass tube containing a liquid, usually mercury or alcohol. Recall that most materials expand when energy is added to them and contract when energy is removed. Glass thermometers use this property to indicate temperature.

Changes in temperature affect the level of the liquid in the thermometer. When thermal energy is added to the liquid, it expands and rises in the tube. When thermal energy is removed from the liquid, it contracts and goes down. Temperature is indicated by the scale next to the liquid.

 **MAIN IDEA** What is temperature?

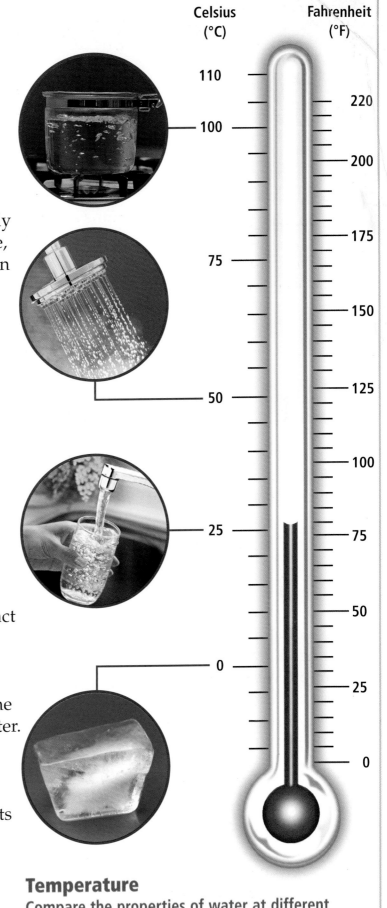

Temperature
Compare the properties of water at different temperatures. What is water like at 23°C (75°F)?

▲ Although temperature is the same in the small cup and the large urn, the cocoa in the urn has 30 times more thermal energy.

Heat

Thermal energy is often produced when other forms of energy go through a transformation. For example, a large amount of thermal energy is produced when solar energy, or sunlight, strikes objects and warms them. Other sources of thermal energy include chemical reactions, friction, and electricity.

Look at the large urn of hot cocoa and the cup of hot cocoa next to it. The cocoa in the cup was just poured from the urn, so it has the same temperature as the cocoa in

the urn. However, the urn contains more cocoa, which means it has more particles in motion. Thus, it has more thermal energy than the cocoa in the cup.

Thermal energy can move through matter. The movement, or transfer, of thermal energy from warmer regions of matter to cooler regions is called **heat.**

Because the liquid in the cup has less thermal energy, it will cool more quickly than the liquid in the urn. The liquid cools as its thermal energy is transferred as heat to the air, the cup, and the table.

Before a hot liquid is poured into a cup, the cup will feel cool to the touch. After the hot liquid is poured, the cup will feel warm. That change in temperature is a result of the transfer of thermal energy.

Recall that thermal energy is the total kinetic energy of the particles that make up a sample of matter. Particles of the hot liquid will collide with particles in the cold cup, transferring some of their kinetic energy to the cup. So, the average kinetic energy of the particles of the cup increases. The cup gets warmer. The liquid loses some thermal energy and gets cooler.

Just as thermal energy of the liquid is passed on to the cup, this energy can be transferred to all matter in contact with the cup, including the air. Eventually, the liquid, the cup, the air, and the part of the tabletop touching the cup will all have the same temperature.

Thermal energy always travels from a region at higher temperature to a region of lower temperature—from warmer to cooler matter. In the photo below, the snowball has a lower temperature than the boy's hand. Therefore, thermal energy moves from the hand to the snowball. The hand gets cold because it loses thermal energy. Cold does not travel from the snowball to the hand.

In the other hand, the pretzel is the warmer object. Thermal energy is transferred to the boy's hand. The hand becomes warmer. As the pretzel loses thermal energy, it cools. Its temperature approaches the temperature of the hand and the air.

▲ Hand warmers generate their own thermal energy, either from an electrical battery or from the reaction of chemicals in the warmer. What happens to this thermal energy?

 **MAIN IDEA** What is heat?

Snow

Since the snowball is colder than the hand, thermal energy moves from the hand to the snow. The snowball gets warmer and starts to melt. ▼

Hot Pretzel

The pretzel is warmer than the hand. So, thermal energy moves from the pretzel to the hand. The hand gets warm and the pretzel cools. ▼

Specific Heat Capacity

Different materials heat up at different rates. For example, if you placed 10 g of copper and 10 g of lead in a hot oven for one minute, the lead would be hotter than the copper.

Look at the picture below. The water and the concrete walkway have been exposed to the same amount of sunlight for the same amount of time. Yet, if you walk across the concrete and jump in the pool, you'll find that the water is much cooler than the concrete. In fact, on a very sunny day, the concrete could burn your feet.

Why do the water and the concrete have different temperatures while receiving the same amounts of energy from the Sun? Part of the answer is that they have different specific heat capacities. The amount of thermal energy it takes to raise the temperature of 1 g of a given material by 1°C is called the specific heat capacity of that material.

Scientists measure all kinds of energy in units called Joules (J). The chart below shows the specific heat capacities for several common materials. The unit is Joules per gram and °C.

As you can see, water has a very high specific heat capacity. It takes a lot more energy to heat the water in the pool than it does to heat the concrete around it.

▶ **MAIN IDEA** What is specific heat capacity?

Compare the specific heat capacities of water and concrete. These values explain why the concrete walkway is warmer than the water on a sunny day. ▼

Specific Heat Capacity

Substance	Specific Heat Capacity (J/g °C)
water	4.18
ice	2.05
wool	1.38
concrete	0.88
copper	0.39
mercury	0.14
lead	0.13

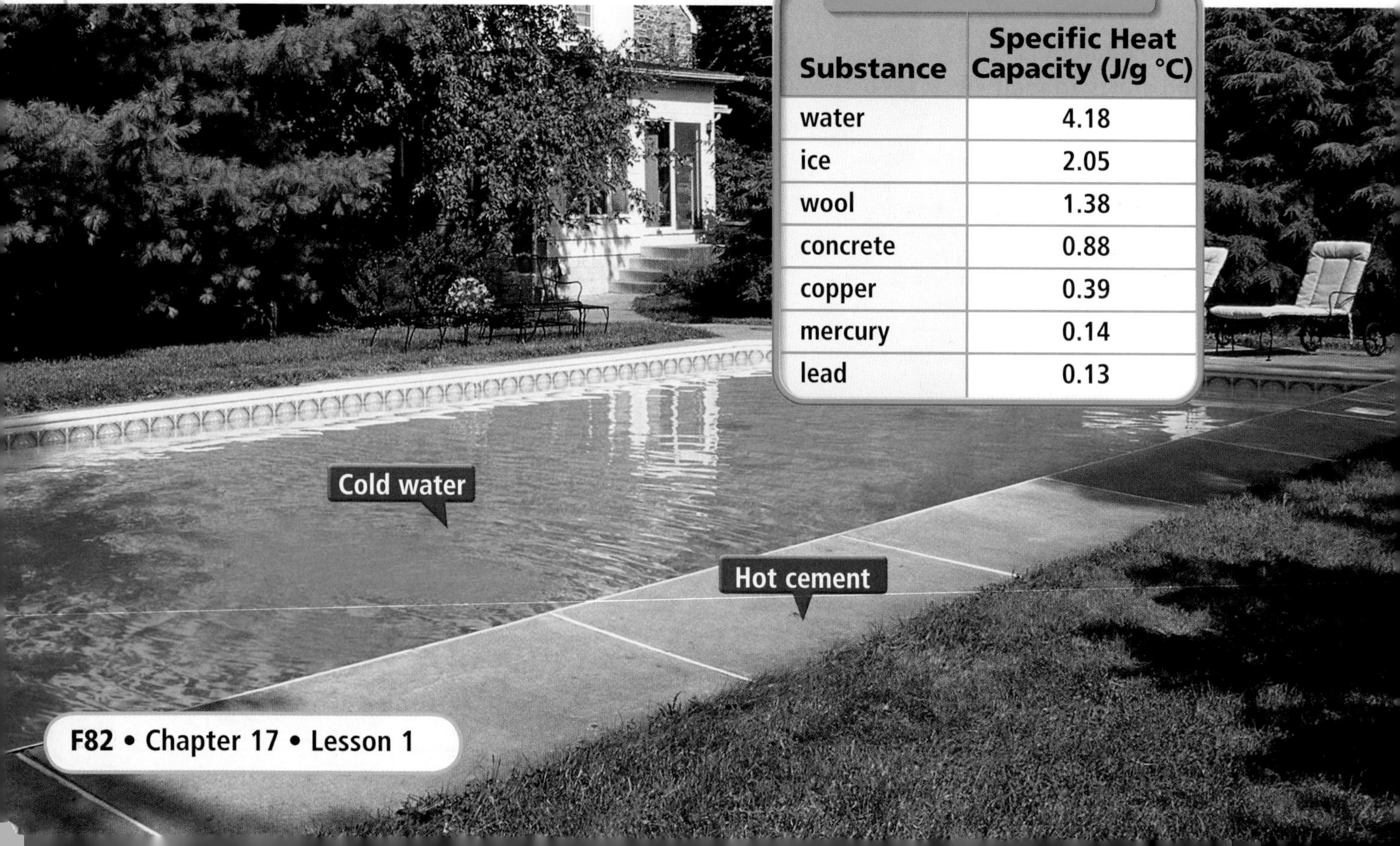

Cold water

Hot cement

Visual Summary

Thermal energy is the *total* kinetic energy of the particles that make up a substance. Temperature is the *average* kinetic energy of the particles.

Heat is the transfer of thermal energy from warmer to cooler regions of matter.

Cold water

Hot cement

Different materials absorb thermal energy at different rates. The amount of energy needed to raise the temperature of 1 g of a material by 1°C is its specific heat capacity.

LINKS for Home and School

MATH Calculate Look at the table of specific heat capacities on page F82. How many times greater is the specific heat capacity of copper than that of lead?

WRITING Expository Research the discoveries of James Joule, whose experiments showed that heat is produced by motion, or kinetic energy. Write a report about his work.

Review

1 MAIN IDEA What is thermal energy? Describe two objects that have different amounts of thermal energy.

2 VOCABULARY How are thermal energy and heat related?

3 READING SKILL: Compare and Contrast How does the thermal energy of a tubful of hot water compare to that of a glass of water at the same temperature? Explain.

4 CRITICAL THINKING: Apply Why can you quickly become chilled in a swimming pool, even if the temperature of the water is only a little lower than the air temperature?

5 INQUIRY SKILL: Infer Why isn't water used as a liquid in a thermometer?

 TEST PREP

When an ice cube is placed in a glass of water, thermal energy

A. increases.

B. moves from the ice to the water.

C. moves from the water to the ice.

D. decreases.

 Technology

Visit **www.eduplace.com/scp/** to find out more about thermal energy.

Cooling Off

Do you ever call a refrigerator an "ice box"? One hundred years ago, that name was more accurate than it is today. Before electricity, people kept food cold in cabinets that housed large blocks of ice. In many cities, workers delivered ice from insulated warehouses to homes and businesses.

People's lives changed for the better when electric refrigerators became available. Refrigerators use a special substance, called a coolant, that cycles through tubes on the inside and outside of the refrigerator. The coolant absorbs thermal energy from the inside of the refrigerator and releases it to the outside.

Would you believe that ice was once a valuable resource? During winter in cold places, people cut ice and stored it for the summer. Sometimes the ice was shipped to warmer places in insulated containers.

1

Compressor

This is the motor of the cooling system. It compresses the coolant gas, raising its pressure. As a result, the gas warms.

2

Outside Heat-Exchanging Coils

The coolant loses thermal energy as it flows through coils on the outside of the refrigerator. As it cools, it condenses from a gas to a liquid.

3

Expansion Valve

Here the coolant expands and evaporates into a gas. This process absorbs thermal energy, so the coolant becomes even colder.

4

Inside Heat-Exchanging Coils

Now a cold gas, the coolant takes up thermal energy from the inside of the refrigerator. The inside becomes cold!

Sharing Ideas

1. **READING CHECK** Describe the cycle of events that keep a refrigerator cold.

2. **WRITE ABOUT IT** Compare a refrigerator to an old-fashioned ice box.

3. **TALK ABOUT IT** How do you think refrigerators have changed how people live?

How Does Thermal Energy Spread?

Why It Matters...

Sometimes you want things hot, and sometimes you want things cold. Many devices control the transfer of thermal energy. Some examples include refrigerators, toasters, hair dryers, blankets, ovens, and fans.

PREPARE TO INVESTIGATE

Inquiry Skill

Use Variables When you use variables, you change one factor of the experiment to see how that change affects the results. The controls of the experiment do not change.

Materials
- plastic knife
- stick of butter
- ruler
- thin metal rod
- low, wide bowl
- hot water
- stopwatch

Science and Math Toolbox
For step 3, review **Measuring Elapsed Time** on page H14.

The Melting Point

Procedure

Safety: Be careful when using hot water.

1 **Collaborate** Work in a small group. Create a chart like the one shown in your *Science Notebook.*

2 **Use Variables** Use the plastic knife to cut three equal pats of butter. Use the ruler to measure distances along the metal rod. Place the first pat of butter at one end of the rod. Place the second pat 8 cm from that end, and place the third pat 16 cm from the same end.

3 **Experiment** Fill the bowl to a height of 3 cm with hot tap water. As one group member holds the bowl in place, carefully slide the unbuttered end of the metal rod into the bowl. Cover as much of the rod as possible with water, but keep the butter out of the water. Start the stopwatch when the rod enters the water.

4 **Observe** Time how long it takes for each butter pat to begin to melt and slide off the rod.

5 **Record Data** Record the times in your *Science Notebook.*

Conclusion

1. **Infer** Why did the butter pats begin to melt at different times?

2. **Use Variables** What part of the experiment could you change to test your inference?

STEP 1

Sample	Placement	Melting Time
1	end of rod	
2	8 cm from end	
3	16 cm from end	

STEP 2

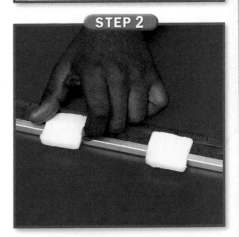

STEP 3

Investigate More!

Design an Experiment
Will using cardboard, plastic, or cloth melt a butter pat as quickly as using a metal rod? Form a hypothesis, then test it with an experiment.

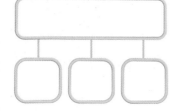
Transfer of Thermal Energy

MAIN IDEA Thermal energy is transferred by conduction, convection, and radiation.

Conduction

Thermal energy is spread, or transferred, through three different processes: conduction, convection, and radiation. Transfer of thermal energy through direct contact is called **conduction.** Conduction occurs mainly in solids, when rapidly vibrating particles cause nearby particles to vibrate more rapidly.

Remember that particles in a solid do not move from place to place, but vibrate back and forth. As they vibrate, they collide with and pass some of their kinetic energy to nearby particles. In this way, thermal energy can spread throughout a solid object or among solid objects in contact with each other.

In the picture below, thermal energy from the burner is transferred to the bottom of the pan through conduction. This happens because vibrating particles in the burner pass some of their kinetic energy to the bottom of the pan. As the process continues, thermal energy is conducted throughout the pan and into the food it contains. The pan and its contents become warmer.

◄ Conduction
Thermal energy from the burner is transferred through the metal by the process of conduction. Conduction happens when particles transfer their vibrations to neighboring particles.

◄ **Convection**
Currents of water or air created by the process of convection are called convection currents.

Convection

As you have learned, gases and liquids are not rigid like solids. Their particles move much more freely. When a gas or liquid is in contact with a hot object, it expands and becomes less dense as its temperature increases. A warmer, lighter liquid will rise, while the surrounding cooler, denser liquid will sink.

This process is called **convection.** Convection is the process for transfer of thermal energy in liquids and gases.

The aquarium above uses a heater to warm the water. Water becomes warmer as it touches the heater, causing it to expand and rise. As the warm water rises to the top of the aquarium, it carries thermal energy with it. Some of that energy is transferred to other water particles by collisions.

When the warm water reaches the surface, it continues to lose thermal energy to the surrounding water and the air. As the water cools, it becomes denser and sinks. Eventually, it reaches the heater and starts the journey again.

▲ The heater at the bottom of the balloon creates convection currents that fill the balloon with hot air, causing it to rise.

 **MAIN IDEA** How do conduction and convection compare?

Radiation

Thermal energy can also be transferred by radiation. **Radiation** is the transfer of energy by electromagnetic waves. All objects emit thermal radiation. Even Earth's polar ice caps emit a little. Living things, including your body, emit some radiation. A hot burner on a stove emits much more.

When an object absorbs thermal radiation, its particles vibrate faster. This increases their kinetic energy and raises the temperature.

Radiation

The fire emits infrared waves, which radiate in all directions and warm the campers. ▼

Here on Earth, the most important source of radiation is the Sun. The Sun emits radiation of different wavelengths. Some are waves of visible light. Others are infrared (ihn fruh REHD) light, which have a longer wavelength. Most of the heating power of the Sun comes from infrared radiation.

A campfire is similar in some ways to the Sun, only on a smaller scale. Both emit waves of visible light and infrared light. After sunset, the campers will use the fire as a source of light and heat.

You feel infrared radiation as heat because the specific wavelengths of this radiation affect the motions of the particles of your body. Longer infrared wavelengths cause particles to move faster and increase their thermal energy. Shorter infrared wavelengths, such as those used in

The special bulb in the picture emits infrared light. These light waves heat the inside of an incubator, helping to keep newborn animals warm. ▼

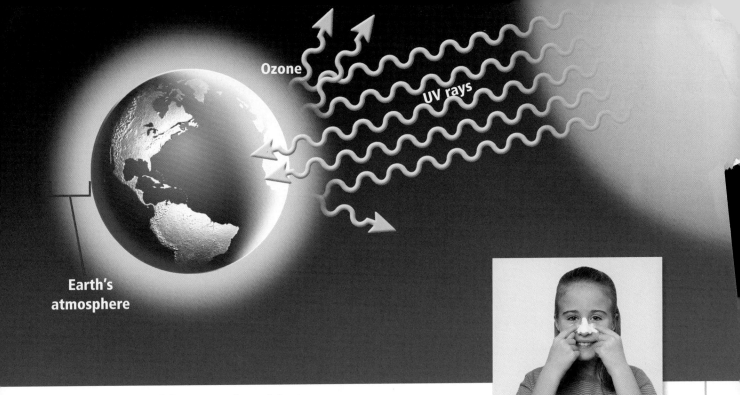

Ozone

UV rays

Earth's atmosphere

▲ Ozone in Earth's atmosphere blocks some of the harmful ultraviolet rays from the Sun.

▲ Sunscreen can help reduce the harmful effects of ultraviolet rays.

remote control devices, do not cause particles to speed up very much. So, they do not increase thermal energy.

All electromagnetic waves carry energy. Matter can absorb some of the waves in infrared, ultraviolet, and visible light. Any waves that are absorbed will add thermal energy to whatever absorbs them.

This is the reason certain colors of clothing feel warmer or cooler on a hot summer day. Lighter colors reflect more solar radiation than they absorb. Wearing lighter-colored clothes will keep you cooler. Darker colors absorb more solar radiation than they reflect. Wearing darker-colored clothes on a cold, sunny day will keep you warmer.

Ultraviolet (UV) rays are electromagnetic waves with shorter wavelengths than visible light. The rays penetrate your skin and are absorbed. Too much UV radiation can cause a sunburn. This is why you should wear a sunscreen to block out UV rays.

Fortunately, a layer of ozone in the upper atmosphere blocks much of the Sun's UV rays. Even so, a certain amount of the radiation always passes through.

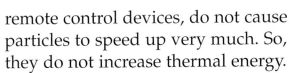 **MAIN IDEA** What kinds of infrared waves are felt as heat?

▲ The metal spoon transfers thermal energy better than the wooden spoon. Metal is a better conductor than wood.

Conductors and Insulators

Some materials transfer thermal energy better than other materials. These materials are called **conductors.**

Most solids are better conductors than liquids or gases. The particles in solids are close together, making it easier for vibrations to be transferred from one particle to the next.

Most metals are excellent conductors of heat. Other solids, such as wood, contain "pockets" of air trapped between their particles. These materials conduct heat at a much slower rate than most metals.

Look at the spoons in the picture to the left. The boiling water has a lot of thermal energy. This energy gets transferred into both spoons by conduction. The metal spoon on the right will soon be too hot to touch. The wooden spoon on the left will be warm, but not too hot to handle.

Materials that are poor conductors of heat are called **insulators.** Plastic is a good insulator. When you heat water in a pot, the pot and the water can get very hot, but the plastic handle stays relatively cool.

Air is also a good insulator. In air, thermal energy is transferred through collisions between molecules, and air molecules are far apart.

A bird's feathers trap air, which acts as insulation. Some winter coats are lined with a type of feather called down.

33°C

28°C

◄ This infrared photo reveals radiated energy from a house. Red areas show the most radiation—places where the homeowner might add insulation.

▼ Keeping windows sealed with caulk prevents heat from escaping.

How do thick blankets and heavy coats keep you warm in the winter? They do not keep cold out. They keep thermal energy from escaping into the air. Recall that thermal energy is transferred from warmer regions to colder regions.

Without a coat, your body heat would be transferred to the cooler air around you. You might want this on a warm summer day, but not on a cold winter one. Insulators, such as coats and blankets, trap the thermal energy that your body generates. This helps keep you warm.

Houses and buildings are also designed with heat transfer in mind. In cold places, most houses and buildings burn natural gas or use electric heaters to warm the air inside. To trap that energy, walls are lined with pockets of non-moving air. The pockets act as insulation.

Fiberglass insulation traps heat even better than air. Adding this kind of insulation can save hundreds of dollars in energy bills every year.

Glass windows help to heat homes by transmitting radiant energy. Glass allows sunlight to pass through into your house, but it is a relatively poor conductor of heat. So, much of the thermal energy stays inside the house.

To increase the insulating effect of a glass window, many homeowners cover windows with clear plastic during the winter. The plastic adds a layer of air between the house and the glass. Plastic caulking and weather stripping can also help seal the frames of windows and doors.

▶ MAIN IDEA How does an insulator help keep something warm?

Home Heating

You won't be surprised to learn that the movement of thermal energy plays an important role in the way homes, schools, and other buildings are heated. Different types of heating are based on the three types of thermal energy transfer that you have learned about.

Some buildings have radiators, which are metal structures with ribs. Hot water is pumped through the radiators to heat them. Then, as the name implies, they radiate heat into the room. Some thermal energy from the radiator warms the air by conduction. However, a cat lying on a rug in front of the radiator will get much warmer than the air because of the radiant energy it absorbs.

Some buildings have forced air heating. This method involves using a fan to force heated air through ducts into all parts of a building. The warm air moving into each room heats the room through convection.

Some heating systems involve more than one type of energy transfer. For example, the baseboard heater shown below uses all three.

First, electricity passing through the heater warms long rows of thin metal vanes through conduction. The vanes then warm the air in the narrow spaces between them through radiation. Finally, the warm air inside the heater expands and becomes less dense. This warm air exits through the open space in the frame and rises.

As warm air rises, cool, denser air moves in to take its place. This cooler air is then warmed by the baseboard heater. Eventually, a continuous convection current of warm air is circulating through the room, and the room is nice and cozy.

▶ **MAIN IDEA** How do radiators heat a room? Is only radiation involved?

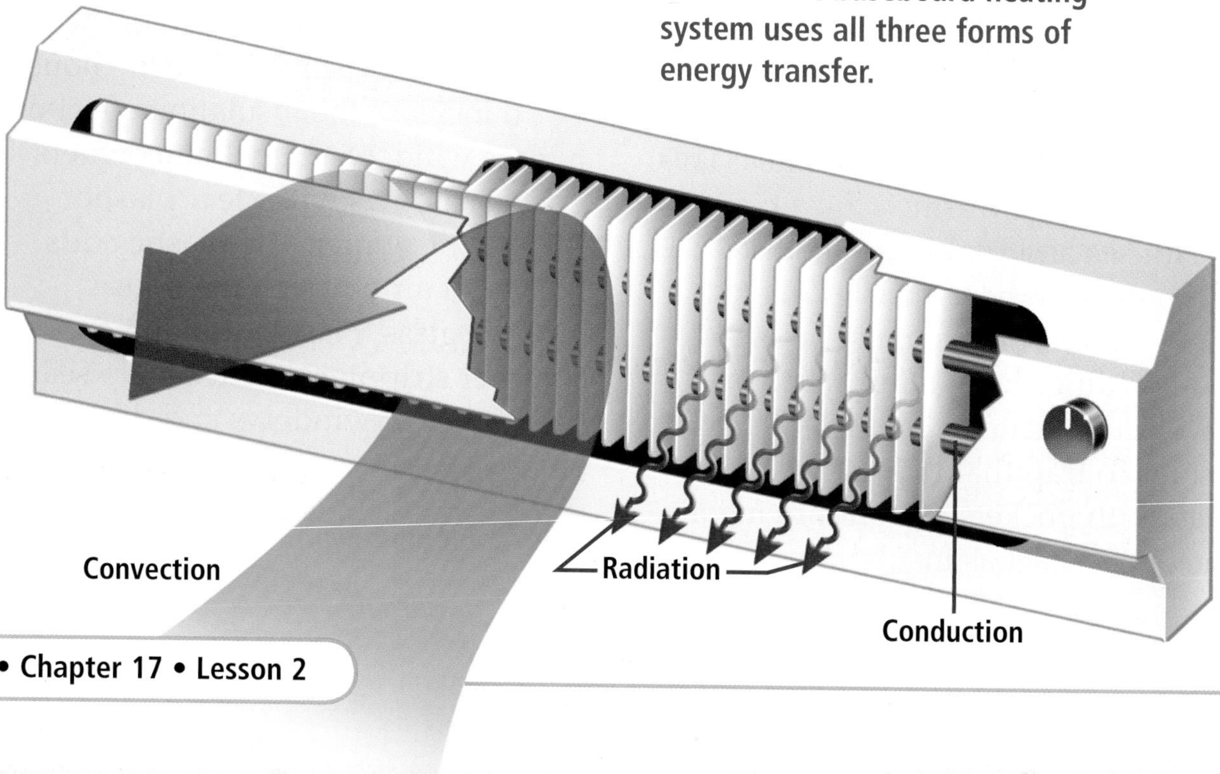

This electric baseboard heating system uses all three forms of energy transfer.

Convection

Radiation

Conduction

Visual Summary

Thermal energy is transferred through solids by conduction. In liquids and gases both conduction and convection occur.

Electromagnetic radiation can change into thermal energy. Radiation may travel through empty space.

Conductors easily transfer thermal energy. Insulators transfer thermal energy poorly.

LINKS for Home and School

MATH **Solve a Problem** Suppose that adding insulation to a home will cost $3,000, but will save an average of $8 per day in energy costs. Determine whether adding the insulation will result in a net savings over two years.

TECHNOLOGY **Be a Smart Consumer!** Research different products designed to improve home insulation, such as window caulking and weather stripping. Find out how they work and how they help homeowners save money.

Review

❶ **MAIN IDEA** Name and describe the three ways that thermal energy is transferred.

❷ **VOCABULARY** What is the difference between conduction and convection?

❸ **READING SKILL: Main Idea and Details** Why do some materials make good conductors while others make good insulators?

❹ **CRITICAL THINKING: Apply** How might you determine if a material is a conductor or an insulator?

❺ **INQUIRY SKILL: Use Variables** How would you design an experiment that shows which of three materials is the best conductor of thermal energy? Identify the variables in your experiment.

✓ **TEST PREP** Infrared rays emitted by a fire are an example of

A. radiation.

B. convection.

C. insulation.

D. conduction.

Technology Visit **www.eduplace.com/scp/** to find out more about conduction, convection, and radiation.

F95

Extreme Science

Almost Not There!

Hey! Why aren't those crayons melting? The answer can be found in that strange stuff they're sitting on. It looks like blue smoke, but it's actually a solid called aerogel. Aerogel is the lightest solid in the world and is 99.8% air!

The porous, sponge-like structure of aerogel traps pockets of air. This trapped air is what makes aerogel so useful. Trapped air is a good insulator. Aerogel insulates for the same reason that a puffy jacket does—because the air between the fibers is a poor conductor of thermal energy. Someday, aerogel may line the inside of your walls to keep you warm. It may also line the inside of your refrigerator to keep your food cold.

How light is aerogel? If an average-sized 10-year-old sat on a seesaw, it would take a cube of aerogel 20 feet by 20 feet to balance his or her weight.

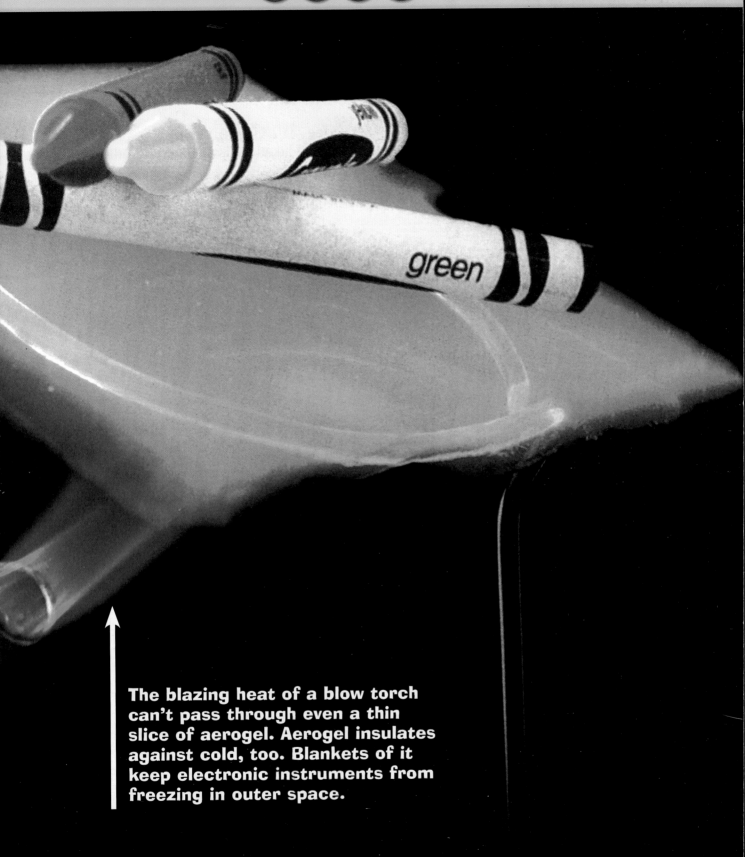

The blazing heat of a blow torch can't pass through even a thin slice of aerogel. Aerogel insulates against cold, too. Blankets of it keep electronic instruments from freezing in outer space.

Vocabulary

Complete each sentence with a term from the list. You may use terms more than once.

1. The transfer of thermal energy through the movement of a liquid or gas is _____.

2. _____ is the transfer of thermal energy from warmer regions to cooler regions.

3. A material that easily transfers thermal energy is a(n) _____.

4. The transfer of thermal energy by _____ does not require matter.

5. The average kinetic energy of the particles in a sample of matter is its _____.

6. A material that transfers thermal energy poorly is a(n) _____.

7. The transfer of thermal energy from one particle to another is _____.

8. The _____ of a substance may rise as thermal energy is absorbed.

9. Infrared light is a form of _____.

10. The total kinetic energy of the particles of a substance is its _____.

conduction F88
conductor F92
convection F89
heat F80
insulator F92
radiation F90
temperature F78
thermal energy F78

Test Prep

Write the letter of the best answer choice.

11. Thermal energy is a form of _____.

    A. electrical energy
    B. chemical energy
    C. kinetic energy
    D. gamma radiation

12. When your skin absorbs too much _____, you get a sunburn.

    A. visible light
    B. infrared light
    C. UV light
    D. sunscreen

13. Thermal energy is often transferred in gases and liquids by _____.

    A. convection
    B. conduction
    C. radiation
    D. electromagnetic waves

14. A good example of a conductor is _____.

    A. air
    B. copper
    C. plastic foam
    D. wood

Inquiry Skills

15. Measure What tool would you use to measure the average kinetic energy of particles in a sample of matter?

16. Use Variables Create an experiment that would test the ability of different materials to prevent heat loss. Identify the variables in the experiment.

Map the Concept

Write the terms from the Word Bank in their proper position in the concept map.

conduction
conductor
convection
insulator
radiation
thermal energy

Critical Thinking

17. Applying Why might damage to the ozone layer in Earth's atmosphere be dangerous?

18. Synthesizing What could you conclude from an experiment that measured the temperature of three amounts of the same substance and showed each to have the same temperature?

19. Evaluate How might you decide if a material would make a good conductor? Describe a test you might perform.

20. Analyzing How is conduction similar to convection? How are the two processes different? Give examples to support your answer.

Performance Assessment

Make a Diagram

Draw a diagram that shows how a simple convection current transfers heat through water in a tea kettle. Label the heat source, the direction that the heated water travels, and what happens as it moves along the current.

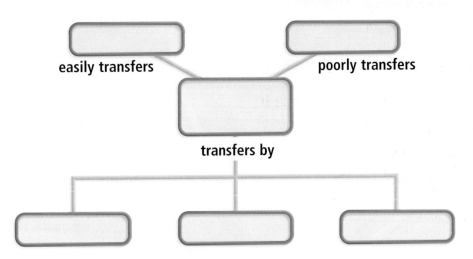

easily transfers   poorly transfers

transfers by

Chapter 18

Electrical Energy

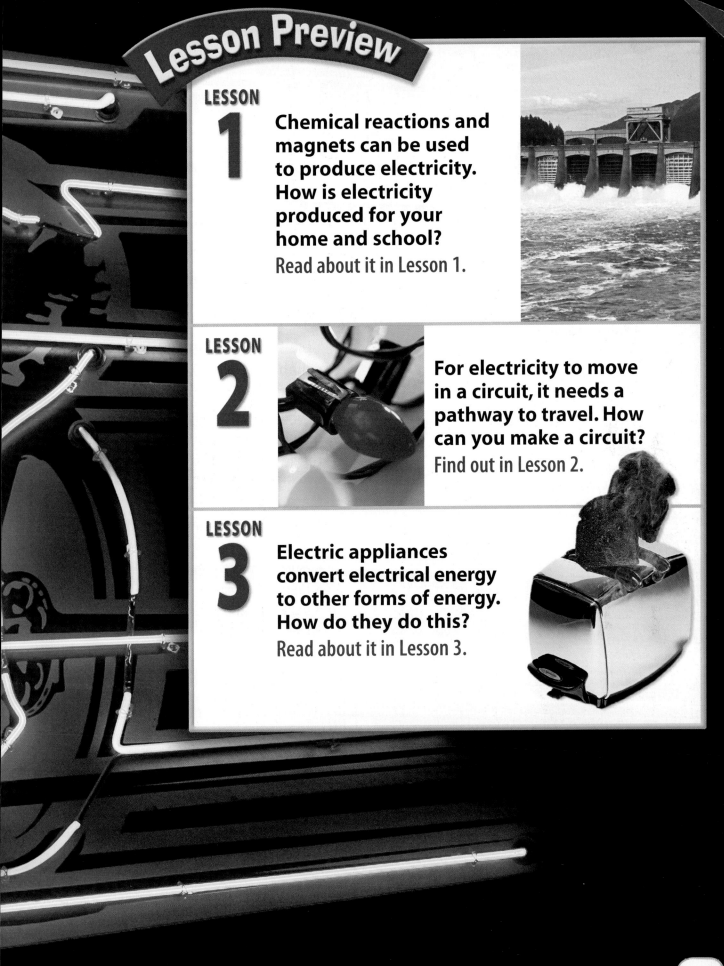

Lesson Preview

LESSON 1

Chemical reactions and magnets can be used to produce electricity. How is electricity produced for your home and school?

Read about it in Lesson 1.

LESSON 2

For electricity to move in a circuit, it needs a pathway to travel. How can you make a circuit?

Find out in Lesson 2.

LESSON 3

Electric appliances convert electrical energy to other forms of energy. How do they do this?

Read about it in Lesson 3.

How Is Electricity Produced?

Why It Matters...

Many things use electricity—from alarm clocks to refrigerators to stereos and computers. Electricity can be produced in many ways, some of which are better for the environment than others. Maybe someday you will develop new technology for producing or using electricity.

PREPARE TO INVESTIGATE

Inquiry Skill

Collaborate When you collaborate, you work in a team to plan and make investigations, share observations, and consider the ideas of others.

Materials

- large plastic foam plate
- wool cloth
- aluminum pie pan
- foam cup
- masking tape
- LED light

Store a Charge!

Procedure

STEP 1

1. **Collaborate** Work with a partner. Tape the foam cup upside down onto the middle of an aluminum pan. Bend the two prongs of the LED gently apart.

2. **Experiment** Place the foam plate upside down on a tabletop. Rub the plate with the wool cloth for one minute.

3. **Experiment** Using the cup as a handle, place the aluminum pan on top of the foam plate, then lift it off again. Be careful not to touch the pan itself! Continue to hold the pan through step 4.

STEP 3

4. **Observe** If possible, darken the room. Holding one prong of the LED between your thumb and index finger, touch the other prong to the aluminum pan. Record your observations in your *Science Notebook.*

5. Repeat step 4. Record your observations.

Conclusion

1. **Infer** What did you observe when you touched the LED to the aluminum pan the first time? How could you explain what you observed?

2. **Compare** What did you observe when you touched the LED to the aluminum pan the second time?

3. **Hypothesize** Develop a hypothesis to explain the difference in your observations between steps 4 and 5. How could you test your hypothesis?

Investigate More!

Design an Experiment Repeat the procedure you used to store a charge using other materials. Predict how each material might respond. How can you account for differences in the way various materials store charges?

Electricity

VOCABULARY

electric current   p. F105
electric generator   p. F107
static electricity   p. F104

READING SKILL

Text Structure Organize information about the forms of electricity discussed in this lesson.

MAIN IDEA Electricity is the movement of electrons from one place to another. It can be produced by transforming other forms of energy.

Static and Current Electricity

Have you ever rubbed a balloon on a carpet, then placed it against a wall? The balloon might stay on the wall for a minute or longer! This happens because of **static electricity**—an electric force between non-moving electric charges.

When you rub a balloon against certain kinds of carpet, electrons from the carpet will jump to the balloon. The balloon acquires an overall negative charge because of the extra electrons. Rub a balloon against plastic, however, and the electrons will jump off the balloon. The balloon is left with an overall positive charge because it now has fewer electrons.

Rubbing helps electrons move from the carpet to the blue balloons, which gain a negative charge. Electrons move from the orange balloon to the plastic, so this balloon gains a positive charge.

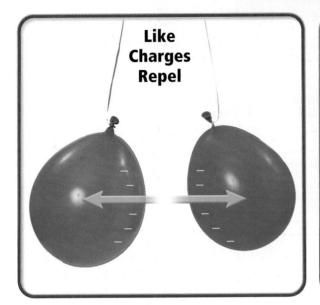

The two negatively-charged balloons repel each other.

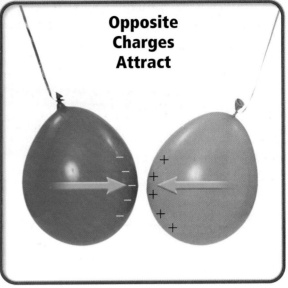

The negatively and positively-charged balloons attract each other.

Charged objects exert a force on one another. Two objects with the same charges repel, or push away from each other. Study the photo of the two blue balloons. Both have a negative charge, so they repel each other. Two positively-charged balloons would repel each other, too.

Two objects with opposite charges attract, or pull toward each other. Look at the photo of the blue and orange balloons. They have opposite charges, so they attract each other.

Have you ever walked across a thick carpet, then touched a metal doorknob? The doorknob might have given you a slight shock! You may have even seen a spark. This is a discharge, or release, of static electricity. Electrons will move between you and the doorknob. Lightning is another example of a discharge, only on a larger scale.

A discharge of static electricity can release a lot of energy, but only for a very brief amount of time. To provide a steady flow of electric charge, you need to create an electric current. An **electric current** is a continuous flow of electric charge through a pathway.

 **TEXT STRUCTURE** What is an electric current?

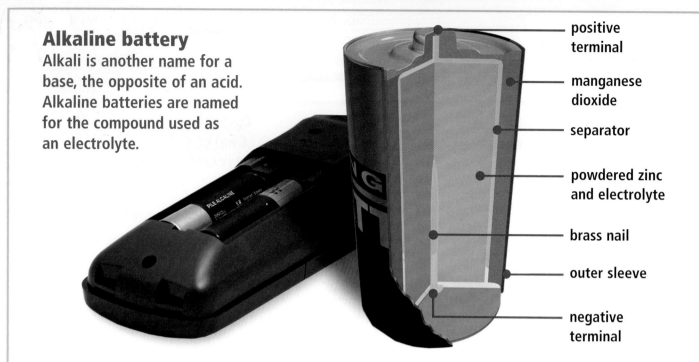

Alkaline battery

Alkali is another name for a base, the opposite of an acid. Alkaline batteries are named for the compound used as an electrolyte.

- positive terminal
- manganese dioxide
- separator
- powdered zinc and electrolyte
- brass nail
- outer sleeve
- negative terminal

Batteries and Fuel Cells

A battery contains one or more electrochemical cells. The cells use chemical reactions to create an electric current.

The cell shown here uses manganese dioxide, powdered zinc, and a paste called an electrolyte (ih LEHK truh lyt). When wires connect the battery to a load, such as a light bulb, the chemical reactions begin and electric current flows. Zinc loses electrons, which move through the brass nail and out the negative terminal. They travel through the wires and light bulb, then return to the positive terminal. The electrons are picked up by the manganese dioxide.

Notice that the cell separates the zinc and the manganese dioxide. If the two came into contact, the electrons would flow inside the battery instead of through the wires and light bulb.

Eventually either the zinc or the electrolyte will be used up. The chemical reactions will stop and the battery will no longer work.

Bring used batteries to a battery-recycling center. Batteries contain chemicals that are toxic to humans and can harm the environment.

There are many different types of batteries. Car batteries use lead and acid, and can be recharged for use over and over again.

In the future, fuel cells may replace some batteries. Fuel cells run by combining oxygen and hydrogen to form water, creating an electric current in the process. Their advantage is that they keep running so long as they have enough fuel.

NASA space missions have used a type of fuel cell since the 1960s. The fuel cells provide both electricity and drinking water for the astronauts! Fuel cell technology for everyday use is still being researched. One problem is how to supply the hydrogen.

Generator

In an electric generator, a loop of wire is rotated in a magnetic field, generating a current in the wire. ▶

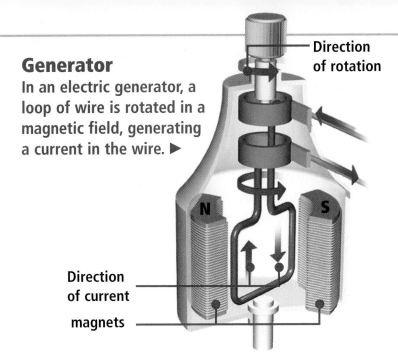

Direction of rotation

N   S

Direction of current

magnets

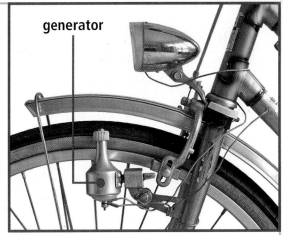

generator

The bicycle light is powered by a generator. The turning bicycle wheel turns the ridged wheel, providing mechanical energy for the generator. ▲

Making Electricity

What makes the electricity that powers your home and school? The answer is an **electric generator,** a device that converts mechanical kinetic energy to electrical energy. A friction generator, such as the one shown on the bicycle, converts the mechanical kinetic energy of the spinning wheel into electrical energy.

In an electric generator, a loop of wire is turned very rapidly through a magnetic field. This produces an electric current in the wire.

What turns the loop of wire? The mechanical energy to turn the wire can come from many sources, including the turning wheels of a bicycle. As you will read on the next page, at electric power plants the energy to turn the wires may come from burning fossil fuels, moving water, wind, or even splitting atoms!

Solar cells provide another way to generate electricity. Solar cells are made of semiconductors, such as silicon. When sunlight strikes, electrons are knocked out of silicon atoms, allowing an electric current to flow.

Solar cells

Some roadside signs are powered by solar cells. ▼

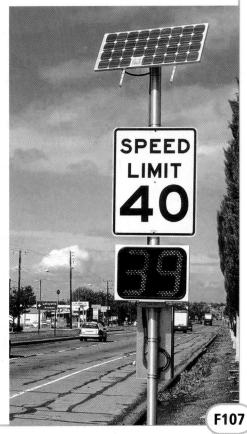

SPEED LIMIT 40

TEXT STRUCTURE How does a generator work?

Electric Power Plants

The electricity that powers your home comes from a power plant. At almost all power plants, electricity is made using the same type of electric generators. But the energy sources used to power the generators differ.

Many power plants burn coal or other fossil fuels. The burning coal is used to heat water and make steam. The steam turns turbines, which are like large fans. The turning turbines power electric generators.

Hydroelectric power plants use running water to turn turbines. These plants rely on river dams to channel the water to the turbines.

Nuclear power plants use the energy found inside an atom! In a process called nuclear fission, uranium nuclei are split apart. The energy released is used to heat water and make steam, which turns turbines just as in a coal-burning power plant.

Unfortunately, each of these technologies has drawbacks. Fossil fuels are limited. Burning them can pollute the environment. Hydroelectric dams can damage ecosystems around them. Spent fuel from nuclear power plants creates dangerous waste.

For these reasons, scientists are studying alternative energy sources. Most of these are used to a small extent today. Windmills harness wind energy. Solar cells and panels use the Sun's energy, and geothermal power relies on heat from Earth's interior. With new technology and financial support, all these alternatives could provide the electricity of the future.

▶ **TEXT STRUCTURE** **What supplies the kinetic energy to a hydroelectric power plant?**

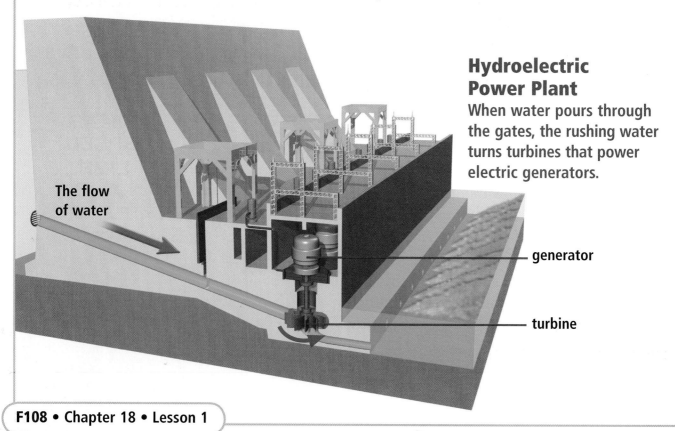

Hydroelectric Power Plant

When water pours through the gates, the rushing water turns turbines that power electric generators.

The flow of water

generator

turbine

Visual Summary

Objects with opposite charges attract each other. Objects with like charges repel each other.

Inside alkaline batteries, chemical reactions release and take up electrons. This can make an electric current.

Mechanical kinetic energy is converted to electrical energy in a generator. Generators rotate loops of wire through a magnetic field to produce electric current.

LINKS for Home and School

MATH **Draw a Bar Graph** Which brand of alkaline battery lasts the longest in a flashlight? Design and conduct an experiment to find out. Present your findings in a bar graph.

TECHNOLOGY **Create a Display**
Research how solar power is used to heat homes or generate electricity. Create a display showing some of the uses of solar power.

Review

1 MAIN IDEA What is electric current?

2 VOCABULARY Write a statement that defines the term *static electricity*.

3 READING SKILL: Text Structure Describe how a generator produces electricity.

4 CRITICAL THINKING: Apply Describe the advantages and disadvantages of using batteries to create electricity. Why do you think fuel cells are used on the space shuttle instead of batteries?

5 INQUIRY SKILL: Collaborate Work with classmates to research wind power, geothermal power, or another alternative energy source. Describe its benefits and drawbacks, and how it may be used in the future.

 TEST PREP
Fuel cells use _____ to produce electrical energy.

A. zinc and an alkaline electrolyte

B. mechanical energy

C. copper and zinc

D. hydrogen and oxygen

 Technology
Visit **www.eduplace.com/scp/** to find out more about electricity.

What Is an Electric Circuit?

Why It Matters...

When you flip the switch on a lamp, the light comes on. Plug in an electric heater, and it will radiate heat into the room. Push a button on a doorbell, and you hear the chimes. How do these devices work? All rely on electric current.

Inquiry Skill

Record Data Store your science observations in a form that will be understandable to you and others in the future.

Materials

- flashlight battery
- battery holder
- 2 light bulbs and fixtures
- 4 wires

◄ A circuit box contains circuit breakers, which are designed to break the connection of an electric circuit if too much current flows through it.

Light Bulb Circuit

Procedure

1. **Collaborate** Work with a partner to connect the battery, wires, and two bulbs, as shown in the photo. Leave one wire unconnected.

2. **Record Data** In your *Science Notebook*, draw a diagram of the incomplete circuit.

3. **Observe** Connect the loose end of the third wire to the negative terminal of the battery. Observe and record the results.

4. **Experiment** Disconnect one wire from the battery or a bulb, then reconnect it. Test the effects of disconnecting different wires from the circuit. Record the results.

5. **Collaborate** Take apart the circuit. Reassemble the parts as shown in the photo. Draw a diagram of the new circuit. Record your observations.

6. **Experiment** Repeat steps 3 and 4 for the new circuit. Record your observations.

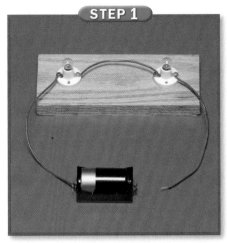

STEP 1

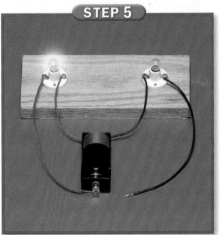

STEP 5

Conclusion

1. **Compare** Describe how the light bulbs were connected differently in the two types of circuits. What effect did this have on the electric current?

2. **Use Models** Which of the two circuits would be better for powering appliances in your home?

Investigate More!

Design an Experiment
How would you connect two batteries to increase the current flowing through the light bulbs? How would you connect the batteries to have one battery keep the light bulbs lit if the other battery failed? Draw diagrams. With your teacher's approval, do the experiment.

Electric Circuits

MAIN IDEA An electric circuit is a pathway for electrons to travel. The energy of moving electrons can be changed into different forms, including light, heat, and sound.

READING SKILL

Draw Conclusions Use a graphic organizer to draw conclusions about the way electricity travels through circuits.

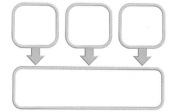

Circuits

To complete a *circuit* means to start at a beginning, travel away, then return by a different route. It is related to the word *circle*.

Think about a water park ride. The boats start at the high point of the track, flow with the water down a pathway, then climb to the high point again to take on new passengers. What would happen if a section of the ride were blocked or taken away, or if the motor that lifted the boats stopped working? The ride would stop because the boats could not complete their circuit.

The pathway for an electric current is called an **electric circuit.** The electric charges are like the boats in the ride. The battery in the circuit is like the motor that lifts the boats to the top of the track. The motor does work lifting each boat, giving it higher gravitational potential energy. The battery does work to "lift" each charge, giving it higher electric potential energy. The amount of electric potential energy per unit charge is called the **voltage** of the battery.

This amusement park ride is a circuit. A circuit is a closed loop. ▶

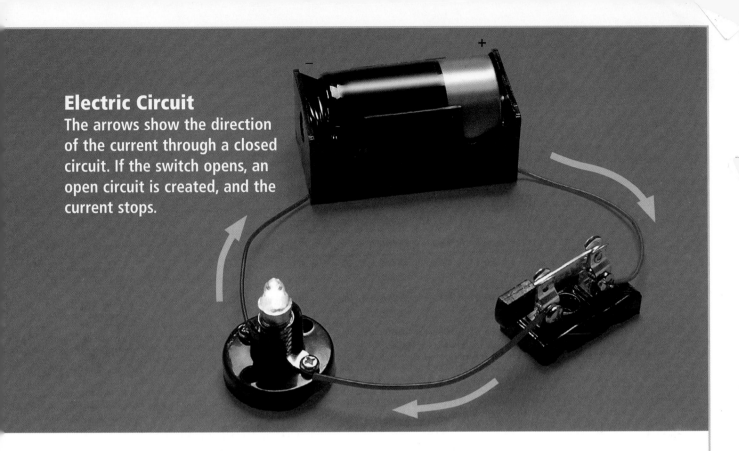

Electric Circuit
The arrows show the direction of the current through a closed circuit. If the switch opens, an open circuit is created, and the current stops.

Like the boats in the ride, electric current flows only through a certain path. This path for an electric current is determined by substances called conductors and insulators.

A **conductor** is a substance that carries electricity well. Most wires used in electric circuits are made of copper, which is an excellent conductor. Other metals make good conductors, too.

An **insulator** is a substance that does not carry electricity very well. Plastic is a good insulator, which is why most wires are coated with plastic. Wood and air are also good insulators.

Do you think water is a better conductor or insulator? If you chose conductor, you are correct. Electricity travels quite easily through water. This is why you should keep water away from electric appliances.

When an electric current can travel through conductors in a complete circuit, the circuit is called a closed circuit. When insulators, such as wood or air, block this path, the circuit is called an open circuit.

A simple device called a switch changes a circuit from open to closed or from closed to open. A **switch** is a movable section of a circuit that can open or close a path for electricity.

Look closely at the electric circuit above. When the switch is closed, electric current flows readily through the battery, wires, and light bulb.

How does electricity light a light bulb? In many light bulbs, current flows through a thin tungsten wire called a filament. The tungsten heats up and glows as it resists the current.

▶ **DRAW CONCLUSIONS** Why must you keep electric appliances away from showers and swimming pools?

Series Circuit

The photograph shows a closed circuit that includes batteries and three light bulbs. Notice that you can trace only one path for the electric current to follow. If any of the wires were cut, the entire circuit would become open. Electricity would stop flowing and no bulbs would light.

This circuit is an example of a series circuit. In a **series circuit,** only a single path for electricity connects two or more different light bulbs or other devices. The light bulbs are said to be "wired in series."

To open a series circuit, you could disconnect one of the wires or remove one of the bulbs from its socket. Or, if one of the bulbs burned out, current would stop flowing as well.

What would happen if you added more and more light bulbs in series? The circuit would remain closed, but the light bulbs would become dimmer and dimmer. The reason is that the battery can deliver only a certain amount of voltage. When the voltage is divided among many light bulbs, there is less voltage to push the current through each bulb.

Look at the schematic diagram of the circuit. The light bulbs are represented by jagged lines, which are symbols for resistors. The symbol for the battery is a group of long and short dashes.

Diagrams like these are simple ways to illustrate circuits. They are used by people who work with circuits, including electricians, computer technicians, and scientists.

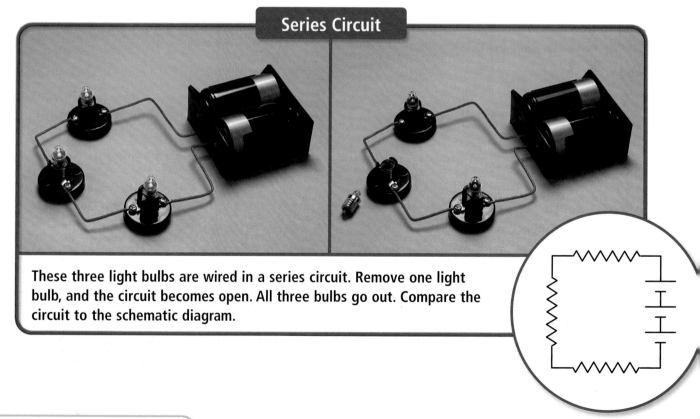

Series Circuit

These three light bulbs are wired in a series circuit. Remove one light bulb, and the circuit becomes open. All three bulbs go out. Compare the circuit to the schematic diagram.

Parallel Circuit

The photograph on this page shows the same three light bulbs and a battery. But notice that the light bulbs are wired in a different way. Each bulb is part of a unique path that can form a circuit with the battery.

This is an example of a parallel circuit. In a **parallel circuit,** electric current can follow two or more different paths. The light bulbs in this example are said to be "wired in parallel."

What happens if you disconnect one of the bulbs from its socket in a parallel circuit? The other bulbs will stay lit! The reason is that you opened only one path of the circuit, not the paths that connect the other bulbs.

Light bulbs are also brighter when connected in parallel than when they are connected in series. The reason is that, in a parallel circuit, all bulbs receive the full voltage from the battery. Each bulb will be as bright as if it were the only bulb in the circuit.

The circuits in your home are arranged in parallel, not in series. When you turn off the switch on a lamp, only that lamp goes out—not all the electrical appliances in the room!

Even strings of holiday lights are often arranged in parallel. If they were arranged in series, all would go out when a single bulb burned out.

▶ **DRAW CONCLUSIONS** How do parallel circuits and series circuits differ?

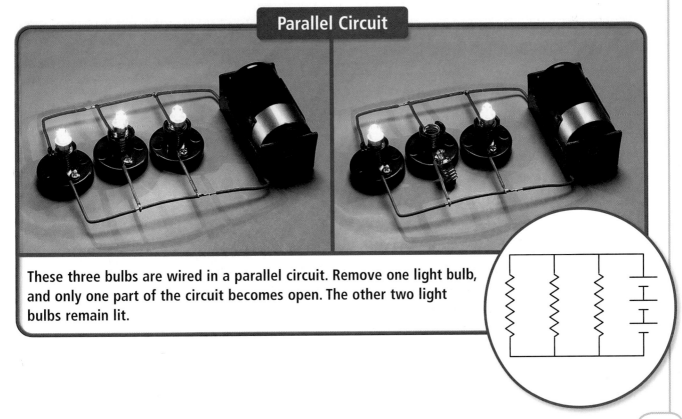

Parallel Circuit

These three bulbs are wired in a parallel circuit. Remove one light bulb, and only one part of the circuit becomes open. The other two light bulbs remain lit.

Electrical Safety

Electricity can be dangerous. You should insert only the plugs to electric appliances into household outlets, never anything else. You could get shocked!

Electricity is also dangerous because it can change into thermal energy. This means that lamps and other appliances can overheat, as can current-carrying wires. Accidental fires often start this way.

The higher the current flowing in the same circuit, the more heat is produced. To stop circuits from overheating and causing fires, most homes use either fuses or circuit breakers.

At the heart of a fuse is a thin metal strip that is part of an electric circuit. When too high a current flows through the strip, it melts. The circuit opens as a result.

A circuit breaker works a lot like a fuse. The difference is that too much current trips a switch, which in turn opens the circuit. The advantage of circuit breakers is that they can be used again and again, while fuses must be replaced after they stop electricity just once. For this reason, most new homes are built with circuit breakers.

▶ **DRAW CONCLUSIONS** What events do fuses and circuit breakers prevent?

◀ In wall outlets like this, the red button is connected to a special kind of circuit breaker. The button pops out to break the circuit and prevent an electric shock.

Circuit breakers respond to overloading by throwing a switch to break the circuit. Unlike fuses, they can be used over and over again. ▲

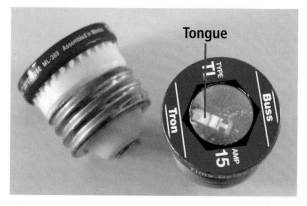

Tongue

When a fuse is overloaded, the tongue melts, breaking the circuit. The fuse has to be replaced to close the circuit. ▲

Visual Summary

Circuits are unbroken pathways. Electric circuits must be closed for electricity to flow.

Series circuits have only one pathway for current to follow. Parallel circuits have multiple pathways.

Fuses and circuit breakers are designed to break the pathway of a circuit and prevent overloading.

LINKS for Home and School

MATH **Calculate Voltage** In a series circuit, the voltage across the circuit is divided among the devices in the circuit. If you use a 1.5-volt battery to power three lights of the same type in a series circuit, how many volts will each bulb receive?

SOCIAL STUDIES **Make a Poster**
Research the inventions and discoveries of Thomas Edison, the inventor of the light bulb. Make a poster explaining one of his inventions.

Review

① MAIN IDEA Why does an electric circuit have to be closed for it to work?

② VOCABULARY In your own words, define *parallel circuit*.

③ READING SKILL: Draw Conclusions You plug in a string of lights and none of them lights up. You test the outlet and verify that it works. What might be the problem?

④ CRITICAL THINKING: Evaluate What would you suggest to a person who complained about having to replace fuses all the time?

⑤ INQUIRY SKILL: Record Data How are series circuits and parallel circuits similar and different? Draw diagrams.

✓ TEST PREP
Which of the following produces a voltage?

A. light bulb

B. battery

C. wires

D. a closed switch

Technology

Visit **www.eduplace.com/scp/** to find out more about electric circuits.

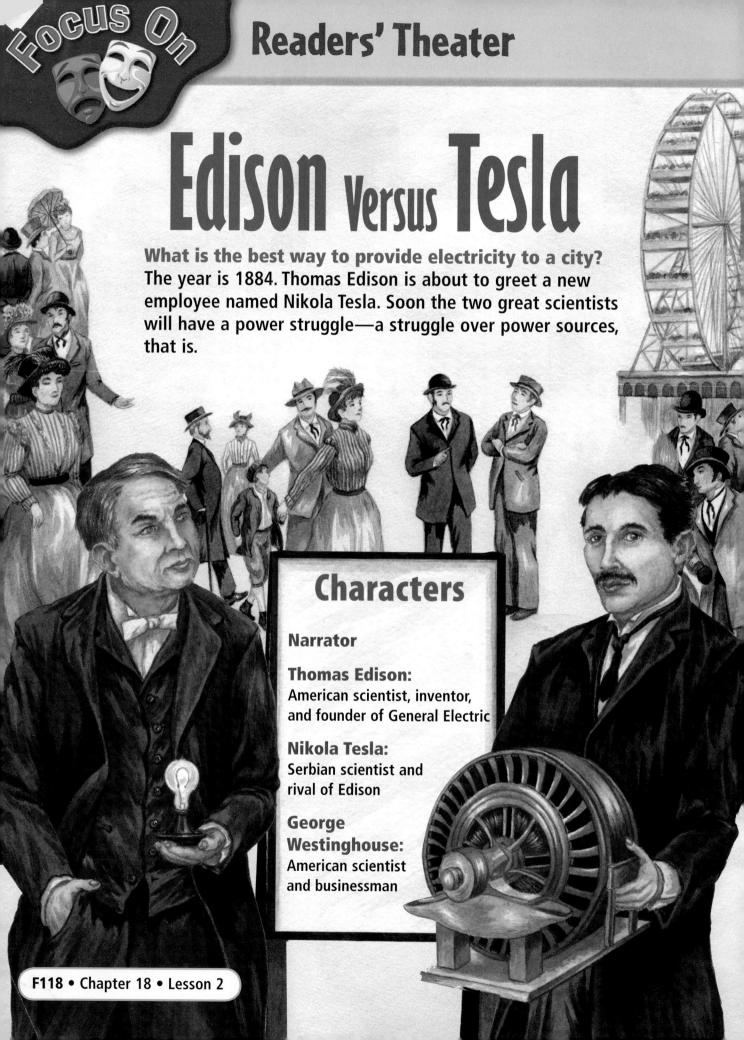

Edison versus Tesla

What is the best way to provide electricity to a city? The year is 1884. Thomas Edison is about to greet a new employee named Nikola Tesla. Soon the two great scientists will have a power struggle—a struggle over power sources, that is.

Characters

Narrator

Thomas Edison: American scientist, inventor, and founder of General Electric

Nikola Tesla: Serbian scientist and rival of Edison

George Westinghouse: American scientist and businessman

Narrator: Thomas Alva Edison invented the light bulb, the phonograph, the microphone, and many other products that use electricity.

Edison: Some might call me a genius. But as I always say, genius is 1 percent inspiration and 99 percent perspiration.

Narrator: Nikola Tesla was another great scientist of Edison's time. In the year 1884, Tesla immigrated to the United States from Serbia and began working for Edison.

Edison: What do you think of New York City, Mr. Tesla? Electricity is available here to the general public, thanks to me and my company.

Tesla: That is truly wonderful, Mr. Edison, except . . .

Edison (upset): Except what?

Tesla: So many wires carry the electricity, Mr. Edison, and they are so huge. They sag from pole to pole.

Edison: Well, I'm afraid that can't be helped. The wires carry a great deal of electricity. If they were thinner, they would overheat.

Tesla: The wires carry direct current, don't they?

Edison: Yes. DC, we call it. The electric current moves directly along the wires, in one direction. I invented the system myself.

Tesla (thoughtfully): Hmmm . . . I wonder if the city could be powered by electric current that moves back and forth.

Edison: Are you suggesting alternating current, or AC? Don't make me laugh!

Tesla: Why is that so ridiculous? With AC, current could travel farther and waste less energy. That would make it less expensive.

Edison: Spare me that nonsense! No one's complaining. Besides, no one has figured out how to make a reliable AC motor.

Narrator: In fact, Tesla already had an idea for such a motor. But Edison had heard quite enough about Tesla's ideas. Every conversation between the two scientists led to argument. Finally, Tesla decided to quit Edison's company.

Tesla (to himself): That bullheaded Edison. He wouldn't know a good idea if it bit him on the nose. But what will I do now?

Westinghouse (entering): No need to worry, Mr. Tesla! For years I've been looking for ways to use alternating current. I'll buy your AC devices for my company.

Tesla: Why, I can use the money to open my own laboratory!

Narrator: So which system would prove to be the better way to power cities: Edison's direct current or Tesla's alternating current?

Edison: The answer is obvious. My system came first, it's safe, and it has my name on it.

Tesla: My system is just as safe, it costs less, and it requires far fewer electrical wires. Our cities won't look like they're caught in giant spider webs!

Narrator: In 1893, both Edison and Westinghouse bid to supply electrical power to the Columbian Exposition, a huge fair in Chicago, Illinois.

New York City in 1888

These thick wires provided DC electricity throughout the city. The wires sagged from pole to pole—especially during a snowy winter.

World's Columbian Exposition

World's First Ferris Wheel

Edison: I'll power the entire fair for one million dollars. I'll string heavy copper wires all over the fairgrounds.

Westinghouse: With Tesla's system, we can power the fair for half that cost—and without a heavy web of wires!

Narrator: Not surprisingly, Tesla and Westinghouse won the rights to power the fair. They also ran a booth at the fair, and Tesla impressed visitors with demonstrations of AC electricity.

Edison: Hmmff. What about me?

Narrator: Well, your demonstrations didn't go so well.

Tesla: Don't feel bad, Mr. Edison. You'll always be remembered for your many accomplishments.

Edison (under his breath): Whippersnapper. Ah well. Back to the drawing board.

Narrator: A short time later, AC generators were chosen for a power plant in Niagara Falls. In 1896, Buffalo, NY, became the first city to be totally wired for AC. Today, Tesla's AC system is the standard all over the world.

Sharing Ideas

1. **READING CHECK** Why was the Columbian Exposition important to Westinghouse and Tesla?

2. **WRITE ABOUT IT** What were the advantages of Tesla's AC system?

3. **TALK ABOUT IT** Discuss the conflict between Edison and Tesla. Does it remind you of conflicts today?

How Do People Use Electricity?

Why It Matters...

When you pluck the strings on an electric guitar, the vibrations of the strings are sensed by electric pickups. The pickups send signals to an amplifier and speakers. Making music is just one of countless ways people use electricity in daily life.

PREPARE TO INVESTIGATE

Inquiry Skill

Predict When you predict, you use observations, patterns, data, or cause-and-effect relationships to anticipate results.

Materials

- plastic propeller
- motor
- switch
- 1.5-volt battery
- battery holder
- 3 wires

Motorized Electricity

Procedure

STEP 1

1. **Collaborate** Work in a small group. Attach the propeller to the axle on the motor. Make sure that the switch is in the off position. Then make a circuit using the battery, switch, motor, and three wires. Use the photo as a guide.

2. **Observe** Hold the motor so the propeller can turn. Turn the switch on. Observe the response of the motor's propeller. In your *Science Notebook,* record your observations.

STEP 3

3. **Experiment** Turn the switch off to stop the motor. Disconnect the wires that are attached to the battery and reattach them to the opposite battery terminals.

4. **Observe** Turn the switch back on. Observe the response of the motor's propeller. Record your observations.

Conclusion

1. **Compare** What change did you notice in the response of the motor's propeller?

2. **Predict** What would change, if anything, if you reversed the order of the switch and the motor in the original circuit? Explain your answer.

Investigate More!

Be an Inventor What else could be attached to the motor's axle? Invent a device that is useful, entertaining, or artistic. Draw a diagram to show your design.

Using Electricity

MAIN IDEA Electrical energy is transformed into light, mechanical energy, and thermal energy for a variety of everyday uses.

Energy Transformations

One of the first popular electric devices was the telegraph machine. To send messages, a telegraph operator used a simple switch, called a key. The switch was connected to a circuit that spanned long distances. Pressing down on the switch closed the circuit temporarily. At the other end, some receivers used a pointer that moved back and forth, converting the electrical energy to kinetic energy. Other receivers used a buzzer.

Both types of receivers used electromagnets to convert the electrical energy into another form. The buzzer made its sound because an electromagnet rapidly vibrated a piece of metal against another material. The pointer was also operated by an electromagnet.

Telegraph key ▲

The monitor on the computer converts electrical energy into light energy. The disk drive converts electrical energy to kinetic energy to spin the drive. ▶

Look at the headlamp the student pictured on the right is wearing. It consists of a simple series circuit made from a battery, a switch, and a light bulb. The filament in a light bulb resists the flow of current. As a result, the filament heats up and gives off light. Electrical energy changes into light and thermal energy.

Radiant Energy
The light bulb in the headlamp converts electrical energy into light—radiant energy.

The hair dryer also converts electrical energy into thermal energy. Coils of thin wire inside the hair dryer resist the electric current. The coils are made of an alloy, or mixture, of nickel and chromium. This material has very high resistance.

The coils produce a lot of thermal energy as current flows through them. A fan that converts electrical energy into mechanical kinetic energy pushes the hot air out of the hair dryer. Switches on the hair dryer allow the user to vary the temperature and the airflow.

Thermal Energy
The heating coils in the hair dryer convert electrical energy into thermal energy.

The saw also converts electrical energy into mechanical kinetic energy. It has a switch for varying the speed of the saw. The switch works by changing the voltage to the electric motor in the saw. When pushed a little, less voltage is applied to the motor. Less current flows and the motor runs at a lower speed. When the switch is pushed all the way, the full voltage is applied. More current flows and the motor runs faster.

▶ **CAUSE AND EFFECT** Why does a light bulb filament glow?

Mechanical Energy
The saw uses a motor to convert electrical energy into mechanical kinetic energy.

Electric Motors

An **electric motor** changes electrical energy into mechanical kinetic energy. To do this, a motor uses both an electromagnet and a permanent magnet. Thanks to clever construction, the poles of the electromagnet constantly exchange positions, which allows it to keep spinning.

The diagram shows the parts of a DC motor, meaning a motor that runs on direct current only. Here is how it works:

The axle holds a kind of frame called an armature. The armature includes a set of coils wound around a metal rod. Also attached to the axle is the commutator, which is a pair of springy metal pieces with small gaps between them. The commutator is connected to the coils of the armature. Resting on the commutator are brushes, which are connected to the motor's power supply.

When current is supplied to the motor, the current flows through the brushes, the commutator, and the coils of the armature. This makes the armature act as an electromagnet. The poles of the permanent magnet repel like poles of the electromagnet. This causes the armature to rotate half a turn, bringing the like poles closer together.

The armature continues to rotate because of the gaps in the commutator. The gaps are positioned where the magnets attract each other and would stop the motion. The gaps break the circuit, briefly turning the electromagnet off.

When the commutator contacts the brushes again, its two metal pieces receive the opposite polarity. This reverses the current through the coils, which reverses the poles of the electromagnet. The armature completes the other half turn.

Different motors drive each set of wheels. This allows the wheelchair to turn or move straight. ▶

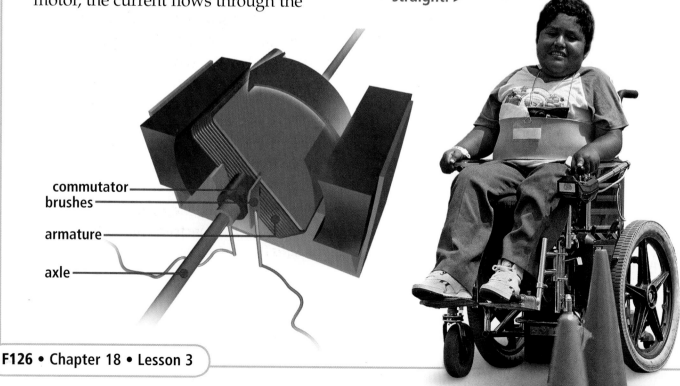

commutator
brushes
armature
axle

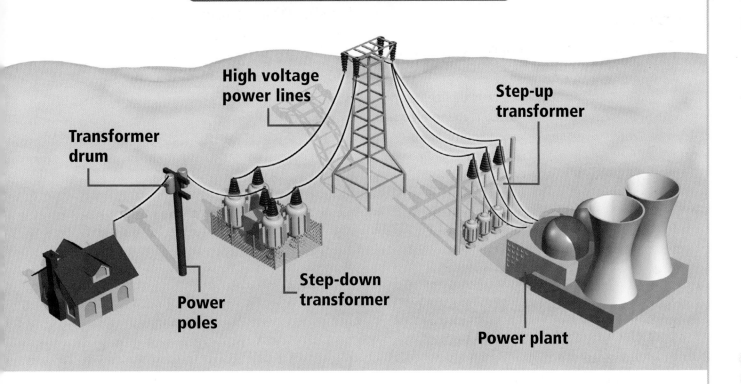

High voltage power lines

Step-up transformer

Transformer drum

Power poles

Step-down transformer

Power plant

Power Distribution

Large generators at power plants produce the electricity that travels to your community. This often is a long journey, sometimes covering hundreds of kilometers.

Electric power can be lost to heat. This is why long-distance power lines carry electricity at low current but very high voltage, as high as 500,000 volts or more. Such wires typically are strung high above the ground, as they are dangerous if touched or disturbed.

To raise or lower voltage, power companies use devices called transformers. A step-up transformer increases the voltage. This is done as electricity leaves the power plant. A step-down transformer lowers voltage. Voltage is lowered before entering your home.

If you look up at a power line in your neighborhood, you may see a drum-shaped can. This houses a step-down transformer that reduces the voltage to 240 volts, the level that enters your home.

In homes in North America, most household appliances, including televisions, lamps, and computers, run on 120 volts. However, major appliances such as water heaters, clothes dryers, and air conditioners run on 240 volts. Household circuits can be wired either to the 240-volt or 120-volt supply.

▶ **CAUSE AND EFFECT** Why do power plants distribute electricity at high voltages?

Visual Summary

Electric devices work by converting electrical energy into other forms of energy, such as thermal, light, and mechanical energy.

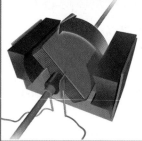

A motor converts electrical energy to mechanical energy by using the properties of magnets and electromagnets.

Electric power plants produce electricity that is distributed over power lines.

LINKS for Home and School

MATH Ratios A pole transformer reduces the voltage from the power line from 7,200 volts to 240 volts. Write a ratio in simplest form to describe the reduction in voltage.

WRITING Narrative Write about the ways that electricity is part of your daily life. Include at least four examples.

Review

1 MAIN IDEA What are two ways that electrical energy is converted to other forms of energy?

2 VOCABULARY Write a short paragraph explaining how an electric motor works.

3 READING SKILL: Cause and Effect Electricity can be changed into radiant energy, thermal energy, and mechanical energy. Give examples of devices that use each kind of change.

4 CRITICAL THINKING: Analyze If you buy a television or computer in another country, why might you have trouble using it in the United States?

5 INQUIRY SKILL: Predict A student builds a motor from a kit, but wraps the coils of wire much more loosely than the instructions suggest. How would the motor be affected? Explain.

✓ TEST PREP
The parts of a motor that are attached to a battery are the

A. commutators.

B. armatures.

C. brushes.

D. permanent magnets.

Technology
Visit **www.eduplace.com/scp/** to find out more about how electrical power is produced.

Acoustical Engineer

The next time you enjoy the music at a live concert, give some of the credit to the acoustical engineers. These professionals are experts in sound. They help design concert halls, theaters, and auditoriums.

Acoustical engineers may also work to block out sounds. They design features in cars to block road noise. They also find ways to reduce noise from airports and construction sites.

What It Takes!

- A degree in engineering or physics
- An understanding of architecture and electronics related to sound production

Gaffer

Special lighting effects thrill audiences of movies, television shows, and plays. They are created by electricians known as gaffers. Gaffers work with light fixtures, color filters, and many other kinds of equipment. They sometimes set up portable electrical generators and transformers at remote filming locations, such as a desert—far from any commercial power source.

What It Takes!

- In some places, being a licensed electrician
- An understanding of electricity and electrical equipment related to lighting
- Artistic talent and judgment

EXTREME Science

BIG static!

Crackle! Flash! Those wool socks you just pulled out of the drier are full of imbalanced electrical charges. Pull them apart in a dark room and watch the sparks fly!

Believe it or not, lightning itself is an example of static electricity. The big difference is size. A single bolt of lightning carries enough electrical current to light up a small city!

Like static electricity in your home, lightning is produced by a build-up of charge. Parts of a thundercloud become positively or negatively charged. A static charge jumps from one part to another, or down to the ground. Ba-boom!

From sparks in your socks to flashes in the sky, it's all static discharge.

When objects in your dryer tumble and rub together, electrical charges become separated. The imbalance causes things to cling—and crackle!

BIG Static! Here lightning strikes the Empire State Building in New York City. A lightning rod conducts the electricity safely away from the inside of the building.

Vocabulary

Complete each sentence with a term from the list.

1. A(n) _____ converts electrical energy to mechanical energy.

2. A(n) _____ is a substance that carries electricity well.

3. An electrical force between nonmoving charges is called _____.

4. A(n) _____ can be used to open and close an electric circuit.

5. A circuit that is wired in one direct pathway is a(n) _____.

6. Electric potential energy per unit charge is called _____.

7. A flow of electric charges moving through a pathway is called _____.

8. For electricity to flow, wires must complete a closed _____.

9. A(n) _____ converts mechanical energy to electrical energy.

10. A(n) _____ has multiple pathways through which electricity can flow.

conductor F113
electric circuit F112
electric current F105
electric generator F107
electric motor F126
insulator F113
parallel circuit F115
series circuit F114
static electricity F104
switch F113
voltage F112

 Test Prep

Write the letter of the best answer choice.

11. A _____ is used to raise or lower voltage.

   A. generator
   B. motor
   C. transformer
   D. fuse

12. A(n) _____ is a material that conducts electricity poorly.

   A. conductor
   B. substation
   C. motor
   D. insulator

13. A _____ does not use a turbine to operate a generator.

   A. fuel cell
   B. hydroelectric dam
   C. windmill
   D. nuclear reactor

14. A _____ is a device that breaks a circuit when the current becomes too high.

   A. fuse
   B. switch
   C. wire
   D. transformer

Inquiry Skills

15. **Compare** Describe similarities and differences between series circuits and parallel circuits. Use the diagrams below as a reference.

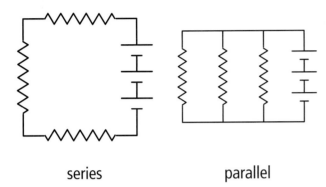

series   parallel

16. **Infer** You reach out to shake someone's hand and feel a static electric spark. What can you infer about the charges on you and on the other person?

Map the Concept

Write the terms below where they belong in the concept map. One of the terms can be used twice.

circuit   electricity
electric cell   parallel
electric current   series
electric generator   static electricity

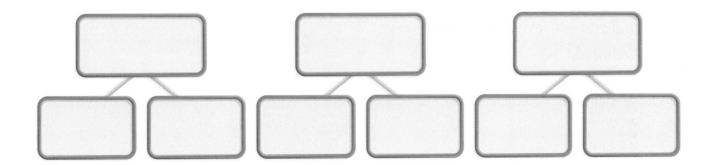

Critical Thinking

17. **Predict** Fossil fuels are the main source of energy used to produce electricity. What might happen when fossil fuels are used up? Are there alternatives? Explain.

18. **Apply** How might you improve a set of decorative lights that are wired in series, so that the rest of the lights would stay on if one of them went out? What would be a possible disadvantage of doing that?

19. **Evaluate** Are fuses a necessary part of a household electric circuit? What are the alternatives? Explain.

20. **Analyze** What are the parts of an electric motor? Describe what they do.

Performance Assessment

Make a Diagram

Draw a diagram to explain how a generator works. Add labels and a caption to the diagram.

Write the letter of the best answer.

1. Which is the best title for the diagram below?

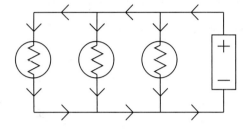

   A. open circuit

   B. series circuit

   C. parallel circuit

   D. circuit switch

2. Jane made an electromagnet with a 1.5 volt battery, a nail, and some wire. Which is MOST likely to increase the magnet's strength?

   A. using a much longer nail

   B. adding a switch to the circuit

   C. adding more coils of wire to the nail

   D. using a nail with a greater diameter

3. Eyeglass lenses work because of _____ .

   A. absorption.

   B. reflection.

   C. refraction.

   D. total internal reflection.

4. Which sound wave will produce the loudest sound with the lowest pitch?

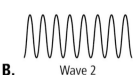

   A.   Wave 1

   B.   Wave 2

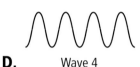

   C.   Wave 3

   D.   Wave 4

5. A motor uses the properties of magnets and electromagnets to convert _____ .

   A. electrical energy to magnetism.

   B. magnetism to mechanical energy.

   C. mechanical energy to electrical energy.

   D. electrical energy to mechanical energy.

6. Which power-generating technology produces both electricity and water?

   A. solar cells

   B. fuel cells

   C. geothermal power

   D. alkaline batteries

7. The handle of a spoon gets hot when the bowl of the spoon sits in some hot soup. Which method of thermal energy transfer explains why?

   A. radiation

   B. convection

   C. insulation

   D. conduction

8. Which playground equipment is an example of a wheel and axle?

A.

B.

C.

D.

Answer the following in complete sentences.

9. A ball rolling across a grass lawn slows down and eventually stops. Why is this NOT a violation of Newton's First Law?

10. On a hot day, you are standing at the edge of a pool. The concrete beneath your feet is very warm, but the water in the pool is cool. Explain this in terms of specific heat capacity.

Discover!

You're standing in a forest at night, and it's so dark that you can't even see your own hand. Yet when you look through special goggles, suddenly you can see the trees all around you. In one tree, you spot an owl staring back at you. Welcome to the world of night vision!

Image-intensifier tube

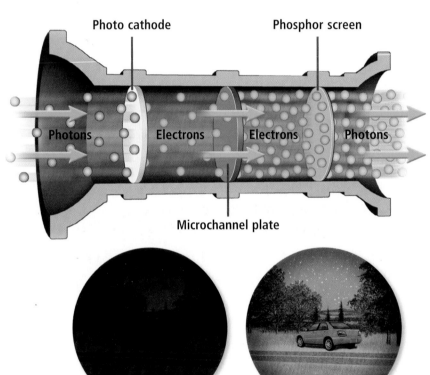

Photo cathode
Phosphor screen
Photons
Electrons
Electrons
Photons
Microchannel plate

Before

After

Night-vision goggles work by applying a high voltage to an image-intensifier tube. The added energy and special plates allow a few photons of light to be multiplied many times.

All night-vision equipment needs some source of light, even if it is very faint. Some equipment includes an infrared light built onto the glasses or eye scope. Infrared light cannot be seen by an unaided eye, but it can provide enough light to allow the night-vision equipment to work.

Learn more about seeing in the dark. Go to **www.eduplace.com/scp/** to see examples of how night-vision technology is being used in everyday life.

Science and Math Toolbox

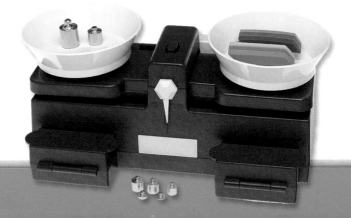

Using a Microscope

A microscope makes it possible to see very small things by magnifying them. Some microscopes have a set of lenses that magnify objects by different amounts.

Examine Some Salt Grains

Handle a microscope carefully; it can break easily. Carry it firmly with both hands and avoid touching the lenses.

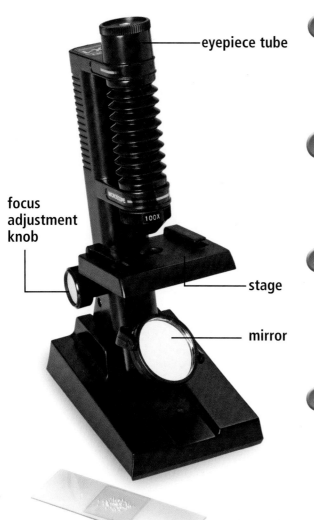

eyepiece tube

focus adjustment knob

stage

mirror

microscope slide

1. Turn the mirror toward a source of light. **NEVER** use the Sun as a light source.

2. Place a few grains of salt on the slide. Put the slide on the stage of the microscope.

3. Bring the salt grains into focus. Turn the adjustment knob on the back of the microscope as you look through the eyepiece.

4. Raise the eyepiece tube to increase the magnification; lower it to decrease magnification.

Making a Bar Graph

A bar graph helps you organize and compare data. For example, you might want to make a bar graph to compare weather data for different places.

Make a Bar Graph of Annual Snowfall

For more than 20 years, the cities listed in the table have been recording their yearly snowfall. The table shows the average number of centimeters of snow that the cities receive each year. Use the data in the table to make a bar graph showing the cities' average annual snowfall.

Snowfall	
City	Snowfall (cm)
Atlanta, GA	5
Charleston, SC	1.5
Houston, TX	1
Jackson, MS	3
New Orleans, LA	0.5
Tucson, AZ	3

1. Title your graph. The title should help a reader understand what your graph describes.

2. Choose a scale and mark equal intervals. The vertical scale should include the least value and the greatest value in the set of data.

3. Label the vertical axis *Snowfall (cm)* and the horizontal axis *City*. Space the city names equally.

4. Carefully graph the data. Depending on the interval you choose, some amounts may be between two numbers.

5. Check each step of your work.

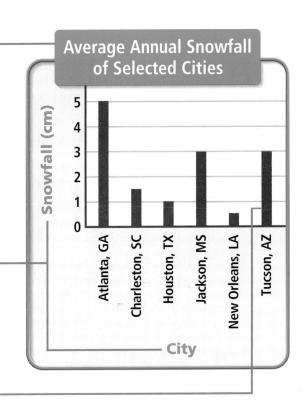

Average Annual Snowfall of Selected Cities

Using a Calculator

After you've made measurements, a calculator can help you analyze your data. Some calculators have a memory key that allows you to save the result of one calculation while you do another.

Add and Divide to Find Percent

The table shows the amount of rain that was collected using a rain gauge in each month of one year. You can use a calculator to help you find the total yearly rainfall. Then you can find the percent of rain that fell during January.

Rainfall	
Month	**Rain (mm)**
Jan.	214
Feb.	138
Mar.	98
Apr.	157
May	84
June	41
July	5
Aug.	23
Sept.	48
Oct.	75
Nov.	140
Dec.	108

1. Add the numbers. When you add a series of numbers, you need not press the equal sign until the last number is entered. Just press the plus sign after you enter each number (except the last).

2. If you make a mistake while you are entering numbers, press the clear entry (CE/C) key to erase your mistake. Then you can continue entering the rest of the numbers you are adding. If you can't fix your mistake, you can press the (CE/C) key once or twice until the screen shows 0. Then start over.

3. Your total should be 1,131. Now clear the calculator until the screen shows 0. Then divide the rainfall amount for January by the total yearly rainfall (1,131). Press the percent (%) key. Then press the equal sign key.

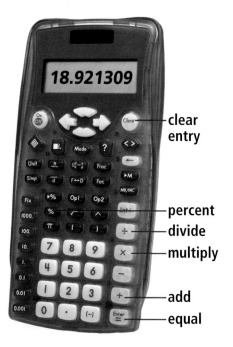

214 ÷ 1131 % =

The percent of yearly rainfall that fell in January is 18.921309, which rounds to 19%.

Finding an Average

An average is a way to describe a set of data using one number. For example, you could compare the surface temperature of several stars that are of the same type. You could find the average surface temperature of these stars.

Add and Divide to Find the Average

Suppose scientists found the surface temperature of eight blue-white stars to be those shown in the table. What is the average surface temperature of the stars listed?

1 First find the sum of the data. Add the numbers in the list.

```
  7,200
  6,100
  6,000
  6,550
  7,350
  6,800
  7,500
+ 6,300
───────
 53,800
```

2 Then divide the sum (53,800) by the number of addends (8).

```
        6,725
    8 ) 53,800
      − 48
       ───
        58
      − 56
       ───
         20
       − 16
        ───
         40
       − 40
        ───
          0
```

3 $53,800 \div 8 = 6,725$
The average surface temperature of these eight blue-white stars is 6,725°F.

Using a Tape Measure or Ruler

Tape measures, metersticks, and rulers are tools for measuring length. Scientists use units such as kilometers, meters, centimeters, and millimeters when making length measurements.

Use a Meterstick

1. Work with a partner to find the height of your reach. Stand facing a chalkboard. Reach up as high as you can with one hand.

2. Have your partner use chalk to mark the chalkboard at the highest point of your reach.

3. Use a meterstick to measure your reach to the nearest centimeter. Measure from the floor to the chalk mark. Record the height.

Use a Tape Measure

1. Use a tape measure to find the circumference of, or distance around, your partner's head. Wrap the tape around your partner's head.

2. Find the line where the tape begins to wrap over itself.

3. Record the distance around your partner's head to the nearest millimeter.

Measuring Volume

A graduated cylinder, a measuring cup, and a beaker are used to measure volume. Volume is the amount of space something takes up. Most of the containers that scientists use to measure volume have a scale marked in milliliters (mL).

▲ This measuring cup has marks for each 25 mL.

▲ This beaker has marks for each 50 mL.

▲ This graduated cylinder has marks for every 1 mL.

Measure the Volume of a Liquid

1. Measure the volume of some juice. Pour the juice into a measuring container.

2. Move your head so that your eyes are level with the top of the juice. Read the scale line that is closest to the surface of the juice. If the surface of the juice is curved up on the sides, look at the lowest point of the curve.

3. Read the measurement on the scale. You can estimate the value between two lines on the scale to obtain a more accurate measurement.

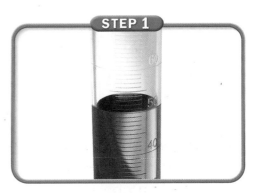

STEP 1

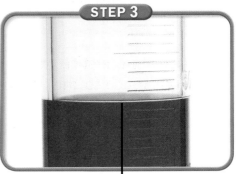

STEP 3

The bottom of the curve is at 35 mL.

Using a Thermometer

A thermometer is used to measure temperature. When the liquid in the tube of a thermometer gets warmer, it expands and moves farther up the tube. Different scales can be used to measure temperature, but scientists usually use the Celsius scale.

Measure the Temperature of a Liquid

1 Half fill a cup with water or another liquid.

2 Hold the thermometer so that the bulb is in the center of the liquid. Be sure that there are no bright lights or direct sunlight shining on the bulb.

3 Wait until you see the liquid in the tube of the thermometer stop moving. Read the scale line that is closest to the top of the liquid in the tube. The thermometer shown reads 22°C (about 71°F).

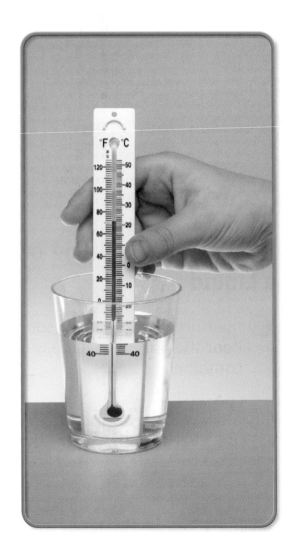

Using a Balance

A balance is used to measure mass. Mass is the amount of matter in an object. To find the mass of an object, place the object in the left pan of the balance. Place standard masses in the right pan.

Measure the Mass of a Ball

1 Check that the empty pans are balanced, or level with each other. When balanced, the pointer on the base should be on the middle mark. If it needs to be adjusted, move the slider on the back of the balance a little to the left or right.

2 Place a ball in the left pan. Then add standard masses, one at a time, to the right pan. When the pointer is at the middle mark again, each pan is holding the same amount of matter, and the same mass.

3 Each standard mass is marked to show its number of grams. Add the number of grams marked on the masses in the pan. The total is the mass of the ball in grams.

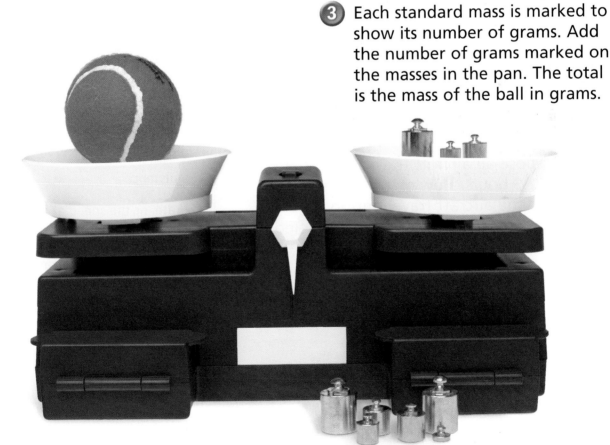

Using an Equation or Formula

Equations and formulas can help you to determine measurements that are not easily made.

Use the Diameter of a Circle to Find Its Circumference

1 Find the circumference of a circle that has a diameter of 10 cm. To determine the circumference of a circle, use the formula below.

$C = \pi d$

$C = 3.14 \times 10 \text{ cm}$

$C = 31.4 \text{ cm}$

The circumference of this circle is 31.4 cm.

π is the symbol for pi. Always use 3.14 as the value for π, unless another value for pi is given.

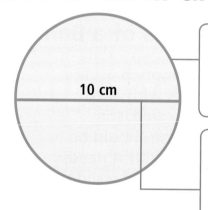

10 cm

The circumference (C) is a measure of the distance around a circle.

The diameter (d) of a circle is a line segment that passes through the center of the circle and connects two points on the circle.

Use Rate and Time to Determine Distance

2 Suppose an aircraft travels at 772 km/h for 2.5 hours. How many kilometers does the aircraft travel during that time? To determine distance traveled, use the distance formula below.

$d = rt$

$d = 772 \times 2.5 \text{ km}$

$d = 1,930 \text{ km}$

The aircraft travels 1,930 km in 2.5 hours.

d = distance

r = rate, or the speed at which the aircraft is traveling.

t = the length of time traveled

Making a Chart to Organize Data

A chart can help you record, compare, or classify information.

Organize Properties of Elements

Suppose you collected the data shown at the right. The data presents properties of silver, gold, lead, and iron.

You could organize this information in a chart by classifying the physical properties of each element.

My Data

Silver (Ag) has a density of 10.5 g/cm^3. It melts at 961°C and boils at 2,212°C. It is used in dentistry and to make jewelry and electronic conductors.

Gold melts at 1,064°C and boils at 2,966°C. Its chemical symbol is Au. It has a density of 19.3 g/cm^3 and is used for jewelry, in coins, and in dentistry.

The melting point of lead (Pb) is 328°C. The boiling point is 1,740°C. It has a density of 11.3 g/cm^3. Some uses for lead are in storage batteries, paints, and dyes.

Iron (Fe) has a density of 7.9 g/cm^3. It will melt at 1,535°C and boil at 3,000°C. It is used for building materials, in manufacturing, and as a dietary supplement.

Create categories that describe the information you have found.

Give the chart a title that describes what is listed in it.

Make sure the information is listed accurately in each column.

Properties of Some Elements

Element	Symbol	Density g/cm^3	Melting Point (°C)	Boiling Point (°C)	Some Uses
Silver	Ag	10.5	961	2,212	jewelry, dentistry, electric conductors
Gold	Au	19.3	1,064	2,966	jewelry, dentistry, coins
Lead	Pb	11.3	328	1,740	storage batteries, paints, dyes
Iron	Fe	7.9	1,535	3,000	building materials, manufacturing, dietary supplement

Reading a Circle Graph

A circle graph shows the whole divided into parts. You can use a circle graph to compare parts to each other or to compare parts to the whole.

Read a Circle Graph of Land Area

The whole circle represents the approximate land area of all of the continents on Earth. The number on each wedge indicates the land area of each continent. From the graph you can determine that the land area of North America is 16% × 148,000,000 km², or about 24 million square kilometers.

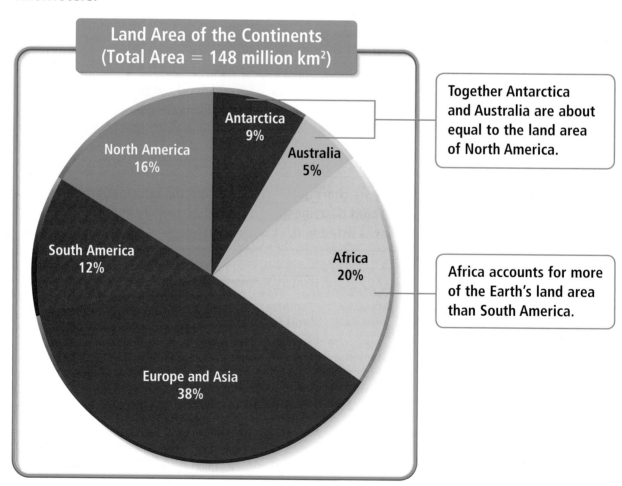

Land Area of the Continents (Total Area = 148 million km²)

Antarctica 9%
Australia 5%
North America 16%
South America 12%
Africa 20%
Europe and Asia 38%

Together Antarctica and Australia are about equal to the land area of North America.

Africa accounts for more of the Earth's land area than South America.

Making a Line Graph

A line graph is a way to show continuous change over time. You can use the information from a table to make a line graph.

Make a Line Graph of Temperatures

The table shows temperature readings over a 12-hour period at the Dallas-Fort Worth Airport in Texas. This data can also be displayed in a line graph that shows temperature change over time.

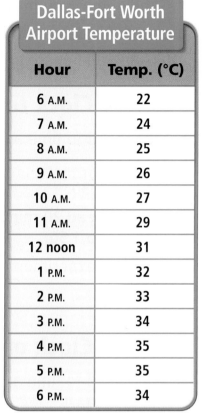

Dallas-Fort Worth Airport Temperature	
Hour	**Temp. (°C)**
6 A.M.	22
7 A.M.	24
8 A.M.	25
9 A.M.	26
10 A.M.	27
11 A.M.	29
12 noon	31
1 P.M.	32
2 P.M.	33
3 P.M.	34
4 P.M.	35
5 P.M.	35
6 P.M.	34

1. Choose a title. The title should help a reader understand what your graph describes.

2. Choose a scale and mark equal intervals. The vertical scale should include the least value and the greatest value in the set of data.

3. Label the horizontal axis *Time* and the vertical axis *Temperature* (°C).

4. Write the hours on the horizontal axis. Space the hours equally.

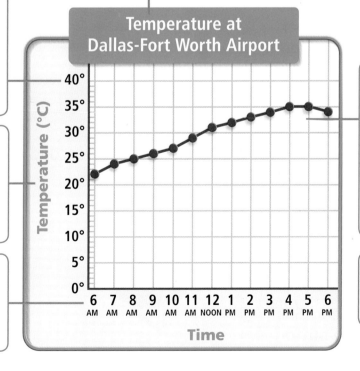

5. Carefully graph the data. Depending on the interval you choose, some temperatures will be between two numbers.

6. Check each step of your work.

Measuring Elapsed Time

Sometimes you may need to find out how much time has passed, or elapsed. A clock is often used to find elapsed time. You can also change units and add or subtract to find out how much time has passed.

Using a Clock to Find Elapsed Minutes

You need to time an experiment for 20 minutes. It is 1:30.

- Start at 1:30.
- Count ahead 20 minutes, by fives to 1:50.
- Stop the experiment at 1:50.

Using a Clock or Stopwatch to Find Elapsed Seconds

You need to time an experiment for 15 seconds. You can use a second hand on a clock.

1. Wait until the second hand is on a number. Then start the experiment.
2. Stop the experiment when 15 seconds have passed.

You can also use a stopwatch to figure out elapsed seconds.

1. Press the reset button on the stopwatch so you see 0:00₀₀.
2. Press the start button to begin.
3. When you see 0:15₀₀, press the stop button on the watch.

Changing Units and Then Adding or Subtracting to Find Elapsed Time

If you know how to change units of time, you can use addition and subtraction to find elapsed time.

1 To change from a larger unit to a smaller unit, multiply.

2 d = ■ h

2 × 24 = 48

2 d = 48 h

2 To change from a smaller unit to a larger unit, divide.

78 wk = ■ yr

$78 \div 52 = 1\frac{1}{2}$

$78 \text{ wk} = 1\frac{1}{2} \text{ yr}$

Another Example

Suppose it took juice in an ice-pop mold from 6:40 A.M. until 10:15 A.M. to freeze. How long did it take for the juice to freeze? To find out, subtract.

```
   9 h      75 min
  10 h      15 min
  − 6 h      40 min
   3 h      35 min
```

Rename 10 hr 15 min as 9 h 75 min, since 1 hr = 60 min.

You can also add to find elapsed time.

```
   3 h      30 min     14 s
 + 1 h      40 min     45 s
   4 h      70 min     59 s = 5 h 10 min 59 s
```

Units of Time
60 seconds (s) = 1 minute (min)
60 minutes = 1 hour (hr)
24 hours = 1 day (d)
7 days = 1 week (wk)
52 weeks = 1 year (yr)

Measurements

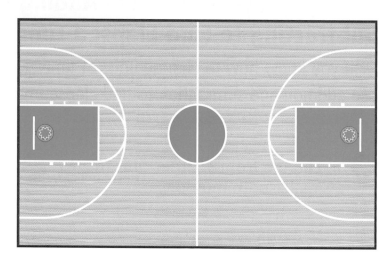

Volume

1 L of sports drink is a little more than 1 qt.

Area

A basketball court covers about 4,700 ft². It covers about 435 m².

Metric Measures

Temperature

- Ice melts at 0 degrees Celsius (°C)
- Water freezes at 0°C
- Water boils at 100°C

Length and Distance

- 1,000 meters (m) = 1 kilometer (km)
- 100 centimeters (cm) = 1 m
- 10 millimeters (mm) = 1 cm

Force

- 1 newton (N) = 1 kilogram × 1 (meter/second) per second

Volume

- 1 cubic meter (m³) = 1 m × 1 m × 1 m
- 1 cubic centimeter (cm³) = 1 cm × 1 cm × 1 cm
- 1 liter (L) = 1,000 milliliters (mL)
- 1 cm³ = 1 mL

Area

- 1 square kilometer (km²) = 1 km × 1 km
- 1 hectare = 10,000 m²

Mass

- 1,000 grams (g) = 1 kilogram (kg)
- 1,000 milligrams (mg) = 1 g

Temperature

The temperature at an indoor basketball game might be 27°C, which is 80°F.

Length/Distance

A basketball rim is about 10 ft high, or a little more than 3 m from the floor.

Customary Measures

Temperature

- Ice melts at 32 degrees Fahrenheit (°F)
- Water freezes at 32°F
- Water boils at 212°F

Length and Distance

- 12 inches (in.) = 1 foot (ft)
- 3 ft = 1 yard (yd)
- 5,280 ft = 1 mile (mi)

Weight

- 16 ounces (oz) = 1 pound (lb)
- 2,000 pounds = 1 ton (T)

Volume of Fluids

- 8 fluid ounces (fl oz) = 1 cup (c)
- 2 c = 1 pint (pt)
- 2 pt = 1 quart (qt)
- 4 qt = 1 gallon (gal)

Metric and Customary Rates

- km/h = kilometers per hour
- m/s = meters per second
- mph = miles per hour

Health and Fitness Handbook

Who is in charge of your health? You! Doctors, nurses, your parents or guardian, and teachers can all help you stay healthy. However, it's up to you to make healthful choices. What are some healthful choices you can make? In this section you'll learn:

- how to keep your body systems strong and healthy
- how to choose healthful foods
- how to exercise your heart and lungs every day
- how to be prepared for emergencies
- the benefits of avoiding alcohol, tobacco, and other drugs

The Muscular System

Your muscular system has three types of muscles.

- *Skeletal muscles* pull on bones to move them. You use them whenever you move your body.

- *Cardiac muscles* make up the walls of your heart and keep it beating.

- *Smooth muscles* line the blood vessels, the stomach, and other organs.

Most skeletal muscles are *voluntary muscles.* You can control them. Cardiac and smooth muscles are *involuntary muscles.* They work without you even having to think about them!

Many skeletal muscles work in pairs. When the biceps muscle in your arm contracts (gets shorter), the triceps muscle relaxes (gets longer). As a result, the elbow bends. How would the muscles work together to straighten the arm?

FACTS

- Your muscles receive about 50 messages from your brain every second.
- You have more than 650 muscles.

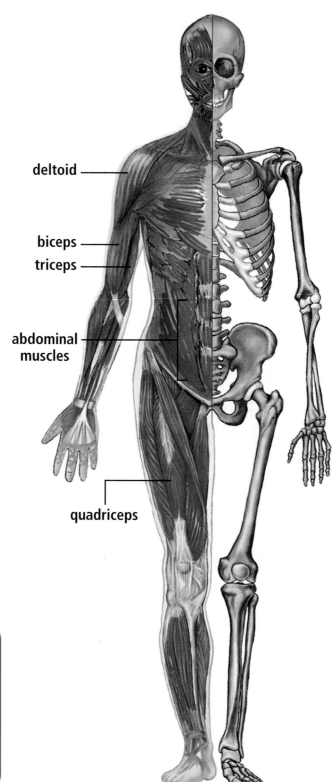

deltoid

biceps

triceps

abdominal muscles

quadriceps

The Skeletal System

Joints connect bones. If you had no joints, you could not bend or move. Each type of joint allows different kinds of movement. Your elbow has a hinge joint. The arm bends only one way at the elbow. Think about your shoulder. It has a ball-and-socket joint. What movement does it allow?

Your skeletal system gives your body strength and support. It works with your muscular system to move body parts. Your bones also protect your organs.

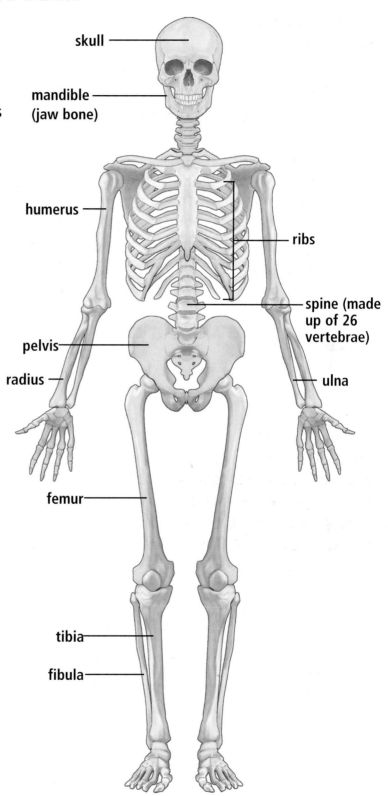

skull

mandible (jaw bone)

humerus

ribs

spine (made up of 26 vertebrae)

pelvis

radius

ulna

femur

tibia

fibula

FACTS

• You have 206 bones in your body. More than half of them are found in your hands and feet!

• Your bones come in all shapes and sizes. There's even a bone in your ear shaped like a hammer!

Exercise Your Heart and Lungs

Exercise that makes your heart and lungs work hard is called aerobic exercise. *Aerobic* means "with oxygen." Any kind of steady exercise that raises your heart and breathing rates is aerobic exercise. Jogging, swimming, bicycling, and playing soccer are all good ways to get aerobic exercise.

Five steps toward a great aerobic workout.

1 **Choose your activity.** Pick an activity you enjoy. Do you like exercising with others? Basketball might be a good choice. Do you like exercising to music? Maybe you'd like dancing!

2 **Get the equipment you need.** Make sure you have the right clothes and shoes for your activity. Wear any safety gear you need. Your clothes and safety gear should fit correctly. Ask a parent, guardian, or physical education teacher for help.

3 **Warm up.** Do gentle activity such as walking for five minutes. Then stretch your muscles.

4 **Exercise.** It's best to exercise for at least 20 minutes. Exercise at a level that makes your heart and lungs work. Stop right away if you are injured.

5 **Cool down.** Exercise at a lower level for five to ten minutes to let your heart and breathing rates come back down. Then stretch your muscles again.

Food Labels

The United States Food and Drug Administration (FDA) requires most companies that sell food to label their packages. The facts shown on food labels can help you make smart food choices. Food labels list the ingredients in the food. They are in order by weight. This means that the food contains the most of the first ingredient listed. The label also tells you the name of the company that makes the food and the total weight or volume of the food in the package.

Food labels also include the Nutrition Facts panel. The panel on the right is for a can of chicken soup.

Nutrition Facts
Serving Size 1 cup (246g)
Servings Per Container About 2

Amount Per Serving

Calories 110   Calories from Fat 20

	% Daily Value*
Total Fat 2.5g	4%
Saturated Fat 0.5g	3%
Cholesterol 25mg	8%
Sodium 960mg	40%
Total Carbohydrate 15g	5%
Dietary Fiber 1g	5%
Sugars 2g	
Protein 9g	

Vitamin A 30%	•	Vitamin C 0%
Calcium 2%	•	Iron 4%

*Percent Daily Values are based on a 2,000 calorie diet.

▲ What nutrients are in the food you eat? Read the Nutrition Facts panel to find out! Calories measure the energy in food.

FACTS

Get Enough Nutrients
- Carbohydrates provide energy. Fiber helps the digestive system.
- Your body uses protein for growth and development.
- Vitamins and minerals are important for many body functions.

FACTS

Limit Some Nutrients
- A healthful diet includes a limited amount of fat. Saturated fats and trans fats can increase the risk of heart disease. Cholesterol is a fat-like substance that can clog arteries.
- Too much sodium can increase the risk of high blood pressure.

Emergency Safety

Earthquakes, hurricanes, and tornadoes are all examples of natural disasters. You can plan ahead so you know what to do when a disaster happens.

Plan Ahead

You might not have fresh running water or electricity during a natural disaster. Here are some items you might want to have on hand.

- flashlights with batteries
- candles or lanterns with matches
- at least two gallons of fresh water
- canned or packaged food that does not need to be cooked
- radio with batteries
- first-aid kit

What To Do

Earthquake Get under something solid like a desk or doorway. Stay away from windows. Also stay away from anything that might fall on you. If you are outdoors, get to a wide open area.

Hurricane If there is some warning that a hurricane is coming, you may be told to evacuate. Tape all windows. Your parents or guardian will probably shut off the gas, water, and electricity.

Tornado If you are inside, go to a storm shelter or basement if you can. If there is no basement, go to an inside room with no windows. If you are outside, lie down in a low area and cover your head.

Tobacco, Alcohol, and Other Drugs

A drug is any substance, other than food, that changes how the body works. Drugs are swallowed, smoked, inhaled, or injected.

Helpful Drugs

Some drugs are helpful. Medicines can treat diseases and relieve pain. Drugs people can buy without a doctor's order are called *over-the-counter medicines.* Medicines that need a doctor's order are called *prescription medicines.*

Medicines can harm you if you use them incorrectly. Only take medicine when your parent, guardian, or doctor tells you to. Follow your doctor's instructions or the instructions printed on the package.

Harmful Drugs

Some drugs can harm your health.

Tobacco is a leaf that is smoked, sniffed, or chewed. Tobacco contains many harmful substances, including nicotine which speeds up the heart. Tobacco is addictive. This means that it is very hard to stop using tobacco once a person starts. Tobacco increases your risk of heart disease and lung disease.

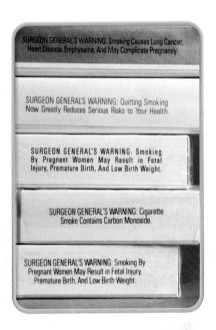

Alcohol is a drug found in drinks such as beer and wine. Alcohol slows brain activity and muscle activity. Heavy drinking can lead to addiction and can damage the liver and other organs. People who drink alcohol are more likely to get into accidents.

Illegal drugs include marijuana, cocaine, ecstasy, LSD, and amphetamines. These drugs can cause serious physical, emotional, and social problems.

Glossary

A

acceleration (ak sehl uh RAY shuhn), change in velocity (F9)

acquired trait (uh KWYRD trayt), characteristic that an organism develops after it is born (A84)

adaptation (ad ap TAY shuhn), a trait or characteristic that helps an organism survive in its environment (A102, B40)

air mass (air mas), huge volume of air responsible for types of weather (D18)

analyze data (AN uh lyz DAY tuh), to look for patterns in collected information that lead to making logical inferences, predictions, and hypotheses

angiosperms (AN jee uh spurmz), plants with seeds covered by protective fruits (A70)

asexual reproduction (ay SEHK shoo uhl ree pruh DUHK shuhn), production of offspring from only one parent (A96)

ask questions (ask KWEHS chunz), to state questions orally or in writing to find out how or why something happens

asteroid (AS tuh royd), small, rocky object that orbits the Sun (D58)

atmosphere (AT muh sfihr), mixture of gases that surrounds Earth (D16)

atom (AT uhm), the smallest particle of an element that still has the properties of that element (E6)

autumnal equinox (aw TUHM nuhl EE kwuh nahks), September 22 or 23, when the number of hours of daylight and darkness are the same (D34)

axis (AK sihs), imaginary line that goes through the center of Earth from the North Pole to the South Pole (D32)

B

biome (BY ohm), large group of similar ecosystems (B12)

boiling point (BOY lihng point), temperature at which a substance changes from a liquid to a gas (E45)

C

cell (sehl), the basic structural unit of a living thing (A6)

chemical change (KEHM ih kuhl chaynj), change in matter that results in new substances being formed (E53)

chemical formula (KEHM ih kuhl FAWR myuh luh), a shorthand way to describe the chemical makeup of a compound (E29)

chemical property (KEHM ih kuhl PRAHP uhr tee), ability of a material to change its chemical makeup (E43)

chemical reaction (KEHM ih kuhl ree AK shuhn), a process in which one or more substances are changed into one or more different substances, or a specific example of one or more chemical changes (E28, E53)

chemical symbol (KEHM ih kuhl SIHM buhl), a letter or letters that abbreviates an element's name (E16)

chlorophyll (KLAWR uh fihl), the green pigment in leaves that collects energy from sunlight (A51)

chloroplasts (KLAWR uh plastz), plant organelles inside which photosynthesis takes place (A51)

chromosome (KROH muh sohm), short, thick coil of DNA (A86)

cilia (SIHL ee uh), small structures that look like hairs (A16)

classification (klas uh fih KAY shuhn), process of sorting things based on similarities and differences (A24)

classify (KLAS uh fy), to sort objects into groups according to their properties to order objects according to a pattern

climate (KLY miht), normal pattern of weather that occurs in an area over a long period of time (B12, D7)

collaborate (kuh LAB uh rayt), to work as a team with others to collect and share data, observations, findings, and ideas

comet (KAHM iht), small orbiting body made of dust, ice, and frozen gases (D59)

communicate (kah MYOO nuh kayt), to explain procedures or share information, data, or findings with others through written or spoken words, actions, graphs, charts, tables, diagrams, or sketches

community (kuh MYOO nih tee), group of living things of different species found in an ecosystem (B7)

compare (kuhm PAIR), to observe and tell how objects or events are alike or different

compound (KAHM pownd), a substance that is made up of two or more elements that are chemically combined (E26)

condensation (kahn dehn SAY shuhn), change of state from a gas to a liquid as energy is removed (E85)

conduction (kuhn DUHK shuhn), transfer of thermal energy between two substances or between two parts of the same substance (F88)

conductivity (kuhn duhk TIHV ih tee), ability to carry energy (E46)

conductor (kuhn DUHK tuhr), material that easily transfers thermal energy or electricity (F92)

conservation (kahn sur VAY shuhn), efficient use of resources (C78)

consumer (kuhn SOO muhr), organism that gets energy by eating food, not producing it (B24)

contour lines (KAHN tur lynz), lines on a topographic map that indicate areas with the same elevation, or height above sea level (C10)

convection (kuhn VEHK shuhn), transfer of thermal energy by the flow of liquids or gases (F89)

core (kohr), Earth's innermost structure (C41)

crust (kruhst), the thin, rocky outer layer of Earth that makes up the continents and the ocean floor (C7, C40)

density (DEHN sih tee), mass per unit volume of a substance (E44)

deposition (dehp uh ZIHSH uhn), [1] constructive force in which sediments that have been moved from one place are dropped or released in another place, or [2] change of state from a gas to a solid (C24, E86)

desert (DEHZ uhrt), a very dry area (B14)

diffusion (dih FYOO zhuhn), movement of particles from an area of higher concentration to an area of lower concentration (A17)

DNA molecule found in the nucleus of a cell and shaped like a double helix; associated with the transfer of genetic information (A86)

dome mountains (dohm MOWN tuhnz), mountains that form when magma pushes up on Earth's crust but does not break through (C64)

dominant trait (DAHM uh nuhnt trayt), trait that is expressed when an organism receives genes for two different forms of a trait (A99)

earthquake (URTH kwayk), violent shaking of Earth's crust as built-up energy is released (C54)

ecosystem (EHK oh sihs tuhm), all the living and nonliving things that interact with one another in a given area (B6)

El Niño (ehl NEE nyo), periodic change in the direction of warm ocean currents across the Pacific Ocean (D10)

electric cell (ih LEHK trihk sehl), device that uses a chemical reaction to produce electricity

electric circuit (ih LEHK trihk SUR kiht), pathway for an electric current (F112)

electric current (ih LEHK trihk KUR uhnt), continuous flow of electric charge along a pathway

electric generator (ih LEHK trihk JEHN uh ray tuhr), device that converts kinetic energy to electricity (F107)

electric motor (ih LEHK trihk MOH tuhr), device that converts electrical energy into kinetic energy (F126)

electromagnet (ih lehk troh MAG niht), a magnet that is powered by electricity (F32)

electron (ih LEHK trahn), a particle in an atom that has a negative charge (E7)

element (EHL uh muhnt), a substance that cannot be broken down into other substances (E6)

endangered species (ehn DAYN juhrd SPEE sheez), a species close to becoming extinct (B59)

energy (EHN uhr jee), ability to do work (F44)

epicenter (EHP ih sehn tuhr), point on Earth's surface directly above the focus of an earthquake (C54)

erosion (ih ROH zhuhn), destructive force in which pieces of rock are moved by water, wind, or moving ice (C16)

experiment (ihks SPEHR uh muhnt), to investigate and collect data that either supports a hypothesis or shows that it is false while controlling variables and changing only one part of an experimental setup at a time

extinction (ihk STIHNGK shuhn), when all members of a species die out (B51)

fault (fawlt), crack in Earth's crust along which movement takes place (C52)

fault-block mountains (fahwlt blahk MOWN tuhnz), mountains that form along fault lines where blocks of rock fall, are thrust up, or slide (C63)

flagellum (fluh JEHL uhm), whip-like tail that helps single-celled organisms move by spinning like a propeller (A17)

focus (FOH kuhs), point underground where the faulting in an earthquake occurs (C54)

fold mountains (fohld MOWN tuhnz), mountains that form where two plates collide and force layers of rock into folds (C62)

food chain (food chayn), description of how energy in an ecosystem flows from one organism to another (B25)

food web (food wehb), description of all the food chains in an ecosystem (B26)

force (fawrs), push or pull acting on an object (F7)

fossil (FAH suhl), physical remains or traces of a plant or animal that lived long ago (C44)

fossil fuel (FAHS uhl fyool), nonrenewable resource formed from ancient plants and animals (C75)

friction (FRIHK shuhn), force from rubbing (F12)

front (fruhnt), narrow region between two air masses that have different properties (D19)

fungi (FUHN jee), kingdom of living things; its organisms are multicellular, have nuclei, and often feed on decaying matter (A26)

galaxy (GAL uhk see), an enormous system of gases, dust, and stars held together by gravity (D78)

gas (gas), state of matter that has no definite shape or volume (E78)

gene (jeen), short segment of DNA that determines an organism's inherited traits (A87)

grasslands (GRAS landz), land covered by grasses with few trees (B14)

gravity (GRAV ih tee), pulling force between objects (F12)

gymnosperms (JIHM nuh spurmz), plants with seeds that are not covered by protective fruits (A69)

habitat (HAB ih tat), the natural environment where an organism lives (B38)

heat (heet), transfer of thermal energy from warmer areas to cooler areas (F80)

heredity (huh REHD ih tee), genetic transfer of characteristics from parent to offspring (A84)

hybrid (HY brihd), organism that has two different genes for the same trait (A99)

hypothesize (hy PAHTH uh syz), to make an educated guess about why something happens

inertia (ih NUR shuh), resistance to a change in motion (F7)

infer (ihn FUR), to use facts, data, and observations to draw a conclusion about a specific event

inner planets (IHN uhr PLAN ihtz), the four planets of the solar system that are closest to the sun — Mercury, Venus, Earth, and Mars (D64)

insulator (IHN suh lay tuhr), material that does not easily transfer thermal energy or electricity (F92)

invertebrate (ihn VUR tuh briht), animal that has no internal skeleton or bones (A28)

kinetic energy (kih NEHT ihk EHN uhr jee), energy of a moving object (F46)

kingdom (KIHNG duhm), largest group of organisms that share traits in common (A24)

life cycle (lyf SY kuhl), sequence of life events beginning with a seed and ending with the next generation of seeds (A68)

light-year (LYT yihr), unit of measurement for distances outside the solar system and equal to about 9.5 trillion km (D75)

liquid (LIHK wihd), state of matter that has a definite volume, but no definite shape (E77)

lithosphere (LIHTH uh sfihr), shell formed from Earth's solid upper mantle and crust (C41)

lunar eclipse (LOO nuhr ih KLIHPS), when Earth passes directly between the Sun and the Moon, casting a shadow on the Moon (D46)

magma (MAG muh), melted rock below Earth's surface; called lava at the surface (C56)

magnitude (MAG nih tood), brightness of a star as perceived from Earth (D75)

mantle (MAN tl), thick layer of Earth's structure just below Earth's crust (C41)

measure (MEHZH uhr), to use a variety of measuring instruments and tools to find the length, distance, volume, mass, or temperature using appropriate units of measurement

mechanical wave (mih KAN ih kuhl wayv), wave that can travel only through matter (F52)

melting (MEHL tihng), change of state from a solid to a liquid as energy is added (E84)

melting point (MEHL tihng point), temperature at which a substance changes from a solid to a liquid (E45)

mesosphere (MEHZ oh sfeer), layer of the atmosphere above the stratosphere and below the thermosphere (D17)

metal (MEHT l), any one of the elements located on the left and bottom of the periodic table, which are usually shiny, can be bent or stretched, and conduct electricity (E17)

meteor (MEE tee uhr), chunk of matter that enters Earth's atmosphere and is heated by friction with the air (D60)

meteorites (MEE tee uh rytz), chunks of meteor matter that fall to the ground (D60)

mixture (MIHKS chuhr), physical combination of two or more substances (E60)

molecule (MAHL ih kyool), two or more atoms joined by chemical bonds (E10)

moon phases (moon FAYZ ihz), shapes created by the changing amounts of the visible lighted areas of the Moon (D44)

motion (MOH shuhn), change in an object's position (F6)

mutation (myoo TAY shuhn), change in the genes of an organism (A89)

natural resource (NACH uhr uhl REE sawrs), resource found in nature, such as air, water, minerals, and soil (C74)

neutron (NOO trahn), a particle in the nucleus of an atom that has no charge (E8)

newton (NOOT n), unit to measure force, it is equal to the force required to accelerate a 1 kg mass by 1 m/s^2 (F11)

niche (nihch), the role of an organism in its habitat (B39)

noble gas (NOH buhl gas), any one of the elements located in the far right column of the periodic table, which generally do not combine with other elements to form molecules (E20)

nonmetal (nahn MEHT l), elements that are usually dull, brittle, and do not conduct electricity (E17)

nonrenewable resource (nahn rih NOO uh buhl REE sawrs), resource that is difficult to replace (C75)

nonvascular plant (nahn VAS kyoo luhr plant), a simple plant that lacks true leaves, stems, and roots (A62)

nucleotide (NOO klee uh tyd), basic structural unit of DNA (A87)

nucleus (NOO klee uhs), storehouse of the cell's most important chemical information, or the central core of an atom (A8, E7)

observe (UHB zuhrv), to use the senses and tools to gather or collect information and determine the properties of objects or events

ocean current (OH shuhn KUR uhnt), moving stream of water created by winds pushing against the ocean's surface (D10)

organ (AWR guhn), group of one or more kinds of tissues that work together to perform the same function (A33)

organ system (AWR guhn SIHS tuhm), group of interconnected organs that perform related life functions (A33)

organelle (AWR guh nehl), cell structure that performs specific functions (A8)

osmosis (ahz MOH sihs), type of diffusion in which water passes through a cell membrane (A17)

outer planets (OW tuhr PLAN ihtz), the five planets of the solar system farthest from the Sun—Jupiter, Saturn, Uranus, Neptune, and Pluto (D66)

parallel circuit (PAR uh lehl SUR kiht), circuit where electric current can follow two or more different paths (F115)

penumbra (pih NUHM bruh), large partial shadow in an eclipse (D46)

periodic table (pihr ee AHD ihk   TAY buhl), a table that organizes the elements by their properties (E15)

phloem (FLOH ehm), specialized tissue within roots, stems, and leaves that moves materials (A63)

photosynthesis (foh toh SIHN thih sihs), the process by which plants use light energy to convert water and carbon dioxide into sugars and oxygen (A50)

physical change (FIHZ ih kuhl   chaynj), change in the size, shape, or state of matter with no new matter being formed (E52)

physical property (FIHZ ih kuhl   PRAHP uhr tee), characteristic that can be measured or detected by the senses (E43)

pitch (pihch), perceived highness or lowness of a sound (F56)

planet (PLAN iht), large bodies that revolve around the Sun (D56)

plate tectonics (playt   tehk TAHN ihks), theory that giant plates of crust are moving slowly across Earth's surface (C42)

pollination (pahl ih NAY shuhn), process of delivering pollen (male) to the egg (female) in a plant (A69)

pollution (puh LOO shuhn), addition of harmful substances to the environment (B60)

population (pahp yuh LAY shuhn), all the members of the same type of organism living in an ecosystem (B8, B46)

population density (pahp yuh LAY shuhn DEHN sih tee), number of individuals in a population in a given area (B47)

potential energy (puh TEHN shuhl   EHN uhr jee), energy stored in an object (F46)

predator (PREHD uh tuhr), animal that hunts and eats other animals (B47)

predict (prih DIHKT), to state what you think will happen based on past experience, observations, patterns, and cause-and-effect relationships

prey (pray), animal that is hunted and eaten by predators (B47)

producer (pruh DOO suhr), organism that makes its own food from raw materials and energy (B24)

protist (PROH tihst), kingdom of living things; its organisms are mostly one-celled but have nuclei and other organelles (A25)

proton (PROH tahn), a particle in the nucleus of an atom that has a positive charge (E8)

protostar (PROH tuh stahr), first stage in the formation of a star (D76)

radiation (ray dee AY shuhn), transfer of thermal energy through electromagnetic waves (F90)

recessive trait (rih SEHS ihv   trayt), trait that is not expressed when an organism receives genes for two different forms of a trait (A99)

record data (rih KAWRD   DAY tuh), to write, draw, audio record, video record, or photograph to show observations

recycling (ree SY klihng), process of recovering a resource from one item and using it to make another item (C92)

reflection (rih FLEHK shuhn), bouncing of a wave off a material (F66)

refraction (rih FRAK shuhn), changing of the path of a wave as it moves between materials of different densities (F66)

renewable resource (rih NOO uh buhl   REE sawrs), resource that is easily replaced or renewed (C76)

research (rih SURCH), to learn more about a subject by looking in books, newspapers, magazines, CD-ROMS, searching the Internet, or asking science experts

residual soil (rih ZIHJ oo uhl   soyl), soil formed directly from the bedrock below it (C85)

revolution (rehv uh LOO shuhn), one full trip, or orbit, around the Sun (D33)

scientific inquiry (sy uhn TIH fik IN kwih ree), method scientists use to ask and answer questions about the world around them (S3)

sediment (SEHD uh muhnt), small pieces of rock (C14)

seismic waves (SYZ mihk wayvz), waves of energy sent through Earth's crust when parts of the crust move suddenly (C53)

selective breeding (suh LEHK tihv BREE ding), practice of breeding plants and animals for desirable traits (A100)

semi-metal (SEHM ee meht l), elements that have some properties of metals and some properties of nonmetals (E17)

series circuit (SIHR eez SUR kiht), circuit where only a single path for electricity connects two or more devices (F114)

sexual reproduction (SEHK shoo uhl ree pruh DUHK shuhn), production of offspring by the union of male and female gametes (A98)

simple machine (SIHM puhl muh SHEEN), a machine that has few or no moving parts (F17)

soil (soyl), natural resource made up of small rocks, minerals, water, gases, and organic matter (C84)

soil profile (soyl PROH fyl), all of the soil horizons, or layers, in a soil sample (C86)

solar eclipse (SOH luhr ih KLIHPS), when the Moon passes directly between the Sun and Earth, casting a shadow on Earth (D46)

solar system (SOH luhr SIHS tuhm), the Sun and all bodies that revolve around it (D56)

solid (SAHL ihd), state of matter that has a definite shape and volume (E76)

solubility (sahl yuh BIHL ih tee), measure of how much of one substance can dissolve in another substance (E46)

solute (SAHL yoot), substance that is dissolved in a solution (E62)

solution (suh LOO shuhn), mixture of two or more substances that are evenly distributed throughout the mixture (E62)

solvent (SAHL vuhnt), substance that dissolves the solute in a solution (E62)

speed (speed), measure of the distance an object moves in a given unit of time (F8)

spores (spawrz), reproductive structures found in fungi and simple plants (A68)

stars (stahrz), giant sphere of glowing gases (D74)

state of matter (stayt uhv MAT uhr), physical form that matter takes; gas, liquid, and solid (E74)

static electricity (STAT ihk ih lehk TRIHS ih tee), electrical force between nonmoving electric charges (F104)

stomata (STOH muh tuh), small openings through which gases move in and out of leaves (A52)

stratosphere (STRA tuh sfeer), layer of the atmosphere above the troposphere and below the mesosphere (D17)

sublimation (suhb luh MAY shuhn), change of state from a solid to a gas (E86)

subsoil (SUHB soyl), layer of soil beneath the topsoil (C86)

summer solstice (SUHM uhr SAHL stihs), June 21 or 22, the longest day of the year in the Northern Hemisphere (D34)

switch (swihch), movable section of a circuit that can open or close a path for electricity (F113)

symbiosis (sihm bee OH sihs), close, long-lasting relationship between species (B42)

taiga (TY guh), area that has long, severe winters and short, cool summers (B15)

technology (tehk NAH luh jee), tools, things built with tools, or methods used to accomplish a practical purpose (S11)

temperate forests forests that experience four distinct seasons: summer, fall, winter, and spring (B13)

temperature (TEHM puhr uh chur), measure of the average kinetic energy of the particles that make up a substance (F78)

thermal energy total kinetic energy of the particles of a substance (F78)

thermal expansion (THUHR muhl ihk SPAN shuhn), increase in size of a substance due to a change in temperature (E87)

thermosphere (THUHR muh sfeer), the outermost layer of the atmosphere, above the mesosphere (D17)

threatened species (THREHT nd SPEE sheez), a species close to becoming endangered (B59)

tissue (TIHSH oo), group of one or more kinds of specialized cells that perform the same function (A33)

topographic map map that shows the shape of surface features and their elevations above sea level (C10)

topsoil uppermost layer of soil (C86)

transpiration (tran spuh RAY shuhn), evaporation through the leaves of a plant (A64)

transported soil (trans PAWRT ihd soyl), soil that has been carried from one place to another by erosion (C85)

tropical rain forests forests in regions that are very hot and very rainy (B13)

troposphere (TROH puh sfihr), layer of Earth's atmosphere closest to Earth's surface and containing about three-quarters of the atmosphere's gases (D17)

tundra Earth's coldest biome (B15)

umbra (UHM bruh), small, dark shadow in an eclipse (D46)

use variables (yooz VAIR ee uh buhlz), to keep all conditions in an experiment the same except for the variable, or the condition that is being tested

vaporization (vay puh rih ZAY shuhn), change of state from a liquid to a gas as energy is added (E85)

vascular plant a plant with specialized tissues and organs for transporting materials (A63)

velocity (vuh LAHS ih tee), measure of speed and direction (F8)

vernal equinox (VUR nuhl EE kwuh nahks), March 20 or 21, when the number of hours of daylight and darkness are the same (D34)

vertebrate (VUR tuh briht), animal that has an internal skeleton or backbone (A26)

vibration (vy BRAY shuhn), rapid back-and-forth movement (F54)

visible light portion of the electro-magnetic spectrum humans can see (F65)

voltage (VOHL tihj), measure of the force that moves electrons (F127)

volume (VAHL yoom), loudness of a sound, or the space an object takes up (F57)

weathering destructive force that breaks down rocks into smaller pieces (C14)

winter solstice (WIHN tuhr SAHL stihs), December 21 or 22, the shortest day of the year in the Northern Hemisphere (D34)

work (wurk), result of a force moving an object a certain distance (F16)

xylem (ZY luhm), specialized plant tissue that moves materials (A63)

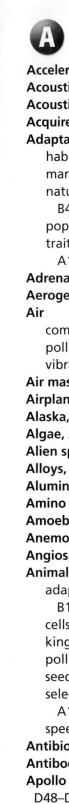

Index

Index

Literature:

Excerpt from *The River of Grass* from *Everglades: Buffalo Tiger and the River of Grass,* by Peter Lourie. Copyright © 1994 by Peter Lourie. Reprinted by permission of Caroline House, Boyds Mills Press, Inc.

Some Rivers from *Sawgrass Poems: A View From the Everglades,* by Frank Asch. Copyright © 1996 by Frank Asch. Reprinted by permission of Harcourt, Inc. This material may not be reproduced in any form or by any means without the prior written permission of the publisher.

Excerpt from *Salt Marshes and Protector of Land and Animals* from *The Florida Water Story: From Raindrops to the Sea,* by Peggy Sias Lantz and Wendy A. Hale. Copyright © 1998 by Peggy Sias Lantz and Wendy A. Hale. Reprinted by permission of Pineapple Press, Inc.

Excerpt from *Comets, Meteors, and Asteroids,* by Seymour Simon. Copyright © 1994 by Seymour Simon. Reprinted by permission of William Morrow and Company, an imprint of HarperCollins Publishers.

Earth Changed in Meteor's Fiery Death from *Earth Shake: Poems From the Ground Up,* by Lisa Westberg Peters, Illustrated by Cathie Felstead. Text copyright © 2003 by Lisa Westberg Peters, illustrations copyright 2003 by Cathie Felstead. Reprinted by permission of Harper-Collins Publishers.

Photography:

Front and back cover (tiger) © Joe McDonald/Corbis. (front cover bkgd) © Randy Wells/Corbis. **Spine** © PhotoDisc, Inc./Getty Images. **Page iv** © Mark Tomalty/Masterfile Stock Photo Library. **v** © Corbis/Punch Stock. **vi** © William Manning/Corbis. **vii** Courtesy of NASA. **viii** © Dorling Kindersley Picture Library. **ix** © Fukuhara, Inc./Corbis. **ix** © Fukuhara, Inc./Corbis. **S1** © LB Goodman/Omni-Photo Communications. **S2** Courtesy of Dr. Dale Brown Emeagwali. **S2-3** © Microfield Scientific Ltd./Photo Researchers, Inc. **S3** (r) © Alamy Images. **S4-5** (bkgd) © Picimpact/Corbis. Ocelot © Pete Oxford/Nature Picture Library. **S6** (bkgd) © Marc Muench/Muench Photography, Inc. **S9** (bkgd) © HMCo. **S10** (b) © Cassandra Wagner. **S10** (t) © Mitsuhiko Imamori/Minden Pictures. **S11** © Janet Hostetter/AP/Wide World Photos. **S12-13** (b) © Brand X Pictures/Punch Stock. **S12-13** (bkgd) © PhotoDisc, Inc./Punch Stock. **S14** © Stephen Frink/Corbis. **Unit A Opener pages** © Tom Adams/Visuals Unlimited, Inc. **A2-3** © David McCarthy/Science Photo Library/Photo Researchers, Inc. **A3** (1) © Leonard Lessin/Peter Arnold, Inc. **A3** (2) © VVG/Science Photo Library/Photo Researchers, Inc. **A3** (3) © Edward AM Snijde/Lonely Planet. **A3** (4) © Ariel Skelley/Corbis. **A4-5** © Mitsuaki Iwago/Minden Pictures. **A6** (l) © Omikron/Photo Researchers, Inc. **A6** (r) © The Granger Collection, New York. **A7** (b) © Dennis Kunkel Microscopy, Inc. **A7** (t) © Mark Tomalty/Masterfile Stock Photo Library. **A8** © Andrew Syred/Science Photo Library/Photo Researchers, Inc. **A9** © Dr. Gopal Murti/Photo Researchers, Inc. **A10** (b) © CNRI/Science Photo Library/Photo Researchers, Inc. **A10** (c) © Professors P. Motta & T. Naguro/Science Photo Library/Photo Researchers, Inc. **A10** (t) © Dr. Jeremy Burgess/Science Photo Library/Photo Researchers, Inc. **A11** (1) © Omikron/Photo Researchers, Inc. **A11** (2) © Leonard Lessin/Peter Arnold, Inc. **A11** (3) © Dr. Gopal Murti/Photo Researchers, Inc. **A11** (4) © Andrew Syred/Science Photo Library/Photo Researchers, Inc. **A12** © VVG/Science Photo Library/Photo Researchers, Inc. **A12- 13** © Brandon D. Cole/Corbis. **A14** © WG/Science Photo Library/Photo Researchers, Inc. **A15** (b) © Science Photo Library/Photo Researchers, Inc. **A15** (t) © SciMAT/Photo Researchers, Inc. **A16** (b) © Andrew Syred/Science Photo Library/Photo Researchers, Inc. **A16** (t) © Michael Abbey/Visuals Unlimited, Inc. **A17** © Andrew Syred/Science Photo Library/Photo Researchers, Inc. **A18** © Andrew Syred/Photo Researchers, Inc. **A19** (b) © Andrew Syred/Photo Researchers, Inc. **A19** (c) © Andrew Syred/Science Photo Library/Photo Researchers, Inc. **A19** (t) © SciMAT/Photo Researchers, Inc. **A19** © SciMAT/Photo Researchers, Inc. **A20** (b) © The Granger Collection, New York. **A20** (b) © Popperfoto/Alamy Images. **A21** (b) © Index Stock Imagery, Inc. **A21** (t) © Larry Lefever/Grant Heilman Photography. **A22** © Digital Vision/Punch Stock. **A22-23** (bkgd) © Ian Cartwright/PhotoDisc, Inc./Getty Images. **A23** (c) © PhotoDisc, Inc. **A23** (l) © PhotoDisc, Inc. **A23** (r) © PhotoDisc, Inc. **A24** © Duncan Usher/Foto Natura/Minden Pictures. **A25** (1) © SciMAT/Photo Researchers, Inc. **A25** (2) © WG/Science Photo Library/Photo Researchers, Inc. **A25** (3) © RO-MA Stock/Index Stock Imagery. **A25** (4) © Goodshoot/Punch Stock. **A25** (5) © Corbis/Punch Stock. **A26** (b) © Corbis/Punch Stock. **A26** (t) © Kim Taylor and Jane Burton/Dorling Kindersley Picture Library. **A27** (b) © Nick Garbutt/Nature Picture Library. **A27** (t) © Peter Johnson/Corbis. **A28** (b) © Gary Bell/Getty Images. **A28** (t) © Dave Roberts/Science Photo Library/Photo Researchers, Inc. **A30-31** © Dr. David M. Phillips/Visuals Unlimited, Inc. **A32** © Innerspace Imaging/Photo Researchers, Inc. **A35** (b) © Jerry Young/Dorling Kindersley Picture Library. **A35** (t) © Ron Boardman; Frank Lane Picture Agency/Corbis. **A38** © Chris Hellier/Corbis. **A40** © Ariel Skelley/Corbis. **A42- 43** © Steve Gschmeissner/Science Photo Library/Photo Researchers, Inc. **A45** (l) © SciMAT/Photo Researchers, Inc. **A45** © Andrew Syred/Science Photo Library/Photo Researchers, Inc. **A46-47** © Steve Hopkin/Getty Images. **A47** (b) Paul McCormick/The Image Bank/Getty Images. **A47** (c) © Eduardo Garcia/Taxi/Getty Images. **A47** (t) © Barry Runk/Stan/Grant Heilman Photography, Inc. **A48-49** © Medford Taylor/National Geographic Society. **A50** © David Sieren/Visuals Unlimited, Inc. **A51** © Barry Runk/Stan/Grant Heilman Photography, Inc. **A52** (l) © Runk/Shoenberger/Grant Heilman Photography, Inc. **A52** (r) © Runk/Shoenberger/Grant Heilman Photography, Inc. **A53** (b) © Andrew Syred/Science Photo Library/Photo Researchers, Inc. **A54** © Claus Meyer/Minden Pictures. **A55** (b) © Claus Meyer/Minden Pictures. **A55** (t) © David Sieren/Visuals Unlimited, Inc. **A57** (l) © PhotoDisc, Inc./Punch Stock. **A57** (r) © Inga Spence/Visuals Unlimited, Inc. **A58** (1) © Alex Kerstitch/Visuals Unlimited, Inc. **A58** (2) © Norbert Wu/Peter Arnold, Inc. **A58** (3) © Ed Reschke/Peter Arnold, Inc. **A58** (4) © Inga Spence/Visuals Unlimited, Inc. **A59** (b) © The Granger Collection, New York. **A59** (t inset) © Patrick Johns/Corbis. **A59** (tr) © Mario Tama/Getty Images. **A60-61** © Peter Marbach/Grant Heilman Photography, Inc. **A62** (l) © Richard Cummins/Corbis. **A62** (r) © Dr. Jeremy Burgess/Photo Researchers, Inc. **A63** (b) © Alfred Pasieka/Science Photo Library/Photo Researchers, Inc. **A63** (t) © Sheila Terry/Science Photo Library/Photo Researchers, Inc. **A65** (c) © Alfred Pasieka/Science Photo Library/Photo Researchers, Inc. **A65** (t) © Richard Cummins/Corbis. **A66** © Ed Degginger/Bruce Coleman, Inc. **A66-67** © Digital Vision/Punch Stock. **A68** © Gerald and Buff Corsi/Visuals Unlimited, Inc.

A69 (b) © Brad Mogen/Visuals Unlimited, Inc. **A69** (r) © James Morgan/Dorling Kindersley Picture Library. **A69** (t) © Brad Mogen/Visuals Unlimited, Inc. **A72** (b) © Dwight Kuhn/Bruce Coleman, Inc. **A72** (t) © Peter Steyn/Photo Access/Taxi/Getty Images. **A73** © Georgette Douwma/The Image Bank/Getty Images. **A73** (br) © Steve Maslowski/Photo Researchers, Inc. **A73** (t) © Lynn Ponto-Peterson. **A74** (bl) © Inga Spence/Visuals Unlimited, Inc. **A74** (br) © Davies & Starr/Stone/Getty Images. **A74** (cl) © Mark Tomalty/Masterfile Stock Photo Library. **A74** (cr) © Rick Souders/Food Pix. **A74** (tl) © Dwight Kuhn. **A74** (tr) © Lois Ellen Frank/Corbis. **A76-77** © Dr. Jeremy Burgess/Science Photo Library/Photo Researchers, Inc. **A76** (c) © Claude Nuridsany & Marie Perennou/Science Photo Library/Photo Researchers, Inc. **A80-81** © Allen Russell/Index Stock Imagery. **A81** (b) © George Grall/National Geographic Image Collection **A81** (t) © Rod Williams/Nature Picture Library. **A82** © Paul Eekhoff/Masterfile Stock Photo Library. **A82-83** © ImageState/Alamy Images Ltd. **A84** © Robert Stock **A85** (b) © Rod Williams/Nature Picture Library. **A85** (t) © Buzz Pictures/Alamy Images. **A86** © Carolina Biological Supply Company/PhotoTake USA. **A89** (inset) © Kaj R. Svenson/Science Photo Library/Photo Researchers, Inc. **A89** © PhotoDisc, Inc. **A90** © Eye of Science/Photo Researchers, Inc. **A91** (b) © Kaj R. Svenson/Science Photo Library/Photo Researchers, Inc. **A91** (t) © Rod Williams/Nature Picture Library. **A92** (b) © Omikron/Photo Researchers, Inc. **A92** (t) © Photo Researchers, Inc. **A93** © Luis Rico **A94** © Yva Momatiuk/John Eastcott/Minden Pictures. **A94-95** © Prenzel, Fritz/Earth Scenes. **A96** © Wally Eberhart/Visuals Unlimited, Inc. **A97** (b) © Dennis Kunkel Microscopy, Inc. **A97** (t) © Andrew J. Martinez/Photo Researchers, Inc. **A99** (l) © Corel/FotoSearch. **A99** (r) © Ulf Wallin/The Image Bank/Getty Images. **A100** (c) © Davies & Starr/The Image Bank/Getty Images. **A100** (l) © Brand X Pictures/Punch Stock. **A100** (r) © Ed Young/Corbis. **A101** (l) © Peter Cade/Stone/Getty Images. **A101** (r) © PhotoDisc, Inc./Punch Stock. **A102** (bl) © Ruth Cole, Animals Animals. **A102** (br) © Peter Blackwell/Nature Picture Library. **A102** (t) © Jeffrey L. Rotman/Peter Arnold, Inc. **A103** (c) © Zigmund Leszczynski/Animals Animals. **A103** (l) © Mark Moffett/Minden Pictures. **A103** (r) © Gerold and Cynthia Merker/Visuals Unlimited, Inc. **A104** (b) © Gerold and Cynthia Merker/Visuals Unlimited, Inc. **A104** (c) © Peter Cade/Stone/Getty Images. **A104** (t) © Wally Eberhart/Visuals Unlimited, Inc. **A105** (t) © Jim Whitmer. **A105** (b) © Patrick Olear/PhotoEdit, Inc. **A106** © Stephen Green-Armytage. **Unit B Opener first page** ©Tom and Pat Leeson. **Unit B Opener spread** ©Gary Kramer. **B2-3** © Kevin Schafer Photography. **B3** (b) © Dwight Kuhn. **B3** (c) © David Mendelsohn/Masterfile Stock Photo Library. **B3** (t) © Dwight Kuhn. **B4** © George McCarthy/Corbis. **B4-5** © Gary Braasch/Corbis. **B6** © Mark Barrett/Index Stock Imagery. **B6-7** (bkgd) © David Muench/Corbis. **B7** (c) © Jeff Lepore/Photo Researchers, Inc **B7** (l) © Frans Lanting/Minden Pictures. **B7** © Dwight Kuhn Photography. **B8** © Alexis Rosenfeld/Photo Researchers, Inc. **B9** (b) © Alexis Rosenfeld/Photo Researchers, Inc. **B9** (c) © Dwight Kuhn Photography. **B9** (t) © Mark Barrett/Index Stock Imagery. **B10** © W. Perry Conway/Corbis. **B10-11** © National Geographic Society. **B13** (b) © Darrell Gulin/Corbis. **B13** (deer) © Stephen J. Krasemann/Photo Researchers, Inc. **B13** (t) © Kevin Schafer Photography. **B13** (toucan) © Cyril Laubscher/